Oracle Solaris 11
System Administration:
The Complete Reference

Michael Jang and Harry Foxwell
with Christine Tran and Alan Formy-Duval, Contributing Writers

New York   Chicago   San Francisco
Lisbon   London   Madrid   Mexico City   Milan
New Delhi   San Juan   Seoul   Singapore   Sydney   Toronto

The McGraw·Hill Companies

Cataloging-in-Publication Data is on file with the Library of Congress

McGraw-Hill books are available at special quantity discounts to use as premiums and sales promotions, or for use in corporate training programs. To contact a representative, please e-mail us at bulksales@mcgraw-hill.com.

Oracle Solaris 11 System Administration: The Complete Reference

Copyright © 2013 by The McGraw-Hill Companies, Inc. (Publisher). All rights reserved. Printed in the United States of America. Except as permitted under the Copyright Act of 1976, no part of this publication may be reproduced or distributed in any form or by any means, or stored in a database or retrieval system, without the prior written permission of Publisher, with the exception that the program listings may be entered, stored, and executed in a computer system, but they may not be reproduced for publication.

Oracle is a registered trademark of Oracle Corporation and/or its affiliates. All other trademarks are the property of their respective owners, and McGraw-Hill makes no claim of ownership by the mention of products that contain these marks.

Screen displays of copyrighted Oracle software programs have been reproduced herein with the permission of Oracle Corporation and/or its affiliates.

Excerpts of copyrighted Oracle user documentation have been reproduced herein with the permission of Oracle Corporation and/or its affiliates.

1 2 3 4 5 6 7 8 9 0   DOC DOC   1 0 9 8 7 6 5 4 3 2

ISBN   978-0-07-179042-0
MHID   0-07-179042-X

Sponsoring Editor
Amy Jollymore

Editorial Supervisor
Janet Walden

Project Editor
Howie Severson,
Fortuitous Publishing Services

Acquisitions Coordinator
Ryan Willard

Contributing Writers
Christine Tran, Alan Formy-Duval

Technical Editors
Sharon Veach, Sam Nicholson,
Alta Estad, Jeff Savit, Jeff Victor,
Juanita Heieck

Copy Editor
Bart Reed

Proofreader
Paul Tyler

Indexer
Jack Lewis

Production Supervisor
James Kussow

Composition
Cenveo Publisher Services

Illustration
Cenveo Publisher Services

Art Director, Cover
Jeff Weeks

Cover Designer
Pattie Lee

Information has been obtained by Publisher from sources believed to be reliable. However, because of the possibility of human or mechanical error by our sources, Publisher, or others, Publisher does not guarantee to the accuracy, adequacy, or completeness of any information included in this work and is not responsible for any errors or omissions or the results obtained from the use of such information.

Oracle Corporation does not make any representations or warranties as to the accuracy, adequacy, or completeness of any information contained in this Work, and is not responsible for any errors or omissions.

Contents at a Glance

Contents

Foreword

If you're reading this, you probably care about operating systems. Some would say that's an unusual thing to care about, especially today. I've been caring about operating systems for quite a while; in fact, I'm writing this on my 23rd anniversary of joining Sun (now Oracle), and the 20th anniversary of Solaris, but it's been even longer that I've cared about UNIX and what has now become Solaris.

Weird, huh?

Not really—at least, not as long as you also care about computing systems working the way they ought to. The operating system sits at a strategic position, between the software and hardware of any solution, and it's there that you can make significant investments in performance, security, reliability, and observability. That's where our investments in Solaris have paid off for our customers for two decades now, and why Solaris has become synonymous with "UNIX" for a large number of people.

Solaris, of course, is now incredibly sophisticated in its features, but still retains the fundamental concepts of UNIX that made it so flexible and powerful from the beginning. UNIX was a natural for companies such as Sun that were trying something completely different from the conventional wisdom of '80s computing: It was open, modular, and incredibly flexible because of this.

By choosing to embrace and invest in UNIX from the beginning, Sun was able to make its original mark in technical computing as well as later make the leap to the data center with Solaris, one of the key technologies behind the explosive growth of the Internet computing era.

The success of Solaris was driven not only by innovation, but by the enthusiasm of Sun's field technologists, the "OS Ambassadors" such as Harry Foxwell who were able to take the unique features of SunOS/Solaris and translate them to the needs of Sun's customers and partners.

Thanks to this virtuous circle of excitement over SunOS's capabilities among Sun's developers, evangelists, and user community, SunOS and Solaris became synonymous with UNIX, and UNIX became the "go-to" platform for pushing the boundaries of technical and business computing.

UNIX and its descendants have become the backbone of innovation in IT.

If you're using an iPhone, you're using UNIX, and it's in turn talking to Solaris in the world's data centers. And Android and other Linux-based platforms also extend the legacy of innovations that grew from UNIX—and most notably Solaris.

This book gives you a chance to explore the most recent advances in Solaris technology as well as the solid foundation that Oracle Solaris 11 is built on and continues to extend. Solaris has a long track record of introducing game-changing capabilities—from the introduction of networked file sharing and directory services with NFS and NIS, to new approaches to filesystems and observability with ZFS and DTrace, and on to the advanced provisioning and network virtualization capabilities of Oracle Solaris 11 that you can learn about here.

Each new release of Solaris has had a habit of changing the way people—including our competitors—think about operating systems. In this book, Michael, Harry, Christine, and Alan amply demonstrate that we haven't given up that habit.

–Larry Wake
Senior Principal Product Director, Oracle Solaris
Redwood City, California (July 2011)

Acknowledgments

This book would not have been possible without the dedication of people from the team behind Solaris 11. Starting with Shirpad Patki, Sr. Director, Solaris Info Development & Globalization (IDG) at Oracle America, Oracle has provided the management commitment that was needed.

The commitment continued with Isaac Rozenfeld, the Solaris Product Manager. He took our questions, and answered them in expansive detail. Kathy Slattery helped us work through the mounds of Solaris documentation, pointing out discrepancies as they appeared.

The technical reviewers brought wonderful care to their work. It's clear that they're passionate about Solaris 11, and want to bring the best possible information to all who read our book. Sharon Veach is a consummate professional in her work, and her background as an author of the *Solaris 10 Security Essentials* book was helpful. Sam Nicholson did an excellent job bringing us up to speed with the latest developments in NFS. Alta Estad's passion emerges in the way she checks every detail.

It takes a large, active, and dedicated community to build, extend, support, and promote a major operating system such as Solaris. So we are indebted not only to Jeff Savit and Jeff Victor's roles as reviewers but for their earlier contributions as members of Sun's Solaris Ambassador community and as authors of their own excellent blogs, articles, and books, along with literally thousands of unsung technical heroes who have made Solaris 11 what it is today. And Oracle's Solaris engineering and documentation organizations, which include many former Sun contributors such as tech reviewers Juanita Heieck and Sharon Veach, have reinvigorated interest in what is demonstrably today's best implementation of the UNIX operating system. We thank them all.

Of course, this book would not have been possible without the hard work and dedication of the publishing team at McGraw-Hill Professional. Amy Jollymore had the vision to make this book happen. Ryan Willard took care of the day-to-day needs of the book, coordinating four authors and a myriad of editors. Howie Severson and Bart Reed took detailed care to make the text readable for the widest possible audience.

–Michael Jang and Harry Foxwell

I have the opportunity to be part of this wonderful book because Harry and Mike were kind enough to include me. Thank you, Harry and Mike. The technical reviewers, Sharon Veach and Jeff Savit, kept me humble and honest.

Over the years, many people have contributed to the beautiful thing that is Solaris. It was the privilege of my life to have worked with these brilliant people, received their guidance, and reaped the rewards of their knowledge. My part of the book is dedicated to them and the work that they've done.

–Christine Tran, contributing writer

It is a real privilege to be asked to contribute to this book by Harry and Mike. I found the creative and educational process to be so rewarding. I'd also like to acknowledge my wife and daughter for inspiration and giving me the time away from them to write.

–Alan Formy-Duval, contributing writer

Introduction

Oracle Solaris 11 is the operating system for the cloud. Because it has been optimized to work more quickly with multiple applications, it's quite the attractive choice for the enterprise. As such, anyone with an interest in the high-paying jobs in the enterprise world associated with UNIX will want to get up to speed with Solaris 11.

The Oracle Solaris 11 Information Library at http://docs.oracle.com/cd/E23824_01 consists of several thousand pages of detailed documentation on all aspects of the operating system and is the authoritative source for how features work. This book hits the major features of the Solaris 11 11/11 release; when you're finished with this book, you'll be up to speed on different methods for installation and configuration of those key features. You'll understand how to make the image packaging system work for a variety of systems in the enterprise. You'll be able to work the Service Management Facility to configure needed systems securely. You'll be able to use Solaris zones to set up multiple virtual environments, without the overhead associated with many alternative solutions. Finally, you'll be able to set up the major network services associated with Solaris 11.

Oracle plans to update Solaris 11 periodically, approximately once per year. Readers should frequently check Oracle's website at oracle.com/solaris to learn of any new releases or features. Readers can learn more by visiting www.mhprofessional.com to browse and purchase other McGraw-Hill Professional computer networking titles, as well as visit this book's page on the site to review or report errata.

About the Command Conventions in This Book

Commands in this book are shown in several different ways. Sometimes, a command such as **ls** is shown in bold, within the main text. Sometimes, longer lines of command text and output are broken out separately, such as the following:

```
# svcs -a
STATE           STIME    FMRI
legacy_run      Jan_02   lrc:/etc/rc2_d/S47pppd
. . .
```

Although Solaris is normally administered by users with various levels of privilege, Solaris 11 still includes a root administrative user. Commands run by that user are prefaced by the following prompt:

```
#
```

Be careful. The hash mark (#) is also used as a comment character in many scripts and programs. When logged in as a regular user, you will see a slightly different prompt; for user michael, for example, it would typically look like this:

```
michael@solaris11:~$
```

In a similar fashion, such commands run by a regular user may be abbreviated as follows:

```
$
```

Sometimes, the differences are subtle. Sometimes, you'll need to actually type in a command or a response to a question at a command line. In that case, you'll see an instruction such as type **y**. Alternatively, some menus require a keypress; for instance, you may be asked to press c to access a command line. In that case, the letter c is not added to the screen when you press that letter. In addition, the c, despite its appearances, is in lowercase. In contrast, C is the uppercase version of that letter.

Finally, some lines of code and even a few commands get long. In that case, the line may appear on two or more lines. If you see the following character at the end of a line

```
¬
```

the target line, along with the line that follows, should be read as if it were a single line.

CHAPTER
1

The Basics of
Oracle Solaris 11

Welcome to Oracle Solaris 11

For those who have worked with Sun Microsystems' flagship operating system for many years, the pairing of the Solaris and Oracle trademarks may seem a bit odd and unfamiliar. And although many mourned the acquisition of Sun by Oracle—and some even questioned its wisdom—the result of the merger has produced an OS that is true to the tradition and original vision of Solaris and yet is modernized to meet the scalability and feature requirements of both traditional enterprise IT and new cloud computing infrastructures.

As you will see, Solaris 11's advanced features help system administrators quickly and easily install, configure, update, and manage the OS and its applications. They provide for secure administration of users, data, and system access, and include unique technologies for virtualization, resource management, and system stability.

In this complete reference we explain Solaris 11's key capabilities for those new to this modern implementation of UNIX as well as for those with prior Solaris experience. We show you how to install Solaris 11 on your desktop PC or laptop for learning, experimentation, and development, and how to deploy it on production servers in your data centers.

Linux users and developers will find in Solaris 11 a familiar and quickly productive working environment; we point out similarities and differences between the Linux and Solaris kernels and system administration tools, and describe how typical open source Web development tasks are accomplished in this OS.

We think you will like what you learn here about what Oracle calls "the #1 enterprise operating system."

So, Why Should You Use Oracle Solaris 11?

If you are a longtime Solaris end user, developer, or administrator, you already know many of the features and benefits provided by this operating system as well as its generally excellent reputation for performance, security, stability, and scalability. Even still, every OS has its faults and annoyances, and Solaris is no exception. Historically, patching and updating the Solaris kernel has been a difficult and time-consuming process, with a bothersome lack of user-friendly tools to help with these tasks. Users of GNU/Linux environments might have found the open source utilities delivered with later Solaris versions buried in some subdirectory, but the default behavior of Solaris' common UNIX tools did not match their user experience on modern Linux systems. And even new and potentially useful technologies such as containers were often incompletely implemented and supported until late in the Solaris 10 release cycle. Oracle Solaris 11 addresses these deficiencies and improves upon the solid OS kernel capabilities that make Solaris a powerful application deployment platform.

But if you consider yourself primarily a "Linux developer," what's in it for you? Well, first we must remind you that virtually *all* of your familiar development tools—from Apache, MySQL, and PHP, to Java, Perl, Python, gcc, and Ruby—are easily available. Some even come preinstalled on Solaris 11. You'll also find typical open source user utilities such as the Firefox web browser, the Thunderbird e-mail client, OpenOffice, GIMP, and many others. In fact, referring to all these as "Linux applications" is inaccurate because they were long ago ported to Solaris and run equally well or even better on this OS. True, there is no longer a comparable community development approach for Solaris 11 as there is for Linux, but that does not negate the value of its innovative features.

Solaris 11 runs on SPARC servers and on a wide variety of Intel- and AMD-based x86 systems, including servers, workstations, and laptops, as you will see in the next chapter. Moreover, Solaris 11 has been optimized to produce superior performance on SPARC and Intel hardware from Oracle, as well as optimized for Oracle's application software such as Weblogic, Oracle Database, and other products.

For developers needing extreme scalability, virtualization, security, and elasticity features required for safe web-based and cloud computing solutions, Solaris 11 provides these capabilities, along with management tools that help administrators install, configure, monitor, and maintain their systems and ensure the integrity and availability of their data.

So, if you're ready to try Solaris 11, read on, and we'll tell you how to obtain, install, license, and use this newest version of the venerable Solaris OS.

A New Name, a New Owner, a Familiar Operating System

Oracle Solaris 11 inherits its features from three major sources: from Solaris 10 (introduced by Sun Microsystems in 2005), from the earlier work by Sun and the OpenSolaris community, and from the ongoing work of the combined Oracle and Sun OS engineering teams.

Solaris 10 introduced innovative and valuable OS capabilities, including the following:

- **Hardware and software fault and service management**   Solaris 10's Fault Management Architecture, consisting of hardware fault monitoring and software service management, reduces system downtime by proactively reporting and correcting problems without the need to shut down the operating system or interrupt applications. It automatically diagnoses hardware failures, taking faulty components out of service and alerting the system administrator; it replaces the manually created and maintained individual software service configuration files with a common framework and execution environment that reacts to and corrects software faults, and provides a better understanding of the interrelationships and dependencies among the services.

- **Extreme multiprocessor/multicore performance and scalability**   Solaris has been designed to take advantage of multiple CPUs, managing and scheduling thousands of processes and execution threads, hundreds of terabytes of system memory, and hundreds of gigabits per second of I/O. Solaris 10 continued to enhance its performance and scalability with the introduction of multicore SPARC *and* x86 processors, allowing multichip systems to efficiently serve very demanding application workloads, large numbers of users, and complex distributed system architectures.

- **The ZFS filesystem**   ZFS, first introduced with Solaris 10, was designed to eliminate file and directory size limitations, to reduce the burden of storage management, and to guarantee data integrity. It enhanced and extended the capabilities of system management, patching, and upgrading, and has become an essential technology component of Solaris virtualization. ZFS includes features such as file system snapshotting and rollback, fast file system cloning, and root/boot file system support.

- **Built-in virtualized workload containment**   Solaris 10 introduced an efficient form of OS virtualization that does *not* require a hypervisor—*containers* (also called *zones*). This feature provides for the secure and safe hosting of multiple application environments on a single instance of Solaris, supporting separate security and performance domains for development, testing, and production. Solaris containers—because they are *not* full virtual machine guest operating system kernels—have negligible system impact and can scale to many hundreds of efficiently isolated execution environments. Additionally, Solaris 10 includes workload and resource management capabilities that allow allocation of memory, CPU, storage, and bandwidth limits and guarantees for applications, users, and virtualized environments.

■ **Integrated observability**   The ability to observe and quickly diagnose production system problems is essential to business operations. Solaris 10 is fully instrumented with nonintrusive observation points that include the entire execution path from application function calls through hardware interrupts, enabling performance analysts using the DTrace tools to rapidly identify application design defects and bugs, system performance bottlenecks, and configuration errors.

■ **Enhanced security**   Solaris is already very well known for its high level of OS security. Solaris 10 introduced significant enhancements and new technologies for secure operation, including Role-Based Access Control (RBAC), management of root privileges, safe initial configuration and installation, support for processor-based encryption technologies, and labeled security domains using Trusted Extensions. Solaris 10 also introduced support for key security features such as digitally signed files, installation packages, and executables.

■ **Hypervisor-based virtualization for SPARC processors**   Along with the multicore SPARC processors introduced earlier by Sun, Solaris 10 added support for a SPARC-based hypervisor that enables a single processor chip to be partitioned into multiple Solaris 10 domains (originally called LDoms, or Logical Domains, and now called Oracle VM for SPARC). This provides virtualization features for SPARC servers comparable to those based on Intel processors such as VMware and Microsoft Hyper-V.

■ **A familiar user and developer environment**   Solaris 10 standardized on the GNOME user interface, and included popular open source applications such as the Firefox browser and the Thunderbird e-mail client, along with available GNU utilities, the gcc compiler, web development tools, Java support, NetBeans, and the StarOffice desktop suite. This approach was introduced in part to attract the growing number of Linux users and web developers by providing a working environment nearly identical to their open source workspaces. Additionally, Sun emphasized that popular open source application and developer tools such as Apache, Perl, and MySQL had long been available on Solaris and in fact ran equally well or even better on the Solaris 10 alternative to the Linux kernel.

Solaris Now "Goes to 11"

In November 2010, Oracle released Solaris 11 Express, which gave a preview of the new Oracle Solaris 11 operating system. This gave end users, administrators, and developers an opportunity to learn about new OS features. This preview was fully tested and quality reviewed, and even offered subscription software support for use in production environments, although not all of the planned OS features were fully implemented. Also, several recently introduced Oracle products, such as the Sun ZFS Storage Appliances and the Exalogic Elastic Cloud system, include Solaris 11 among their foundation operating systems.

The complete/production version of Oracle Solaris 11 (Figure 1-1), released in November 2011, is supported by both legacy Sun OS engineers and Oracle software developers; it runs on SPARC, Intel, and AMD processors, as well as on servers, workstations, and even laptops manufactured

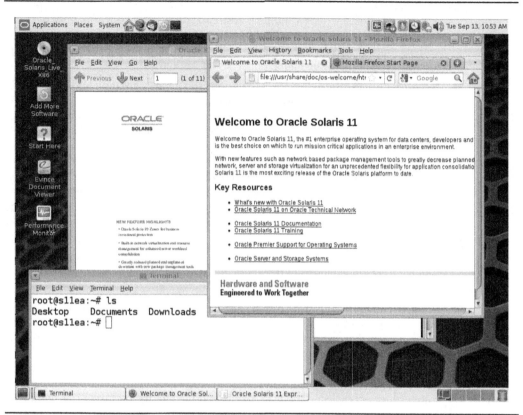

FIGURE 1-1. *Welcome to Oracle Solaris 11*

by Oracle, IBM, HP, Dell, and others. It enhances and adds to the impressive Solaris 10 features listed previously, and we'll be covering many of these new Solaris 11 features in more detail in subsequent chapters:

■ **A new patching and updating facility, the Image Packaging System (IPS)** Adding OS kernel and application patches are essential administrative tasks, which have historically been difficult and error prone on earlier versions of Solaris. IPS is a network repository–based service that enables easy updates to new kernel versions and patches, as well as application installation, updating, and removal, including installation of any needed dependencies. These updates can be accomplished using Oracle and third-party repositories over the Internet, or using locally installed and managed repositories. IPS can be accessed through command-line utilities, enabling inclusion in your custom scripts, or through an easy-to-use graphical interface. It also retains compatibility with the legacy SVR4 package utilities.

- **Automated installation**   The new Automated Installer (AI) for Solaris 11 helps server administrators easily deploy multiple customized OS kernel environments over their local networks. AI interfaces with IPS image repositories to allow for software installation without manual intervention, automatically recognizing and locating installation profiles for each type of hardware client, either SPARC or x86.

- **Network virtualization**   Solaris 11 supports the flexible creation and configuration of virtual network interface controllers (VNICs) and virtual LANs (VLANs), along with virtual switches and routing protocols. This enables modeling and testing of network environments within a single Solaris server in preparation for wider deployment. Additionally, both VNICs and NICs can be configured to control both bandwidth limits and CPU resources assigned to network traffic, allowing administrators to enforce quality of service (QoS) policies and to minimize the effects of network-based denial of service (DoS) attacks. Solaris 11's full network virtualization capabilities now permit administrators of individual containers to configure complete, exclusive, IP stacks for each container instead of allocating a full hardware NIC from the server.

- **Built-in CIFS support**   Solaris 11 includes kernel-based support for the Common Internet File System (CIFS) to provide file-sharing services for Microsoft Windows client systems. This service includes the ability to manage network connection and file access restrictions.

- **Security enhancements**   Solaris 11 adds many security features to the already well-known earlier capabilities of Solaris. For example, the root user is no longer a default super-privileged account; root is now simply a role whose privileges are managed through the Role-Based Access Control (RBAC) service. This eliminates the traditional approach of giving full root privileges to applications; now they can be granted only what they need in order to run. Additionally, direct root logins are disabled, requiring users to log in without special privileges and then explicitly asking for the root role. This permits control and monitoring of privileged actions. And Solaris 11 initial installations are "secure by default," meaning that no network-based services are activated automatically during the first system setup; only local console access is active. This prevents accidental exposure of the system to network-based intrusions during installation.

- **Enhanced GNOME and GNU user and developer environments**   The default GUI environment for Solaris 11 is the well-known GNOME interface, and includes by default common user applications such as Thunderbird, Firefox, and many utilities familiar to Linux users. For developers, the command-line PATH defaults to include /usr/gnu/bin, containing familiar GNU utilities rather than pointing to the System V binaries traditionally provided by Solaris. This creates a user and developer experience matching that of Linux environments because it is paired with the **bash** shell for standard users and **ksh** for the root user.

- **New ZFS features**   The ZFS file system is an integral technology of Solaris 11, supporting data integrity, easy storage management, patching and updating services, and virtualized environment configuration. New ZFS features in Solaris 11 include file system encryption, compression, and deduplication for security and for conserving disk space. The new **zfsdiff** command assists in identifying changes between file system snapshots, and the new TimeSlider utility allows users to manage their own home directory snapshots with an easy-to-use GUI that can recover deleted files or earlier file versions.

■ **CUPS printing system**   The legacy LP printing services used in earlier Solaris versions have been replaced with the widely used Common UNIX Printing System (CUPS). This service uses a web interface to discover, install, configure, and manage both local and remote printers and queues.

■ **Distribution Constructor**   System administrators who need to configure and deploy customized Solaris 11 OS server environments can now use the new Distribution Constructor to create "golden images" of operating systems and guest virtual machines and then install them over their local networks. These images can include customizations of OS parameters, application configurations, and policy implementations, as well as support the creation of bootable media on files, USB memory devices, or other media that can be used with the Automated Installer service (described earlier).

■ **New boot features**   Enabled by ZFS snapshots, Solaris 11 supports the instant creation of multiple boot environments. Administrators who make changes to the configurations or patches of an OS installation can first take a snapshot of that instance and then proceed with any needed updates or changes. A simple reboot to the snapshotted previous boot environment leaves everything unchanged in the event that there were problems with the changes made. This feature is what enables the Solaris 11 Live Upgrade service to easily install revisions to the OS. And to reduce the impact of OS restarts, Solaris 11 enables fast reboots that bypass previously successful hardware tests and initializations from earlier system startups.

■ **New container features**   Although containers have been in Solaris 10 from its introduction, new container features and services continue to be added to the OS. Solaris 11 now supports Solaris 10 branded containers that can run applications in a Solaris 10 environment, assisting developers and administrators with updating their applications to the next OS level. Additionally, new container administration tools have been introduced, including the **zonestat** program, which allows full observation of container resource utilization. The creation of new boot environments, mentioned previously, clones nonglobal containers along with the global container.

■ **Observability enhancements**   Solaris 11 now includes improved network observation utilities such as **dlstat**, **wireshark**, and **snoop** that can monitor traffic on both real and virtual network interfaces, including those assigned to containers. Moreover, the well-known DTrace utility has been enhanced to provide better observability of caches, network protocols, and **iscsi** I/O traffic, as well as general system latencies.

■ **Network auto-magic**   Wired and wireless network connection availability is now automatically detected and connected by default upon system startup. This is particularly useful for Solaris 11 installations on laptops dependent on wireless networks, and for newly installed servers within a DHCP environment.

■ **Multicore processor support**   On both x86 and SPARC systems that implement multiple-CPU cores and execution threads, Solaris 11 recognizes each hardware thread as a separately schedulable CPU. For example, on the new SPARC T4 processor, which has eight cores and eight threads per core, Solaris 11 sees 64 CPUs, and automatically recognizes and uses each core's crypto stream processors for applications requiring high-performance encryption services.

These are just a few of the innovative technologies introduced or enhanced in Solaris 11. In subsequent chapters, we explain many of these features, how to use them, and why they are important to end users, developers, and system administrators.

A Short Review of Solaris' Long History

The early history and evolution of UNIX is well known; it originated in the late 1960s at AT&T's Bell Laboratories, developed by researchers Ken Thompson and Dennis Ritchie. Later, at the University of California at Berkeley, Bill Joy, eventual Sun Microsystems cofounder, extended UNIX virtual memory management on the DEC VAX systems and contributed important development tools such as the **vi** editor and the **csh** command shell. By the early 1990s Sun had licensed the distribution rights to the UNIX SVR4 source code, derivatives, and kernel binaries. Eventually, in response to growing interest in community-developed open source solutions on the x86 architecture, Sun announced plans to release Solaris under an open source license and to reverse its decision to end-product development of Solaris on the x86 platform. Finally, in 2005, Sun introduced Solaris 10 for both SPARC and x86 systems, including release of the Solaris 10 kernel source code under an OSI-approved open source license, and founded the OpenSolaris.org developer community. An OpenSolaris binary distribution was released in 2008 with an update in 2009, but by that time Sun was starting to feel the effects of competition and the general downturn in IT spending and evolved into an acquisition target.

Initially, IBM showed interest in acquiring Sun Microsystems but ultimately declined, at which point Oracle announced its intention in early 2009 to purchase Sun, declaring its interest in Sun's key intellectual properties and technologies—SPARC, Java, and Solaris. Then, following nearly a year of wrangling with the European Union (EU) over concerns about Oracle's plans for the popular open source database MySQL that Sun had acquired earlier, Oracle basically completed its purchase of Sun in early 2010 (with the exception of some non-U.S. assets that followed later).

Because Sun was well known for strongly supporting open source software and Oracle was definitely not known for such support, users of Sun's open source products such as MySQL, OpenOffice, NetBeans, Lustre, Java, and of course Solaris, along with open source competitors and supporters such as Red Hat, were worried and critical of Oracle's ownership of these technologies. Oracle eventually met the EU's concerns about MySQL, but then discontinued its support of the OpenSolaris community development model and decided to focus on internal Solaris development and to take a more traditional, monetized approach to its newly acquired operating system. The general open source community and Oracle's competitors widely criticized the apparent abandonment of the Solaris community's development process, even claiming "Solaris is dead." Oracle insisted, however, that Solaris' value was worth the price it was now charging for development and support of a world-class operating system. Nevertheless, Oracle does provide source code to limited, GPL-licensed components of Solaris, and much of the original CDDL-licensed OpenSolaris source is still available for study at http://src.opensolaris.org/source, with helpful OS design discussions at www.solarisinternals.com.

The Future of Solaris

In spite of what may have been said by those concerned and critical about Oracle's acquisition of Sun Microsystems, Solaris, along with other legacy Sun technologies such as Java software and SPARC hardware, indeed has a future. Oracle is generally not very open and detailed about future product plans, but the company has publicly revealed its general operating systems strategy and direction, and has backed it up by incorporating Solaris 11 into key products such as Exadata, Exalogic, the SPARC SuperCluster, and the ZFS-based storage appliances.

Oracle's current public roadmap for Solaris includes additional updates for Solaris 10 (the most recently released version is the Solaris 10 8/11 update, sometimes referred to as "Update 10" in the series) and future updates for Solaris 11 that track the evolution of Intel chips and especially new SPARC processors through at least 2015, as these chips increase their number of cores, core clock speeds, and multichip capabilities. Oracle's general OS strategy, having acquired Solaris after initially competing against it with significant Linux development and support, now encompasses *two* major operating systems—Linux *and* Solaris. Oracle is expected to continue to develop and evolve *both* of these operating systems and the application products and systems based on each of them, positioning each OS as appropriate to specific markets and solutions.

Solaris 11 Licensing

Prior to Oracle's acquisition of the company, Sun Microsystems provided unlimited free downloads and use of its software, including Solaris. The intent behind this approach was to encourage use and distribution of Solaris in order to increase its user base and market share. And although Oracle still provides free software downloads at www.oracle.com/technetwork/indexes/downloads/index. html, the company only permits "use of full versions of the products at no charge while developing and prototyping your applications, or for strictly self-educational purposes." All other uses require a software support license, including any use of applications and operating systems in production environments. Additionally, whereas Sun provided certain Solaris OS patches for free, Oracle now requires a software support subscription to download any Solaris patches, including those addressing security issues. Sun/Oracle servers, both SPARC and x86, include a Solaris 11 usage license and subscription with the cost of the server support contract; a separate Solaris 11 subscription is not needed for Sun/Oracle hardware because it is included at the point of sale when the customer purchases Premier Support. However, support for Solaris 11 on *non-Oracle hardware*, such as that manufactured by Dell, IBM, or HP, requires a separate OS support contract that can be purchased through Oracle's online store at http://shop.oracle.com. The cost of such subscriptions depends on the number of processor chips, or "sockets," in the system to be supported, and includes 24/7 problem reporting and resolution services, access to the Oracle Solaris knowledge base and patches, and upgrades to future Oracle Solaris releases and enhancements. And although distribution of Solaris is intended primarily through downloads from Oracle's website at www.oracle.com/technetwork/server-storage/solaris11/downloads/index.html, media packs with installation DVDs will also be available for extra cost.

Solaris Communities

Numerous technical user and developer communities can be found on the Web for Oracle and legacy Sun technologies, including many that address Solaris tutorials, hints and tricks, and best practice recommendations. The largest such community originated with Sun Microsystems' BigAdmin site, now subsumed by the Oracle Technology Network (OTN) at www.oracle.com/ technetwork/systems/index.html (see Figure 1-2). This site is an excellent resource of solutions and advice for system administrators working not only with Solaris but with Linux as well.

At the time of this publication, parts of the OpenSolaris.org community website are still active, with ongoing contributions around the earlier OpenSolaris release and derivatives. It still hosts active discussions and solutions related to ZFS, containers, DTrace, and other technologies directly relevant to those in Oracle Solaris 11, so it is worth a visit, especially for the best practice FAQs on zones and ZFS (see Figure 1-3).

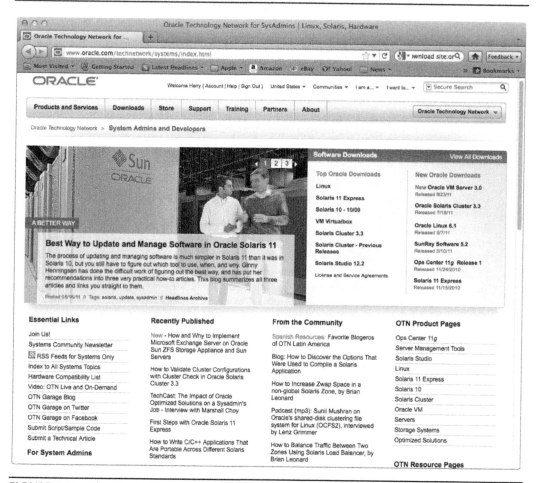

FIGURE 1-2. *The Oracle Technology Network (OTN) website*

As a response to Oracle's changes to its involvement with OpenSolaris, several derivative efforts were initiated by contributors to that community, including Illumos (www.illumos.org), a fork of the original OpenSolaris kernel intended to replace any proprietary components with open source equivalents, and the OpenIndiana project (www.openindiana.org), based on the Illumos kernel. Oracle has no involvement in these efforts, although some corporations such as Nexenta and Joyent have provided some support and use of these derivatives in their products.

Another spinoff of the original Solaris and OpenSolaris technologies is DTrace.org (www.dtrace.org), formed by DTrace developer Adam Leventhal and other former Sun engineers. Although independent of Oracle, contributors to this website include Sun DTrace experts such as

FIGURE 1-3.   *The OpenSolaris.org community website*

Brendan Gregg, developer of the DTrace Toolkit, and ZFS developers Brian Cantrill and Erick
Schrock. As such, it hosts much valuable information about how to use the powerful DTrace tools
for performance diagnostics.

There are, however, several Solaris 11 community web resources worth highlighting. Brian
Leonard, one of Oracle's Solaris Product Managers, blogs regularly at The Observatory (http://blogs.
oracle.com/observatory/), where he posts valuable instructions on how to use various features of
Solaris 11 (see Figure 1-4). Readers of this book and any Solaris administrator will gain valuable
knowledge about the operating system by frequently checking Leonard's website.

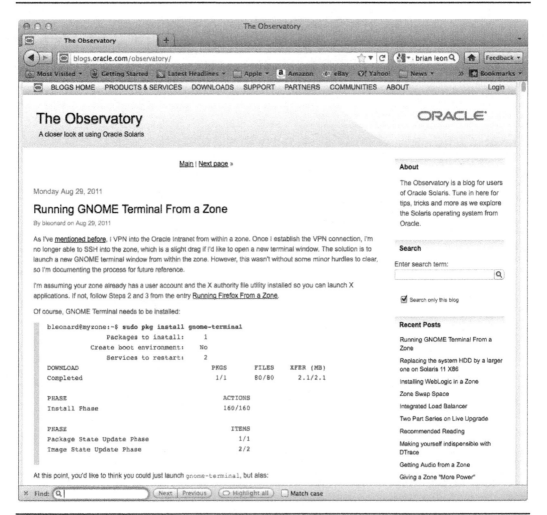

FIGURE 1-4. *Brian Leonard's "The Observatory" Solaris 11 blog*

No modern technology would be complete without a presence in popular social media, and Solaris 11 is no exception. Readers should check out Oracle's Solaris 11 group on Facebook (www.facebook.com/oraclesolaris), where product managers and others post announcements and technical product discussions with group members (see Figure 1-5).

And for immediate, live updates from Solaris engineers and users, you can even follow the action on Twitter at @ORCL_Solaris, currently with more than 1,100 followers.

FIGURE 1-5. *The Oracle Solaris group on Facebook*

Solaris 11 Documentation

Sun users were long accustomed to using http://docs.sun.com for all documentation related to Sun hardware and software. That link now redirects to the Oracle Technology Network (OTN), which includes not only Oracle's collection of software references but also the legacy and current Sun hardware and software documentation. Downloadable Solaris 11 references in English and other major languages are available at www.oracle.com/technetwork/documentation/solaris-11-192991. html, including the all-important Release Notes, What's New announcements, and End-of-Feature notices, along with documentation on installation, administration, security, and developer tools. Here, you will also find pointers to related Solaris resources such as articles and whitepapers, training videos, podcasts and webcasts, feature demos, and links to Solaris 11 training offerings (see Figure 1-6).

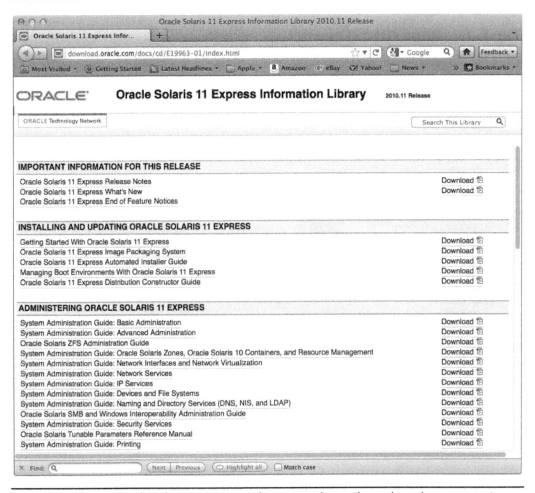

FIGURE 1-6.   *The Oracle Solaris 11 Express Information Library (formerly at docs.sun.com)*

For Those Moving from Solaris 10 to Solaris 11

Any time a vendor makes major changes to operating systems, administrators and developers need to learn how to use the new features and to relearn how to do routine tasks differently. Solaris 11 is no exception—there are significant changes (assuming most are for the better!) to how you install, configure, maintain, patch, monitor, and upgrade the OS. We detail these changes in the following chapters, but be forewarned—there are many things you will do much differently in Solaris 11, such as the following, to name but a few:

- Update and patch the OS and applications using IPS instead of patch tools
- Boot by default from a ZFS filesystem instead of UFS
- Boot over the Net with Automated Installer instead of JumpStart
- Use Distro Constructor instead of Flash Archive
- Manage printers with CUPS instead of LP services
- Create and manage alternate boot environments with ZFS and **beadm**
- Configure real and virtual network interfaces with **ipadmin** instead of **ifconfig**

Additionally, some familiar tools and procedures will change or go away, including these:

- Basic security module auditing
- Cryptographic services and tools
- **rdist** distributed file management

Summary

Oracle Solaris 11 continues to evolve as the leading implementation of UNIX on multiple hardware platforms from laptops to enterprise servers, exploiting modern multicore processors and a range of virtualization technologies. It has a long and rich history, a well-defined future supported by Oracle, and a large and active community of end users, system administrators, and application developers. We encourage Linux users and developers to complement their UNIX skills by learning more about Solaris 11 in the following chapters, not to replace Linux but to enhance their skills and to expand their repertoire of technical solutions. And current users of Solaris 10 will find both new capabilities and significant enhancements to existing features. So, let's get started!

NOTE
Unfortunately, as of this publication, no administrator tools are available to automate your upgrade from Solaris 10 to 11—you must perform a new installation and then manage movement of your data files separately. There are, however, some utilities to help you convert Solaris 10 procedures to those used in Solaris 11, such as the JumpStart to Automated Installer utility.

Reference

Information on licensing Oracle Solaris 11 can be found at www.oracle.com/technetwork/ licenses/solaris-cluster-express-license-167852.html.

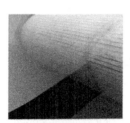

CHAPTER
2

Getting Ready
for Solaris 11

odern computers no longer achieve their performance solely through high clock rates on single-CPU microprocessors. In fact, you *can't* improve processor performance only in that way, due to the limitations of cooling and electrical power consumption. Instead, today's general-purpose microprocessors for servers, workstations, and even for laptops use a combination of *parallelism* and *multilevel caching* to reduce latency and to run multiple instruction streams simultaneously.

Oracle Solaris 11 is an ideal operating system for such microprocessors. In the next two chapters, we show you how to determine whether Solaris 11 can run on your x86 laptop, desktop, and servers, as well as on your SPARC systems, and how to install the OS using DVDs, files, and network repositories. We also explain how to install Solaris 11 as a "guest virtual machine" on top of a host operating system.

Where Solaris 11 Runs: Hardware Requirements

Typical "multicore" processors today from Oracle, Intel, AMD, IBM, and others have multiple CPU units on a single chip; each CPU generally has private and/or shared caches for instructions and data, along with dedicated memory management circuitry. Some processor cores, like those in the SPARC T4 and the Intel i7, include components for special purposes such as encryption, Ethernet packet processing, or I/O acceleration, as shown in Table 2-1.

Each core's CPU is designed to execute several instruction streams, or "threads," either simultaneously or in rapid succession; this is called *hyperthreading* or *chip multithreading*. A typical microprocessor core is shown in Figure 2-1.

Feature	SPARC T4	Intel Xeon E7-8800
Cores	8	10
Threads/core	8	2
Maximum core speed	3.0 GHz	2.4 GHz
L1 cache	$8 \times 16 + 16$KB	32KB
L2 cache	8×128KB	256KB
L3 cache	4MB	30MB
Crypto stream processors (CSPs)	1/core	1/core
Special-purpose circuits	Dual PCI Express, dual multithread 10GbE	Intel-VT virtualization acceleration, streaming SIMD extensions

TABLE 2-1.   *Features of Modern Processors Supported by Oracle Solaris 11*

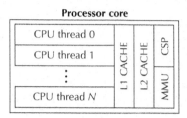

FIGURE 2-1. *Typical microprocessor "core" architecture, using multiple execution threads, L1 and L2 caches, a crypto stream processor (CSP), and memory management unit (MMU)*

The chips themselves include multiple copies of such cores, as well as caches shared by all the cores and additional memory management units, as shown in Figure 2-2. Collectively, the cores and caches on such chips may use nearly *one billion* transistors, all devoted to running multiple instructions in parallel and ensuring that data is close to the CPU when it is needed. Moreover, system manufacturers can build servers with more than one of such multicore chips. For example, Oracle's SPARC T4-4 server uses *four* multicore T4 processors, each with eight eight-thread cores, for a total of 256 CPU threads.

Although Solaris 11 is designed to run on a range of SPARC and x86 processors, Oracle has focused considerable attention to optimizing its performance on their newest multicore SPARC chip family, the T4. Solaris 11 has special awareness of the eight-core T4 architecture, its shared and dedicated instruction and data caches, its crypto acceleration hardware, and its on-chip

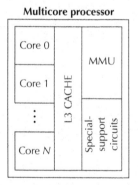

FIGURE 2-2. *Typical multicore processor architecture, using multiple CPU cores, a shared L3 cache, and additional memory management unit*

memory management units. Because of this hardware knowledge built into the operating system, Solaris 11 performs and scales extraordinarily well on T4-based systems, dynamically reallocating more CPU resources to "critical threads" as needed. Oracle and Sun also have worked closely with Intel to include similar optimizations of OS performance on x86 multicore processors.

A key piece of this processor technology is, of course, the operating system, which must recognize and make use of all that parallelism, caching, and special-purpose circuitry. In fact, Solaris was designed from its beginning to take advantage of multiple CPUs, eventually including multicore/ multithread processors such as the SPARC T3 and T4 and the Intel i3, i5, and i7. Additionally, Solaris automatically recognizes special-purpose components when they are present on the chip, such as the crypto stream processors; no application program changes are needed to exploit these hardware features.

The kinds of processors and systems that Solaris 11 runs on have implications not only for performance, but also for software licensing. Many software sellers license their applications according to the number of CPUs on the host's system. Generally, the greater number of chips or cores, the higher the cost of support, although more often such OS support costs are built into the base price and support subscription costs for the server hardware. But more about Solaris licensing later.

Oracle Solaris 11 can be installed and run on a wide variety of Oracle SPARC systems, from the smallest rack-mounted servers to the multinode, enterprise-class SPARC SuperCluster, as well as on a great range of x86 laptops, workstations, and servers from Oracle and from other x86 system vendors.

The *minimum* memory and disk space hardware requirements for Solaris 11 installation are listed in Table 2-2. Generally, nearly all *recent* 64-bit SPARC and x86 processors from Intel and from AMD will run this OS version.

	SPARC	X86 (64-bit Only)
Processor Architecture	Sun 4v (SPARC T series); SPARC64	Intel Xeon, i3, i5, i7; AMD Opteron
Minimum Memory	1GB	1GB
Recommended Memory	1GB	1GB
Minimum Disk Space	Live Media: 5GB Text Installer: 2.5GB Automated Installer: 2.5GB	Live Media: 5GB Text Installer: 2.5GB Automated Installer: 2.5GB
Recommended Disk Space	Live Media: 7GB Text Installer: 4.5GB Automated Installer: 13GB	Live Media: 7GB Text Installer: 4.5GB Automated Installer: 13GB

TABLE 2-2.   *Minimum Hardware Specifications for Oracle Solaris 11*

NOTE
SPARC processors have come in a variety of "architectures" over time, all supporting the same basic instruction set. However, Solaris 11 runs only on the SPARC 4v processor versions, and on later releases of Fujutsu's SPARC64 microprocessors; it will not run on older Sun systems using the UltraSPARC-I, UltraSPARC-II, UltraSPARC-IIe, UltraSPARC-III, UltraSPARC-III+, UltraSPARC-IIIi, UltraSPARC-IV, and UltraSPARC-IV+ architectures.

The Application Guarantee Program

Sun Microsystems has always promised binary compatibility of earlier Solaris applications on current OS versions, providing the application was built with standard Solaris interfaces and libraries. Oracle has continued this guarantee program for both SPARC and x86 Solaris applications, including those running in guest virtual machines. This means that applications that run on Solaris 2.6, 7, 8, 9, or 10 will run on Solaris 11 without the need to recompile, within each processor family. If there is a compatibility problem for a qualified application running on Solaris 11, the guarantee programs states that Oracle will analyze the problem and provide an appropriate remedy.

Additionally, the Solaris Source Code Guarantee states that qualified application code that meets the program guidelines and was developed and compiled on either SPARC or x86 platforms will successfully recompile and run on the other processor architecture. See the Oracle Application Guarantee Program website for details on how to check your applications for compliance with the compatibility guidelines.

Testing Your x86 System for Solaris 11 Compatibility

Oracle Solaris 11 will run on a wide variety of x86 systems from many different vendors; the Hardware Compatibility List (HCL), shown in Figure 2-3, catalogs the systems that have been shown to run the OS as well as details the supported devices and storage media.

CAUTION
"Runs on" or "reported to work" is not the same as "is fully supported by Oracle." For non-production purposes you can install Solaris 11 on many different laptops, workstations, and servers, but only systems manufactured by Oracle and by select other "non-Oracle systems" qualify for support contracts. Such systems have been tested with the Oracle Solaris and Hardware Certification Test Suite (HCTS) and the results reviewed, audited, and approved by Oracle for listing.

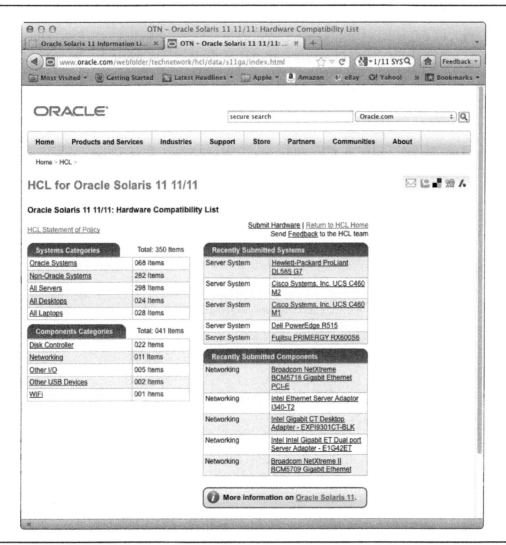

FIGURE 2-3.   *The Oracle Solaris Hardware Compatibility List website*

Also on the HCL site is the Java-based Oracle Device Detection Tool (www.oracle.com/webfolder/technetwork/hcl/hcts/device_detect.html), which lets you test your system for Solaris 10 or Solaris 11 compatibility (see Figure 2-4). This tool downloads, installs, and runs a Java program that detects your system's devices and lets you know whether there are drivers for your installed components; this tool runs on Solaris, Windows, Linux, Mac OS X, and FreeBSD operating systems.

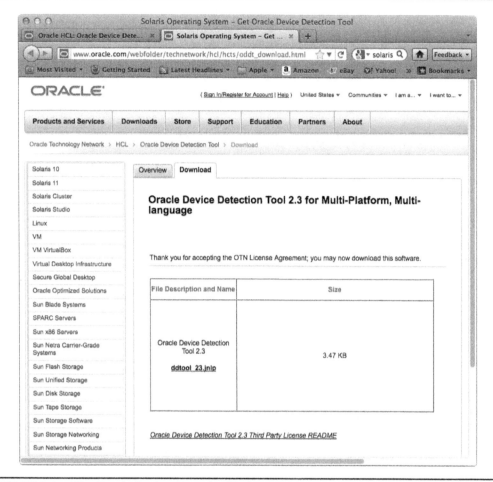

FIGURE 2-4.   *The Oracle Device Detection Tool*

To run the Device Detection Tool, first click the Accept License Agreement button to agree to its download and execution restrictions and then click the ddtool_23.jnlp link. The tool downloads a Java Web Start program to your system; you do not need to have Java installed on your system for this to work because a Java runtime program is included with the download (see Figure 2-5). Select the Open with Java Web Start Launcher option and then click OK. The tool will execute and display the screen shown in Figure 2-6. Click the Start button; the Java program will probe your system's hardware and will report whether device drivers are included with Solaris 11 or available for the devices it finds.

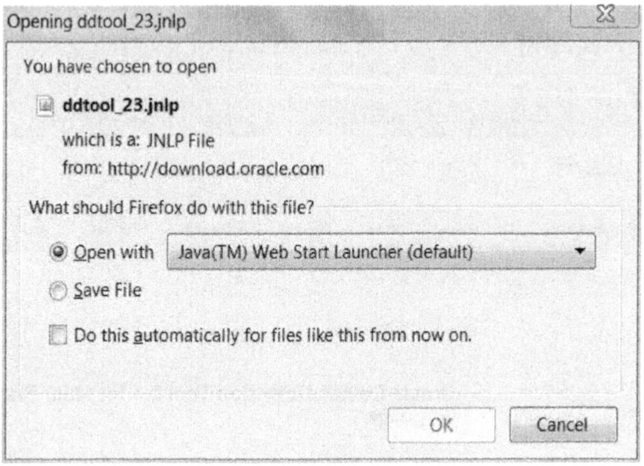

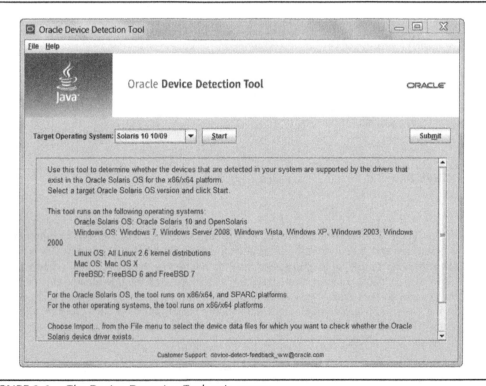

FIGURE 2-5. *The Java Web Start for the Device Detection Tool*

FIGURE 2-6. *The Device Detection Tool main screen*

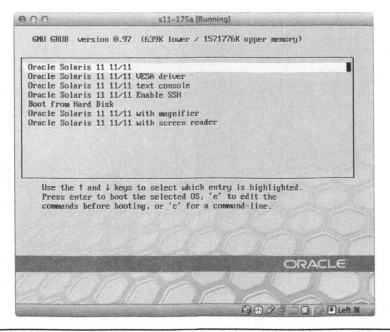

FIGURE 2-12.   *The Solaris 11 Live Media startup screen*

The first screen shows a list of several boot choices, all controlled by the GRUB boot loader program, which enables systems to use more than one OS. Select the first item, Oracle Solaris 11 11/11. The Live Media will start to boot, probe and recognize your system's devices, and then ask you to select the number of your preferred keyboard (see Figure 2-13); the default is "47. US-English."

NOTE
If the Live Media fails to boot, it may be due to your system's graphics subsystem not being recognized; if so, try the VESA or Text install modes. Also, do not try to "Boot from Hard Disk" at this time.

Next, select the number for your preferred language; the default is "3. English." If all goes well, after a few minutes, the next screen you see will be the Solaris 11 graphical environment, and you can start exploring (see Figure 2-14). If you were connected to the Internet when you booted the Live Media, Solaris 11 should have recognized that and configured its network connection automatically so that you can use the Firefox browser and other network programs. Remember, however, that this Live Media environment is not intended for any permanent work; it is merely a test/demo OS instance with no permanence. Removing the DVD and rebooting your system will return you to your original OS.

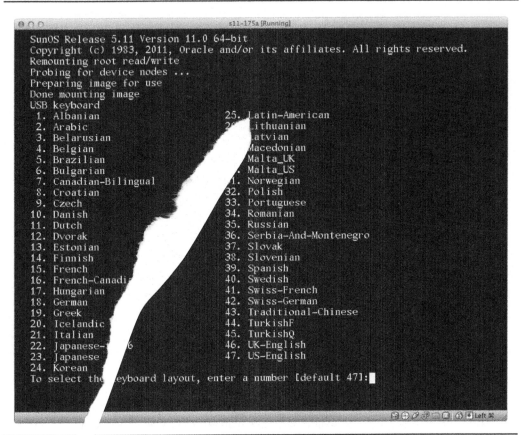

```
○ ○ ○                              s11-175a [Running]
SunOS Release 5.11 Version 11.0 64-bit
Copyright (c) 1983, 2011, Oracle and/or its affiliates. All rights reserved.
Remounting root read/write
Probing for device nodes ...
Preparing image for use
Done mounting image
USB keyboard
   1. Albanian                     25. Latin-American
   2. Arabic                       2  Lithuanian
   3. Belarusian                      Latvian
   4. Belgian                         Macedonian
   5. Brazilian                       Malta_UK
   6. Bulgarian                       Malta_US
   7. Canadian-Bilingual           1. Norwegian
   8. Croatian                     32. Polish
   9. Czech                        33. Portuguese
  10. Danish                       34. Romanian
  11. Dutch                        35. Russian
  12. Dvorak                       36. Serbia-And-Montenegro
  13. Estonian                     37. Slovak
  14. Finnish                      38. Slovenian
  15. French                       39. Spanish
  16. French-Canadi                40. Swedish
  17. Hungarian                    41. Swiss-French
  18. German                       42. Swiss-German
  19. Greek                        43. Traditional-Chinese
  20. Icelandic                    44. TurkishF
  21. Italian                      45. TurkishQ
  22. Japanese-     6              46. UK-English
  23. Japanese                     47. US-English
  24. Korean
To select the  eyboard layout, enter a number [default 47]:█
```

FIGURE 2-1   *The Live Media keyboard selection screen*

...ther exploration of the Live Media environment, you may want ...ecome the "root" user. If so, the password is **solaris**.

...eparing Your x86 System for Solaris 11 Installation

.fter experimenting with the Live Media environment for a while, you can select the Install Solaris 11 icon from the main screen and install the OS along with included application software onto your hard disk; that option allows you to select a target install disk, partition the disk if desired, and set up initial user accounts. We'll cover this and other installation processes in more detail in the next chapter. But if you are planning to install Solaris 11 on a laptop or PC that already has

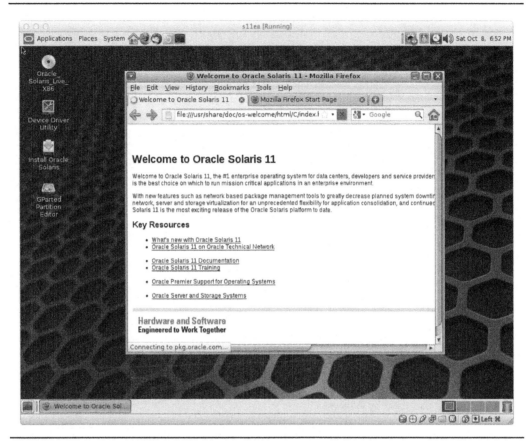

FIGURE 2-14.   *The Solaris 11 Live Media main screen*

Windows installed (we will assume you use Windows 7 in our examples), you will need to do a bit of preparation to make room for a second OS for your system. If you have no more need for your Windows environment, you can simply replace it with Solaris.

Your first task is to reserve space on your hard disk for Solaris 11. In order to do this, you should remove any unwanted files from your Windows system, clean up the Windows environment, and defragment your disk (move all files up near the start of the physical disk). Therefore, select the My Computer option from your Windows main screen; you should see a display of your disk devices like that shown in Figure 2-15.

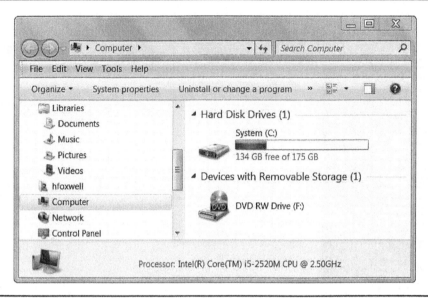

FIGURE 2-15. *A system's disk devices*

Double-click the hard disk displayed and you will then see the Properties display for that disk (see Figure 2-16); from the General tab, click the Disk Cleanup button. This will remove some temporary files used by Windows.

Next, select the Tools tab (see Figure 2-17), select the Defragment Now button, and then click Defragment Disk. This will start a possibly many-minutes-long process of moving all Windows files up near the beginning sector of your hard disk, leaving no gaps between the files, and expanding contiguous unused disk space at the end of the hard disk for your Solaris 11 installation to use (see Figure 2-18).

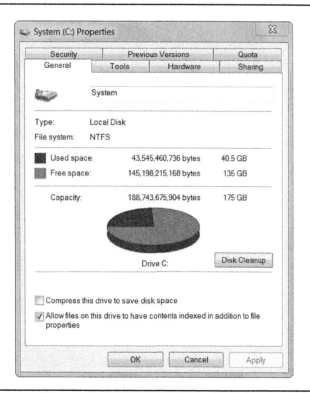

FIGURE 2-16.   *The Windows System (C:) Properties display*

Disk Partitions

When the disk defragmentation process is finished, you will have some free space at the end of the section of the disk where Windows is installed. Hard disks are generally divided into sections called "partitions." The first partition on most laptop and PC hard disks is the "boot partition," whose first block of data tells the system how to boot up. The next partition usually contains the Windows OS; there may be additional partitions for data or other operating systems (see Figure 2-19).

FIGURE 2-17.   *The Windows System Properties Tools screen*

Once you have completed your Windows disk cleanup and defragmentation, you are ready to install Solaris 11. Therefore, reboot your system using the Live Media disk. On the main screen is an icon for the GParted Partition Editor. You will use this tool to reallocate space on your hard disk. Double-click the GParted icon and you will see a display similar to that shown in Figure 2-20.

You can then use GParted to resize the Windows partition (and any empty or data partition) to accommodate Solaris 11. Be sure to leave extra space for future Windows files as well as sufficient space for future Solaris 11 files. Note that Solaris 11 needs at least 3GB of space, but you will probably want to allocate much more than that if it is available (see Figure 2-21).

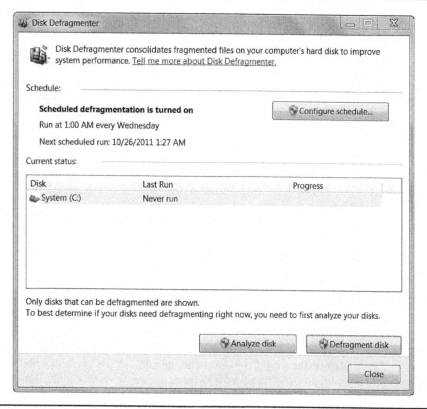

FIGURE 2-18.   *The Windows Disk Defragmenter screen*

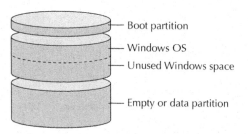

FIGURE 2-19.   *Typical hard disk partitions*

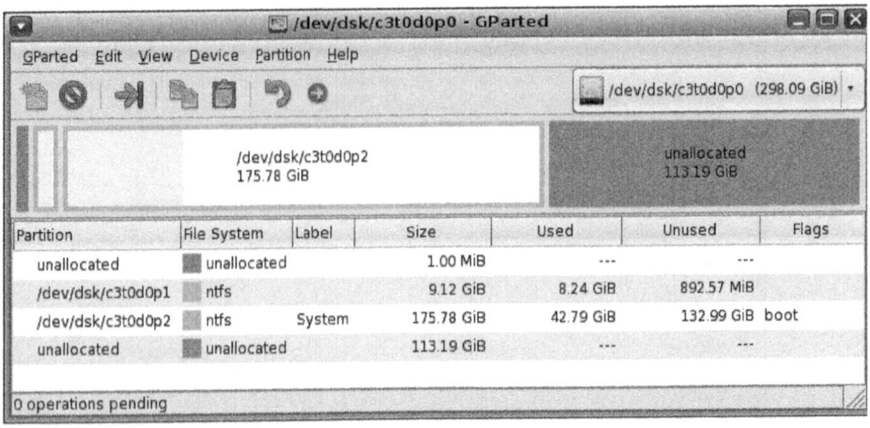

FIGURE 2-20.   *The GParted Partition Editor*

Now click the Install Solaris 11 icon on the main Live Media screen. You will see the Oracle Solaris Installer window (see Figure 2-22); select the empty partition you created with GParted, select Solaris2 for the partition type, and then click Next to begin your Solaris 11 installation. Chapter 3 will provide more detail about the installation process from this point.

After the installation has completed, you can then reboot your system. The GRUB boot loader will offer you a menu of operating systems to boot, including your original Windows OS and your newly installed Solaris 11 OS. Select which one you wish to boot, wait for it to start, log in, and start working. Note, however, that this "dual-boot" method only lets you use one OS at a time; to use the other OS, you must shut the current one down and then reboot to the other.

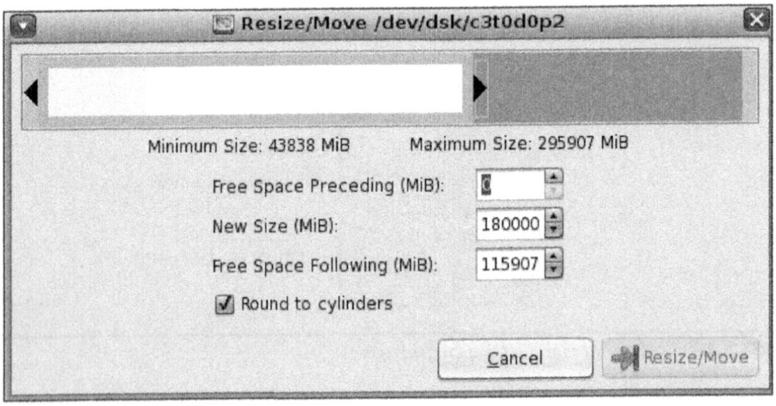

FIGURE 2-21.   *Resizing your hard disk partitions*

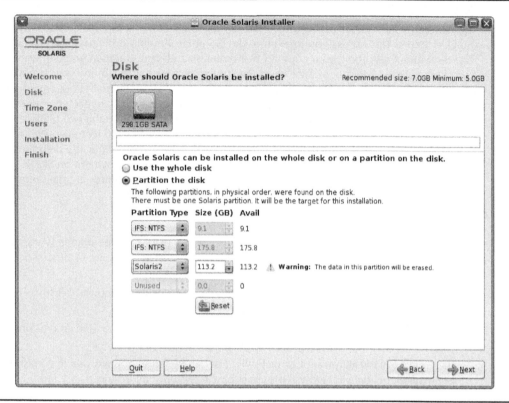

FIGURE 2-22. *Starting the Solaris Installer*

Other Installation Methods

The Interactive Text Installer is designed for server systems and others that either lack a graphical display or have an incompatible display. It provides a nongraphical, text-based installation interface that requires simple, keyboard-based responses, and has the same basic capabilities as the graphical installer. The files included with the Text Install download package are generally directed at servers, so the desktop environment is not included (although it can be installed later).

The Automated Installer feature of Solaris 11 allows for noninteractive, network-based OS installations onto one or more target systems, and includes support for customized install profiles for both SPARC and x86 systems as well as install-time selection of applications to be included.

You can also install Oracle Solaris 11 as a virtual machine (VM) image on x86 systems running Solaris, Windows, or OS X, by using hypervisor programs such as VirtualBox, VMware, Parallels, or other virtualization software; this lets you install, try out, and use Solaris 11 on your base operating system without replacing it.

We'll tell you more about these installation options in the next chapters.

Summary

You can start your familiarization with Solaris 11 using your x86 laptop or PC simply by booting the Live Media. This allows you to explore the OS environment and learn about some of its features without disturbing your current OS installation and data. But then you will want to install a working Solaris 11 instance. After checking your system for compatibility, you can install the OS either as a replacement for your current environment or as an alternate boot environment.

Because the Solaris 11 versions for SPARC and for x86 processors are each compiled from the same source code base, virtually all Solaris 11 features are identical on the two platforms, other than drivers for server-specific hardware. This means that *all* the key OS features—IPS, containers, ZFS, DTrace, SMF (all of what makes Solaris 11 so valuable)—work identically on both processor architectures. This lets you learn and develop on x86 systems for deployment on SPARC systems, and vice versa. And many of the installation and configuration procedures are the same as well.

References

Features and specifications for Oracle's SPARC T4 Processor can be found at www.oracle.com/us/products/servers-storage/servers/sparc-enterprise/t-series/sparc-t4-processor-ds-497205.pdf

www.oracle.com/technetwork/server-storage/solaris11/documentation/o11-136-sol11-sys-reqs-524534.pdf

The Oracle Application Guarantee Program can be found at www.oracle.com/us/products/servers-storage/solaris/solaris-guarantee-program-1426902.pdf.

The Oracle Solaris Hardware Compatibility List can be found at www.oracle.com/webfolder/technetwork/hcl/data/s11ga/systems/views/oracle_systems_all_results.page1.html.

CHAPTER
3

Installation Options

his chapter is for those of you who want to install Solaris 11 on a system for one or more individual users. In most cases, such users will want to log into a desktop, a laptop, or a workstation. In today's world of computing, all three systems are, for our purposes, essentially the same thing. Whatever the differences in hardware, you can use the same basic steps to install Solaris 11 on a system configured for one or more individual users.

Chapter 2 described the basic hardware requirements for Solaris 11 installations. In this chapter, you'll see how to get Solaris 11. As some of you may be using Solaris for the first time, it may be helpful to set up a "dual-boot" with another operating system such as Linux or Microsoft Windows. If you prefer, Solaris 11 can be configured on a number of virtual machine (VM) solutions.

Because users who are installing Solaris on the desktop for the first time might not yet be experts, this chapter describes the installation of Solaris 11, step by step, from the Live Media. Finally, this chapter includes an analysis of the bootloader, to help you understand how it boots Solaris 11 and other operating systems configured on the local machine.

For the most part, this chapter assumes you're using an x86 system. The Live Media is available only for x86 systems. The GRUB boot menu described in this chapter can be used only for x86 systems.

How to Get Solaris 11

Oracle welcomes you to download and install Solaris 11 for test purposes. Once testing is complete, Oracle requires the purchase of a valid license before you use Solaris 11 in production. With those provisos in mind, you can download Solaris 11 in a number of formats, including the Live Media described in Chapter 2.

Solaris 11 retains its advantages as an operating system for workstations. It's an excellent platform for sophisticated applications that can help you create detailed models of physical systems. For example, CATIA, which is extensively used in both the automotive and aerospace industries, has been ported to Solaris. The power of Solaris is useful when a designer wants to depict what are literally millions of parts used to build a commercial airplane.

Downloads

As noted in Chapter 2, you can download installation images associated with Solaris 11 from www.oracle.com/technetwork/server-storage/solaris11/downloads/index.html. Once you accept the license agreement, select the desired download, and log into an Oracle account, the download should begin. Just remember, these are big files that are practical to download only over a high-speed connection.

With that in mind, the available downloads are listed in Table 3-1. Just remember, available downloads vary with architecture. For example, the Live Media for DVD and USBs are available only for x86 systems. In addition, except for the file designed for the USB and the Preflight application checker, the files are available in ISO format.

Licensing

Before downloading Solaris 11, you should have accepted a license agreement. You can read a copy at http://www.oracle.com/technetwork/licenses/solaris-cluster-express-license-167852.html. In essence, Oracle allows you to use Solaris 11 for "developing, testing, prototyping,

Download	Description
Text install	CD-sized download. Available for both SPARC and x86 systems.
Automated installation	CD-sized download. Supports "hands-free" network-based minimal installations. Available for both SPARC and x86 systems.
Live Media	DVD-sized download. Boots a "Live" version of Solaris 11 directly, along with an installation program. Available only for x86 systems.
Repository image	Two DVD-sized downloads. Includes the files required to set up a local repository.

TABLE 3-1. *Basic Solaris 11 Media Downloads*

and demonstrating your applications, and not for any other purpose." Although some software included with Solaris was released under the Common Development and Distribution License (CDDL), Oracle's current licensing is more restrictive. In essence, even though you can test for an indefinite period, you're not allowed to use Solaris 11 for production purposes, unless you have an Oracle support contract.

The authors of this book are not lawyers. The descriptions in this section are not intended as legal advice. If you have any questions on the meaning of the license shown at http://www.oracle.com/technetwork/licenses/solaris-cluster-express-license-167852.html, consult appropriate legal counsel.

Write to DVD

Once you've downloaded one of the media files just described, you can "burn" that file to a CD or DVD. In other words, you can use available tools to take the contents of the ISO file and write them to appropriate media.

If you want to install Solaris 11 on a virtual machine (VM), you may not even need to burn that file to CD/DVD media. Most VM solutions can be configured to read ISO files directly as if they were CDs or DVDs. Furthermore, such virtual media is read at hard drive speeds. However, not all Solaris 11 installations are performed on VMs.

If you already have a Solaris 11 GUI desktop system available, you can burn a CD/DVD file with the Brasero Disc Burner, available from the Applications menu. As shown in Figure 3-1, it supports various methods for writing files to CD/DVD media, including the Burn Image option appropriate for ISO files. The same tool is available on most major Linux distributions. Most Microsoft CD/DVD-burning tools can also be used to burn ISO files to CD/DVD media in a similar fashion.

TIP
Avoid the **cdrecord** *command with DVDs on Solaris. Proper operation of DVD recorders is easier to manage with the* **cdrw** *command.*

Of course, this operation can be run from the command line with the **cdrw** command. First, you'll need to identify a list of available CD/DVD writers with the following command:

```
$ cdrw -l
```

FIGURE 3-1. *The Brasero Disc Burner*

The relevant output from our system is as follows:

```
Looking for CD devices...
    Node                        Connected Device                    Device type
---------------------+----------------------------------+------------------
  cdrom0             | PHILIPS  DVD+-RW SDVD8820 AD20 | CD Reader/Writer
```

That tells us the relevant node is cdrom0. To burn the Solaris 11 DVD ISO file to blank media on that node, we'd run the following command, where the **-d** represents the device and the **-i** specifies the ISO file:

```
$ cdrw -d cdrom0 -i sol-11-1111-live-x86.iso
```

If successful, it should proceed with messages such as this:

```
Initializing device...done.
Formatting media...done
Writing track 1...
```

Write to a USB Key

If you want to use Solaris 11 to write a .usb file to an USB key, you'll want to use the **usbcopy** command. It's available from the distribution-constructor package. The following command, as the root administrative user, installs that package from the command line. For more information on the **pkg** command, see Chapter 11.

```
# pkg install distribution-constructor
```

Once this package is installed, you can "burn" the files from the downloaded .usb package to a connected USB stick. The following command burns the appropriate Solaris 11 Live Media file to a USB stick:

```
# usbcopy sol-11-1111-live-x86.usb
```

If multiple USB devices are connected, you're prompted to select the desired device.

A Focus on Workstations

New features in Solaris 11 include a renewed focus on the workstation. Oracle has included the GNOME desktop environment, described in Chapter 5. Because it's the same desktop environment in common use on Linux, it can ease the transition for such users. The Solaris HCL includes a number of desktop and laptop systems. It even works with some wireless network adapters. For the latest information, see www.oracle.com/webfolder/technetwork/hcl/data/s11ga/index.html.

Just be aware, Oracle hasn't tested Solaris 11 against the full range of available workstations. If you want support for a system that has not been officially tested, follow the procedures associated with the Oracle Hardware Certification Test Suite, available from www.oracle.com/webfolder/technetwork/hcl/hcts/index.html.

A Range of Installation Scenarios

In this section, you'll review some tips and tricks associated with installing Solaris 11 on the same machine as a different operating system.

In many cases, administrators will install Solaris 11 on a wide variety of VMs. That's sufficient for a large number of users. However, there are situations where direct access to hardware is appropriate. CAD applications commonly used on Solaris such as CATIA require direct hardware access. Administrators who want to set up Solaris 11 as a VM host will also want to install directly on physical hardware.

Of course, in production, Solaris 11 would be the only operating system on a machine. However, users who haven't yet purchased an Oracle support contract will want to be able to use it on a machine that may also be used for different operating systems.

New Systems

It's simplest to set up Solaris 11 on a new computer, with empty hard drives. If you plan to designate part or all of a hard drive to a different operating system, just be sure to leave that space free for those operating systems during the installation process described later in this chapter. And if you're planning to install either Windows or Linux after installing Solaris 11, take care with the bootloader.

Linux

Many Linux users in the job market may find themselves wanting to learn Solaris. Such users may be motivated to set up Solaris 11 in a "dual-boot" with Linux. With that in mind, one Solaris problem associated with a Linux partition scheme is based on the Linux swap partition. If you're familiar with **fdisk**, you may realize that the Linux swap partition is actually labeled "Linux swap / Solaris." As such, the Solaris installation program recognizes the Linux swap partition as a Solaris native partition. This is especially important where the swap partition comes before the designated Solaris partition.

During the installation process, you'll need to deactivate the swap partition in order to keep the installation program from trying to install Solaris 11 on that partition.

NOTE
When installing Oracle Solaris on a system that also has a Linux swap partition, you may need to deactivate that swap partition during the Solaris 11 installation process.

Because the Solaris 11 installation process does not recognize Linux, you'll have to follow up after installation is complete. Save the appropriate entries from the GRUB bootloader in Linux. Shortly, you'll see where to write those entries in the Solaris version of GRUB.

Microsoft Windows

The Solaris 11 installation program recognizes Microsoft-formatted partitions, including the partition with the actual Windows operating system. It automatically includes appropriate entries in the bootloader, supporting access to Windows from the GRUB menu.

However, if you install Microsoft Windows after installing Solaris, you'll need to restore the bootloader. The process involves booting from Live Media such as the DVD. The basic steps are as follows:

1. Boot from Live Media (either the DVD or USB drive).

2. From the GRUB menu that appears, select Oracle Solaris 11/11 text console.

3. Because direct logins as the root user are disabled, you'll have to log in as the standard Solaris 11 Live Media user, jack. The designated password is also jack.

4. You can now assume root administrative privileges with the **su** command, with the designated password, solaris.

5. Now check the status of ZFS pools with the following command (for more information, see Chapter 9):

   ```
   # zpool status
   ```

6. You should see output similar to the following:

   ```
     pool: rpool
    state: ONLINE
     scan: none requested
   config:

           NAME        STATE     READ WRITE CKSUM
           rpool       ONLINE       0     0     0
           c5d0s0      ONLINE       0     0     0
   ```

The device file is shown at the end of the output. The c5d0s0 represents "controller 5, disk 0, slice 0." If this were a SATA or SCSI device, the file would be something like c5t0d0s0, where t0 represents target 0. If you don't see this type of output, or see an error message such as "no pools available," you'll need to bring the pool into the configuration. The **zpool import** command lists the pools available to import; the **zpool import -D** command can frequently recover lost pools.

7. You can now write the pointer to the GRUB bootloader with the **installgrub** command. The following command is based on the pool named rpool, with the c5d0s0 device as shown in the output to the **zpool status** command:

    ```
    # installgrub /boot/grub/stage1 /boot/grub/stage2 /dev/rdsk/c5d0s0
    ```

8. If successful, you'll see messages associated with the writing of both stage 1 and stage 2 of the GRUB bootloader.

Solaris 10

Oracle encourages administrators to set up Solaris 10 as virtual machines within Solaris 11 zones. In that way, enterprises can still use Solaris 10 during any transition period. However, the "Installing Oracle Solaris 11 Systems" document suggests the following: "If you need to preserve a specific Solaris Volume Table of Contents (VTOC) slice in your current operating system, use the text installer." You can read more about the text installation in Chapter 4.

Notes on Virtual Machines

Solaris 11 can be tested on a variety of VM solutions. Unfortunately for those who have only x86 hardware, there is no low-cost way to emulate the SPARC CPUs closely associated with Solaris. However, there are a variety of virtual machine solutions for x86 systems that can be used for testing.

 NOTE
Although there is a SPARC hypervisor for the Kernel-based Virtual Machine (KVM) software associated with Linux, it is not recognized by the Solaris 11 SPARC installation.

Oracle makes a preconfigured virtual machine image available for users who run VirtualBox. You can download it from www.oracle.com/technetwork/server-storage/solaris11/downloads/virtual-machines-1355605.html. Uncompress the download, and then open VirtualBox. Click File | Import Appliance to use the associated wizard to import that appliance.

In this chapter, although we used the KVM solution common on Linux systems, early in our testing, Solaris 11 was not installable on KVM. Today, it leads to minor device driver problems, as illustrated in Figure 3-2. To access this tool, click Applications | System Tools | Device Driver Utility.

We also tested these installations on Oracle's VirtualBox system. For more information on the virtual machines that can be installed on Solaris 11, see Chapter 4.

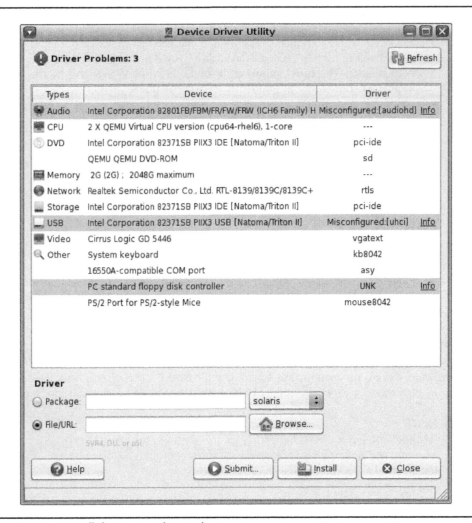

FIGURE 3-2.   *Not all devices are detected.*

The GUI Interactive Installation

Earlier in this chapter, you reviewed methods for creating different forms of Live Media. From the resulting media, you can start a fully functional version of Solaris 11. It includes a complete GUI desktop environment described in Chapter 5. Once booted, you can start the interactive installation process. In this section, you'll review the boot and installation process, step by step. Live Media is limited to x86 systems.

TIP
If you're currently running Linux, and are preparing a system for a "dual-boot" with Solaris 11, save the stanza associated with your GRUB configuration. If you're running a system with GRUB 1 (or 0.97), it's available in the /boot/grub/grub.conf file. If you're running a system with GRUB 2, you'll have to get that information from the GRUB menu shown during the boot process. More information on how to set up GRUB for Solaris and Linux is shown later in this chapter.

Boot the Live Media

Most modern computers support booting from either the CD/DVD drive or connected USB media. The instructions that follow are general, and depend on the initial process for powering up a system.

When most computers are powered up, they run a Power On Self Test (POST) to check for connected hardware such as RAM, hard drives, network cards, and more. Once the POST is complete, you may be able to directly access a boot menu with a key such as F12. If a boot menu is not available, you may need to access the BIOS (Basic Input/Output System) or UEFI (Universal Extensible Firmware Interface) menus for the system with a key such as F1, F2, DEL (or others). Because these are general instructions, you may need to consult hardware documentation for details.

If successful, you'll see a Grand Unified Bootloader (GRUB) menu similar to that shown in Figure 3-3. If you're booting from the Live USB, the Boot From Hard Disk option does not appear. The GRUB options shown are described here:

- **Oracle Solaris 11 11/11**　Boots the standard Live Media to a GUI desktop.
- **Oracle Solaris 11 11/11 VESA Driver**　Uses the low-level graphics driver associated with the Video Electronics Standards Association (VESA), which is an option if a GUI does not appear from the regular Live Media option.
- **Oracle Solaris 11 11/11 Text Console**　Boots the standard Live Media to a text console; see the note for configured users and associated passwords.
- **Oracle Solaris 11/11 Enable SSH**　Boots the standard Live Media; enables the SSH service for remote access.
- **Boot From Hard Disk**　Normally passes control to the Master Boot Record (MBR) of the first or second local hard drive.
- **Oracle Solaris 11/11 With Magnifier**　Includes a magnifier for those who just need a bit of help reading the GUI screen.
- **Oracle Solaris 11/11 With Screen Reader**　Adds a screen reader for help with the GUI screen.

As of this writing, the last two options add a **-B assistive_tech=magnifier** or a **-B assistive_tech=reader** command. However, neither option is relevant to the functions specified. They make no changes to the GUI during the installation process.

However, both a magnifier and a screen reader are available through a component of the default GNOME desktop, the Orca Screen Reader. Orca's screen reader is based on GNOME speech services. Orca's magnifier supports user focus on a specific part of the screen, at a default magnification of 4x.

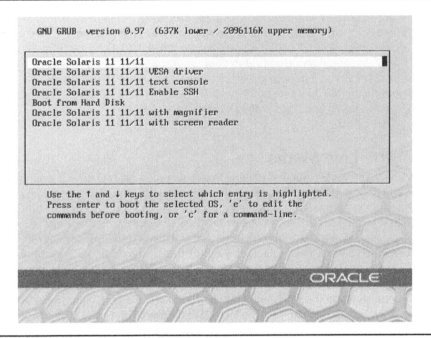

FIGURE 3-3. *The Live DVD GRUB menu*

Answer Basic Questions

Unless you've told GRUB to hand over control to the MBR of a hard disk, you're prompted next with two basic questions. First, you're prompted to select one of 47 keyboards and then to select one of 10 languages, as shown in Figure 3-4.

These answers are used to set language and keyboard parameters, not only for the Live version of Solaris, but also as prerequisite entries for the interactive GUI installation.

Start the Interactive GUI Installation

Now you'll install Solaris 11 with the program available from the Live Media. The GUI desktop that appears includes an Install Oracle Solaris link to the installation program, as shown in Figure 3-5. Select it to run the **gui-install** program with administrative privileges. In the subsections that follow, you'll explore the different steps associated with the interactive installation.

Basic Parameters

When you start the Live Media–based installation program, it opens the window shown in Figure 3-6. The basic steps are listed in the left pane; the figure is the welcome screen. As suggested by the comments, it includes a hyperlink to the current release notes. Those notes include an overview of installation requirements, known installation bugs, runtime problems, and update issues.

```
 4. Belgian                     28. Macedonian
 5. Brazilian                   29. Malta_UK
 6. Bulgarian                   30. Malta_US
 7. Canadian-Bilingual          31. Norwegian
 8. Croatian                    32. Polish
 9. Czech                       33. Portuguese
10. Danish                      34. Romanian
11. Dutch                       35. Russian
12. Dvorak                      36. Serbia-And-Montenegro
13. Estonian                    37. Slovak
14. Finnish                     38. Slovenian
15. French                      39. Spanish
16. French-Canadian             40. Swedish
17. Hungarian                   41. Swiss-French
18. German                      42. Swiss-German
19. Greek                       43. Traditional-Chinese
20. Icelandic                   44. TurkishF
21. Italian                     45. TurkishQ
22. Japanese-type6              46. UK-English
23. Japanese                    47. US-English
24. Korean
To select the keyboard layout, enter a number [default 47]:47

 1. Chinese - Simplified
 2. Chinese - Traditional
 3. English
 4. French
 5. German
 6. Italian
 7. Japanese
 8. Korean
 9. Portuguese - Brazil
10. Spanish
To select the language you wish to use, enter a number [default is 3]: █
```

FIGURE 3-4. *Select a keyboard layout and language.*

FIGURE 3-5. *Access the installation program from the Live Media desktop.*

FIGURE 3-6. *Starting the graphical installation*

Risks

Before proceeding, you should be aware of a few risks. If you're installing Solaris 11 on a system where the data matters, back it up! If needed, stop the installation now and make appropriate backups. Steps taken from this point forward may change local partitions or even entire hard drives, and may make it at best difficult to recover any data on that system.

If you're installing Solaris 11 in a dual-boot configuration with another operating system, make sure you know how partitions are currently configured on local drives. You should know the position and size of each partition on each hard drive. That information is readily available with tools such as Microsoft's Disk Administrator and Linux's **fdisk**.

Partitions for Solaris and More

The installation program allows you to create partitions. You'll need to set up at least one Solaris partition for installation. If desired, you could set up that partition to span the entire hard drive. However, if multiple Solaris partitions are configured from the GUI, the installation process will stop with an error message.

TIP
If you want to set up a logical volume or RAID array, you'll need to use the tools associated with the ZFS filesystem described in Chapter 9.

Although the installation program supports the creation of Solaris partitions, it recognizes a whole variety of partition types. Figure 3-7 illustrates the response of the installation program to one of our systems that is also configured with Linux and Microsoft Windows, on the "149.0GB ATA" drive shown near the top of the screen. If desired, you can also configure partitions on any other detected drives. You may recognize NTFS as the current standard Microsoft filesystem, FAT32 as the older Microsoft filesystem, and so on. The Linux native filesystems are somewhat generic since they may be associated with any number of Linux formats.

If you have a map of the current filesystem configuration, you can use this information to identify those partitions you want to keep, such as those with an alternative operating system or a user home directory.

If there's already an existing Linux swap partition on a local hard drive, it can fool the Solaris GUI installation program. A partition that has the Linux swap label is also read as a Solaris partition. Although the format is different from the Solaris2 partition shown in Figure 3-7, it is still recognized as a Solaris partition. If it comes before the actual Solaris partition, it takes precedence. The solution is to set up the Linux swap partition as "Unused." Even though you'll see a warning that "The data in this partition will be erased," permanent data should not be stored in Linux swap partitions.

Once you've configured a single partition for Solaris 11 installation, click Next to continue. From Figure 3-7, we've configured the last partition with 61.6GB of space. While that is well

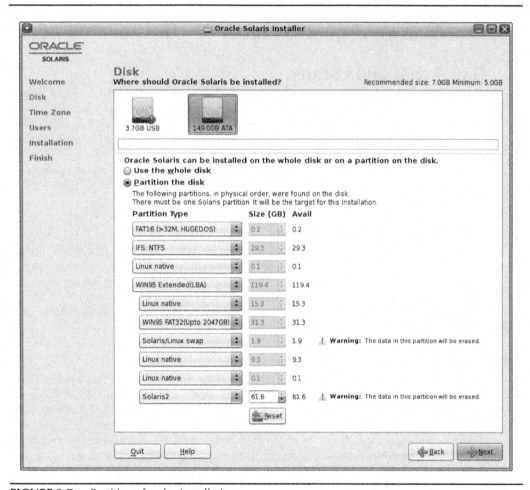

FIGURE 3-7. *Partitions for the installation*

above the recommended and minimum partition sizes shown above (7.0GB and 5.0GB, respectively), it leaves room for services, databases, and user files. If you set a Solaris partition below the minimum size, the installation process stops with an error message. If you set a Solaris partition between the recommended and minimum sizes, the installation program prompts you with an error message.

TIP
The Solaris installation program does not recognize the standard virtual disks associated with the QEMU hypervisor. If you do install Solaris 11 on such a VM solution, you'll need to have that VM emulate a more standard storage device such as IDE (SATA) or SCSI.

NOTE
If you're running the installation program on a system with less than 900MB of RAM, the recommended and minimum partition sizes are 8.0GB and 6.0GB, respectively.

Time Zones and Locales

In the next step shown in Figure 3-8, you'll set the time zone associated with the local system. The dots shown each specify a major city associated with every available time zone. If you're not sure which dot to pick, select options sequentially. You can select a region, associated with a continent or ocean. You can then select a location, typically a country. For larger countries, you can then select an appropriate time zone.

After installation is complete, you can check the result with the **date** and the **date -u** commands, which displays the local time, along with Greenwich Mean Time. Click Next to continue.

Users and Hostnames

The standard user you create in Figure 3-9 is important. Because Solaris 11 does not normally allow direct logins by the root administrative user, the first user gets "sudo" level privileges (described in Chapter 12). In other words, that user is allowed to access administrative utilities with nothing more than his password and username. The designated computer hostname is seen by directory services. Information from this screen is added to the /etc/passwd, /etc/sudoers, and the /etc/hosts files.

Final Step

The final step is to review the settings configured so far. One configuration is shown in Figure 3-10. It specifies the size of the partition to be erased and then formatted with the ZFS filesystem. It includes information on the amount of data to be written to the formatted partition during the installation process. The software for the operating system was developed by Oracle Solaris. The time zone should match that for the local system. The locale of default language and language (keyboard) support was determined when you answered the related questions during the boot process for the Live DVD.

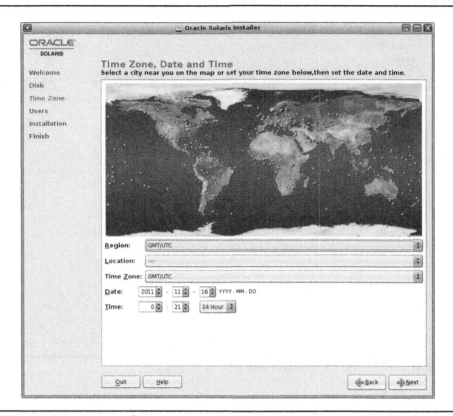

FIGURE 3-8. *Time zone configuration*

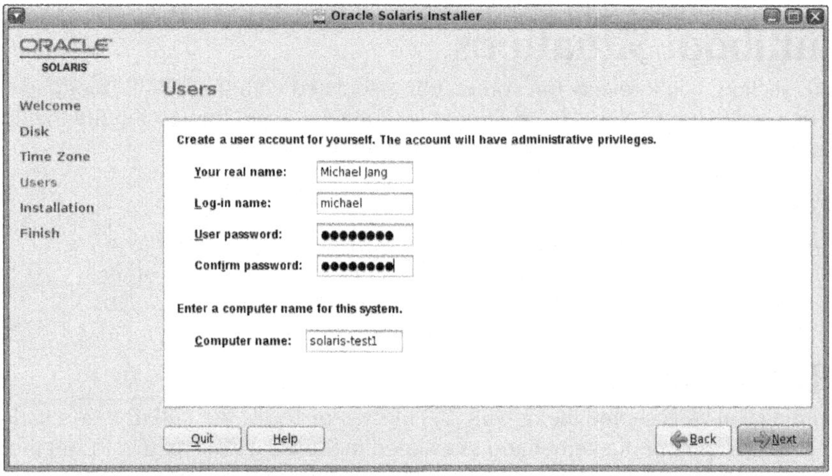

FIGURE 3-9. *Users and hosts*

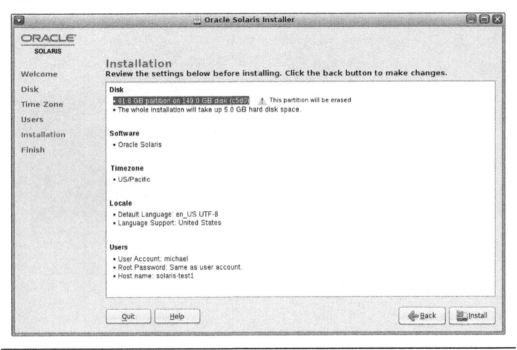

FIGURE 3-10. *Before installation begins*

Finally, the user and host information should match what you just configured in the previous section. When complete, click Install to begin the installation process. The speed of the installation depends on local hardware.

Multiboot Situations

In this section, you'll review the commands associated with the GRUB bootloader and how they can be used to boot Solaris. In addition, you'll review if and how to modify the GRUB bootloader to support access to Microsoft and Linux operating systems.

NOTE
If you're a Linux user, be aware that the Solaris GRUB package has been enhanced to boot the default Solaris 11 ZFS filesystem. In other words, you can't use the Linux GRUB package to directly boot Solaris.

GRUB on Solaris

Assuming you've accepted the default ZFS filesystem pools, the GRUB menu includes commands that load the appropriate kernel and associated modules. It's instructive to run these commands from the **grub>** prompt. Print out a copy of the GRUB commands in the menu.lst file. The one that's used for ZFS-based systems can be found in the /boot directory of the local pool. The standard ZFS pool, which you can confirm with the **zfs list** command, is rpool. Specifically, the output includes the following entry, which lists the pool associated with the top-level root directory:

```
NAME                   USED   AVAIL  REFER  MOUNTPOINT
rpool/ROOT/solaris     3.59G  54.2G  3.19G  /
```

Based on that bit of data, you can find the menu.lst file in the /rpool/boot/grub directory. The relevant stanza from one of our systems is shown here:

```
title Oracle Solaris 11 11/11
     bootfs rpool/ROOT/solaris
     kernel$ /platform/i86pc/kernel/amd64/unix -B $ZFS-BOOTFS,console=graphics
     module$ /platform/i86pc/amd64/boot_archive
```

The options shown in your Solaris installation may vary. With that information in hand, reboot the system. When the GRUB menu shown in Figure 3-11 appears, you may see more than one option. In that case, select Oracle Solaris 11 11/11. Note how that option matches the **title** entry from the associated stanza in the menu.lst file.

Press E to edit the commands associated with the Oracle Solaris 11 11/11 option. The commands that appear should be familiar; they're the commands from the menu.lst file.

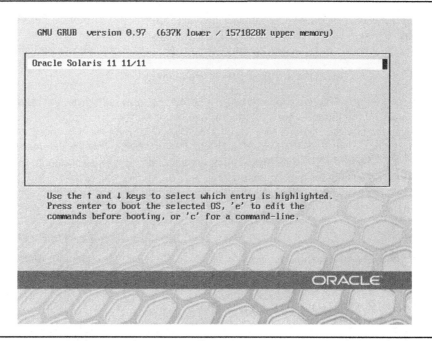

FIGURE 3-11. *GRUB from a Solaris 11 installation*

Now press c to open a **grub>** prompt. At the prompt, run the first command in the stanza. For the configuration shown previously, it's as follows:

```
grub> bootfs rpool/ROOT/solaris
```

The **bootfs** command sets the current ZFS boot filesystem to the one associated with the top-level root directory. For more information on **bootfs**, run the **help bootfs** command from the **grub>** prompt.

Next, run the full **kernel$** directive. For those of you who know the Linux version of GRUB, the **kernel** directive doesn't recognize Solaris kernels. The **kernel$** directive has been enhanced. With the options shown next, it is designed to load the image of the Solaris 11 kernel (**unix**) from the noted directory. The **i86pc** refers to generic PC platforms, compiled for 64-bit systems (**amd64**).

```
grub> kernel$ /platform/i86pc/kernel/amd64/unix
```

That's the command used for the default boot process from the Live DVD. But that's not enough for a Solaris 11 system installed on the hard drive. The following options are added to this command to provide boot support for ZFS filesystems: **-B $ZFS-BOOTFS**. The **console=graphics** includes a splash screen during the boot process. If you omit this option, the boot process will scroll all messages visibly to the screen.

```
grub> kernel$ /platform/i86pc/kernel/amd64/unix -B $ZFS-BOOTFS,console=graphics
```

When run from the **grub>** prompt, the full **kernel$** command (just shown) returns several messages. They specify where the kernel is to be loaded into memory, include the path to the PCI (Peripheral Component Interconnect) device (normally the hard drive), and set an ID for that device.

The next command specifies the module image to be loaded, from a similar directory:

```
grub> module$ /platform/i86pc/amd64/boot_archive
```

Because the hard drive should now be a known, the messages from the **module$** directive specify where the modules are loaded into memory.

From the standard Solaris 11 installation, the size of the kernel is about 2MB, quite a bit smaller than the modules in the boot_archive (at over 40MB). That's a statement on the nature of Solaris 11, which includes a relatively small kernel, coupled with a substantial number of modules for device drivers, filesystems, and more.

Once the modules are loaded, you can proceed directly to the boot process with the following command at the **grub>** prompt:

```
grub> boot
```

If you want to make a permanent change, you'll have to edit the menu.lst file directly after the system has booted.

A GRUB Option for Windows

GRUB doesn't boot Microsoft operating systems directly. When a user selects an option for a Windows operating system, the commands specified in the associated GRUB stanza hands off responsibility to the Microsoft bootloader, whether it be the older NTLDR or the current BOOTMGR system. To that end, Solaris identifies the partition with the bootable Microsoft format and then hands off responsibility to the Microsoft bootloader with the following two commands:

```
rootnoverify (hd0,1)
chainloader +1
```

The **rootnoverify** command itself identifies the bootable partition (**root**), but does not try to mount it (**noverify**). The options identify the partition on a hard drive (**hd**), on the first drive, on the second partition.

The **chainloader +1** command identifies the second bootloader on the first sector of the noted partition.

A GRUB Option for Linux

If as a Linux user, you choose to install Solaris 11 in a dual-boot setup with Linux, you may be in for a surprise, as Solaris 11 uses GRUB 0.97. You might think, "Ah hah! It's the same GRUB that's used on several popular Linux distributions, such as Red Hat Enterprise Linux. But that would be a mistake. GRUB for Solaris has been enhanced with the ability to boot and read the ZFS filesystem. Therefore, although the GRUB commands used to boot Solaris may be unfamiliar, Linux stanzas do work in Solaris GRUB.

If you're installing Solaris 11 in a dual-boot configuration with Linux, save the options for the preferred GRUB entry. Red Hat Enterprise Linux (RHEL) includes a GRUB configuration file, grub.conf, in the Linux /boot/grub directory. For example, the following is an appropriate stanza to save from an installed version of RHEL 6:

```
title Red Hat Enterprise Linux Server (2.6.32-131.17.1.el6.x86_64)
        root (hd0,5)
        kernel /vmlinuz-2.6.32-131.17.1.el6.x86_64 ro root=UUID=781a1bb4-
        6956-49bb-8a98-fca5e58a355b rd_NO_LUKS rd_NO_LVM rd_NO_MD rd_NO_DM
        LANG=en_US.UTF-8 SYSFONT=latarcyrheb-sun16 KEYBOARDTYPE=pc KEYTABLE=us
        crashkernel=128M rhgb quiet
        initrd /initramfs-2.6.32-131.17.1.el6.x86_64.img
```

If you're running GRUB version 2, as is typical for newer releases of Ubuntu or Debian Linux, the menu.lst file does not exist. Two options are available in this case:

- *Write down the information from the active GRUB menu.* Reboot the system; when the Linux-based GRUB menu appears, make selections to review the details of the desired Linux kernel to be booted. The options shown should be similar to the Red Hat GRUB stanza just shown.

- *Translate the information from the grub.cfg file.* Linux distributions, which use GRUB 2.0, build the boot menu from the grub.cfg file. It's written in a special scripting language.

TIP
*If you just want to use GRUB to hand over control to a second bootloader, use the **rootnoverify** and **chainloader** commands. For example, it can give control to an option such as the Linux Loader (LILO), written to the first sector of a specified partition. It can even pass control to Linux GRUB version 0.97 or 2.0 on a specified partition.*

Configure a GRUB Password

By default, GRUB is not password protected. A black-hat hacker could conceivably power-cycle a system, access GRUB commands for editing, and gain root administrative privileges by booting in single-user mode.

NOTE
In the UNIX and Linux communities, there are differences of opinion concerning the term hacker. For this book, users who are doing good computer work are "white-hat hackers." In contrast, users who are working with computers for malicious purposes are "black-hat hackers."

Therefore, any Solaris administrator who is interested in security will want to set up a GRUB password. And that's possible with the help of the **grub>** prompt. With the **grub** command in the /boot/grub/bin directory, you can access the **grub>** prompt from within Solaris. The process relies on the **md5crypt** command, which is available only from within GRUB. One weakness of the **md5crypt** command is that it prompts for a password only once. In addition, it "salts" the hashed password that appears in a random fashion. In other words, if you run the **md5crypt** command twice, the hashed password that appears will vary.

To set up a GRUB password, take the following steps:

1. Open a command-line interface.

2. Run the **/boot/grub/bin/grub** command.

3. When the **grub>** prompt appears, run the **md5crypt** command.

4. When the password prompt appears, type in a password carefully. Because the password prompt appears only once and is obscured by asterisks, there's no way to know at this point if you make a mistake in typing. When we typed in solaris as the password, the following hash appeared:

   ```
   $1$G7nnN0$tBPrihh2TAjRqO5Rx1woK1
   ```

5. Copy the hashed password. The one sign associated with the password is $1, which is the default prefix for Message Digest 5 (MD5) encryption.

6. Exit from GRUB with the **quit** command.

7. Open the menu.lst file in the /rpool/boot/grub directory. Before the first **title** command, enter the following:

   ```
   password --md5 $1$G7nnN0$tBPrihh2TAjRqO5Rx1woK1
   ```

8. Save the changes. If successful, the next time you access the GRUB menu, it should include the following statement:

   ```
   Press enter to boot the selected OS or 'p' to enter a password to unlock
   the next set of features.
   ```

With the GRUB password in place, black-hat hackers are "stuck" booting one of the options configured in your menu.lst file.

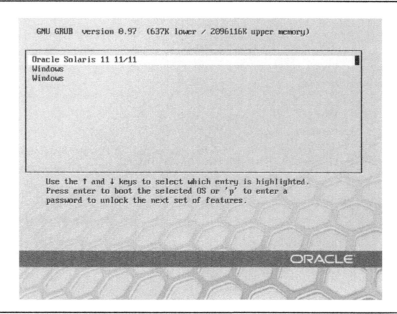

GNU GRUB version 0.97 (637K lower / 2096116K upper memory)

Oracle Solaris 11 11/11
Windows
Windows

Use the ↑ and ↓ keys to select which entry is highlighted.
Press enter to boot the selected OS or 'p' to enter a
password to unlock the next set of features.

ORACLE

FIGURE 3-12. *A troubled triple-boot*

A Triple-Boot Scenario

In the process of creating this book, we set up a triple-boot on a Dell e1405 laptop system. CentOS Linux 5.4 and Windows XP were already installed on that system before we added Solaris 11. When installation was complete, we saw the menu shown in Figure 3-12.

CentOS Linux is built on the source code released by Red Hat for its Enterprise Linux product. It's strange to think that Solaris recognizes Microsoft but does not recognize its sister UNIX-based operating system. You might think the option was mislabeled. But that is not so. The Solaris 11 installation process specifies the second "Windows" option on the partition with the Linux swap partition.

The final result that works on our triple-boot system is based on the menu.lst file shown in Figure 3-13. The figure is slightly modified to group the active commands together, which are explained here, starting with the **default** directive.

In this case, **default 0** points to the first available stanza to boot, based on the title directives. In other words, based on Figure 3-13, if you wanted to configure Windows as the default during the boot process, you'd set **default 1**. If you wanted to configure CentOS Linux as the default during the boot process, you'd set **default 2**.

The **timeout 30** directive specifies that unless some action is taken within 30 seconds after the GRUB menu appears, GRUB will automatically boot the default stanza.

The **splashimage** directive includes the default screen included with GRUB. It works with the colors assigned to the **foreground** and **background** directives.

Every stanza starts with a **title** directive. The value of that directive is shown in the GRUB menu that boots in Figure 3-14. The details under each **title** directive were described earlier in this chapter.

```
#
#   kernel /platform/i86pc/kernel/amd64/unix <boot-args> -B prop=value,...
#
#
#
default 0
timeout 30
splashimage /boot/grub/splash.xpm.gz
foreground 343434
background F7FBFF
#
title Oracle Solaris 11 11/11
        bootfs rpool/ROOT/solaris
        kernel$ /platform/i86pc/kernel/amd64/unix -B $ZFS-BOOTFS,console=graphics
        module$ /platform/i86pc/amd64/boot_archive
title Windows
        rootnoverify (hd0,1)
        chainloader +1
title CentOS 5
        root (hd0,2)
        kernel /vmlinuz-2.6.18-164.11.1.el5 ro root=LABEL=/ rhgb nofb quiet
        initrd /initrd-2.6.18-164.11.1.el5.img
```

FIGURE 3-13.   *The GRUB menu configuration file*

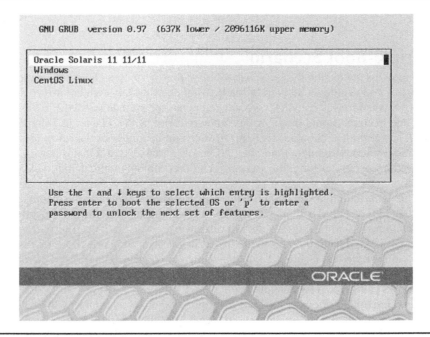

FIGURE 3-14.   *The modified GRUB menu*

Summary

This chapter focused on the installation of Solaris 11 on systems for individuals. Because such systems are primarily based on x86 Intel/AMD CPUs, it illustrated the installation process for these systems.

The chapter started with a description of available downloads, which include text as well as automated installations for both x86 and SPARC systems. The downloads are freely available for non-production uses. Advanced installations in many of those cases are covered in Chapter 4. The focus of installations in this chapter is based on the Live Media that can be copied to a DVD disc or a USB key. Once you're ready to put Solaris 11 in production, you will need to purchase a support contract.

As you evaluate Solaris 11, you may be configuring it with a variety of other operating systems. There are ways to set up Solaris 11 on the same system with Linux, Microsoft Windows, and even Solaris 10 systems. Of course, some of you may install Solaris 11 on a virtual machine solution, essentially isolated from the rest of a system.

The heart of the chapter is in the interactive installation. Whether you boot a system from the Live DVD or the USB key, the steps are essentially the same. You'll get a fully functional desktop environment from where you can start the Solaris 11 installation process. It recognizes the partitions configured for a variety of operating systems. Since the root user is not allowed to log in directly, Solaris 11 gives the first user "sudo" privileges.

If you want to configure multiple operating systems on the same machine, you can use the last part of this chapter as guidance for how to configure the Solaris 11 GRUB bootloader. Although it's based on the same GRUB as is used on Linux, Solaris includes additional features to work with the ZFS filesystem. With a few tweaks, you can use Solaris GRUB to boot both Linux and Microsoft Windows.

References

The article that describes the availability and installation of Solaris 11 can be found at www.oracle.com/technetwork/articles/servers-storage-admin/o11-112-s11-first-steps-524819.html.

The basic installation process is documented in the "Installing Oracle Solaris 11 Systems" document, available online from http://docs.oracle.com/cd/E23824_01/html/E21798/index.html.

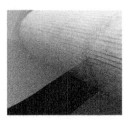

CHAPTER
4

Alternative Oracle
Solaris 11 Installation
Methods

n the previous two chapters, we showed interactive graphical installations from the x86-based Live Media DVD. Several other installation options are available, including a text-based install designed primarily for both x86 and SPARC servers without graphics cards, and an automated non-interactive installation process suitable for deployment over a network to one or more remote servers. In this chapter, we'll describe these alternative installation methods, including installing Solaris 11 as a guest OS, along with a method for creating customized OS boot images and application environments for servers. We'll also review how to reconfigure a system after it has been installed.

SPARC and x86 Systems

The Solaris operating system (rebranded from the original SunOS) was first introduced by Sun Microsystems nearly 20 years ago on the SPARC microprocessor, which was first introduced in 1987. Since its initial release, Solaris has always been offered on the SPARC systems, and many people associate Solaris only with SPARC. Sun introduced an x86 version in 1993, considered dropping it around 2001, and then reconsidered as the x86 Linux market continued to grow. Today, Oracle fully supports and develops Solaris 11 for Intel x86 processors, as well as for SPARC processors from Oracle and from Fujitsu, offering the OS on its extensive line of servers and engineered systems, which includes the SPARC SuperCluster T4-4. Nearly all of what we describe in this book applies to Solaris 11 on either platform, but there are some differences, particularly related to installation and booting.

Solaris 11 on x86 and SPARC Systems: What's the Same?

Solaris 11 for both x86 and SPARC processors is produced from the same source code base, with more than 95 percent of the code being identical for each architecture. This means that *all* of Solaris 11's important features—ZFS, IPS, DTrace, SMF, security, multi-core and multi-processor scalability—are the same on both platforms. Oracle fully tests these and other OS components and offers premier OS software support for both x86 and SPARC systems, including support for servers purchased from Oracle. Also, support is made available for a subscription fee for x86 servers from Dell and HP through the Oracle Store (see Figure 4-1).

Solaris 11 on x86 and SPARC Systems: What's Different?

Because x86 and SPARC processors and the servers built with them are indeed different, there are some obvious and some not-so-obvious differences in how Solaris 11 is installed and booted. Most of these differences generally do not impact day-to-day system administration tasks; for example, internal kernel and data structures differ between the two processor architectures, and Intel and SPARC chips have opposite endian-ness (byte order). Oracle's SPARC systems use the OpenBoot architecture and commands, whereas their x86 systems use the GNU GRUB boot loader. Essentially, this means that boot command syntax and some configuration options will differ between the two architectures, but nearly all other setup tasks will be the same. For example, all SPARC systems are booted using **OpenBoot** commands, whereas the boot sequence for x86 systems is controlled from the system BIOS that controls the order of potential boot devices (disk, USB, or network). For SPARC systems, there is no Live Media option; systems must be booted directly from Text Install media or booted over a network using the Automated Installer.

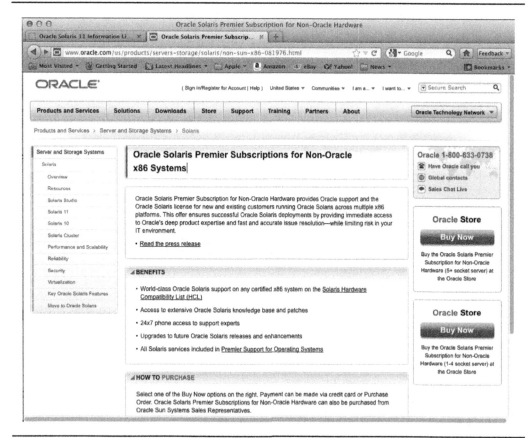

FIGURE 4-1. *Oracle Solaris premier subscriptions for non-Oracle x86 systems*

The Text Install Method

The Text Install method is generally used to install Solaris 11 interactively on servers with no attached monitors, often using a remote virtual console. Text-based installation is also for systems with lower disk space, servers where you don't need a GUI desktop environment, and any SPARC systems that are not being installed with the Automated Installer.

In contrast to the graphical installation described in the previous chapter, the Text Install method requires a different install image; a sample version is available from the Solaris 11 Downloads site (see Figure 4-2).

Note that Solaris 11 Text Install files are available for both x86 systems and SPARC systems. Although you can use the x86 Text Install file for a laptop or desktop workstation, its contents are targeted at servers and includes a different collection of applications than that for the desktop environment. You could install the desktop packages later if you wish, using the **pkg** command to install the **solaris-desktop** package (see Chapter 7 for how to use the package management system);

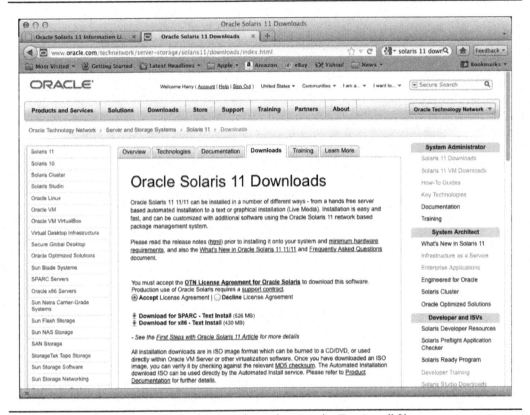

FIGURE 4-2.   *The Solaris 11 Downloads website showing the Text Install files*

that package is one of several preconfigured "group" packages that contain application collections suitable for different system configuration environments:

- group/system/solaris-desktop
- group/system/solaris-large-server
- group/system/solaris-small-server (used for zones)

NOTE
There is no Live Media distribution for installing Solaris 11 on SPARC systems; you must use SPARC Text Install files or Automated Installer files.

The configuration information required for a Text Install is similar to that needed when you installed Solaris 11 from the Live Media files. First, download one of the Text Install sol-11-1111-text-x86.iso or sol-11-1111-text-sparc.iso files from the Oracle Solaris 11 Downloads website. As described in Chapter 2, one option is to create a DVD from one of these files for use as an initial

```
SunOS Release 5.11 Version 11.0 64-bit
Copyright (c) 1983, 2011, Oracle and/or its affiliates. All rights reserved.
Remounting root read/write
Probing for device nodes ...
Preparing image for use
Done mounting image
USB keyboard
  1. Albanian              25. Latin-American
  2. Arabic                26. Lithuanian
  3. Belarusian            27. Latvian
  4. Belgian               28. Macedonian
  5. Brazilian             29. Malta_UK
  6. Bulgarian             30. Malta_US
  7. Canadian-Bilingual    31. Norwegian
  8. Croatian              32. Polish
  9. Czech                 33. Portuguese
 10. Danish                34. Romanian
 11. Dutch                 35. Russian
 12. Dvorak                36. Serbia-And-Montenegro
 13. Estonian              37. Slovak
 14. Finnish               38. Slovenian
 15. French                39. Spanish
 16. French-Canadian       40. Swedish
 17. Hungarian             41. Swiss-French
 18. German                42. Swiss-German
 19. Greek                 43. Traditional-Chinese
 20. Icelandic             44. TurkishF
 21. Italian               45. TurkishQ
 22. Japanese-type6        46. UK-English
 23. Japanese              47. US-English
 24. Korean
To select the keyboard layout, enter a number [default 47]:█
```

FIGURE 4-3. *The initial Text Install screen. Select your keyboard type.*

boot device for your server. The Text Install steps for x86 systems and for SPARC systems are nearly identical.

Boot the system from the DVD; the Text Installer will begin the initial install process, locating your system's devices and beginning a series of questions, starting with your keyboard layout (see Figure 4-3).

Select the number for your keyboard and then press the RETURN key to continue. Next, select your desired language (see Figure 4-4).

```
  1. Chinese - Simplified
  2. Chinese - Traditional
  3. English
  4. French
  5. German
  6. Italian
  7. Japanese
  8. Korean
  9. Portuguese - Brazil
 10. Spanish
To select the language you wish to use, enter a number [default is 3]: █
```

FIGURE 4-4. *Select your language.*

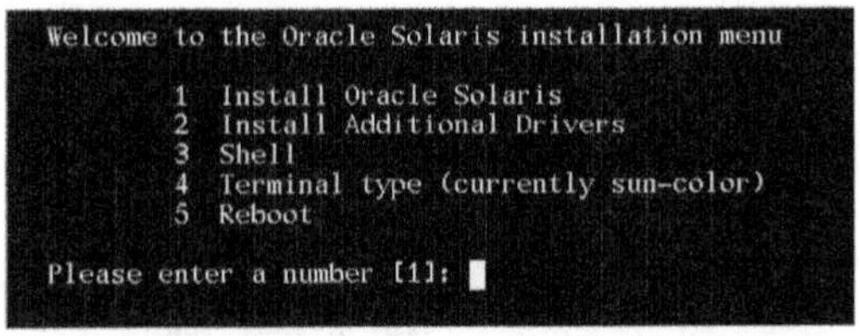

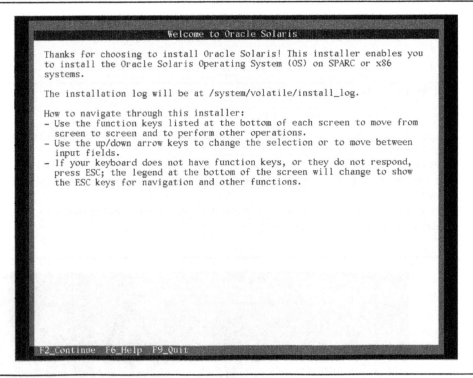

FIGURE 4-5. *The Text Install installation menu*

The installer will configure your devices, assign a default hostname (solaris) that you can change later, and then display a menu of options (see Figure 4-5).

Select the first (default) option to continue; the installation Welcome screen will be displayed (see Figure 4-6). Note that the message indicates this process is the same for both x86 and SPARC systems. Also note that navigating subsequent screens requires the use of your connected terminal's keyboard function keys; if they do not respond as required for numeric selections, the ESC key followed by the desired number will work. That is, ESC-2 will be used for the F2 key.

FIGURE 4-6. *The Text Installer Welcome screen*

The next sequence of steps in the installation process configure the system. First, select the disk and partition where the OS is to be written to, as shown in Figures 4-7 and 4-8, and then set your system's time, date, and time zone.

Next, enter a hostname and select a network connection method (see Figure 4-9); you can automatically configure your host's IP address, assuming you have a DHCP server enabled on your network, or you can manually enter an IP address.

The next screen, shown in Figure 4-10, asks you to select a root password and to assign an initial user ID and password (be sure to record that user and password information for later use). The initial user ID you assign will have system administration privileges. And note that after installation, you will not be able to log in directly as the root ID; this is to enforce monitoring of the root (superuser) role.

After these configuration settings have all been entered, the installation process will ask you to review all your choices (see Figure 4-11). Now you can begin copying the OS files from the install media; this process will take several minutes, and a progress bar will be displayed. When the copying is complete, a new window will display that information (see Figure 4-12).

Upon reboot, for x86 systems, the GRUB boot menu will be displayed (see Figure 4-13); a similar boot menu will be shown for SPARC systems.

As your newly installed Solaris 11 server boots for the first time, the Service Management Facility (described in Chapter 6) initializes and starts up a number of services, recognizes and configures devices, and finally displays a login prompt (see Figure 4-14).

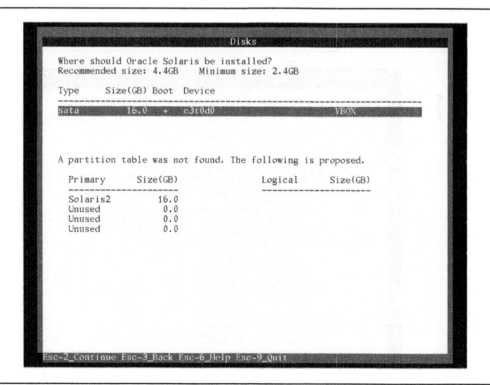

FIGURE 4-7.   *Select the destination disk for the OS.*

FIGURE 4-8. *Select the destination partition of the disk.*

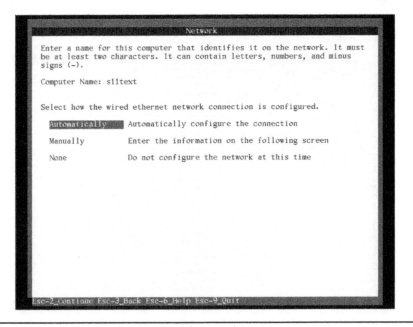

FIGURE 4-9. *Configuring your hostname and network*

FIGURE 4-10. *Selecting a root password and initial user ID*

FIGURE 4-11. *Reviewing your configuration choices*

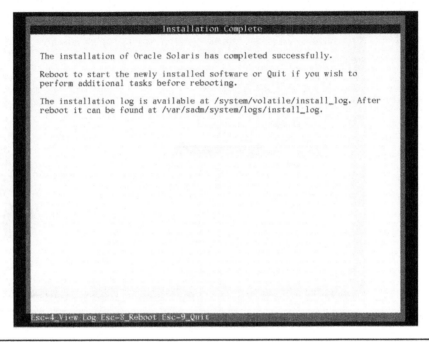

FIGURE 4-12. *Installation is complete; ready to reboot.*

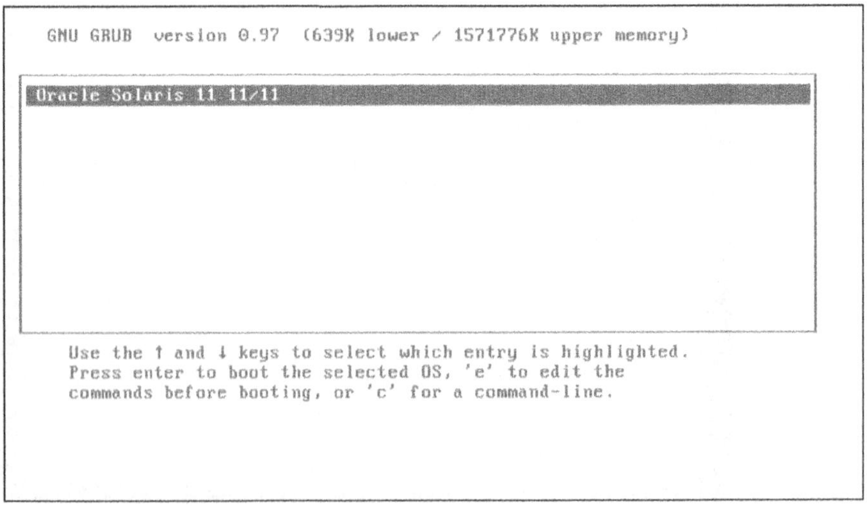

FIGURE 4-13. *The GRUB boot menu (x86)*

```
SunOS Release 5.11 Version 11.0 64-bit
Copyright (c) 1983, 2011, Oracle and/or its affiliates. All rights reserved.

Loading smf(5) service descriptions: 191/191
Configuring devices.
Hostname: s11text

s11text console login: root
Password:
Roles can not login directly
Login incorrect
Mar 21 18:17:51 s11text login: login account failure: Permission denied

s11text console login: hfoxwell
Password:
Oracle Corporation      SunOS 5.11      11.0      November 2011
hfoxwell@s11text:~$
hfoxwell@s11text:~$ su
Password:
Mar 21 18:20:14 s11text su: 'su root' succeeded for hfoxwell on /dev/console
root@s11text:~#
```

FIGURE 4-14.   *Logging into the system from the console*

In this example, notice that we attempted to log in as the root user; however, direct root logins are not permitted by default, so that attempt is rejected. Instead, we log in with the user ID specified earlier; later that user can assume the root role using the **su** command.

The Automated Installer

The Automated Installer (AI) is designed for non-interactive network installation of Solaris 11 onto one or more client systems. It allows administrators to design and deploy custom OS images for such servers using installation profiles for each type of system to be provisioned. AI can use images created using the Distribution Constructor, as we show in the following examples. AI requires a DHCP server on the network, an AI install server, and access to a Solaris 11 package repository (as described in Chapter 7, this is either a public repository or a locally installed repository). AI replaces the JumpStart network installation utility used in earlier versions of Solaris. In this section, we show you how to create a bootable Solaris 11 image and how to set up a boot server.

If you have installed Solaris 11 11/11 using the Live Media distribution, you will need to install the **solaris-auto-install** package using the IPS **pkg** command (see Chapter 7 for how to use IPS):

```
# pkg install pkg:/system/install/auto-install
        Packages to install: 1
     Create boot environment: No
Create backup boot environment: No
        Services to change: 1

DOWNLOAD                 PKGS      FILES    XFER (MB)
Completed                 1/1      11/11    0.0/0.0$<3>
```

```
PHASE                    ACTIONS
Install Phase              35/35

PHASE                    ITEMS
Package State Update Phase         1/1
Image State Update Phase           2/2
# pkg list auto-install
NAME (PUBLISHER)                 VERSION          IFO
system/install/auto-install           0.5.11-0.175.0.0.0.2.1482 i--
```

The Distribution Constructor

In order to create bootable Solaris 11 AI images, you can use the Distribution Constructor (DC). This utility is a CLI tool for creating customized Solaris 11 installation media. It allows you to customize these media to include or exclude installation packages. Pre-built AI images for SPARC and for x86 systems can also be downloaded from the Solaris 11 Downloads website (see Figure 4-15); here, we will show you how to create and use your own AI images.

The Distribution Constructor software is not installed on Solaris 11 by default; you must install it using IPS (how to do this is described in Chapter 7):

```
# pkg install distribution-constructor
        Packages to install: 3
    Create boot environment: No
Create backup boot environment: No

DOWNLOAD              PKGS    FILES   XFER (MB)
Completed             3/3     65/65   0.2/0.2
```

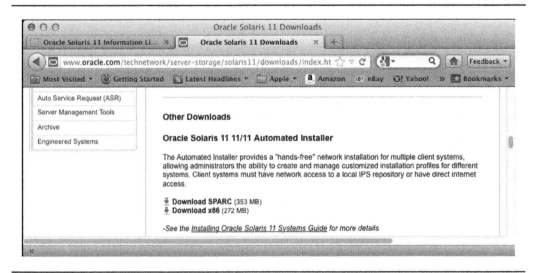

FIGURE 4-15.   *Preconfigured AI files on the Solaris 11 Downloads website*

```
PHASE                    ACTIONS
Install Phase                127/127

PHASE                    ITEMS
Package State Update Phase           3/3
Image State Update Phase             2/2
#
```

You will need root role privileges to run the **distro_const** command. Also note that you can only construct SPARC images on a SPARC system, and only construct x86 images on an x86 system. Additionally, the release version of the AI images you create will match that of the Solaris 11 release used to create them. DC images can also be used without using the Automated Installer.

The Distribution Constructor uses customized configuration files, or *manifests,* to build its images. Sample manifest files for both x86 and SPARC servers are installed, along with the **distribution-constructor** package, in the /usr/share/distro_const directory. It's good practice to copy and modify these manifest files instead of trying to create your own; manifests are XML files and need to be edited carefully. For example, make a copy of an existing manifest:

```
# cp /usr/share/distro_const/dc_ai_x86.xml s11image01.xml
```

You will need to modify several key lines in this manifest file:

```
<distro name="Oracle_Solaris_AI_X86" add_timestamp="false">

<origin name="http://pkg.oracle.com/solaris/release/"/>

<software_data action="install">

<zpool name="rpool" action="use_existing">
```

Search for these lines in your manifest. First, modify the name of the distribution; any character string name may be used here. Second, if desired, modify the publisher repository location to be used when creating the image and installing applications; you may use network-based or locally based repositories here. Third, edit the list of software to be installed (or uninstalled). Finally, indicate the name of the ZFS storage pool where DC will do its work; DC will create several work and output directories in the specified **zpool**.

After you have modified your manifest file to your specifications, use the **distro_const** command to create your AI image (see Listing 4-1); this command is used to read the specifications in your manifest and build a bootable kernel along with the packages you specified. This program also allows you to define checkpoints that can be used to restart the build process from known-good steps instead of redoing the entire build. Creating an AI image can produce a lot of output and take many minutes to complete, depending on the speed of your system and network and on your specified software installs.

Listing 4-1: Creating an AI image

```
# distro_const build s11image01.xml
23:15:58   Build datasets successfully setup
23:15:58   Simple log: /rpool/dc/ai/logs/simple-log.2012-03-23.23:15
23:15:58   Detail Log: /rpool/dc/ai/logs/detail-log.2012-03-23.23:15
23:15:59   Creating IPS image
```

(Continued)

```
23:16:06  Installing packages from:
23:16:06    solaris
23:16:06      origin: http://pkg.oracle.com/solaris/release/
23:16:06      mirror: http://pkg-cdn1.oracle.com/solaris/release/
DOWNLOAD              PKGS    FILES  XFER (MB)
Completed            334/334 32936/32936 214.2/214.2$<3>

PHASE                    ACTIONS
Install Phase            49282/49282

PHASE                      ITEMS
Package State Update Phase        334/334
Image State Update Phase          2/2
23:27:13  Setting post-install publishers to:
23:27:13    solaris
23:27:13      origin: http://pkg.oracle.com/solaris/release/
23:27:15  === Executing Pre-Package Image Modification Checkpoint ===
23:27:15  Preloading SMF repository
23:27:55  Applying SMF profile: /etc/svc/profile/generic_limited_net.xml
23:27:57  Applying SMF profile: /usr/share/distro_const/profile/generic.xml
23:28:00  Applying SMF profile: /usr/share/distro_const/profile/ai.xml
23:28:01  Applying SMF profile: /etc/svc/profile/ns_files.xml
23:28:26  === Executing ba-init Checkpoint ===
23:28:28  Transferring files to /rpool/dc/ai/build_data/boot_archive
23:28:31  Transferring files to /rpool/dc/ai/build_data/boot_archive
… (output deleted)
23:47:14  === Executing Create ISO Checkpoint ==
23:47:14  Making final ISO image: /rpool/dc/ai/media/s11image01.iso
23:48:12  === Executing Create USB Checkpoint ===
23:48:12  Making final USB image: /rpool/dc/ai/media/s11image01.usb
23:50:35  === Executing AI Publish Packages Checkpoint ===
23:50:35  Creating repository
23:50:46  Publishing pkg://ai-image/install-image/solaris-auto-install@5.11-0
.175.0.0.0.2.1482
23:51:58  pkg://ai-image/install-image/solaris-auto-install@5.11,5.11-0.175.0.
0.0.2.1482:20120324T035048Z
PUBLISHED
#
```

This sample Distribution Constructor process has created two bootable AI files, as specified in the s11image01.xml manifest—an s11image.iso DVD image and an s11image.usb USB image—and written them to the /rpool/dc/ai/media directory:

```
# pwd
/rpool/dc/ai/media
# ls -l
total 1125417
drwxr-xr-x  3 root    root        4 Mar 23 23:50 ai_image_repo
-rw-r--r--  1 root    root 276957184 Mar 23 23:48 s11image01.iso
-r--r--r--  1 root    root 332348928 Mar 23 23:50 s11image01.usb
#
```

But wait, there's more! All we have done up to this point is create a bootable image of Solaris 11; now we need to set up a network distribution service that client systems can use to boot from. Fortunately, that's easy, using the **installadm** command to generate the image you have defined.

The **installadm** command is used to manage AI install services. You use it to create and enable install services, to set up the required DHCP server, to add custom client installation and configuration instructions, and to set criteria for clients' custom installation and configuration instructions.

Use the **installadm create-service** subcommand to specify the service name and the location of the installation image:

```
# installadm create-service -n my_S11_AI_service -s ¬
/rpool/dc/ai/media/s11image01.iso
Creating service from: /rpool/dc/ai/media/s11image01.iso
OK to use default image path: /export/auto_install/my_S11_AI_service? [y/N]: y
Setting up the image ...
Creating service: my_S11_AI_service
Image path: /export/auto_install/my_S11_AI_service
Refreshing install services
```

Your AI boot image and service is now ready to deploy to client servers on your network:

```
# installadm list
Service Name      Alias Of      Status Arch   Image Path
------------      --------      ------ ----   ----------
default-i386   my_S11_AI_service on    x86   /export/auto_install/my_S11_AI_service
my_S11_AI_service -            on    x86   /export/auto_install/my_S11_AI_service
```

Note that when the first install service of a given architecture is created on an install server, an alias of that service, **default-i386** or **default-sparc**, is automatically created. This default service is used for all installations to clients of that architecture that were not added to the install server explicitly with the **create-client** subcommand. Also note that if you don't provide an AI manifest, a default will be used. And if you don't provide a configuration profile, the System Configuration Interactive tool will be displayed—the install is then interactive.

Booting Client Systems from the AI Server

The final step for network installations of Solaris 11 is to identify the system(s) that will use the AI service. These systems can be x86 or SPARC servers, and must have sufficient memory and disk space to install and run the OS. They must also be connected to the AI service's network so that they can locate the service and obtain a network address; for this you need to know the MAC address of each client, and enable each client to boot from the network. Again, the **installadm** program is used to define clients allowed to boot from the service:

```
# installadm create-client -e 00:1b:21:10:aa:f1 -n my_S11_AI_service
```

The client system with that specific MAC address (00:1b:21:10:aa:f1) will now be able to boot from the my_S11_AI_service using the non-interactive AI file, s11image01.iso, which we created earlier. For x86 systems, their BIOS should be configured to search for and boot from the network. Boot files on the AI server reside in its /etc/netboot directory, and they include a GRUB menu.lst file for each client that will be invoked at bootup.

Just as the install server provides GRUB files for x86 clients, it also provides system.conf and wanboot.conf files for SPARC clients. SPARC clients can now boot and install from the client's **ok** prompt. The net boot sequence will begin, starting with the client system locating the boot server and then, as with all installation scenarios, probing for devices, starting the AI process, copying files from the specified repository, and finally completing. The "Installing Oracle Solaris 11 Systems" document (file E21798.pdf) lists the following sample output sequence:

```
ok boot net:dhcp - install
SPARC Enterprise T5120, No Keyboard
Copyright 2008 Sun Microsystems, Inc. All rights reserved.
OpenBoot 4.29.1, 16256 MB memory available, Serial #81036844.
Ethernet address 0:14:4f:d4:86:2c, Host ID: 84d4862c.
Boot device: /pci@0/pci@0/pci@1/pci@0/pci@2/network@0:dhcp File and args: -
install
… (output abbreviated)
14:49:05 Automated Installation succeeded.
14:49:05 You may wish to reboot the system at this time.
Automated Installation finished successfully
The system can be rebooted now
Please refer to the /system/volatile/install_log file for details
After reboot it will be located at /var/sadm/system/logs/install_log
```

Similarly, the x86 client system net boot sequence begins with the client discovering the net boot server, configuring devices, starting the AI process, installing application packages, and completing with the same AI success message.

Deleting a client system on x86 and SPARC AI servers is the same—identify the MAC address of the client(s) to be deleted and then use the following command:

```
# installadm delete-client {MAC address}
```

This will delete the client system from its assigned install service; the client can still use the default install service.

Transitioning from JumpStart to Automated Installer for Solaris 10 Administrators

Solaris 10 administrators familiar with JumpStart tools must now learn to use the Automated Installer. Fortunately, a transition tool called **js2ai** (JumpStart to Automated Installer) is available to help with this transition. The **js2ai** command converts JumpStart profile files to an AI manifest file and converts sysidcfg files to AI configuration profiles. But first, that application must be installed using IPS:

```
# pkg install install/js2ai
        Packages to install: 1
    Create boot environment: No
Create backup boot environment: No

DOWNLOAD            PKGS    FILES   XFER (MB)
Completed           1/1     20/20   0.1/0.1$<3>
```

```
PHASE                       ACTIONS
Install Phase                45/45

PHASE                        ITEMS
Package State Update Phase          1/1
Image State Update Phase            2/2
```

You can then use **js2ai** to translate JumpStart rules and profiles for use with the Automated Installer; it creates an AI manifest and system configuration profile containing "best effort" conversions of JumpStart parameters.

Configuring Oracle Solaris 11

There may be occasions after you have installed an instance of Solaris 11 when you need to reconfigure how it is installed, or need to reset the system back to an unconfigured state. Or, you may want to pre-build system configuration files, called *profiles,* for later use with other systems. For these tasks, you will use the **sysconfig** command, which we review next.

Unconfiguring a Solaris 11 System

In order to return a previously configured Solaris 11 system to a state with no users, hostname, or net addresses defined, use the **sysconfig** command with the **unconfigure** subcommand:

```
# sysconfig unconfigure
This program will unconfigure your system.
The system will be reverted to a "pristine" state.
It will not have a name or know about other systems or networks.
Do you want to continue (y[n])?
```

Notice that the default selection if you accidentally hit an extra RETURN key is **[n]** or **NO**. Additional flags to this subcommand can be specified; use **-s** to shut the system down after the unconfiguration process completes, and use the **--destructive** flag to specify that no earlier system configuration settings should be kept as backup.

> **NOTE**
> *Solaris 10 has a **sys-unconfig** command; this command has been replaced in Solaris 11 by the **sysconfig unconfigure** command.*

As a result of this unconfiguration process, the next time the system is booted, it will display the startup and configuration menus we discussed earlier in this chapter.

(Re)configuring a Solaris 11 System

Another capability of the **sysconfig** command is to create a system configuration profile using the **create-profile** subcommand. You can use the resulting profile with the **sysconfig configure** subcommand to configure systems non-interactively. Profiles are XML documents and must have an .xml extension, and they can be used as configuration files for AI server installations:

```
# sysconfig create-profile -o s11prof1.xml
```

This command writes the file s11prof1.xml to the current directory for use with other systems and AI installations. This file can be modified and used to non-interactively configure other systems. Here's an example:

```
# sysconfig configure -c s11prof1.xml
```

The file /etc/svc/profile/site/profile_sc_manifest.xml is the default configuration profile for each Solaris 11 system. This file is created at installation time.

Installing Solaris as a Virtual Machine Guest

In addition to installing Solaris 11 directly on a hardware platform (laptop, workstation, or server), you can install it as a virtual machine guest on other OS environments that support hypervisors. For x86 systems from Intel and AMD that are running Microsoft Windows, Linux, Oracle Solaris, or Apple OS X, hypervisor applications are available from several sources:

- **Oracle VM VirtualBox** https://www.virtualbox.org/ and www.oracle.com/us/technologies/virtualization/061976.html
- **Parallels** www.parallels.com
- **Xen** www.xen.org/
- **VMware** www.vmware.com/
- **Oracle VM for x86** www.oracle.com/us/technologies/virtualization/oraclevm/index.html
- **Oracle VM Server for SPARC** www.oracle.com/us/technologies/virtualization/oraclevm/oracle-vm-server-for-sparc-068923.html
- **Linux KVM** www.linux-kvm.org

Not all of these products officially support Solaris 11 guest VMs, although they *might* work; check their websites for details. Oracle's VirtualBox does support Solaris guest VMs on Windows, Linux, Solaris, and on OS X hosts. In general, such hypervisor programs all have similar architectures and installation requirements. You typically need to allocate sufficient memory and virtual disk space for the Solaris VM from your host, and you must specify the usual requirements for an OS installation, including a hostname, root and user passwords, and network addresses. In the following example, we'll show the installation of Solaris 11 as a guest VM onto VirtualBox; we use this Oracle product as an example because it is freely downloadable from VirtualBox.org (see Figure 4-16).

Select the version of VirtualBox for your particular host OS; then download and install it according to your system's usual application installation procedure (see Figure 4-17).

After you have downloaded and installed VirtualBox on your host system, start it up using your system's usual method for starting applications (for example, selecting a VirtualBox menu item or clicking a VirtualBox icon; appearances will vary depending on your host OS—Linux, Windows, Solaris, or OS X). Start the Solaris 11 VM creation sequence by clicking the New icon (see Figure 4-18).

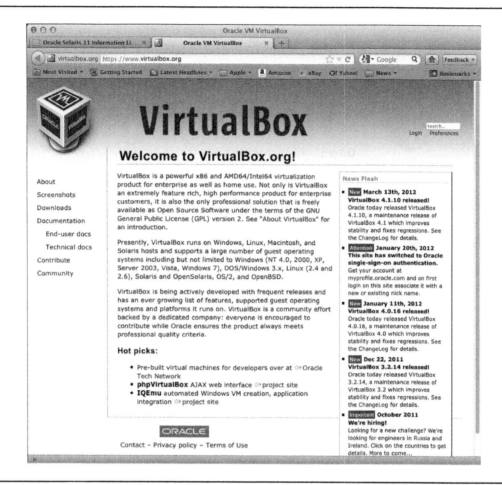

FIGURE 4-16. *The VirtualBox website*

Next, enter what you want to name your VM and specify its type (see Figure 4-19).

The next several steps are typical of most virtualization software; you need to allocate sufficient memory for your VM and need to create a virtual disk of sufficient size for the VM's root filesystem (see Chapter 2 for required memory and disk space for Solaris 11). Be sure to allocate sufficient memory and disk space, but recall that you are using resources from your host. Be sure to reserve working memory and disk space for your host system! Figures 4-20 through 4-24 detail these configuration options.

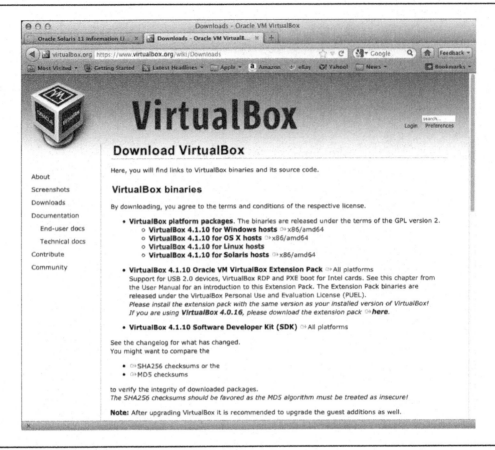

FIGURE 4-17.   *The VirtualBox Download website*

After these steps, VirtualBox will present you with a summary of your disk and VM choices (see Figures 4-25 and 4-26).

After you click the Create button, VirtualBox will display a window of VM parameters that you can change (see Figure 4-27). The location of your install image must be specified; this will generally be a DVD or an .iso disk image that you have created or have downloaded from Oracle's website (see Figure 4-28).

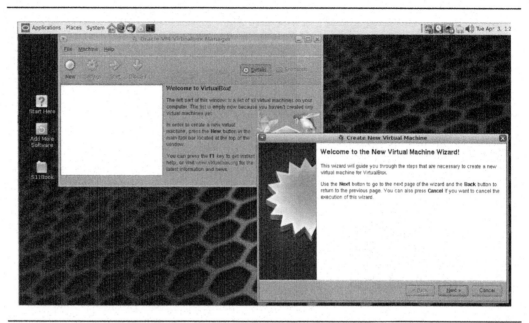

FIGURE 4-18. *Starting the Solaris 11 VM creation sequence*

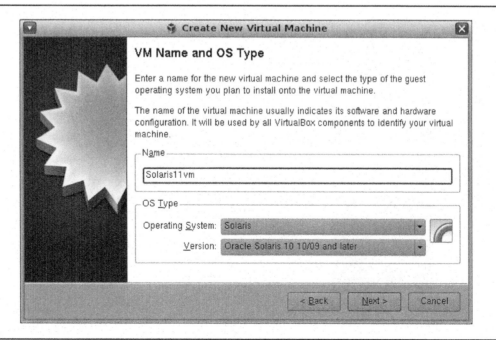

FIGURE 4-19. *Naming your Solaris 11 VM and type*

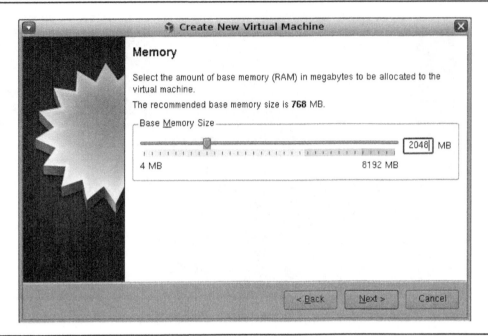

FIGURE 4-20. *Specifying your VM's memory*

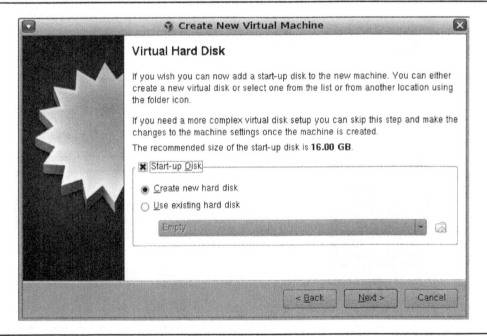

FIGURE 4-21. *Creating your VM's startup disk*

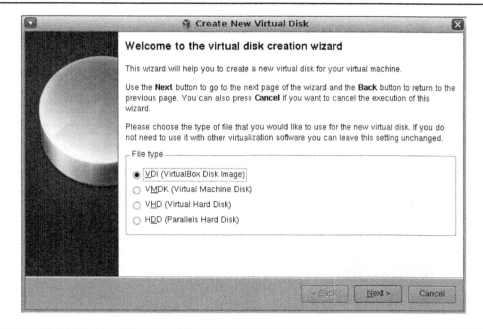

FIGURE 4-22. *Choosing your VM's startup disk type*

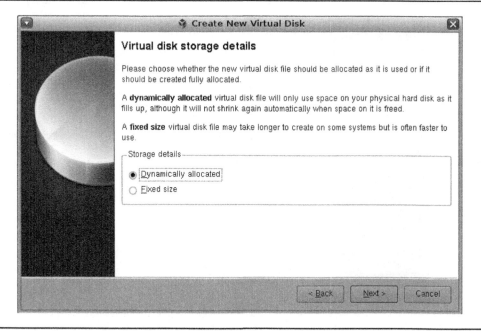

FIGURE 4-23. *Selecting the type of your virtual disk*

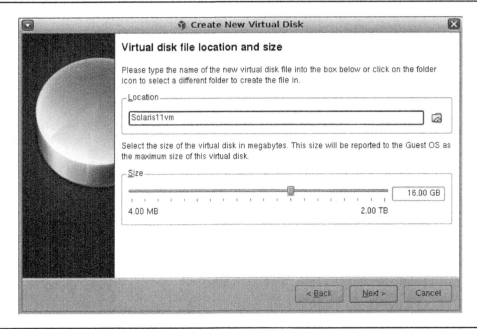

FIGURE 4-24. *Specifying the size of your VM's virtual disk drive*

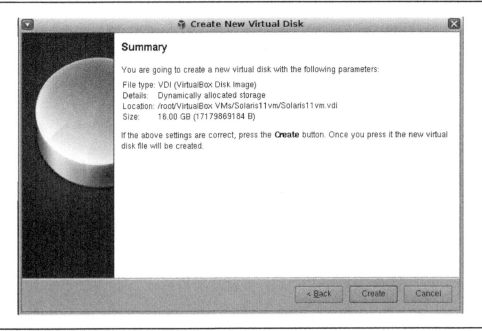

FIGURE 4-25. *Summary of your virtual disk choices*

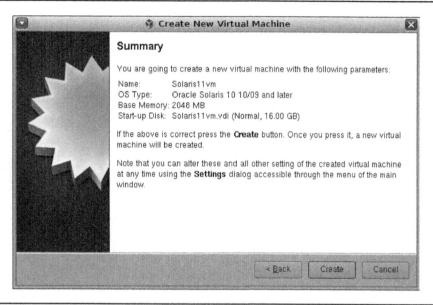

FIGURE 4-26. *Summary of your virtual disk choices (continued)*

At this point, you can click VirtualBox's Start button for this VM; installation will then proceed as we described in Chapter 2 and earlier in this chapter.

VirtualBox can also be used to install Solaris 11 Text Install images onto x86 servers. Additionally, VirtualBox installs several CLI utilities that can be used in a non-graphical environment. For example, the VBoxManage utility lets you configure and install a VM from the command line:

```
# VBoxManage createvm --name "Solaris 11" --ostype Solaris –register
```

VirtualBox allows you to configure other parameters of your Solaris 11 virtual machines, including the VM's boot order (disk or net), network type for the VM (NAT, Bridged, or Internal), number of virtual CPUs, and folders shared between the VM and your host OS. See the *VirtualBox User Manual,* included with your VirtualBox file downloads, for additional details about these choices.

The Oracle Solaris 11 VM for Oracle VM VirtualBox

The Oracle Solaris VM Downloads website (see Figure 4-29) provides several types of preconfigured VM images of Solaris 11 for both x86 and SPARC environments, including the following:

- x86 and SPARC Solaris 11 container templates for running Solaris 10 applications on a Solaris 11 server (see Chapter 14 for details about containers)
- A SPARC Solaris 11 container for running Oracle's Siebel CRM environment
- An Oracle Solaris VM template for OVM (Linux based)
- An Oracle Solaris 11 VM for Oracle VM VirtualBox

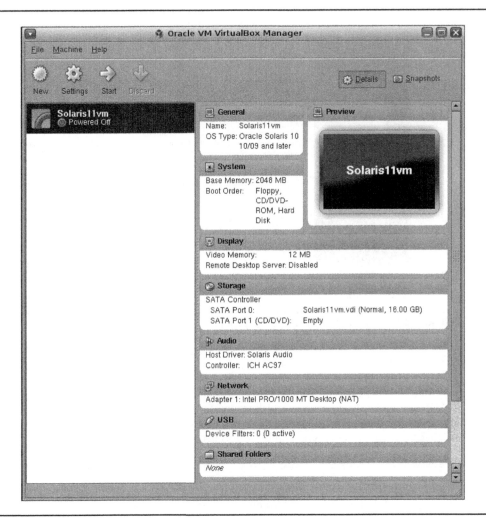

FIGURE 4-27. *The VirtualBox Manager for the new VM*

This VM image is a preinstalled virtual machine ideal for learning about and evaluating the Oracle Solaris 11 operating system and its development environment.

Oracle VM for SPARC

The Oracle VM for SPARC product is designed for the SPARC T-series processors; it uses a SPARC-based hypervisor and allows multiple Solaris VMs to be installed on segments, or *cores,* of these processors. Prior to Oracle's acquisition of Sun Microsystems, this technology was called *Logical*

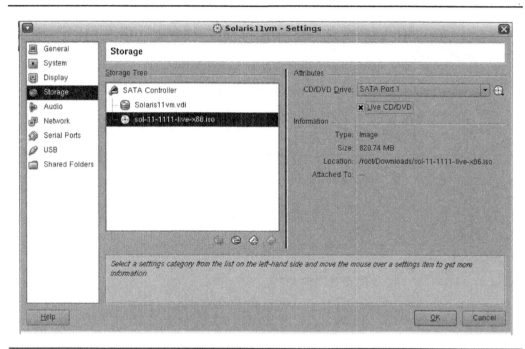

FIGURE 4-28. *Specifying the location of the VM's installation file*

Domains or *LDoms*. It provides features very similar to those in x86 hypervisor environments, including VM creation and management and live migration of VMs from one T-series server to another. The complete documentation library for Oracle VM for SPARC is at http://docs.oracle .com/cd/E23120_01/index.html, and there is a related Wiki page at https://wikis.oracle.com/ display/oraclevm/Oracle+VM+Server+for+SPARC. Once the Oracle VM for SPARC has been installed and configured on a server, installation of Solaris on each of the domains can be accomplished using the methods we have described so far—installation from a DVD device, using Text Install, or, more typically for such systems, using Automated Installer over your network.

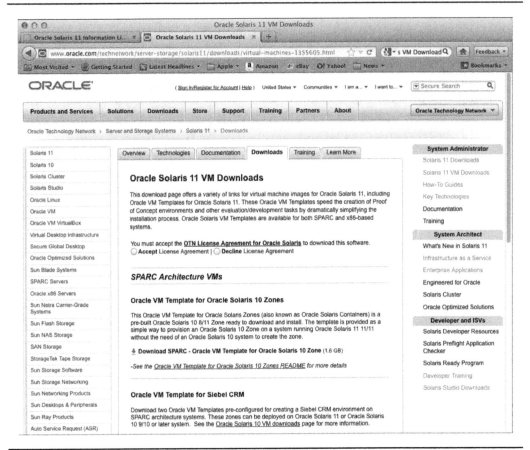

FIGURE 4-29. *The Oracle Solaris 11 VM Downloads website*

Summary

In this chapter, we provided an overview of several alternate types of Solaris 11 installations on both x86 and SPARC systems—text-based installs, automated network installations, and virtual machines on host operating systems. We showed how to create an AI install server that installs Solaris OS images created using the Distribution Constructor. And we reviewed how to reconfigure a Solaris 11 system after it has been installed. We also reviewed installing Solaris 11 as a guest VM on VirtualBox, using that software as an example of how to use such hypervisor applications.

References

The document "Installing Oracle Solaris 11 Systems" (March 2012, E21798–03) can be found at http://docs.oracle.com/cd/E23824_01/html/E21798/index.html.

The document "Creating a Custom Oracle Solaris 11 Installation Image" (November 2011, E21800–01) can be found at http://docs.oracle.com/cd/E23824_01/html/E21800/index.html.

The Oracle Solaris Premier Subscriptions for Non-Oracle x86 Systems website is located at www.oracle.com/us/products/servers-storage/solaris/non-sun-x86-081976.html.

The Oracle Solaris 11 VM Downloads website is located at www.oracle.com/technetwork/server-storage/solaris11/downloads/virtual-machines-1355605.html.

The document "Transitioning from Oracle Solaris 10 JumpStart to Oracle Solaris 11 Automated Installer" can be found at http://docs.oracle.com/cd/E23824_01/html/E21799/index.html.

The Oracle VM VirtualBox User Manual is included with VirtualBox software download.

The book *Oracle Solaris 10 System Virtualization Essentials* is available from www.amazon.com/Oracle-Solaris-Virtualization-Essentials-Administration/dp/013708188X/.

CHAPTER
5

The Solaris Graphical
Desktop Environment

y reputation, the most skilled administrators of UNIX-based operating systems have always worked just from the command-line interface. That is no longer the case. With appropriate GUI tools, expert users can perform most standard administrative tasks. With appropriate GUI tools, regular users can operate the multimedia applications expected on today's networks.

In this chapter, you'll examine the Solaris 11 implementation of the GUI. Because it uses the GNOME desktop environment, it uses the same basic GUI installed on many Linux systems. Yes, many administrators can be found running a whole bunch of command-line interfaces on their GUI systems. Nevertheless, a wide variety of excellent graphical tools is available for UNIX-based operating systems, including Solaris.

Those of you familiar with the history of Solaris understand that its engineers are interested in more than just a server environment. With their work on the OpenOffice.org suite, Solaris includes a viable alternative to Microsoft Office. In fact, this book was drafted, in part, using OpenOffice.org Writer. It is so compatible with Microsoft-based document tools that publishers such as McGraw-Hill are able to use OpenOffice.org Writer files almost without a hitch.

In many cases, this chapter is just an overview. For those administrative tools covered in other chapters, the tools described here are just a preview. For example, if you want a detailed discussion of the Printer Configuration tool, you'll want to read Chapter 15. In addition, tools such as the Firefox web browser are trivial for most people who've even heard of Solaris as an operating system. Such tools also won't be covered in detail in this chapter or this book.

The Default Solaris GUI

The default Solaris GUI is the GNOME desktop environment. GNOME stands for the GNU Network Object Model Environment. Yes, it's part of a network. The way GUIs are configured on UNIX-based operating systems support the use of graphical clients on one system and a graphical server on a second system.

The default Solaris 11 implementation of the GUI is shown in Figure 5-1. Despite our personal opinion of the wallpaper, it's deceptively simple. The desktop includes three icons:

- **Start Here**   Links to introductory information about Solaris 11.
- **Add More Software**   Opens the Package Manager tool, with links to the configured Solaris repository.
- **DVD icon**   Exists only if there's a CD/DVD, or an ISO file, connected to the appropriate drive.

The action on the Solaris desktop is in the panels. The top panel includes menus that can start applications, open a file browser associated mostly with local or remote directories ("Places"), and support local and system administration ("System"). You can click these menus for yourself. In a moment, this chapter covers each of these menus in more detail.

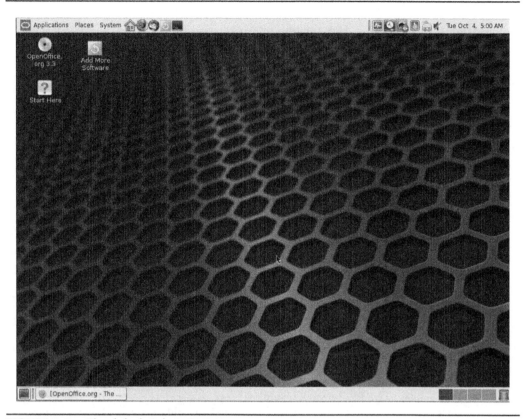

FIGURE 5-1. *The default Solaris GUI*

Though the details vary by configuration, Table 5-1 lists the icons shown in the default version of the Solaris 11 GUI. These icons are known as *launchers,* and they serve as shortcuts to different applications. For more information, right-click the shortcut. In the pop-up menu that appears, you may see a Properties option. If so, it'll include the command associated with the shortcut. Depending on the options on your system, you may not see all of these icons, or you may see additional icons.

A Fully Featured Desktop Environment

This chapter explores the full range of applications and applets associated with the GNOME desktop environment, based on what's available for Solaris 11. To get that full range of features, you'll need to install a few more packages. For those of you who are new to Solaris 11, you can use the Package Manager tool noted in Table 5-1. Open it and then click Applications in the left pane. To review some of the applications in this chapter, we added certain options from this category.

Icon	Description
Nautilus	Primarily used as a file browser
Firefox	The well-known web browser
Thunderbird	The well-known e-mail manager
Package Manager	Front end to the **pkg** command for package installation; manages packages by categories
Terminal	A terminal command-line interface
Time Slider	Configuration tool for zone backups
Network Preferences	Configuration tool for network adapters
Accessibility	Tool with different options for universal access, often used to customize desktops for disabled users
Power Management	Tool with power management options
Sound	Volume control
Time	Clock preferences

TABLE 5-1. *Typical GNOME Desktop Icons*

The options with the dark gray box in the status category are applications and packages that are not installed. If you want to install one or more of these options, activate the check box in a fashion similar to what's shown in Figure 5-2.

Once you've selected the desired packages, click Install/Update and follow the prompts. The Package Manager tool identifies any dependent packages and then installs them all together.

Later in this chapter, you'll examine the process for installing the OpenOffice.org suite on Solaris 11. Although the OpenOffice.org suite is also developed by Oracle, the associated packages are not part of standard Solaris 11 package repositories.

TIP
*If you don't see an option for a newly installed application in the Applications menu, log out and log back into the Solaris 11 GUI. If it still doesn't appear, review the Main Menu application, which you can start with the **alacarte** command.*

The UNIX Client Server Model for GUIs

Because UNIX-based operating systems use a client/server model, you can access GUI-based applications from remote systems. The local system is the GUI server because it includes hardware engines such as graphics cards. You can find configuration files in the /etc/X11 directory. Some of you may be a bit surprised at this directory, because the xorg.conf file is normally no longer used. Default settings associated with that file suffice for the great majority of configurations. That's a testament to the usability of the GUI on UNIX-based operating systems.

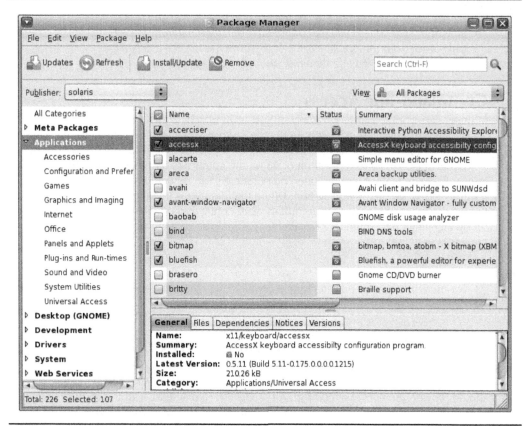

FIGURE 5-2. *Selecting packages to be installed*

Customized options can be configured in the /etc/X11/xorg.conf.avail directory. For example, some systems may include a fairly simple file, 90-zap.conf, in that directory. The contents of that file add one nonstandard option to the Solaris 11 GUI configuration:

```
Section "InputClass"
    Identifier "keyboard zap by default"
    MatchIsKeyboard "on"
    Option "XKbOptions" "terminate:ctrl_alt_bksp"
EndSection
```

This option allows users to "zap" or stop the processes associated with the GUI with the noted CTRL-ALT-BACKSPACE key combination. As the GUI is set to run by default, the system will automatically restart and take you back to the login screen.

NOTE
Solaris doesn't support the separate virtual terminals seen in Linux. However, given the availability of the GNOME terminal from the top taskbar (or from the Applications | Accessories menu), the availability of different command line terminals shouldn't be a problem.

Command-line Access

In many cases, Solaris administrators will just want to access the command-line interface. If the Terminal icon doesn't already exist on the top taskbar, you can access the command-line interface by clicking Applications | Accessories | Terminal or selecting Applications | System Tools | Xterm.

Up to Solaris 8, there was a limit of 48 on the number of terminals. Ever since terminals were allocated dynamically, there has been no practical limit. By definition, a "pseudo terminal" requires 192 bytes on a 64-bit system. While that number is trivial today, it was significant during the development of UNIX, when terminals were configured on teletypes. Nevertheless, you can set up a ceiling on the number of available terminals by configuring the pt_max_pty variable in the /etc/system file.

NOTE
For more information on /etc/system variables, see the Oracle Solaris Tunable Parameters Reference Manual.

The GNOME Desktop Environment

If you're already familiar with GNOME on the Solaris or most Linux environments, this section should be quite familiar to you. If your main experience is with Microsoft Windows, this section should provide some level of comfort. All readers should at least scan this section to learn how to open a command-line interface and access administrative tools from the System Tools submenu. After a brief discussion of generic desktop features, this section examines the basic Applications and Places menus systematically. For the purpose of this chapter, additional relevant packages were installed to maximize the components found and available from the menus.

TIP
If an application does not open from the GUI menu, start a command-line interface. Use the command associated with the application. Frequently, descriptive error messages appear that point to the problem. Many commands that start GNOME applications are included in this section.

The Desktop Pop-up Menu

One strength of any UNIX-based operating system comes from the way it can be controlled. Part of that comes from the detail available in text configuration files. Part of that is also due to the detail available from the utilities and scripts you can execute from the command-line interface. Right-click an open area of the desktop. The pop-up menu that appears is shown in Figure 5-3.

The options are straightforward, as summarized in Table 5-2.

FIGURE 5-3. *Desktop pop-up menu*

Applications Menu

To open the Applications menu, click the Oracle icon in the upper-left corner of the desktop. The menu shown in Figure 5-4 should appear. If you haven't installed some of the applications shown in the menus, they may not appear on your desktop. For example, unless you've installed the gnome-games package (or another package in the same category), the Games submenu won't appear.

Option	Description
Create Folder	Creates an "Untitled Folder" in the current home directory, in the Desktop/ subdirectory.
Create Launcher	Sets up a link to an executable file, normally to launch a program.
Create Document	Adds a file in the current user's Desktop/ subdirectory; may specify options such as OpenOffice.org document types, if installed.
Open Terminal	Opens the default GNOME Terminal command-line interface.
Clean Up by Name	Sorts the icons on the desktop.
Keep Aligned	Keeps icons aligned.
Paste	Pastes, if you've copied an icon.
Run Application	Opens a window to run an application from the command line. This is equivalent to ALT-F2.
Desktop Appearance	Starts the Appearance Preferences tool, also available by clicking System	Preferences	Appearance.
Screen Resolution	Opens the Monitor Preferences tool, also available by clicking System	Preferences	Monitors.

TABLE 5-2. *Options from the Desktop Pop-up Menu*

FIGURE 5-4.   *The Applications menu*

In other words, the Applications menu includes a variety of everyday programs. Except for the System Tools submenu, administrative utilities are reserved for the Systems menu, described later in this chapter. The options shown in the Applications submenus are described in the following sections.

Accessories

Under the Accessories submenu, you have access to a wide variety of applets. Perhaps most significant among them are the gedit Text Editor and the Terminal, which provides one more way to open a GNOME Terminal. These and other options are shown in Figure 5-5 and are summarized in Table 5-3. The table includes the commands you can use to access these applets. Given the

FIGURE 5-5.   *The Accessories submenu*

Applet	Description
Archive Manager	Supports the viewing and unpacking of files from a number of archived and compressed formats; also accessible with the **file-roller** command.
Avant Window Navigator	When the Compiz compositing manager is running, the Avant Window Navigator supports an Apple OS X–style dock on the desktop; also accessible with the **avant-window-navigator** command.
Calculator	Opens a calculator tool that can be configured in several modes. Accessible with the **gcalctool** command.
Character Map	Enables the use of special characters from a variety of different languages; can be started with the **gucharmap** command.
Find Files	Supports access to the GNOME file name search tool, a front end to the **find** command. It's also accessible with the **gnome-search-tool** command.
gedit Text Editor	Opens a text editor that works in the GUI; can be opened with the **gedit** command.
PDA Synchronization	Starts a tool that syncs local data to handheld Palm Pilot devices; as such, it may be obsolete. Accessible with the **gnome-pilot** command.
StarDict	Opens a GUI-based dictionary lookup tool. You can start it with the **stardict** command.
Take Screenshot	Runs the screenshot tool associated with GNOME. Although you can start it with the **gnome-screenshot** command, the option specifies **gnome-screenshot --interactive**, which includes screenshot options.
Terminal	Starts the GNOME Terminal, something that you can also open with the **gnome-terminal** command.
Terminator	Starts an application that supports multiple command-line terminals in a single window.

TABLE 5-3.   *Options from the Accessories Submenu*

client/server nature of the UNIX GUI, you can open these accessories (and other GUI applications) remotely.

Developer Tools

Though it may seem odd to think of the emacs text editor as a developer tool, it respects those who use emacs to change, modify, configure, and, yes, develop the operating system. Other developer tools, shown in Figure 5-6, are detailed next:

- ■ **Bluefish Editor**   Starts an editor designed for users of scripts and code.
- ■ **Emacs**   Opens a GUI version of the emacs text editor in the GUI; you can start it with the **emacs** command.

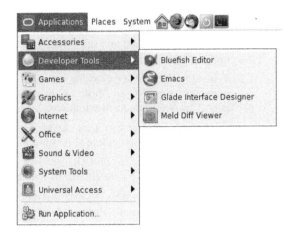

FIGURE 5-6. *The Developer Tools submenu*

- **Glade Interface Designer** Supports the development of user interfaces with the GTK+ toolkit, primarily for GNOME. You can open it with the **glade-3** command. (GTK stands for the GIMP Tool Kit; GIMP stands for the GNU Image Manipulation Program.)

- **Meld Diff Viewer** Allows you to compare text files, side by side; related to the **diff** command. Can be started with the **meld** command.

Games

The games listed in the Games submenu shown in Figure 5-7 are the options associated with a standard GNOME Games package.

Graphics

The options shown in Figure 5-8 illustrate the variety of graphics-related applications available on GNOME for Solaris 11. (One of the authors used the GIMP to take screenshots for this book.) The applications shown are summarized in Table 5-4, including the utilities you can use to open these applications from the command line.

Internet

There are few surprises with the Internet submenu shown in Figure 5-9. The applications available from that menu are associated with basic online communication.

- **Drivel Journal Editor** Opens a tool that aids in blogging for sites such as LiveJournal. You can also start it with the **drivel** command.

- **Evolution Mail and Calendar** Invokes the noted personal information manager (PIM) for e-mails, contacts, and scheduling functionally similar to Microsoft Outlook. You can open it with the **evolution** command.

- **Firefox Web Browser** Starts the well-known GUI web browser; accessible with the **firefox** command.

FIGURE 5-7.   *The Games submenu*

FIGURE 5-8.   *The Graphics submenu*

Option	Description
Dia Diagram Editor	Opens a drawing program similar to Microsoft Visio; can be started with the **dia** command.
GQview	Runs the GQview image viewer, which defaults to a view of graphical images in the local directory; you can open it with the **gqview** command.
gThumb Image Organizer	Initiates an image viewer that facilitates the movement of images between directories; can be started with the **gthumb** command.
Image Editor	Starts the GIMP, the UNIX image-editing program presented as an alternative to Photoshop; you can run it with the **gimp** command.
Image Viewer	Runs the Eye Of GNOME image viewer, which can open images individually; associated with the **eog** command.
XSane – Scanning	Runs the application that can read information from scanners; you can also start it with the **xsane** command.

TABLE 5-4. *Options from the Graphics Submenu*

FIGURE 5-9. *The Internet submenu*

- **gFTP**   Runs a graphical FTP client; you can run it with the **gftp** command.

- **Pidgin Internet Messenger**   Accesses an instant messaging client that can communicate on a variety of networks; can be started with the **pidgin** command.

- **Remote Desktop Viewer**   Opens a Virtual Network Computing (VNC) client; accessible with the **vinagre** command.

- **Terminal Server Client**   Opens a remote desktop client associated with several different protocols. You can open it with the **tsclient** command.

- **Thunderbird Mail/Calendar**   Runs an e-mail manager with an integrated calendar. You can start it with the **thunderbird** command.

- **Transmission BitTorrent Client**   Starts a GUI application that supports uploads and downloads for peer-to-peer file sharing; may not be legal in all jurisdictions. You can start it with the **transmission** command.

- **Video Conference**   Opens the video conference application known as Ekiga, which you can also start with the **ekiga** command.

- **XChat IRC**   Supports access to Internet Relay Chat (IRC). Preloaded with access to IRC networks. You can start it with the **xchat** command.

Command-line alternatives to Firefox and Thunderbird are still popular among many in the Solaris community. For example, the **elinks** web browser can access web pages and the **mutt** e-mail manager can review text-based e-mails. In a command line, try the following command:

```
$ elinks mheducation.com
```

To exit from the elinks browser, press Q to open an exit dialog and confirm by selecting yes and pressing ENTER.

Office

The standard applications available in the Office submenu are fairly simple. They include the following:

- **Dictionary**   Starts the GNOME dictionary tool, accessible with the **gnome-dictionary** command.

- **Evince**   Supports the Evince document viewer for PDFs; it's an alternative to Acrobat Reader. You can start it with the **evince** command.

- **Project Management**   Runs the Serena Open Project application, which supports the scheduling of projects where jobs have to be run in some sequence. Accessible with the **planner** command.

This is just a snippet of what's available; later in this chapter, you'll add applications associated with the OpenOffice.org suite to this submenu.

Sound and Video

The Sound and Video submenu supports access to a variety of recording and playback applications. As shown in Figure 5-10, two different applications are available to burn ISO files to CD/DVD media. Table 5-5 provides an overview of each application shown in that submenu. The Brasero Disc Burner is also accessible from the System Tools submenu as the CD/DVD Creator.

FIGURE 5-10. *The Sound and Video submenu*

Option	Description
Brasero Disc Burner	Runs the disc management application that can create audio, video, or data CD/DVDs. It can also copy CD/DVDs, or burn an image from an ISO file. The menu item specifies **brasero**, which opens Brasero with administrative privileges.
CD Ripper	Starts an application that plays tracks from a CD, and can write them to appropriate files. The menu item is also associated with the **gksu** option, in this case to the **sound-juicer** command.
Cheese Webcam Booth	Supports access to a connected web camera; you can start it with the **cheese** command.
Jokosher Audio Editor	Enables access to the Jokosher Audio Editor, for multi-track audio management.
Sound Recorder	Opens a sound-recording application, if the local sound card is properly detected. You can run it with the **gnome-sound-recorder** menu.
Totem Movie Player	Starts a movie player that can be configured to play many formats; associated with the **totem** command.

TABLE 5-5. *Options from the Sound and Video Submenu*

System Tools

The System Tools submenu shown in Figure 5-11 allows you to run tools that can manage files, disks, performance, and more. These are administrative applications of significant interest. As such, this section includes additional detail on these tools in the following subsections. The one exception is the CD/DVD Creator, which was already covered earlier in this chapter as the Brasero Disc Burner.

Device Driver Utility   The Device Driver Utility shown in Figure 5-12 searches and lists detected hardware on the local system. If there are problems, they're highlighted. If you have drivers that may address problems or enhance features, you can install them from a package, a file, or a remote URL. You can start this tool from the command line with the **ddu** command.

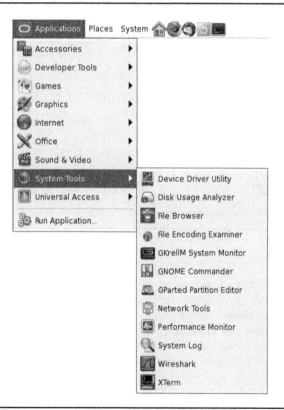

FIGURE 5-11.   *The System Tools submenu*

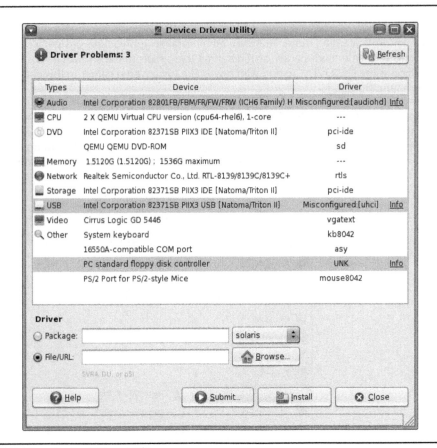

FIGURE 5-12.   *Device Driver Utility*

Before the Device Driver Utility starts, you're prompted to run the program as the root user. If you've configured a different user with appropriate privileges, you can substitute accordingly. You're then prompted for that user's password. For more information on Role-Based Access Control, see Chapter 12. The misconfigured drivers shown in Figure 5-12 relate to the limited support from Solaris 11 for certain types of hardware. For advice on how to handle such problems, consult other users on the Oracle Technology Network, described in Chapter 1, or the Oracle Solaris professional associated with your support contract.

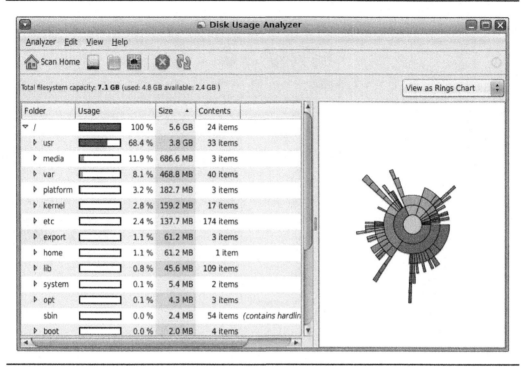

FIGURE 5-13. *Disk Usage Analyzer*

Disk Usage Analyzer   If you need to know what's taking up space on various folders, volumes, or drives, the Disk Usage Analyzer can help. Figure 5-13 illustrates a view of the filesystem, after Analyzer | Scan Filesystem was selected. You can also scan the current user's home directory or a specific local or remote folder. You can start this tool from the command line with the **baobab** command.

File Browser   The File Browser is the Solaris implementation of Nautilus. As shown in Figure 5-14, it includes a current list of files with thumbnails, the current free space, along with access to other folders. This file browser is also what's opened when you select most options in the Places menu. You can open a standard File Browser window with the **nautilus** command.

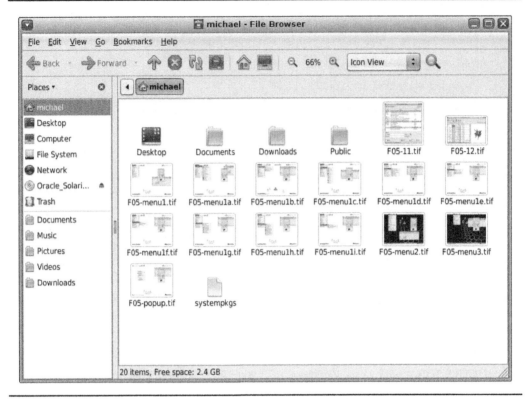

FIGURE 5-14. *The Solaris file browser*

File Encoding Examiner   The File Encoding Examiner is designed to help developers convert the name and contents of an older text file to the standard character encoding format, known as UTF-8, which is short for UCS Transformation Format for 8-bit characters. You can open this utility with the **fsexam** command.

GKrellM System Monitor   The GKrellM System Monitor can help you keep tabs on the status of the target system. As shown in Figure 5-15, it can help you monitor the current activity related to CPUs, processes, disk usage, network devices, and more. You can also open it with the **gkrellm** command.

FIGURE 5-15.   *A GNOME System Monitor*

GNOME Commander   GNOME Commander is an implementation of the older Midnight Commander file browser. Whereas Nautilus may be more familiar to users who are converting from operating systems such as Microsoft Windows, GNOME Commander may be more familiar to users coming from older versions of Solaris and other UNIX-based operating systems.

GParted Partition Editor   The GParted Partition Editor is a front end to the **parted** command. As such, it can help administrators manage the partitions configured for Solaris. However, even though it's accessible from the Applications menu, you can't start it as a regular user. To start GParted, you'll need to open a command-line interface and run **gparted** as the root administrative user. The editor is shown in Figure 5-16.

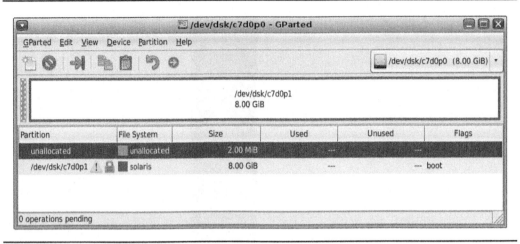

FIGURE 5-16. *The GParted Partition Editor*

Network Tools The Network Tools utility serves as a front end to a number of command-line options, in the following areas:

- **Devices** Examines the state of current network devices; a front end to the **ifconfig** command.
- **Ping** Supports a front end to the **ping** command to test network connectivity.
- **Netstat** Works with the **netstat** command for routing tables and more.
- **Traceroute** Supports a front end to the **traceroute** command for a topology of the routing of a network packet.
- **Port Scan** Enables a look at the status of a group of ports on remote systems; don't do this without the approval of the administrator of the remote system.
- **Lookup** Sets up a search of a DNS database for a variety of different items.
- **Finger** Supports user lookups, locally and remotely, with a front end to the **finger** command.
- **Whois** Enables searches of official domain name databases, with the **whois** command.

Performance Monitor As suggested by the command you can use to start it (**gnome-system-monitor**), the Performance Monitor starts the GNOME System Monitor. As shown in Figure 5-17, it includes four tabs of information. The following describes a bit about what you can see under each tab:

- **System** Includes basic system status, including RAM and available storage.
- **Processes** Shows information on processes. Also available from the **ps** command.
- **Resources** Identifies current usage levels for CPU, RAM, and network transfers.
- **File Systems** Displays information on currently mounted filesystems. The same information is available from the **df** command.

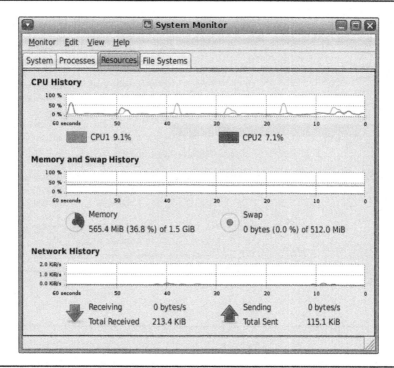

FIGURE 5-17. *The GNOME System Monitor*

System Log   The GNOME System Log viewer can be especially useful for administrators who are converting from Linux. As Solaris has a somewhat different structure for log files, the viewer shown in Figure 5-18 provides an easy view of the range of available log files. Although the filenames may seem a bit cryptic to Microsoft administrators, many of these files will be described in more detail in future chapters. The current log information shown is based on the file in the title bar.

As suggested by the name, you can start this utility from the command line with the **gnome-system-log** command.

Wireshark   The Wireshark utility, formerly known as Ethereal, is a protocol analyzer. Colloquially known as a "sniffer," Wireshark can help you identify information about network packets that are transmitted. In fact, if passwords are transmitted in clear text, as is typical for protocols such as Telnet, Wireshark can display those passwords. You can start Wireshark from the command line with the **wireshark** command. As shown in Figure 5-19, the prompts make it relatively easy to capture network packets from specific interfaces.

XTerm   The XTerm utility is one more command-line interface that you can start in the GNOME desktop environment.

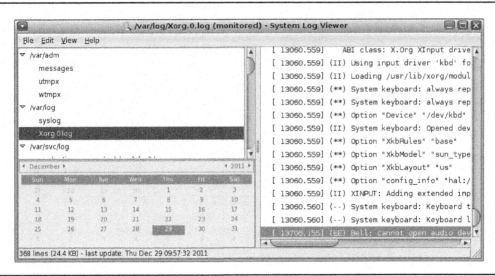

FIGURE 5-18. *The GNOME System Log viewer*

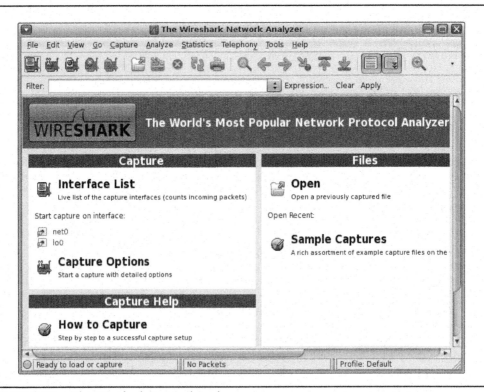

FIGURE 5-19. *The Wireshark Protocol Analyzer*

Universal Access   The Universal Access submenu supports tools that can help those with disabilities of various sorts. Two options are shown in Figure 5-20. The Orca Screen Reader can help those with visual disabilities. The Predictive Text Entry can help those on smaller systems where keyboards are more difficult to use.

The options associated with Universal Access work hand in hand with the Assistive Technologies applet in the System | Preferences menu.

NOTE
The GNOME Onscreen Keyboard has been made obsolete for Solaris 11. Even though it appears to be available from the Solaris 11 repositories, you won't be able to install it. For some situations, its functionality has been replaced by Dasher, the Predictive Text Entry tool.

More Help from Orca   As suggested by the tabs shown in Figure 5-21, Orca is an impressive tool. While it's not appropriate to go into too much detail, the tab titles are descriptive of its capabilities: General, Speech, Braille, Key Echo, Magnifier, Key Bindings, Pronunciation, and Text Attributes. You can start it from the command line with the **orca** command.

Dasher, the Predictive Text Entry Tool   Dasher can help users set up different types of predictive text entries, based on different languages, alphabets, and other custom features.

Run Application
Those of you who are paying attention may note one more entry under the Applications menu: Run Application. This opens a Run Application window where you can use the commands described earlier to open a selected application without opening a command-line interface.

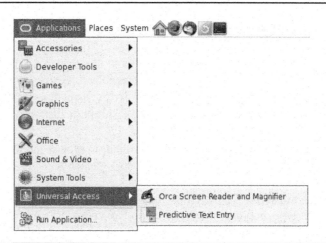

FIGURE 5-20.   *The Universal Access submenu*

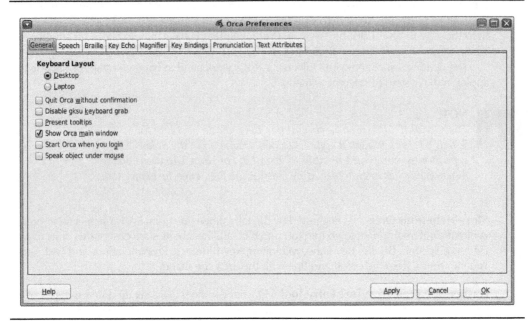

FIGURE 5-21. *More assistance from Orca*

Places Menu

In general, the options associated with the Places menu shown in Figure 5-22 opens the Nautilus file browser in the specified location. The first few options are the home directory of the current user, along with major subdirectories. Although the subdirectory names are descriptive, there's no requirement to have music files in the Music/ subdirectory.

We describe the options that follow in more detail:

- **Computer**   Opens Nautilus in a window similar to Figure 5-14. It includes a link to "File System," which moves Nautilus to a view of the top-level root directory.

- **Oracle_Solaris_Live_X86**   This entry will vary, depending on the CD/DVD or other media that might be installed or attached. This particular entry is based on the Live DVD associated with this release.

- **Network**   The Network entry opens Nautilus in browse mode, for Samba-based browsing. It works in a fashion similar to My Network Places on Microsoft operating systems.

- **Connect to Server**   Opens the Connect to Server window shown in Figure 5-23. The Service Type drop-down text box supports access to SSH, user-based and anonymous FTP, Samba/CIFS shared directories, files shared via web servers using WebDAV (HTTP) and Secure WebDAV (HTTPS), along with custom file sharing services.

- **Find Files**   Starts the Find Files utility described earlier in this chapter.

- **Recent Documents**   Opens a list of the 10 most recently accessed files.

FIGURE 5-22.   *The Places menu*

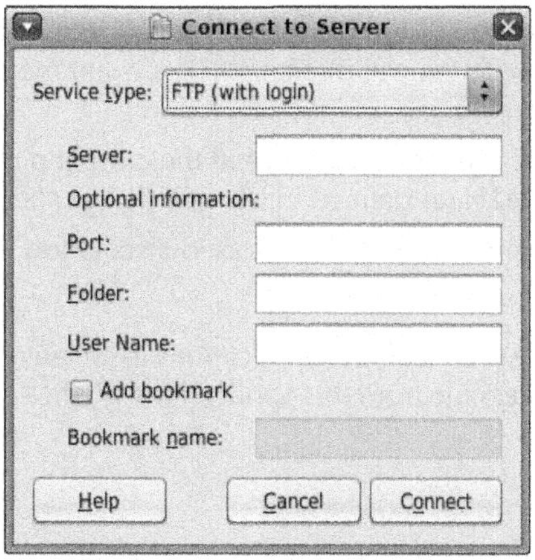

FIGURE 5-23.   *Connect to Server options*

Installing the OpenOffice.org Suite

The latest version of the OpenOffice.org suite is available online from OpenOffice.org. When you navigate to that web page from Solaris, make sure to download a package suitable for this operating system. Before proceeding, make sure sufficient space is available on the volume. All told, with the download and installation, you may need around 2 GB of free space.

While the main download is a tarball in tar.gz format, you can also download it in other formats such as an ISO image. In fact, many administrators will want to do just that, to facilitate its installation from a CD/DVD drive. In some of the tests we ran on Solaris 11 virtual machines, the installation of OpenOffice.org from an ISO image frequently got stuck, unless we copied the relevant directories to some partition or zone on the hard drive.

The installation process is relatively simple. The following steps are one method that worked at the time of this writing:

1. Navigate to OpenOffice.org from within Solaris.

2. Find and click a download link to the OpenOffice.org suite.

3. Make sure the download is associated with the Solaris operating system and then start the download. Because the download is around 200MB, it may take some time.

4. Once the download is complete, open a command line and navigate to the download directory, normally the Download/ subdirectory of the current user's home directory.

5. Run the **ls -ltar** command in the download directory to confirm the downloaded file. Normally, it's available as a compressed tarball, in .tar.gz format.

6. Unpack the tarball. The following command is just an example. The version you download will likely be different. The compression scheme may also be different, so adjust what you do accordingly:

   ```
   # tar xzvf Ooo_3.3.0_Solaris_x86_install-wJRE_en-US.tar.gz
   ```

7. The compressed package will be downloaded into a subdirectory, as depicted in the output. Navigate to that subdirectory. If you want more information, see the files in the readmes/ subdirectory.

8. As the root user, run the **setup** script in the current directory. Assuming the local directory is not in your **PATH** (as defined in Chapter 9), run the **./setup** command.

9. The command should open a GUI-based installation wizard on the desktop. Follow the prompts.

If the installation is successful, the applications associated with the OpenOffice.org suite should now also be accessible from the Applications | Office submenu, as shown in Figure 5-24.

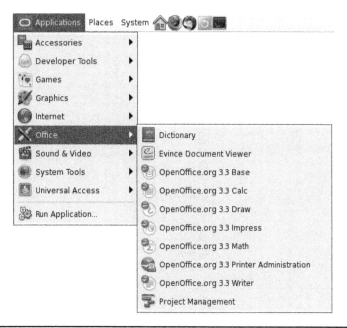

FIGURE 5-24.   *OpenOffice.org applications in the Office submenu*

System Menu

The System menu is perhaps the most important GUI menu for administrators. With exceptions, the Preferences submenu is used to configure the local system. The Administrative menu is used to configure and control a variety of services. As an administrator, you'll be expected to understand each of these tools in some detail in order to configure the system. In several cases, administrative tools will be covered in more detail in future chapters.

System Preferences

In the following subsections, you'll review the options associated with the Preferences submenu. In a few cases, the programs are described in more detail in different chapters. In addition, because the Printers applet is not normally active under the Preferences submenu, it is not described in this book. The submenu is shown in Figure 5-25.

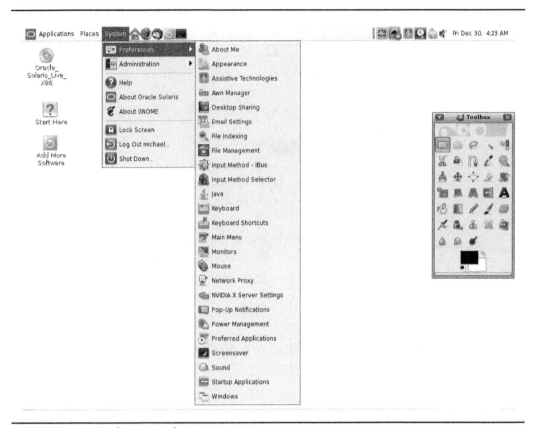

FIGURE 5-25. *Preferences submenu*

About Me

The About Me applet provides a straightforward way for users to include more information about themselves on the local system. It includes entries for contact information, addresses, and more personal information. It also includes a front end to the **passwd** command; if a user asks you how he or she can change their passwords, you can tell that user to open the About Me tool, shown in Figure 5-26, and click the Change Password button. This tool can also be started from the command line with the **gnome-about-me** command.

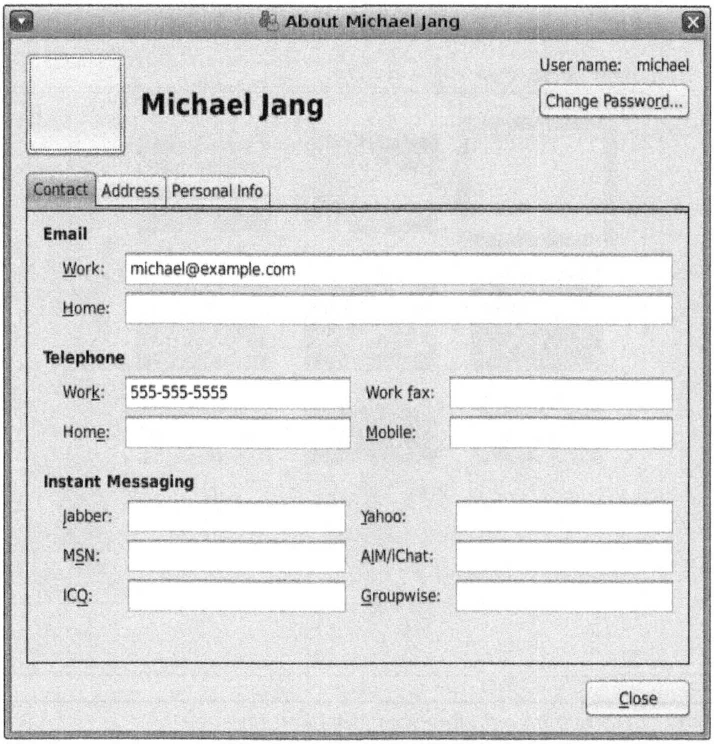

FIGURE 5-26.   *Information "About Me"*

Appearance
The Appearance applet supports changes to the "look and feel" of the local desktop. Since many organizational environments support a common background in GUI desktop environments, you may want to select the Background tab shown in Figure 5-27 to add the background of your choice. You can also open this applet with the **gnome-appearance-properties** command.

Assistive Technologies
Except for the Enable Assistive Technologies check box, this applet is a front end to several others, described shortly. Specifically, it starts the Preferred Applications, Keyboard Accessibility, and Mouse Accessibility tools. And that makes sense. Assistive technologies provide shortcuts of various types to preferred applications such as browsers, keyboard shortcuts, and mouse functionality. You can open this tool with the **gnome-at-properties** command.

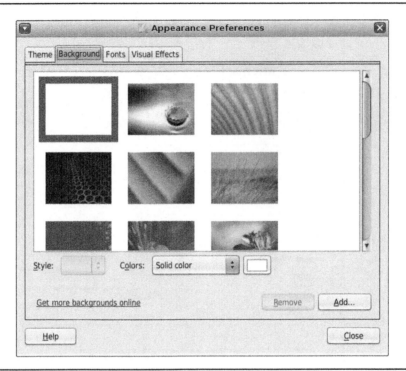

FIGURE 5-27. *Appearance Preferences – Background*

Awn Manager
The Awn Manager applet, shown in Figure 5-28, can help you customize the look and feel of the bottom taskbar, also known as the dock. You can start it from the command line with the **awn-manager** command.

Desktop Sharing
The Desktop Sharing option opens the Remote Desktop Preferences tool. If you're trying to help a user who is having a problem, this tool can help you get a view of their desktop. As shown in Figure 5-29, remote access is disabled by default. And that is how it should be, as you don't want black-hat hackers to see what you or your users are doing.

NOTE
The sharing associated with the Remote Desktop Preferences tool is different from the access associated with the Secure Shell discussed in Chapter 20. It is a different service that communicates on different ports. If you need to activate sharing with the Remote Desktop Preferences tool, make sure the appropriate ports are open. The default ports for this purpose are 5900 and 5901.

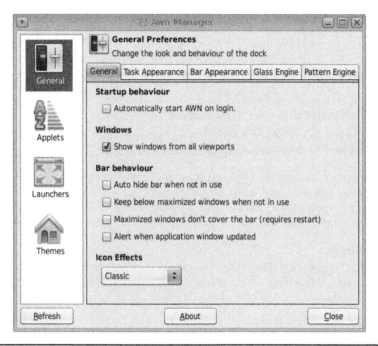

FIGURE 5-28. *The Awn Manager for the bottom taskbar*

FIGURE 5-29. *Remote Desktop Preferences*

If you need to help a user and don't have time to go to their desk, tell them to take the following steps:

1. Click System | Preferences | Desktop Sharing.

2. In the Remote Desktop Sharing window that appears, activate the top option: Allow Other Users to View Your Desktop.

3. Tell the user to confirm that the desktop is reachable over the local network, over a certain IP address. Ask the user to confirm that address.

4. If you're on a remote network, you'll need to tell the user to activate one more security setting: Configure Network Automatically to Accept Connections.

These actions activate the VNC server on the local system, enabling access from administrators like yourself—and potentially others. For that reason, you should tell your user to deactivate the Allow Other Users to View Your Desktop option when the help session is complete. If you need to open this tool from the command line, run the **vino-preferences** command.

Email Settings

The Email Settings option starts the Evolution Account Assistant. As noted earlier, Evolution is the PIM for e-mails, scheduling, and contacts. The Account Assistant supports the configuration of additional contacts.

File Indexing

The File Indexing option opens the Tracker Preferences tool. It's associated with a local search database. You can confirm that the Tracker daemon is running with the **ps aux | grep trackerd** command that the associated service is running by default. The tool shown in Figure 5-30 allows you to set up the database to be tracked.

TIP
If the Tracker daemon is not running, you can make sure it's active the next time you log into the GUI with the help of the Startup Application Preferences tool, described later in this chapter.

As suggested by the tabs, you can configure the local database as follows:

■ Under the General tab, you can set up indexing under basic conditions.

■ With the Files tab, you may specify whether Tracker searches the contents of files, and in specific directories.

■ When you select the Ignored Files tab, you are allowed to configure directories and file patterns to ignore in the index, to save time and space.

■ Under the Email tab, if you use the Evolution personal information manager (PIM), you can set up Tracker to include e-mails in the index.

■ With the Performance tab, given the demands of Tracker, you can regulate its usage of RAM and drive space.

If desired, you can open the Tracker Preferences window with the **tracker-preferences** command.

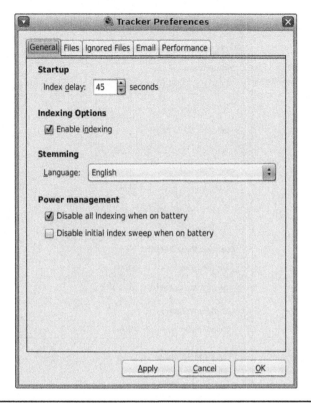

FIGURE 5-30. *Tracker Preferences*

File Management

If you're converting from some versions of Linux, what you see in the Nautilus file browser may appear quite different. That's because of the custom settings associated with the File Management tool. In essence, the tool shown in Figure 5-31 can be used to make Nautilus appear more like other file management tools.

You can configure Nautilus in different ways, associated with the following tabs:

- **Views**   Supports the configuration of new folders, icons, and file views.

- **Behavior**   Customizes behavior for clicks, executable files, and the Trash folder.

- **Display**   Includes the information associated with each icon inside Nautilus.

- **List Columns**   Specifies information to be included with a file in a list. Files can be ordered in a dozen different categories.

- **Preview**   Allows you to include different preview information for each icon, such as thumbnails and text.

- **Media**   Supports automatic access to applications when media such as CDs and USB cameras are inserted while the system is running.

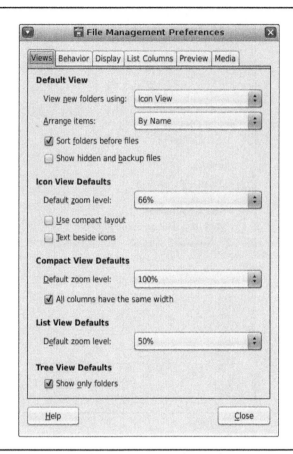

FIGURE 5-31. *File Management Preferences to control Nautilus*

As befits its role in controlling the Nautilus File Manager, you can start this tool with the **nautilus-file-management-properties** command.

Input Method – IBus

Some of you may have seen keyboards with multiple sets of characters. These hybrid keyboards are typically configured to support input in English and another language, perhaps with a different alphabet or character set. Those of you who use a keyboard associated with more than one set of characters should take note of the Input Method – IBus option. It opens the Input Method Preference Editor. It's associated with the **ibus-setup** command. However, this tool doesn't change anything unless the Input Method applet is properly configured.

Input Method Selector

The Input Method Selector applet opens the Input Method Framework Selector tool. If the packages associated with the Input Method – IBus applet are installed, you should be able to activate that Enable Input Method Framework. It's associated with the **imf-selector** command.

Java

A few Linux users actually avoid the use of Java applets. However, because Java is an Oracle product, Solaris users should have no reason to hesitate to use Java. The Java applet opens the Java Control Panel shown in Figure 5-32. It's also accessible with the **jcontrol** command.

There are several ways to configure Java using this control panel. The options are associated with the following tabs:

- **General**   Supports the configuration of network settings and temporary files
- **Java**   Enables access to specific Java Runtime Environment files
- **Security**   Allows the configuration of secure user and system certificates
- **Advanced**   Supports the customization of a variety of settings

Keyboard

The Keyboard Preferences tool, which you can also start with the **gnome-keyboard-properties** command, allows you to configure the behavior of a keyboard. Options include the control of repeat keys, sticky keys, mouse control from the keypad, and a periodic lock on the screen to enforce disabling the keyboard, which forces the user to take periodic breaks from typing.

Keyboard Shortcuts

The Keyboard Shortcuts tool includes a list of functions as well as key combinations that run those functions. You can select and change the key combination as desired. To open the Keyboard Shortcuts tool from the command line, run the **gnome-keybinding-properties** command.

FIGURE 5-32.   *Java Control Panel*

Main Menu

If desired, you can use the Main Menu tool to customize those items shown in the menus. For example, as shown in Figure 5-33, you might deselect those items that can't even be started from the menu unless the root user (or a user with appropriate privileges) has logged into the GUI.

You can start this tool from a terminal with the **alacarte** command.

Monitors

Because the developers behind the X server no longer include a GUI-based configuration tool, the GNOME Monitors applet is more important. You can start it from System | Preferences | Monitors or with the **gnome-display-properties** command.

As shown in Figure 5-34, you can use the tool to deactivate access as well as change the resolution, refresh rate, and rotation. If you've just added a monitor, click Detect Monitors. If successful, you'll see the two connected monitors depicted side by side in the window.

NOTE

In some cases, GUI applets include the name of the host system in parentheses. For example, the GNOME Monitor Preferences applet was opened from a system with a hostname of solarisdel.

FIGURE 5-33. *The Main Menu panel*

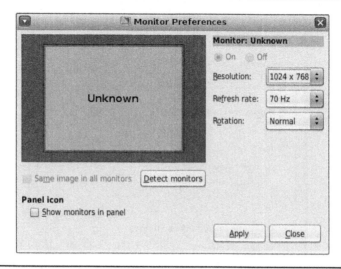

FIGURE 5-34. *GNOME Monitor Preferences*

Mouse

The mouse preferences applet works just as well for touchpads. It allows you to configure options for right- and left-handed users, along with actions associated with different kinds of "clicks." It's also accessible with the **gnome-mouse-preferences** command.

TIP

By default, highlighted text is copied to the cursor location with the middle mouse button. For users with two-button mice (or trackpads), click the left and right buttons simultaneously to simulate a middle mouse click.

Network Proxy

Communication between network clients and remote systems can be controlled with the Network Proxy tool, shown in Figure 5-35. Given its impact on the network, the associated command is **gnome-network-properties**. If you've configured a proxy server such as Squid, this is where you configure a client to use that proxy.

Although clients are configured to connect directly by default, Figure 5-35 supports the same or different proxy servers for three different protocols: HTTP, secure HTTP, and FTP. The reference to the SOCKS Host field is independent. If you create a SOCKS Proxy, an entry in that field is sufficient. Independent entries in the other fields would confuse network clients.

If you want to still support direct connections to the Internet for certain hosts or domains, you can enter that information under the Ignored Hosts tab.

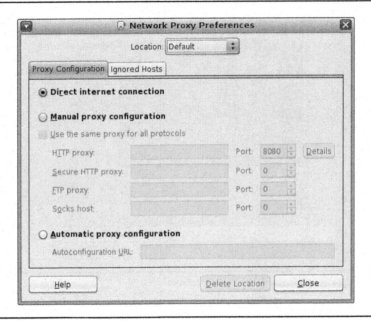

FIGURE 5-35. *Network Proxy Preferences*

NOTE
Make sure all network clients use the proxy server. After using the Network Proxy tool, test each client.

NVIDIA X Server Settings

NVIDIA is a popular manufacturer of graphics cards. As such, they've included custom settings for the system in the nvda.cfg file in the /usr/X11/lib/X11/getconfig directory. Any changes you make with the NVIDIA X Server Settings tool can be saved by default to the hidden .nvidia-settings-rc file in user home directories.

Pop-Up Notifications

The Pop-Up Notifications tool supports configuration options for pop-up notifications associated with different applications and utilities on the Solaris desktop.

Power Management

The Power Management tool may be especially important on systems with batteries, such as laptop computers. They determine system behavior associated with power buttons, the closing of laptop lids, and when battery power is low. The On Battery Power tab isn't shown unless the local system may be powered by a battery. See Figure 5-36 for more information. The screenshot was taken from a laptop system where Solaris 11 was directly installed, with the help of the **gnome-power-preferences** command.

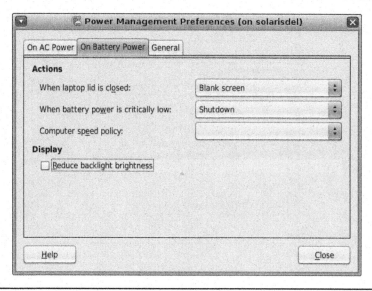

FIGURE 5-36. *Power Management Preferences*

Preferred Applications

Files from the Nautilus file browser, as well as files listed in the Places | Recent Documents submenu (or the **gnome-default-applications** command), are frequently linked to certain applications. The link is driven by settings in the Preferred Applications utility shown in Figure 5-37. As suggested by the tabs in this window, preferred applications are available in four different categories:

- ■ **Internet**   Selects applications for web browsing and e-mail reading
- ■ **Multimedia**   Determines the default multimedia player used for associated files
- ■ **System**   Defines the standard command-line terminal opened in the GUI
- ■ **Accessibility**   Specifies the visual and other utilities associated with disabilities

Screensaver

Screensavers are important for saving energy. Appropriate options can improve security. On older systems, screensavers were used to help prevent monitor "burn-in," where a shadow of the active screen was burned into monitor pixels. Just as many organizations specify a common desktop background, they may also specify a common screensaver. The Solaris Screensaver Preferences window is shown in Figure 5-38. You can open it with the **xscreensaver-demo** command.

Perhaps most important for security is the Lock Screen option. If a user walks away from the machine, the screensaver automatically runs and requires that user's password to return to the desktop. Standard screensaver pictures can be loaded under the Advanced tab.

FIGURE 5-37. *Preferred Applications*

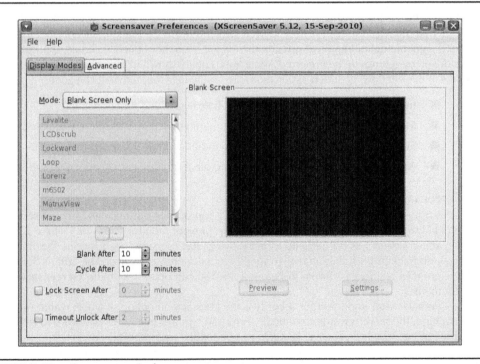

FIGURE 5-38. *Screensaver Preferences*

For security, you could tell users to click System | Lock Screen when they walk away from their desks. That command automatically invokes the screensaver with password protection.

Because options are saved to the .xscreensaver file in user home directories, you can set up a standard version of this file that reflects any policies associated with your organization. When you send a copy of this file to each applicable home directory, each Solaris workstation will comply with appropriate policies with respect to screensavers.

Sound

The Sound option opens a Volume Control window. However, it doesn't work unless the system has a detected sound card. If so, this applet, or the **gnome-volume-control** command, opens volume control options for speakers, headphones, and microphones. It also supports the configuration of sound themes for certain actions.

Startup Applications

You can configure a standard set of applications to start when you log into a Solaris 11 system. That's made possible with the help of the Startup Applications Preferences applet shown in Figure 5-39. It's also accessible with the **gnome-session-properties** command. The list of programs shown are automatically started upon a successful login. If desired, you can add or remove startup items with appropriate buttons, and information on the full path to a program, such as **/usr/bin/firefox** for the Firefox Web Browser.

Windows

The Windows applet supports different actions associated with cursors, title bars, and window movement.

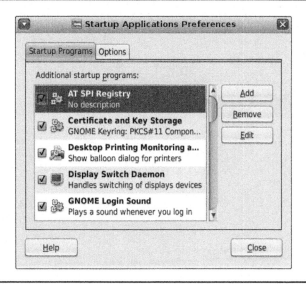

FIGURE 5-39.   *Startup Applications Preferences*

System Administration Menu

The tools available under the System | Administration menu are focused on services. They range from the Apache Web Server tool, which can help you set up the configuration files associated with that service, to the Update Manager, which can help you manage the status of installed packages.

Apache Web Server as a Tool

The Apache Web Server tool included in Solaris 11 is a Java-based configuration tool. As shown in Figure 5-40, it includes options for global settings. The localhost option highlighted in the figure is a local virtual host, which in this case is associated with Apache documentation. It supports the configuration of secure virtual hosts, based on the Secure Sockets Layer (SSL).

As suggested by the figure, it allows you to change the default port, the domain name associated with the local virtual host, whether individual user public_html/ subdirectories can be shared via Apache, as well as different file extensions (MIME types). The SSL tab includes options for appropriate certificates and associated key files.

As a Java applet, the command that starts this GUI tool is **vp apache**.

Although the command appears complex, all but the last word is the same for all such applets, configured in a virtual panel client. Apache configuration is covered in Chapter 22.

Core Files

In essence, a process creates a core file if an error is "bad enough." In that case, the process dumps selected data into a core file as a log for later analysis. Such core files are essentially snapshots of the status of memory when the error occurred. The Core Files applet, as shown in Figure 5-41, supports the configuration of core files locally or in centralized directories or systems.

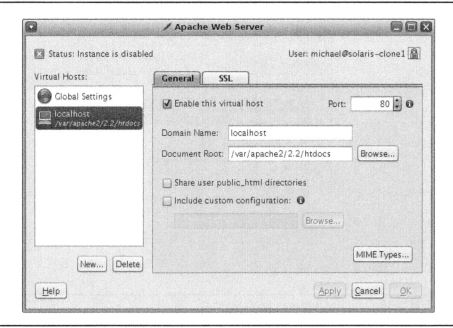

FIGURE 5-40. *The Apache Web Server configuration utility*

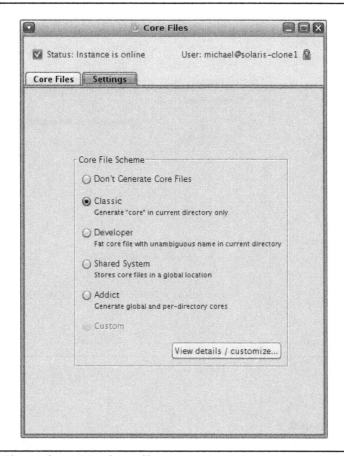

FIGURE 5-41. *The configuration of core files*

It is also a Java applet, which you can start with the **vp coreadm** command.

Network

The Network applet in the System | Administration menu opens the Network Preferences tool. If there's a DHCP server on the local network, great. The network services associated with Solaris 11 in general will configure the network cards on a system automatically. However, there are some in the security community who believe that the most secure systems have static IP addresses. If there are problems, or if you're configuring static IP addresses on a system, get familiar with the Network Preferences tool. A sample view with an active wireless network connection is shown in Figure 5-42.

If you have a dynamically configured network card and want to change it (or vice versa), click the Show drop-down text box that's currently associated with Connection Status. You should see entries associated with all detected (but not necessarily active) network cards. Select that card, and then you can configure it for both IPv4 and IPv6 addresses.

FIGURE 5-42. *The Network Preferences tool*

Package Manager

Package management is an important tool in your arsenal. The Package Manager, shown in Figure 5-43, is a comprehensive front end to various **pkg*** commands, starting with **pkg**. It's configured with default connections to repositories. Packages are collected in categories, which can be selected in the left pane. You can view the status of and select individual packages in the upper-right pane. You can review information about each package, including its contents, in the lower-right pane.

The figure shows a view of the package associated with the Nautilus File Manager. It's part of the Desktop category, in the File Managers subcategory. The Package Manager and associated commands are described in more detail in Chapter 11. You can start it from the command line with the **packagemanager** command.

Print Manager

The Print Manager may seem especially familiar to Linux users. And that's for good reason. With the release of Solaris 11, this operating system now uses the Common UNIX Printing System (CUPS) as the default print service. This tool was originally developed by Red Hat for its Linux releases, and has been adapted for Solaris. You can open the tool shown in Figure 5-44 with the **system-config-printer** command. For more information on CUPS, see Chapter 15.

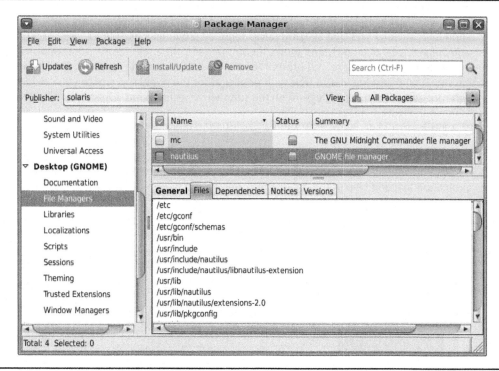

FIGURE 5-43. *The Package Manager*

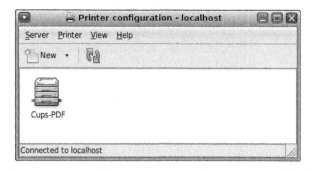

FIGURE 5-44. *The Print Manager*

SMF Services

The Service Management Facility (SMF) is focused on the SMF Services tool. As a front end to commands such as **svcs** and **svcadm**, SMF Services provides a high-level view of the current status of services, daemons, and more. If you open it from a regular account, options such as Enable and Disable require and prompt for administrative access. If you wish to dispense with that step, you could log in as a user with privileges for the noted service, or you could just open it with root administrative privileges with the **sudo vp svcs** command. One view of current services is shown in Figure 5-45.

Options associated with SMF will be described in more detail in Chapter 6.

System Firewall

The System Firewall option starts the Service Firewall configuration tool. It is a Java-based GUI application that can help you manage the configuration of firewalls. As suggested by the options

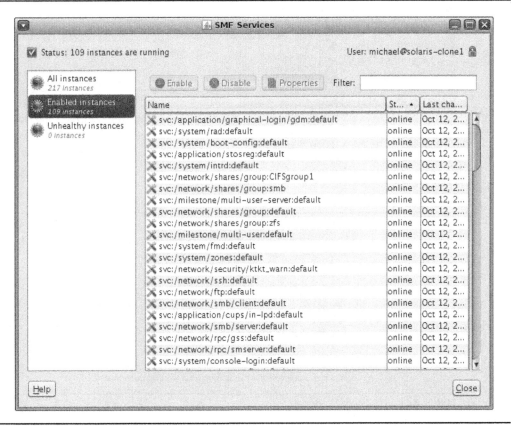

FIGURE 5-45. *The SMF Services tool*

shown in Figure 5-46, you can set up a variety of access policies. Other options include the following:

- **Add Service Policy** Supports the configuration of firewalls by individual services
- **Open Programs tab** Enables the configuration of specific open TCP and UDP ports
- **Override tab** Allows the setup of a system-wide policy that overrides any configured service-specific policy

To start this Java-based tool, you can also run the following command:

```
$ vp firewall
```

Time Slider Tool

The Time Slider Manager is not a clock tool. As shown in Figure 5-47, it can help you configure automatic backups of the ZFS filesystems of your choice. To see the full screen shown in the figure, activate the Enable Time Slider option and click the Advanced Options setting. It supports backups to external drives as well as custom backups of selected filesystems.

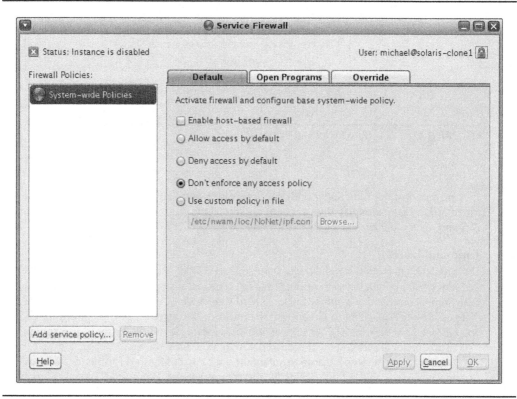

FIGURE 5-46. *The Service Firewall tool*

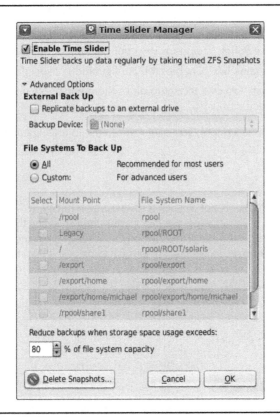

FIGURE 5-47. *The Time Slider setup tool*

You can start the Time Slider with the **time-slider-setup** command. You should be prompted for an appropriate administrative account and the associated password. For more information on ZFS and related backup concepts, see Chapter 8.

Time and Date

The Time and Date utility can help you configure an NTP client. As shown in Figure 5-48, it includes basic information with respect to time on the local system. You can also start it with the **time-admin** command. It assumes the local hardware clock is set to UTC, a non-English acronym that's essentially equivalent to Greenwich Mean Time. As suggested by the options in the left pane, you can set the time zone of your choice, which is useful for mobile systems. In addition, you can make sure the local system is synchronized with remote time servers.

In general, you should be able to select time servers configured for the local organization. Alternatively, you could set up connections to remote servers. Pools of NTP servers are maintained by the NTP public services project.

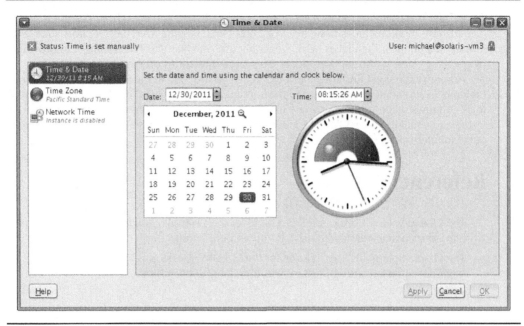

FIGURE 5-48.   *The Time and Date utility*

Because the NTP service is not active by default, you should make sure the ntp.server and ntp.client files in the /etc/inet directory are available and properly configured. You can then activate the client and/or server service with the **svcadm enable network/ntp** command.

Update Manager
When the Update Manager is selected, it checks currently installed packages against the packages stored in configured repositories. If a newer version of a package is available, it downloads and then installs the package, with dependencies. You can start it from the command line with the **/usr/lib/pm-launch pm-updatemanager** command. You should be prompted for an appropriate administrative account and the associated password. For more information on Solaris package management, see Chapter 7.

Summary
In this chapter, you looked at the Solaris 11 GUI in some detail. Because basic Solaris installations include a GUI, it's where most Solaris developers and administrators will do their work. Although that means regular text consoles are not available, you can open as many command-line terminals as needed.

The Solaris 11 GUI is built on the GNOME desktop environment. It includes a variety of menus and preconfigured icons. One menu is directly available by right-clicking the desktop. The Applications menu includes basic everyday programs, ranging from basic editors such as gEdit to multimedia utilities. The Places menu generally uses the Nautilus File Manager to provide a view of key directories. It also supports access to shared directories on remote servers.

Administrators will find the heart of GNOME in the System menu. In general, utilities in the Preferences submenu are dedicated to the configuration of the local desktop environment. Utilities in the Administration submenu can be used to control and configure many of the services you can install and configure on a Solaris 11 server. When appropriate, these utilities are described in more detail in future chapters.

References

The GNOME Project can be found at www.gnome.org.

The Oracle Solaris 11 Accessibility Guide for the GNOME Desktop is available online at http://docs.oracle.com/cd/E23824_01/html/E24675/index.html.

The Oracle Solaris 11 User's Guide for the GNOME Desktop is available online at http://docs.oracle.com/cd/E23824_01/html/E24676/index.html.

CHAPTER
6

Service Management

NIX systems, especially multiuser servers, generally run "background" (noninteractive) processes (also called *daemons*) that provide services such as e-mail receipt and transmission, file sharing, printing, security monitoring, login and identity controls, network connectivity, shared applications, and many more. Such services are started when the system boots and run continuously while the system is up. Some of these services are designed to monitor system hardware health and to take corrective actions if needed—for example, taking a faulty disk offline. As part of Solaris' Fault Management Architecture (FMA), Solaris 10 and 11 include the Service Management Facility (SMF), which is used to monitor the systems' software services. In earlier UNIX implementations, such services were defined and started by varied ad-hoc scripts in the operating system's /etc/rc directory. This approach was haphazard, prone to errors, and provided no unified framework for monitoring services, understanding their interdependencies, or defining and taking corrective actions in case of problems.

In this chapter, we detail SMF's capabilities, structure, and tools. We start by describing Solaris 11 services, how they are named, categorized, and administered using both command-line interface (CLI) and graphical user interface (GUI) tools. We detail how services are defined using manifest files and discuss how to create and customize your own services. We also show you how to troubleshoot service problems using the detailed output that SMF provides.

Solaris Service Concepts

The SMF in Oracle Solaris provides a unified, common framework for creating, monitoring, and managing all system software services, including automated responses and corrections to service software errors and disruptions. It allows unrelated services to be started in parallel, significantly reducing system startup time. In addition, it defines a common state model for all services, along with a single location for service configuration files. SMF also allows you to assign or delegate privileges to services; this enables services to run as specific roles with configurable authorizations.

In this section, we explain the various categories of Solaris 11 services and how they are named. These services have "states" that indicate their current conditions and interactions with the operating system and with other services; we describe these states and how they can change.

What Is a Solaris 11 Service?

In most operating systems, and in particular in Solaris, a *service* is a noninteractive program generally started at boot time that continues to run and provides shared capabilities for all users. Typical examples of such services include web servers (Apache), file sharing (NFS), database programs (Oracle DB, MySQL), and e-mail transfer (sendmail), to name a few. Such services "listen" for user requests and respond as needed; they often run as privileged programs under the "root" user ID permissions so that they can service any user.

UNIX and Linux administrators are familiar with service startup scripts that reside in the /etc/rc* directories; this hierarchy of directories contains files whose names indicate their function and order of execution as the system boots up or shuts down. Such scripts and naming conventions still work as expected in Solaris, but they cannot be managed by SMF.

Service Naming

Services in Solaris are referred to using a structured naming pattern called the Fault Managed Resource Identifier (FMRI), which specifies five components:

- **Scheme**   The type of service (managed or legacy)
- **Location**   The host system where the service runs (usually localhost)
- **Function category**   The service function (Application, System, and so on)
- **Description**   The service name
- **Instance**   Indicates instances of services that may have more than one copy or version running (NFS server, for example)

The general form of an FMRI is as follows:

```
scheme://location/function/description:instance
```

As you can see, it looks very much like a web URI. For example, the FMRI for the sendmail daemon looks like this:

```
svc://localhost/network/smtp:sendmail
```

This is an SMF-managed service (svc) running on the local system (localhost), providing a network service instance of the e-mail utility (smtp) called sendmail. Programs that reference FMRIs can use abbreviated names, such as network/smtp:sendmail, or even simply sendmail.

Services in Solaris are managed by another daemon that starts at boot time, svc.startd, which is responsible for starting, monitoring, restarting, and error state reporting for all services and their dependencies. It also runs any legacy rc scripts at their appropriate run levels *after* SMF-managed services have been started. The svc.startd daemon keeps service status information in files in the /etc/svc directory hierarchy. It keeps a repository of all service instances in a lightweight database file called /etc/svc/repository.db, including backups of earlier repositories. The svcs program reads its service state information from these files. The daemon also stores boot log files in /etc/svc/volatile during the initial system boot stages prior to mounting /var as a writable filesystem. Service configuration definitions common to all system services are defined in the system manifest at /etc/svc/profile/generic.xml.

Service Categories

Services are grouped under several functional categories:

- **Applications**   Programs that provide user services (such as the ZFS TimeSlider program or the CUPS printing service)
- **Network**   Network services (such as login, file sharing, firewall, DNS, and so on)
- **Device**   Device-specific and I/O services (for device availability dependencies)
- **Milestone**   Boot sequence run levels (corresponding to UNIX SVR4 run levels)
- **System**   System services (such as auditing, filesystems, and so on)

Service States

Every service has a *state*—a set of characteristics and data values associated with each service at a given moment in time. Some services' states are listed as "legacy_run." These are services started with the traditional /etc/rc scripts. They are visible to SMF, but that's all; SMF cannot manage their states. SMF-managed services can have the following states:

- **Online**   The service is enabled and running without error, including all its dependencies.
- **Offline**   The service is enabled but not yet running (often waiting for a dependency service to be ready).
- **Disabled**   The service is not running and has been explicitly disabled by the administrator.
- **Maintenance**   svc.startd cannot start the service due to an error or missing dependency.
- **Degraded**   The service is running in a defined limited mode.
- **Legacy_run**   The service is not manageable by SMF but its presence is observable.

SMF Programs

Solaris 11 includes both CLI and GUI programs for observing and administering services. The most common and useful of these are the svcs program for monitoring service states and the svcadm program for manipulating service instances. In general, most administrators manage services using the root role, although that is not strictly necessary; other user roles may be given privileges to start or stop services.

Listing Services

The svcs program is used to display detailed state information about services defined on your system. The **svcs –a** command and flag will list all services for your system, including those that are running as well as those that are disabled or incomplete. The following abbreviated output shows a typical list of some of these services:

```
# svcs -a
STATE          STIME    FMRI
legacy_run     Jan_02   lrc:/etc/rc2_d/S47pppd
legacy_run     Jan_02   lrc:/etc/rc3_d/S99webmin
...
disabled       Jan_02   svc:/system/sar:default
disabled       Jan_02   svc:/network/finger:default
disabled       Jan_02   svc:/network/telnet:default
disabled       Jan_02   svc:/network/rexec:default
...
online         Jan_02   svc:/system/svc/restarter:default
online         Jan_02   svc:/network/smb:default
online         Jan_02   svc:/milestone/multi-user-server:default
...
online         Jan_08   svc:/application/pkg/update:default
maintenance    Jan_02   svc:/network/rpc/keyserv:default
...
```

In this output, we see that the pppd service is of legacy type (started by the /etc/rc2_d/S47pppd script), the telnet service is disabled, the smb file sharing service is online, and the rpc/keyserv service is in the maintenance state and needs attention from the administrator.

The **svcs** command is used to display the *state* of services, but its real value is in the other information it is able to collect and report about a service. The **svcs –l** command and option flag will display all of the properties of a service. Here's an example:

```
# svcs -l svc:/network/nfs/server:default
fmri           svc:/network/nfs/server:default
name           NFS server
enabled        true
state          online
next_state     none
state_time     January  2, 2012 09:44:43 PM EST
logfile        /var/svc/log/network-nfs-server:default.log
restarter      svc:/system/svc/restarter:default
contract_id    125
manifest       /etc/svc/profile/generic.xml
manifest       /lib/svc/manifest/network/nfs/server.xml
dependency     require_any/error svc:/milestone/network (online)
dependency     require_all/error svc:/network/nfs/nlockmgr (online)
dependency     optional_all/error svc:/network/nfs/mapid (online)
dependency     require_all/restart svc:/network/rpc/bind (online)
dependency     optional_all/none svc:/network/rpc/keyserv (maintenance)
dependency     optional_all/none svc:/network/rpc/gss (online)
dependency     optional_all/none svc:/system/filesystem/reparse (online)
dependency     require_all/error svc:/system/filesystem/local (online)
```

This output shows the following characteristics of the "nfs server" instance:

- **fmri**   The full FMRI name of the service
- **name**   An abbreviated service label character string
- **state**   The current state of the service
- **next_state**   If the service is still initializing, the next state beyond the current state
- **state_time**   The timestamp showing the service startup time
- **logfile**   The location of the service's log file
- **restarter**   The system service used to restart the service
- **contract_id**   The process ID of the service's starter
- **manifest**   Configuration file(s) for the service
- **dependency**   Prerequisite service(s) for the service

Therefore, in the preceding example, the state of the nfs server is "online," it started January 2, 2012 09:44:43 P.M. EST, the service's log file is /var/svc/log/network-nfs-server:default.log, its definition and initialization file is /lib/svc/manifest/network/nfs/server.xml, and it is dependent on several prerequisite services such as the network milestone and local filesystems being online. This wealth of information is invaluable in managing system services, especially the listing of dependencies.

You can also list all the services that a particular service *depends on*. Here's an example using **svcs –d**:

```
# svcs -d ssh
STATE          STIME     FMRI
disabled       Jan_02    svc:/network/ipfilter:default
online         Jan_02    svc:/system/cryptosvc:default
online         Jan_02    svc:/network/loopback:default
online         Jan_02    svc:/system/utmp:default
online         Jan_02    svc:/network/physical:default
online         Jan_02    svc:/system/filesystem/local:default
online         Jan_02    svc:/system/filesystem/autofs:default
```

You can also list what services depend on a specified service. The following example uses **svcs –D**:

```
# svcs -D ssh
STATE          STIME     FMRI
online         Jan_02    svc:/milestone/self-assembly-complete:default
online         Jan_02    svc:/milestone/multi-user-server:default
```

In this way, you can easily troubleshoot service problems with your system. Not all the listed dependencies are explicitly required to be online; they can be specified as individually required or as a group. You can also specify exclusionary services (that is, services that must be disabled in order for your service to start).

Starting and Stopping Services

The **svcadm** command is used to manage services on your system. It has several subcommands:

- **enable** Start the service and place it in the online state (if possible)
- **disable** Stop the service and place it in the offline state
- **restart** Restart the service (after some maintenance)
- **refresh** Used to tell svc.startd to reread the service configuration file and notify dependents
- **mark** Set the service state to maintenance (prior to diagnostic work on it)
- **clear** Clear the maintenance state (after some maintenance work)
- **milestone** Set the specified boot-level milestone

When you specify the FMRI for a service, you can give the full FMRI or just a part of it, as shown here:

```
# svcadm enable svc:/network/smtp:sendmail
```

or

```
# svcadm disable sendmail
```

The svcs program allows for wildcards. For example, this command will list all nfs-related services:

```
# svcs -l *nfs*
```

After issuing a command to enable or disable a service, it's usually a good idea to verify the state of the service. Here's an example:

```
# svcs sendmail
STATE          STIME    FMRI
online         17:04:04 svc:/network/smtp:sendmail
# svcadm disable sendmail
# svcs sendmail
STATE          STIME    FMRI
disabled       17:05:05 svc:/network/smtp:sendmail
```

When you enable or disable a service, setting that state persists through reboots. That is, if you execute **svcadm disable sendmail**, that service will remain disabled in subsequent reboots. If, however, you want only to disable a service for the current boot session, use the **-t** option flag:

NOTE
SMF is in charge of services; if you identify a service's process and then kill that process, SMF will attempt to restart the service according to the rules and programs specified in its manifest file.

Here, we have killed rpcbind's process, but the service refuses to die! SMF won't let it because that service has a restarter (a defined process used by the svc.startd daemon to trigger a service restart).

```
# pgrep -l bind
 6856 rpcbind
# kill 6856
# pgrep -l bind
 7241 rpcbind
```

In addition to the svcs and svcadm CLI programs, the Solaris 11 desktop provides a GUI interface for managing services. Select the System | Administration | SMF Services menu option (see Figure 6-1).

This will display the SMF Services GUI, shown in Figure 6-2, which lists all available services, including their states.

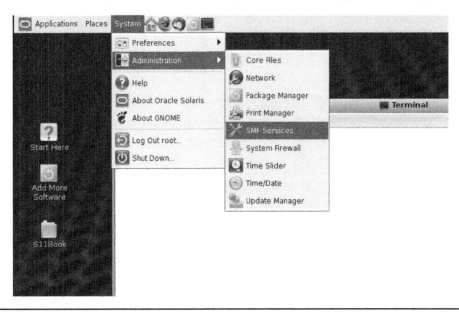

FIGURE 6-1. *The SMF GUI System Administration menu option*

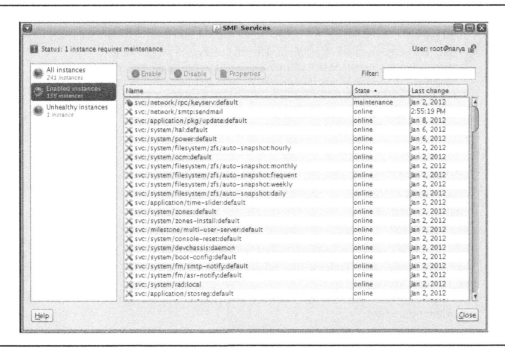

FIGURE 6-2. *The SMF Services management GUI*

From this GUI, you can select a service, enable or disable it, and display its characteristics (shown in Figure 6-3), including its associated log file (shown in Figure 6-4).

Because each service can have its own log file, diagnosing service problems becomes easier than with the earlier UNIX approach, which dumped all service events into a single system log file.

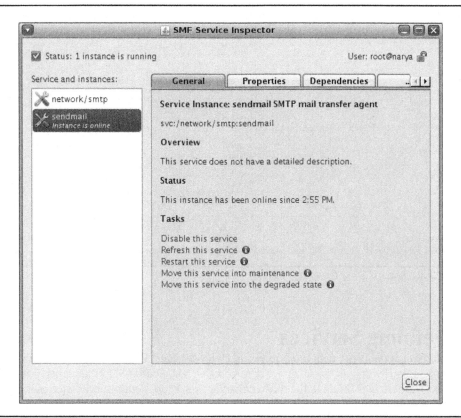

FIGURE 6-3.   *The SMF Service Inspector*

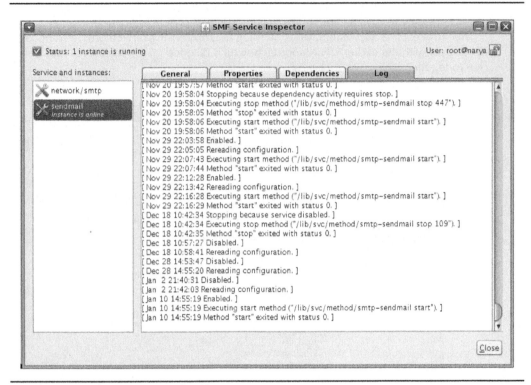

FIGURE 6-4. *The SMF Service log file*

Defining Services

Solaris 11 is delivered with most common UNIX services predefined, although many of them are not enabled by default. Services are defined using a standard file format called a *manifest,* written in XML; these files reside in the /lib/svc/manifest directory within subdirectories for each of the service functional categories.

Service Manifests

A service's manifest file defines all of its properties, behaviors, and actions, including the following:

- Full name (FMRI)
- Dependencies (other services and files)
- Start and stop methods
- Log file where service events are recorded
- Restarters and error condition handling
- Number of allowable instances

Manifest files can be copied and modified to create new services or to change the behavior of existing services. Practically speaking, creating XML manifest files from scratch is difficult and error prone, unless you are adept at XML. You can search the Web for prewritten manifests that you can modify and install (see www.scalingbits.com/solaris/smf/directory or http://hub.opensolaris.org/bin/view/Community+Group+smf/manifests for some examples). Ideally, independent software vendor (ISV) providers should include service manifests instead of rc scripts for installing and managing their software services.

Creating a Service Manifest

Manifest files define dependency, startup, and restart conditions for services. Solaris 11 manifest files reside in the /lib/svc/manifest directory. New services created by the administrator require manifest files if they are to be managed by SMF; scripts in the /etc/rc directories will also work as in earlier Solaris releases, but this approach is not recommended because you lose all the benefits of SMF.

If you are adding a service to the Oracle Solaris OS, you must create a manifest file for that service in the /lib/svc/manifest directory. As mentioned in the previous section, it's easier to simply copy and modify an existing manifest. You must change certain key items in the copied manifest:

- Service Name and Version
- Default Startup Flag (true or false)
- Service Dependency (one or more dependencies on other services)
- Exec Method (script that defines start, stop, and refresh actions)

Your new manifest file (for example MyService.xml) must be readable. Verify that there are no errors in the manifest using svccfg:

```
# svccfg validate MyService.xml
```

Next, you must add the manifest to the repository, tell the svc.startd daemon about the new service, and then enable it:

```
# svccfg import MyService.xml
# svcadm enable myservice
```

Always check the *state* of your service with the svcs program, and examine the *log file* you specified for your service for any startup errors.

For a detailed example showing how to create a manifest file, see "How to Create an Oracle Solaris Service Management Facility Manifest" at www.oracle.com/technetwork/server-storage/solaris/solaris-smf-manifest-wp-167902.pdf.

Boot Services

As Solaris boots up from a "cold start" (from the hardware (HW) power-off state), it runs hardware presence and diagnostic tests and then starts grouped sequences of system services. As the OS completes each group (or milestone), subsequent services can check whether their dependencies have been met and are online before starting up.

Boot Milestone Services

The Solaris boot process goes through several stages that can be individually selected for administrative purposes. These stages (milestones) roughly correspond to UNIX or Linux "run levels" (which are based on earlier UNIX SVR4), and indicate that the set of services and their dependencies associated with a boot milestone have all been completed (see Table 6-1).

In order to set your system to single-user mode, for example, you use the svcadm program:

```
# svcadm milestone svc:/milestone/single-user
```

And here's how to return it to full operation:

```
# svcadm milestone svc:/milestone/all
```

For some diagnostic activities, it's useful to boot the system without *any* services enabled:

```
# svcadm milestone svc:/milestone/none
```

The traditional **init s** and **init 6** commands for single-user mode and reboot still work, but using **svcadm** guarantees proper shutdown and restart of all system services.

NOTE
*Although **init** in Solaris 11 still reads the /etc/inittab file and starts programs listed there, it does not directly execute scripts in the /etc/rc.* directories; those are started by the SMF svc.startd daemon.*

Other SMF Tools

In addition to the svcs and svcadm programs, you will need to use several other service administration tools to manage and configure services (see Table 6-2).

Solaris 11 services have extensive configurable properties defined in the system (generic.xml) and other service manifest files. You can display these properties using svcprop, for example:

```
# svcprop svc:/network/nfs/server:default
nfs-props/device astring ""
nfs-props/listen_backlog integer 32
nfs-props/max_connections integer -1
nfs-props/protocol astring ALL
nfs-props/server_delegation boolean true
nfs-props/server_versmax integer 4
nfs-props/server_versmin integer 2
nfs-props/servers integer 1024
general/complete astring
general/enabled boolean false
...
(output truncated for brevity)
```

These properties can be modified using svccfg. For example, a useful service property to configure is **set-notify**; you use this service property to take an action when a service's state changes.

SVR4 Run Level	SMF Milestone
-	svc:/milestone/none. All services disabled.
s or **S**	svc:/milestone/single-user. Single-user admin mode.
2	svc://milestone/multi-user. Multiuser mode without network services.
3	svc://milestone/multi-user. Multiuser mode with network services enabled.
5	svc://milestone/all. Multiuser mode with all services enabled.

TABLE 6-1. *SMF Boot Milestones and SVR4 Run Levels*

Tool	Description
svcprop	View SMF repository data.
svccfg	Manipulate the SMF repository.
inetadm	View and configure inetd managed services.
inetconv	Convert an inetd.conf entry to an SMF manifest.

TABLE 6-2. *Service Management and Configuration Programs*

The following command tells the svc.startd daemon to send an e-mail to an administrator whenever *any* service (**-g** means it's a *global* setting) changes its state to **maintenance**:

```
# svccfg setnotify -g to-maintenance mailto:admin@hostname
```

Properties for individual services can be set in the same way:

```
# svccfg -s svc:/network/ssh:default set-notify to-offline mailto:admin@hostname
```

The preceding command tells the service daemon to send admin@hostname (or any other e-mail address you specify) a message whenever the ssh service goes offline.

You can also use the svccfg program in interactive mode; once in that mode, you can display usage information on any of the other subcommands using the **help** subcommand:

```
# svccfg
svc:> help
General commands: help set repository end
Manifest commands: inventory validate import export
Profile commands: apply extract
Entity commands: list select unselect add delete describe
Snapshot commands: listsnap selectsnap revert
Instance commands: refresh
Property group commands: listpg addpg delpg
Property commands: listprop setprop delprop editprop
Property value commands: addpropvalue delpropvalue setenv unsetenv
Notification parameters: listnotify setnotify delnotify
svc:> select system/timezone
```

```
svc:/system/timezone> list
:properties
default
svc:/system/timezone> select default
svc:/system/timezone:default> listprop
timezone                           application
timezone/localtime                 astring    US/Eastern
general                            framework
general/complete                   astring
general/enabled                    boolean    true
restarter                          framework              NONPERSISTENT
restarter/logfile                  astring    /var/svc/log/system-timezone:default.log
restarter/start_pid                count      285
restarter/start_method_timestamp   time       1326395214.524943000
restarter/start_method_waitstatus  integer    0
restarter/transient_contract       count
restarter/auxiliary_state          astring    dependencies_satisfied
restarter/next_state               astring    none
restarter/state                    astring    online
restarter/state_timestamp          time       1326395219.155725000
svc:/system/timezone:default>
svc:> exit
#
```

The preceding example shows how to display the properties of the system timezone service. We can interactively change any of the service properties, as shown in the following example:

```
# svccfg
svc:> select system/timezone
svc:/system/timezone> list
:properties
default
svc:/system/timezone> select default
svc:/system/timezone:default> setprop timezone/localtime="US/Central"
svc:/system/timezone:default> exit
#
```

inetd Services

The inetd service daemon (svc:/network/inetd:default) manages SMF's Internet services. Service programs that in earlier UNIX systems were configured from the /etc/inetd.conf file are now managed by SMF. The inetadm program is used to list and configure such services:

```
# inetadm
ENABLED    STATE      FMRI
enabled    online     svc:/application/x11/xvnc-inetd:default
enabled    online     svc:/application/cups/in-lpd:default
enabled    online     svc:/network/rpc/smserver:default
...
disabled   disabled   svc:/network/talk:default
disabled   disabled   svc:/network/tftp/udp6:default
disabled   disabled   svc:/network/login:rlogin
```

```
disabled   disabled         svc:/network/telnet:default
disabled   disabled         svc:/network/rexec:default
disabled   disabled         svc:/network/rpc/wall:default
disabled   disabled         svc:/network/rpc/rusers:default
...
(output truncated for brevity)
```

This output shows several enabled/online services such as VNC and CUPS, along with disabled services such as the talk daemon, rlogin, telnet, and rexec.

The inetadm program is also used to modify service properties. For example, you can list all the system default properties using **inetadm –p**:

```
# inetadm -p
NAME=VALUE
bind_addr=""
bind_fail_max=-1
bind_fail_interval=-1
max_con_rate=-1
max_copies=-1
con_rate_offline=-1
failrate_cnt=40
failrate_interval=60
inherit_env=TRUE
tcp_trace=FALSE
tcp_wrappers=FALSE
connection_backlog=10
tcp_keepalive=FALSE
```

Then to change any of the system default properties, use **inetadm –M**:

```
# inetadm -M tcp_keepalive="TRUE"
# inetadm -p
NAME=VALUE
bind_addr=""
bind_fail_max=-1
bind_fail_interval=-1
max_con_rate=-1
max_copies=-1
con_rate_offline=-1
failrate_cnt=40
failrate_interval=60
inherit_env=TRUE
tcp_trace=FALSE
tcp_wrappers=FALSE
connection_backlog=10
tcp_keepalive=TRUE
```

To change a property for a specific service, use **inetadm –m**. Here's an example:

```
# inetadm -m svc:/application/x11/xvnc-inetd:default tcp_keepalive="FALSE"
```

Service Troubleshooting

When all is well with Solaris, services are somewhat self-correcting and will often restart automatically. But occasionally you will notice (or will be notified) that a service "isn't working." SMF provides useful information to you to diagnose service problems. Quite often (in fact, almost always) the reason a service is not working is due to one or more of its dependencies not being online.

Using the svcs Program for Service Diagnostics

As described earlier, you can observe the state of all services using the **svcs –a** command:

```
# svcs -a
... (output truncated for brevity)
online         12:36:19 svc:/system/filesystem/zfs/auto-snapshot:monthly
online         12:36:24 svc:/system/filesystem/zfs/auto-snapshot:frequent
online         12:36:28 svc:/system/filesystem/zfs/auto-snapshot:daily
online         12:36:28 svc:/application/time-slider:default
online         12:37:55 svc:/application/texinfo-update:default
online         12:52:11 svc:/system/power:default
online         12:52:43 svc:/system/hal:default
offline        12:47:57 svc:/application/cups/scheduler:default
maintenance    12:34:41 svc:/network/rpc/keyserv:default
```

We see in this example that the cups printing scheduler is offline and that the keyserv service is in maintenance mode. The cups scheduler is required to respond to users' print requests, and keyserv manages encryption keys for secure network services such as NFS.

The first diagnostic step is to run **svcs –xv** (you specify **–v** for *verbose* mode):

```
# svcs -xv
svc:/network/rpc/keyserv:default (RPC encryption key storage)
 State: maintenance since January 29, 2012 12:34:41 PM EST
Reason: Start method exited with $SMF_EXIT_ERR_CONFIG.
   See: http://sun.com/msg/SMF-8000-KS
   See: man -M /usr/share/man -s 1M keyserv
   See: /var/svc/log/network-rpc-keyserv:default.log
Impact: This service is not running.

svc:/application/cups/scheduler:default (CUPS Print Spooler)
 State: offline since January 29, 2012 12:47:57 PM EST
Reason: Dependency file://localhost/etc/cups/cupsd.conf is absent.
   See: http://sun.com/msg/SMF-8000-E2
   See: man -M /usr/share/man -s 8 cupsd
   See: /var/svc/log/application-cups-scheduler:default.log
Impact: This service is not running.
```

First, we'll look at why the cups service is not running. The output lists the full name (FMRI) of the service, indicates how long it has been offline, and provides both a reason and some supporting documentation for the problem. In this case, a configuration file dependency (/etc/cups/cupsd.conf) is missing, probably due to some administrator's maintenance work forgetting to replace the file. Additionally, SMF displays a URI pointing to a potential diagnostic message, displays the man page location for the program, and displays the location of the service's log file (be sure to examine this file for error reports). However, we already see the reason for the service being offline—the missing file. Therefore, we replace the required file and then tell SMF to reread the service's configuration information; the SMF svc.startd daemon will then notice that the cups file dependency has been met and has restarted the service:

```
# cp /etc/cups/cupsd.conf.sav /etc/cups/cupsd.conf
# svcadm refresh svc:/application/cups/scheduler:default
# svcs svc:/application/cups/scheduler:default
STATE          STIME    FMRI
online         14:15:55 svc:/application/cups/scheduler:default
```

Earlier we mentioned the SMF Services GUI, started from the GNOME desktop's System | Administration | SMF Services menu. This program also displays information about services that are available, online, and in need of attention (see Figure 6-5).

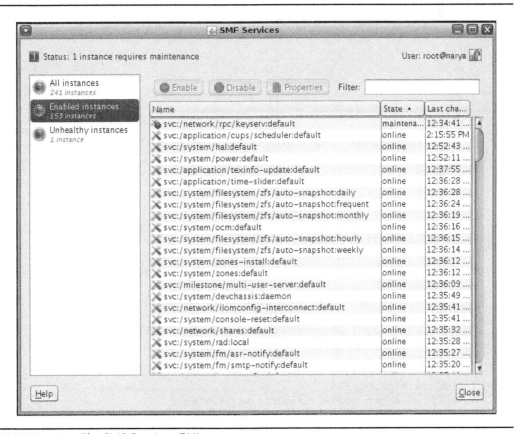

FIGURE 6-5. *The SMF Services GUI*

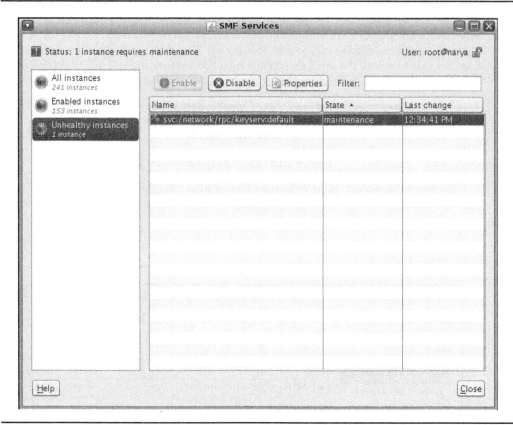

FIGURE 6-6. *SMF Services displaying unhealthy service instances*

Notice that the SMF Services GUI displays one "unhealthy instance." Clicking the Unhealthy Instances button and then clicking the service instance, as shown in Figure 6-6, brings up the SMF Service Inspector (see Figure 6-7). From here, you can display the service's description, dependencies, and log file, as well as select one of the links that attempt to restart the service or disable it.

From either the log file or the referenced man page for the keyserv service, we see that the service is not running because the system's domain name has not been set. Therefore, we identify the appropriate domain name for our system, set it using the domainname program, clear the maintenance state for keyserv, and then observe that svc.startd has noticed the state change and has restarted the service:

```
# domainname dc.cox.net
# svcadm clear svc:/network/rpc/keyserv:default
# svcs svc:/network/rpc/keyserv:default
STATE        STIME    FMRI
online       15:31:00 svc:/network/rpc/keyserv:default
```

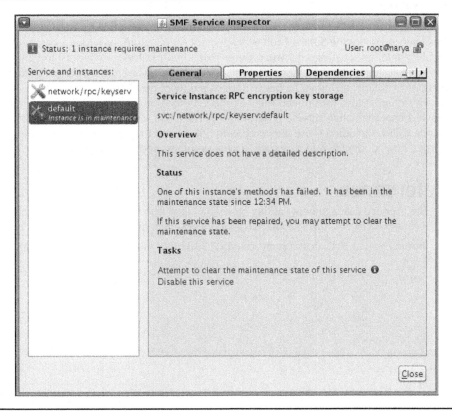

FIGURE 6-7. *The SMF Service Inspector*

NOTE
Because not all service problems are logged by default, you can configure a service's manifest to alter the severity of error messages that get written to the service's log file. The supported message options include **quiet**, **verbose**, *and* **debug**. *The* **quiet** *option sends error messages requiring administrative intervention to the console, syslog, and svc.startd's global log file. The* **verbose** *option sends error messages requiring administrative intervention to the console, syslog, and svc.startd's global log file, as well as information about errors that do not require administrative intervention to svc.startd's global log file. The* **debug** *option sends svc.startd debug messages to svc.startd's global log file, as well as error messages requiring administrative intervention to the console, syslog, and svc.startd's global log file.*

Summary

This chapter introduced one of Solaris 11's most essential components—Service Management. This feature, part of the Solaris Fault Management Architecture, provides a common framework for all system service programs and ensures that administrators can understand and observe service states and interdependencies. SMF replaces the ad-hoc startup scripts used in earlier versions of Solaris, giving you a better understanding of how services interact.

This chapter also introduced the CLI and GUI tools for starting and monitoring services and showed how to change service program properties. You saw how services are defined by their manifest files, including those delivered with Solaris and those created by administrators. And you learned how to identify and diagnose service problems and then restart them.

References

The "Service Management Facility How To Guide" can be found at www.oracle.com/technetwork/server-storage/solaris10/overview/servicemgmthowto-jsp-135655.html.

Introduction to SMF, docs.oracle.com/cd/E23824_01/html/821-1451/dzhgy.html

CHAPTER
7

The Image Packaging
System (IPS)

n spite of the long-recognized high quality of the Solaris operating system itself, the processes of installing software and patching both applications and the kernel have long been a source of difficulty and complaints. Dealing with Solaris patch dependencies, backing out of upgrades, and other software maintenance tasks were time consuming and error prone. Not any more. Three foundation technologies in Oracle Solaris 11—Service Management Facility (SMF), ZFS, and Image Packaging System (IPS) —now all work together to ease system administrators' tasks. The goal of this approach is to provide a common framework for all software management tasks, to reduce the impact of software changes, and to preserve fallback environments when changes are found to be inappropriate.

In this chapter, we show you how to use the Solaris Image Packaging System to locate, install, and update application software and to upgrade and manage OS boot environments, using network-based software repositories. You'll see how IPS automatically takes care of software interrelationships and dependencies, and how it automates the process of creating and testing new OS upgrades. We'll show you how IPS tools help you to keep your applications and Solaris kernel up to date and to minimize the disruption of operating system upgrades.

IPS Basics

The Solaris Image Packaging System is a network-based service for maintaining and upgrading your Solaris OS and its applications. That is, all such upgrades are located, delivered, and installed over your system's network, either from Internet-based software libraries called *repositories* (or *repos)*, from locally configured servers on your own network, or from local package archive files. IPS is designed to account for and include any software dependencies for installation requests, and to ensure safe and secure updates for both SPARC and x86 systems. It provides both CLI and GUI tools to manage both user and system software, including the ability to build your own software repositories.

NOTE
*Many of the SVR4 packages and tools from earlier Solaris versions
will still work, but you will not have the advantage of IPS's ability to
manage package dependencies and compatibility checks.*

Additionally, IPS assists you in managing OS updates. Using ZFS, it first takes a snapshot of the existing root filesystem and then applies any required kernel updates, all while the system is still running, and without disturbing current users. This process creates a new OS image called a *boot environment*. Then, at a convenient time, you can reboot using the updated environment. And if you like the new boot environment, keep it; if not, quickly reboot back to your previous boot environment snapshot without any changes having occurred. All earlier user and OS data remain unchanged.

IPS Repositories

An IPS repository is a library of Solaris 11 software packages; content in these libraries is organized into packages, each containing one or more application directories and files along with configuration and installation information. Repositories are created and maintained by publishers. Oracle is the publisher of both public and subscription-based repositories for Solaris 11. Other repository publishers might include ISVs, Solaris developer communities, or even your own internal IT organization. Repositories can be referenced through the Web using URLs; for example, the default repository for Oracle Solaris 11 is http://pkg.oracle.com/solaris/release (Figure 7-1).

Solaris 11 administrators can locate and install new software or update existing software from this and other repositories, search for new packages, and even copy public repositories onto local servers. Repositories can also be created and referenced on local filesystems or even on removable media.

The IPS pkg Program

Most of the IPS command-line management tasks use the /usr/bin/pkg program. Many administrators will execute **pkg** using the root role, but unprivileged users can also use the program if given appropriate sudo or execution privileges. Table 7-1 lists the **pkg** subcommands used to manage IPS packages and repositories.

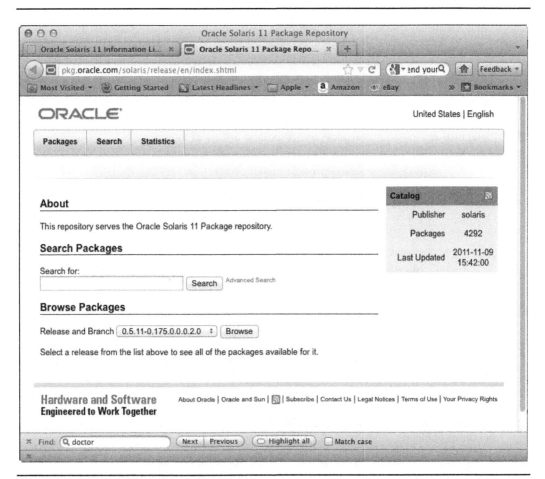

FIGURE 7-1. *The default Oracle Solaris 11 repository website*

Subcommand	Description
pkg publisher	Lists your system's currently active as well as disabled repository publishers.
pkg set-publisher	Adds a publisher to your system's list of publishers.
pkg unset-publisher	Removes a publisher from your system's list of publishers.
pkg list	Lists installed packages.
pkg search	Searches for packages in your system's list of active publishers until a first match is found.
pkg install	Installs and updates packages.
pkg uninstall	Uninstalls a package from your system.
pkg refresh	Updates your system's cached list of packages available from enabled publishers.
pkg update	With no argument, updates all installed packages to their latest installable versions. Alternatively, you can specify a package to be updated.
pkg info	Displays info about packages.
pkg contents	Displays file and directory contents delivered by packages.
pkg verify	Validates the installation and digital signature packages.
pkg history	Displays the command history of the image.
pkg help	Displays the **pkg** usage message; with an argument. displays the subcommand usage message.

TABLE 7-1. *The **pkg** Program Subcommands*

Using the **pkg** program, you can see what *publishers* are configured for the current boot environment:

```
# pkg publisher
PUBLISHER            TYPE     STATUS   URI
solaris              origin   online   http://pkg.oracle.com/solaris/release/
```

This shows only one publisher with only one origin, the default repository for the current Oracle Solaris 11 release. There are other public and Oracle-supported repositories of software for Solaris 11 available on the Web, such as the one published by the OpenIndiana project community at http://pkg.openindiana.org/sfe/en/index.shtml; you can add such a repository to your list of publishers using the **set-publisher** subcommand, and just as easily remove it using the **unset-publisher** subcommand, as shown here:

```
# pkg set-publisher -g http://pkg.openindiana.org/sfe sfe
# pkg publisher
```

```
PUBLISHER          TYPE     STATUS   URI
solaris            origin   online   http://pkg.oracle.com/solaris/release/
sfe                origin   online   http://pkg.openindiana.org/sfe/
# pkg unset-publisher sfe
# pkg publisher
PUBLISHER          TYPE     STATUS   URI
solaris            origin   online   http://pkg.oracle.com/solaris/release/
```

IPS will search configured publisher repositories when you request a software installation or update and then it will list the first package it finds. Be aware, however, that software from community repositories might not be compatible with your current OS environment.

You display additional detail about a publisher using the **pkg publisher** command by adding the publisher name as an argument to the command:

```
# pkg publisher solaris

        Publisher: solaris
            Alias:
       Origin URI: http://pkg.oracle.com/solaris/release/
          SSL Key: None
         SSL Cert: None
      Client UUID: a0d6f60c-094e-11e1-bb60-80144f585782
  Catalog Updated: November  9, 2011 03:34:27 PM
          Enabled: Yes
 Signature Policy: verify
```

This shows the origin of the repository, when it was last updated, and that its contents have been digitally signed.

The **pkg list** subcommand will list all packages available on your system:

```
# pkg list | more
NAME (PUBLISHER)                      VERSION                         IFO
SUNWcs                                0.5.11-0.170                    i-r
archiver/gnu-tar                      1.26-0.175.0.0.0.2.537          i--
audio/audio-utilities                 0.5.11-0.175.0.0.0.2.1          i--
benchmark/x11perf                     1.5.4-0.175.0.0.0.0.1215        i--
codec/flac                            1.2.1-0.175.0.0.0.0.0           i--
codec/libtheora                       1.1.1-0.175.0.0.0.0.0           i--
codec/ogg-vorbis                      2.30.0-0.175.0.0.0.0.0          i--
codec/speex                           1.2-0.175.0.0.0.0.0             i--
communication/im/pidgin               2.10.0-0.175.0.0.0.0.0          i--
communication/pda/gnome-pilot         2.0.17-0.175.0.0.0.0.0          i--
communication/pda/pilot-link          0.12.5-0.175.0.0.0.0.0          i--
compress/bzip2                        1.0.6-0.175.0.0.0.2.537         i--
compress/gzip                         1.3.5-0.175.0.0.0.2.537         i--
compress/p7zip                        9.20.1-0.175.0.0.0.2.537        i--
compress/unzip                        6.0-0.175.0.0.0.2.537           i--
compress/zip                          3.0-0.175.0.0.0.2.537           i--
(output truncated)
```

This lists the name and functional group of each package, along with its current version. The IFO column provides additional information about packages; an **i** in the first (I) column indicates that the package is *installed,* an **f** in the second (F) column indicates that the package is *frozen* and cannot be updated, and an **o** in the third (O) column indicates that the package is *obsolete.*

You display more detailed information on specific packages also with the **pkg list** subcommand; the **–v** (verbose) flag gives more detail:

```
# pkg list gzip
NAME (PUBLISHER)                                  VERSION              IFO
compress/gzip                                     1.3.5-0.175.0.0.0.2.537   i--
# pkg list -v gzip
FMRI                                                                   IFO
pkg://solaris/compress/gzip@1.3.5,5.11-0.175.0.0.0.2.537:20111019T091246Z   i--
```

NOTE
In the verbose output, the package's full FMRI name is given; this includes the FMRI scheme (pkg), the publisher (solaris), the package name (compress/gzip), the full version info (1.3.5,5.11-0.175.0.0.0.2.537), and the package creation timestamp (20111019T091246Z).

To list all available packages of a specific kind, you can use the * wildcard symbol; for example, here's how to list editor programs installable from your configured repositories:

```
# pkg list -a editor*
NAME (PUBLISHER)                     VERSION               IFO
editor/blog/drivel                  3.0.2-0.175.0.0.0.0.0      ---
editor/bvi                          1.3.2-0.169               --o
editor/diagram/dia                  0.97.1-0.175.0.0.0.0.0     ---
editor/gedit                        2.30.4-0.175.0.0.0.2.0     i--
editor/gedit/gedit-plugins          2.30.0-0.175.0.0.0.0.0     i--
editor/ghex                         2.24.0-0.175.0.0.0.0.0     --o
editor/gnu-emacs                    23.1-0.175.0.0.0.2.537     ---
editor/gnu-emacs/gnu-emacs-gtk      23.1-0.175.0.0.0.2.537     ---
editor/gnu-emacs/gnu-emacs-lisp     23.1-0.175.0.0.0.2.537     ---
editor/gnu-emacs/gnu-emacs-no-x11   23.1-0.175.0.0.0.2.537     ---
editor/gnu-emacs/gnu-emacs-x11      23.1-0.175.0.0.0.2.537     ---
editor/gobby                        0.4.12-0.175.0.0.0.0.0     ---
editor/gvim                         7.3.254-0.175.0.0.0.2.537  i--
editor/hexedit                      1.2.12-0.175.0.0.0.2.537   ---
editor/jedit                        4.3-0.169                  --o
editor/nano                         2.0.9-0.175.0.0.0.0.0      i--
editor/vim                          7.3.254-0.175.0.0.0.2.537  i--
editor/vim/vim-core                 7.3.254-0.175.0.0.0.2.537  i--
editor/xedit                        1.2.0-0.175.0.0.0.0.1215   ---
```

Again, note that the **i** in the IFO column indicates that a package is installed.

Installing Application Software

IPS is designed to make it easy to find, install, and update Solaris 11 software. Operating very much like the Linux **yum** command, the IPS **pkg** command allows you to manage both your Solaris applications as well as your system and kernel software. Files are downloaded from external publishers' network repositories, or, as we will show you later in this chapter, from your own local network- or file-based repositories.

Using the pkg Command

Let's first look at a simple example to get started. Suppose you're interested in using the open source gimp image-processing program on your Solaris 11 system. First, you would look to see if it is already installed. Discovering that it isn't, you use the **pkg search** subcommand to locate a version from the configured repositories. You find an installable version and then use the **pkg install** subcommand to install it onto your system; IPS locates the package in the repository and downloads the necessary files and dependencies, reporting its progress. When IPS is finished, you verify that gimp is now installed in the /usr/bin directory (the commands you would use are listed in bold below):

```
# which gimp
no gimp in /usr/bin /usr/sbin
# pkg list editor/gimp
pkg list: no packages matching 'editor/gimp' installed
# pkg search editor/gimp
INDEX     ACTION VALUE                    PACKAGE
pkg.fmri  set    solaris/image/editor/gimp pkg:/image/editor/gimp@2.6.10-0.175.0.0.0.2.0
# pkg install editor/gimp
          Packages to install:  4
      Create boot environment: No
Create backup boot environment: No
          Services to change:  2

DOWNLOAD                              PKGS      FILES    XFER (MB)
Completed                             4/4     2083/2083  14.0/14.0$<3>

PHASE                              ACTIONS
Install Phase                      2402/2402

PHASE                               ITEMS
Package State Update Phase            4/4
Image State Update Phase             2/2
# pkg list gimp
NAME (PUBLISHER)                    VERSION                    IFO
image/editor/gimp                   2.6.10-0.175.0.0.0.2.0     i--
# which gimp
/usr/bin/gimp
```

SMF has not only downloaded and installed the program, it has also restarted and reported any SMF services needed to support the application. Similarly, you use the **pkg uninstall** subcommand to remove a package from your system; SMF will delete all files belonging to that package. In this example, installing gimp did not require a new kernel boot environment (although some applications do); SMF will also create new boot environments if they are needed. More on that later in this chapter.

The **pkg uninstall** command deletes all files that belong to the uninstalled package that are not dependencies of another installed package. For example, the amp package installs Apache, MySQL, and PHP, but when you uninstall amp, those packages might not be uninstalled because some other package might also depend on them.

The package command can also locate software based on the expected contents of the package. For example, if you expected to find the gcc compiler at /usr/bin/gcc but it wasn't there, you can search for it like this:

```
# pkg search /usr/bin/gcc
INDEX       ACTION VALUE         PACKAGE
path        link   usr/bin/gcc pkg:/developer/gcc-45@4.5.2-0.175.0.0.0.2.537
# pkg list developer/gcc-45
pkg list: no packages matching 'developer/gcc-45' installed
```

This tells you which package contains that program, and that the required package is not installed. Then, if you need that software, you can install it:

```
# pkg install developer/gcc-45
           Packages to install:  1
       Create boot environment: No
Create backup boot environment: No
           Services to change:  1

DOWNLOAD                                PKGS       FILES    XFER (MB)
Completed                               1/1      986/986   116.3/116.3$<3>

PHASE                                        ACTIONS
Install Phase                              1111/1111

PHASE                                          ITEMS
Package State Update Phase                      1/1
Image State Update Phase                        2/2
# which gcc
/usr/bin/gcc
```

Updating Application Software

When software changes are made by developers and deposited in their repositories, IPS refreshes its list of packages and makes them available to you for updating your system's programs. The **pkg** program itself is a package and will occasionally need updating. In fact, some package update attempts will warn you that the **pkg** program needs updating before proceeding further. The **pkg list** subcommand will display a package's current version and installation status; the **pkg info** subcommand, as shown in bold in the following example, lists greater detail, including the package's state, publisher, and size.

```
# pkg list pkg
NAME (PUBLISHER)                            VERSION                    IFO
package/pkg                                 0.5.11-0.175.0.0.0.2.2576  i--
# pkg info pkg
          Name: package/pkg
       Summary: Image Packaging System
   Description: The Image Packaging System (IPS), or pkg(5), is the software
```

delivery system used on OpenSolaris systems. This package
contains the core command-line components and depot server.
```
         Category: System/Packaging
            State: Installed
        Publisher: solaris
          Version: 0.5.11
    Build Release: 5.11
           Branch: 0.175.0.0.0.2.2576
   Packaging Date: October 20, 2011 06:36:49 AM
     Size: 7.32 MB
     FMRI: pkg://solaris/package/pkg¬
@0.5.11,5.11-0.175.0.0.0.2.2576:20111020T063649Z
```

Continuing with this example, to update the **pkg** package (or any other named package), use the **pkg update** subcommand. IPS will connect your system to the repository from which the package was originally installed, locate the latest installable version of your specified package, and then download and install it, as you see in this output:

```
# pkg update pkg
            Packages to update:    1
      Create boot environment:   No
DOWNLOAD                         PKGS      FILES     XFER (MB)
Completed                        1/1     118/118     0.6/0.6
PHASE                               ACTIONS
Update Phase                        240/240
PHASE                                 ITEMS
Package State Update Phase             2/2
Package Cache Update Phase             1/1
Image State Update Phase               2/2
PHASE                                 ITEMS
Reading Existing Index                 8/8
Indexing Packages                      1/1
```

If there are no current updates for your requested package, IPS will report that there are no updates available from currently configured publishers:

```
# pkg update gcc-3
No updates available for this image.
```

You can update *all* installed packages in the current image by executing the **pkg update** subcommand with no target package specified; IPS will then update all packages from all publishers to your system. If a new boot environment is required for such an update, IPS will create one for you. If you need the *most recent* version of a package, append **@latest** to the requested package name; for example, here's how to update the evince PDF viewer to the most recent version:

```
# pkg update evince@latest
```

IPS will search for the most recent compatible version of the package and then download and install it for you if it is available.

Other Useful pkg Subcommands

The **pkg** program has many other subcommands that you use to query and control publishers, repositories, and packages. For example, to display the files and directories of a package, use the **pkg contents** subcommand:

```
# pkg list top
NAME (PUBLISHER)                            VERSION                 IFO
diagnostic/top                              3.8-0.175.0.0.0.2.537   i--
# pkg contents top
PATH
usr
usr/bin
usr/bin/amd64
usr/bin/amd64/top
usr/bin/i86
usr/bin/i86/top
usr/bin/top
usr/share
usr/share/man
usr/share/man/man1
usr/share/man/man1/top.1
```

We see here that the **top** program package includes not only the program's executables and installation directory path, but the man pages as well.

It is generally useful for CLI system management programs to keep track of previously executed statements; fortunately, the **pkg** program does this for you. Use the **pkg history** subcommand to display all earlier actions of the **pkg** program; IPS will display a list of operations, when they were run, and whether they succeeded:

```
# pkg history
START                    OPERATION                CLIENT             OUTCOME
2011-07-05T18:09:09      set-property             transfer module    Succeeded
2011-07-05T18:09:09      add-publisher            transfer module    Succeeded
2011-07-05T18:09:09      refresh-publishers       transfer module    Succeeded
2011-07-05T18:09:09      image-create             transfer module    Succeeded
2011-07-05T18:09:20      rebuild-image-catalogs   transfer module    Succeeded
2011-07-05T18:09:30      install                  transfer module    Succeeded
2011-07-05T18:39:30      update-publisher         transfer module    Succeeded
2011-07-22T12:00:55      uninstall                transfer module    Succeeded
2011-07-22T12:02:40      set-property             transfer module    Succeeded
2011-07-22T12:38:06      refresh-publishers       pkg                Succeeded
2011-07-22T12:38:08      rebuild-image-catalogs   pkg                Succeeded
2011-07-22T12:43:08      install                  packagemanager     Succeeded
2011-07-22T12:44:05      refresh-publishers       packagemanager     Succeeded
2011-07-22T12:44:07      rebuild-image-catalogs   packagemanager     Succeeded
2011-07-22T12:46:19      install                  packagemanager     Failed
2011-07-22T12:49:53      install                  packagemanager     Failed
(output truncated)
```

Oracle-provided Solaris 11 packages are digitally signed for security validation. You check the validity of such packages using the **pkg verify** subcommand, either without a package argument (for all packages in the entire system image) or for a specified package (using the **–v** flag for verbose output):

```
# pkg verify -v gzip
PACKAGE                                                    STATUS <3>
pkg://solaris/compress/gzip                                    OK
```

Configuring Local Repositories

Users who are restricted from updating software over the Internet due to security policies or bandwidth restrictions can configure local Oracle Solaris 11 package repositories. Of course, they must first create or obtain the repository files and then validate them according to their own internal procedures. For example, suppose you obtained (via download or otherwise copied) the two repository files from the Solaris 11 11/11 Download site at www.oracle.com/technetwork/server-storage/solaris11/downloads/index.html. Because the repository files are very large (several GB each), they are provided in two parts (-a and -b) that must be reassembled into one file. Assuming the two files are in a common directory, merge the two files to create one full ISO image that can be burned to a dual-layer DVD or directly mounted, as follows:

```
# cat sol-11-1111-repo-full.iso-a sol-11-1111-repo-full.iso-b > ¬
sol-11-1111-repo-full.iso
```

Next, you will create a ZFS filesystem to contain the repository files, mount that filesystem, and copy the files into it:

```
# zfs create rpool/LocalRepo
# zfs set mountpoint=/LocalRepo rpool/LocalRepo
# mv sol-11-1111-repo-full.iso /LocalRepo
```

Next, use the **lofiadm** program or the Solaris 11 File Browser GUI (see Figures 7-2 and 7-3) to mount and extract the repository files into the /LocalRepo directory, resulting in the following files:

```
# ls
COPYRIGHT               README                  sol-11-1111-repo-full.iso
NOTICES                 repo
```

Review the README file for instructions on more ways to prepare the repository; for this next example, we will access a local repository for your system.

First, you must tell the IPS package repo server where the repository resides, set the repository to the read-only property, and then refresh and enable the **pkg** server:

```
# svccfg -s application/pkg/server setprop pkg/inst_root=/LocalRepo
# svccfg -s application/pkg/server setprop pkg/readonly=true
# svcadm refresh application/pkg/server
# svcadm enable application/pkg/server
```

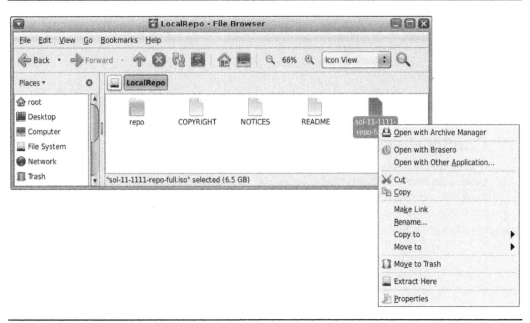

FIGURE 7-2. *Using the file browser GUI to extract repository files (select the Extract Here option)*

You can now set your local server to be a host for this repository:

```
# pkg set-publisher -g /LocalRepo solaris
# pkg publisher
PUBLISHER          TYPE     STATUS    URI
solaris            origin   online    file:///LocalRepo/
solaris            origin   online    http://pkg.oracle.com/solaris/release/
```

FIGURE 7-3. *Extracting files from the .iso archive*

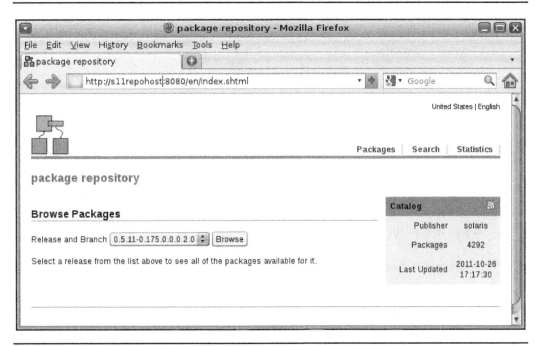

FIGURE 7-4. *Web access to the local system repository*

Your local repository is now ready; searches for packages for installations and updates for the server will be conducted in the publisher order listed. But suppose you want to share that repository to other Solaris 11 servers on your network? Assuming your host is named s11repohost, simply tell the package server to listen to a specified port (for example, port 8080), add that system as a publisher, and then point any other system's browser to the publisher system (see Figure 7-4):

```
# svccfg -s application/pkg/server setprop pkg/port=8080
# pkg set-publisher -g http://s11repohost:8080/ solaris
# pkg publisher
PUBLISHER                           TYPE     STATUS   URI
solaris                             origin   online   file:///LocalRepo/repo/
solaris                             origin   online   http://s11repohost:8080/
```

Boot Environments

As we mentioned earlier, some package updates might include Solaris 11 OS kernel updates as well. Also, you might want to do any package updates (not just a kernel update) in a new environment to make sure you do not disturb the work of current users and to make sure you can always get back to your current state if anything goes amiss with the update. Alternatively, you may simply need to explicitly update Solaris 11 to the next published release. Additionally,

Subcommand	Description
beadm list {bename}	Lists all available boot environments or the specified BE.
beadm create {bename}	Creates a new boot environment named bename that is a clone of the current boot environment. Options enable creation from a current active, inactive, or snapshot BE, with optional specified properties.
beadm create {bename@snapshotname}	Creates a snapshot of the bename boot environment.
beadm activate {bename}	Configures a boot environment to start at the next system reboot.
beadm destroy {bename}	Destroys (erases) a boot environment and all snapshots of that boot environment.
beadm mount {bename}	Mounts an inactive boot environment onto a specified mount point for inspection.
beadm unmount {bename}	Unmounts a mounted inactive boot environment.
beadm rename {bename} {newbename}	Renames an existing inactive boot environment.

TABLE 7-2. *The **beadm** Program Subcommands*

you should preserve your current OS environment before updating the OS or its packages. Here is where IPS and ZFS interact to make such tasks easier.

A Solaris 11 *boot environment (BE)* is a bootable instance of the operating system image plus any other application software packages installed into that image. You can have many boot environments on your systems, each having different package collections and configurations. When you first install Solaris 11, a boot environment named solaris is created for you. Boot environments are then managed using the **beadm** CLI command or through the IPS GUI.

Managing Boot Environments

The **beadm** program has several subcommands for administering boot environments; these are listed in Table 7-2.

In the previous section, we discussed updating your system software using the **pkg** program. In the following example, we update the system and see that several packages have been updated and a new boot environment named solaris-2 has been automatically created:

```
# pkg update
              Packages to update:            28
           Create boot environment:          Yes
     Create backup boot environment:         No
```

```
DOWNLOAD                PKGS     FILES      XFER (MB)
Completed               28/28   389/389     28.0/28.0

PHASE                                     ACTIONS
Removal Phase                               84/84
Install Phase                             100/100
Update Phase                            1950/1950

PHASE                                       ITEMS
Package State Update Phase                  56/56
Package Cache Update Phase                  28/28
Image State Update Phase                      2/2

PHASE                                       ITEMS
Reading Existing Index                        8/8
Indexing Packages                           28/28
```

```
A clone of solaris exists and has been updated and activated.
On the next boot the Boot Environment solaris-2 will be mounted on '/'.
Reboot when ready to switch to this updated BE.
```

We can see that newly created boot environment using the **beadm list** subcommand. Note especially the characters in the Active column; an **N** means the BE is active *now,* whereas an **R** means the BE will be active upon the next *reboot.* After rebooting in this example, the Active column would list **NR** for BE solaris-2.

```
# beadm list
BE          Active Mountpoint Space    Policy Created
--          ------ ---------- -----    ------ -------
solaris     N      /          249.32M  static 2011-07-22 11:50
solaris-2   R      -          77.0K    static 2012-03-04 15:49
```

You can easily create and activate new BEs at any time without disturbing your current running OS environment; simply use the **beadm create** subcommand. Here's an example:

```
# beadm create mynewbe
# beadm activate mynewbe
# beadm list
BE          Active Mountpoint Space    Policy Created
--          ------ ---------- -----    ------ -------
mynewbe     R      -          53.27G   static 2012-03-04 16:05
solaris     N      -          249.32M  static 2011-07-22 11:50
solaris-2   -      -          77.0K    static 2012-03-04 15:49
```

Note that the solaris BE is still active (**N**), and the mynewbe BE will be used the next time the system is booted.

If it is necessary to inspect an inactive BE you created earlier, you mount it like any other ZFS filesystem; you can then read or copy files from any directory of that BE to your current BE, if needed:

```
# beadm mount solaris-3 /tmp/solaris-3
# ls /tmp/solaris-3
bin      devices  home2   mnt       nfs4      rmdisk   sbin     usr
boot     etc      kernel  mypool-1  opt       root     share    var
cdrom    export   lib     mypool-2  platform  rpool    system
dev      home     media   net       proc      save     tmp
```

Updating the Operating System Kernel

To update your Solaris 11 kernel image and all its associated packages, especially when a new release is posted to the Oracle repository, use the **pkg image-update** command. IPS will first create a ZFS clone of the current BE and then apply any necessary package updates to that clone; the new clone will be activated for startup on the next reboot. Be aware that because the entire kernel and all applications are being updated, this process will take many minutes, or even several hours. Note that in the following example, *several thousand files* have been downloaded:

```
# pkg image-update
               Packages to remove:    169
              Packages to install:    189
               Packages to update:    664
Additional filesystem space needed: 4.17 GB
         Filesystem space available: 148.44 GB
              Create boot environment:    Yes
DOWNLOAD                         PKGS        FILES    XFER (MB)
Completed                        1022/1022 57379/57379  937.3/937.3$<3>

PHASE                              ACTIONS
Removal Phase                   17857/17857
Install Phase                   59714/59714
Update Phase                    62021/62021

PHASE                                ITEMS
Package State Update Phase        1686/1686
Package Cache Update Phase          833/833
Image State Update Phase                2/2

A clone of solaris exists and has been updated and activated.
On the next boot the Boot Environment solaris-5 will be
mounted on '/'.  Reboot when ready to switch to this updated BE.
...
-------------------------------------------------------------------------
NOTE: Please review release notes posted at:
http://download.oracle.com/docs/cd/E19963-01/
-------------------------------------------------------------------------
# beadm list
```

```
BE         Active Mountpoint Space  Policy Created
--         ------ ---------- -----  ------ -------
solaris    N      /          53.72M static 2011-07-22 11:50
...
solaris-4  -      -          6.32G  static 2012-01-12 12:01
solaris-5  R      -          24.48G static 2012-03-09 13:55
```

TIP

To save additional administrative time and to reduce downtime, remember that you can use the **reboot –f** *command for a fast reboot. This bypasses firmware and hardware initializations (which presumably have already occurred at your system's power-up) and then loads the new kernel and transfers control to it; this works on both SPARC and x86 systems.*

The IPS GUI

All the IPS tools discussed so far have used the command line, which is very useful for terminal-based management of servers on your network. But the Solaris 11 desktop includes an IPS GUI for those who prefer such an interface; you can manage publishers, application installs and updates, package searchers, as well as the boot environment from this GUI.

Software Installation and Update (Using the GUI)

From the main Solaris 11 GNOME desktop, select the System | Administration | Package Manager menu item (see Figure 7-5); it will display the package content hierarchy for the enabled publisher(s), which can be changed to any other publisher (see Figure 7-6). To change how Package Manager opens, select Edit | Preferences | Remember Current State on Exit.

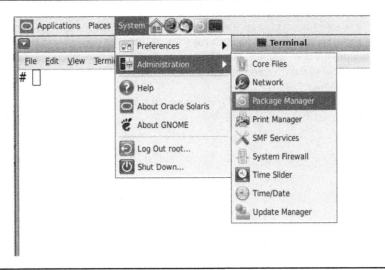

FIGURE 7-5. *Selecting the Package Manager*

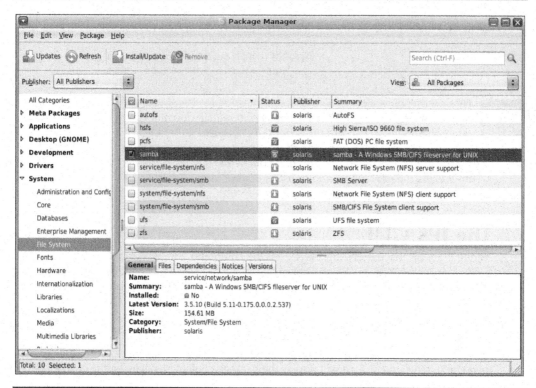

FIGURE 7-6. *The IPS Package Manager interface*

From this interface, you can search and select applications for installation or update; for example, to install the Samba file service for Windows clients, select that package and click the Install/Update icon. You will be asked to confirm your selection in a pop-up dialog box (see Figure 7-7); clicking the Proceed button will start the installation from the default or your selected publisher (see Figure 7-8).

When the installation or update is complete, the IPS GUI will display a status window summarizing its actions (see Figure 7-9).

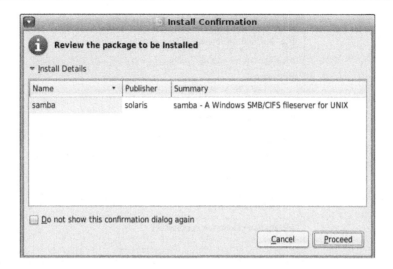

FIGURE 7-7. *The Install Confirmation dialog box*

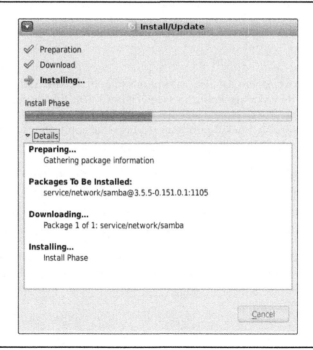

FIGURE 7-8. *The Install/Update status window*

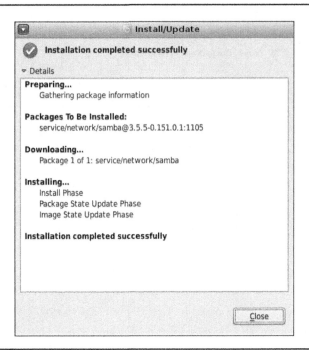

FIGURE 7-9. *Successful installation completion*

The Package Manager GUI also has options to add, modify, and remove publishers; from the GUI select File | Manage Publishers (see Figure 7-10). This displays the Manage Publishers window (see Figure 7-11). Notice whether the Enabled check box is selected, and also notice the Sticky check box. A "sticky" publisher requires that applications be updated from the same publisher that originally installed them.

Boot Environment Management (Using the GUI)

As with the publisher management process, you can use a CLI program to manage your boot environments or select the Manage Boot Environments option from the Package Manager GUI (see Figure 7-12). The Manage Boot Environments window allows you to delete, rename, or activate BEs in the same way you did using the **beadm** program (see Figure 7-13). Notice how the active and next BEs are indicated—with a check mark on the currently active environment and a selectable button for which BE to activate upon the next reboot. Clicking the OK button will pop up a confirmation dialog box and apply the selected changes before returning you to the Package Manager window.

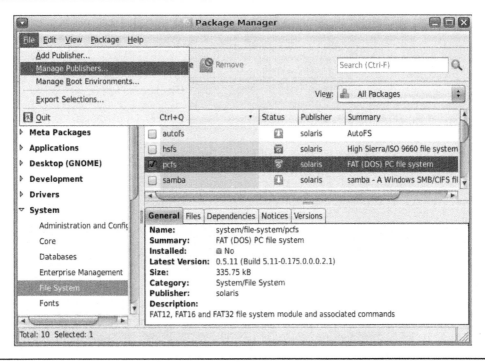

FIGURE 7-10.   *Selecting the Publisher Manager*

FIGURE 7-11.   *The Manage Publishers window*

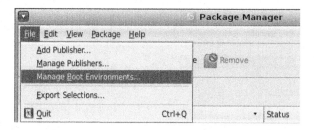

FIGURE 7-12. *The Manage Boot Environments selection*

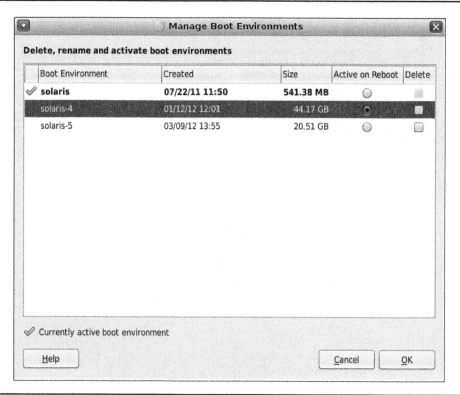

FIGURE 7-13. *The Manage Boot Environments window*

Summary

The Oracle Solaris 11 Image Packaging System is a framework for searching, installing, updating, and removing application and kernel packages. Solaris 11 software is distributed in IPS packages; these packages are stored in repositories that are developed and maintained by both Oracle and independent publishers. Packages are installed into Solaris 11 images, which can be updated in whole or in part from Internet or local package repositories as well as accessed via HTTP or NFS or from package archive or WebInstall files. We reviewed how to manage these packages, repositories, publishers, and boot environments using both CLI and GUI tools. If you are moving from earlier versions of Solaris to Solaris 11, you will see that IPS is a necessary and welcome improvement over previous methods of patching and updating your software.

References

The document "Adding and Updating Oracle Solaris 11 Software Packages" can be found at http://docs.oracle.com/cd/E23824_01/html/E21802/index.html.

The document "Introduction to Managing Boot Environments" can be found at http://docs.oracle.com/cd/E23824_01/html/E21801/index.html.

The document "Image Packaging System Man Pages" can be found at http://docs.oracle.com/cd/E23824_01/html/E21796/index.html.

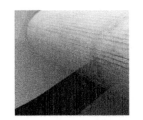

CHAPTER
8

Solaris at the
Command Line

NIX-based systems are most powerful when controlled from the command-line interface. From the command line, you can do more. From the command line, you can configure a variety of services, with details unavailable in even the most comprehensive GUI tools. From the command line, you can set up scripts that can meet the needs of every enterprise. If you're a administrator of Microsoft systems, this may be the chapter you've been most looking forward to. On the other hand, if you're experienced with Linux at the command line, you'll be pleased with how much you can already do with Solaris. But be aware of the differences. Although the standard Solaris command-line interface uses the Bourne Again Shell (bash), some of the differences in commands may surprise you. For more information on shells, see Chapter 10.

This chapter is intended to help users who are new to the command-line interface, in at least a minimal fashion. But because it's important to help you master administrative tasks associated with Solaris, most of these descriptions may be less than complete. It'll be up to you to fill in the blanks. If you're new to UNIX-based operating systems, practice what you see in this chapter. You'll see references to different shell environments described in Chapter 10.

This chapter starts with basic navigation commands, the tools needed to explore what files and directories are present in Solaris. It continues with a view of file management, which gives you the skills needed to create and modify files and directories. Given the focus on text files, this chapter describes the commands needed to read text files and manipulate their contents. Of course, even though you could customize text files with a GUI-based editor, it's best to do so from the command-line interface. To that end, this chapter covers the basics of the vi and nano text editors.

Basic Navigation

It's important to be able to move around the Solaris directory tree. With the commands described in this section, you'll learn to know where you are, how to move to a different directory, how to list the files in the current directory, and how it all relates to a concept known as the **PATH**.

With that information in hand, you'll be able to review what files are available. These tools can help you identify files that help configure services. With these commands, you can identify log files related to different systems. Sometimes, files in home directories should be audited. Sometimes, files in home directories should be analyzed in other ways. In essence, the commands in this section are fundamental skills for any Solaris systems administrator.

If you're comfortable at the Linux command line, just about everything in this section should seem familiar. And that's to be expected, because the commands and associated syntax are based on the same default bash shell.

For those of you who are coming from a GUI-based operating system such as Microsoft Windows, these commands may seem obscure and mundane. You could simulate the functionality of a number of these commands with a GUI file browser such as Nautilus. But be aware: GUI tools such as Nautilus are just front ends. Few GUI tools are even half as capable as their command-line cousins.

One of the key features of the command line is the use of special characters. UNIX-based operating systems include wildcards that are more fine-grained than their Windows cousins.

NOTE
The commands described in this chapter can be modified with a number of quote and related keys described in Chapter 10.

Command Manuals

In general, Solaris and all UNIX-based operating systems include command manuals. For example, to call up the manual for the **pwd** command, type in the following at the command line:

```
$ man pwd
```

You'll be able to scroll down the manual page for the command with the spacebar. Once you're finished, press the Q key to exit from the manual. As with the vi editor, you can search forward in the manual with the forward slash key; for example, if you type in the following, the implicit command searches for the next instance of the word **test**:

```
/test
```

You can then press N to find the next instance of the search term. You can search backward by substituting the question mark for the forward slash.

The Current Working Directory

Before doing anything else, it's important to know where you are. If you're running a command based on a relative directory path, it's important to run it from the right directory. If you're modifying the configuration of a service, you should know that the file is in the correct directory. That's made possible with the **pwd** command. The output is the absolute path to the current directory. The directory at the top of the tree is known as root, signified by the forward slash (/). For example, when we run the **pwd** command after logging in, we get the following output, which confirms that the home directory (michael) is a subdirectory of /home.

```
/home/michael
```

Changing Directories

You can use the **cd** command to change the current directory. By itself, the command navigates to the home directory of the current user. For example, when we log into the michael account, navigate to a different directory, and then run the **cd** command, it directs us to the /home/michael directory. When we run the **cd** command from the main administrative account, it directs us to the /root directory.

As a preview of Chapter 10, the **cd** command can be used to navigate based on the full path of a directory. For example, if you want to navigate to the directory with FTP server files, run the following command:

```
$ cd /etc/ftpd
```

The first forward slash refers to the "absolute path." In other words, you can build the destination from the top-level root directory. In this case, the destination is a subdirectory of /etc, which is a subdirectory of /.

If you navigate to the /etc directory with the **cd /etc** command, you can then use the "relative path." From the /etc directory, you can navigate to the /etc/ftpd subdirectory with the following command:

```
$ cd ftpd
```

However, if this command were run from the /home/michael directory, it would look for and navigate to the /home/michael/ftpd directory, if it exists.

From the /etc/ftpd directory, you can navigate one level up to the /etc directory with the following command:

```
$ cd ..
```

If you repeat this command, you'll go up one more level in the directory tree to the top-level root directory. If desired, you could speed up the process, navigating up two levels in the directory tree with the following command:

```
$ cd ../..
```

If you're in the /etc/apache2 directory, the **cd ../..** command navigates to the top-level root directory.

File Lists

We prefer to use the **ls** command more than any other. It lists the files in a specified directory. With the right switches, it can tell us the permissions associated with each file, the date when each file was last changed, the size of each file, and even display hidden files, in the current directory. After logging in, try the **ls** command by itself. It'll show the files in the current home directory. The following output displays four files on our system:

```
Desktop   Documents   Downloads   Public
```

These files are in fact directories. But there's no way to know that from the output shown. One way to identify these files as directories is with the **ls -l** command, which specifies a "long listing" format. The output shown includes the following default entries:

```
drwxr-xr-x 2 michael staff        6 2012-07-13 21:33 Desktop
drwxr-xr-x 6 michael staff        6 2012-07-13 21:33 Documents
drwxr-xr-x 2 michael staff        2 2012-07-13 21:33 Downloads
drwxr-xr-x 2 michael staff        2 2012-07-13 21:33 Public
```

The first **d** in the output for each file indicates that it's a directory. Some of the more common options for this first letter are listed in Table 8-1. Although you may find several other file types, the identifiers shown in the table are the most common.

The additional letters in the left side, along with the names "michael" and "staff," specify permissions and ownership of each file. For more information, see Chapter 12. The information that follows is the size of the file in bytes, followed by the last date and time the file was revised.

Now let's go a bit further with the **ls** command. Try the **ls -a** command in your home directory. As shown in Figure 8-1, it includes a bunch of additional files, each with a dot in front. The dot hides files from the view of normal commands.

As you can see from the figure, there is a substantial number of hidden files in a typical user's home directory. Try the **ls -la** command. It'll show that a number of these hidden files are actually directories. Because many of these files can help you customize the Solaris shell, you'll explore the contents of such files in Chapter 10. But wait a second; we've specified two different switches with a single command, the **-l** and the **-a**. Yes, we could have specified these switches separately, with the **ls -l -a** command. But the shell allows us to combine these switches.

File Identifier	File Type
-	Regular file
b	Block file
c	
Character special file, commonly associated with hardware devices	Directories
l	Symbolic link
p	Named pipe
P	Port file P

TABLE 8-1.   *Different File Types Shown in the **ls -l** Long Listing Output*

NOTE
*Just be aware there's a hidden .zfs directory that's not normally visible even to the **ls -a** command.*

Perhaps our favorite command is **ls -ltr**. Let's break down the content of that command. It provides information on each file in long listing format, sorted by modification time, in reverse order. The output displays the most recently modified files last. And that can be useful when the list of files is long. Additional switches of interest are shown in Table 8-2.

The PATH

Technically, all commands can be run with the full path. For example, you can list all the files in the current directory with the **/bin/ls** command. That may not seem so bad. But what of those special commands in a directory such as /usr/java/jre/bin? Do you really want to type in the full path to the commands in that directory every time? That's where the **PATH** can provide relief.

```
michael@solarisdel:~$ ls -a
.                 .gnome2              .updatemanager
..                .gnome2_private      .vp
.bash_history     .gstreamer-0.10      .xsession-errors
.bashrc           .gtk-bookmarks       .xsession-errors.old
.cache            .ICEauthority        Desktop
.chewing          .iiim                Documents
.config           .lesshst             Downloads
.dbus             .local               Private
.dmrc             .mozilla             Public
.esd_auth         .nautilus            smb.conf-example
.gconf            .profile             sol-11-exp-201011-live-x86.usb
.gconfd           .profile.swp         test
.gksu.lock        .recently-used.xbel  test1
michael@solarisdel:~$ █
```

FIGURE 8-1.   *The **ls -a** command includes hidden files.*

Command	Description
ls	Lists all non-hidden files.
ls -a	Displays all files, regular and hidden.
ls -p	Adds a forward slash to the end of a file that's used as a directory.
ls -i	Shows files with inode numbers, which identify the location of the file; two different files with the same inode number include identical contents.
ls -l	Lists all regular files in the current directory, in long listing format.
ls -r	Displays files in reverse order.
ls -t	Shows files by the last time they were changed.
ls -u	Displays files by the last time they were accessed (not necessarily changed).

TABLE 8-2. *Options to the ls Command*

The **PATH** is an environment variable that simplifies life at the command line. When you type in a command, the shell automatically searches the directories specified in the **PATH** for the content of your command. To review the current value of **PATH**, run the following command:

```
$ echo $PATH
```

NOTE
In the default Solaris 11 bash shell, environment and shell variables are essentially the same thing.

Special Characters

The command line for UNIX-based operating systems can handle a variety of special characters. Whereas the asterisk can represent anywhere from zero to many alphanumeric characters, the question mark represents a single character. For example, the **ls a*** command could return the following filenames:

```
a ab alpha
```

In contrast, the **ls a?** command would have more limited output; from the list just shown, it would only return the file named ab.

The range of characters can be limited further; for example, the **ls a[a-f]** command could potentially list the following files, if they exist in the current directory:

```
aa ab ac ad ae af
```

The dots are important as well. A single dot is associated with the current directory. When placed in front of a file, a single dot hides that file from view. In contrast, when used in conjunction with the **ls** command, that single dot represents all files in the current directory, regular and hidden.

In contrast, a double dot represents the directory directly above. For example, if you're in the /home/michael directory, the **ls ..** command lists the files in the /home directory.

File Management

You certainly need to know how to do more than just navigate and see what files are available. As an administrator, you need to know how to create, copy, move, and delete files—and more. With the tools described in this section, you'll be able to set up files and directories as needed by any variety of users.

Commands described in this section include **touch**, **cp**, **mv**, **rm**, and **ln**.

The Basic touch Command

The **touch** command has two purposes: It can be used to create a new empty file; it can also be used to modify the date and time associated with a file. First, the following command creates a file named abc with the current date and time:

```
$ touch abc
```

The **touch** command includes a number of switches that can change the time in different ways. For example, the **touch -a** command changes the access time; the **touch -m** command changes the modification time; and the **touch -t** command can be used to modify time in the MMDDhhmm format. For example, the following command sets a modification time of April 13 of the current year, at 4:12 A.M, for the file named abc:

```
$ touch -t 04130412 abc
```

File Copies

The copy command is **cp**. It's more versatile than you think. Not only can it copy files from one name to another, it can copy the contents of entire directories. Just be careful; if the target is an existing file, its contents are automatically overwritten. The simplest use of the command is as follows, where the contents of filename1 are written to filename2:

```
$ cp filename1 filename2
```

The file can be written to a specific directory; for example, the following command makes a copy of filename1 in the directory named dir1:

```
$ cp filename1 dir1
```

Let's dig deeper. There are actually three copies of the **cp** command available on Solaris, in the /bin, /usr/bin, and /usr/xpg4/bin directories. The copies in the /bin and /usr/bin directories are identical. You can confirm this with the **ls -i /bin/cp** and **ls -i /usr/bin/cp** commands, which return the same inode numbers. But the **/usr/xpg4/bin/cp** command is a bit different in its management of extended attributes, such as Access Control Lists (ACLs).

Command	Description
cp *f1 f2*	Copies files from file *f1* to file *f2*
cp *file?* dir1	Copies files such as file1, filea, and fileZ to directory dir1
cp -a dir1 dir2	Copies directory dir1, including its contents, to directory dir2, recursively, while preserving all file links
cp -a dir1/. dir2	Copies just the contents of directory dir1 to directory dir2
cp -i *f1 f2*	Prompts for confirmation before overwriting file *f2*
cp -r dir1 dir2	Copies directory dir1 recursively

TABLE 8-3. *Options to the **cp** command*

NOTE
*If you ran the **echo $PATH** command earlier in this chapter, you should realize that the /usr/xpg4/bin directory is not in the **PATH**. Thus, if you want to run commands from that directory, you'll need to type in the full path to the desired command.*

The **cp** command includes a number of important variations, as described in Table 8-3.

NOTE
*One of the challenges of a command such as **cp** is that it automatically overwrites a file without saving its contents. One way to prevent that result with commands such as **cp** and **mv** is to set up an alias, as described in Chapter 10.*

Moving a File

The command associated with moving a file is **mv**. It's functionally similar to the **cp** command. Once the target file is copied to the new location, the original file is deleted. Unless the file is being moved to a different volume, the file retains the same inode number. Several examples of the **mv** command are illustrated in Table 8-4.

Command	Description
mv *f1 f2*	Changes the name of a file from *f1* to *f2*
mv *f1* dir1	Moves the file named *f1* to the directory dir1
mv dir1 dir2	Renames directory dir1 to directory dir2; the contents of directory dir1 can then be found in directory dir2

TABLE 8-4. *Options to the **mv** Command*

The **mv** command can be used on directories; because it just changes the name of the directory, it automatically includes the files within the directory.

Deleting a File

The command to delete a file is **rm**. It should be used with care; once a file is deleted, it is at best difficult to restore. But it's not as dangerous of a command as it used to be. At one time, a mistake in the following command could be disastrous:

```
# rm -r / tmp
```

With a space between the first forward slash (/) and **tmp**, the noted command would delete all files recursively, starting with the top-level root directory. That would delete all files on the local system. Fortunately, that option is not available, unless you include the **--no-preserve-root** switch.

As just suggested, the **-r** switch is most powerful and dangerous because it can delete files recursively, from all subdirectories. However, the **rm** command without the **-r** switch can't remove a directory. For more examples, see Table 8-5.

File Links

Run the **ls -l /etc** command. You should see a number of files with the **l** in front, which specifies a linked file, along with a redirection arrow that points to a different file. For example, the following excerpt from the **ls -l /etc** output illustrates a soft link between the /etc/aliases and the /etc/mail/aliases file:

```
lrwxrwxrwx 1 root root   14 2011-07-19 10:28 aliases -> ./mail/aliases
```

The reference to /etc/mail/aliases is subtle. Because this is a long listing of files in the /etc directory, Solaris substitutes /etc for the dot in front of /mail/aliases. You can open the /etc/aliases file or the /etc/mail/aliases file in a text editor. The contents are identical, because both are links to the same file.

You can create a link to another file with the **ln** command. The format is as follows:

```
$ ln switch existingfile linkedfile
```

Without a switch, the **ln** command tries to create a hard link. Such files share the same inode number. As suggested earlier with the **/bin/cp** and **/usr/bin/cp** commands, the hard-linked file is

Command	Description
rm f1	Removes file *f1*. Can also be applied to a list of files.
rm -r *dir1*	Removes directory *dir1*, including all files and directories therein, recursively.
rm -f *f1*	Removes file *f1*, in force mode. If permissions are read-only, this command does not prompt for confirmation.

TABLE 8-5. *Options to the **mv** Command*

simply another label for the original file. Hard-linked files are more resilient; if one copy is deleted, the other copy is still fully functional.

But Solaris 11 doesn't allow hard-linked files between different volumes. For example, from our home directory, when we try to create a hard link to the sample Samba configuration file with the command

```
$ ln /etc/samba/smb.conf-example .
```

an error message similar to the following appears:

```
ln: ./smb.conf-example' is on a different file system
```

If you try to create a hard link for a directory, the **ln** command also returns an error message. For such purposes, it's possible to create a soft link. For example, the following command creates a copy of the example Samba configuration file in the local directory:

```
$ ln -s /etc/samba/smb.conf-example .
```

However, if the original file is deleted or moved, the soft link points to a file that no longer exists.

Directory Management

The commands associated with creating and deleting directories are **mkdir** and **rmdir**. The commands are straightforward, with two switches of importance:

- **-m MODE**   Specifies the desired permissions, in numeric format.
- **-p a/b/c**   Supports the creation of a tree of directories; in this case, it creates a directory named a, with a subdirectory named b.

For example, the **mkdir -pm 700 a/b** command creates the a/b subdirectory, with read, write, and execute permissions limited to the user who owns the directory.

NOTE
Executable permissions are required to read the files in a directory.

Naturally, the **rmdir** command can reverse the process associated with the **mkdir** command. As long as the directories are empty, the following command deletes both the a and the a/b subdirectories just created with the **mkdir -pm 700 a/b** command:

```
$ rmdir -p a/b
```

Reading Text Files

It's all well and good to know what files are available on a system. The next step is to learn how you can explore the contents of such files. But not all files are text files, and UNIX files aren't necessarily identifiable by their extensions. Therefore, in this section, you'll explore those commands that can identify file types, how text files can be output to the screen, as well as the commands that you can use to read text files.

Identifying File Types

The aptly named **file** command can identify the types of files listed in a directory. Perhaps the most complete way to list file types in the local directory is with the following command, which includes hidden files:

```
$ file .*
```

A sample of the output is shown in Figure 8-2. Note some of the descriptive categories listed, including directory, data, empty file, ascii text, c program text, and XML document.

Outputting Files to the Screen

On UNIX-based systems, data from text files moves in a flow. Normally, it is output to the screen. The simplest way to display the contents of a text file is with the **cat** command. For example, the following command outputs the contents of the noted file to the screen:

```
$ cat .dmrc
```

In this case, the output is simple—it documents the default language associated with the desktop environment:

```
[Desktop]
Language=en_US.UTF-8
```

But in most cases, there's a lot of information in such files. For example, the sample Samba configuration file described earlier includes about 270 lines, too much to read easily on a screen.

```
.config:          directory
.dbus:            directory
.dmrc:            ascii text
.esd_auth:        data
.gconf:           directory
.gconfd:          directory
.gksu.lock:       empty file
.gnome2:          directory
.gnome2_private:      directory
.gstreamer-0.10:      directory
.gtk-bookmarks: ascii text
.ICEauthority:  data
.iiim:            directory
.lesshst:         [nt]roff, tbl, or eqn input text
.local:           directory
.mozilla:         directory
.nautilus:        directory
.profile:         c program text
.profile.swp:   data
.recently-used.xbel:    XML document
.updatemanager: directory
.vp:              directory
.xsession-errors:       ascii text
.xsession-errors.old:   ascii text
michael@solarisdel:~$ █
```

FIGURE 8-2. *Different file types*

One option is to add numbers to the output with the **-n** switch; the following command can be indexed by line numbers:

```
$ cat -n smb.conf-example
```

Later in this chapter, you'll examine the use of the **grep** command to search by term from the output.

NOTE
For more information on how data and error messages can be redirected from the screen, see Chapter 10.

Top and Bottom File Readers

Especially with the size of many log files, it can be helpful to just glance at the top of a file to identify its contents, and at the bottom of the file to check out the latest information. By default, the **head** *textfile* and **tail** *textfile* commands display the first and last 10 lines of a specified text file.

You can modify the number of lines shown by either command with the **-n** *num* switch; for example, the **head -n 15 smb.conf-example** command shows the first 15 lines of the given file.

If you're monitoring new error messages, the following command can help you monitor them as they appear:

```
$ tail -f /var/adm/messages
```

It lists the last 10 lines of the noted file, and monitors the file for additional input. As new log messages appear, the lines are updated, so you can see what's happening in real time. You'll have to press CTRL-C to exit out of the monitoring mode.

The File Pagers

Sometimes, you've just got to search through a longer text file. Two commands that can help are **more** and **less**. Both commands start at the beginning of a text file. However, the effects are different. For example, if you run the **more smb.conf-example** command and then press the SPACEBAR, you can search through the file, one page at a time.

On the other hand, if you run the **less smb.conf-example** command, you can press the SPACEBAR to search through the file. But you can also use the UP and DOWN ARROW keys to scroll through the file. You can exit from the pager by pressing Q. One useful feature is search; for example, if you type in **/home directory** and press ENTER, the pager searches forward in the file for the "home directory" text. You can search backward by substituting a question mark (?) for the forward slash (/).

Additional features of the **more** and **less** pagers are available; just press H while the pager is active.

File Manipulation

Although it's nice to be able to page through a file, as an administrator, you need to be able to do more. Statistics on elements such as log files can substantively show how much data is being produced, or perhaps how many errors are being generated. You can collect that data with the help of the **wc** command. With the tens of thousands of files on a Solaris system, it's helpful to know how to use the **find** command to identify their locations. Once you've found a list of files, the **grep** command can help isolate that configuration detail needed for other systems. Finally, the output of commands can be redirected with arrows and more.

Lines, Words, and Characters

The **wc** command can do three things. It can count the numbers of lines, words, and characters in a target file. When applied to the aforementioned smb.conf-example file, it leads to the following result (the numbers represent the lines, words, and characters in the noted file):

```
$ wc smb.conf-example
271 1687 9662 smb.conf-example
```

You can isolate the numbers of lines, words, and characters with the **-l**, **-w**, and **-c** switches, respectively. Such statistics can be used in scripts, as described in Chapter 10.

Finding Files Locally

With the tens of thousands of files on a Solaris system, nobody can be expected to remember the location of every file. That's where the **find** command is useful. The following command on a test system revealed nearly 200,000 files:

```
# find / | wc -l
```

This command may take a few seconds or more, depending on the available resources. It takes a little time to count 200,000 files. You can simplify the task. For example, if you're just looking for a specific configuration file in the /etc directory, such as httpd.conf, the following command can work a lot more quickly:

```
# find /etc -name httpd.conf
```

With appropriate wildcards, exact filenames are not required. Given the different types of files, it may be helpful to identify them by type. For example, the following command searches for all directories on the local system:

```
# find / -type d
```

Additional file types are similar to what is shown in the output to the **ls -l** command described earlier in this chapter. Of course, you could be searching for regular files (including directories). That's possible with the following command:

```
# find / -type -f
```

Alternatively, you can search files based on permissions. For example, the following command searches for all files with Super User ID permissions. The 4000 is the numeric representation for a file to which regular users have access with root administrative privileges:

```
# find / -perm 4000
```

You can search for files based on access time; the following command identifies those files that were last accessed more than one day ago:

```
# find / -atime 1
```

Switch	Description
-atime *n*	Identify files last accessed more than *n* days ago.
-group *group*	List files owned by a specific group.
-name *term*	Show files associated with a search term. May be used with wildcards.
-perm *permission*	Display files associated with a given permission, in numeric format.
-user *username*	List files owned by a specific user.

TABLE 8-6. *Switches for the **find** Command*

Some of the important switches for the **find** command are shown in Table 8-6.

TIP
*Linux users won't find an analogue to the **locate** command on Solaris 11. Previous versions of Solaris included a **fastfind** command that was removed for security reasons. If a black-hat hacker can identify the names of key files accessible only to administrative users, he could get a better sense of the potential weaknesses on the system.*

You could go a bit further. For example, the following command finds all files in the local directory (and subdirectories) that have a .pdf extension:

```
# find . -name '*.pdf'
```

Search Within a File

Solaris 11 includes a substantial number of large text files. Text files for databases and logs can frequently grow into the gigabytes. The **grep** command can quickly search in text files for important information. For example, the following command searches through the local database of users for accounts configured with bash as the login shell:

```
$ grep bash /etc/passwd
```

Search utilities such as **grep** can also be used to search through databases of output. If you've just tried commands such as **find / -perm 4000**, described earlier, you might have been overwhelmed by the amount of output. That's where **grep** can be helpful. If you use the "pipe" described next, it'll help you filter that output. For example, the following command filters the output by the /sbin directory, normally associated with administrative commands:

```
$ find / -perm 4000 | grep /sbin
```

File Redirection and More

With all of these text files and filters, it still can be a lot of information to digest on the screen. To help focus this data and make it more useful, six different types of redirection arrows, as well as the pipe just described, are available:

- **>** A forward redirection arrow can move the regular output of a command to a specific file. For example, the **ls > /tmp/filelist** command directs the list of files in the current directory to a file named filelist in the /tmp directory. Just be aware that the command also overwrites any existing content in the target file. Synonymous with **1>**.

- **>>** A double forward redirection arrow appends to a specific file. For example, the **ls -l >> /tmp/runlist** command redirects the output of the **ls -l** command to the end of the target file. Synonymous with **1>>**.

- **2>** When a command or program has errors, it directs them differently. You can isolate those errors with the **2>** arrow. As a simple example, try the **ls abed 2> error1** command. Assuming the abed file does not exist, it should redirect an error message to the local error1 file.

- **2>>** In the same fashion as the regular double forward redirection arrow (**>>**), the **2>>** redirects errors and appends them to a target file, without erasing any contents of the file.

- **<** The backward redirection arrow is one way to use input from a text file.

- **2>&1** Combines the effect of both the **>** and **2>** arrows, redirecting both regular and error output to a target file.

Finally, the pipe ([|] the vertical character above the backslash on most U.S. keyboards) redirects the output of one command as input to a second command. For example, the pipe in the command

```
# find / | wc -l
```

redirects the output of the **find /** command as input to the **wc -l** command. In essence, the pipe is a shortcut. The alternative is to run two separate commands, such as the following:

```
# find / > tempfiles
# wc -l tempfiles
```

Options for File Editing

It's important to learn how to use text editors at the console. Administrators may frequently need to connect to remote systems, using a command-line connection such as the Secure Shell (SSH) described in Chapter 20. Although it's possible to use GUI tools over an SSH connection, it can be slow, especially on a busier network.

For that purpose, you'll explore two different console editors in this section: vi and nano. Although vi is a complex editor, an understanding of vi is a sign of credibility among a number of UNIX gurus. If you can open and edit simple configuration files in vi, you'll seem more credible to such gurus, who may frequently be your supervisors on the job. However, with the availability of other intuitive console editors such as nano, pico, and joe, expert knowledge of vi is not required.

The vi Editor

The easiest way to open the vi editor is with the **vi** command. When you do so, the first screen, as shown in Figure 8-3, notes that this is actually the VIM editor, short for "vi, improved." As noted in the output to the **ls -l /bin/vi** command, the **vi** command is actually linked to the **vim** command. To quit, run the **:q** command.

If you've made any changes and want to quit without saving, type in the following command:

```
:q!
```

Alternatively, if you want to save changes into a specific file, such as file1.txt, run the following command:

```
:w file1.txt
```

You can open up that file from the command line with the following command:

```
$ vi file1.txt
```

You can then run the aforementioned **:q** command to exit from vi. Such commands can be combined. For example, **:wq file1.txt** would combine the intent of the previous two commands. The colon in vi is associated with one of the three modes of vi:

- **Command mode** is the default when the vi editor is open.
- **Insert mode** is where text can be added to and deleted from a file.
- **Execute mode** allows you to run shell commands from within the editor.

The commands described in this section just represent a fraction of the capabilities of the vi editor. But they should be enough for you to show many UNIX gurus that you respect the "old ways" (if that's at all important to you).

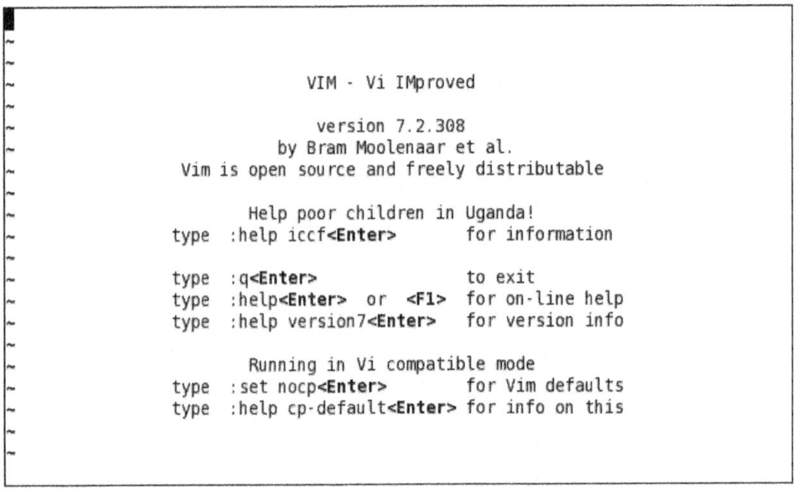

```
VIM - Vi IMproved

               version 7.2.308
             by Bram Moolenaar et al.
       Vim is open source and freely distributable

              Help poor children in Uganda!
       type  :help iccf<Enter>        for information

       type  :q<Enter>               to exit
       type  :help<Enter>  or  <F1>  for on-line help
       type  :help version7<Enter>   for version info

              Running in Vi compatible mode
       type  :set nocp<Enter>         for Vim defaults
       type  :help cp-default<Enter>  for info on this
```

FIGURE 8-3. *The vi editor, improved*

Command Mode

Within command mode, you can search, navigate, and delete. As with the **more** and **less** command pagers, you can use the forward slash (/) and the question mark (?) to search a term further, forward and backward, in a file.

Navigation is straightforward, as the PAGE UP, PAGE DOWN, and ARROW keys work in most terminals. Because older terminals did not have arrow keys, the H, J, K, and L keys were used for the left, down, up, and right-facing arrows, respectively.

Navigation is also possible by line number. But how do you know what line number is what? Enter the **:set nu** command, and line numbers should appear in the left column. With or without labeled line numbers, you can type the **gg** command to go to the first line and the **G** command to navigate to the last line. To go to the tenth line, you could type in **10G** or **10gg**.

Command mode can also include editing features; the **yy** command "yanks" the current line into the buffer. The **2yy** command yanks the current and the next line into the buffer. Once these lines are in the buffer, the **p** command takes the contents of the buffer and inserts them into the next line.

Insert Mode

Once in insert mode, you should be able to type your desired text directly into the file. As described in Table 8-7, there are a number of ways to enter insert mode.

To exit insert mode and return to command mode, press the ESC key.

Execute Mode

Execute mode allows you to run shell commands from within the vi editor. The command is prefaced by the bang character (!), which is also used as the exclamation point in regular English. For example, the following command from within insert mode lists the files in the current directory:

```
:!ls
```

Just a reminder: To exit from the vi editor without saving in command mode, run the **!q** command; to exit from the vi editor while saving changes that have been made, run the **!wq** command.

vi Command	Starting Point for Insert Mode
a	Next character position.
A	End of current line.
i	Current character position.
I	Beginning of current line.
o	Insert and add a new line below the current line.
O	Insert and add a new line above the current line.
cw	Delete the current word and enter insert mode in its position.
cc	Delete the current line and enter insert mode in its position.

TABLE 8-7. *Commands to Enter* **vi** *Insert Mode*

One Other Text Editor

UNIX-based operating systems support a number of other text editors. Entire books have been dedicated to their operation. The nano text editor is one intuitive alternative to vi. To open a local smb.conf-example file in that editor, run the following command:

```
# nano smb.conf-example
```

Once the target text file is open, you're already in "insert mode." The other commands shown at the bottom of Figure 8-4 can be started with the CTRL key. For example, to start the process of exiting from nano, press CTRL-X. If any changes have been made, you'll be prompted with the following question:

```
Save modified buffer (ANSWERING "No" WILL DESTROY CHANGES) ?
```

At this prompt, press Y or N. If you press N, the nano editor exits and returns to the command-line interface. If you press Y, nano prompts you for a filename, suggesting the current name of the file, normally in the local directory. Here's an example:

```
File Name to Write: smb.conf-example
```

If you change the name of the file, you're prompted to confirm, once again by pressing Y or N.

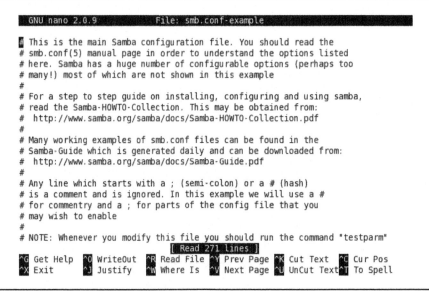

```
  GNU nano 2.0.9             File: smb.conf-example

 This is the main Samba configuration file. You should read the
# smb.conf(5) manual page in order to understand the options listed
# here. Samba has a huge number of configurable options (perhaps too
# many!) most of which are not shown in this example
#
# For a step to step guide on installing, configuring and using samba,
# read the Samba-HOWTO-Collection. This may be obtained from:
#  http://www.samba.org/samba/docs/Samba-HOWTO-Collection.pdf
#
# Many working examples of smb.conf files can be found in the
# Samba-Guide which is generated daily and can be downloaded from:
#  http://www.samba.org/samba/docs/Samba-Guide.pdf
#
# Any line which starts with a ; (semi-colon) or a # (hash)
# is a comment and is ignored. In this example we will use a #
# for commentry and a ; for parts of the config file that you
# may wish to enable
#
# NOTE: Whenever you modify this file you should run the command "testparm"
                        [ Read 271 lines ]
^G Get Help  ^O WriteOut  ^R Read File ^Y Prev Page ^K Cut Text  ^C Cur Pos
^X Exit      ^J Justify   ^W Where Is  ^V Next Page ^U UnCut Text^T To Spell
```

FIGURE 8-4.   *The nano text editor is intuitive.*

Summary

In this chapter, you explored the basic command-line skills used in Solaris. Although these commands are based on the same functional bash shell used on Linux systems, there are subtle differences. If you've never used a command-line interface before, you may need to supplement the knowledge in this chapter with materials from other chapters and related books.

With the skills described in this chapter, you should be able to

- Navigate around the directory tree.
- List files in selected directories, based on variables such as revision time.
- Create, copy, move, delete, and link files.
- Identify file types, scroll text files to the screen, and apply top and bottom file readers as well as pagers to text files.
- Manage the data associated with files, such as word counts, file searches, the contents of a file, as well as redirection of data from a text file.
- Use the vi and nano editors in at least an elementary fashion.

References

For a more detailed introduction to the command line, see *Introduction to Unix and Linux* by John Muster, published by McGraw-Hill Professional, 2002.

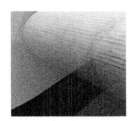

CHAPTER
9

Filesystems and ZFS

our computer systems' data and programs are generally stored on one or more "hard disks." These hardware devices have an internal storage structure that must be mapped to human-readable directories and files. How this is mapped depends on the type and capacity of the disks as well as on the features of the operating system that is used. For much of UNIX (and Solaris) history, the UFS (UNIX File System) has been used to create and support the organization of disks, directories, and files. Although UFS has been extensively enhanced and improved over time, it still has some significant limitations. In UFS, files and directories can only be so large, and there are ways that disks and UFS filesystems can fail that might lose or corrupt data. The ZFS filesystem, introduced in Solaris 10, addresses these issues and adds other important features.

In this chapter, we first review how data is stored on disk devices and how the disk components are named and accessed in Solaris 11. We'll discuss a bit about UFS, but we will focus primarily on Solaris 11's default filesystem, ZFS (originally called the "Zettabyte File System," but now simply called by its trademarked initials). We'll review ZFS's special features, which include easy storage management, data integrity technologies, copying and duplicating data, and compressing and encrypting filesystems.

Because ZFS is the default filesystem used by Solaris 11, you will see in other chapters how it is used to help administrators with patching and upgrading the OS and applications, managing multiple OS boot environments, supporting the creation and management of containers, and backing up and restoring files.

Disk Structure and Naming Conventions

Modern disk drives usually consist of one or more circular platters coated with a magnetic iron oxide compound (some critics call such devices "rotating rust"). The disk platters spin rapidly while a data-access mechanism, called the read/write head, moves across the spinning platters to locate the required data (see Figure 9-1). Data is generally written to or read from the disk in blocks of

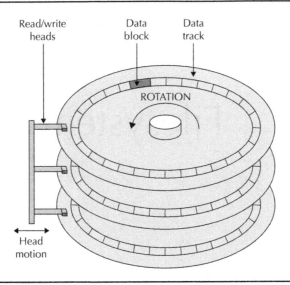

FIGURE 9-1. *The structure of a typical multiplatter hard disk drive*

512 bytes arranged in concentric tracks on the disk's surface; blocks are read or written as each block's location on the platter rotates under the read/write head. Performance and capacity of the disk are determined by the density of the bytes recorded on the magnetic substance, by the physical size and number of disk platters in the drive, by how fast the disk spins, and by how quickly the read/write head can locate the required disk blocks. Today's disk drives are compact and fast, spinning as high as 15,000 rpm, capable of storing many terabytes (trillions of bytes) of data, and transferring data at rates exceeding 1 Gbps.

Additionally, disks are organized into several overlapping and resizable sections called *partitions* for the purpose of separating types of data used by the operating system. Each partition includes a portion of the disk's total capacity (see Figure 9-2). Depending on the operating system used, disk partitions are assigned symbolic names by the OS for use by administrators in order to configure and access portions of the disk storage for the OS and for users. When Solaris 11 is first installed, it probes the system for disk I/O controllers and disk drives, then assigns and activates predetermined symbolic names to the devices it finds. The general naming pattern for Solaris 11 disk devices is basically the same for SPARC and x86 systems. The filename links to the disk devices are contained in the /dev directory; the two special subdirectories there are /dev/dsk and /dev/rdsk. Most file access will occur multiple data blocks at a time, so the /dev/dsk directory contains partition names that are interpreted as block devices, whereas those in the /dev/rdsk directory point to the same data and are interpreted and accessed as character devices (reading and/or writing a byte/character at a time). The symbolic names in the /dev directory are really links to longer device description filenames in the /devices directory, but those are rarely referenced directly by system administrators.

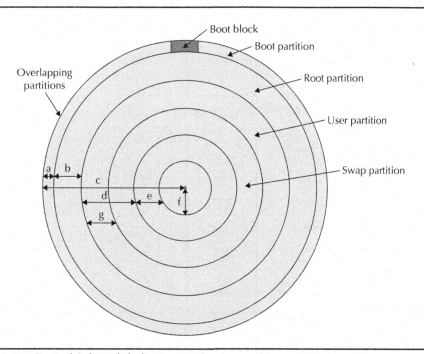

FIGURE 9-2. *Typical Solaris disk device partitions*

Disk names in both the /dev/dsk and /dev/rdsk directories use the following naming convention:

    c?t?d?p?

where **c?** is the number of the disk's controller device, **t?** is the controller's target number, **d?** is the number of the disk on that controller, and **p?** is the partition number (disk partitions are sometimes called *slices,* so the device name might use an *s* instead of a *p*). Counting of components starts with 0 instead of 1, so the device name

    /dev/dsk/c0t0d1p2

is a pointer to the block device on the first controller, first target, second disk, third partition. Figure 9-3 shows how disk device names are organized; only disks that are installed, powered on, and connected to the system are recognized devices and accessible to the operating system.

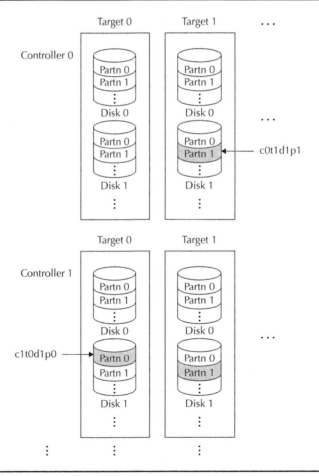

FIGURE 9-3. *Disk device organization*

When configuring disk storage space on Solaris using a UFS filesystem, administrators (using the root ID) must perform several steps:

- Identify the device to be used and its link in /dev/dsk
- Format and divide the disk into partitions
- Create a UFS filesystem on the partition
- Verify the integrity of the UFS filesystem
- Mount the UFS filesystem onto a new or existing directory mount point
- Create user or system directories on the filesystem, including access controls and parameters
- Identify and implement a backup procedure for the filesystem

Typically the system administrator would perform these steps in sequence manually, although several Solaris and third-party tools can be used to help automate this process somewhat. ZFS takes care of nearly all of these tasks automatically, however, thus significantly simplifying storage management.

Introduction to ZFS

The ZFS filesystem, first introduced in Solaris 10, was designed to provide a highly scalable storage management system that guarantees data integrity. Sun and Oracle gradually introduced planned ZFS features into Solaris 10 updates; Solaris 11 now implements all of those earlier planned features, plus the following additional capabilities:

- Easy storage management, able to address multiple disk storage devices as a large contiguous storage block instead of as separate disks and partitions
- 128-bit addressing, eliminating for all practical purposes any size restrictions on filesystems, directories, and files
- Data integrity assurance, by computing and validating 256-bit checksums on all disk operations as well as providing for RAID operations for parity, striping, and mirroring
- Automated detection and repair of data corruption caused by disk hardware errors and failures
- Encrypting ZFS filesystems to protect sensitive data and to comply with privacy regulations
- Compressing and deduplicating data to save disk space
- Configuring and managing user storage quotas
- Copying and transmitting data to other systems with ZFS pools
- Creating snapshots of current filesystem contents for later recovery and use

We'll cover each of these capabilities in this chapter.

ZFS joins multiple disk devices into one view of storage, much like how the operating system merges multiple memory modules into a single addressable block of main memory. Storage can then be managed as a single unit, called a *pool*, from which filesystems of any size can be allocated without being limited by disk or partition boundaries (see Figure 9-4).

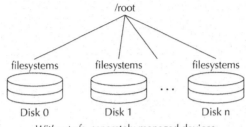

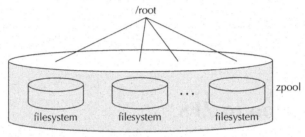

FIGURE 9-4. *ZFS view of disk storage*

Additionally, Solaris 11 now uses ZFS for the root filesystem that is used to boot the OS, including the capability of creating a duplicate, or mirror, of that boot filesystem to guard against boot failures.

NOTE
*There is currently no direct method for converting a UFS filesystem in place to a ZFS filesystem. You must create a new ZFS filesystem and then copy your data from the UFS filesystem into the ZFS filesystem using any of the standard UNIX file tools, such as **tar**, **cpio**, or **cp**.*

Some ZFS Terminology

ZFS is a collection of technologies and commands used to manage storage in Solaris 10 and 11. In order to understand its concepts and implementation, we need to define its terms and naming conventions. Table 9-1 describes the ZFS "vocabulary" we will use in later sections.

ZFS Commands

As we will explain in the following sections, you create ZFS pools using the **zpool** command and then create ZFS filesystems within the pools using the **zfs** command. These commands are also used to configure the features and characteristics of the pools and filesystems.

Term	Description
pool	The basic ZFS storage element consisting of one or more disk devices (partitions) and containing one or more datasets.
filesystem	A dataset managed as a unit containing directories and files.
clone	A copy of a ZFS filesystem.
snapshot	A read-only copy of the state of a ZFS filesystem.
checksum	A 256-bit number derived from a data element, used to validate the data when it is read or written.
compression	Reducing the required storage space by removing and codifying redundant data patterns.
encryption	Encoding data using a password for security and privacy.
deduplication	Removal of duplicate data blocks to conserve storage space.
quota	A maximum allowable storage amount allocated to a user or group.
reservation	A preallocated storage amount reserved for a specific filesystem or user.
RAID-Z	A RAID-5-like storage method used by ZFS to ensure data integrity through mirroring and parity-checking disk writes.
mirror	An exact duplicate of a disk device or partition used to ensure continuous data availability. Writes to a disk are duplicated on its mirror disk.
zpool	The **/usr/sbin/zpool** command used to manage ZFS pools.
zfs	The **/usr/sbin/zfs** command used to manage ZFS filesystems.
raidz2, **raidz3**	Additional parity disks for greater data integrity, striped across multiple disks. Multiple disk failures can be sustained.

TABLE 9-1. *ZFS Terminology*

The zpool Command

The **zpool** command is used to create and configure ZFS storage pools. It is located in the /usr/sbin directory and requires root user privileges to run. Table 9-2 summarizes the **zpool** subcommands you use to configure and manage pool storage.

The zfs Command

After ZFS pools have been created and configured with their desired properties, filesystems can be created within the pools in order to present storage directories to users. The **zfs** command is used for this purpose; it also resides in the /usr/sbin directory and, like the **zpool** command, requires root user privileges. Table 9-3 summarizes the **zfs** subcommands used to configure and manage ZFS filesystems.

Subcommand	Description
create	Creates a ZFS storage pool using a list of disk devices and configures its properties and mount point.
destroy	Destroys a ZFS storage pool, releasing its disk devices for other use.
list	Lists the health status and storage usage of a pool. You can also use **list** to repeatedly monitor the pool by specifying a display interval.
status	Reports the health of a pool, stating whether it is online, offline, degraded, or in an error fault condition.
history	Displays the list of commands issued for a pool since its creation.
add	Adds a disk device to an existing pool.
remove	Removes a disk device from an existing pool.
replace	Replaces an existing pool disk device with another disk device.
get	Retrieves and displays a list of properties for a pool.
set	Sets or resets a property for a pool.
scrub	Verifies the checksums for a pool and repairs any damaged data blocks due to disk failures.

TABLE 9-2. *The **zpool** Subcommands*

Subcommand	Description
create	Creates a ZFS filesystem on a specified pool, sets its properties, and automatically mounts it.
destroy	Destroys a ZFS filesystem or snapshot.
list	Lists the properties and storage usage of a ZFS filesystem.
get	Displays the configured properties of a filesystem.
set	Sets a specific property for a filesystem.
snapshot	Creates a read-only copy of the state of a filesystem.
rollback	Returns a filesystem to the state saved in the specified snapshot.
send	Creates a stream or file from a snapshot for transmission to another ZFS system.
receive	Retrieves a snapshot stream or file created with **zfs send**.
clone	Creates a copy of a snapshot.
promote	Transforms a clone into an independent filesystem.
diff	Displays the file differences between two snapshots or between a snapshot and its parent.
mount	Mounts a ZFS filesystem on a specified mount point.
unmount	Unmounts a ZFS filesystem.

TABLE 9-3. *The **zfs** Subcommands*

Using ZFS

Now that we have shown you the commands and subcommands needed to create and manage ZFS storage, let's look at examples of how they are used. Recall that the reason for using ZFS in the first place (other than the fact that it's the default) is to make storage management easy and to keep data safe.

For the following discussion, we will assume you have an array of eight disk devices, /dev/dsk/c3t0d0p0 through /dev/dsk/c3t0d7p0 (note the disk numbers). ZFS can work with individual disk partitions, but the recommended best practice is to use whole disks. The **zpool** command takes the disk names among its required parameters and assumes that the default directory for the devices is /dev/dsk, although any device directory can be specified explicitly.

In the following example, we first list any existing pools and their status (lines 1 and 4), and then we see **rpool**, which is the system's boot and root environment (more about that later in this chapter).

```
1   # zpool list
2   NAME    SIZE   ALLOC   FREE   CAP   DEDUP   HEALTH   ALTROOT
3   rpool   232G   65.8G   166G   28%   1.00x   ONLINE   -
4   # zpool status
5     pool: rpool
6    state: ONLINE
7     scan: none requested
8   config:
9
10            NAME         STATE      READ WRITE CKSUM
11            rpool        ONLINE        0     0     0
12              c10d0s0    ONLINE        0     0     0
13
14   errors: No known data errors
15   # zpool create mypool-1 c3t0d0p0  c3t0d1p0
16   # zpool list
17   NAME         SIZE   ALLOC    FREE   CAP   DEDUP   HEALTH   ALTROOT
```

Experimenting with ZFS

If you want to experiment with ZFS pools but don't yet have spare disks to play with, you can create files in your HOME or other directory that ZFS can use to create pools and filesystems. Just make a few 300MB files with the **mkfile** program, like this:

```
mkfile 300m {your-dir}/fakedisk1
mkfile 300m {your-dir}/fakedisk2
mkfile 300m {your-dir}/fakedisk3
```

Then you can practice making and configuring pools using these files, like so:

```
zpool create practicepool mirror {your-dir}/fakedisk1 {your-dir}/fakedisk2
```

Other commands (such as those reviewed next) can be used, but pools created on such files are for practice and learning only, not meant for production.

```
18   mypool-1  7.94G   123K   7.94G   0%  1.00x   ONLINE  -
19   rpool      232G  65.8G    166G  28%  1.00x   ONLINE  -
20   # zpool status mypool-1
21     pool: mypool-1
22    state: ONLINE
23     scan: none requested
24   config:
25
26           NAME          STATE     READ WRITE CKSUM
27           mypool-1      ONLINE       0     0     0
28             c3t0d0p0    ONLINE       0     0     0
29             c3t0d1p0    ONLINE       0     0     0
30
31   errors: No known data errors
32   #
```

In line 15, we created a ZFS pool named mypool-1 using two disk devices. Then we again checked the list and status (lines 16 and 20). ZFS has not only created the pool, but has created a default filesystem and mount point, ready to be used to store files.

Recall that one of the ways we can protect data against disk failure is to write it to a duplicate disk, or *mirror*. Thus, we'll destroy our newly created pool (line 1) and re-create it as a mirrored pool (line 2):

```
 1   # zpool destroy mypool-1
 2   # zpool create mypool-1m mirror c3t0d0p0  c3t0d1p0
 3   # zpool list
 4   NAME          SIZE  ALLOC   FREE  CAP  DEDUP   HEALTH  ALTROOT
 5   mypool-1m    3.97G   126K  3.97G   0%  1.00x   ONLINE  -
 6   rpool         232G  65.8G   166G  28%  1.00x   ONLINE  -
 7   # zpool status mypool-1m
 8     pool: mypool-1m
 9    state: ONLINE
10     scan: none requested
11   config:
12
13           NAME          STATE     READ WRITE CKSUM
14           mypool-1m     ONLINE       0     0     0
15             mirror-0    ONLINE       0     0     0
16               c3t0d0p0  ONLINE       0     0     0
17               c3t0d1p0  ONLINE       0     0     0
18
19   errors: No known data errors
20   # zpool add mypool-1m mirror c3t0d2p0  c3t0d3p0
21   # zpool status mypool-1m
22     pool: mypool-1m
23    state: ONLINE
24     scan: none requested
25   config:
26
27           NAME          STATE     READ WRITE CKSUM
28           mypool-1m     ONLINE       0     0     0
```

```
29              mirror-0      ONLINE      0      0      0
30                  c3t0d0p0  ONLINE      0      0      0
31                  c3t0d1p0  ONLINE      0      0      0
32              mirror-1      ONLINE      0      0      0
33                  c3t0d2p0  ONLINE      0      0      0
34                  c3t0d3p0  ONLINE      0      0      0
35
36    errors: No known data errors
```

In line 20, we added disk drives to the pool. Note that we needed to add *two* disks—one for the additional data disk and a second one for its mirror.

ZFS also supports a RAID-5-like capability called RAID-Z. This technique spreads data blocks among several disks and adds a "parity" component used to reconstruct the data in the event of a disk failure. ZFS on Solaris 11 includes several versions of this feature (RAID-Z2 and RAID-Z3) that use multiple parity disks for greater redundancy and protection from as many as three simultaneous pool disk failures. In the following example, we create a RAID-Z3 pool and assign an additional disk device as a spare that can be automatically configured into the pool if one of the other pool drives fails:

```
 1  # zpool create mypool-z3 raidz3 ¬
    c3t0d0p0 c3t0d1p0 c3t0d2p0 c3t0d3p0 spare c3t0d4p0
 2  # zpool list
 3  NAME        SIZE    ALLOC   FREE    CAP   DEDUP   HEALTH   ALTROOT
 4  mypool-z3   15.9G   134K    15.9G   0%    1.00x   ONLINE   -
 5  rpool       232G    65.8G   166G    28%   1.00x   ONLINE   -
 6  # zpool status mypool-z3
 7    pool: mypool-z3
 8   state: ONLINE
 9    scan: none requested
10  config:
11
12          NAME          STATE    READ WRITE CKSUM
13          mypool-z3     ONLINE      0      0      0
14            c3t0d0p0    ONLINE      0      0      0
15            c3t0d1p0    ONLINE      0      0      0
16            c3t0d2p0    ONLINE      0      0      0
17            c3t0d3p0    ONLINE      0      0      0
18          spares
19            c3t0d4p0    AVAIL
20
21  errors: No known data errors
```

The **zpool get** subcommand lists the current properties of a ZFS pool. For the mypool-z3 pool we created in this example, if we display all of its properties (line 1, next), we see that the spare disk we allocated would *not* be automatically used in the event of a disk failure in that pool because the property **autoreplace** is set to **off** (line 11). We can change and verify that property, and any other, using the **zpool set** subcommand (lines 21 and 22).

```
 1  # zpool get all mypool-z3
 2  NAME        PROPERTY     VALUE              SOURCE
 3  mypool-z3   size         15.9G              -
```

```
 4  mypool-z3  capacity      0%                      -
 5  mypool-z3  altroot       -                       default
 6  mypool-z3  health        ONLINE                  -
 7  mypool-z3  guid          11582677798614037519    -
 8  mypool-z3  version       33                      default
 9  mypool-z3  bootfs        -                       default
10  mypool-z3  delegation    on                      default
11  mypool-z3  autoreplace   off                     local
12  mypool-z3  cachefile     -                       default
13  mypool-z3  failmode      wait                    default
14  mypool-z3  listsnapshots on                      local
15  mypool-z3  autoexpand    off                     default
16  mypool-z3  dedupditto    0                       default
17  mypool-z3  dedupratio    1.00x                   -
18  mypool-z3  free          15.9G                   -
19  mypool-z3  allocated     98.5K                   -
20  mypool-z3  readonly      off                     -
21  # zpool set autoreplace=on mypool-z3
22  # zpool get autoreplace mypool-z3
23  NAME        PROPERTY    VALUE    SOURCE
24  mypool-z3   autoreplace on       local
```

If we want to remind ourselves or to document the actions that have been taken for a pool, the **zpool history** subcommand will list all activity since the creation of the pool. Here's an example:

```
# zpool history mypool-z3
History for 'mypool-z3':
2011-11-30.19:41:35 zpool create mypool-z3 ¬
c3t0d0p0 c3t0d1p0 c3t0d2p0 c3t0d3p0 spare c3t0d4p0
2011-12-01.19:10:19 zpool set autoreplace=on mypool-z3
2011-12-01.19:35:42 zpool add mypool-z3 c3t0d5p0
2011-12-01.19:39:03 zpool scrub mypool-z3
```

Although the **zpool** command creates and mounts a default ZFS filesystem for you, the **zfs** command can be used to create ZFS filesystems within pools. In the following example, we create mirrored pool mypool-2 (line 1) and two filesystems within that pool, george and martha (lines 2 and 3):

```
 1  # zpool create mypool-2 mirror c3t0d2p0 c3t0d3p0
 2  # zfs create mypool-2/george
 3  # zfs create mypool-2/martha
 4  # zfs list
 5  NAME                 USED   AVAIL  REFER  MOUNTPOINT
 6  mypool-1             5.53M  3.90G  5.38M  /mypool-1
 7  mypool-2             162K   3.91G    33K  /mypool-2
 8  mypool-2/george       31K   3.91G    31K  /mypool-2/george
 9  mypool-2/martha       31K   3.91G    31K  /mypool-2/martha
10  rpool                66.2G   162G  39.5K  /rpool
11  ...
```

You can set several important and very useful properties on ZFS filesystems. These can be set at creation time on the command line or after the filesystem is created. Two of these properties are focused on saving storage space—**compression** and **deduplication**.

The ZFS compression feature reads data in a filesystem, tokenizes repetitive strings of characters, and stores the data in reduced form. Compressing data in this way is completely transparent to the user, and it can save a significant amount of storage, depending on the nature of the data and how much it can be compressed. For example, you can create a compressed filesystem like this:

```
# zfs create -o compression= on mypool-2/thomas
```

Alternatively, you can set the **compression** property on an existing filesystem like this:

```
# zfs set compression=on mypool-2/george
```

NOTE
Enabling compression on a filesystem with existing data only compresses new data. Existing data remains uncompressed.

You can see the effect of filesystem compression by displaying the **compressratio** property:

```
# zfs get compressratio mypool-1
NAME       PROPERTY      VALUE  SOURCE
mypool-1   compressratio 1.12x  -
```

A ratio of 1.0 means that no compression is active; a value more than 1.0 gives an estimate of the amount of compression achieved. The ratio is calculated using the compressed size and logical size of the filesystem contents, and could be 10 or even higher for some data types.

Another space-saving ZFS property is **deduplication**. This technology understands that some data blocks are identical and stores them only once; that is, it removes duplicate storage blocks. Like other properties, it can be set at filesystem creation time or after the fact. The **zpool list** subcommand will report the storage savings resulting from deduplication:

```
# zfs set dedup=on mypool-2/Martha
# zpool list mypool-2
NAME       SIZE   ALLOC   FREE   CAP   DEDUP   HEALTH   ALTROOT
mypool-2   3.97G  227K    3.97G  0%    2.10x   ONLINE   -
```

Solaris 11 finally introduced ZFS filesystem encryption, a frequently requested feature for data protection and privacy. Unlike **compression** and **deduplication**, the **encryption** property can be enabled only when the filesystem is created. At that time, you must enter a passphrase that will be needed for subsequent actions on that filesystem. The **keysource** property defaults to **prompt**, meaning that you will be asked for the passphrase to access the filesystem, or you can set the **keysource** property to point to a file containing an encrypted wrapping key.

```
# zfs create -o encryption=on mypool-2/john
Enter passphrase for 'mypool-2/john': ********
Enter again: ********
# zfs get encryption mypool-2/john
NAME            PROPERTY     VALUE   SOURCE
mypool-2/john   encryption   on      local
```

```
# zfs get keysource mypool-2/john
NAME            PROPERTY   VALUE              SOURCE
mypool-2/john   keysource  passphrase,prompt  local
```

ZFS as the Root/Boot Filesystem

So far we haven't said anything about that other ZFS pool that keeps showing up in our examples—rpool, the *root pool*. In Solaris 10 and earlier, the default root and boot filesystem was based on UFS; Solaris 11 boots from a ZFS filesystem created at installation time.

```
# zpool list rpool
NAME    SIZE   ALLOC  FREE   CAP   DEDUP   HEALTH   ALTROOT
rpool   232G   65.9G  166G   28%   1.00x   ONLINE   -
# zpool status rpool
  pool: rpool
 state: ONLINE
  scan: none requested
config:

        NAME         STATE    READ WRITE CKSUM
        rpool        ONLINE      0     0     0
          c10d0s0    ONLINE      0     0     0
errors: No known data errors
```

Within the rpool are several filesystems also created at installation time, including rpool/ROOT, which contains the mount points for the current and alternate Solaris 11 boot images, and the /export/home filesystem for users' home directories. By default, installation filesystems are created on this rpool.

```
# zfs list rpool
NAME    USED   AVAIL  REFER  MOUNTPOINT
rpool   66.1G  162G   39.5K  /rpool
# zfs list -r rpool
NAME                          USED   AVAIL  REFER  MOUNTPOINT
rpool                         66.1G  162G   39.5K  /rpool
rpool/ROOT                    46.8G  162G     31K  legacy
rpool/ROOT/solaris            66.2M  162G   8.60G  /
rpool/ROOT/solaris-3          46.7G  162G   40.8G  /
rpool/dump                    4.09G  162G   3.97G  -
rpool/export                  11.1G  162G     32K  /export
rpool/export/home             11.1G  162G     32K  /export/home
rpool/export/home/hfoxwell    11.1G  162G   7.61G  /export/home/hfoxwell
rpool/swap                    4.09G  162G   3.97G  -
#
```

The most common (yet optional) task for system administrators is to create a mirror of the root disk containing the root pool for redundancy, in the event that the primary boot disk fails for some reason, in which case the system can boot from the mirror until the failed disk is replaced. In order to add a mirror disk to the root pool, you must **attach** (not **add**) a duplicate, identically sized device to the pool. Here's an example where c1t0d0 is the root disk and c1t10d0 will be its mirror:

```
# zpool attach rpool c1t0d0 c1t10d0
```

Now you must wait for the primary boot disk's data to be copied (ZFS calls it "resilvering") to the mirror disk. And then you must add the mirror disk to the available boot disks for your system by modifying the BIOS boot order (for x86 systems) or modifying the PROM boot-device variable (using the **setenv** command for SPARC systems).

ZFS for Managing HOME Directories

Creating home directories for an end user is as simple as creating a ZFS filesystem for that user at the time the user is created and specifying the pool, user ID, and login shell. Here's an example:

```
etc# useradd -m -d /mypool-2/thomas -s /usr/bin/bash thomas
etc# zfs list
NAME                      USED   AVAIL   REFER   MOUNTPOINT
mypool-1                 5.53M   3.90G   5.38M   /mypool-1
mypool-2                  274K   3.91G     35K   /mypool-2
mypool-2/george           31K    3.91G     31K   /mypool-2/george
mypool-2/john             33K    3.91G     33K   /mypool-2/john
mypool-2/martha           31K    3.91G     31K   /mypool-2/martha
mypool-2/thomas           35K    3.91G     35K   /mypool-2/thomas
rpool                    66.1G    162G   39.5K   /rpool
...
```

Chapter 11 gives more details on creating and managing user IDs; for now we will use the simplified sample user shown here. Most administrators will want to set disk quotas for users because, by sharing a filesystem, one user could potentially exhaust all available space, thereby blocking other users of that filesystem. Quotas may be set on the parent filesystem or on specific user home directories. Here's an example:

```
# zfs set quota=2G mypool-2/thomas
```

Additionally, if you need to guarantee a predetermined amount of available storage for a user, you can set a reserved amount by setting a *reservation* for that user:

```
# zfs set reservation=1G mypool-2/thomas
```

As before, we can see those properties of user thomas's filesystem (abbreviated output):

```
# zfs get all mypool-2/thomas
NAME             PROPERTY       VALUE                  SOURCE
mypool-2/thomas  type           filesystem             -
mypool-2/thomas  creation       Sun Dec 11 12:18 2011  -
mypool-2/thomas  used           664K                   -
mypool-2/thomas  available      2.00G                  -
mypool-2/thomas  referenced     664K                   -
mypool-2/thomas  compressratio  1.00x                  -
mypool-2/thomas  mounted        yes                    -
mypool-2/thomas  quota          2G                     local
mypool-2/thomas  reservation    1G                     local
mypool-2/thomas  recordsize     128K                   default
mypool-2/thomas  mountpoint     /mypool-2/thomas       local
```

If the user creates files that result in storage greater than their specified quota, they will receive a "Disc quota exceeded" warning, at which point they must remove some files or request the administrator to increase or remove their quota. Unprivileged users can check their quotas using the **zfs** command:

```
thomas@narya:~$ zfs get quota mypool-2/thomas
NAME            PROPERTY VALUE SOURCE
mypool2/thomas  quota    2G    local
```

ZFS Snapshots

One of Solaris 11's most powerful features is ZFS *snapshots*. A ZFS snapshot is a read-only copy of the state of a ZFS filesystem, and one of its benefits is that it consumes virtually no disk space within a pool. After a filesystem snapshot is taken, ZFS keeps track only of changes to the filesystem, rather than making a complete new copy of its data. Therefore, you can create as many snapshots as you like of any filesystem without concern for how much storage might be required. Additionally, Solaris 11 uses snapshots to enable patching and upgrading of applications and the operating system itself, as well as helping with the management of root filesystems needed to support containers. End users as well as administrators can take snapshots of filesystems, resulting in simple, local backups of user and system data.

The format of the subcommand to create snapshots is

```
zfs snapshot poolname@snapshotname
```

where **poolname** is, of course, the name of the pool and **snapshotname** is defined by the user to give a name to the snapshot. For example, the command

```
# zfs snapshot -r mypool-2@snapshot1
```

creates a recursive (**-r**) snapshot of all filesystems in mypool-2, appending a name of shapshot1. Snapshot names can be any character string; it's often useful to name them using the time they were taken. Here's an example:

```
# zfs snapshot -r mypool-2@Sunday-Dec11
```

You can list all the snapshots of a filesystem using the **zfs** command:

```
# zfs list -t snapshot -r mypool-2
NAME                           USED  AVAIL  REFER  MOUNTPOINT
mypool-2@snapshot1                0     -     35K  -
mypool-2@Sunday-Dec11             0     -     35K  -
mypool-2/george@snapshot1         0     -     31K  -
mypool-2/george@Sunday-Dec11      0     -     31K  -
mypool-2/john@snapshot1           0     -     33K  -
mypool-2/john@Sunday-Dec11        0     -     33K  -
mypool-2/martha@snapshot1         0     -     31K  -
mypool-2/martha@Sunday-Dec11      0     -     31K  -
mypool-2/thomas@snapshot1         0     -    743K  -
mypool-2/thomas@Sunday-Dec11      0     -    743K  -
```

After you have taken one or more snapshots of a filesystem, either explicitly or automatically via a snapshot schedule, you can use the **zfs rollback** subcommand to restore the filesystem to the state that existed at the time the most recent snapshot was taken. If there are multiple snapshots and you need to roll back to one earlier than the most recent, all snapshots subsequent to the one you want need to be destroyed:

```
# zfs list -t snapshot -r mypool-2
NAME                            USED   AVAIL   REFER   MOUNTPOINT
mypool-2@snapshot1                 0       -     35K   -
mypool-2@Sunday-Dec11              0       -     35K   -
mypool-2/george@snapshot1          0       -     31K   -
mypool-2/george@Sunday-Dec11       0       -     31K   -
mypool-2/john@snapshot1            0       -     33K   -
mypool-2/john@Sunday-Dec11         0       -     33K   -
mypool-2/martha@snapshot1          0       -     31K   -
mypool-2/martha@Sunday-Dec11       0       -     31K   -
mypool-2/thomas@snapshot1          0       -    743K   -
mypool-2/thomas@Sunday-Dec11       0       -    743K   -
# zfs rollback mypool-2/thomas@snapshot1
cannot rollback to 'mypool-2/thomas@snapshot1': more recent snapshots exist
use '-r' to force deletion of the following snapshots:
mypool-2/thomas@Sunday-Dec11
# zfs destroy mypool-2/thomas@Sunday-Dec11
# zfs rollback mypool-2/thomas@snapshot1
```

The **zfs diff** subcommand lists the differences between two snapshots. For example, if we copy files into the /mypool-2/thomas directory, take a snapshot, copy another file, and then take another snapshot, we can see the changes that occurred to the filesystem at each snapshot:

```
# zfs snapshot mypool-2/thomas@snapshot2
# cp /etc/hosts /mypool-2/thomas
# cp /etc/motd /mypool-2/thomas
# zfs snapshot mypool-2/thomas@snapshot3
# zfs diff mypool-2/thomas@snapshot2 mypool-2/thomas@snapshot3
M        /mypool-2/thomas/
+        /mypool-2/thomas/hosts
+        /mypool-2/thomas/motd
```

The **M** shows that the /mypool-2/thomas filesystem has been modified, and the **+** means that the file has been added and recorded in the last snapshot. Other indicator symbols, **-** and **R**, show that a file has been deleted or renamed, respectively, in the last snapshot.

Recall that ZFS snapshots are read-only. In order to convert a snapshot to a writable filesystem, use the **zfs clone** subcommand. A clone is a writable duplicate of the snapshot, and can be placed within any other pool.

```
# zfs clone mypool-2/thomas@snapshot3 mypool-2/thomas2
# zfs list
NAME                     USED   AVAIL   REFER   MOUNTPOINT
mypool-1                5.53M   3.90G   5.38M   /mypool-1
mypool-2                1.17M   3.91G     37K   /mypool-2
mypool-2/george           31K   3.91G     31K   /mypool-2/george
```

```
mypool-2/john            33K   3.91G    33K  /mypool-2/john
mypool-2/martha          31K   3.91G    31K  /mypool-2/martha
mypool-2/thomas         770K   1.25M   746K  /mypool-2/thomas
mypool-2/thomas2         30K   3.91G   712K  /mypool-2/thomas2
rpool                   66.1G   162G  39.5K  /rpool
```

The new filesystem in this example, mypool-2/thomas2, consumes no space until something is written to it.

NOTE
*Within each filesystem where snapshots have been taken is a hidden directory, .zfs. The .zfs directory is not listed even with the **-a** option of the **ls** command, but you can **cd** to that directory and then read or copy files from any snapshot there, as in the following example:*

```
# cd /mypool-2/thomas/.zfs
# ls
shares     snapshot
# ls snapshot
snapshot1       Sunday-Dec11
# ls -l Sunday-Dec11
total 18
drwxr-xr-x   2 thomas    staff          5 Dec 11 12:29 Desktop
drwxr-xr-x   6 thomas    staff          6 Dec 11 12:29 Documents
drwxr-xr-x   2 thomas    staff          2 Dec 11 12:29 Downloads
-rw-r--r--   1 thomas    staff        165 Dec 11 12:18 local.cshrc
-rw-r--r--   1 thomas    staff        170 Dec 11 12:18 local.login
-rw-r--r--   1 thomas    staff        130 Dec 11 12:18 local.profile
drwxr-xr-x   2 thomas    staff          2 Dec 11 12:29 Public
```

ZFS Devices

You can build ZFS pools on your server's internal disks, on LUNs (Logical Units) on attached storage arrays, and on SAN-based storage, and it's both recommended and easier to use whole physical disks as **zpool** elements. You should be familiar with your storage device configuration, especially any redundancy features offered on those devices. In general, it's best practice to use ZFS to provide those features, such as mirroring and RAID configurations, so that ZFS can automatically report and repair any bad data it detects.

Time Slider

Time Slider is a graphical tool for managing snapshots. You select it from the System | Preferences menu from the Solaris 11 desktop (see Figure 9-5).

FIGURE 9-5. *Selecting the Time Slider GUI*

The Time Slider tool allows you to select those filesystems that will be snapshotted regularly (see Figure 9-6); snapshots are taken on a predetermined schedule every 15 minutes, daily, weekly, or monthly.

After you have selected the filesystems that Time Slider will manage, any directory in that filesystem that a user displays using the graphical desktop will include a small clock icon on its toolbar; this is the Time Slider icon. When the user clicks that icon, a timeline will display below the toolbar, representing a sequence of snapshots up to the present contents (labeled "Now"), as shown in Figure 9-7.

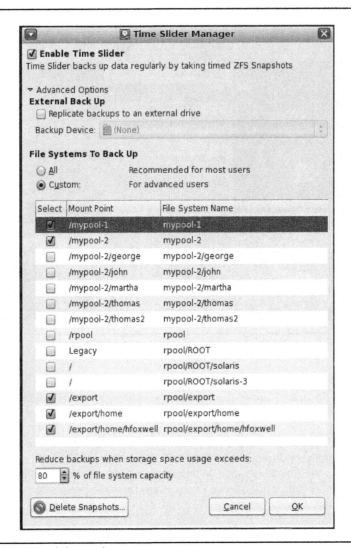

FIGURE 9-6. *The TimeSlider configuration manager*

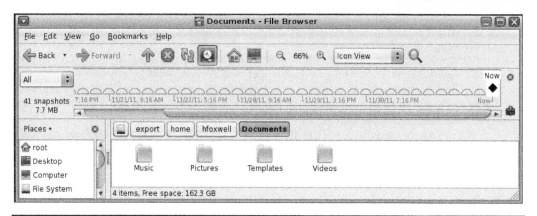

FIGURE 9-7. *The TimeSlider directory display*

For example, suppose that user hfoxwell has inadvertently deleted a file, TestDoc.odt, from his current directory. Clicking the series of snapshot icons on the timeline, he will eventually find an earlier snapshot that contains his missing file (see Figure 9-8); he can then simply drag and drop the file from the displayed snapshot into his current directory to retrieve it (recall that the snapshot files are really available in his read-only .zfs/snapshot directory—TimeSlider is simply displaying the contents of the previously scheduled snapshots).

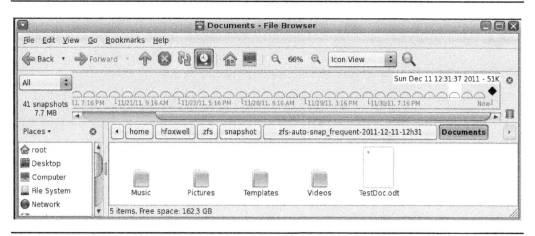

FIGURE 9-8. *Recovering a file from a TimeSlider snapshot*

Summary

We have reviewed the key capabilities of the ZFS filesystem in Solaris 11, including how to create and manage device pools and filesystems using the **zpool** and **zfs** commands and subcommands for both end user filesystems and those needed for booting and supporting the operating system itself (**rpool**). We've shown how to display (**get**) and change (**set**) the properties of ZFS filesystems, including how to enable key features such as mirroring, compression, deduplication, and encryption. And we demonstrated how to create and use ZFS snapshots to back up and retrieve files, along with the TimeSlider graphical tool.

However, this is only part of the ZFS story. In later chapters, you will see how ZFS supports patching and updating applications and OS images, and how it makes managing Solaris 11 virtualized environments (containers) much easier. In summary, ZFS empowers many of Solaris 11's key capabilities; learn it well because it is an essential component of OS administration.

References

Oracle Solaris Administration: ZFS File Systems can be found at http://docs.oracle.com/cd/E23824_01/html/821-1448/index.html.

ZFS Best Practices Guide can be found at http://www.solarisinternals.com/wiki/index.php/ZFS_Best_Practices_Guide.

CHAPTER
10

Customize the
Solaris Shells

he essence of UNIX-based operating systems is in the shell, which includes the command-line interface. It is a custom window into the UNIX operating system and its programs. A shell provides an interactive window to run commands. It supports commands that are combined into scripts. It defines how configuration files work with different services. It allows administrators to customize scripts to meet the needs of enterprise-level networks. Although this chapter focuses on bash, which is the default shell for Solaris 11, several other shells are available.

Most users who are coming from Linux will be comforted by the familiarity of bash. It works in essentially the same way in Solaris, modified to support more enterprise-ready features. In this chapter, you'll examine the options for shells, along with how they work with different commands and configuration files. Then you'll examine how the bash shell works, with different special characters and aliases. Lastly, the meat of the shell comes when you create your own scripts. You'll get a chance to dissect and create sample scripts toward the end of this chapter.

Shell Management

Although bash is the new default shell, Oracle Solaris 11 comes with a variety of ways to control the system from the command-line interface. Each of these shells supports some measure of interactivity. Command completion can help when you don't remember the exact spelling of a long command. If you've run some long command sometime in the recent past, the history can help you remember and run that command. The standard options associated with a shell can be customized in appropriate configuration files.

A Choice of Shells

You can choose between several different shells on Solaris 11. Although bash is the default, users who are coming from Solaris 10 or other UNIX-based operating systems may not be so anxious to convert. The shells available in Solaris 11 repositories as of this writing are listed in Table 10-1.

The standard four shells—bash, ksh, tcsh, and zsh—are available directly from Solaris 11 repositories from packages of the same name, and are all installed by default. A number of scripts refer to a construct known as the *system shell*, /bin/sh. Apply the **ls -l** command to that construct.

Shell	Description
bash	The "Bourne-Again" shell, the new default for Solaris 11. It's in common use on Linux and is available from /usr/bin/bash.
csh	The C shell is one of the original UNIX shells, available from /usr/bin/csh.
ksh	The Korn shell is a common option for many UNIX users; also known as ksh93 in the /usr/bin directory.
tcsh	The enhanced C shell comes with command-line completion features.
zsh	The Z shell includes a number of additional features.

TABLE 10-1. *Solaris 11 Command-Line Shells*

You'll see that it's linked to the Korn shell, specifically ksh93. With that in mind, perhaps a majority of the shell scripts configured for Solaris 11 are processed through that shell.

In general, the differences between shells are subtle, indistinguishable to most regular Solaris 11 users. The developers of each shell are best qualified to describe the features and benefits of their command-line interfaces.

Each shell in Oracle Solaris is associated with a "profile shell," as signified by *pf*. For example, bash is associated with pfbash. The advantage of the profile shell is that it can interpret RBAC authorizations and privileges. With profile shells, you can set up scripts with custom privileges and therefore limited risks.

Even though bash is the default, it's easy enough to change shells, in defaults, or on the fly. From the command line, run the command associated with the shell, such as bash, ksh, tcsh, or zsh. Except for ksh, the options lead to a different prompt. Try out some of the regular commands described in Chapter 8. Observe how commands may work differently. In all cases, commands are case sensitive. You can then return to the bash shell with the **exit** command.

TIP

To change the default login shell for a user, change the last field for that user in the password authentication database. For local users, that database is in the /etc/passwd directory. If a user is configured to log into the default bash shell, you should find the /usr/bin/bash shell in the entry associated with that user; Korn shell devotees may want to change that to /usr/bin/ksh93.

Interactivity

In a shell, *interactivity* is the ability to work with current and previously executed commands. It allows you to use the HOME, DELETE, and the four arrow keys on the keyboard. The function of the left- and right-arrow keys is straightforward. The function of the up- and down-arrow keys can help you scroll through the history of commands that have been executed in the current shell.

Interactivity and the History of Commands

Recently executed commands are stored by default. In the default bash shell, you can find these commands in the .bash_history file in your home directory. Except for the regular C shell, you can list the files in the history of the current shell with the **history** command.

NOTE

Despite what's suggested in the current man page for the **history** *command (128), the default history of stored commands is 500 lines.*

Normally, you can repeat commands in the history buffer in several different ways:

- **Up arrow**   Moves backward through the history of commands
- **Down arrow**   Goes forward through the history of commands
- **!***num*   Runs the command associated with **num** in the history
- **!***abc*   Executes the last command in the history that starts with *abc*

To change the number of stored commands, you'll need to set the **HISTSIZE** variable in the profile. For example, the following directive sets the number of stored commands to 100:

```
HISTSIZE=100
```

To change the number of stored commands for a single user, add the noted directive to the .profile file in that user's home directory. To change the number for all users, add the directive to the /etc/profile file. Just be aware that the change is not implemented until the next time that user logs into the subject system.

Interactivity and Editing Commands

Many UNIX users are devotees of the vi text editor. It includes a number of handy shortcuts that can help you navigate and change text in a file. To demonstrate, run the following command to set vi editor mode for the current shell:

```
$ set -o vi
```

At this point, you can use various vi options to navigate in a long command. If you've set vi editor mode, call up a command and press B. The cursor should automatically move left one word, just as it would in the vi editor. Try it again; this time press W. It's a more precise way to navigate through and edit a command, especially with the help of options such as **cw** to change a word or **dw** to delete a word.

To reverse the process, use the **set +o vi** command.

Command Completion

You'll run into a lot of long commands in Solaris 11. Even if you're an extremely fast and accurate keyboardist, command completion can save time and effort. For example, if you want to run a command that starts with an *l* and don't precisely remember the spelling of the full command, just go to a command-line interface and type in **l**. Then press the TAB key once. If nothing happens, you'll know that more than one command at the shell starts with an *l*. Press the TAB key a second time. You should see a result similar to Figure 10-1, which lists all available commands that start with *l*.

```
michael@solaris11-ea:~$ l
labelit              let                   lkbib               lorder
lari                 lex                   ln                  lp
last                 lgrpinfo              loadkeys            lpadmin
lastcomm             libart2-config        local               lpc
latencytop           libassuan-config      locale              lpinfo
ld                   libgcrypt-config      localedef           lpmove
ldapadd              libglade-convert      locator             lpoptions
ldapaddent           libIDL-config-2       lockfs              lppasswd
ldapclient           libpng-config         lockstat            lpq
ldapdelete           libpng10-config       lofiadm             lpr
ldaplist             libpng12-config       logadm              lprm
ldapmodify           libpng14-config       logger              lprsetup.sh
ldapmodrdn           libusb-config         login               lpstat
ldapsearch           linc-cleanup-sockets  logname             ls
ldd                  line                  logout              lshal
less                 link                  logresolve          luit
lessecho             list_devices          look                luxadm
lesskey              listusers             lookbib
michael@solaris11-ea:~$ l
```

FIGURE 10-1. *Commands That Start with* l

Just be aware that the list shown in Figure 10-1 may not be complete. It is limited to those commands in the **PATH** as defined for the current active user, as discussed in Chapter 8. However, the directories associated with the **PATH** are defined in /etc/bash/bashrc and the .profile file in each user's home directory.

Configuration Files

For the shell, there are two sets of configuration files. One set resides in the /etc directory and is applied to all users. A second set usually exists in the subject user's home directory, with settings that can be customized by that user. The basic configuration files that apply to all users, independent of their shells, are /etc/profile and .profile in each user's home directory. Additional configuration files are shell specific.

/etc/profile

The following is a brief analysis of the default /etc/profile that comes with Solaris 11. It starts with a **trap** function, shown next, which prevents users from accidentally sending interrupt or kill signals while the profile is being established. (For more information on the numbers, see the man page for the **kill** command.)

```
trap 2 3
```

The **export** directive makes the variables that follow into global variables consistent among the different shells:

```
export LOGNAME PATH
```

The loop that follows defines a terminal variable, depending on whether the system is based on an Intel or some other (SPARC) CPU:

```
if [ "$TERM" = "" ]
then
        if /bin/i386
        then
                TERM=sun-color
        else
                TERM=sun
        fi
        export TERM
fi
```

The next loop applies to shells available to Solaris 11. It applies some basic settings to all users, including quotas, and checks for e-mail sent internally, which in this case is normally associated with administrative messages. It also allows users to skip past any configured message of the day.

NOTE
*The **jsh** refers to a job control shell, not to be confused with the Java application launcher shell. In any case, it's a legacy variable, as its functionality has been assumed by the Korn shell. The reference to **rsh** should not apply, as long as you don't use the clear-text Remote Shell server for remote connections.*

The final directives in /etc/profile set a default value of **umask** and reenable the ability to interrupt and quit a process:

```
umask 022
trap 2 3
```

User's .profile

In this section, you'll look at the standard .profile file that's included with each user's home directory. You can also find the .profile file in the /etc/skel directory. Any changes that you want incorporated for new users should be edited into /etc/skel/.profile. Once the .profile file is copied, each user has the right to change it in their home directories.

The top of the file defines components of the default value of **PATH**, along with the default pager, depending on the availability of the **less** and **more** commands. If you want a more complete set of directories in your **PATH**, the place to configure it is here.

NOTE
*The pager is associated with commands that allow a user to review the contents of a text file, one screen at a time. As noted in Chapter 8, the corresponding commands are **more** and **less**.*

```
export PATH=/usr/bin:/usr/sbin

if [ -f /usr/bin/less ]; then
    export PAGER="/usr/bin/less -ins"
elif [ -f /usr/bin/more ]; then
    export PAGER="/usr/bin/more -s"
fi
```

These files work with hidden files in each user's home directory, specifically the username, hostname, current directory, and the familiar $ prompt:

```
case ${SHELL} in
*bash)
    typeset +x PS1="\u@\h:\w\\$ "
    ;;
esac
```

If you want to add the **HISTSIZE** variable for a nonstandard number of commands to add to the history, this file is appropriate. Just remember, if you use multiple shells, you may want to add the **export** directive to make the setting global:

```
export HISTSIZE=100
```

Configuration Files Specific to bash

You can find generic configuration files for the bash shell in the /etc/bash directory. But note that the files have .example extensions. To implement these options for users who run the bash shell, you'll have to remove the .example extension.

Because there are nearly 10,000 lines in the /etc/bash/bash_completion file, detailed coverage is beyond the scope of this book. It includes detailed instructions to the shell on many common commands and programs. This section covers the other files in that directory in some detail.

Basic Settings in the bashrc File   The first line in the file sets the value of **umask**:

```
umask 022
```

But wait, there was also a **umask** directive in the /etc/profile file. If there's a conflict, the profile governs the result. Fortunately, this value of **umask** happens to be the same as shown in /etc/profile.

The next directives specify the directory with utilities and commands developed under the GNU project. In most cases, they don't have all of the capabilities of the commands of the same name developed for Solaris. For example, GNU commands don't work with Solaris ACLs.

```
GNU=/usr/gnu/bin
X11=/usr/X11/bin
```

NOTE
GNU stands for "GNU's Not UNIX." It's a recursive acronym.

The **GNU** and **X11** variables are then used to specify the **UTIL_PATH**, in contrast to the **STANDARD_PATH**:

```
UTIL_PATH=$GNU:$X11
STANDARD_PATH=/bin:/usr/bin:/sbin:/usr/sbin
```

For those user home directories with executable files in a bin/ subdirectory, the following **if** loop adds that subdirectory to the **PATH**:

```
if [ -d $HOME/bin ]; then
    MY_PATH=$MY_PATH:$HOME/bin
fi
```

The three directives associated with the **PATH** (**UTIL_PATH**, **STANDARD_PATH**, and **MY_PATH**) are combined. Be aware that this option prioritizes GNU-based commands and utilities over those developed for Solaris 11, and that can cause problems:

```
export PATH="$MY_PATH:$UTIL_PATH:$STANDARD_PATH"
```

The directives afterward relate to when a shell is allowed to quit, what to do for users who run the emacs text editor, notifications related to jobs that are completed while running in the background, along with a failsafe from **exec** commands that don't work:

```
set -o ignoreeof
auto_resume=exact
set -o notify
shopt -s execfail
```

Next comes the definition for a login shell as well as two directives that set a different value for the number of commands to be stored in history, along with a check for new mail every 60 seconds:

```
if [ -z "$LOGIN_SHELL" ] ; then
    PS1="[\u@\h]:[\#]:[\w]:\$ "
fi

HISTSIZE=256
MAILCHECK=60
```

The following stanza supports the configuration of file colors in either the .dir_colors or .dircolors file, in user home directories:

```
if [ -x /usr/bin/dircolors ] ; then
    if [ -f ~/.dir_colors ] ; then
        eval "`/usr/bin/dircolors -b ~/.dir_colors`"
    elif [ -f ~/.dircolors ] ; then
        eval "`/usr/bin/dircolors -b ~/.dircolors`"
    fi
fi
```

The line that follows refers to the rules listed in the bash_completion file, also in the /etc/bash directory. As with bashrc, the bash package includes a bash_completion.example file. If you want to apply the rules in the file, you'll have to remove the .example extension from the file.

```
[ -f /etc/bash/bash_completion ] && . /etc/bash/bash_completion
```

The loops that follow look for scripts with .sh and .bash extensions. If they exist in the /etc/bash file, they are executed:

```
for s in /etc/bash/*.sh ; do
    test -r $s && . $s
done

for s in /etc/bash/*.bash ; do
    test -r $s && . $s
done
```

The final directives look for custom bash settings in user home directories, in the .bash_expert and .bash_aliases files. If they exist, the options in those files are included in the configuration.

```
[ -f ~/.bash_expert ] && . ~/.bash_expert
[ -f ~/.bash_aliases ] && . ~/.bash_aliases
```

Configured Key Bindings in the inputrc File   At over 300 lines, the inputrc.example file is difficult to cover in much detail. Suffice it to say that it includes a number of options for key bindings at the bash command line. If you want to activate the options in this file, you'll need to remove the .example extension. Because we prefer vi as a text editor, we prefer to just set vi mode at the shell with the following command, described earlier:

```
$ set -o vi
```

To set it up for our own account, we add it to the .profile file in our home directory.

User-Specific bash Configuration Files   Two configuration files directly related to the bash shell are included in user home directories: .bash_history and .bashrc. The .bash_history file is in essence a buffer of previously run commands, limited to the number of lines specified in the aforementioned **HISTSIZE** variable.

The .bashrc file is one designated file for users who want to customize their bash shell. Users can also store aliases and expert settings in .bashrc. However, the .bash_aliases and .bash_expert files are also available for that purpose.

Configuration Files Specific to ksh

The standard configuration file associated with the Korn shell is ksh.kshrc, in the /etc directory. The following is a brief analysis of that file. The first loop provides an editing mode for the command line:

```
if [[ "$(set +o)" != ~(Er)--(gmacs|emacs|vi)( .*|) ]] ; then
        set -o gmacs
        # enable multiline input mode
        set -o multiline
        # enable globstar mode (match subdirs with **/)
        set -o globstar
fi
```

Although the remainder of the file includes a complex algorithm for the command-line prompt, it's just the prompt, and is superseded by any setting in the local /etc/profile or .profile file. Even though there's a reference to gmacs (the GNU version of the emacs text editor), it's obsolete because it is not included in the Solaris 11 repositories.

Shell Tips and Tricks

Anyone who is serious about Solaris should already know something about the command-line shell. For many such users, it can help to go back to basics. Data flows in streams, in and out of commands and utilities. If you're administering a system remotely, you may have access to only one command line. To optimize what you do, it helps to understand the functionality of different shell characters. Of course, it can be useful to set up groups of commands in scripts, but that's something for later in this chapter.

Data Flows In and Out

Data flows into and out of UNIX commands in three basic streams: standard input, standard output, and standard error. The meaning is straightforward. Standard input may come from a keyboard entry to a command. In some cases, it can come from a text file of prepackaged data that is processed through a utility. For example, with the following command, **cat** is the utility and /etc/passwd is the input:

```
$ cat /etc/passwd
```

Based on the same command, standard output is what happens after a command processes input. In this case, the standard output is the contents of the /etc/passwd file.

In contrast, standard error is the message output from a command when there's an error. For example, if we misspell the /etc/passwd file, there's a standard error stream, something like the following:

```
cat: /etc/passw: cannot open [No such file or directory]
```

Standard input, output, and error normally are shown at the command line. Nominally, they're associated with the file descriptors 0, 1, and 2, respectively.

Standard Output

While standard output from a command such as **cat /etc/passwd** normally is sent to the screen, that output can be redirected. For example, the following command redirects that standard output stream to a file named passwd_text1:

```
$ cat /etc/passwd > passwd_text1
```

Since standard output is associated with file descriptor 1, the following command would work in the same way:

```
$ cat /etc/passwd 1> passwd_text1
```

Standard Input

The normal form of standard input—data typed in with a command—is trivial. It's more significant when prepared data is stored in a file. Call that file data1. If you have set up a script named script 1 to process data from that file, you can set up standard input with either of the following commands:

```
$ script1 < data1
$ script1 0< data1
```

Sometimes, standard input comes from a prompt; for example, when logging into a remote system, you may be prompted for a password. That password entry is standard input. Finally, a pipe character (|) may be used to redirect standard output from one command as standard input to a second command. For example, the following command redirects the standard output from the **cat /etc/passwd** command as standard input to the **wc -l** command:

```
$ cat /etc/passwd | wc -l
```

NOTE
*Standard input in a script is normally associated with the $1 variable. For example, if you've included the **start** switch to the **sendmail** command, that switch is processed by the **sendmail** script in the /etc/ init.d directory to start the noted e-mail service.*

Standard Error

If there are errors, from a command or a script, related error messages are sent through file descriptor 2. For example, if you run a script and something goes wrong, the **2>** redirects that message. For instance, the following command, run in a directory where the noted file does not exist, sends the error message to the noted file named err1:

```
$ ls 2> err1
```

When There's Only One Command Line

You can open up a whole bunch of command-line interfaces at a local terminal, especially in a GUI desktop environment. It's easy with the right selections. And it's helpful when you're running multiple tasks. It's a bit more problematic if you're working from a remote system. Two options can help. First, you can run a command with the ampersand character (&) at the end. It continues running the program in the background and returns you to the command-line interface. For example, if you are running a script that's updating 100 packages, the download and installation of those packages will take some time. Add an **&** at the end of the command, and you'll be returned to the command line. If desired, you can return the job to the foreground with the **fg** command.

If you've executed a command and want to send it to the background, while making the command line available again, take the following steps:

1. Press CTRL-Z to suspend the job.
2. Type in the **bg** command to restart the job in the background.

Alternatively, if you're running a remote session in an application such as GNOME Terminal, you can open up multiple tabs in the same window. To do so, take the following steps:

1. Connect to the remote system from a GUI terminal, using X11 forwarding.
2. Run the **gnome-terminal &** command to open up a GNOME Terminal from the remote system.
3. Press CTRL-SHIFT-T to open a second terminal, under a different tab. The result is shown in Figure 10-2. You can repeat this, as desired, to open additional terminals from the same remote system.

All Manner of Shell Characters

A *shell character* is a group of one or more character constructs that can regulate how data flows on the shell. In general, most UNIX-based operating systems, including Solaris, already have a predetermined set of shell characters. To see for yourself, run the **stty -a** command. The output on our system is shown in Figure 10-3.

The characters shown are somewhat descriptive. For example, the intr character is set to ^C, which happens to be the CTRL-C key combination. In other words, the caret (^) represents the CTRL key, and the ^C shell character will interrupt a running program. The functionality of some of these characters is listed in Table 10-2.

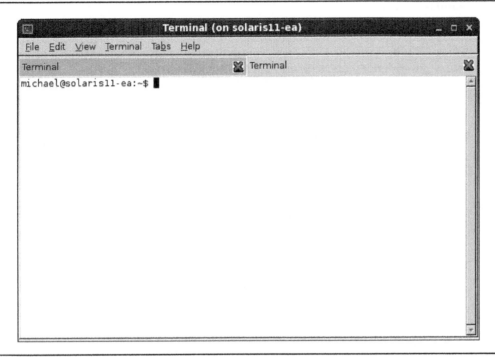

FIGURE 10-2. *Remote GNOME Terminals*

Closely related are the other settings shown in the second part of the output to the **stty -a** command. If there's a dash in front, the option is negated. For example, the **-parenb** setting does not generate a parity bit, nor does it expect a parity bit in input. Other options are listed in the man page for the **stty** command.

```
michael@solarisdel:~$ stty -a
speed 38400 baud; rows 15; columns 80;
intr = ^C; quit = ^\; erase = ^?; kill = ^U; eof = ^D; eol = M-^?; eol2 = M-^?;
swtch = <undef>; start = ^Q; stop = ^S; susp = ^Z; dsusp = ^Y; rprnt = ^R;
werase = ^W; lnext = ^V; flush = ^O;
-parenb -parodd cs8 -hupcl -cstopb cread -clocal -crtscts
-ignbrk brkint -ignpar -parmrk -inpck -istrip -inlcr -igncr icrnl ixon -ixoff
-iuclc ixany imaxbel
opost -olcuc -ocrnl onlcr -onocr -onlret -ofill -ofdel nl0 cr0 tab3 bs0 vt0 ff0
isig icanon iexten echo echoe echok -echonl -noflsh -xcase -tostop -echoprt
echoctl echoke
michael@solarisdel:~$ 
```

FIGURE 10-3. *Shell characters*

Shell Character	Description
^C	CTRL-C. Interrupts and stops a running program.
^\	CTRL-\. Quits from a program and dumps related information from the memory core.
^?	CTRL-?. Erases the current contents of the command line.
^D	CTRL-D. Exits from the current shell.

TABLE 10-2. *Shell Characters*

Scripts and the Shell

Because UNIX is based on text commands, administration in Solaris 11 is based on a variety of different scripts. To see what's available just in the /usr/sbin directory, run the following command:

```
$ file /usr/sbin/* | grep script
```

We count over 50 shell scripts in this directory. Some of these scripts are shown in Figure 10-4. Note the detail. Many of these scripts are based on Perl or the Korn shell. But wait. If you apply the

```
/usr/sbin/install:      executable /usr/sbin/sh script
/usr/sbin/installboot:  executable shell script
/usr/sbin/mountall:     executable /usr/sbin/sh script
/usr/sbin/mvdir:        executable /usr/sbin/sh script
/usr/sbin/netservices:  executable shell script
/usr/sbin/nscfg:        executable /usr/bin/python2.6 script
/usr/sbin/ntptrace:     executable /usr/bin/perl script
/usr/sbin/projadd:      executable /usr/perl5/bin/perl script
/usr/sbin/projdel:      executable /usr/perl5/bin/perl script
/usr/sbin/projmod:      executable /usr/perl5/bin/perl script
/usr/sbin/psrinfo:      executable /usr/perl5/bin/perl script
/usr/sbin/rc0:  executable /usr/sbin/sh script
/usr/sbin/rc1:  executable /usr/sbin/sh script
/usr/sbin/rc2:  executable /usr/sbin/sh script
/usr/sbin/rc3:  executable /usr/sbin/sh script
/usr/sbin/rc5:  executable /usr/sbin/sh script
/usr/sbin/rc6:  executable /usr/sbin/sh script
/usr/sbin/rcS:  executable /usr/sbin/sh script
/usr/sbin/root_archive: executable /bin/ksh script
/usr/sbin/setmnt:       executable shell script
/usr/sbin/shareall:     executable /usr/sbin/sh script
/usr/sbin/shutdown:     executable /usr/sbin/sh script
/usr/sbin/stmsboot:     executable /usr/sbin/sh script
/usr/sbin/swapadd:      executable /bin/ksh script
/usr/sbin/sysconfig:    executable /usr/bin/python2.6 script
/usr/sbin/trapstat:     executable /usr/bin/sh script
/usr/sbin/umountall:    executable /usr/sbin/sh script
/usr/sbin/unshareall:   executable /usr/sbin/sh script
/usr/sbin/wanbootutil:  executable /usr/bin/pfsh script
/usr/sbin/ypinit:       executable /usr/sbin/sh script
/usr/sbin/zonep2vchk:   executable /bin/ksh script
michael@solaris11-ea:~$
```

FIGURE 10-4. *A variety of scripts in the /usr/sbin directory*

ls -l command on the **sh** shell in the /usr/bin and /usr/sbin directories, you'll find these scripts are also linked to the Korn shell. That suggests quite the database of scripts that depend on a shell that's no longer the default for Solaris 11.

In the sections that follow, you'll take a look at some of these scripts and how they work. With that knowledge, you'll be more able to write and modify scripts to administer a variety of Solaris systems. With this information in hand, you'll be able to write scripts suited to the cron and at daemons, which can be automatically run on a scheduled or regular basis.

The Basics of Shell Scripts

A shell script is a combination of commands that could be run at the command prompt. Developers write scripts in the shell to automate the process of running such groups of commands. Sometimes scripts include commands that are run in loops, based on certain conditions. In the following subsections, you'll look at some basic loop constructs, as well as some conditional operators normally found in Solaris scripts.

In general, you can test a script in your home directory. Just create a new text file and start it with a pointer to the desired shell. For example, the following directive points to the bash shell:

```
#!/usr/bin/bash
```

To users who are newer to UNIX-based operating systems, this construct may be confusing. Even though the pound sign (#) is normally a comment character, the pound sign with the bang (which looks like an exclamation point) is an active directive, which is associated with the full path to a shell. The following are two alternatives for the first line in a script:

```
#!/usr/bin/ksh93
#!/usr/bin/zsh
```

Once you include desired commands in the file, save it and make sure it's executable. For example, assume the file is named script1, and it is owned by your account. In that case, you can add the execute bit and then run it from the current directory with the following commands:

```
$ chmod u+x script1
$ ./script1
```

In general, you could include a bunch of commands in a script and execute that script if needed. But the power of a script comes with conditional expressions such as **if**, **test**, **while**, **do**, **until**, **case**, and more. With these expressions, you can set up a script to run commands only if specified conditions are met.

The if Conditional

In a number of scripts, commands are run only if given files exist or meet certain other conditions. For example, the following **if** conditional checks to see if the /etc/inet/hosts file exists:

```
if [ -e /etc/inet/hosts ];
```

Of course, the question is then what do you want to do if the file exists. The **then** construct is useful, followed by desired commands. The **fi** at the end closes the loop and tells the shell to expect no more commands associated with the noted conditional:

```
if [ -e /etc/inet/hosts ]; then
      command_1
      command_2
fi
```

The options associated with the **if** and related script commands are listed in Table 10-3.

You can review several examples of the **if** conditional in the **addgnupghome** script in the /usr/sbin directory. The following directive in that file checks for the existence of a home directory for a user:

```
if [ -z "$home" ]; then
```

The next line looks for an entry, and specifically a username, in the local /etc/passwd file:

```
if ${cat_passwd} | awk -F: -v n="$user" '$1 == n {exit 1}'; then
```

Just remember, each **if** conditional is not complete without an **fi** at the end. It's common to have script stanzas start with an expression and end with that same expression spelled backward.

Script Option	Description
-b	Checks if a file is a block file
-d	Verifies that the file is a directory
-e	Checks if the file exists
-f	Tests if a file is a regular file
-r	Checks a file for read permission
-w	Inspects a file for write permission
-x	Reviews a file for execute permission
-z	Checks the expression for an existing value
!	Designates the expression as "anything but"
==	Equal to (in contrast to !=, which means "not equal to")
-eq	Reviews the values before and after for equality
-ge	Checks if the first value is greater than or equal to the second
-lt	Checks if the first value is less than the second
-le	Checks if the first value is less than or equal to the second
-ne	Checks if the first value is *not* equal to the second

TABLE 10-3. *Options for the **if** construct in a script*

The test Operator

One more basic conditional operator is **test**. When used with the conditionals shown with the **if** command, it checks to see if a condition is true. For example, in the **gparted** script in the /usr/sbin directory, the following line checks for an executable hal-lock file in a directory defined by the **$k** variable:

```
if test -x "$k/hal-lock"; then
```

The for and do Loops

Now take a different loop, where tests are done numerically. The following directive essentially counts to three:

```
for n in 1 2 3
```

But you need to do something with that count. The following directive takes a simple approach, using **n** as a variable:

```
do
     echo "this is test number $n"
done
```

Unlike stanzas with the **if** directive, the end of a **do** directive is not "od," but **done**.

Once you save the script, activate the execute bit, and then run the script, the output you see should look like the following:

```
this is test number 1
this is test number 2
this is test number 3
```

A case Conditional

The **case** command is another conditional, which tries to match a specified value against one or more patterns. A **case** stanza includes the following pattern of directives:

```
case
     value in
     pattern)
     command command;;
esac
```

One example is shown in the check-hostname script in the /usr/sbin directory, which uses the **accept_if_fully_qualified()** function to review input, such as from /etc/inet/hosts. Each entry is associated with the **$1** variable and is checked for a dot, which is one standard for fully qualified domain names. Note how the stanza starts with a **case** directive and ends with the **esac** directive (the word *case* spelled backward).

```
accept_if_fully_qualified() {
        case $1 in
        *.*)
                echo "Hostname $myhostname OK: fully qualified as $1
                exit 0"
```

```
            ;;
      esac
}
```

The while and until Options

The **while** directive allows a script to run commands in a stanza as long as the condition is true. In contrast, the **until** directive allows a script to run commands in a stanza as long as the condition is false. The following directive from the cups-config script in the /bin directory shows how the **while** directive works, coupled with the **test** directive, to run the commands in the stanza as long as the noted variable (**$#**) is greater than (**-gt**) zero:

```
while test $# -gt 0; do
```

Study Available Scripts

You might realize by now that a substantial number of scripts and executable files exist in Solaris 11 that are text scripts of various sorts. The **file** command can help you identify the types of files available in a specified directory. For example, the following command identifies the different scripts in the /usr/sbin directory:

```
$ file /usr/sbin/* | grep script
```

One example of the output, shown in Figure 10-5, illustrates the different scripts available in the directory normally reserved for system tools, commands, and daemons.

You might note the different types of scripts available. All of the scripts are listed as "executable." Some refer to other scripting languages such as Perl and Python. The scripts shown are based on the first line of each file, which is typically one of those listed in Table 10-4.

```
/usr/sbin/accept:        executable /usr/perl5/bin/perl script
/usr/sbin/addgnupghome: executable shell script
/usr/sbin/applygnupgdefaults:   executable shell script
/usr/sbin/auditrecord:  executable /usr/perl5/bin/perl script
/usr/sbin/beadm:        executable /usr/bin/python2.6 script
/usr/sbin/check-hostname:        executable shell script
/usr/sbin/check-permissions:     executable shell script
/usr/sbin/cups-genppdupdate:     executable /usr/perl5/bin/perl script
/usr/sbin/dmesg:        executable /usr/bin/sh script
/usr/sbin/etrn: executable /usr/perl5/bin/perl script
/usr/sbin/exportfs:     executable /sbin/sh script
/usr/sbin/ftpaddhost:   executable /usr/bin/ksh script
/usr/sbin/ftpconfig:    executable /usr/bin/ksh script
/usr/sbin/gdm:  executable shell script
/usr/sbin/getmajor:     executable shell script
/usr/sbin/gkadmin:      executable shell script
/usr/sbin/gparted:      executable shell script
/usr/sbin/growfs:       executable shell script
/usr/sbin/ikecert:      executable /usr/bin/pfsh script
/usr/sbin/install:      executable /sbin/sh script
/usr/sbin/installboot:  executable shell script
/usr/sbin/k5srvutil:    executable shell script
/usr/sbin/kclient:      executable /bin/ksh93 script
/usr/sbin/kdcmgr:       executable /usr/bin/ksh script
:
```

FIGURE 10-5.   *Scripts in the /usr/sbin directory*

Shell Processor	Description
#!/bin/sh	Standard shell (linked to ksh93)
#!/sbin/sh	Standard shell (linked to ksh93)
#!/usr/bin/pfsh	Standard profile shell (supports limited user privileges for scripts)
#!/bin/ksh	Standard Korn shell (linked to ksh93)
#!/usr/bin/bash	Default bash shell for Solaris 11 (hard linked to #!/bin/bash)
#!/bin/bash	Default bash shell for Solaris 11
#!/usr/perl5/bin/perl	Script based on the Perl language

TABLE 10-4. *Shell Scripts*

These are just the scripts shown from standard executable text files listed in the /usr/bin and /usr/sbin directories. Others are available, depending on what scripting languages may be installed.

Sample Scripts

With all of this information in mind, you should now feel more able to read some of the scripts on a Solaris 11 system. Take a simple example, the sendmail script in the /etc/init.d directory. As is true on other UNIX-based operating systems such as Linux, some of the scripts in this directory can be used to start and stop different services. You can review the essence of the script in Figure 10-6.

```
# compatibility with previously documented init.d script behaviour.

case "$1" in
'restart')
        # The previous init.d/sendmail restart behaviour matches
        # the smf(5) 'refresh' semantics.

        svcadm refresh network/smtp:sendmail
        svcadm refresh network/sendmail-client:default
        ;;

'start')
        svcadm enable -t network/smtp:sendmail
        svcadm enable -t network/sendmail-client:default
        ;;

'stop')
        svcadm disable -t network/smtp:sendmail
        svcadm disable -t network/sendmail-client:default
        ;;

*)
        echo "Usage: $0 { start | stop | restart }"
        exit 1
        ;;
esac
```

FIGURE 10-6. *Scripts in the /usr/sbin directory*

The sendmail script is relatively straightforward; the **$1** is associated with standard input. The three valid **case** directives for input are **'restart'**, **'stop'**, and **'start'**, respectively. This script essentially translates the functionality of these options to various **svcadm** commands, to refresh, enable, and disable both the sendmail server and client services.

Summary

This chapter focused on the management of the shell in Solaris 11. It shows you some of the different methods you can use to set up the command-line interface. Although the default shell for Solaris 11 is now bash, other shells, including ksh, zsh, and tcsh, are still prominent options. In fact, perhaps a majority of scripts in Solaris 11 are based on some form of the Korn shell.

Each of these shells features some form of interactivity and command completion. Basic parameters for Solaris shells are configured in the /etc/profile file. Individual shells may have their own general configuration files in the /etc directory. For example, whereas the bash shell supports configuration files in the /etc/bash directory, the Korn shell can be configured through /etc/ksh.kshrc. Each of these files can be further modified with the help of hidden files in each user's home directory.

In general, shells are designed to help an operating system manage the flow of data. This chapter described some of the ways a shell can handle standard input, standard output, and standard error. You can also configure shell characters to designate functions for certain key combinations.

This chapter provided a basic introduction to shell scripts. Although it's relatively easy to set up a script with a bunch of regular commands, the power of a script comes from the use of conditional expressions that support customized commands in different situations. This chapter described some typical conditionals, along with a description of how they work in some sample scripts. Many text scripts are available in directories such as /usr/bin and /usr/sbin.

References

Advanced Bash-Scripting Guide: The Linux Documentation Project. Although Linux is not UNIX, they are clones. Therefore, the commands and scripts available for the bash shell do work just as well in Solaris. Available online from http://tldp.org/LDP/abs/html/.

KornShell Documentation, developed by David Korn. Available online from www.kornshell.com. Although the documentation is from the year 2000, the Korn shell is still an excellent way to communicate with UNIX-type operating systems such as Solaris 11.

The home page for tcsh, available online at www.tcsh.org. As documented on that page, tcsh is an enhanced version of the original C shell, with command completion features.

Z-Shell Frequently Asked Questions, available online at http://zsh.sourceforge.net/FAQ/.

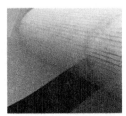

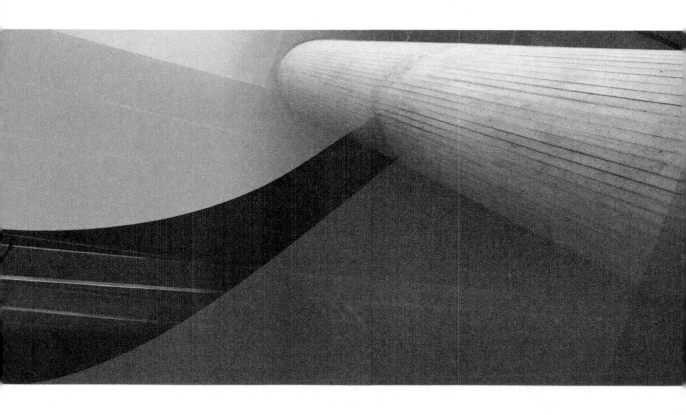

CHAPTER
11

Users and Groups

ser management is one of the most important aspects of any system administrator's job. The UNIX principle of managing users and groups has not fundamentally changed in decades, regardless of vendor or distribution. The functionality is well designed and powerful. Oracle Solaris 11 maintains this benefit and brings new enhancements and features to the user and group model. In this chapter, we'll cover the basics and then expand on the enhancements and management capabilities that are built into Oracle Solaris 11, such as the Role Based Access Control (RBAC) feature of Oracle Solaris and the integration of other technologies, such as the Lightweight Directory Access Protocol (LDAP).

User Concepts

Every user of a UNIX system must have a login account. A user's login account includes several components, each of which will be discussed in detail in this chapter. There is a special type of user account, called a *role*. Roles allow users to act as fictitious users. Those fictitious users might or might not have extra privileges, or they might exist only to allow a group of users to act as a single user when necessary.

User names, also called *login names,* allow users to access their own systems and any remote systems on which they have the appropriate access privileges. A user name is usually made of a simple string, often some derivative of the user's actual name. User names are publicly known and must be accompanied by a password, which should be kept secret. For security reasons, user passwords should be changed according to your organization's security policy.

What the user sees as their user name is really just the name of their account. The user's account is represented by a number, called a user identification (UID) number. This number is unique and is what the system uses to recognize each user account. UID numbers are required for regular user accounts and also for special system accounts. There are certain UIDs that cannot be assigned to regular user accounts. Table 11-1 describes how UIDs are allocated.

NOTE
UID 0 is always the root account.

When a user account is created, it can be assigned to a group. A *group* provides a way to organize user accounts based on its members having something in common. A group should be

UID	Login Account	Description
0–99	**root**, **daemon**, **bin**, **sys**, and so on	Reserved for use by the operating system
100–2147483647	Regular users	General-purpose accounts
60001 and 65534	**nobody** and **nobody4**	NFS anonymous users
60002	**noaccess**	Non-trusted users

TABLE 11-1.   *UID Allocation and Ranges*

predefined based on the user's type, location, or any shared relationship with other users within the context of the server system. The most common criteria for maintaining a group is for a collection of users who can share files and directories. The administrator can set permissions on directories and files that only those users who belong to the same group can access.

A user can belong to two kinds of groups: a primary group and a supplemental group. Each user must belong to a primary group. If not specified at the time of creation, new users are assigned to the default group, which is staff (group 10). In Oracle Solaris 11, users can belong to up to 1,024 supplemental groups. Use the **groups** command to list the groups for a user. For example, the user carla only belongs to the default group, staff, as shown here:

```
# groups carla
staff
```

Like user accounts, groups are also identified by a name and group identification (GID) number.

Users, groups, and roles comprise a powerful tool for administering the users of the Oracle Solaris 11 system.

NOTE
The maximum number for UIDs and GIDs is 2147483647. As you can see, we can have a lot of users and groups on a system! Why 2147483647? This is the largest number that can be stored within an integer (int) data type, which is 32 bits in length.

Standard Users

A *standard user* is an account that is generally used interactively by a human user of the system. These accounts are typically named based on the user's real name or perhaps some identification string that is assigned by their employer. Standard user accounts are interactive in the sense that the user can log into the system locally or remotely. Once logged in, the standard user can use a command line or graphical user interface such as the GNOME Desktop. The user can issue commands, edit documents, browse the World Wide Web, check e-mail, and all of those things humans like to do on their computer. Restrictions can also be placed on user accounts to limit a standard user's access to certain parts of the system.

A standard user account will have a home directory associated with it. The home directory can be created at the same time that the user's account is created, or later. The home directory is the portion of a filesystem that is allocated to a user for storing private files. Home directories can be located either on the user's local system or on a remote file server.

System Accounts

A *system account* is one that is used by the system, rather than a standard user. System accounts are often associated with an application process that is installed and running on the system. These running processes need a way to operate on the system just as standard users do. Like with standard users, restrictions can be in place to limit what parts of the system can be accessed by the system account. However, some system accounts do require special access to network ports, or ranges of network ports, to listen for incoming connections to the service they provide. There are differences, though. A system account usually does not require a home directory. They are also very rarely accessed from remote locations.

NOTE
An application process that listens on a network port for service requests is also referred to as a daemon.

Sometimes an account is used by both a standard user and a system account. For instance, the Oracle Database Server might be installed under an account called *oracle*. The database administrator might log into the oracle account to administer the database, and the Oracle database services will run on the system as the oracle account.

A system account also provides a basic level of security to the system by protecting it in the event that the service associated with the account is violated and someone with malicious intent (referred to as a *mal-actor* in security circles) gains access to the account. In this scenario, the mal-actor might be able to damage the service, the account, and any data and files that it owns, but the damage will not spread to other users or services running on the system—given that proper permissions and other protections are in place. This isn't a total solution, because it might be possible for the mal-actor to modify the vulnerable service to consume excessive or all resources on the server, causing it to grind to a halt. This at least provides some protection, which is generally more than would be available to a service running as the root user because it would have much more access to sensitive parts of the system.

The Root Account

Like all UNIX systems, Oracle Solaris 11 has a root account. The root account, called *super user* in previous Solaris releases, is generally the owner of most binaries and many configuration files. The root account can also make changes to any part of the system, because the account runs with all privileges and has all Oracle Solaris authorizations. The root account in Oracle Solaris 11 is generally configured as an RBAC role, which means it cannot be logged into directly (even on the console), and users must be explicitly granted access to the account. When you're authenticating to a role, the password must be that of the role. We'll discuss the root role further in the next section.

Role Based Access Control (RBAC) and Administrative Privileges

The RBAC feature is used to control user access to tasks that would normally be restricted to the root role. The biggest driver for the usage of RBAC is the need for privilege delegation and separation of duties. RBAC components and concepts include roles, rights profiles, authorizations, privileges, and security attributes.

Process rights management is implemented through privileges. Both RBAC and privileges work to provide a more secure alternative to administering a system as the root user.

Various super user capabilities are collected into a *rights profile,* which can be broadly or narrowly defined. Predefined rights profiles are included in the Oracle Solaris software. Rights profiles are assigned to special user accounts, called *roles*. The administrator creates these roles and then assigns the profiles to the roles. Roles can be assigned with either broad or narrow capabilities, or both. You can base roles on rights profiles that have the same name—for example, the root role, which is equivalent to the root account, and the system administrator profile, which is used for nonsecurity types of administration.

In Oracle Solaris 11, users and roles can also run privileged applications from a *profile shell,* which is a special shell that recognizes the security attributes included in a rights profile. A profile shell can be assigned to a specific user as a login shell, or it can be started by using the **su** command to assume a role. In Oracle Solaris 11, every shell has a profile shell counterpart (for example, bash and pfbash).

A user can assume a role that includes those capabilities required to perform a specific job. Different users can be assigned different roles so that no one user has the ability to perform all operations on a system. A role can be tailored to fit a required task, depending on which authorizations might be necessary for the user to perform that task. For instance, you might want to give one of your standard users the ability to manage the smb server daemon. We'll explore this scenario more in the next section.

The Root Role

During the installation of Oracle Solaris 11, if you created an initial user account, that account was assigned the root role. For instance, suppose the initial account created during the installation is named alan:

```
# roles alan
root
```

We can assign the privileges of the root role to other users, as well as enable them to assume the root role, so they can also administer the server. For example, the following command modifies the user james, adding the root role:

```
# usermod -R +root james
```

Creating a Role

Let's look at the process of creating a role. The **roleadd** command is used to create a role. The **roleadd** command has a similar syntax to that of the **useradd** command. For example, both offer the **–D** argument for displaying the default settings for a new role or user (refer to the man pages for **roleadd** for complete details of its usage):

```
# roleadd -D
group=staff,10   project=default,3   basedir=/export/home
skel=/etc/skel   shell=/usr/bin/pfbash   inactive=0
expire=  auths=  profiles=All  limitpriv=
defaultpriv=  lock_after_retries=  roleauth=role
```

If we wanted to enable a standard user to manage a particular service on our Oracle Solaris 11 system, we first need to add a role that has the authorizations for managing that service. The role can then be assigned to a standard user. Let's step through an example. Suppose we want to enable a standard user, james, to be able to stop, start, and restart the Server Message Block (SMB) service, svc:/network/smb:default.

```
# svcs smb
STATE          STIME    FMRI
online         March_21   svc:/network/smb:default
```

Start by determining what management authorizations are necessary to perform these operations. We can do this by using the **svcprop** command from the Oracle Solaris 11 Service Management Facility (SMF) and using **grep** to search for the word **manage**, as shown here:

```
# svcprop svc:/network/smb |grep manage
general/action_authorization astring solaris.smf.manage.smb
general/value_authorization astring solaris.smf.manage.smb
```

This shows that the management authorization for SMB is called **solaris.smf.manage.smb**.

Take a look at a few other services, such as the Network Time Protocol or Apache HTTP Server:

```
# svcprop svc:/network/ntp |grep manage
general/action_authorization astring solaris.smf.manage.ntp
# svcprop svc:/network/http:apache22 |grep manage
general/action_authorization astring solaris.smf.manage.http/apache22
```

You can see that each of them has a similarly named authorization for management purposes. Services generally have two different authorizations, as shown. The **general/action** authorization allows someone to manage the service, such as starting, stopping, or restarting, whereas the **general/value** authorization allows changes to configuration settings to be made.

Now use the **roleadd** command to create a role with the management authorizations assigned.

We will call our sample role smbmgr, because it will be used for SMB management. The following **roleadd** command creates the role and assigns the management authorizations:

```
# roleadd -A solaris.smf.manage.smb -c "SMB Management" smbmgr
```

After the role is created, it can be assigned to users. Those users will be able to assume the role and perform the operations allowed by the assigned authorizations. Verify the new role with the **auths** command. The management authorization for SMB will be listed.

```
# auths smbmgr
solaris.admin.wusb.read,solaris.device.mount.removable,solaris.mail.
mailq,solaris.smf.manage.smb
```

Also, an entry will be placed in the user database, which can be shown with the **getent** command:

```
# getent passwd smbmgr
smbmgr:x:101:10::/home/smbmgr:/usr/bin/pfbash
```

Set a password for the new smbmgr role:

```
# passwd smbmgr
New Password:
Re-enter new Password:
passwd: password successfully changed for smbmgr
```

NOTE
The password must contain at least one numeric or special character.

Finally, assign the role to the standard user:

```
# usermod -R +smbmgr james
```

The role assignment can be verified using the **roles** command:

```
# roles james
smbmgr
```

Before the user james can begin using this new role, the system administrator must provide him with the password that was set for the role. Using this password, james can now assume the role of smbmgr. Upon logging in, james can also verify that he has access to the smbmgr role using the **roles** command:

```
james@elevenvm:~$ roles
smbmgr
```

The user james can view the status of the smb service as a standard user. However, until he assumes the smbmgr role, he will not be permitted to manage this service.

```
james@elevenvm:~$ svcs smb
STATE          STIME    FMRI
online         21:46:51 svc:/network/smb:default
james@elevenvm:~$ svcadm disable smb
svcadm: svc:/network/smb:default: Permission denied.
```

If james issues the **auths** command at this point, he will not see the authorizations for SMB management listed:

```
james@elevenvm:~$ auths
solaris.admin.wusb.read,solaris.device.mount.removable,solaris.mail.mailq
```

To manage the smb service, james must assume the smbmgr role by using the **su** command and entering the password provided by the system administrator:

```
james@elevenvm:~$ su smbmgr
Password:
smbmgr@elevenvm:~$
```

If james issues the **auths** command now, he will see the authorizations for SMB management listed:

```
smbmgr@elevenvm:~$ auths
solaris.admin.wusb.read,solaris.device.mount.removable,solaris.mail.mailq,solaris.smf.
manage.smb
```

The user james has now become the smbmgr role and can issue service management commands successfully, such as the **svcadm** command to disable and enable the smb service:

```
smbmgr@elevenvm:~$ svcadm disable smb
smbmgr@elevenvm:~$ svcs smb
STATE          STIME    FMRI
disabled       21:52:56 svc:/network/smb:default
smbmgr@elevenvm:~$ svcadm enable smb
smbmgr@elevenvm:~$ svcs smb
STATE          STIME    FMRI
online         21:53:35 svc:/network/smb:default
```

The smbmgr role has been specifically assigned to the user james. Any other user who tries to assume this role will not be permitted. Even if the user discovers what the password is for the smbmgr role, the system will prevent the user from executing the **su** command. Suppose user edward has learned the password and attempts to **su** to smbmgr. He will not be allowed to become smbmgr. Edward is only allowed to view the service status.

```
edward@elevenvm:~$ svcs smb
STATE          STIME    FMRI
online         21:53:35 svc:/network/smb:default
```

If the user edward attempts to **su** to the smbmgr role, using the actual password, he will receive an error and will be prevented from continuing:

```
edward@elevenvm:~$ su smbmgr
Password:
Roles can only be assumed by authorized users
su: Sorry
```

The role can also be unassigned using the **usermod** command. When the role was assigned, the role name was preceded by a plus (+) symbol. To unassign the role, the role name should be preceded by a minus (–) symbol:

```
# usermod -R -smbmgr james
```

We can verify again with the **roles** command:

```
# roles james
No roles
```

A role can be deleted using the **roledel** command:

```
# roledel smbmgr
```

Using a role in this manner allows the system administrator to give several users the ability to manage a system service or daemon. One example might be in a development environment where a group of developers are assigned a role that has the ability to manage an application server. This way, each time the developers need to restart the application server following a deployment, they don't need to call on the system administrator.

Local Configuration Files

A set of important files, referred to as *administrative databases,* stores information about local users and groups on the system. Table 11-2 lists these files.

Oracle Solaris 11 stores local user information in the file /etc/passwd. This file is used by the system and its processes for user lookups and authentication; for this reason, the user database file is given broad read permissions.

```
# ls -l /etc/passwd
-rw-r--r-- 1 root sys 1230 2011-09-15 15:22 /etc/passwd
```

The **getent** command is used to display the users stored in the user database file. The following is an excerpt:

```
# getent passwd
root:x:0:0:Super-User:/root:/usr/bin/bash
daemon:x:1:1::/:
bin:x:2:2::/usr/bin:
sys:x:3:3::/:
adm:x:4:4:Admin:/var/adm:
lp:x:71:8:Line Printer Admin:/:
uucp:x:5:5:uucp Admin:/usr/lib/uucp:
nuucp:x:9:9:uucp Admin:/var/spool/uucppublic:/usr/lib/uucp/uucico
dladm:x:15:65:Datalink Admin:/:
netadm:x:16:65:Network Admin:/:
netcfg:x:17:65:Network Configuration Admin:/:
alfalfa:x:100:10::/home/alfalfa:/usr/bin/bash
```

Each colon-delimited line contains certain information about its corresponding user. Table 11-3 describes each field for the user alfalfa (from the last line shown in the preceding excerpt).

NOTE
The Bourne-again shell, bash, is now the default shell. This might be a welcome change by many UNIX users.

Oracle Solaris 11 stores local group information in the file /etc/group. This file is used by the system and its processes for group lookups and authentication; for this reason, the group database file, like the user database file, is given broad read permissions.

```
# ls -l /etc/group
-rw-r--r-- 1 root     sys         461 Apr 16 23:33 /etc/group
```

File	Purpose
/etc/passwd	User database file (a database of users)
/etc/group	Group database file (a database of groups)
/etc/shadow	Shadow database file (a password database)

TABLE 11-2. *Local Administrative Database Files*

User Name	Password Information	UID	Primary GID	Comment	Home Directory	Shell
Alfalfa	X	60009	60009	Little Rascal	/home/alfalfa	/usr/bin/bash

TABLE 11-3. *Fields of the User Entry Within the Administrative Database*

The **getent** command is also used to display the groups stored in the group database file. The following is an excerpt:

```
# getent group
root::0:
other::1:root
bin::2:root,daemon
sys::3:root,bin,adm
adm::4:root,daemon
uucp::5:root
mail::6:root
tty::7:root,adm
lp::8:root,adm
nuucp::9:root
staff::10:james,jane
daemon::12:root
```

Oracle Solaris 11 stores user password information in the /etc/shadow file, which is only readable by root. The /etc/shadow file doesn't actually contain the users' passwords; it contains hashes of each user's password. Permissions are stricter on this file.

```
# ls -l /etc/shadow
-r-------- 1 root root 758 2011-09-15 15:22 /etc/shadow
```

As we can see, the password database file only has read access for the owner, which is root. The shadow database functions to abstract and isolate users' passwords from the user database file, which we saw has more read access because many processes might need to refer to it regularly.

Commands Used for Managing Users and Groups

Table 11-4 details the set of commands used for configuration and management of users and groups on a UNIX system in Oracle Solaris 11.

Command-line Account Management

The **useradd** command is used to add a new user. Its most basic form is **useradd james**. This usage results in the james account being added to the user database file. By default, the **useradd** command creates the user account for the user name that is requested using the next available UID and assigns it to group 10, staff. When a new user is added to the system, the password and shadow databases

Command	Purpose
getent	Queries administrative databases
groupadd	Adds a group
grpck	Checks the integrity of the group database
groupdel	Deletes a group
groupmod	Modifies a group
login	Logs a user into the system
newgrp	Logs a user into a new group
passwd	Changes a password, password attributes, and other password attributes
pwck	Checks the integrity of the user database
pwconv	Creates or updates the shadow database based on the user database
su	Assumes the root role, or another user account or role
useradd	Adds a user
userdel	Deletes a user
usermod	Modifies a user

TABLE 11-4.   *User and Group Administration Commands*

are updated with the user's information. The user database receives a line for the new user, as described in the section "Local Configuration Files."

```
# useradd james
# getent passwd james
james:x:60010:10::/home/james:/usr/bin/bash
```

The shadow database also receives an update for the new user:

```
# grep james /etc/shadow
james:UP:::::::
```

Notice that initially in the password field is "UP," which means that the account is not yet activated and useable. Once a password is set for the user, the field will change to contain the user's password hash. Table 11-5 lists the other possible password entries. Refer to the passwd(1M) man page for complete information.

The **groupadd** command is used to create a new group. A common convention among UNIX administrators is to create a group with the same name as the user, to be assigned as the user's primary group. Here, we create a group to assign to our sample user, james, as the primary group:

```
# groupadd james
```

Because the group was created after the user in this example, the user's primary group must be changed from staff to james. The **usermod** command with the –**g** argument is used to do this.

Entry	Description
LK	The account is locked.
NP	The account has no password.
PS	The account has a password.
UP	The account is not yet activated and useable.

TABLE 11-5. *User Account States*

We'll use the **id** command to clearly demonstrate. Before the change, james's primary group was the default, staff.

```
# id -a james
uid=60010(james) gid=10(staff) groups=10(staff)
# usermod -g james james
# id -a james
uid=60010(james) gid=60010(james) groups=60010(james)
```

Now, james's primary group is james. This result can be achieved more efficiently with a bit of planning. If you can determine each user's needs ahead of time, their account can be created correctly in one step. This is quicker than having to modify your users' accounts as shown in the preceding example. You should refer to the man page of the **useradd** command for full usage, but some of the more commonly used options are covered next. Just as with the primary group, several other account parameters are generally set at the time of user creation. The more common ones are primary and supplementary group memberships, home directory path, and a descriptive comment. Most system administrators prefer to have some conventions decided ahead of time. This allows users to be created correctly using the **useradd** command with appropriate command-line options. This way, only two commands are required to create an account for our sample user, james.

We can create the james account with a primary group called james with the **useradd** command. We can also set staff as his supplementary group. The **–g** and **–G** arguments are used for these respective tasks. A descriptive comment is also commonly provided by using the **–c** argument. The second line of the following example combines all of these arguments into one command:

```
# groupadd james
# useradd -c "Example" -g james -G staff james
```

The result of these two commands shows that the james account is created with the primary group of james, and staff is now a supplementary group. The comment can be verified with the **getent** or **finger** command:

```
# id -a james
uid=60010(james) gid=60010(james) groups=10(staff)
# getent passwd james
james:x:60010:60010:Example:/home/james:/usr/bin/bash
# finger james
```

```
Login name: james                          In real life: Example
Directory: /home/james                     Shell: /usr/bin/bash
```

Another important item to set is the location of the user's home directory. The **useradd** command in Oracle Solaris 11 does not create the user's home directory by default, even though this field in the user database is set to /home/<username>. Therefore, upon login, the user will be alerted that login could not change to the home directory. Furthermore, the user will be placed in the system root (/), where very limited access is available. In practice, the system administrator generally should specify a home directory for standard users. Continuing with our sample user, we could modify the james account using the **usermod** command, like this:

```
# usermod -d /export/home/james -m james
```

The **–d** option specifies the location of james's home directory, and the **–m** option forces the directory to be made since it doesn't already exist. As was demonstrated in the last example, it would have been easier (and is recommended) to pass the appropriate arguments with the **useradd** command when initially creating the user account. To include the creation of the home directory, simply use the **–m** argument. That way, there is no need to specify the home directory.

```
# useradd -c "James" -g james -G staff -m james
```

In previous versions of Oracle Solaris, a new directory /export/home/james would have been created with ownership assigned to james. In Oracle Solaris 11, home directories are created as ZFS datasets. Including the **–m** option will actually create a ZFS dataset for james. The filesystem is located in the rpool/export/home/james directory and has a mount point of /export/home/james, as shown in the following output of the **zfs list** command:

```
# zfs list |grep james
rpool/export/home/james   35.5K   2.22G   35.5K   /export/home/james
```

NOTE
Refer to Chapter 9 for more information on the ZFS filesystem and datasets.

User and Group Security

One of the most important aspects of managing user accounts relates to passwords. System administrators should be familiar with their corporate security policy governing passwords. If no policy exists, due diligence should be used to establish a policy to promote good password management. Most importantly, all users, especially any interactive login account, should have a password assigned. You can assign a password for a user when you create the user's account, or force the user to specify a password at the first login. Most organizations today require password complexity and regular password change intervals.

The /etc/default/passwd file contains a number of variables for enforcing a password-aging and complexity policy for the users of a given system. These settings are documented in detail in the passwd(1) man page. Often-used variables include **MAXWEEKS** and **MINWEEKS**, which are used for password aging, and **PASSLENGTH**, which specifies the number of characters required for a password. The password length must at least match the value identified by the **PASSLENGTH** variable in /the etc/default/password file, which is set to 6 by default.

One significant change in Oracle Solaris 11 is that the default password-hashing algorithm is now SHA256. The benefit of this change is that passwords are no longer limited to eight characters as they were in older editions of Oracle Solaris which used the crypt command. Thus, if you were using **crypt**, and entered a 20-character password, it only matches the complexity rules within the first eight characters. Oracle Solaris 11 replaces crypt with encrypt that enables password complexity to apply to the full length.

Password complexity is set further in the file using several other variables; some examples of these are **MINLOWER**, **MINUPPER**, and **MAXREPEATS**. Consult the man pages for the password command for complete details.

Here's an example of manually setting a password policy for a user:

```
# passwd -n 1 -x 60 -w 14 james
```

This usage of the password command will prevent James from changing his password more than once a day, will force his password to expire after 60 days, and begin warning him of password expiration when he only has 14 days left. We can verify this with the command **passwd -s**, as shown here:

```
# passwd -s james
james     PS   01/01/12     1    60    14
```

The date that appears is not the date that the james account was created. It is the date of the last password change, known as **LASTCHG**. Based on what we now know about the **LASTCHG** and **MAX** fields, we can determine that James's password will expire at the end of February 2012.

See the "Password Management" section of Chapter 12 for a discussion of password-change policies.

Who Am I

"Who am I" isn't simply the title of this section, it is the command that users can run to view some of the information about their account on the system:

```
# who am I
alan      pts/3        Mar 19 21:13     (:0.0)
```

Or perhaps:

```
# who am Iz
alan       pts/1       March 29 22:32    (:0.0)
jaideep    pts/2        Jun  2 21:50     (jnode1.example.net)
```

Oracle Solaris 11 provides several different commands for users to view information about who is logged into the system. In addition, there are several commands that users can use to change the information about their accounts.

The **who** command can tell you who is logged into the system. There is also the **w** command, as well as the **finger**, **id**, and **users** commands. The command **id** is useful for viewing group membership information.

If you've used previous versions of Linux or other UNIX operating systems, you might be familiar with the **chfn** command. Oracle Solaris 11 doesn't include this command. Instead, one of the command's operations is available from the –**g** argument to the **passwd** command. But it can only be used by the root user. Previously, all users could use the **chfn** command to change the comment field and what is known as the *gecos* information for their account. Now, only the root user can use the **passwd –g** command to change a user's comment field, which is stored in the user database.

```
# getent passwd james
james:x:60010:60010:Example:/home/james:/usr/bin/bash
# passwd -g james
Default values are printed inside of '[]'.
To accept the default, type <return>.
To have a blank entry, type the word 'none'.

Name [Example]: James
passwd: password information changed for james
# getent passwd james
james:x:60010:60010:James:/home/james:/usr/bin/bash
```

GUI Account Management

Oracle Solaris 11 does not include a graphical user interface (GUI) for managing users and groups, as of the Oracle Solaris 11/11 release. Open source software packages, such as Webmin, provide some of the functionality needed to manage users, groups, and roles. However, this functionality isn't as fully featured as the built-in Oracle Solaris command-line utilities. Oracle also offers user and group management through the Enterprise Manager family of products, such as Oracle Identity Manager.

Basic LDAP User Database

Similar to the basic UNIX user database that is maintained in the shadow and password databases discussed earlier in this chapter, other database types are available for storing user information. Although the local shadow and password files can serve a single system for authentication and authorization, it isn't possible to serve this information to other hosts or applications across the network. For this, we need a service that is network accessible and can provide the performance, robustness, and security required by any service that acts as a network daemon for other servers to query. The service that has come to fill this role is the Lightweight Directory Access Protocol (LDAP), pronounced the way it looks *(el dap)*. LDAP has become the de facto standard for user database storage. An LDAP directory can be used to store any type of organized data, such as information about users and systems. Extended attributes, such as permissions and roles, can be stored as well. LDAP is not only used for authentication to servers within a network, but also for applications that require login access to various services and functions.

LDAP and NIS

Before LDAP, there was the yp service, which was later renamed the Network Information Service (NIS). NIS (later NIS+) is an information service that provides network-wide access to user and system information. NIS+ was released in 1992 as an improvement to NIS, but both were ultimately replaced by LDAP as the more popular technology for distributed information services. In Oracle Solaris 11, NIS+ is no longer supported. NIS is still available, although the NIS services are not installed by default. LDAP has certain advantages over NIS, but an organization will need to evaluate these to determine which route to take. Although not exhaustive, Table 11-6 shows some of the more compelling reasons to choose LDAP over NIS.

	LDAP	**NIS**
Namespace	Hierarchical	Flat
Scale	Global	LAN
Security	Kerberos, SSL, TLS	None
Transport	TCP/IP	RPC

TABLE 11-6. *Information Services Comparison: LDAP vs. NIS*

NOTE
A more detailed comparison of LDAP and NIS is available in the Oracle Solaris 11 online documentation.

NIS is limited to local area network communications and is not securable. These are big drawbacks against it for most modern enterprise environments. Plus, NIS uses a flat file storage structure that, along with the LAN/RPC requirement, limits its scalability to small organizational networks or segments.

LDAP has neither of these limitations. It supports several methods for securing its communications and can be scaled to large networks. LDAP can even be used across the Internet because it relies on TCP/IP.

Nevertheless, there could be a time and place for either, so this chapter covers both of them in the Oracle Solaris 11 operating environment.

The NIS Software

More than likely, your organization has already moved to or is planning to move to a directory services system based on LDAP, but there are a few relying on NIS. In the following section, we'll show how to get an NIS master server running on Oracle Solaris 11. There are a few hurdles related to some changes in the way other services and files are installed compared to previous operating system versions. As we said, NIS is not installed by default on an Oracle Solaris 11 system. First, the lack of NIS should be confirmed, followed by installation if necessary:

```
# pkg info service/network/nis
```

If NIS is not found, install it:

```
# pkg install service/network/nis
```

Now verify again:

```
# pkg info service/network/nis
          Name: service/network/nis
       Summary: NIS Server
   Description: Network Information Service (NIS) Server software
      Category: System/Administration and Configuration
         State: Installed
     Publisher: solaris
```

```
        Version: 0.5.11
 Build Release: 5.11
         Branch: 0.175.0.0.0.2.1
Packaging Date: October 19, 2011 06:29:04 AM
           Size: 541.05 kB
           FMRI: pkg://solaris/service/network/nis@0.5.11,5.11-
                 0.175.0.0.0.2.1:20111019T062904Z
```

NOTE
We could have also used the graphical version of the Oracle IPS packaging system to accomplish the location and installation of the NIS service package.

Setting Up an NIS Client
The NIS client can be configured for one of two lookup methods: broadcast or server-list. Ensure that the NIS services have the correct domain name with the following command.

```
# svcprop -p config/domainname svc:/network/nis/domain:default
```

If the domain name isn't displayed as expected, use the following command to set it:

```
# svccfg -s nis/domain setprop config/domainname = example.net
# svcadm refresh nis/domain
```

Verify that NIS knows the domain name with the same command as before:

```
# svcprop -p config/domainname svc:/network/nis/domain:default
example.net
```

Configure the name server switch to use NIS:

```
# svccfg -s system/name-service/switch
svc:/system/name-service/switch> setprop config/host = astring: "files nis"
svc:/system/name-service/switch> quit
# svcadm refresh name-service/switch
```

Verify that the name service search order is configured properly:

```
# svcprop -p config/host svc:/system/name-service/switch
files\ nis
```

Setting Up an NIS Server
Start by editing the /etc/inet/hosts file by adding a "master" entry and ensuring the server's fully qualified domain name is specified. Here's an example:

```
10.0.4.15 elevenvm elevenvm.example.net master
```

Ensure that the NIS services have the correct domain name with the following command:

```
# svcprop -p config/domainname svc:/network/nis/domain:default
```

If the domain name isn't displayed as expected, use the following command to set it:

```
# svccfg -s nis/domain setprop config/domainname = example.net
# svcadm refresh nis/domain
```

Verify that NIS knows the domain name with the same command as before:

```
# svcprop -p config/domainname svc:/network/nis/domain:default
example.net
```

The command **ypinit** is used to initialize the NIS server, but before it will succeed, the source directory needs to be created. This directory will contain all the user database files necessary for building the NIS information database. The path to this directory is configured in the file /var/yp/Makefile. Edit this file and change the following lines as shown:

```
DIR =/var/yp/etc
PWDIR =/var/yp/etc
RBACDIR =/var/yp/etc/security
```

Then create the directories:

```
# cd /var/yp
# mkdir -p etc/security
```

Copy the source files into the newly created source directories:

```
# cp /etc/auto_home /var/yp/etc
# cp /etc/auto_master /var/yp/etc
# cp /etc/group /var/yp/etc
# cp /etc/hosts /var/yp/etc
# cp /etc/netmasks /var/yp/etc
# cp /etc/networks /var/yp/etc
# cp /etc/passwd /var/yp/etc
# cp /etc/protocols /var/yp/etc
# cp /etc/rpc /var/yp/etc
# cp /etc/shadow /var/yp/etc
# cp /etc/user_attr /var/yp/etc
# cp /etc/TIMEZONE /var/yp/etc/timezone
# cp /etc/inet/ipnodes /var/yp/etc
# cp /etc/inet/services /var/yp/etc
# cp /etc/security/exec_attr /var/yp/etc/security
# cp /etc/security/auth_attr /var/yp/etc/security
# cp /etc/security/prof_attr /var/yp/etc/security
```

NIS expects several files that are deprecated in Oracle Solaris 11. To prevent errors during the initialization process, create dummy versions of these files:

```
# touch /var/yp/etc/ethers
# touch /var/yp/etc/netgroup
# touch /var/yp/etc/bootparams
# touch /var/yp/etc/publickey
```

After all the source files are copied, several important changes should be made to them. First, and definitely most important, is to remove all entries for the root user and group from the password, group, and shadow files. Second, clean up the files by removing all comment lines from the files.

NOTE
Due to changes in the way Oracle Solaris 11 stores RBAC roles, profiles, and authorizations, the files in the /etc/security directory that are copied in the previous example will be empty, unless the server administrator has created additional new roles and role assignments. In order for NIS to include Oracle Solaris 11's default RBAC information, these files need to be edited with the consolidated RBAC data, which is now stored in separate files in the following directories:

- /etc/security/auth_attr.d
- /etc/security/exec_attr.d
- /etc/security/prof_attr.d

For the sake of this example, this step has been omitted. For additional information, refer to the "Role Based Access Control (RBAC)" section of Chapter 12.

Now we can initialize and enable the NIS service. First, use the **ypinit -m** command to initialize and install the NIS database. The first prompt asks for additional NIS hosts; because we only have one host, which is already shown, we'll press CTRL-D as instructed. Type **y** at the second prompt to confirm the hostname. The next prompt asks whether to quit on nonfatal errors; type **y** for this as well. The following is a transcript of a successful NIS initialization:

```
# /usr/sbin/ypinit -m
In order for NIS to operate successfully, we have to construct a list of the
NIS servers.  Please continue to add the names for YP servers in order of
preference, one per line.  When you are done with the list, type a <control D>
or a return on a line by itself.
        next host to add:  elevenvm
        next host to add:  <ENTER>
The current list of yp servers looks like this:

elevenvm

Is this correct?  [y/n: y]  y

Installing the YP database will require that you answer a few questions.
Questions will all be asked at the beginning of the procedure.

Do you want this procedure to quit on non-fatal errors? [y/n: n]  y
OK, please remember to go back and redo manually whatever fails.  If you
don't, some part of the system (perhaps the yp itself) won't work.
The yp domain directory is /var/yp/example.net
Can we destroy the existing /var/yp/example.net and its contents? [y/n: n]  y
There will be no further questions. The remainder of the procedure should take
```

```
5 to 10 minutes.
Building /var/yp/example.net/ypservers...
Running /var/yp /Makefile...
updated passwd
updated group
updated hosts
updated ipnodes
updated ethers
updated networks
updated rpc
updated services
updated protocols
updated netgroup
updated bootparams
/var/yp/example.net/mail.aliases: 12 aliases, longest 10 bytes, 138 bytes total
/usr/lib/netsvc/yp/mkalias /var/yp/`domainname`/mail.aliases /var/yp/`domainname`/
mail.byaddr;
updated aliases
updated publickey
updated netid
/usr/sbin/makedbm /var/yp/etc/netmasks /var/yp/`domainname`/netmasks.byaddr;
updated netmasks
updated timezone
updated auto.master
updated auto.home
updated ageing
updated auth_attr
updated exec_attr
updated prof_attr
updated user_attr

elevenvm has been set up as a yp master server without any errors.

If there are running slave yp servers, run yppush now for any data bases
which have been changed.  If there are no running slaves, run ypinit on
those hosts which are to be slave servers.
```

Now start the NIS service:

```
# svcadm enable nis/domain
# svcs nis/domain
STATE          STIME    FMRI
online         23:08:43     svc:/network/nis/domain:default
```

Oracle Solaris 11 doesn't include a graphical tool for managing the NIS server, but the open source Webmin software includes an "NIS Client and Server" module.

The LDAP Software

Solaris 11 provides packages for the open source LDAP server OpenLDAP and a package for LDAP utilities. An IPS search shows the available packages. From Figure 11-1, you can see that both LDAP-related packages are already installed. These packages were installed by default.

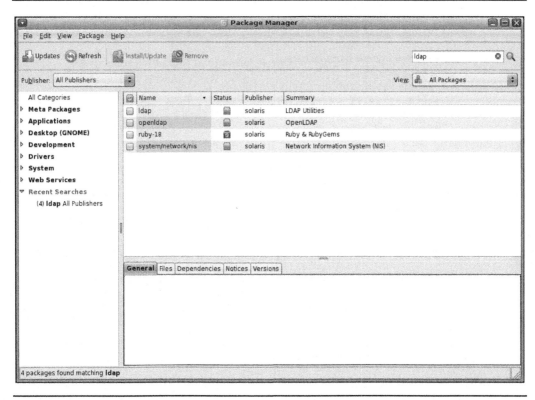

FIGURE 11-1. *Package Manager*

We can also view the details of these packages from the command line with the **pkg** command:

```
# pkg info -r ldap
          Name: naming/ldap
       Summary: LDAP Utilities
   Description: LDAP server search and modification utilities, including
                ldapsearch(1), ldapdelete(1), ldapmodify(1), ldapadd(1), and
                ldapmodrdn(1)
      Category: System/Administration and Configuration
         State: Installed
     Publisher: solaris
       Version: 0.5.11
 Build Release: 5.11
        Branch: 0.175.0.0.0.2.1
Packaging Date: October 19, 2011 06:12:35 AM
          Size: 294.16 kB
          FMRI: pkg://solaris/naming/ldap@0.5.11,5.11-0
.175.0.0.0.2.1:20111019T061235Z
# pkg info -r openldap
```

```
          Name: library/openldap
       Summary: OpenLDAP
   Description: OpenLDAP is an open source implementation of the Lightweight
                Directory Access Protocol.
      Category: System/Libraries
         State: Installed
     Publisher: solaris
       Version: 2.4.25
 Build Release: 5.11
        Branch: 0.175.0.0.0.2.537
Packaging Date: October 19, 2011 10:44:58 AM
          Size: 12.02 MB
          FMRI: pkg://solaris/library/openldap@2.4.25,5.11-0
.175.0.0.0.2.537:20111019T104458Z
```

Setting Up an LDAP Client

Oracle Solaris 11 includes an LDAP client. Begin by initializing with the **ldapclient** command:

```
# ldapclient init -a profileName=exprof -a domainName=enode3.example.net 10.0.3.17
```

This initialization includes the specification of a profile name, the domain name, and the IP address of the LDAP server. This process copies the file /etc/nsswitch.ldap to /etc/nsswitch.conf. It also creates or edits the file /etc/defaultdomain. Any files that are modified during initialization are first backed up to the directory /var/ldap/restore. As a result of this process, your system will no longer be configured for DNS resolution. This can be changed back. Refer to the documentation for DNS configuration to set up DNS resolution.

Setting Up an LDAP Server

Configurations for the LDAP server are located in the directory /etc/openldap. The OpenLDAP server and client are controlled through SMF. The services aren't enabled by default:

```
# svcs -a |grep ldap
disabled       Mar_28    svc:/network/ldap/client:default
disabled       22:56:29  svc:/network/ldap/server:openldap_24
```

Enabling the LDAP server is similar to any other service that's managed through SMF:

```
# svcadm enable svc:/network/ldap/server:openldap_24
```

At the time of this writing, it appears there is a problem with the openldap_24 service. The service transitions to maintenance mode and shuts down after running for a few minutes. Another way to start the ldap server is to call it directly without the use of SMF. This will hopefully be addressed and resolved in upcoming releases of Oracle Solaris 11.

```
# /lib/svc/method/ldap-olslapd start
```

Oracle Solaris 11 doesn't include a graphical tool for managing the LDAP server, but the open source Webmin software includes the "LDAP Users and Groups" and "LDAP Server" modules.

An LDAP Data Interchange Format File

The LDAP Data Interchange Format (LDIF) file contains directory information or a description of a set of changes made to the entries stored in an LDAP directory. The information in the LDIF file may be information about the users, servers, printers, or other items existing on a network. It is a plain-text file that can be used to export data records from or input data records into the LDAP server. Because it is plain text, it can be hand-edited and is fairly easy to understand. This allows for quick and easy manipulation of the records without need of complicated management tools. Of course, both command-line and graphical LDAP management tools are available. There are quite a few graphical tools for browsing and editing an LDAP directory. These tools can certainly relieve administrators from needing to manually edit LDIF files because they can get very large. However, understanding the fundamental format and contents of an LDIF file is a recommended skill for any enterprise systems or security administrator. The LDIF file describes entities using a set of description fields containing the user's attributes. The LDIF fields are as follows:

- **dn** Distinguished Name
- **dc** Domain Component
- **ou** Organization Unit
- **cn** Common Name

The following is a sample entry in an LDIF file:

```
dn: uid=alan,ou=People,dc=example,dc=net
uid: alan
cn: Alan Formy-Duval
```

Here's an example of a standard user on an Oracle Solaris system. The entry contains information needed to add the user jford and much of the usual UNIX account attributes with which any system administrator should be familiar:

```
dn: uid=jford,ou=people,dc=example,dc=net
cn: jford
uidNumber: 1107
gidNumber: 1
gecos: Jim Ford
homeDirectory: /export/home/jford
loginShell: /bin/bash
creatorsName: cn=directory manager,ou=profile,dc=example,dc=net
createTimestamp: 20120219152758Z
objectClass: posixAccount
objectClass: shadowAccount
objectClass: account
uid: jford
userPassword: {crypt}$1$Q6wQlx04$lgbtnNmPDR3Mjgn6IMgNus
shadowMin: 7
shadowMax: 45
shadowWarning 7
```

Now, if we wanted to change the login shell for the user jford, we can use the following ldif file:

```
dn: uid=jford,ou=people,dc=example,dc=net
changetype: modify
replace: loginShell
loginShell: /bin/csh
```

Importing an Object

Let's look at a brief example of how we can import the data that is stored in an ldif file into the LDAP directory. First, an ldif file is created:

```
# cat ch11.ldif
dn: dc=example,dc=net
objectclass: dcObject
objectclass: organization
o: elevenhome
dc: example

dn: cn=Manager,dc=example,dc=net
objectclass: organizationalRole
cn: Manager
```

Now, use the **ldapadd** command:

```
# ldapadd -v -D "cn=Manager,dc=example,dc=net" -w secret -f ch11.ldif
ldapadd: started Fri Apr 13 00:48:48 2012

ldap_init( localhost, 389 )
add objectclass:
        dcObject
        organization
add o:
        elevenhome
add dc:
        example
adding new entry dc=example,dc=net
modify complete

add objectclass:
        organizationalRole
add cn:
        Manager
adding new entry cn=Manager,dc=example,dc=net
modify complete
```

The **ldapsearch** command can be used to verify the contents of the LDAP directory:

```
# ldapsearch -x -b 'dc=example,dc=net' '(objectclass=*)'
version: 1
dn: dc=example,dc=net
objectClass: dcObject
```

```
objectClass: organization
o: elevenhome
dc: example

dn: cn=Manager,dc=example,dc=net
objectClass: organizationalRole
cn: Manager
```

Another command to be familiar with is **ldaplist** for performing searches from an LDAP directory.

Client Profiles

A client profile for each server operating system on your network can be added and stored in the directory server. This simplifies client setup by centralizing the configuration. A client profile can be generated using the **idsconfig** command. The **idsconfig** tool is interactive. It first asks for server host information of an existing instance of Directory Server Enterprise Edition (DSEE). It then connects to the DSEE and prepares it to be populated with data and serve LDAP clients. The **idsconfig** tool can be used to maintain a set of attributes for each client host. These attributes must be specified by the system administrator.

A complete list of the attributes can be viewed by consulting the Oracle System Administration Guide: Naming and Directory Services. To run the **idsconfig** command, specify the full path (it isn't located in the default path). The full path is /usr/lib/ldap/idsconfig.

/usr/lib/ldap/idsconfig

```
It is strongly recommended that you BACKUP the directory server
before running idsconfig.

Hit Ctrl-C at any time before the final confirmation to exit.

Do you wish to continue with server setup (y/n/h)? [n]
```

Upon invoking **idsconfig**, you must set a name for the new client profile. A list of default servers should also be assigned using one of the following attributes:

- **preferredServerList**
- **defaultServerList**

The **ldapclient** command is used to set the local LDAP client attributes. These include the administrators' Distinguished Name (an attribute called **adminDN**) and their password (called **adminPassword**). The clients' domain name should also be set using the attribute **domainName**. If the client needs to use a proxy, those attributes can be set as well.

Extend LDAP to a Network

Now that the LDAP server is up and running, it can be accessed by other systems and applications across the network. Services that are capable of querying the LDAP service will do so using an LDAP URL of the form: ldap://host:port/DN?attributes?scope?filter?extensions.

For instance, in the URL, **host** would be the hostname of the LDAP server; **port** is the listening port. The remaining portion of the URL is the reference to the specific details of the entity you are querying within the directory tree. Refer to the Oracle Solaris 11 documentation and also that of the OpenLDAP open source software project for further details on configuration of LDAP communications. There are many different applications from different software vendors on the market that can take advantage of LDAP authentication. The Oracle Solaris 11 system hosting an LDAP server should be compatible with most, if not all.

LDAP and Other Services

LDAP has become the de facto standard for user authentication for many types of applications. Many companies that have web-based application services, such as Apache Tomcat or Oracle WebLogic, maintain a backend connection to an internal LDAP server for authentication and lookups for logins.

Summary

Oracle Solaris 11 is often employed in high-security environments due to its robust user and group management capabilities. This chapter covered the aspects of managing users and groups that give Oracle Solaris 11 an advantage in these demanding environments by showing how users, groups, and processes can be restricted through the use of Role Based Access Control. Oracle Solaris 11 makes obsolete the old "all or nothing" model, where allowing a user to perform sensitive tasks required pretty much giving their account full root privileges. The chapter concluded by illustrating how Oracle Solaris 11 also provides a stable base for running various information services such as NIS and LDAP.

References

The document "Oracle System Administration Guide: Naming and Directory Services" can be found at http://docs.oracle.com/cd/E23824_01/html/821-1455/ldapsecure-103.html.

The home page for OpenLDAP is www.openldap.org/.

Oracle Solaris 11 Information Library is located at http://docs.oracle.com/cd/E23824_01/index.html.

A Wikipedia article on the LDAP protocol can be found at http://en.wikipedia.org/wiki/Lightweight_Directory_Access_Protocol#LDAP_URLs.

The Internet Engineering Task Force Network Working Group Request for Comments: 2849 – The LDAP Data Interchange Format (LDIF) – Technical Specification can be found at http://www.ietf.org/rfc/rfc2849.txt.

Comparisons of LDAP to NIS can be found in the Oracle Solaris 11 Information Library at http://docs.oracle.com/cd/E23824_01//html/821-1455/intro2ns-5.html#scrolltoc.

CHAPTER
12

Solaris 11 Security

he Solaris operating system has a long and well-deserved reputation as one of the most secure general-purpose versions of UNIX. But as IT infrastructures are evolving to accommodate very-large-scale, virtualized, and distributed systems implementing cloud computing services, OS security features need to evolve as well, because many applications leave access and data protection tasks to the operating system. Oracle Solaris 11 is one of the first operating systems to meet the needs of cloud computing security; it includes such features as secure-by-default installation, built-in secure virtualization, limiting the privileges of the root user, securing data with encryption, auditing of all system events, and protection against common hacking exploits. In addition, it supports traditional UNIX file protections, password management, and network access controls.

In this chapter, we review the essential security features of Solaris 11, starting with the installation process and continuing with basic file access controls, password policy enforcement, user roles and privileges, auditing system activity, and controlling remote access.

Installation and Initial Configuration Security

At the initial installation steps, Solaris 11 provides a "secure by default" environment. This means that unlike earlier versions of UNIX that assumed a server's network services would always need to be immediately available, Solaris 11 by default recognizes only safe, local **ssh** communications during the install process, requiring all other incoming network services to be explicitly activated only after installation using the Service Management Facility tools.

root Is a Role

One of the first things you will notice after you install Solaris 11 is that you can no longer log in directly to the root account. The root ID (**UID=0**) is now a "role" whose privileges can be constrained; users who access that role can be monitored. Additionally, only explicitly authorized users can assume the privileged root role so that all actions under that role can be audited and attributed to a real user. The initial user you created at installation is assigned the root role; in that role, one can perform all the system admin tasks such as installing and managing software.

More about managing roles and privileges later in this chapter.

Hardening and Minimizing the OS Installation

Hardening an OS instance generally refers to reviewing and enhancing the default security configuration of the system—for example, by removing default execution privileges for certain programs or by removing default read permissions from sensitive files. *Minimizing* refers to completely removing files and services not explicitly needed for the specific purpose of the system—for example, by deleting web server software from a system that will not provide that service. Minimizing is performed to reduce the risk that inactive software that may have vulnerabilities could be used to compromise a system.

Every IT organization has unique, individual security needs and policies that can be applied to operating system environments. The U.S. Federal Government's Department of Defense (DoD), for example, has very strict security policies that must be enforced and are published as Security Technical Implementation Guide (STIG) checklists and Security Readiness Review (SRR) scripts for various operating systems, including Solaris 10; these have not yet been updated for Solaris 11, although an informal blog commentary on how the OS conforms to the guide can be found at https://blogs.oracle.com/jimlaurent/entry/solaris_11_compliance_with_disa. It's worth reviewing, even if your organization does not require security controls as strict as those for the DoD.

Oracle does not claim that Solaris 11 needs no hardening or minimizing; that decision is left to your organization's security policies. However, if you do need to modify Solaris 11's default security configuration, you can use the Service Management Facility tools described in Chapter 6 to disable unneeded or unwanted services, and the Image Packaging System tools described in Chapter 7 to delete unwanted application packages. You should display your organization's security policy and legal access warnings by placing appropriate messages in the /etc/issue and /etc/motd files that will be displayed when users first connect and log in. Other Solaris 11 security-related tasks are described in the following sections.

NOTE
The Solaris Security Toolkit (SST), also known as the JumpStart Architecture and Security Scripts (JASS), used to harden and minimize Solaris installations, has long been available for versions through Solaris 10. This toolkit is not compatible with Solaris 11 and should not be run on Solaris 11 systems.

Managing File Access

One of the traditional ways to secure UNIX systems such as Solaris is to control access permissions to files—restricting or allowing read, write, and execute rights. We review the basics of file access in this section, along with other protection mechanisms such as encryption and other access controls.

Basic UNIX File Access Permissions

For the purpose of controlling access to files, all UNIX-based operating systems categorize file ownership into three classes:

- **user (u)** The owner, usually the creator of a file, who has control over who else can use the file
- **group (g)** A named collection of users on the system who may be given access to a set of files
- **others (o)** All other system users not members of the group

Additionally, three access permissions are defined:

- **read (r)** Permission to open a file and read its contents
- **write (w)** Permission to modify a file
- **execute (x)** Permission to run a file (if it is a program) or to see the contents of a file (if it is a directory)

The combination of the type of user category and access permissions defines how a file can be accessed and who can access it. The **ls** program is typically used to display the contents of a directory; adding the **-l** flag will list the files' owners and access permissions. Access permissions are indicated using a 10-character string; the first (leftmost) character indicates the file type (using **d** for a directory), followed by three sets of three permissions each, the first set indicating file access permissions for the user (owner), the second for the file's group assignment, and the third for all other users. For example, in the listing

```
# ls -l
.:
total 11544
-rw-rw-rw-  1 hfoxwell staff     1823 Dec 18 11:41 cal2012.txt
-rw-rw-r--  1 hfoxwell staff      914 Apr 10 13:41 matrix.c
drwxr-xr-x  2 hfoxwell staff        3 Apr 10 14:06 MyJavaProgs
-rw-r--r--  1 hfoxwell staff  5773824 Sep 6 2011 Presentation.ppt
-r-x------  1 root     root        24 Apr 10 13:57 test.sh
```

the file cal2012.txt is owned by user hfoxwell, and is readable and writable by user hfoxwell, all members of the staff group, and anyone else on the system (generally a very bad practice). File matrix.c can be read but not written by any system users other than the owner and his group members. The file Presentation.ppt can only be modified by user (owner) hfoxwell, and program test.sh, owned by root, can only be read and executed by the root user. The file MyJavaProgs is a directory (indicated by the initial **d**) and is owned by hfoxwell; all other users can view the contents of that directory but are not allowed to write to it.

File ownership, group, and access permissions are modified using the **chown**, **chgrp**, and **chmod** programs, and only a file's owner or the root role can change its ownership or permissions. In the following sample listing, as root, we first change the owner of file matrix.c to user thomas and then change that file's group to mysql:

```
# ls -l matrix.c
-rw-rw-r--  1 hfoxwell staff      914 Apr 10 13:41 matrix.c
# chown thomas matrix.c
# ls -l matrix.c
-rw-rw-r--  1 thomas   staff      914 Apr 10 13:41 matrix.c
# chgrp mysql matrix.c
# ls -l matrix.c
-rw-rw-r--  1 thomas   mysql      914 Apr 10 13:41 matrix.c
```

Changing the owner and/or group of a directory uses the same syntax; to recursively change the owner or group of *all* files in a directory, use the **–R** flag on either command:

```
# chmod -R thomas MyJavaProgs
# chgrp -R mysql MyJavaProgs
```

We can combine these commands into one by specifying the required group along with the owner using the **chmod** command:

```
# chmod -R thomas:mysql MyJavaProgs
```

Changing file access permissions can use one of two different syntaxes: absolute mode, which uses octal numeric values, or symbolic mode, which uses letters. Table 12-1 shows the octal values and meanings for the absolute mode.

Octal Value	Meaning
400	Allow read by owner.
200	Allow write by owner.
100	Allow execute (search in directory) by owner.
700	Allow read, write, and execute (search) by owner.
040	Allow read by group.
020	Allow write by group.
010	Allow execute (search in directory) by group.
070	Allow read, write, and execute (search) by group.
004	Allow read by others.
002	Allow write by others.
001	Allow execute (search in directory) by others.
007	Allow read, write, and execute (search) by others.

TABLE 12-1. *Absolute Mode Permission Values for File Access*

Octal values for permissions are additive. For example, if you want a file to have read and execute permission for the owner and only read permission for the group, you add the corresponding octal values from the table (400 + 100 + 040 = 540) and then use that number to set the permissions:

```
# chmod 540 test.sh
```

Symbolic mode uses letters to indicate permission values:

- **u** The user's permissions
- **g** The group's permissions
- **o** The others' permissions
- **a** All permissions (user, group, and other)

Using the symbolic mode with **chmod**, you can indicate the user type(s) and the permissions. For example,

```
# chmod ug+rx test.sh
```

will add read and execute permissions to the test.sh file for the owner and group, and

```
# chmod o-w test.sh
```

will remove write permission for all others from that file. That is, the **+** symbol adds permissions, and the **–** symbol removes permissions.

In addition to the CLI tools for changing file permissions, the GUI File Browser lets you inspect and change a file's owner, group, and permissions (see Figure 12-1).

Additional File Protections: umask

Whenever you create a new file, it has a default set of file permissions. This set comes from the configurable system parameter **umask**, which is specified in the /etc/profile file. This parameter uses the same octal values as **chmod** and is subtractive; that is, permissions indicated by the **umask** octal values are disabled. The default system **umask** value is **022**; this means new files

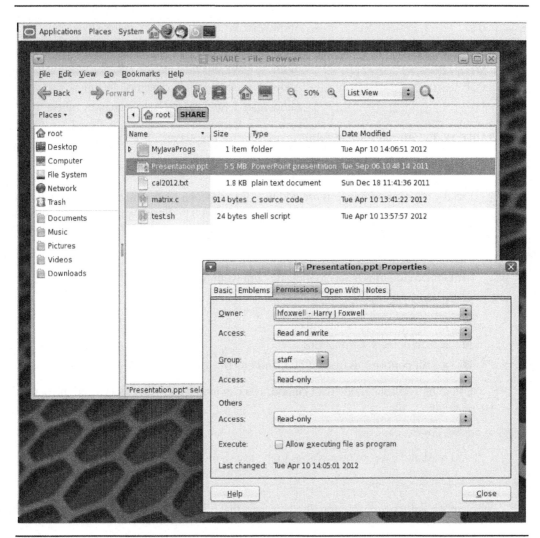

FIGURE 12-1. *The File Browser can be used to change the file owner and permissions.*

are created with write permissions for group (**020**) and for others (**002**) disabled. To see your default **umask** value, run the **umask** command with no arguments. To change your current **umask**, specify the octal values for permissions you want disabled. Here's an example:

```
# umask
0022
# touch newfile.txt
# ls -l newfile.txt
-rw-r--r--  1 root    root        0 Apr 11 17:23 newfile.txt
# umask 026
# touch newfile2.txt
# ls -l newfile2.txt
-rw-r-----  1 root    root        0 Apr 11 17:25 newfile2.txt
```

Notice that the default **umask** value is **022**; when we created file newfile.txt, it had no write permissions for group or other. When the admin changed the **umask** to **026** and created newfile2.txt, only group had read permission and other had no access permissions.

Additional File Protections: encryption

In addition to controlling access to a file, you can protect its contents using encryption. To protect a file in this way, use the **encrypt** command. First, you must decide what encryption algorithm to use; the **-l** flag will list available encryption algorithms:

```
# encrypt -l
Algorithm     Keysize: Min  Max (bits)
----------------------------------------
aes             128   256
arcfour           8  2048
des              64   64
3des            128   192
```

For example, you can use the **aes encryption** algorithm:

```
# encrypt -a aes -i Resume.pdf -o Resume.cry
Enter passphrase: #####
Re-enter passphrase: #####
# ls -l Resume.*
-rw-r--r--  1 root    root     1856 Apr 10 18:07 Resume.cry
-rw-r--r--  1 root    root     1823 Apr 10 17:53 Resume.pdf
```

The **encrypt** program will ask you to specify a passphrase and to verify it; be sure to record this passphrase for later decryption of the file:

```
# decrypt -a aes -i Resume.cry -o Resume.pdf
Enter passphrase: #####
```

This form of encryption protection is for individual files; see Chapter 9 for how to use ZFS filesystem encryption.

NOTE
*The **crypt** command found in earlier versions of Solaris is not supported in Solaris 11.*

Password Management

Passwords are the basic access protection mechanism for nearly all operating system and network service access. Choosing good passwords—and avoiding poor passwords—enhances system security. Here are some typical requirements for choosing good passwords:

- Avoiding simple words found in a dictionary
- Using passwords of sufficient length (usually six or more characters)
- Including a mix of upper- and lowercase letters, numbers, and special characters
- Restricting the reuse of old passwords

Whether or not passwords should be changed frequently is a matter of your local policy, although some security professionals claim that too frequent changing reduces security. Solaris 11 includes tools for using and changing passwords, as well as tools for enforcing password policies.

Changing Passwords

When a user is logged in and needs/wants to change their password, they can use the **passwd** program. This program does not echo back the characters entered by the user; however, the examples shown here reveal that input (designated by a bold gray color):

```
hfoxwell@narya:~$ passwd
passwd: Changing password for hfoxwell
Enter existing login password: S11forME
New Password: S11forME
passwd: The first 256 characters of the old and new passwords must differ ¬
by at least 3 positions.
Please try again
New Password: MyS11pwd
Re-enter new Password: MyS11pwd
passwd: password successfully changed for hfoxwell
```

The root user's password is changed in the same way; if you are already logged in as root, execute the **passwd** program:

```
# passwd root
New Password: r00t
passwd: Password too short - must be at least 6 characters.

Please try again
New Password: 123456
passwd: The password must contain at least 2 alphabetic character(s).
```

```
Please try again
New Password: S11r00t
Re-enter new Password: S11r00t
passwd: password successfully changed for root
```

The root user can change passwords for other users:

 # passwd hfoxwell
```
New Password: Sec.r3t
Re-enter new Password: Sec.r3t
passwd: password successfully changed for hfoxwell
```

NOTE
Only the root user/role can change the password for another role;
a role cannot change its own password.

Setting Password Policies

Password policies are configured in the file /etc/default/passwd; typical enforceable parameters
that can be changed are shown in Table 12-2.

Password Parameter	Meaning
MAXWEEKS	Maximum time period the password is valid.
MINWEEKS	Minimum time period before the password can be changed.
PASSLENGTH	Minimum length of password, in characters; good practice recommends at least eight characters.
HISTORY	Maximum number of prior password history to keep for a user.
MINDIFF	Minimum differences required between an old and a new password.
MINALPHA	Minimum number of alpha characters required.
MINNONALPHA	Minimum number of non-alpha characters (including numeric and special) required.
MINUPPER	Minimum number of uppercase letters required.
MINLOWER	Minimum number of lowercase letters required.
MINSPECIAL	Minimum number of special (non-alpha and non-digit) characters required.
MINDIGIT	Minimum number of digits required.
MAXREPEATS	Maximum number of allowable consecutive repeating characters.
WARNWEEKS	Time period until warning of date of password's ensuing expiration.

TABLE 12-2. *Configurable Password Policy Parameters*

Role Based Access Control (RBAC)

Early versions of UNIX had two types of users—unprivileged and root. Any task not able to be performed by an unprivileged user, such as creating system directories or allocating devices, had to be done by the root user. This user model resulted in administrators and developers using the root ID for nearly all tasks requiring special privileges, such as for installing and configuring software, and even for running general-purpose server applications such as web servers and databases. Unfortunately, this led to the abuse of the privileged root account as well as difficulty in accounting for who used it and for what purpose. It also provided a very tempting target for black-hat hackers to exploit.

A better approach to managing systems is to use the principle of *least privilege*—granting a user only the access rights needed for the task at hand and no more. Role Based Access Control (RBAC) implements this access model, and most modern versions of UNIX, including Solaris 10 and Solaris 11, now include it. In this section, we explain user roles, how to define them, and how to use them.

The All-Powerful root User

The root user in UNIX systems is assigned user ID 0. Earlier UNIX systems would check to see if a process was running under **UID 0**; if it was, it had full permission to perform any action on the system. This is why some application programs were often installed and run under the root ID, so that they could create and access files sharable among many users. Additionally, a special file permission called **setuid** could be used to execute a program as if the root user was running it. And although there are still applications installed in Solaris using this technique, their use is now being minimized through the use of roles and the allocation of least privilege (assigning only the process privileges required to perform a task).

The root user in Solaris 11 is now a role like any other user whose privileges can be explicitly defined and limited.

NOTE
*To find all programs on your system that are set to run as root (**setuid 0**), you can use the **find** program:*

```
find / -user root -perm -4000 -exec ls -l {} \;
```

Because creating or exploiting such programs is a favorite target of black-hat hackers, you should periodically review the output of this search for unusual entries.

What's a Role?

A *role* is a named collection of access privileges associated with an administrative job function, such as database administrator, printer manager, file backup operator, or password assigner; a *privilege* is a permission to perform some action on the system, such as modifying a file. Often these functions require privileged access to create or modify system files or to perform sensitive operations. In Solaris 11, roles are defined by named *rights profiles* that explicitly list the privileges for each system job function. Solaris 11 defines more than 80 such privileges controlling access to files, directories, network devices, and special applications such as **dtrace**. To list all the possible privileges and their meaning, use the **ppriv** command with the **-l** (list) flag, or additionally add the **-v** (verbose) flag to the command. Some of the key access privileges for each job function that will be listed include the following:

```
file_chown
    Allows a process to change a file's owner user ID.
    Allows a process to change a file's group ID to one other than
    the process' effective group ID or one of the process'
    supplemental group IDs.
...
file_read
    Allows a process to read objects in the filesystem.
...
file_write
    Allows a process to modify objects in the filesystem.
...
net_access
    Allows a process to open a TCP, UDP, SDP or SCTP network endpoint.
```

Roles are very similar to user IDs in that they have "login" names and passwords; roles are assigned rights profiles that define their list of administrative capabilities. Information on system roles can be found in the /etc/user_attr.d directory in the core-os file, which defines each system role's general privileges and specifies its profile. The root role in Solaris 11 by default has all "solaris.*" administrative privileges, although any of these can be removed if needed. Predefined rights profiles that may be assigned to roles include the following:

- **lp**   Printer management
- **adm**   Log management
- **netadm**   Network autoconf admin, network management, service management
- **netcfg**   Network autoconf user
- **zfssnap**   ZFS filesystem management

These roles allow authorized users, for example, to configure printers and print files, or to choose wireless or wired networks when they start up their Solaris 11 laptops. Additional end-user roles are defined in the local-entries file, which includes an entry for the first system user that was specified at installation time; this user is assigned to the root role. The **usermod** program is used to add a user to a role. For example, here's how to add user thomas to the root role:

```
# usermod -R root thomas
Found user in files repository.
```

Now user thomas can become the root role:

```
thomas@narya:~$ roles
root
thomas@narya:~$ su
Password: #####
root@narya:~#
```

New roles can easily be created using the **roleadd** program, which works much like the **useradd** program. Chapter 11 reviewed how to assign roles to users as their user ids are created or afterward.

Privileged Execution with sudo

Another solution to the problem of how to permit unprivileged users to run commands normally requiring special permissions comes from the open source community—**sudo**—and is now included in Solaris 11. This command, well known to Linux administrators, allows specified users to run applications as the root user. Such users must be listed along with their specific program permissions in the /etc/sudoers file. The **sudo** program also reports unauthorized usage attempts to the system console.

Suppose user thomas wanted to change the owner of one of his files, cal2012.txt, to user hfoxwell, an action normally prohibited:

```
thomas@narya:~$ ls -l cal2012.txt
-rw-r--r-- 1 thomas staff    1823 Apr 20 18:59 cal2012.txt
thomas@narya:~$ chown hfoxwell cal2012.txt
chown: cal2012.txt: Not owner
thomas@narya:~$ sudo chown hfoxwell cal2012.txt
Password: #####
Sorry, try again.
sudo: 1 incorrect password attempt
Password: #####
thomas is not in the sudoers file. This incident will be reported.
```

The system reports this unauthorized attempt to the system console and to the /var/adm/ messages log file:

```
# Apr 20 19:00:33 narya sudo: [ID 702911 auth.alert]  ¬
thomas : 1 incorrect password attempt ; TTY=pts/4 ; PWD=/home/thomas ; ¬
USER=root ; COMMAND=/usr/bin/chown hfoxwell cal2012.txt
```

But now the system admin adds user thomas to the /etc/sudoers file, and user thomas tries again:

```
thomas@narya:~$ sudo chown hfoxwell cal2012.txt
Password: #####
thomas@narya:~$ ls -l cal2012.txt
-rw-r--r-- 1 hfoxwell staff    1823 Apr 20 19:05 cal2012.txt
```

This time the change of ownership of the file is successful.

The **sudo** program predates RBAC by many years, and UNIX/Linux admins still use it instead of RBAC. Although both approaches are nearly equivalent—allowing users to execute programs with extended privileges—we recommend RBAC for Solaris 11 for its integration with the Service Management Facility. However, system admins who use both Solaris and Linux systems might prefer using the same tool (**sudo**) on both systems rather than different implementations of RBAC on each OS. Both **sudo** and RBAC on Solaris 11 require you to learn how to express extended user permissions and roles using special command syntax, so the learning effort is about the same.

System Auditing

Solaris 11's auditing system is enabled by default and keeps a log of security-related system activity, including especially the identities of users' actions such as all login/logout events. Auditing can be configured to log nearly every action or to log only specified sensitive actions. With the introduction of roles, auditing is now especially critical because users may assume new roles to perform privileged tasks; monitoring all actions of the root role *and who has performed them* is now both possible and essential.

NOTE
Anonymous use of the root login is no longer the default (and shouldn't be tolerated!) in order to administer the system.

The auditd Daemon

The **auditd** system daemon is a service that monitors and reports on system activity; it is enabled by default on Solaris 11 systems and is managed via the **audit** and **auditconfig** commands:

```
# svcs -l auditd
fmri      svc:/system/auditd:default
name      Solaris audit daemon
enabled   true
state     online
next_state none
state_time  March 23, 2012 10:08:01 PM EDT
logfile   /var/svc/log/system-auditd:default.log
restarter  svc:/system/svc/restarter:default
contract_id 117
manifest  /lib/svc/manifest/system/auditd.xml
dependency  require_all/none svc:/system/filesystem/local (online)
dependency  require_all/none svc:/milestone/name-services (online)
dependency  optional_all/none svc:/system/system-log (online)
```

Because auditing activity on a busy server can generate large amounts of data, you need to carefully plan and select what to audit, and decide where to store the audit log(s) and how often to review them according to your organization's policies.

Although auditing can be started and stopped via the **svcadm** command, the preferred method uses the **audit** command executed within the root role:

```
# svcadm system/auditd enable
# svcadm system/auditd disable
```

or

```
# audit -s
# audit -t
```

Unlike earlier Solaris versions, no reboot is required for Solaris 11 when stopping or restarting auditing. The **auditd** writes its files to the /var/audit directory using a compressed data format and using filenames that indicate the start and end of the auditing period. The following example shows an audit log file that started March 24, 2012 and concluded April 20, 2012 for server narya:

```
root@narya:/var/audit# ls -l 20120324020800.20120420192527.narya
-rw-r-----  1 root   root    7284 Apr 20 15:25 20120324020800.20120420192527.narya
```

To inspect the contents of these log files, use the **praudit** program, which interprets the compressed audit log date and prints it in human-readable format:

```
# praudit 20120324020800.20120420192527.narya
file,2012-03-23 22:08:00.917 -04:00,
header,64,2,system booted,na,narya,2012-03-23 22:05:01.357 -04:00
text,booting kernel
header,81,2,login - ssh,,narya,2012-03-23 22:08:33.061 -04:00
subject,root,root,root,root,root,988,3065907404,10160 5632 192.168.1.208
return,success,0
... (output truncated)
subject,thomas,thomas,staff,thomas,staff,9887,2272114335,10293 71168 192.168.1.208
return,success,0
header,132,2,sudo(1M) execution,fe,narya,2012-04-20 14:21:11.084 -04:00
subject,thomas,root,staff,thomas,60005,10179,134509924,10293 71168 192.168.1.208
exec_args,3,chown,hfoxwell,cal2012.txt
...
```

Notice that the earlier **chown** attempt by the thomas user has been logged. Audit log files should be periodically (frequently) reviewed for unauthorized activity according to your organization's security policies.

The IP Filter Firewall

Solaris 11 implements a version of the open source **ipfilter** firewall software. This software is used to control inbound and outbound TCP/IP network traffic to your system, typically to filter (or block) unwanted network packets from entering or leaving your system, thus reducing the risk of network-based system attacks. IP Filter can filter by IP address, port, protocol, network interface, and traffic direction; it can also filter by an individual source IP address, a destination IP address, or by a range of IP addresses. Solaris 11 provides both CLI and GUI tools to configure and manage the IP Filter firewall.

Configuring IP Filter

The IP Filter firewall service is not enabled in Solaris 11 by default; it can be started using SMF:

```
# svcs ipfilter
STATE      STIME  FMRI
disabled   16:44:25 svc:/network/ipfilter:default
# svcadm enable ipfilter
```

As we have seen with other services, you can list details of the **ipfilter** firewall, as done next. You can see its full FMRI, state, logfile, configuration manifest, and dependencies.

```
# svcs -l ipfilter
fmri    svc:/network/ipfilter:default
name    IP Filter
```

```
enabled    true
state      online
next_state none
state_time April 22, 2012 04:49:06 PM EDT
logfile    /var/svc/log/network-ipfilter:default.log
restarter  svc:/system/svc/restarter:default
contract_id 492
manifest   /lib/svc/manifest/network/ipfilter.xml
manifest   /lib/svc/manifest/network/network-location.xml
dependency optional_all/none svc:/network/location:default (online)
dependency require_all/none svc:/system/filesystem/minimal (online)
dependency require_all/restart svc:/network/physical:default (online)
dependency require_all/restart svc:/system/identity:node (online)
dependency require_all/restart svc:/system/identity:domain (online)
# ps -ef | grep ipf
  root 6382 1149  0 16:49:33 pts/3    0:00 grep ipf
  root 6366    1  0 16:49:06 ?        0:00 /lib/svc/bin/svc.ipfd
```

Starting it in this way from the command line starts up the **svc.ipfd** daemon, which is the firewall packet filter itself. The configuration rules for the firewall are usually read from the /etc/ipf/ipf.conf file, which initially has no entries; they must be specified according to your organization's network access policies.

The IP Filter **firewall** can be easily started and managed by the administrator using the Service Firewall GUI, accessed from the main GNOME window, by selecting the System | Administration | System Firewall menu option (see Figure 12-2).

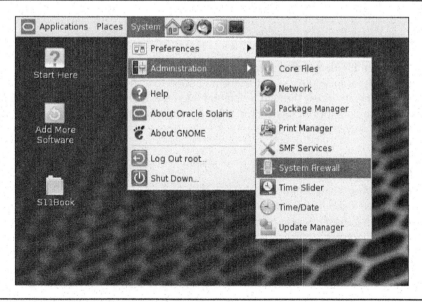

FIGURE 12-2. *The System Firewall menu option*

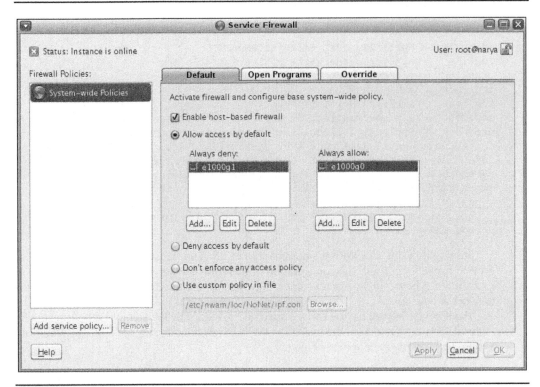

FIGURE 12-3. *The Service Firewall GUI*

Firewall allow/deny rules for inbound and outbound traffic are specified using the Service Firewall GUI; for example, you can deny all access to a specific network interface (e1000g0) while allowing all access through a different interface (e1000g1), as shown in Figure 12-3. You can configure port-specific access for applications through this interface as well as specify rules for common network protocols.

Remote Access

Most access to systems will not be through the physical console of each machine but through remote logins. It should be common practice by now to avoid the use of **telnet** and similar programs that transmit system passwords "in the clear" (that is, unencrypted). Remote access should use encrypted services such as **ssh**, the secure remote login client. Such access requires the destination system to enable an **ssh** server that listens for **ssh** client connections.

NOTE
*The **telnet** and **ftp** services are disabled (part of Solaris's "Secure by Default" design); the administrator can enable them if necessary but should only do so when **ssh** and other methods are not available or are incompatible with the task to be performed.*

The ssh Server

The Secure Shell daemon (**sshd**) is the program on a destination system for serving remote **ssh** clients. It provides secure encrypted communications between two untrusted hosts over assumed insecure networks. This daemon manages password authentication and enables safe remote execution of programs as well as encrypted data transfers. This service is enabled by default on Solaris 11 and is managed by SMF:

```
# svcs -l ssh
fmri        svc:/network/ssh:default
name        SSH server
enabled     true
state       online
next_state  none
state_time  March 23, 2012 10:07:49 PM EDT
logfile     /var/svc/log/network-ssh:default.log
restarter   svc:/system/svc/restarter:default
contract_id 108
manifest    /etc/svc/profile/generic.xml
manifest    /lib/svc/manifest/network/ssh.xml
dependency  require_all/none svc:/system/filesystem/local (online)
dependency  optional_all/none svc:/system/filesystem/autofs (online)
dependency  require_all/none svc:/network/loopback (online)
dependency  require_all/none svc:/network/physical:default (online)
dependency  require_all/none svc:/system/cryptosvc (online)
dependency  require_all/none svc:/system/utmp (online)
dependency  optional_all/error svc:/network/ipfilter:default (disabled)
dependency  require_all/restart file://localhost/etc/ssh/sshd_config (online)
```

Note that among the listed dependencies (the last line of the preceding output) is the /etc/ssh/sshd_config configuration file, which enforces remote login permissions. If this file is missing, the **sshd** service will not start.

The ssh Client

The **ssh** (Secure Shell) program is used to log into a remote system for the purpose of executing commands on that system. The syntax for remote login is

```
$ ssh username@remotehost
```

or

```
$ ssh username@IPaddress
```

Here's an example:

```
$ ssh thomas@narya
```

or

```
$ ssh thomas@192.168.1.201
```

The **sshd** service at the destination will require that you have an ID on the system and will prompt for your password; upon login, you can access and execute whatever your privileges on that system permit. It's often useful to log in remotely and run GUI applications on the server that display back to the client; in that case, you should include the **-X** flag:

```
$ ssh -X thomas@narya
```

Additionally, you can use the **sftp** program to transfer files between your client and a remote server; **sftp** replaces the older (unencrypted) **ftp** service:

```
thomas@vilya:~$ sftp thomas@narya
Connecting to narya...
The authenticity of host 'narya (::1)' can't be established.
RSA key fingerprint is 52:ce:0e:df:14:42:6b:12:3a:b1:58:09:97:0e:27:2a.
Are you sure you want to continue connecting (yes/no)? yes
Warning: Permanently added 'narya' (RSA) to the list of known hosts.
Password: #####
sftp> put cal2012.txt cal2012a.txt
Uploading cal2012.txt to /home/thomas/cal2012a.txt
cal2012.txt                    100% 1823   1.8KB/s   00:01
sftp> bye
thomas@narya:~$
```

Logging in Directly as Root—Since You Asked

Okay, you know the risks and policy issues, but you *still* want to log into your system directly as root. *Bad* sysadmin! So, since you asked, here's how:

1. Edit the /etc/ssh/sshd_config file to include the following line:

   ```
   PermitRootLogin=yes
   ```

2. Edit the /etc/default/login file and comment out this line (insert # at the start-of-line):

   ```
   CONSOLE=/dev/login
   ```

3. Make root a normal user like it has always been:

   ```
   rolemod -K type=normal root
   ```

Okay, now you can log in as root. But we warned you! The person logging in as root cannot be audited and the audit record will not include a regular user's name.

The first time a user connects to a remote system using **ssh** or **sftp**, the **sshd** daemon authenticates the connection and records it as one of the user's "known hosts" in the user's $HOME/.ssh/known_ hosts file; that step does not need to be repeated upon subsequent connections.

Another Security Feature

Modern UNIX operating systems such as Solaris 11 have additional features to enhance system security and to reduce the risk of malicious usage, such as preventing buffer overflow exploits.

One of the most common system attacks is the buffer overflow. This technique writes more input into a program's data input area than the original programmer intended, seeking to place executable code into a privileged area of memory, thereby gaining special or even root privileges. Some programming languages such as Java have the means to prevent this, but some, such as C, do not. And some operating systems, notably Solaris 10 and 11 and modern Linux kernels, include a feature that reduces the risk of buffer overflow attacks by preventing execution of code in stack memory. To enable this protection feature, edit the /etc/system file to include the following line:

```
set noexec_user_stack=1
```

The kernel normally logs all stack execution attempts in the /var/adm/messages file; you can disable such logging by including this line in the /etc/system file:

```
set noexec_user_stack_log=0
```

Both of these changes to the /etc/system file require a reboot to take effect.

Summary

Obviously much more can be said about Solaris 11 security than we have briefly covered in this chapter. We reviewed some essentials—file protections, password management, and the all-important features of roles and privilege control. We also discussed how to audit system activity. You should review your organization's security policies to understand how they would be implemented in Solaris 11; the "Oracle Solaris Administration: Security Services" document (referenced next) provides further assistance with that task.

References

The "Oracle Solaris Administration: Security Services" document can be found at http://docs. oracle.com/cd/E19963-01/html/821-1456/.

The Oracle Solaris 11 Security website is located at www.oracle.com/technetwork/server-storage/solaris11/technologies/security-422888.html.

The IP Filter is available from http://coombs.anu.edu.au/~avalon/ip-filter.html.

You can find the Oracle Solaris Security Guidelines at http://docs.oracle.com/cd/E23824_01/pdf/819-3195.pdf.

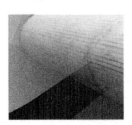

CHAPTER
13

System Performance

ystem administrators are generally responsible for ensuring that the servers under their care are operating correctly and efficiently. Therefore, they must be reasonably fluent in the tools needed for observing and managing system performance. Solaris has a long history of excellent performance as well as literally dozens of programs for monitoring CPU, memory, I/O, and network activity. In this chapter, we review some basic principles of system performance and introduce some essential tools for monitoring and tuning the Solaris 11 operating system, including a brief introduction to DTrace.

First, Know Your System!

You can't manage and optimize what you don't understand; you need to know the hardware and software components of your system and their capabilities. And you need to use the tools available on each system to discover those components and capabilities; if you believe you have purchased a system with 32GB of memory and a dual-core 3.0 GHz processor, then such tools will confirm that belief. Then, if your system does not perform according to your expectations, you can take informed actions—address the problems by tuning/adjusting the system or by replacing underperforming components. In this section, we discuss some of the tools for displaying your system's hardware and software characteristics.

NOTE
If you are running Solaris 11 on an Oracle server, additional documentation and specifications for these can be found at http://oracle.com/servers.

What Hardware Do I Have?

Solaris 11 includes two programs that can be used to list hardware components: **psrinfo**, which displays information about processors, and **prtconf**, which prints the system configuration. Each of these programs has a version that runs on x86 systems and SPARC systems, providing information appropriate for each architecture. Use the **-v** (verbose) flag to get detailed information. Here's an example on an x86 system:

```
# psrinfo -v
Status of virtual processor 0 as of: 04/24/2012 22:25:12
  on-line since 03/23/2012 22:05:00.
  The i386 processor operates at 2000 MHz,
        and has an i387 compatible floating point processor.
Status of virtual processor 1 as of: 04/24/2012 22:25:12
  on-line since 03/23/2012 22:05:05.
  The i386 processor operates at 2000 MHz,
        and has an i387 compatible floating point processor.
```

Here, **psrinfo** reports the speed and type of the processor; it will report multiple "virtual processors" for chips that have multiple cores.

```
# prtconf -v | more
System Configuration:  Oracle Corporation i86pc
Memory size: 8128 Megabytes
System Peripherals (Software Nodes):

i86pc
    System properties:
        name='#size-cells' type=int items=1
            value=00000002
(output truncated)
```

Here, **prtconf** reports voluminous output about all devices and interfaces recognized by the OS.

For a multicore SPARC T3 system, for example, you'll see many more virtual processors; Solaris 11 recognizes eight cores with eight threads each as 64 separate CPUs:

```
# psrinfo -v
Status of virtual processor 0 as of: 04/24/2012 22:47:24
  on-line since 03/28/2012 16:09:28.
  The sparcv9 processor operates at 1415 MHz,
      and has a sparcv9 floating point processor.
Status of virtual processor 1 as of: 04/24/2012 22:47:24
  on-line since 03/28/2012 16:09:31.
  The sparcv9 processor operates at 1415 MHz,
      and has a sparcv9 floating point processor.
Status of virtual processor 2 as of: 04/24/2012 22:47:24
  on-line since 03/28/2012 16:09:31.
  The sparcv9 processor operates at 1415 MHz,
      and has a sparcv9 floating point processor.
… (output abbreviated)
Status of virtual processor 63 as of: 04/24/2012 22:47:24
  on-line since 03/28/2012 16:09:32.
  The sparcv9 processor operates at 1415 MHz,
      and has a sparcv9 floating point processor.

# prtconf -v | more
System Configuration:  Oracle Corporation  sun4v
Memory size: 16256 Megabytes
System Peripherals (Software Nodes):

SUNW,Sun-Blade-T6320
    System properties:
        name='fm-capable' type=int items=1
            value=00000009
…(output truncated)
```

Often, when you call Oracle for hardware support, they will ask you for the output of the **prtconf** command for your system.

What OS Software Do I Have?

Solaris operating systems are periodically updated to include new features, bug fixes and patches, and to add support for new hardware. The first thing you'll be asked about your OS is what version of Solaris are you running. On either an x86 or SPARC system, you can use the **uname** command (adding the **-a** flag for *all* detail). Additional detail is recorded at install time in the /etc/release file:

```
# uname -a
SunOS narya 5.11 11.0 i86pc i386 i86pc
# cat /etc/release
                         Oracle Solaris 11 11/11 X86
  Copyright (c) 1983, 2011, Oracle and/or its affiliates.  All rights reserved.
                         Assembled 18 October 2011
```

The IPS system also provides details about the operating system's current kernel package:

```
# pkg info kernel
          Name: system/kernel
       Summary: Core Kernel
   Description: Core operating system kernel, device drivers and other modules.
      Category: System/Core
         State: Installed
     Publisher: solaris
       Version: 0.5.11
 Build Release: 5.11
        Branch: 0.175.0.0.0.2.1
Packaging Date: October 19, 2011 07:57:11 AM
          Size: 32.33 MB
          FMRI: pkg://solaris/system/kernel@0.5.11,5.11-0.175.0.0.0.2.1:20111019T075711Z
```

Observing Your System

Administrators are usually made aware of system problems when users call and complain that their response time is too long, they can't find something that should be there, or they can't connect to a service. More often than not, such complaints are due to end-user error, but when there is a real system problem, the admin must diagnose and correct it in a timely manner…usually "immediately." In this chapter, we discuss what to look for and the tools needed to observe and correct system performance problems.

What to Look For

The task of a system performance analyst is to identify and to eliminate or correct impediments to efficient system operation. Performance problems can arise from individual hardware components—disk, memory, CPU, and network—and from interactions among them, as well as from misconfigured applications or operating systems. Typical issues causing performance problems include the following:

■ Single-threaded applications
■ Too much locking/synchronization (especially with Java apps)
■ Too much context switching
■ Too many CPU interrupts

- CPU over-utilization
- Too many blocked/waiting processes in the run queue
- Insufficient physical memory (leading to paging/swapping)
- Too much or unbalanced disk I/O
- Slow or overloaded networks

To know when something is "too much" or "too slow" requires an understanding of what a "normal" or acceptable baseline level of performance is so that extremes or outliers of system metrics can be recognized. Then, when investigating performance issues, admins need to follow some basic performance and troubleshooting principles:

1. Characterize the symptoms.

   - Are they chronic, intermittent, or periodic?
   - Is the system/application just slow or has it crashed?
   - Is the problem reproducible?

2. Identify what *changed* before the problem occurred.

   - "Nothing" is usually the *wrong* answer!

3. When attempting to correct the problem(s):

   - Don't change more than one thing at a time.
   - Document what you change!
   - Be patient! Change one thing, measure, and repeat.
   - Tune before replacing. Know your system's capabilities and limits.
   - Work on the greatest return for your time investment. For example, don't spend too much time on an application's compiler options when the real problem is too much disk I/O.

Many system problems often arise from misconfigurations, missing items, or from incorrect or incompatible software versions; therefore, hardware and software installations need to be checked and verified for correctness.

How to Look: Observability Tools

First, you need to know who is using the system and what they are doing; your goal is to know exactly what the OS is doing. The **who** command will let you know what users are currently logged in, when they logged in, and from where they logged in:

```
# who
root        pts/1        Apr 25 18:12    (192.168.1.208)
hfoxwell    pts/2        Apr 25 18:12    (192.168.1.208)
thomas      pts/3        Apr 25 18:15    (192.168.1.208)
thomas      pts/4        Apr 25 18:17    (localhost:10.0)
```

The **uptime** command will list when the system was booted and how long it has been up, how many users are logged in, and three load averages for the system for the past 1 minute, 5 minutes, and 15 minutes:

```
# uptime
  5:28pm  up 40 min(s),  3 users,  load average: 0.92, 0.94, 0.68
```

The **w** command combines the output from **who** and **uptime**, and it includes additional detail about what users are doing (or not doing, indicating how long they've been idle). What's more, it's much easier to type.

```
# w
  5:31pm  up 53 min(s),  3 users,  load average: 0.93, 0.93, 0.72
User       tty            login@  idle   JCPU   PCPU  what
root       pts/1          6:12pm                  1         w
hfoxwell   pts/2          6:12pm    17                      top
thomas     pts/3          6:15pm    13                      bash
thomas     pts/4          6:17pm    14                      bash
```

The "workhorse" command for understanding what's happening on your system is **ps** (report process status); it has myriad options and variations, depending on the option flags and even their format. Here are perhaps the most useful flags:

- **-e** Lists every process
- **-f** Lists full details for each process
- **-L** Lists process threads

For example, the following abbreviated output of the **ps -ef** command shows key information about what's running on the system, including process IDs and their parents, user names associated with those processes, how much CPU time has been consumed by each process, and the name of the command that created the process:

```
# ps -ef
     UID    PID   PPID  C    STIME TTY        TIME CMD
    root      0      0  0 18:08:31 ?         0:01 sched
    root      5      0  0 18:08:28 ?         0:11 zpool-rpool
    root      6      0  0 18:08:35 ?         0:00 kmem_task
    root      1      0  0 18:08:36 ?         0:00 /usr/sbin/init
    root      2      0  0 18:08:36 ?         0:00 pageout
    root      3      0  0 18:08:36 ?         0:02 fsflush
    root      7      0  0 18:08:36 ?         0:00 intrd
    root      8      0  0 18:08:36 ?         0:00 vmtasks
(output abbreviated)
webservd    893    891  0 18:12:25 ?         0:00 /usr/apache2/2.2/bin/httpd -f
hfoxwell   1050   1042  0 18:12:53 pts/2     0:00 -bash
  thomas   3060   2056  0 18:17:36 pts/3     0:00 xterm
hfoxwell   1784   1050  0 18:14:18 pts/2     0:01 top
    root   1041    701  0 18:12:47 ?         0:00 /usr/lib/ssh/sshd
  thomas   3115   3060  0 18:17:45 pts/4     0:00 bash
  thomas   1934   1933  0 18:14:52 ?         0:00 /usr/lib/ssh/sshd
(output truncated)
```

Notice that user thomas is logged in remotely using **ssh** and running **xterm** (process ID 3060); should you decide that his process needs to be terminated, use the **kill** command, as follows:

```
# kill -1 3060
```

Two additional programs for actively monitoring system activity are **prstat**, a native Solaris tool for reporting active process statistics, and **top**, an open source tool familiar to Linux admins and now a part of Solaris 11. As with **ps**, both **top** and **prstat** have a great many command options for selecting process types and the ordering of processes in the constantly updating display. **prstat** is a bit more lightweight and has a lower observation effect on the system than **top**, but **top** provides a wealth of information in a compact, single-screen format. In Figure 13-1, we see an instant capture of the **top** command; it shows process and memory usage statistics, along with a constantly updating display of user processes. We immediately notice that user thomas is running a program, matrix (PID 5961), that is consuming a large amount of memory and CPU time. The **prstat** program displays similar information (see Figure 13-2).

Another command useful for observing multicore systems is **mpstat**, which reports a separate line for each virtual processor. Here's an example running **mpstat** every 4 seconds:

```
# mpstat 4
CPU minf mjf xcal  intr ithr  csw icsw migr smtx  srw syscl  usr sys  wt idl
  0    0   0  112   467  198 6648    4   17    4    0 12175    5  27   0  68
  1    0   0   58   286   46 5941    4   17    3    0 10406    4  18   0  79
```

```
last pid:  5962;  load avg:  1.01,  0.95,  0.62;  up 2+05:11:01          20:19:08
76 processes: 74 sleeping, 2 on cpu
CPU states: 49.8% idle, 48.2% user,  1.9% kernel,  0.0% iowait,  0.0% swap
Kernel: 218 ctxsw, 104 trap, 479 intr, 4917 syscall, 74 flt
Memory: 8127M phys mem, 6425M free mem

   PID USERNAME NLWP PRI NICE  SIZE   RES STATE    TIME    CPU COMMAND
  5961 thomas      1   1    0   12M   11M cpu/0    0:01 12.79% matrix
  5941 root        1  59    0 4636K 2664K cpu/1    0:00  0.03% top
  1138 hfoxwell    1  59    0   19M 7564K sleep    0:00  0.01% sshd
  1178 thomas      1  59    0   10M 4464K sleep    0:02  0.01% bash
  5535 hfoxwell    1  59    0   18M 7928K sleep    0:00  0.01% xclock
   420 root        1  29    0 7788K 4020K sleep    0:03  0.00% cupsd
   533 root        4   1    0   11M 9240K sleep    0:38  0.00% hald
   789 root       16  29    0   12M 8504K sleep    0:09  0.00% smbd
  1003 root        1   1    0   18M 7448K sleep    0:00  0.00% sshd
   891 root        1  44    0   18M 5380K sleep    0:04  0.00% httpd
   352 root        1  59    0 2584K 1396K sleep    0:02  0.00% dhcpagent
   653 root        4   1    0 6440K 3660K sleep    0:01  0.00% inetd
    77 netadm      8  29    0 4292K 2960K sleep    0:01  0.00% ipmgmtd
    11 root       12  59    0   15M   12M sleep    0:05  0.00% svc.startd
   790 root       29  29    0 7644K 4184K sleep    0:19  0.00% nscd
   260 root        7  29    0 4688K 3300K sleep    0:02  0.00% devfsadm
   895 webservd    1  59    0   17M 2136K sleep    0:00  0.00% httpd
    13 root       28  29    0   22M   21M sleep  147:33  0.00% svc.configd
```

FIGURE 13-1. *The **top** command display*

PID	USERNAME	USR	SYS	TRP	TFL	DFL	LCK	SLP	LAT	VCX	ICX	SCL	SIG	PROCESS/LWPID
6496	thomas	95	5.1	0.0	0.0	0.0	0.0	0.0	0.0	0	71	17K	0	matrix/1
6355	root	0.0	0.1	0.0	0.0	0.0	0.0	100	0.0	23	0	530	0	prstat/1
5	root	0.0	0.1	0.0	0.0	0.0	0.0	100	0.0	95	0	0	0	zpool-rpool/7
5	root	0.0	0.1	0.0	0.0	0.0	0.0	100	0.1	94	0	0	0	zpool-rpool/137
1178	thomas	0.0	0.0	0.0	0.0	0.0	0.0	100	0.3	3	0	67	0	bash/1
1138	hfoxwell	0.0	0.0	0.0	0.0	0.0	0.0	100	0.0	5	0	40	0	sshd/1
5535	hfoxwell	0.0	0.0	0.0	0.0	0.0	0.0	100	0.0	5	0	25	0	xclock/1
158	root	0.0	0.0	0.0	0.0	0.0	0.0	100	0.0	15	0	0	0	zpool-mypool/7
158	root	0.0	0.0	0.0	0.0	0.0	0.0	100	0.0	14	0	0	0	zpool-mypool/9
790	root	0.0	0.0	0.0	0.0	0.0	0.0	100	0.0	22	0	132	0	nscd/24
533	root	0.0	0.0	0.0	0.0	0.0	0.0	100	0.0	1	0	6	0	hald/1
1003	root	0.0	0.0	0.0	0.0	0.0	0.0	100	0.0	1	1	13	0	sshd/1
789	root	0.0	0.0	0.0	0.0	0.0	0.0	100	0.0	5	0	5	0	smbd/5
891	root	0.0	0.0	0.0	0.0	0.0	0.0	100	0.0	5	0	10	0	httpd/1
1002	noaccess	0.0	0.0	0.0	0.0	0.0	100	0.0	0.0	1	0	1	0	smtp-notify/4
1012	root	0.0	0.0	0.0	0.0	0.0	100	0.0	0.0	1	0	1	0	rad/3
786	root	0.0	0.0	0.0	0.0	0.0	100	0.0	0.0	1	0	1	0	fmd/27
337	netadm	0.0	0.0	0.0	0.0	0.0	100	0.0	0.0	1	0	1	0	nwamd/3
260	root	0.0	0.0	0.0	0.0	0.0	100	0.0	0.0	3	0	6	0	devfsadm/3
77	netadm	0.0	0.0	0.0	0.0	0.0	100	0.0	0.0	1	0	1	0	ipmgmtd/6
13	root	0.0	0.0	0.0	0.0	0.0	100	0.0	0.0	1	0	1	0	svc.configd/3
5	root	0.0	0.0	0.0	0.0	0.0	0.0	100	0.0	0	0	0	0	zpool-rpool/22

Total: 84 processes, 722 lwps, load averages: 1.01, 1.00, 0.86

FIGURE 13-2. *The prstat command display*

CPU	minf	mjf	xcal	intr	ithr	csw	icsw	migr	smtx	srw	syscl	usr	sys	wt	idl
0	0	0	0	308	103	99	10	12	0	0	3028	60	2	0	37
1	0	0	2	178	49	165	9	8	0	0	1697	36	2	0	62
CPU	minf	mjf	xcal	intr	ithr	csw	icsw	migr	smtx	srw	syscl	usr	sys	wt	idl
0	0	0	0	312	105	81	14	12	1	0	3186	69	3	0	28
1	0	0	1	193	50	196	8	14	1	1	1551	27	1	0	72
CPU	minf	mjf	xcal	intr	ithr	csw	icsw	migr	smtx	srw	syscl	usr	sys	wt	idl
0	0	0	82	567	312	345	52	26	8	0	5980	82	7	0	11
1	0	0	19	307	56	483	30	31	7	0	3245	32	8	0	61
CPU	minf	mjf	xcal	intr	ithr	csw	icsw	migr	smtx	srw	syscl	usr	sys	wt	idl
0	0	0	0	313	104	51	19	12	0	0	3992	83	4	0	13
1	0	0	2	222	59	228	6	12	0	0	730	13	1	0	86

(output truncated)

This shows statistics for the two virtual processors on the system; we see both CPUs are busy, and the number of system calls (**syscl**) seems quite high.

One of the most commonly used observability tools is **vmstat**, which displays details about the number of processes in the run queue (**r**), the number of blocked threads waiting for I/O (**b**), and the number of swapped-out processes (**w**). **vmstat** also reports context switches (**cs**), user (**us**) and system (**sy**) times, and CPU idle time (**id**), thus giving a high-level picture of system activity.

```
# vmstat 4
kthr      memory            page               disk          faults       cpu
r b w   swap    free   re  mf pi po fr de sr cd s0 s2 --   in   sy   cs us sy id
0 0 0 5966504 7005324 1546 1084 0 0 0 0 3 40  0  0  0  752 22552 12569 5 22 73
0 0 0 5539292 6584240 1400 5375 0 0 0 0 0 121 0  0  0 1181 9035   915 55  7 37
0 0 0 5548644 6590020 12 338 0 0  0  0  0  8  0  0  0  628 5002   291 50  2 47
0 0 0 5548952 6590328 9  92  0 0  0  0  0  0  0  0  0  545 4854   321 48  2 50
0 0 0 5549272 6590648 10 92  0 0  0  0  0  0  0  0  0  552 4741   264 48  2 50
0 0 0 5549584 6590960 9  92  0 0  0  0  0  0  0  0  0  515 4723   271 48  2 50
0 0 0 5549892 6591268 10 92  0 0  0  0  0  0  0  0  0  488 4734   285 48  2 50
0 0 0 5550080 6591460 10 92  0 0  0  0  0  0  0  0  0  530 4734   275 48  2 50
(output truncated)
```

Typically, an admin will first inspect these **vmstat** statistics and decide if they are abnormal in some way compared to a baseline for a well-behaved system. Here are some examples:

- **Low or zero CPU idle time (id)**   The CPU is very busy; not always a problem, but could indicate an overloaded system.

- **High number of context switches (cs) or interrupts (i)**   The OS is too busy switching among programs and doing no useful work, or being too frequently interrupted (typically to service device access requests).

- **High number of processes in the run queue (r)**   Processes are waiting to execute (but this number may be high on multicore systems).

- **Low value of free memory (free)**   Processes are consuming memory; may result in excessive paging/swapping.

After the admin gets a rough idea of where performance issues are occurring, if the cause is not obvious, then more powerful diagnostic tools can be used, such as DTrace.

CAUTION
If you are running Solaris 11 (or any other operating system for that matter) as a virtual machine guest, traditional observability tools such as these will generally not report accurate values for CPU utilization and memory allocation because the guest VM might be sharing these resources with other VMs.

Log Files

As we discussed in Chapter 6, services managed by SMF have their own log files that admins can inspect for diagnostic messages. For example, the **ssh** service's log file is /var/svc/log/network-ssh:default.log. Other OS messages are logged by the syslogd daemon; the /etc/syslog.conf file specifies what types of messages are logged and the location of the system log files, typically in the /var/log and /var/adm directories. For example, kernel events (such as new device attachments or hardware errors) are typically logged in the /var/adm/messages file; admins should inspect this file for indications of system problems. Some service log files are kept in the /var/log directory; for example, activity logs for the CUPS printing service are in /var/log/cups. Other log files such as sulog, which records root logins, are kept in /var/adm.

System Tuning

The Solaris 11 OS is fully multithreaded and highly scalable; it typically needs little or no help adjusting itself to increasing system loads and therefore requires minimal "system tuning," except for very specific types of application environments. Additionally, administrators should focus on ensuring sufficient memory resources and balancing disk I/O to get the greatest return on system optimization efforts, because changing kernel parameters rarely has any dramatic effect on performance.

CAUTION
Do not copy the /etc/system file from one system to use on another system, especially if they are not identical hardware architectures! Parameters set on one system are generally not relevant to other systems. Also, each new release or update of Solaris from Oracle might modify, add, or delete tunable kernel parameters, thus rendering existing optimizations irrelevant or incorrect.

Kernel Parameters

Some configurable kernel parameters are specified in the /etc/system file, which may be edited as needed to add or modify entries; any changes you make to this file require a system reboot to take effect. Each parameter has a name, data type, and range, which are specified in the *Oracle Solaris Tunable Parameters Reference Manual* (see the "References" section of this chapter), along with a description of the parameter's purpose and some advice on when it might be useful to alter it. For example, you could reduce the **physmem** parameter to test how the system performs using less memory.

Here are some parameters that might be appropriate to experiment with:

- **maxusers**   The maximum allowable number of active users. This parameter is also used to derive the maximum number of processes supported. Increase this parameter from the default of 2048 if you get "out of processes" system messages.

- **max_nprocs**   The maximum *total* number of processes (user and system) that can be created on the system. Derived from **maxusers**.

- **maxuprc**   The maximum number of *user* processes that can be created on the system. Derived from **maxusers**.

- **shminfo_shmax**   The maximum size of shared memory. Set this according to specified application requirements, such as Oracle Database.

- **zfs_arc_max**   The maximum size of the ZFS cache. Reduce this if the system is running low on memory for application workloads.

Other Resource Controls

Solaris 11 includes the ability to observe and change running kernel and process resource controls. This capability is typically used to constrain processes to a limited amount of memory or CPU utilization. The **rctladm** command is used to list available resources that can be set, and the **prctl** command is used to change their values. For example, here's how to limit process ID 2345 to a maximum of 30 seconds of CPU time:

```
# prctl -n process-max-cpu-time -s -v 30 -p 2345
```

This is handy for processes with an uncertain running time when you want to terminate them if they run too long. Additional changes of this type can be made, but consult the requirements of your application software before altering such OS behavior.

DTrace

Dynamic Tracing (DTrace) for Solaris was introduced with Solaris 10 in 2005; since then it has become an indispensible performance analysis tool as well as a foundation for usage analytics on Oracle's ZFS Storage Appliance. DTrace is built into Solaris 10 and Solaris 11; it is a powerful technology that enables administrators to observe every aspect of operating system behavior—from application function calls, all the way down to hardware interrupts. And because it is already an integral part of the Solaris OS, it can be used without impact on production systems to investigate performance issues. It is like an MRI brain scan for your Solaris environment…no invasive surgery required.

The primary administrative component of DTrace is the **dtrace** command, which can be used directly on the command line or can be used to run DTrace script files. It usually requires root permissions to run, although normal users' privileges can be augmented so that they can use it as well, which is particularly useful for developers. DTrace scripts are written in the D scripting language; this language's syntax is much like C and another UNIX tool, **awk**. And although becoming proficient in DTrace does require learning D, there are many prewritten **dtrace** scripts, books, and other resources contributed by Oracle and others in the Solaris user communities that administrators can use right away while they are still learning.

Some DTrace Tools

Solaris 11 includes a collection of DTrace scripts known as the DTrace Toolkit. This collection, originally developed by former Sun kernel engineer Brendan Gregg, is preinstalled as IPS package pkg://solaris/system/dtrace in the /usr/dtrace/DTT directory, and consists of more than 200 sample scripts for observing kernel behavior, disk and network I/O activity, detailed CPU utilization, application system calls, and many other OS actions. Additionally, Gregg has contributed several dozen DTrace "one-liners"—short, **dtrace** CLI commands that observe and display common performance diagnostics; these and other DTrace tools and learning examples are all on Gregg's website, www.brendangregg.com/dtrace.html, with even more on the DTrace developer community's site, http://dtrace.org/blogs/about/.

Some DTrace Examples

We will not delve deeply into all that DTrace can do in this book; see the "References" section of this chapter for more learning resources. But we will show a few examples that highlight DTrace's utility in observing system activity, taken from Gregg's one-liners.

To run a DTrace script, execute the command line, wait a while for it to collect some data from your running system, and then terminate the script with CTRL-C. DTrace will then display the performance information captured while it was running and stored in its run buffer.

For example, the following "one-liner" traces file-open system calls (when the call code is entered, which is a good time to catch it), and prints out the parent process ID (**ppid**) and name of the program (**execname**) that made the system call, along with its arguments (**arg1**):

```
# dtrace -n 'syscall::open*:entry ¬
{ printf("%d %s %s",ppid,execname,copyinstr(arg1)); }'
```

So when might such a trace be useful? When you are trying to determine what processes are opening certain files. To find this out, we execute this trace and see the following (abbreviated) output:

```
# dtrace -n 'syscall::open*:entry ¬
{ printf("%d %s %s",ppid,execname,copyinstr(arg1)); }'
dtrace: description 'syscall::open*:entry ' matched 2 probes
CPU   ID      FUNCTION:NAME
  0  141        openat:entry 26594 bash /lib/libgen.so.1
  0  141        openat:entry 26595 cat /var/ld/ld.config
  0  143     openat64:entry 26595 cat /etc/hosts
  . . .
  1  143     openat64:entry 26595 cat /etc/passwd
  0  141        openat:entry 26602 gcc /var/ld/ld.config
  0  141        openat:entry 26669 ld matrix
  . . .
```

Here we see that process 26602 (user hfoxwell's shell) is using **gcc** to compile the user's matrix program, which seems harmless enough. However, process 26585 (user thomas's shell) has used the **cat** program to display the system's host and password files. Hmmm, wonder what thomas is doing?

Another useful one-liner watches and reports processes that are writing to filesystems, a handy tool to determine who is consuming disk space:

```
# dtrace -n 'sysinfo:::writech { @bytes[execname] = sum(arg0); }'
dtrace: description 'sysinfo:::writech ' matched 4 probes
^C
  dtrace                                                    1
  in.mpathd                                                 1
  readlink                                                 70
  hald                                                     72
  svcprop                                                 160
  Xserver                                                 230
  bash                                                    331
  hald-addon-acpi                                         403
  sshd                                                    708
  Xorg                                                   1385
  gdm-binary                                             5641
```

```
gdm-simple-slave                                              20789
dbus-daemon                                                   33715
mkfile                                                   465567745
```

This short script listens for the **writech** (write character) system call, counts the bytes written to the disk, and displays a sorted array of process names. Again, recall that the script is started, allowed to run for a while, and then interrupted with CTRL-C, at which point it reports its data. We see in the preceding output that the **makefile** program has written millions of bytes. Who is doing this? The **ps** program will easily tell us:

```
# ps -ef | grep mkfile
hfoxwell 21402 15818    1 20:03:42 pts/3         0:00 mkfile 1G onegigfile
```

We can see that user hfoxwell is creating a 1GB file; we might want to ask him, what for?

Some Performance-Monitoring Guidelines

DTrace will usually not be the first tool you select when attempting to diagnose system performance issues. First, use **vmstat** and **iostat** to determine sufficiency of memory and balance of I/O among multiple disks—these are the major factors related to performance. After narrowing down potential problem areas, if necessary, call upon DTrace to identify the specific issue, using the prewritten **dtrace** scripts if possible.

NOTE
Admins who manage multiple system types should be aware of some differences between the output of Solaris 11 performance-monitoring tools and that of Linux systems. For example, the Solaris 11 version of **vmstat** *shows a column for swapped-out processes, whereas the Linux version does not.*

The Performance Monitor GUI

The GNOME GUI of the Solaris 11 desktop includes a handy visual performance monitor that displays utilization for multiple CPUs, memory and swap usage, and network I/O (see Figure 13-3). With this tool, you can check your system's basic health at a glance.

The Performance Monitor also includes a visual display of all filesystem components, including users' home directories. You can easily spot problem areas, like in Figure 13-4 where user thomas has run out of his allocated disk space.

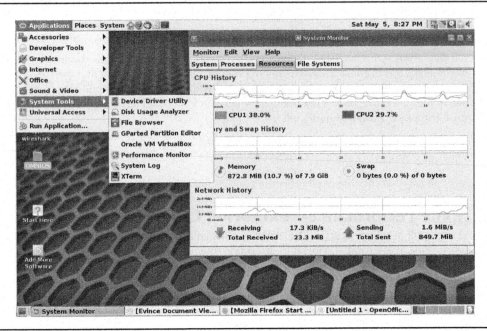

FIGURE 13-3. *The GNOME Performance Monitor*

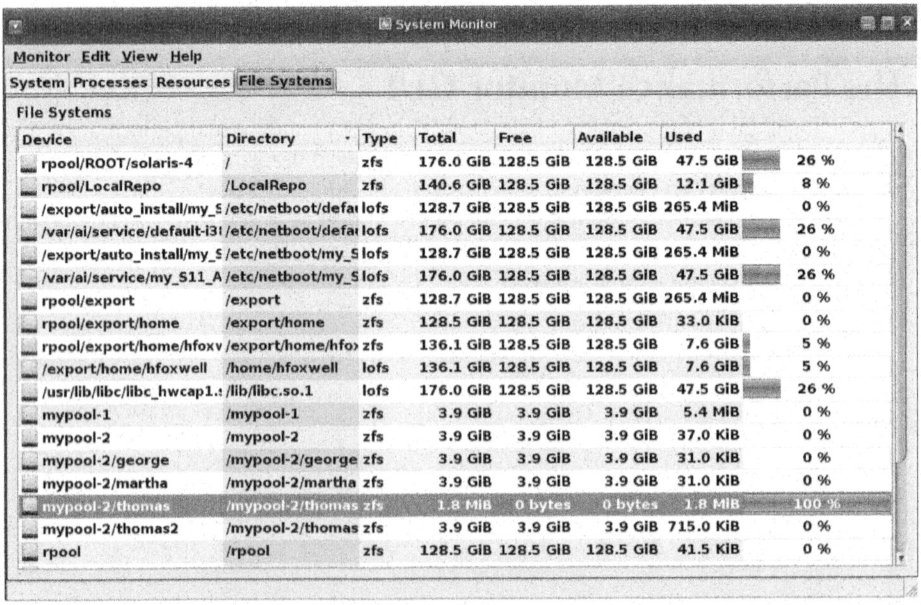

FIGURE 13-4. *The GNOME Performance Monitor disk usage display*

Oracle Hardware and Software Support

Oracle provides subscription support for its hardware and software customers, including "24×7" technical assistance to subscribers. This includes "Premier" support for all Oracle software—databases, middleware, applications, and both Solaris and Oracle Linux operating systems. This software support includes required patches and updates; *no such patches are provided without a support contract.* Operating system software support is included with Oracle hardware servers; details on these support services are available at the following websites:

- Oracle Premier Support for Software, www.oracle.com/us/support/premier/software/overview/index.html

- Oracle Premier Support for Systems, www.oracle.com/us/support/premier/servers-storage/overview/index.html

In addition, customers who have a valid Oracle support agreement can register, log in, and report bugs through My Oracle Support, at https://support.oracle.com (see Figure 13-5).

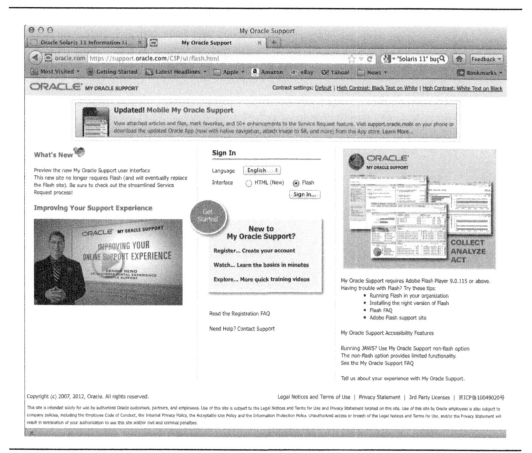

FIGURE 13-5.   *The Oracle Support website*

Summary

We have covered some very basic performance guidelines and system tools for Solaris 11 administrators. In this chapter, we emphasized understanding the capabilities of your hardware and software as well as discussed what to watch for when a system is not performing as expected. We briefly covered tuning kernel parameters, but emphasized that admins should focus first on changes that have the greatest effect and should allow Solaris to adjust itself to changing workloads. Also, we briefly introduced DTrace, a powerful OS observation tool that requires some practice and study to master. Together, all these tools let you observe and diagnose the key performance characteristics of your Solaris 11 systems—CPU, memory, disk I/O, and network traffic. Correcting performance problems might require altering configuration parameters of the OS or its applications, or might even require replacement or upgrade of hardware components.

References

Oracle Solaris Tunable Parameters Reference Manual (February 2012) can be found at http://docs.oracle.com/cd/E23824_01/html/821-1450/index.html.

Oracle Solaris Dynamic Tracing Guide can be found at http://docs.oracle.com/cd/E23824_01/html/E22973/index.html.

Information on the book *Solaris™ Performance and Tools: DTrace and MDB Techniques for Solaris 10 and OpenSolaris*, by R. McDougall, J. Mauro, and B. Gregg, can be found at www.pearsonhighered.com/educator/product/Solaris-Performance-and-Tools-DTrace-and-MDB-Techniques-for-Solaris-10-and-OpenSolaris/9780131568198.page.

Information on the book *DTrace: Dynamic Tracing in Oracle Solaris, Mac OS X, and FreeBSD*, by Brendan Gregg and Jim Mauro, can be found at www.dtracebook.com.

CHAPTER
14

Solaris Virtualization

irtualization has been a buzzword since at least 2006—virtualized services, virtualized network stack, virtualized OS—we can't read a new product or service pitch without hearing the virtualization angle. Zones are the Solaris implementation of one method of virtualization, and they have been present since the release of Solaris 10 in 2005. Zones in Solaris 11 have matured, as the network stack underneath them matured in the six years it took for Solaris 10 to "go to 11." We say "one method" of virtualization, because…well, let's back up a bit.

Introduction: Zones and Virtualization

Without getting pedantic, virtualization is a way of abstracting a set of physical components. As hardware improves in speed and power while occupying the same footprint, the need to have administrative control and ownership over what runs on the hardware remains the same. We still work in a world where dev guys want their own dev box, and the QA guys and testers can stay out. DB guys want their machine configured a certain way, but that configuration isn't standard for the web-dev guys. Production, well, production just *has* to have their own servers—they are everybody's bread and butter. And there's the security audit guy who says there's *no way* the forward-facing web servers are ever sharing a network with the storage backend, and *nobody*, but nobody messes with the security audit guy. Computing power (and budget) for five or six organizations now comes in one box, and virtualization is a way to abstract the physical so as to easily divide it up.

One way is to *really* divvy it up; a class of Oracle servers comes with firmware logic to allow components, processors, network cards, and HBAs (host bus adapters) to be grouped in a way that they are electronically isolated from other groups. An OS is laid on top of this group of components, and from this point of view, each OS "owns" its own hardware components. Software such as VMware runs in the space just above the hardware to present a set of abstracted resources to the OS running on top of the resources. Zones are something else; they are an abstraction of an OS instance. Zones present a nearly perfect simulacrum of the Solaris operating environment for applications. Applications behave similarly whether running on Solaris 11 in a zone or on Solaris 11 on bare metal.

A word of caution: Zones are not full virtual machines with their own instance of the kernel. All zones running on the same hardware, including the global zone, share the same kernel. The kernel provides the separation and the enforcement, as we will explain in Chapter 18. For this reason, live migration similar to VMotion cannot be performed on Solaris zones. If they need to move from one host to another, zones must be shut down and detached from their host.

Zones are fast and flexible, and they don't depend on a specific type of hardware or additional software. They are the virtualization silver bullet for an admin short on time and low on budget. They are quickly set up, torn down, configured, and corralled into shape. On SPARC or x86, regardless of the hardware, if it can run Solaris 11, virtualization is possible using zones.

Quick Tour with Zones

"You are in the server room. There is a table here. On the table is a terminal and keyboard. The cursor glows menacingly. It is cold in here."

Pardon the nerd name check. So you are at terminal on a host known to be running Solaris 11; you know nothing else about the box. Let's have a look around, shall we?

```
# zoneadm list -cv
  ID NAME           STATUS      PATH                          BRAND    IP
   0 global         running     /                             solaris  shared
   4 db             running     /zonefs/db                    solaris  excl
   - zclone         installed   /zonefs/zclone                solaris  excl
   - alpha          installed   /export/alpha                 solaris  shared
   - web            installed   /zonefs/web                   solaris  excl
   - backup         configured  /zonefs/backup                solaris  excl
```

With one command you already know a lot more than you did about this box. There is only one zone named "global" on any machine running Solaris; global is the "real" OS, the box, the host you are on. The rest of the zones are by default called "non-global" zones. They are all virtual. If you only see one line listing the global zone, that means no virtual zones are currently configured on this box. The global zone has knowledge of all the other non-global zones, but the reverse is not true.

The STATUS column is quite self-explanatory. A status of "running" means the OS instance is running—you can log into it, and it's ready for action. "Configured" is a state where you've articulated the name of the zone, its network information, and where its files are to live, but you haven't put packages into it so it can boot and run. "Installed" is the next state, where the zone has been installed but not booted. If a zone is being installed while this command is being run, you will see an "incomplete" status next to the zone being installed.

As to the zone ID, we don't need to care too much about that. That's the order in which a running zone has been booted. If there are gaps in the numbering, that just means other zones have booted and been shut down sometime in the past. On the right side, you see the BRAND and IP columns. For now, suffice it to say that all these zones are running an instance of Solaris 11. Here, "excl" stands for *exclusive-ip* and "shared" stands for *shared-ip* type zones, the two kinds that you can have. An exclusive-ip zone is one where the zone exclusively controls its IP stack, whether that stack sits on top of a physical NIC or a virtual NIC. A shared-ip zone is one that shares its IP stack with the global zone and possibly other non-global zones; in this case, the interface is usually a physical NIC. For our purposes, we'll be working with exclusive-ip zones.

Basic Zones Administration

We begin with some basic commands for zone administration: creating zones, checking zone configuration, installing zones, and the procedures to boot and shut them down.

Creating Zones

To create a zone, first we configure it. We give it a zone name, a place to put its files, and assign a network interface to it. That information is recorded as the zone configuration. Then we install the zone.

Zone Configuration

Let's imagine a very unoriginal scenario of web hosting with a matching unoriginal name. Caveat: Each zone is allocated its own dataset (see Chapter 9 for more on datasets), and its dataset cannot be in the rpool/ROOT dataset or immediately under the global zone filesystem root ("/") dataset.

zonepath specifies where the zone will have its files, and straight away specifying a zonepath in /web is a no-no; in fact, **zoneadm** will refuse. However, you can create a separate ZFS filesystem and mount it on /web—that would be no problem. To start off on the right foot, let's create a specific filesystem just for zones.

```
# zfs create -o mountpoint=/zonefs rpool/zonefs
# zonecfg -z web
web: No such zone configured
Use 'create' to begin configuring a new zone.
zonecfg:web> create
create: Using system default template 'SYSdefault'
zonecfg:web> set zonepath=/zonefs/web
zonecfg:web> set autoboot=true
```

zonepath specifies the filesystem hierarchy where the zone's root filesystem lives. Setting **autoboot** to **true** tells the zone to boot every time the platform is started or rebooted.

info will give you a rundown of what you've set so far, as well as what the /etc/zones/SYSdefault.xml template has filled in for you. Some resources are not configured.

```
zonecfg:web> info
```

Note that the **ip-type** is **exclusive** by default. An exclusive-ip zone requires a dedicated network interface, which could be a physical or a virtual NIC.

```
ip-type: exclusive
anet:
        linkname: net0
        lower-link: auto
```

net0 is a virtual NIC created automatically via the anet resource; it goes away when the zone is shut down. You can attach the linkname to another physical or virtual NIC presented in the global zone.

On my laptop there is only one active NIC, net0, which **zonecfg** has conveniently selected for me. If you are working on a box with more than one active NIC and you want to assign a different NIC, for example net1, to the zone, do the following:

```
zonecfg:web> select anet linkname=net0
zonecfg:web:anet> set linkname=net1
zonecfg:web:anet> end
zonecfg:web> verify
zonecfg:web> exit
```

verify does a configuration check (actually, it's more of a template check). For example, if you specify a net1, it doesn't check that you in fact have a net1, just that your "anet" resource has a linkname set to something. **end** denotes the closing block of a resource (in this case, "anet"). **exit** means you're done with the configuration.

So far, all you need to provide to **zonecfg** is the zonepath; setting autoboot is optional.

Zone Installation

For those of you who have worked with Solaris 10 zones, there are some significant changes under the hood. Solaris 11 has a new packaging system very different from Solaris 10. Packages can now be installed from remote repositories, so it's no longer a matter of copying and **pkgadd**-ing, but rather fetching. IPS caches packages, so the first zone install, in my experience, takes a bit longer than the rest, which can be done in a matter of minutes.

```
# zoneadm -z web install
Progress being logged to /var/log/zones/zoneadm.20120406T230221Z.web.install
       Image: Preparing at /zonefs/web/root.
 Install Log: /system/volatile/install.23014/install_log
 AI Manifest: /tmp/manifest.xml.T7aG7S
  SC Profile: /usr/share/auto_install/sc_profiles/enable_sci.xml
    Zonename: web
Installation: Starting ...
              Creating IPS image
              Installing packages from:
                  solaris
                      origin:  http://pkg.oracle.com/solaris/release/
DOWNLOAD                                PKGS      FILES    XFER (MB)
Completed                           167/167 32062/32062  175.8/175.8$<3>
PHASE                                         ACTIONS
Install Phase                             44313/44313
PHASE                                           ITEMS
Package State Update Phase                    167/167
Image State Update Phase                         2/2
Installation: Succeeded
Done: Installation completed in 194.554 seconds.
Log saved in non-global zone as /zonefs/web/root/var/log/zones/
zoneadm.20120406T230221Z.web.install
```

Zone Login, Boot, and Shutdown

Boot the zone and log into the virtual console using the **–C** switch. You'll be connected, you'll see SMF manifest import messages, and you'll be presented with the screen and prompt for system identification, as shown here.

```
# zoneadm -z web boot
# zlogin -C web
```

You are now connected to the web zone's console.

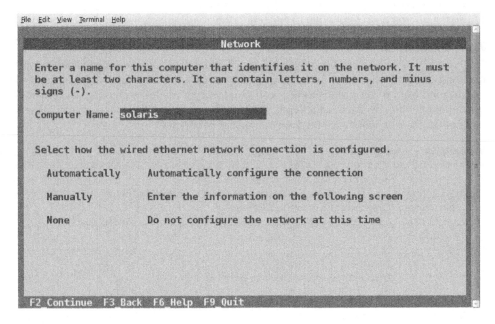

Zone Identification

Follow the prompts and supply the hostname, IP, default router, timezone, root password, and so on, when asked.

NOTE
You can bypass this step for a noninteractive zone installation if you use sc_profile.xml, the counterpart to the /etc/sysidcfg file that's been used up until now for system identification. See the "Tips, Tricks, and Pitfalls" section near the end of the chapter.

When done, you'll come to a console prompt. Ignore spurious error messages about sendmail, if any.

```
Exiting System Configuration Tool. Log is available at:
/var/tmp/install/sysconfig.log
Hostname: web
web console login:
```

Incidentally a zone can be booted into single-user mode:

```
# zoneadm -z web boot -- -s
# zlogin -C web
Enter user name for system maintenance (control-d to bypass): root
Enter root password (control-d to bypass): ********
```

```
single-user privilege assigned to root on /dev/console.
Entering System Maintenance Mode
root@web:~# who -r
    .       run-level S  Apr  7 02:04     S     0  0
root@web:~# exit
logout
svc.startd: Returning to milestone all.
```

Have a look around: **hostname**, **pwd**, **df**, **ls**, **ps –ef**, **ifconfig –a**, **svcs –a**. See anything different? You may find you have no disks if you run **format**, though. You're now working inside a zone; it looks just like Solaris, because it is Solaris. It's the same kernel running underneath.

The non-global zone is only aware of itself; it does not know that it's a non-global zone running on a platform with other non-global zones. It has its own process space, hostname, network identity, users, and timezone. Although it can shut down and reboot, it cannot change its configuration, resources, and privileges assigned to it, nor can it manage other zones. Nested zones are not possible. The only place to configure and install zones is the global zone.

Quit the **zlogin** console connection by typing **~.** (just a tilde then a dot) at the prompt. You'll be back at your working shell in the global zone.

There's a quick way to log into the zone without having to go through the console, using the safe login mode. You will automatically be connected as root. This connection is more like an **rlogin** connection, and you close it by exiting, not with a tilde-dot. You need to be root in the global zone to do this, though—or more precisely, the user needs to have the "solaris.zone.manage" RBAC authorization.

```
# zlogin -S web
[Connected to zone 'web' pts/5]
@web:~$ id
uid=0(root) gid=0(root)
@web:~$ exit
[Connection to zone 'web' pts/5 closed]
```

For non-root users, provided they have been created in the zone, use the following:

```
# zlogin -l <username> web
```

To shut down a zone from the global zone, use any of the following, although **shutdown** is preferred to **halt**:

```
# zoneadm -z web shutdown
# zoneadm -z web halt
# zoneadm -z web reboot
```

Resources and Zones

By *resources,* we mean things that can be allocated to a zone, which includes disks, devices, filesystems, physical or virtual network interfaces, memory, and processors. This is a good spot for a detour into the zone's child dataset. You may have heard the term *container* used interchangeably with *zones*. To be more specific, containers are resource-managed zones.

Zones and ZFS Datasets

In this section we introduce a zone called "db." A **zlogin** to a zone, followed by a command, is equivalent to executing the command from within the zone. Here are the datasets we see from inside the zone:

```
# zlogin db zfs list
NAME                         USED   AVAIL  REFER  MOUNTPOINT
rpool                        76.8M  163G   31K    /rpool
rpool/ROOT                   76.7M  163G   31K    legacy
rpool/ROOT/solaris-0         76.7M  163G   393M   /
rpool/ROOT/solaris-0/var     210K   163G   25.2M  /var
rpool/export                 21K    163G   32K    /export
rpool/export/home            1K     163G   31K    /export/home
```

No other dataset is visible, although we know that there are other zones and other datasets at the global zone level. From inside the zone, we create a dataset and call it rpool/database to distinguish it from the rpool/zonefs/db dataset:

```
# zlogin db zfs create -o mountpoint=/opt/mysql rpool/database
# zlogin db zfs list
NAME                         USED   AVAIL  REFER  MOUNTPOINT
rpool                        76.8M  163G   31K    /rpool
rpool/ROOT                   76.7M  163G   31K    legacy
rpool/ROOT/solaris-0         76.7M  163G   393M   /
rpool/ROOT/solaris-0/var     210K   163G   25.2M  /var
rpool/database               31K    163G   31K    /opt/mysql
rpool/export                 21K    163G   32K    /export
rpool/export/home            1K     163G   31K    /export/home
```

From the global zone, we see the following:

```
# zfs list -r rpool/zonefs/db
NAME                                     USED   AVAIL  REFER  MOUNTPOINT
rpool/zonefs/db                          76.8M  163G   34K    /zonefs/db
rpool/zonefs/db/rpool                    76.8M  163G   31K    /zonefs/db/root/rpool
rpool/zonefs/db/rpool/ROOT               76.7M  163G   31K    legacy
rpool/zonefs/db/rpool/ROOT/solaris-0     76.7M  163G   393M   /zonefs/db/root
rpool/zonefs/db/rpool/ROOT/solaris-0/var 211K   163G   25.2M  /zonefs/db/root/var
rpool/zonefs/db/rpool/database           31K    163G   31K    /zonefs/db/root/opt/
                                                               mysql
rpool/zonefs/db/rpool/export             21K    163G   32K    /zonefs/dbroot/export
rpool/zonefs/db/rpool/export/home        1K     163G   31K    /zonefs/db/root/export/
                                                               home
```

What we see from inside the zone as rpool/database is actually a child of the zone dataset rpool/zonefs/db; the mountpoint is similarly expanded from the zonepath.

The advantage of using a dataset is that you can take a snapshot of its contents and save it to a file. This is an efficient and simple way to back up any application or user data, independent from zone data, if that data lived on a child dataset.

Adding a Directory from the Global Zone

Zones have their own datasets that they can modify and manipulate. If you have data that is the same across different zones (for example, a common software or document location), it's not necessary to copy it into every zone. You can make the directory and everything below available to a zone by using an LOFS (loopback file system) mount.

NOTE
*Do not mount a directory from the global zone using NFS. For example, if the global zone's directory is global#:/docdir, do not issue a **mount −F nfs global:/docdir /my_docdir** from the non-global zone. The LOFS mount was created specifically for this purpose. You can be an NFS client of any other NFS server, just not of your own global zone.*

In our global zone we have a directory called /opt/helpdoc, which we want to mount into zone web instead of copying it and duplicating the information. You can mount this on the fly while the zone is running:

```
# mkdir -p /zonefs/web/root/opt/helpdoc
# mount -F lofs /opt/helpdoc /zonefs/web/root/opt/helpdoc
```

If the zone is shut down or rebooted, the LOFS mount will disappear. To make it permanent, you must modify the zone configuration to specify that directory as a zone resource. If /opt/helpdoc contains data you do not want modified or deleted, you can instruct the zone to mount the directory read-only:

```
# zonecfg -z web
zonecfg:web> add fs
zonecfg:web:fs> set dir=/opt/helpdoc
zonecfg:web:fs> set special=/opt/helpdoc
zonecfg:web:fs> set type=lofs
zonecfg:web:fs> add options [ro,nodevices]
zonecfg:web:fs> end
zonecfg:web> exit
```

```
# zlogin web ls /opt/helpdoc
help.index
# zlogin web touch /opt/helpdoc/foo
touch: cannot create /opt/helpdoc/foo: Read-only file system
```

In the previous snippet, you are telling **zonecfg** to add a resource, fs. Use **add** to add a resource, and use **set** to specify the value pair. **dir** is the directory point in the non-global zone, and **special** is the directory path in the global zone. In our example, we've mounted the directory onto a mountpoint of the same name, perhaps because users of the system expect to find the help documentation in /opt/helpdoc. You can mount the global zone's /opt/helpdoc into the web zone's /data or any directory path you chose, if you remember that from inside the zone, the **dir** is the directory name and the **special** is the special device (in this case, a read-only LOFS) you are mounting.

Zone Access to the DVD-ROM Drive

Using this same method, you can allow access to the global zone's DVD-ROM drive, or any other directory. For example, we have a Solaris 10 Release 10/09 CD in the CD tray, and we wish to grant read access to zone web:

```
# ls -l /cdrom
lrwxrwxrwx   1 root      root            19 Apr 21 17:59 cdrom0 -> ./sol_10_1009_sparc
lrwxrwxrwx   1 root      root            24 Apr 21 17:59 sol_10_1009_sparc /media/
SOL_10_1009_SPARC
# zlogin web mkdir /mycdrom
# zonecfg -z web
zonecfg:web> add fs
zonecfg:web:fs> set dir=/mycdrom
zonecfg:web:fs> set special=/cdrom/cdrom0
zonecfg:web:fs> set type=lofs
zonecfg:web:fs> add options [ro,nodevices]
zonecfg:web:fs> end
zonecfg:web> exit
# zoneadm -z web reboot
# zlogin web ls /mycdrom
Copyright                    boot
JDS-THIRDPARTYLICENSEREADME  installer
License                      platform
```

Be careful if you make a DVD-ROM LOFS mount permanent with **zonecfg**, because you will not be able to eject the DVD until the mount becomes free:

```
# eject cdrom
eject of cdrom /dev/dsk/c4t1d0s2 failed: umount: /media/SOL_10_1009_SPARC busy
```

Removing a Resource

To remove the LOFS mount, specify the fs resource and use **remove**:

```
# zonecfg -z web
zonecfg:web> info fs
fs:
        dir: /opt/helpdoc
        special: /opt/helpdoc
        raw not specified
        type: lofs
        options: [ro,nodevices]
fs:    <-- We want to remove this fs resource
        dir: /mycdrom
        special: /cdrom/cdrom0
        raw not specified
        type: lofs
        options: [ro,nodevices]
```

Specify the resource attribute: the resource is fs and the identifying attribute is **dir=/mycdrom**:

```
zonecfg:web> remove fs dir=/mycdrom
zonecfg:web> exit
# zonecfg -z web reboot
```

Incidentally, to change a resource attribute instead of removing it, use the keyword **select**. For example, here's how to change the mountpoint instead of removing it:

```
zonecfg:web> select fs dir=/mycdrom
zonecfg:web> set dir=/myother_cdrom
zonecfg:web> exit
```

Now we can eject the DVD:

```
# eject cdrom
cdrom /dev/dsk/c4t1d0s2 ejected
```

As a backup strategy, you can create in the global zone a /backup directory, with subdirectories corresponding to each zone. You can LOFS mount these subdirectories into the zone, with read-write privileges. The zone administrator can copy what he wants into this location, and the Enterprise Backup Software can back up from the global zone's directory /backup.

Adding an NFS Mount

Non-global zones can be NFS servers and NFS clients. The cardinal rule to remember is this: Don't be in an NFS relationship if you have a global/non-global relationship on the same box. Technically, non-global zones on the same box can be NFS servers and clients to each other, because technically they are not aware of each other and their location in the "universe." However, we don't advocate this practice. If you're working with zones on the same box, stay away from NFS. If you must share, use LOFS.

Mounting NFS in a Non-Global Zone

Suppose we want to mount my home directory from my Mac (192.168.0.4) on the fly:

```
root@web:~# mkdir /machome
root@web:~# mount -F nfs 192.168.0.4:/Users/christinetran /machome
root@web:~# ls /machome
Desktop        gr            Movies        Public        work
...
```

This mount disappears after reboots. To make this persistent and automatic on every reboot, we need to add the NFS mount to /etc/vfstab and enable the NFS client. Add a line like this to the web zone's /etc/vfstab:

```
# NFS
192.168.0.4:/Users/christinetran - /machome nfs - yes rw,soft
```

However, the NFS client is dependent on several other services, and if we only enable nfs/client, we will get a service that is offline. (See Chapter 6 for a definition of dependencies and service states.)

```
root@web:~# svcadm enable nfs/client
root@web:~# svcs -a|grep nfs
disabled       18:56:06 svc:/network/nfs/status:default
disabled       18:56:06 svc:/network/nfs/nlockmgr:default
disabled       18:56:06 svc:/network/nfs/cbd:default
disabled       18:56:06 svc:/network/nfs/mapid:default
disabled       18:56:07 svc:/network/nfs/server:default
disabled       18:56:15 svc:/network/nfs/rquota:default
offline        18:56:06 svc:/network/nfs/client:default
```

Recall that a service in the offline state means it's waiting on another service to become enabled. We need to find SMF services that nfs/client is dependent on, and enable those that are disabled.

```
root@web:~# svcs -d nfs/client
STATE          STIME    FMRI
disabled       18:56:06 svc:/network/nfs/nlockmgr:default
disabled       18:56:06 svc:/network/nfs/cbd:default
disabled       18:56:06 svc:/network/nfs/mapid:default
disabled       18:56:06 svc:/network/rpc/keyserv:default
online         18:56:11 svc:/milestone/network:default
online         18:56:12 svc:/milestone/name-services:default
online         18:56:14 svc:/network/rpc/bind:default
online         18:56:15 svc:/network/rpc/gss:default

root@web:~# svcadm enable nfs/nlockmgr
root@web:~# svcadm enable nfs/cbd
root@web:~# svcadm enable nfs/mapid
root@web:~# svcadm enable rpc/keyserv
```

nfs/nlockmgr also depends on nfs/status, so we'll need to enable that too:

```
root@web:~# svcadm enable nfs/status
```

We discover that rpc/keyserv is in maintenance, and that nfs/client is still offline. The reason is that the domain name, a relic of old RPC exchanges, is not set. Set the domain name, restart system/identity, and clear the maintenance state from rpc/keyserv. We made up the domain name solaris11.com, but it can be anything for our purposes.

```
root@web:~# domainname solaris11.com
root@web:~# svcadm restart svc:/system/identity:domain
root@web:~# svcadm clear svc:/network/rpc/keyserv:default
root@web:~# svcs -x
```

Notice that rpc/keyserv is no longer in maintenance. The next time the zone boots, we will have the NFS mount automatically. Reboot and log back into the web zone.

```
root@web:~# reboot
root@web:~# df -k|grep machome
192.168.0.4:/Users/christinetran   488050672   46842892   440951780   10%   /machome
```

NFS Sharing from a Non-Global Zone

nfs/server is automatically started on execution of an NFS share:

```
root@web:~# mkdir /var/webdata
root@web:~# share -F nfs /var/webdata
root@web:~# svcs -a |grep nfs
online         19:05:26 svc:/network/nfs/status:default
online         19:05:26 svc:/network/nfs/cbd:default
online         19:05:26 svc:/network/nfs/mapid:default
online         19:05:27 svc:/network/nfs/nlockmgr:default
online         19:51:38 svc:/network/nfs/rquota:default
online         19:51:38 svc:/network/nfs/server:default
online         19:51:57 svc:/network/nfs/client:default
root@web:~# showmount -e
export list for web:
/var/webdata (everyone)
```

Unlike NFS mount, NFS share survives reboots. The /etc/dfs/dfstab file is deprecated.

```
root@web:~# reboot
# zlogin web
root@web:~# showmount -e
export list for web:
/var/webdata (everyone)
```

Here's how to remove an NFS share:

```
root@web:~# unshare /var/webdata
root@web:~# showmount -e
no exported file systems for web
```

You can also disable SMF nfs/server and other NFS services for good measure.

Advanced Zones Administration

Now we're ready to wade hip-deep into zones. In this section we discuss allocating different resources to zones, and how to verify that we actually have those resources. We also walk through some tools to observe zone statistics and performance.

CPU Allocation

You can choose how much processing power to allocate to a zone, and whether that allocation is fixed or dynamic. You can allocate one CPU or a range of CPUs. For an unmanaged zone, all system processors are visible and available to the zone.

```
# zlogin web psrinfo -v
Status of virtual processor 0 as of: 04/21/2012 21:57:52
  on-line since 03/11/2012 11:06:20.
  The i386 processor operates at 2400 MHz,
        and has an i387 compatible floating point processor.
Status of virtual processor 1 as of: 04/21/2012 21:57:52
```

```
on-line since 03/11/2012 11:06:25.
The i386 processor operates at 2400 MHz,
        and has an i387 compatible floating point processor.
```

After we allocate one dedicated CPU to this zone, it shows one processor, with cpuid 0:

```
# zonecfg -z web
zonecfg:web> select dedicated-cpu
zonecfg:web:dedicated-cpu> set ncpus=1
zonecfg:web:dedicated-cpu> end
zonecfg:web> exit
# zoneadm -z web reboot
# zlogin web psrinfo -v
Status of virtual processor 0 as of: 04/21/2012 22:32:35
  on-line since 03/11/2012 11:06:20.
  The i386 processor operates at 2400 MHz,
        and has an i387 compatible floating point processor.
```

Dedicated CPUs will not be visible to other non-global zones on the system. We have another zone called db; after we allocate a CPU to zone web, zone db shows that it only has one CPU to work with, cpuid 1:

```
# zlogin db psrinfo -v
Status of virtual processor 1 as of: 04/21/2012 22:39:21
  on-line since 03/11/2012 11:06:25.
  The i386 processor operates at 2400 MHz,
        and has an i387 compatible floating point processor.
```

This system has a total of two CPUs. What happens when we try to give another dedicated CPU to zone db?

```
# zonecfg -z db
zonecfg:db> add dedicated-cpu
zonecfg:db:dedicated-cpu> set ncpus=1
zonecfg:db:dedicated-cpu> end
zonecfg:db> exit
# zoneadm -z db reboot
zone 'db': libpool(3LIB) error: Invalid configuration
zone 'db': dedicated-cpu setting cannot be instantiated
```

The db zone will not be able to boot; the same thing happens if we try to set **dedicated-cpu** equal to or greater than the total number of processors present on the system. If the other zone on the system shuts down and relinquishes its claim on the dedicated CPU, then db zone can boot, but subsequently the web zone will have the same problem.

```
# zoneadm -z web halt
# zoneadm -z db boot
# zoneadm -z web boot
zone 'web': libpool(3LIB) error: Invalid configuration
zone 'web': dedicated-cpu setting cannot be instantiated
zoneadm: zone 'web': call to zoneadmd failed
```

For this reason, you may want to use a range of CPUs instead of a fixed number. A range of CPUs means a number between a minimum and a maximum number of assigned CPUs will be dedicated to the zone when it boots, if those CPUs are available. For example. if your system has a total of eight processors, and you specify a range of CPUs as **ncpus=2–4**, when the zone boots, the system will attempt to allocate two, three, or four CPUs to your zone, if they are available. A range of CPUs allows some flexibility so a system can boot if a number of CPUs are available. You specify a range of CPUs as follows:

```
zonecfg:web> add dedicated-cpu
zonecfg:web:dedicated-cpu> set ncpus=2-4
zonecfg:web> end
```

The drawback to using dedicated CPUs is that once they are grabbed by a zone, even if the zone is idle, no other zone can use those processors, thus wasting CPU power. You can choose to manage CPUs by using a hard cap instead of dedicating a full CPU to a zone. The resource is **capped-cpu**, and the **ncpus** value is expressed as a rational number with significant digits—for example, 1.00, 1.25, 1.90. These translate to percentages—respectively, 100%, 125%, and 190%, with 100% meaning one full CPU. If you assign a capped-cpu resource, the zone can consume up to the cap without monopolizing any processing power when the zone is idle. For a machine with eight processors, a value of **ncpus=8.00** means the zone can use as much CPU power as is physically available—for all intents and purposes, no limit. A value of **ncpus=2.00** means the zone can use up to two full CPUs, and no more.

NOTE
When you assign a dedicated CPU, you are indirectly creating a resource pool underneath and attaching that to the zone. You can see a pool created for zone web, with output similar to this:

```
# poolcfg -c 'info' -d
                pool SUNWtmp_web
                int     pool.sys_id 3
                boolean pool.active true
                boolean pool.default false
                int     pool.importance 1
                string  pool.comment
                boolean pool.temporary true
                pset    SUNWtmp_web
                cpu
                        int     cpu.sys_id 0
                        string  cpu.comment
                        string  cpu.status on-line
```

The dedicated-cpu and capped-cpu resources are mutually exclusive; use one or the other. Remove the dedicated-cpu resource from your zone:

```
# zonecfg -z web "remove dedicated-cpu"
# zonecfg -z db "remove dedicated-cpu"
# zonecfg -z web
zonecfg:web> add capped-cpu
```

```
zonecfg:web:capped-cpu> set ncpus=1.25
zonecfg:web:capped-cpu> end
zonecfg:web> exit
# zonecfg -z db
zonecfg:db> add capped-cpu
zonecfg:db:capped-cpu> set ncpus=1.25
zonecfg:db:capped-cpu> end
zonecfg:db> exit
```

You can see the total **ncpus=2.50**, which is greater than the total number of processors this system has (two). This is possible because we are adding a cap, not a guaranteed minimum. It's possible that zone db is active when zone web is idle, so there's always one and a quarter of the CPU power for either zone. If both zones are active and competing for CPU resources, the cap still applies; obviously it cannot be 1.25 concurrently, since we are only operating on two processors.

NOTE
When you set the CPU limit, you are indirectly manipulating another zone resource called rctl (resource control). Here's the result of using a CPU cap, which we've previously set at 125%:

```
# zonecfg -z web info rctl
rctl:
        name: zone.cpu-cap
        value: (priv=privileged,limit=125,action=deny)
```

CPU Shares and the Fair Share Scheduler

A very sophisticated mechanism for allocating CPU resource is to use CPU shares. Unlike a dedicated or capped CPU, a CPU share provides proportional access to a CPU. It can be viewed simplistically as a guaranteed minimum. If a system is idle and no zone or process is contending for resources, a zone and its processes can consume all available CPU power. When a system is busy and other zones and processes queue up for the CPU, the system throttles down each zone to its guaranteed minimum. For this to work, you need the zone to use the Fair Share Scheduler (FSS), and you need to allocate shares to all zones on the system, including the global zone.

Shares are calculated in context of each other. On our system, we have the global zone, and the zones web and db. If we allocate one CPU share to each zone, we would have effectively divided the entire system's processing power into thirds. The same result is achieved if we allocate 10, 20, or 100 CPU shares to each zone. If we allocate two CPU shares to global, one share to web and one share to db, we would have effectively given 50-percent processing power to the global zone, and 25 percent to the web and db zone each. We could have made the math easier and more intuitive by allocating 50 CPU shares to global, and 25 shares each to web and db. The Fair Share Scheduler apportions CPU resources according to the weighting of shares as a ratio.

It's important to remember that share allocation is like a guaranteed minimum; if the system is idle, any zone can consume up to system's CPU maximum without penalty. No CPU cycle is wasted.

Using CPU shares is an all or nothing proposition. If you elect to use them, *all* zones must use them. It's not like a dedicated CPU where one zone can be managed and other zones not. If we allocate 20 CPU shares to zone web, and neglect to allocate any shares to zones global and db, effectively the ratio of global:web:db would be 1:20:1. The default CPU share is one, if not modified.

In the next example, we allocate a 50:25:25 ratio to global:web:db, and we demonstrate the result with a CPU consumer. First, we set the FSS as the default scheduling class on the machine and the zones and then reboot:

```
# dispadmin -d FSS
# dispadmin -l
CONFIGURED CLASSES
==================
SYS     (System Class)
TS      (Time Sharing)
SDC     (System Duty-Cycle Class)
FX      (Fixed Priority)
IA      (Interactive)
FSS     (Fair Share)
# zonecfg -z web "set scheduling-class=FSS"
# zonecfg -z db "set scheduling-class=FSS"
# init 6
```

Add 50:25:25 CPU shares to global:web:db, respectively. Incidentally this is one of the few times you can manipulate the global zone using **zonecfg** (remember that the global zone is really the mother ship).

```
# zonecfg -z global
zonecfg:global> set cpu-shares=50
zonecfg:global> exit

# zonecfg -z web
zonecfg:web> set cpu-shares=25
zonecfg:web> exit

# zonecfg -z db
zonecfg:db> set cpu-shares=25
zonecfg:db> exit
```

Observing CPU Allocation

We have a CPU consumer whose job it is to consume as much CPU as it can. We run it in each zone and observe that the Fair Share Scheduler throttles each process down so its CPU consumption is equal to the CPU shares ratio we've allocated to each zone.

```
# prstat -Z
   PID USERNAME  SIZE   RSS STATE   PRI NICE      TIME  CPU PROCESS/NLWP
  4963 root       22M   11M run       1    0   0:00:30  44% web.spin/1
  4964 root       22M   11M cpu1     27    0   0:00:22  38% db.spin/1
   307 daemon     14M 2868K sleep    49    0   0:00:01 0.3% rcapd/1
  1569 ctran      83M   48M sleep    59    0   0:00:07 0.2% Xorg/4
  1981 ctran     198M  127M sleep    58    0   0:00:09 0.1% java/23
```

Although only the web and db zones are contending for resource, their CPU consumption can be greater than the allotted 25 percent, because nothing in the global zone is competing.

After the global zone becomes a competitor for resources, the statistics settle toward the guaranteed minimum.

```
# prstat -Z
  PID USERNAME   SIZE   RSS STATE   PRI NICE    TIME  CPU PROCESS/NLWP
 8903 root        22M   11M cpu1     30    0  0:01:35  47% global.spin/1
 9099 root        22M   11M run       1    0  0:00:56  26% db.spin/1
 9086 root        22M   11M run       6    0  0:00:54  24% web.spin/1
  307 daemon      14M 2868K sleep    59    0  0:00:10 0.3% rcapd/1
 1981 ctran      198M  135M sleep    58    0  0:00:13 0.1% java/23
 8532 root        17M   15M sleep    59    0  0:00:07 0.0% svc.configd/17
```

Memory Allocation

Like CPU power, memory must also be shared among zones. You can enforce a memory cap, using one, two, or three limits: physical memory, locked memory, and swap.

A cap on physical memory limits the total memory footprint used by the zones and their processes. When a zone exceeds this cap, memory pages for its processes are paged out until the footprint is smaller than the cap.

Applications can lock memory—that is, prevent its text and code data from being paged out to a backing store, keeping it in memory. You can prevent memory-greedy applications from locking everything they use, to the detriment of everyone else, by setting a limit on how much memory a zone can lock. Keep in mind that not all applications lock memory, and some applications require the ability to lock memory to work. Know your application before setting this limit.

The third limit is swap, which limits swap space and tmpfs mount for the zone. If you decide to use **memory-cap**, you must specify at least one of these limits.

Here we set a 100MB hard memory cap for zone web:

```
# zonecfg -z web
zonecfg:web> add capped-memory
zonecfg:web:capped-memory> set physical=100m
zonecfg:web:capped-memory> end
zonecfg:web> exit
# zonecfg -z web info capped-memory
capped-memory:
        physical: 100M
```

Zone Performance and Statistics

Frequently used admin tools such as **vmstat**, **mpstat**, **iostat**, and **netstat** work the same way they do in the global zone, with the caveat that they present a view limited to the operating resources available to the zone. For example, **iostat –xnp** will not show the real device name. From the global zone, we want a bird's-eye view of how things are going in each zone. We've set several resource controls; we would like to know that they work. Even better, we should find the operating baseline before we set these limits. For this, you'll find three commands very useful: **zonestat**, **rcapstat**, and **prstat**.

zonestat by itself produces a comprehensive view of resource consumption broken down by each zone, and a total of what's consumed as a percentage of system resources. The format of the command follows all the other ***stat** commands, frequency followed by an interval.

To have **zonestat** produce one output every second, run the following:

```
# zonestat 1
Collecting data for first interval...
Interval: 1, Duration: 0:00:01
SUMMARY                    Cpus/Online: 2/2   PhysMem: 4027M  VirtMem: 5051M
                 ---CPU----  --PhysMem--  --VirtMem--  --PhysNet--
          ZONE  USED %PART  USED %USED  USED %USED  PBYTE %PUSE
       [total]  0.10 5.21%  2083M 51.7%  2815M 55.7%      0 0.00%
      [system]  0.01 0.80%   978M 24.2%  1578M 31.2%      -     -
        global  0.08 8.33%   991M 24.6%  1141M 22.5%      0 0.00%
            db  0.00 0.22%  55.2M 1.37%  44.2M 0.87%      0 0.00%
           web  0.00 0.24%  58.9M 1.46%  51.2M 1.01%      0 0.00%
```

For statistics taken every five seconds, use

```
# zonestat 5 1
```

For three iterations every five seconds, use

```
# zonestat 5 3
```

You can get a summary of memory usage, or specify physical, virtual, or locked memory, like so:

```
# zonestat -r memory -z web 1
```

or

```
# zonestat -r physical-memory -z web 1
```

A finer-grained tool to look at resource consumption is **rcapstat**:

```
# rcapstat -z 1
    id zone          nproc    vm   rss   cap    at avgat    pg avgpg
    59 web              -     48M   65M  100M    0K    0K    0K    0K
    59 web              -     48M   65M  100M    0K    0K    0K    0K
    59 web              -     48M   65M  100M    0K    0K    0K    0K
```

Wondering why there are two zones, web and db, and only zone web shows up in the statistics? It's because there's no cap assigned to the db zone: **rcapstat** only reports on zones where caps are in place.

We've capped the physical memory for zone web at 100MB. Here's a simple Perl program to allocate 200MB of memory. Cut and paste the following code snippet into a file, in a zone. Let's call it **grabmem**. Save and **chmod +x** it. Move it to a non-global zone. Open two terminal windows: one in the global zone, one in the non-global zone.

```
#!/usr/bin/perl
my $chunk = "1" x (1024 * 1024 * 200);
print "Grabbed " . length($chunk) . " byte memory chunk.\n";
sleep(900); # sleep so we can CTRL-C when we want
```

In the global zone, run **rcapstat –z 1**. In the non-global zone, run **grabmem**. What we're doing is mimicking an application running in a zone grabbing 200MB of memory.

```
root@web:/var/tmp# ./grabmem
Grabbed 209715200 byte memory chunk.
```

You will see **rcapstat** report the following:

```
# rcapstat -z 1
    id zone              nproc    vm   rss   cap    at avgat    pg avgpg
    59 web                   -   50M   70M  100M    0K    0K    0K    0K
    59 web                   -   50M   70M  100M    0K    0K    0K    0K
```

eventually changing to

```
    59 web                  38  450M  470M  100M 4496K    0K 3464K    0K
    59 web                   -  450M  470M  100M    0K    0K    0K    0K
    59 web                   -  450M   84M  100M    0K    0K    0K    0K
    59 web                   -  450M   84M  100M    0K    0K    0K    0K
```

There are a few things to observe. Most important, despite the physical cap at 100MB, the allocation for 200MB succeeded. The vm (virtual memory) and the rss (resident set size) column both increased by 400MB, then the rss column went down below 100MB but the vm column remained at 450MB.

Solaris memory allocation requires a reservation of equal size in swap; that's why you see rss and vm first went up by 400MB instead of 200MB: 200MB of real and 200MB of swap. The resource cap daemon kicks in, and you see rss size decrease to below the cap, but vm remains the same, because we did not cap swap. There's enough swap space to page out 200MB, so the total virtual memory consumed by **grabmem** is about 400MB, including 84MB of real and the rest in swap. Solaris pages to handle memory shortage.

If you were to add a swap cap, the result will be different:

```
zonecfg:web> select capped-memory
zonecfg:web:capped-memory> set swap=100m
zonecfg:web:capped-memory> end
# zoneadm -z web reboot
# zonecfg -z web info capped-memory
capped-memory:
        physical: 100M
        [swap: 100M]

root@web:/var/tmp# ./grabmem
Out of memory!
```

grabmem is unable to grab any memory because there's not enough virtual memory to guarantee Solaris can page out what's in memory.

NOTE
Know what your application's memory footprint is before you cap the zone. It's a good idea to cap swap and physical memory so the zone doesn't deplete the virtual memory or all available RAM.

Zones and Discrete Privileges

If you attempt to set the system time from inside a zone, you'll be prevented from doing so. We can see the logic of removing from a zone the ability to do some things. Zones are execution environments bounded by privileges. There's a default set of things a zone can do, another set of things a zone can be allowed to do, and another set of things a zone is absolutely forbidden to do. The first is the zone default privileges. You can see this by running

```
# zlogin web ppriv -l zone
```

sys_time is a privilege that allows a process to set the system time; you can see this is not among the default zone privileges, but it can be added. The privileges **dtrace_proc** and **dtrace_user** enable *some* DTrace providers, although these privileges are not in the default set of zone privileges. If you try to run a simple DTrace one-liner in a zone (in our example, we use a one-liner that counts system calls for each process), you will get an error:

```
root@web:~# dtrace -n 'syscall:::entry { @num[execname] = count(); }'
dtrace: invalid probe specifier syscall:::entry { @num[execname] = count(); }:
probe description syscall:::entry does not match any probes
```

You can grant *some* DTrace privileges to the zone by modifying the zone's set of privileges:

```
# zonecfg -z web 'set limitpriv="default,dtrace_proc,dtrace_user"'
# zoneadm -z web reboot
```

Now log in and try the previous command again, let it run for a second or two, and then press CTRL-C. You should get an output count.

You can add or remove privileges by overwriting with a new set of resource definitions; a zone reboot makes the new limit set effective. Here's how to allow a zone to modify the system time:

```
# zonecfg -z web 'set limitpriv="default,sys_time"'
# zonecfg -z web info limitpriv
limitpriv: default,sys_time
```

It should be noted that not all privileges are available to non-global zones by a matter of granting them. Some privileges are prohibited to zones—for example, **dtrace_kernel** (the ability to use DTrace to look at the kernel), **sys_config** (the ability to configure the global zone's sysid), and others.

More Zones Administration

Still with us? Terrific! We're ready to wade into even deeper waters for bigger fish. In the admin's tackle box there are tricks to clone, rename, and move a zone, and some options on how to back them up.

Cloning

The fact that zones have their own ZFS dataset means that zones can be cloned the same way ZFS datasets are cloned, and the new zone appears almost instantaneously. This reduces provisioning time, saves disk space, and ensures configuration consistency if you were building several zones from one clone. First, create a prototype zone from which you'll clone all others. Cloning preserves all the customizations made to the source zone, for packages and files.

```
# zonecfg -z prototype
prototype: No such zone configured
Use 'create' to begin configuring a new zone.
zonecfg:prototype> create
create: Using system default template 'SYSdefault'
zonecfg:prototype> set zonepath=/zonefs/prototype
zonecfg:prototype> set autoboot=true
zonecfg:prototype> verify
zonecfg:prototype> commit
zonecfg:prototype> exit
```

At this point, you'll want to boot the zone so that the zone's SMF manifests get imported. But to keep the configuration state pristine, do not proceed to the interactive **sysconfig** tool.

```
# zoneadm -z prototype boot
# zlogin -C prototype
[Connected to zone 'prototype' console]
(SMF manifest import)
```

At the System Configuration Tool prompt, type ~. (tilde-dot) and return to the global zone. Halt the prototype zone. The zone being cloned cannot be in the running state.

```
# zoneadm -z prototype halt
```

See the "Profile for Automatic Installer" section under "Tips, Tricks and Pitfalls" for how to create an XML profile. Modify that file to match the node name, IP address, root password, and so on, or find an old-style /etc/sysidcfg and run **js2ai** to convert it.

NOTE
js2ai is a script that converts the familiar sysidcfg file to an XML format, used to configure zones.

Configure a new zone using the prototype's template. Modify the new zone's configuration so it doesn't overlap with the source. For example, the source's zonepath is /zonefs/prototype, and you have to modify the new zone's zonepath so it doesn't collide with /zonefs/prototype. Then invoke the **zoneadm clone** command and specify the path to the profile XML. In the following example, we clone a new zone called data-silo from prototype:

```
# zonecfg -z data-silo "create -t prototype"
# zonecfg -z data-silo "set zonepath=/zonefs/data-silo"
# zoneadm -z data-silo clone -c /tmp/myprofile.xml prototype
A ZFS file system has been created for this zone. ...
```

Boot the zone and log in normally; you should not need the **sysconfig** tool if you've provided a valid profile.xml.

```
# zoneadm -z data-silo boot
# zlogin -S data-silo
```

Show Zone Information

Let's consider the configuration for the zone we've just created. It should look very much like the configuration for our prototype zone.

```
# zonecfg -z data-silo info
```

You can also specify a specific resource to show:

```
# zonecfg -z data-silo info zonepath
zonepath: /zonefs/data-silo
# zonecfg -z data-silo info anet
anet:
        linkname: net0
        lower-link: auto
...
```

Commands from the Global Zone

As you have discovered previously, you can run commands in the zone without having to log into the zone, using a variation of **zlogin**:

```
# zlogin data-silo ifconfig -a
lo0: flags=2001000849<UP,LOOPBACK,RUNNING,MULTICAST,IPv4,VIRTUAL> mtu 8232 index 1
        inet 127.0.0.1 netmask ff000000
net0: flags=1000843<UP,BROADCAST,RUNNING,MULTICAST,IPv4> mtu 1500 index 2
        inet 192.168.0.119 netmask ffffff00 broadcast 192.168.0.255
        ether 2:8:20:3b:2f:98
# zlogin data-silo ping 192.168.0.1
192.168.0.1 is alive
```

Removing Zones

Shut down or halt the zone from the global zone. Then uninstall it and remove its configuration, as shown here:

```
# zoneadm -z data-silo halt
# zoneadm -z data-silo uninstall
Are you sure you want to uninstall zone data-silo (y/[n])? y
# zonecfg -z data-silo delete -F
```

Changing a Zone's Name and Its Root Dataset

Let's say six months ago you built a zone called sas-dev for a specific purpose. Now it's being repurposed, renamed, and turned over to another administrative group. You could leave everything the way it is and just change the zone's hostname, which can be different from the zonename. But look what happens when you list the zones—it's as if nothing has changed.

```
# zoneadm list -cv
  ID NAME            STATUS       PATH                   BRAND      IP
   0 global          running      /                      solaris    shared
   9 sas-dev         running      /zonefs/sas-dev        solaris    excl
```

Knowing that what used to be sas-dev is now data-silo would be mentally jarring, not to mention potentially disastrous when the new guy uninstalls it because everybody knows sas-dev is retired. The zonename, the zone's hostname, the zone's zonepath, and its dataset can all have different names, but it's in the interest of the admin's sanity to keep them all together. Solaris provides the zonename resource, but it's trickier than you think. The zone cannot be in the running state when you're changing these properties, so shut it down:

```
# zoneadm -z sas-dev shutdown
# zonecfg -z sas-dev "set zonename=data-silo"
# zoneadm list -cv
  ID NAME            STATUS       PATH              BRAND    IP
   0 global          running      /                 solaris  shared
   - data-silo       installed    /zonefs/sas-dev   solaris  excl
```

That's not exactly what we want—that is, to change the dataset underneath the zone and the mountpoint as well. ZFS will not unmount the dataset to change the mountpoint, and it will not allow renaming of a dataset being used by a non-global zone. We can try **zoneadm move**:

```
# zoneadm -z data-silo move /data-silo
```

However, this will give an error because **zoneadm** will not allow a zonepath to be on the global zone's root filesystem, as mentioned before. If we try to preemptively create the dataset and mountpoint, we'd encounter another error that the dataset is already created. The only choice left is to move the zone to a location *not* directly under the / directory:

```
# zoneadm -z data-silo move /zonefs/data-silo
# zoneadm list -cv
  ID NAME            STATUS       PATH               BRAND    IP
   0 global          running      /                  solaris  shared
   - data-silo       installed    /zonefs/data-silo  solaris  excl
```

Zone Backup and Restore

The number of books and papers that have been written on backup and recovery strategies could easily fill a library shelf. As storage mediums get smarter, the number of tools and ways to back up and restore your data has only proliferated. Ah, the good old days of a **ufsdump** or a **cpio cronjob**, inserting a tape cartridge, running **ufsrestore**, and waiting an hour for the tape to seek to the right marker. I'm just kidding; those days were bad. It was good only in that the process was simple, the OS was a monolith composed of files and directories, and the hierarchy could be copied and reproduced as a whole or in parts. Now that other instances of an OS are living on the platform (perhaps with shared LOFS mounts, perhaps with some duplication of data), the backup sweet spot can be harder to find.

By the *backup sweet spot,* we mean that tradeoff between a simple one-size-fits-all, complete backup versus the storage cost and time spent pulling out of backed-up piles of data the things you actually need. You have to envision a few scenarios where you want to recover data: Disaster recovery is one, moving or consolidating zones onto new hardware is another, and saving application or user data is another.

You can back up the entire platform, the OS, the global zone, and every zone on the box. However, if the failure scenario is that a zpool that contains a zone's dataset is corrupted, then an enterprise backup solution might not be the best in this case. We're going to show you some ways to recover what you need from a non-global zone.

A zone is made up of its configuration, the resources manipulated by **zonecfg**, and the data that lives in it. To recover a zone, you need its configuration and its data.

Back Up the Applications

If your zones are fungible—that is, they are simple containers only used for applications—you can choose to back up only the application and its data using an Enterprise Backup Software (EBS) suite. From the global zone, the absolute path to the data directory is prepended with /$ZONEPATH/root/. For example, the /opt/mysql directory in a zone named db, which has a zonepath of /zonefs/db, has the absolute path of /zonefs/db/root/opt/mysql, when viewed from the global zone. Add the absolute directory path to your EBS.

An alternate method is to create a child dataset inside the zone and put your application on that. You can then take a ZFS snapshot of the dataset and send its stream to a file. This file then can be written onto an LOFS mounted directory from the global zone. If this directory is organized to subdirectories writable by assigned zones, then the global zone's admin can specify the directory path to the EBS, which will back up everything each non-global zone's admin deems to be important, without backing up the entire zone. See the "Adding a Directory from the Global Zone" section for details on how use LOFS mounts.

To recover or re-create a zone with saved application data, first create the zone from a saved configuration, clone or install it, and then put the application data back in place.

A Backup Example Using ZFS Snapshot

In the following example, we'll be working to save and restore a zone named db and its data. Here's how to save a zone's configuration:

```
# zonecfg -z db export -f db.config
```

The content of db.config is text—in fact, it looks like the batched command input to **zonecfg** to create a zone. Save this file; it's a good candidate for EBS.

```
# cat db.config
create -b
set zonepath=/zonefs/db
set brand=solaris
set autoboot=true
set ip-type=exclusive
add anet
set linkname=net0
set lower-link=auto
set configure-allowed-address=false
set link-protection=mac-nospoof
set mac-address=random
set auto-mac-address=2:8:20:4:79:72
end
```

It will be helpful but not imperative to get a copy of the sc_profile.xml used to build this zone. If the XML is not available, you'll have to interact with a system identification tool after the zone is installed. You'll need to have the zone's original hostname, IP, and netmask information. Having the XML file makes this process faster.

Refer back to our previous example of a zone child dataset under "Resources and Zones." We have a zone called db, with a child dataset mounted on the zone's /opt/mysql. The dataset to the application data is rpool/zonefs/db/rpool/database. In the dataset is a file called DBdump; we take a digest to compare later.

```
@database:~$ digest -a md5 /opt/mysql/DB.dump
05ee92b2fedb0722f8d8ab24eda6e589
```

Take a snapshot of the dataset:

```
# zfs snapshot -r rpool/zonefs/db/rpool/database@now
```

List it:

```
# zfs list -r -t snapshot rpool/zonefs/db
NAME                                      USED  AVAIL  REFER  MOUNTPOINT
rpool/zonefs/db/rpool/database@now          0      -   204M   -
```

Send it to a file:

```
# zfs send -rc rpool/zonefs/db/rpool/database@now > /backup/mysql.snap
# ls -al /backup
-rw-r--r--   1 root     root      214600360 Apr  7 17:16 mysql.snap
# file /backup/mysql.snap
/backup/mysql.snap:    ZFS snapshot stream
```

Now that you have a saved copy of the snapshot, you can delete the original snapshot:

```
# zfs destroy rpool/zonefs/db/rpool/database@now
```

You can back up /backup/mysql.snap with whatever backup software you choose. If you have other Solaris 11 machines with ZFS, you can send the ZFS stream to the other host and store the snapshot there.

Along the same principle, you can also choose to snapshot the entire dataset under the zonepath (in our case, rpool/zonefs/db mounted on /zonefs/db) and preserve the entire zone and its application content. Here's an example:

```
# zfs snapshot -r rpool/zonefs/db@now
# zfs send -rc rpool/zonefs/db@now > /backup/db.snap
```

Restoring a Zone

Disaster has struck! Your zone called db, and even the server that contained it, is gone. You wrangle up another similar server, and armed with nothing but the backup you've managed to save, you are going to recover what you lost.

We have to hedge our bets a little and say something in our best radio-announcer fine-print reader voice. The idea that any Solaris 11 zone can be saved, stored, and shuffled around and then snapped together indiscriminately like Lego pieces is enticing. Within the confines of this book, our examples use simplistic scenarios to illustrate a concept. In the real world, where there are more than five variables, with a mix of hardware from new to old to ancient, with different shop practices and naming conventions, trying to find "another similar server" on which to recover your zone can be a formidable task. When a zone is first built, like anything else, it's clean, pristine, orderly, and everyone knows where everything is and why it's supposed to be there. After 12 months go by, with drive corruptions and zpool renames and directory changes and new mountpoints, your current zone configuration may not look anything like the configuration you've saved.

For example, if your old zone had a DVD-ROM device allocated to it, or other disks, disk quotas, a specific network device, or a number of processors, and you move it to a different server, with different network drivers, fewer processors, and disk devices that don't match, you may be able to restore the snapshot but the zone may fail the configuration verification check or fail to boot. This is pertinent, especially to zones that have been saved in their entirety using snapshot.

Back to our example. We are re-creating the zone and then restoring the data in /opt/mysql. First, restore the zone using the configuration and profile you've saved:

```
# zonecfg -z db -f db.config
# zoneadm -z db install -c /tmp/dbprofile.xml
```

The previous step can be replaced by a **zoneadm clone** operation if you've managed to save the prototype zone.

```
# zoneadm -z db boot
# zfs receive rpool/zonefs/db/rpool/database < /backup/mysql.snap
```

The following is from inside the db zone:

```
@db:~$  zfs list
NAME                     USED   AVAIL  REFER  MOUNTPOINT
rpool                    568M   162G    31K   /rpool
rpool/ROOT               363M   162G    31K   legacy
rpool/ROOT/solaris       363M   162G   337M   /
rpool/ROOT/solaris/var   26.1M  162G   25.1M  /var
rpool/database           204M   162G   204M   /opt/mysql
rpool/export             63K    162G    32K   /export
rpool/export/home        31K    162G    31K   /export/home
```

Nice. Notice that ZFS has helpfully made the dataset available to the zone, and kept the mountpoint, an attribute of the dataset.

```
@db:~$  cd /opt/mysql
-bash: cd: /opt/mysql: No such file or directory
```

It's not mounted yet. We can mount it, verify the content, ensure that it's a writeable copy, and make sure it mounts automatically the next time the zone boots.

```
@db:~$  zfs mount rpool/database
@db:~$  digest -a md5 /opt/mysql/DB.dump
05ee92b2fedb0722f8d8ab24eda6e589
# zoneadm -z db reboot
# zlogin db ls -l /opt/mysql
-rw-r--r--   1 root     root        214001243 Apr  7 19:16 DB.dump
```

And, we're back.

Notice that we didn't create any child dataset for the zone yet; we used rpool/zonefs/db/rpool/ database because we know it to be our dataset from before. If you don't remember the hierarchy for the dataset, no matter: Simply restore to a temporary dataset, mount that and grab the data, or allocate the temporary dataset to the zone, like this:

```
# zfs receive rpool/zonefs/tmp < /backup/mysql.snap
# zfs set mountpoint=/test rpool/zonefs/tmp
# ls -l /test
-rw-r--r--  1 root     root     213954491 Apr  7 16:51 DB.dump
```

There remains one thing we need to clean up—the snapshot from which the dataset was restored:

```
@db:~$ zfs list -r -t snapshot -o name rpool/database
rpool/database@now
```

We can destroy it now or keep it; at this point it takes up no extra space. However, in the interest of tidiness, we'll delete it. There's already a backed-up stream copy, and the file will be modified and we will be taking another clean snapshot.

```
@db:~$ zfs destroy rpool/database@now
```

Zone Rehosting

Expanding on the theme, we will now try to recover an entire zone on a new system. We can also think of this process as zone migration, the process of moving a non-global zone from one platform to another. The underlying process is the same. Save the zone configuration and the content of **zonepath**, and move it onto another system.

We've already covered in depth the procedure to save a zone configuration and sc_profile. xml. Here it is again in short form:

```
#  zonecfg -z db export -f db.config
```

Verify the zonepath and the underlying dataset:

```
# zonecfg -z db info zonepath
zonepath: /zonefs/db
# zfs list /zonefs/db
NAME                USED  AVAIL  REFER  MOUNTPOINT
rpool/zonefs/db     577M   162G  33.5K  /zonefs/db
```

The next step is to halt and detach the zone on the old server:

```
# zoneadm -z db halt
# zoneadm -z db detach
```

A detached zone status is marked as "configured," although we haven't uninstalled anything.

```
# zoneadm list -cv
  ID NAME           STATUS     PATH                        BRAND    IP
   0 global         running    /                           solaris  shared
   - db             configured /zonefs/db                  solaris  excl
```

Now we need to transfer the content of the old zonepath to the new server. There are many ways to do this. The simplest would be to use **tar** (or one of any number of available archiving tools, such as **cpio** or **gzip**) for the entire zonepath and then transport the tar file. Because we're on a ZFS filesystem, we can snapshot the zone's dataset and send it to a file and then transport the file. If the backing store is shared storage such as a NAS or a SAN, it's a matter of rezoning the SAN or reconfiguring the NAS to reveal the volume to the new server while hiding it from the old server.

Method 1: Using tar

If you choose to take a manual backup of the zonepath, you *must* take the backup *before* you detach the zone—the reason being that detached zones have their dataset unpinned. Nothing appears below the zonepath, even though the dataset and content have not been deleted.

Here's how the zonepath of a detached zone looks (there's not much there):

```
# ls -R /zonefs/db
/zonefs/db:
dev                 root                SUNWdetached.xml
/zonefs/db/dev:
/zonefs/db/root:
```

If you take a manual backup, the order of work is as follows: halt the zone, take the backup, and *then* detach.

```
# zoneadm -z db halt
# cd /zonefs/db/root; tar -cpf database.tar ./*
# zoneadm -z db detach
```

CAUTION

It is written elsewhere that the archive directory is the zonepath; this is incorrect. Archive the content of the $zonepath/root directory. This is important. The attach logic assumes $zonepath/root; if you archive the zonepath, during attach you will get errors about missing or incompatible libc.so.1 and attach will fail.

Transfer the tar file to the new host and then use the configuration file to configure the zone on the new server:

```
# zonecfg -z db -f db.config
```

This is the time to change any configuration resources to match what is available on the new platform (for example, the zonepath, mountpoints, name of physical network interface, and any resource allocations). Attach the zone. A successful attach will have output similar to this:

```
# zoneadm -z db attach -a /backup/database.tar
A ZFS file system has been created for this zone.
Progress being logged to /var/log/zones/zoneadm.20120408T024708Z.database.attach
Attaching...
    Installing: This may take several minutes...
      Zone BE root dataset: rpool/zonefs/db/rpool/ROOT/solaris-0
                    Cache: Using /var/pkg/publisher.
```

```
Updating image format
  Updating non-global zone: Linking to image /.
  Updating non-global zone: Auditing packages.
No updates necessary for this image.

  Updating non-global zone: Zone updated.
                    Result: Attach Succeeded.
Log saved in non-global zone as /zonefs/db/root/var/log/zones/
zoneadm.20120408T024708Z.db.attach
```

Method 2: Using ZFS Snapshot

With this method, you don't need to worry about backing up before detaching. You are taking a snapshot of a dataset, which is possible whether or not it's mounted.

```
# zfs snapshot -r rpool/zonefs/db@migration
# zfs send -rc rpool/zonefs/db@migration > /backup/db.snap
```

Transfer the snapshot stream to the new host, configure the new zone, and then attach the zone using the ZFS snapshot stream. If successful, you will see output similar to the following:

```
# zonecfg -z db -f db.config
# zoneadm -z db attach -a /backup/db.snap
A ZFS file system has been created for this zone.
Progress being logged to /var/log/zones/zoneadm.20120408T020829Z.db.attach
Attaching...
    Installing: This may take several minutes...
      Zone BE root dataset: rpool/zonefs/db/rpool/ROOT/solaris-0
                      Cache: Using /var/pkg/publisher.
Updating image format
  Updating non-global zone: Linking to image /.
  Updating non-global zone: Auditing packages.
No updates necessary for this image.
  Updating non-global zone: Zone updated.
                    Result: Attach Succeeded.
Log saved in non-global zone as /zonefs/db/root/var/log/zones/
zoneadm.20120408T020829Z.db.attach
```

The previous examples assume that the source and destination server are running the same Solaris 11 release and have the same packages on both. If you find yourself migrating a zone from an older release, or one installed with a smaller set of packages than the new server, the attach may not work. Use the **–u** switch to force an upgrade while attaching and bring the non-global zone up to par with the global zone:

```
# zoneadm -z db attach -a /backup/db.tar -u
```

Failing that, try to force an attach, but be warned that if you bypass validation, the new zone may not play well on its new home:

```
# zoneadm -z db attach -F -a /backup/db.tar
```

The attached zone will be in the "installed" state. Boot the zone and then log in to verify the place looks like how you last left it.

Solaris10 Branded Zones

Recall in the "Quick Tour with Zones" section that we encountered a column called "brand" when we run **zoneadm list –cv**. This column describe a runtime environment for applications different from the native Solaris 11. There are three supported brands: solaris, solaris10, and labeled. We've been working with solaris zones—a Solaris 11 runtime environment. solaris10 branded zones create a Solaris 10 runtime environment for applications. The labeled zone is a creation of Trusted Extensions, which we will explore in Chapter 18.

If an application requires the operating environment to be Solaris 10, you can run it in a solaris10 branded zone, where the global zone is Solaris 11. You can migrate a bare-metal Solaris 10 environment, or a non-global zone off a Solaris 10 environment, onto a solaris10 branded zone.

The migration of a Solaris 10 operating environment onto a solaris10 branded zone is beyond the scope of this chapter, but the procedure is similar to moving a zone, which was described earlier:

1. Take a flash-archive of a Solaris 10 system and move it onto to a Solaris 11 machine:

    ```
    # flarcreate -S -n s10box -L cpio /some/dir/s10.flar
    ```

NOTE
*There's no **flarcreate** on Solaris 11; flash archive, or FLAR, is no longer supported in Solaris 11 due to the change to the IPS packaging system.*

2. On the Solaris 11 machine, configure a solaris10 branded zone:

    ```
    # zonecfg -z s10box
    s10box: No such zone configured
    Use 'create' to begin configuring a new zone.
    zonecfg:s10box> create -t SYSsolaris10
    zonecfg:s10box> set zonepath=/zonefs/s10box
    zonecfg:s10box> exit
    ```

3. Install the solaris10 branded zone using the flash archive:

    ```
    # zoneadm -z s10box install -u -a /location/of/s10.flar
    ```

NOTE
This command is very similar to our previous example of attaching a zone using a ZFS stream backup.

Tips, Tricks, and Pitfalls

Here are a few tips to keep up your sleeves to make zone administration more efficient.

hostid

Non-global zones do not have a unique hostid; they take the hostid of the global zone. If your system is an x86 or x64 platform, the hostid changes every time the server is installed. If you are moving applications from a physical server to a non-global zone, and these applications have licenses tied to the hostid, you can assign a hostid to the zone to satisfy this requirement, like so:

```
# zonecfg -z data-silo "set hostid=0006c0d0"
```

In place of 0006c0d0, use the original hostid that's tied to the license.

Profile for Automatic Installer

Solaris 10 and previous versions used an /etc/sysidcfg file to provide system-identifying values such as primary network interface, IP, netmasks, root password, and locale. If this file exists, Solaris will not run the interactive **sysconfig** tool—the Solaris 11 counterpart to /etc/sysidcfg is sc_profile.xml. It's written in XML and is therefore not easy for humans to read and modify. You invoke **sysconfig**,

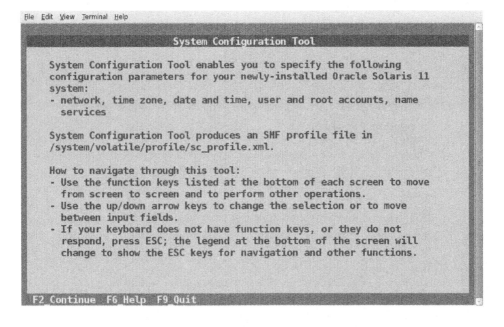

walk through the interactive question and answer,

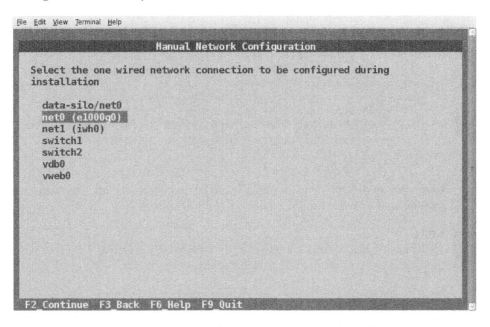

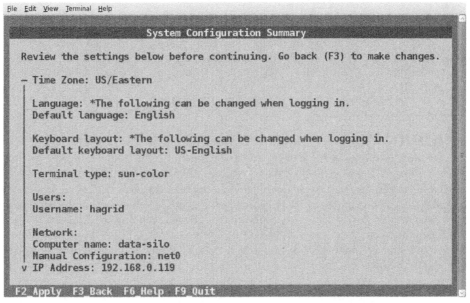

and save your response in an XML file, which you provide at the time of zone installation.

```
# sysconfig create-profile -o myprofile.xml
```

Interactive sysconfig to Create Profile XML

Here's a snippet of the XML file created:

```
<!DOCTYPE service_bundle SYSTEM "/usr/share/lib/xml/dtd/service_bundle.dtd.1">
<service_bundle type="profile" name="sysconfig">
  <service version="1" type="service" name="system/config-user">
    <instance enabled="true" name="default">
      <property_group type="application" name="root_account">
        <propval type="astring" name="login" value="root"/>
        <propval type="astring" name="password" value="uQkGf325B75ik"/>
        <propval type="astring" name="type" value="role"/>
      </property_group>
  . . .
```

If you have an old-style /etc/sysidcfg, you can use a tool called **js2ai** (JumpStart to AI converter) to convert it to an XML file that the Automated Installer can use.

NOTE
*The format of **sysidcfg** may need tweaking; some value pairs have been deprecated or their format changed slightly.*

cd to the directory containing the **sysidcfg** tool and run the following:

```
# js2ai -s
```

This will look for **sysidcfg** in the current directory and produce a file called sc_profile.xml, which you can rename to something more descriptive.

After zone configuration and during installation, specify the full path to the XML file. On first boot, the zone will not go into the interactive **sysconfig** routine, provided the sc_profile is complete and correct.

```
# zoneadm -z web install -c /tmp/sc_profile.xml
```

Summary

Zones provide a powerful and flexible virtualization tool that allows you to create a virtual OS without special hardware or third-party software. Zones are isolated from each other and from the real OS, so failures in a zone are confined to that zone. Isolation also allows different groups to manage each zone the way they prefer, without impacting other users of the system.

Because Solaris 11 zones are built on ZFS datasets, cloning, backup, and migration are efficient and fast.

Zone management is scriptable, thus making building, moving, and deleting zones well suited for automation. You can allocate different resources to a zone, such as disk and network devices, filesystems, and a whole number or percentage of processors and memory. When used in conjunction with resource management, many zones can co-exist harmoniously on the same server with maximum use of available resources.

Reference

The Oracle Solaris Zones, Oracle Solaris 11 Zones, and Resource Management, March 2012 Revision is found at http://docs.oracle.com/cd/E23824_01/pdf/821-1460.pdf.

CHAPTER
15

Print Management

ith the release of Solaris 11, the default print service is now CUPS, formerly known as the Common UNIX Printing System. It's essentially the same service used on both the Linux and Apple operating systems. Because CUPS communicates via the Internet Printing Protocol (IPP), it's also compatible with the latest iteration of the Microsoft printing service.

Solaris 11 no longer supports the Line Print (LP) service. The Solaris 11 print service is CUPS. And that promotes interoperability. In a network of mixed operating systems, CUPS is more compatible. It can be administered with a web-based interface. It is less complex than LP. Although you may want to retain LP servers for printing, the transition to CUPS should not be difficult.

This chapter is focused on the configuration of CUPS. Because it is the default print service for Solaris 11, newer administrators should consider CUPS first.

Print Service Options

While Solaris 11 Express supported LP, Solaris 11 does not. If you have printers connected via LP, you'll have to take some time to convert them to CUPS. Fortunately, CUPS supports many standard LP-based commands, including **lp, lpr, lpc, lpstat,** and more. In addition, CUPS can be used to administer LP-based printers on remote systems.

If this is the first time you're configuring a dedicated print server, you'll want to make sure sufficient space is available for spool files. In general, 1GB is more than sufficient, unless users are printing complete books on a regular basis. And in that case, you'll either want high-capacity printers or want to manage and even limit those kinds of jobs, as discussed later in this chapter.

CUPS, the Print Service

Although the default protocol associated with CUPS is IPP, CUPS can handle printers configured to a variety of protocols. As shown next, it primarily works with printers set up through IPP or shared with CIFS/Samba.

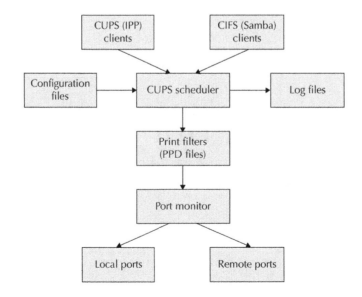

CUPS can also be used as the server for printers connected locally as well as through a variety of other print protocols, as shown in Table 15-1.

The basic steps required to configure servers that use each of these network print protocols are the same. These steps are covered later in this chapter.

NOTE
The acronyms associated with CUPS reflect its open source heritage. For example, GNU is a recursive acronym that stands for GNU's Not Unix. The other acronyms were covered in Chapter 5.

Related Packages

CUPS is more than just the configuration files in the /etc/cups directory along with the libraries and binaries that run the service. CUPS includes the hal-cups-utils package, which helps set up the print queue. It includes the ipp and related packages for client interaction with CUPS servers. In essence, besides the print driver packages previously described, you may be interested in the packages described in Table 15-2.

Protocol	Description
IPP	The Internet Print Protocol has become the standard for network printing. Although it communicates over TCP/IP port 631, some IPP-configured printers are set up over port 80.
CIFS/Samba	The Common Internet File System (CIFS) is the standard for networking on Microsoft-based systems. Solaris 11 uses Samba to communicate on such networks.
LP	Not only can CUPS connect to LP-configured printers, CUPS includes a limited degree of LP functionality, based on **lp*** commands.
AppSocket/ HP JetDirect	The AppSocket/HP JetDirect protocol works through TCP/IP port 9100. Originally designed for printers built by Tektronix and HP, it is also used by some hardware-based print servers.
Bluetooth	Although Bluetooth is, strictly speaking, a network protocol, it is a short-range packet-based serial protocol associated with local printers.

TABLE 15-1. *CUPS Network Printer Protocols*

CUPS Package	Description
cups	Main package for CUPS.
cups-libs	Runtime libraries for CUPS.
foomatic-db	Basic database of CUPS drivers developed through openprinting.org.
foomatic-db-engine	Driver database management tools.
ipp	Open Printing application programming interface (API) print service module.
ipp-listener	Apache module to listen for HTTP requests on port 631.
libipp	Core libraries for IPP.
open-printing	Application programming interface (API) from the Free Standards Group.
print-client-commands	Package with desktop tools such as the desktop monitor as well as the print-service management tool.
pycups	Python language binding for CUPS. Supports a GUI management tool.

TABLE 15-2. *CUPS Print Packages*

The Internet Print Protocol (IPP) and CUPS

IPP was developed by a number of companies as a standard network printing protocol. As a part of the TCP/IP protocol suite, it allows users to send jobs to remote printers, even on Internet print servers so configured. CUPS has emerged as the dominant UNIX implementation of print services. In this section, you'll examine the commands, management tools, and configuration files for that service.

Before proceeding, back up the files in the /etc/cups directory. A number of actions suggested in this chapter will change the content of these files. When you use the Printer Configuration or web-based tools, compare new versions of these files with the originals. The differences can help you learn more about CUPS.

NOTE
CUPS goes a little beyond IPP in terms of network communication. Whereas IPP uses TCP port 631, CUPS uses UDP port 631.

Basic Components

As is true on other UNIX-based operating systems, the CUPS service includes most of its configuration files in the /etc/cups directory. It includes the same message templates in the /usr/share/cups/templates directory. It includes libraries in the /usr/lib/cups directory. It also includes log files in the /var/log/cups directory. Linux users may be pleased to see a Printer Configuration tool similar to that used on several major Linux distributions. Users who are converting from other operating systems should be pleased to see the same web-based CUPS interface.

However, there are differences. For XML information on how CUPS is configured on Solaris 11, examine the cups.xml file in the /lib/svc/manifest/application directory. It includes the services and executables associated with the CUPS server on Solaris.

Basic Commands

In this section, you'll examine the utilities that can be used from the command-line interface to manage CUPS.

Those of you who are converting from LP should take heart. CUPS also includes some of the same functionality, based on commands with many of the same names. These commands are summarized in Table 15-3. The LP-based commands listed work just fine on CUPS servers. Just be aware that commands such as **lpc** on CUPS include fewer features than **lpc** on the LP service.

In many cases, these command-line tools will "get the job done" more quickly. For example, the **lpc status** command shows the status of all currently configured printers, including messages such as the following if there is a problem:

```
printing is disabled
```

Command	Description
cups-calibrate	Supports printer color calibration.
cups-config	Provides basic parameters such as versions and key directories.
cups-genppd.5.2	Generates Gutenprint PPD drivers.
cups-genppdupdate	Updates Gutenprint PPD drivers based on updates in the /usr/share/cups/model/gutenprint directory.
cupsaddsmb	Exports CUPS printers to Samba servers.
cupsctl	Configures some CUPS options. Changes are written to the cupsd.conf configuration file.
lp, lpr	Submits a print request, based on filenames that follow. No more than 52 files are allowed per request.
lpadmin	Allows configuration of printer options, even on CUPS systems.
lpc	Supports a command line where you can check printer status. Less capable than the LP version of this command.
lpmove	Enables a print administrator to move a job between printers.
lpoptions	Configures or lists printer options for the current user.
lppasswd	Adds passwords for specified users. Does not create CUPS administrators.
lpq	Queries the current print queue.
lpr	Prints a specified file.
lprm	Removes a specified print job.
lprsetup.sh	Creates a Ghostscript filter.
lpstat	Details status of current print jobs.

TABLE 15-3. *Commands for CUPS*

In that case, you can move a print job. For example, the following command moves print job number 5, currently assigned to printer1, to printer2:

```
# lpmove 5/printer1 printer2
```

Job numbers are listed in the output to the **lpq** command.

Set Up a Printer Administrator

Of course, you'll want to set up a dedicated user as a print administrator. It's actually a two-part process. First, based on the options described in Chapter 11, you can set up dedicated users with the Users and Groups tool, or with the **roleadd** and **usermod** commands. For example, the following command sets up a new user, dickens, as a print administrator:

```
# roleadd -P "Printer Management" dickens
```

In contrast, the following command adds such privileges to an existing user named donna:

```
# usermod -P "Printer Management" donna
```

If successful, you'll see the users configured as printer administrators in the /etc/user_attr file. However, to set up such users with CUPS administrative privileges, you'll need to set them up as members of an appropriate administrative user group. That's set up in the main CUPS configuration file, cupsd.conf, in the /etc/cups directory. Specifically, it's based on the following directive:

```
SystemGroup sys root
```

In other words, you'll need to set up print administrators as members of one of the groups associated with the **SystemGroup** directive. You could make them members of the sys or root groups, but that could come with risks. Alternatively, you could add a group already configured for printers, lp, to the directive. You'd then add the print administrator(s) as members of the group in the /etc/group file. Once you restart the CUPS service with the command

```
# svcadm restart cups/scheduler
```

those print administrators will have full privileges to the CUPS tools described in this chapter.

The Printer Configuration Tool

If you are familiar with Linux, you may be pleasantly surprised by the GUI Print Manager used on Solaris 11. In fact, you can start the tool from a GUI-based command-line interface with the same **system-config-printer** command used on many Linux systems. The tool has been modified to work with the Solaris 11 implementation of CUPS. Although the tool shown in Figure 15-1 looks simple, it is rich with features.

To demonstrate, we'll illustrate the configuration of a new networked printer. To set that up on your system, take the following steps from the Solaris 11 GUI. First, click System | Administration | Print Manager. The Printer Configuration tool shown in Figure 15-1 should appear.

NOTE
New printers, along with custom configuration options associated with such printers, are written to individual stanzas in the /etc/cups/ printers.conf file.

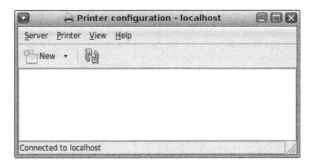

FIGURE 15-1. *The Solaris Printer Configuration tool*

Next, click New. (You can also press CTRL-N or click Server | New | Printer.) If you haven't logged in as the root administrative user, you'll be prompted for the root password, as shown in Figure 15-2. If desired, you can substitute a print administrator, as long as she's a member of the one of the groups specified by the **SystemGroup** directive in the cupsd.conf configuration file.

The configuration tool looks for connected printers. If it doesn't find any, it'll present the New Printer window, as shown in Figure 15-3. The window shows a variety of local and remote options for printers. If a printer was detected, or if a different port such as Bluetooth is available, it could be included in the list. The options shown in the figure are further described in Table 15-4. Depending on configuration, you may see variations on the available devices.

To review available options, temporarily select some of the options listed in Table 15-4. Note how the prompts change with each option. Be aware that the URI listed in the table is the Uniform Resource Identifier, a superset of the Uniform Resource Locator. For the purpose of this section, select Internet Printing Protocol (IPP). You'll have to enter the hostname or IP address of a print server. By default, configured CUPS printers can be found in a /printers/ subdirectory.

If successful, you'll see a list of printers shared from the server specified, similar to that shown in Figure 15-4. If you select a printer from this list, it's entered in the Queue Name text box, with the associated URI. Here's the URI for one of our home printers:

```
ipp://server1.example.com:631/printers/OfficePrinter
```

FIGURE 15-2. *The root user is just one print administrator.*

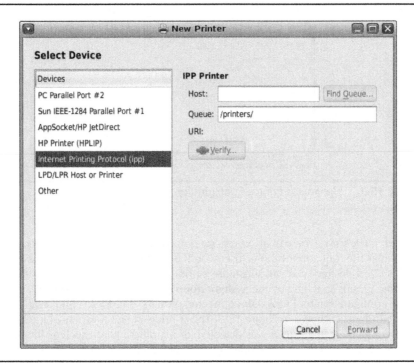

FIGURE 15-3. *A variety of print options*

Device	Description
PC Parallel Port #2	Associated with device file /dev/lp*n*, where *n* is the device number.
Sun IEEE-1284 Parallel Port #1	Associated with device file /dev/ecpp*n*, where *n* is the device number. In most cases, this is a second name for PC Parallel Port 2.
AppSocket/HP Jet Direct	Works with systems networked through port 9100.
HP Printer (HPLIP)	Uses the HP Linux Imaging and Printing database.
Internet Printing Protocol (IPP)	Configures a connection to a printer shared over IPP, generally through port 631.
LPD/LPR Host or Printer	Enables a connection to a remote printer configured to the Line Print Daemon (LPD), also known as Line Printer Remote (LPR).
Other	Supports a connection to a nondefined networked print server.

TABLE 15-4. *Add Printer Device Options*

FIGURE 15-4. *A list of shared printers*

TIP
If you've already configured printers in CUPS, the associated URI
should be defined in the printers.conf file in the /etc/cups directory.
*When properly configured, it's defined with the **DeviceURI** directive.*

Next, you'll get a chance to specify the name, printer location, and description, as shown in Figure 15-5. Although you're not allowed to include spaces in the name of the printer, you can use multiple words for the location and description, as shown.

The printer is now added to the main Printer Configuration screen. Right-click the printer and select Properties from the pop-up menu that appears. It'll open a Printer Properties window, similar to that shown in Figure 15-6.

You might note the error message associated with the printer. If there's a problem with the printer connection, it may appear here, in the Printer Properties window. In fact, Figure 15-6 illustrates a processing error; you'll see how this error is addressed with the configuration of a local print driver. The following subsections explore options associated with Printer Properties, in turn. The options shown in the left pane often vary based on the capabilities of the printer.

Settings

Note that the description and location are as specified in the previous screen. The Device URI points to how the system can access the printer, using the IPP, over port 631. If you click Change on the Device URI line, it restarts the configuration process for the printer, based on the window shown in Figure 15-3. Alternatively, if you click Change on the Make and Model line, it opens the Change Driver window shown in Figure 15-7.

At this point, you have two choices. You can use the so-called "foomatic" print driver database collected by the people behind OpenPrinting.org, but the database is not complete. Alternatively, you could load a PPD file. Some printer manufacturers include PPD files in their Macintosh or Microsoft-based drivers, which potentially could be used here.

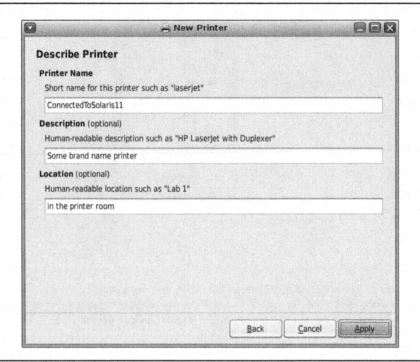

FIGURE 15-5. *Printer name, location, description*

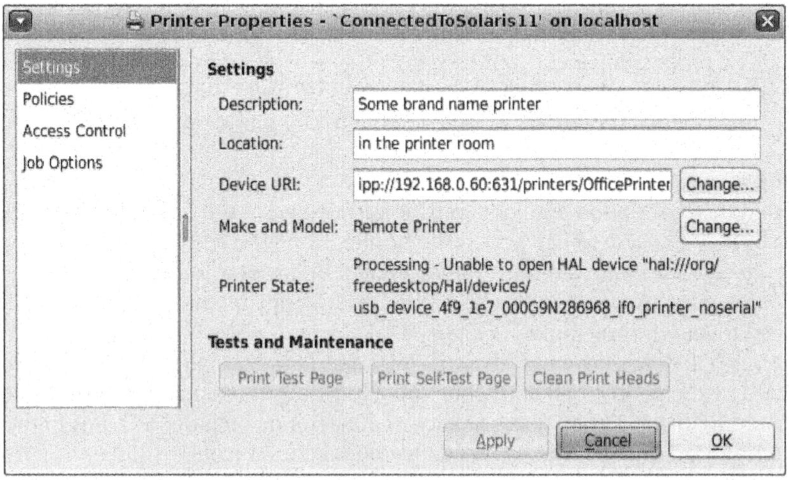

FIGURE 15-6. *Printer properties*

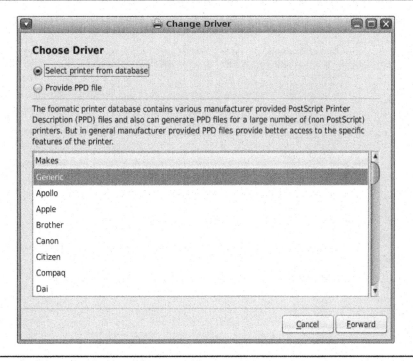

FIGURE 15-7. *Changing a printer driver*

Assuming you use the foomatic database, select a printer manufacturer and click Forward to continue. You'll then see the window shown in Figure 15-8, where you can select a printer model and specific driver. Sometimes different drivers are available for text and graphics, and they should be labeled as such. In most cases, there will be a "recommended" driver. Select a driver and click Forward to continue.

Next, you'll see two options based on the changes you're about to make. If you've customized the printer in some fashion, you'll want to select the Try to Copy the Option Settings Over from the Old PPD radio button. Otherwise, you may accept the defaults associated with the PPD file. Make a selection and then click Apply. The make and model of the revised printer should appear in the Printer Properties window.

Policies

You can configure policies for individual printers. Select the Policies option in the left pane. The policy options shown in Figure 15-9 should appear. They allow you to configure whether printers are in operation, how they are shared, how they respond when an error is encountered, and so on, as detailed here:

- **Enabled** Deselecting this option stops the printer and adds a **State Stopped** directive to the /etc/cups/printers.conf file.

- **Accepting Jobs** Deselecting this option blocks new jobs that a user might try to send to the printer.

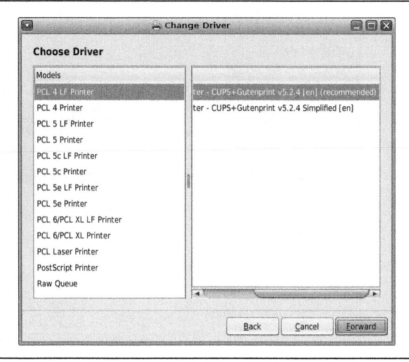

FIGURE 15-8. *Selecting a new printer driver*

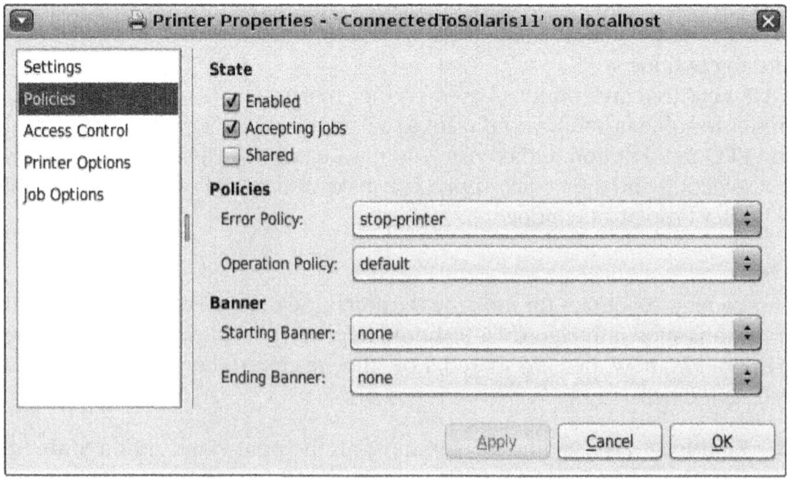

FIGURE 15-9. *Printer policies*

- **Shared**   Selecting this option allows this printer to be shared on the network; however, the change isn't implemented unless sharing is enabled in the CUPS configuration file.
- **Error Policy**   Customizes what happens when a job can't be sent to a printer. The job can be aborted (abort-job), retried (retry-current-job), or retried after a defined number of seconds (retry-job). Alternatively, the printer can be stopped altogether (stop-printer).
- **Operation Policy**   If this policy is set to authenticated, users are then required to enter their passwords before a print job is accepted.
- **Banner**   You're allowed to set a banner header and footer, as described in the associated drop-down text boxes.

Access Control

You can configure user-based access control, by printer. Select the Access Control option in the left pane. The access control options shown in Figure 15-10 should appear. They allow you to access policies for the printer, by user.

As suggested by the figure, you can limit access to specific users, or you can deny access to other specific users. The process is straightforward; for example, to limit access to just user michael, select the radio button Deny Printing for Everyone Except These Users and then click Add. When implemented, this adds the following directive to the printers.conf file:

```
AllowUser michael
```

If any other user then tries to use the subject printer, the following error message should appear:

```
Not allowed to print.
```

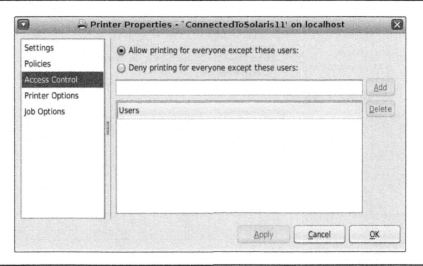

FIGURE 15-10.   *Printer access control*

Printer Options

Not all printers have printer options. If they're available to you, they can help you customize features associated with the printer, such as color, resolution, and print quality.

Job Options

You can configure what happens with print jobs as well. Select Job Options in the left pane. The options shown in Figure 15-11 should appear. They allow you to configure how print jobs are processed, such as the number of copies, orientation, scaling, text options, and more. When you've completed the review, click Apply or Cancel to close the window.

A Printer Class Is a Group of Printers

If you have a group of printers in a dedicated location, it's often appropriate to distribute the load, to make sure every print job isn't automatically sent to "printer1." That's one reason why you should set up a printer class. In CUPS, a class is a group of previously configured printers represented by a single name. To set this up from the Printer Configuration tool, click Server | New | Class. The basic steps are the same as for a single printer, except for Figure 15-12, where you select the printers that are part of the class.

Once configured, the printer class can be selected like any other single printer. Jobs that are sent to a printer class are sent to individual printers in that class randomly.

Print Server Configuration

Back in the Printer Configuration tool, it is now time to see what you can do to configure the server. Click Server | Settings. The Basic Server Settings window shown in Figure 15-13 should now appear.

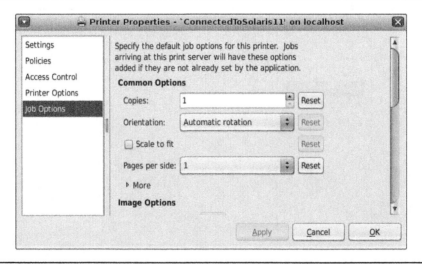

FIGURE 15-11. *Job options*

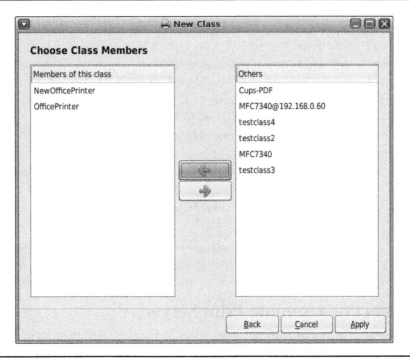

FIGURE 15-12. *Selecting printers to be members of a print class*

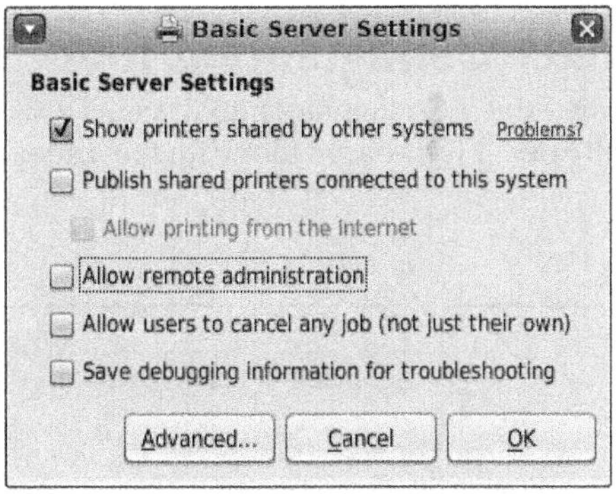

FIGURE 15-13. *Basic print server settings*

The options shown are described here:

- **Show Printers Shared by Other Systems**   If printers are shared by other CUPS servers, and are detected, this option allows them to be shown in the Printer Configuration tool.
- **Publish Shared Printers Connected to This System**   This option shares printers with others on the local network. Uses the **Allow @LOCAL** directive.
- **Allow Printing from the Internet**   Supports access from all systems, regardless of network. Changes **Allow @LOCAL** to **Allow all**.
- **Allow Remote Administration**   Enables access to the web-based CUPS administrative tool from remote systems.
- **Allow Users to Cancel Any Job (Not Just Their Own)**   As suggested, it gives users more control over printer jobs.
- **Save Debugging Information for Troubleshooting**   Changes the log level associated with CUPS to debug.

Of course, the Advanced button opens another window that supports additional configuration. Specifically, it allows you as a print administrator to control what happens to print jobs after they're complete. It also allows you to specify print servers to help search for desired printer queues.

Connect to a Remote Print Server

If a remote CUPS server has been configured to "allow remote administration" from the local system (per Figure 15-13), and you have print administrator privileges, you can connect to that service directly from the Printer Configuration tool. Click Server | Connect. The Connect to CUPS Server window shown in Figure 15-14 should appear.

The default is the local CUPS server, associated with the local /var/run/cups-socket file. To connect to a remote CUPS server, you'd enter the hostname or IP address in the CUPS server text box. If the connection is successful, all actions that follow would affect the CUPS server of the remote system.

The Other Printer Configuration Tool

If it's still open, close the Printer Configuration tool. Open a web browser and navigate to http://localhost:631. This will open a web-based tool with the same basic functionality as the Printer Configuration tool.

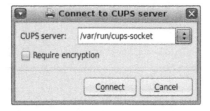

FIGURE 15-14.   *Connecting to a CUPS server*

Here are two additional features of use from the web-based tool:

- **Online help** It's available on CUPS servers. Navigate to http://localhost:631/help.
- **Developer documentation** For example, the following URI provides an introduction to CUPS programming: http://localhost:631/help/api-overview.html.

Although the same information is also available online, the help and documentation are also part of the standard CUPS packages and are therefore available locally.

The Files of CUPS

Configuration files in the CUPS directory are stored in the /etc/cups directory. The main configuration file is cupsd.conf. When printers are configured, they're set up in the printers.conf file. The function of each CUPS configuration file is summarized in Table 15-5.

There's one additional related file, /etc/printers.conf. CUPS develops it from the /etc/cups/printers.conf file, and writes the output in LP format. It's available for sharing with LP and Samba services. Important elements of these configuration files are summarized in the following sections.

The Main CUPS Server Configuration File: cupsd.conf

The following is an analysis of the default version of the main CUPS configuration file, /etc/cups/cupsd.conf. It starts with the **LogLevel**, a measure of the amount of logging information sent to the error_log file in the /var/log directory:

```
LogLevel warn
```

One of the options associated with CUPS servers in the Printer Configuration tool can change this value to and from debug. The next directive is associated with groups of users who have

File	Description
classes.conf	Defines printer names that represent groups of printers
command.types	Supports the use of print filters
cupsd.conf	Notes the CUPS server configuration file
interfaces/	Specifies the subdirectory for CUPS scripts
pdftoraster.convs	Includes filters that convert PDFs to raster format
ppd/	Specifies the subdirectory with PPD driver files
printers.conf	Defines current options for configured printers
pstoraster.convs	Includes the Ghostscript file filter that converts PDF files to raster format
snmp.conf	Notes options associated with SNMP printer discovery
ssl/	Specifies the subdirectory with secure certificates
subscriptions.conf	Includes data for user-based printer subscriptions

TABLE 15-5. *Add Printer Device Options*

administrative privileges with CUPS. The **SystemGroup** directive was described earlier in this chapter.

The following directives limit access to the local system. By default, clients on remote systems don't have access to local printers.

```
Listen localhost:631
Listen /var/run/cups-socket
```

The Printer Configuration removes the localhost limitation, focusing access via port 631 and supporting access from remote clients:

```
Listen 631
```

Although you could set up a specific IP address for the **Listen** directive, that would cause problems with SNMP-based printer discovery.

TIP

If you see a problem with the SNMP service, you may need to disable and then reenable the service.

As suggested by the comment, the **Browsing*** directives define how printers configured locally are shared. The first directive is straightforward:

```
# Show shared printers on the local network.
Browsing On
```

The two directives that follow support browsing on all systems:

```
BrowseOrder allow,deny
BrowseAllow all
```

By default, the following directive searches for CUPS-configured printers on the local system:

```
BrowseLocalProtocols CUPS
```

Alternatively, the following directive accommodates a system that searches external systems for printers:

```
BrowseLocalProtocols CUPS
```

The default for authentication can be risky because it allows print administrators to transmit their usernames and passwords in clear text:

```
DefaultAuthType Basic
```

To set up a level of encryption for such usernames and passwords, you could change **Basic** to **Digest**; CUPS would then look for passwords in the passwd.md5 file in the /etc/cups directory. You can create new passwords in that file with the **lppasswd -a *username*** command. You could have custom **AuthType** directives in stanzas that follow, to specify different authentication schemes for the server, administrative access, and configuration files.

The following stanza is the default limitation on the server:

```
<Location />
     Order allow,deny
</Location>
```

If you want to support access from other systems on the local network, you'd add the following directive to the stanza, after the **Order allow,deny**:

```
Allow @LOCAL
```

This corresponds to the Publish Shared Printers Connected to This System option described earlier. Here, **@LOCAL** is shorthand for the current local network. Alternatively, you could specify the hostname, domain, or IP address of the desired network, such as:

```
Allow 192.168.0.0/24
```

Alternatively, if you want to allow any connected network client to print, you could change the directive to the following:

```
Allow all
```

This corresponds to the Allow Printing from the Internet option described earlier.

The two stanzas that follow define access parameters on administrative pages, along with associated configuration files. The default version of the stanzas should look familiar:

```
<Location /admin>
     Order allow,deny
</Location>

<Location /admin/conf>
     Order allow,deny
     Require user @SYSTEM
</Location>
```

There's one additional directive in the configuration file stanza: **Require user @SYSTEM**, which requires that administrative users be members of the **@SYSTEM** group, defined by the **SystemGroup** directive earlier in the file.

The **Allow** directive that you can add to these stanzas follows the same guidelines as that just described for shared printers. In general, you'll want to limit access to a local network, or perhaps just the hostname or IP address of the computer used by the printer administrator.

The directives that follow are more straightforward than they look. They relate to the operational policies associated with printers and print jobs. The directives within each stanza are descriptive; for more information, see the Managing Operation Policies document. If you've installed CUPS, it should be available on your system at http://localhost:631/help/policies.

Additional CUPS Configuration Options

"Real" printer administrators may want to go beyond the defaults and basic directives just listed. The directives discussed in this section all apply to the main CUPS configuration file, cupsd.conf.

One directive of interest is **MaxClients**. By default, a standard CUPS server is limited to 100 simultaneous clients. The CUPS documentation suggests that you could expand that by including the following directive:

```
MaxClients 1024
```

Related directives, as described in Table 15-6, allow you to configure other limits on users and servers.

Configured Printers in printers.conf

As noted earlier, there are two versions of the printers.conf file. The version in the /etc directory is a simplified form of the file formerly used by the LP service. It's still used to share printers on some services such as Samba. Note the following information from the top of the file:

```
# This file was automatically generated by cupsd(8) from the
# /etc/cups/printers.conf file.
```

The description of the printer is straightforward, relative to the full version of LP:

```
OfficePrinter:\
        :bsdaddr=solarisdel,OfficePrinter:\
        :description=in the office:
```

The directives are configured in LP service format, beyond the scope of CUPS. Because the file is automatically generated by CUPS, you should not have to modify the options found within it. In any case, when a printer is configured on a CUPS system, it's documented in the /etc/cups/printers.conf file. One version of that file, with one configured printer, is shown in Figure 15-15. It includes one configured printer, in one stanza. Many systems include several configured printers, connected locally and remotely. Each printer would be configured in its own stanza in /etc/cups/printers.conf.

Directive	Function
FilterLimit	Maximum number of print jobs; disabled by default. Set this to a reasonable number to avoid overloading or abuse.
MaxClients	Limit on number of clients; 100 is the default.
MaxCopies	Limit on the number of copies per print job; 100 is the default.
MaxJobs	Limit on the number of jobs in cache, normally stored in the /var/spool/cups directory; 500 is the default.
MaxJobsPerPrinter	Limit on the number of jobs per printer; disabled by default. Set this to a reasonable number to avoid overloading of a specific printer.
MaxJobsPerUser	Limit on the number of jobs per user; disabled by default.
MaxLogSize	Upper bound on the size of log files; set to 1MB by default.
PreserveJobHistory	Job history is saved by default. You can set it to Off to enhance privacy.

TABLE 15-6. *CUPS Capacity-Related Directives*

```
# Printer configuration file for CUPS v1.4.2
# Written by cupsd on 2011-08-17 14:30
# DO NOT EDIT THIS FILE WHEN CUPSD IS RUNNING
<DefaultPrinter ConnectedToSolaris11>
AuthInfoRequired none
Info Some brand name printer
Location in the printer room
MakeModel Generic PCL 4 LF Printer - CUPS+Gutenprint v5.2.4
DeviceURI ipp://192.168.0.60:631/printers/OfficePrinter
State Idle
StateTime 1313542499
Type 12595206
Filter application/vnd.cups-raw 0 -
Filter application/vnd.cups-raster 100 rastertogutenprint.5.2
Accepting Yes
Shared No
JobSheets none none
QuotaPeriod 0
PageLimit 0
KLimit 0
AllowUser michael
OpPolicy authenticated
ErrorPolicy stop-printer
</Printer>
```

FIGURE 15-15. *The CUPS printers.conf file*

Although the file is pretty generic, you may recognize the first three directives from Figure 15-5. Because the **Info** and **Location** directives are essentially comments, the content doesn't matter except to help your users identify the purpose and location of the printer. Perhaps the most important directive is the **DeviceURI**, which identifies the protocol and location of the printer. In this case, it specifies the IPP protocol, on the given IP address, in the queue named printers. The name of the printer on the remote system is the ever-generic OfficePrinter. Important directives from the file are summarized in Table 15-7, and are listed in the order shown in Figure 15-15. Additional directives not shown are listed at the end of the table.

You'll note that a number of directives are associated with current printer operation; in fact, it's one place to find more information about the current status of a printer. If there's a problem, it may appear here, such as a printer that's not currently accepting print jobs, a printer with an unexpected error policy, a printer with a URI that's unacceptable, and so on.

NOTE
The UNIX epoch is the first moment of January 1, 1970. UNIX time is defined relative to this epoch, in seconds.

If you've configured access restrictions by user, they'll appear in this file for each printer. For example, the following directive limits access to one user:

```
AllowUser michael
```

Directive	Description
AuthInfoRequired	Possible requirement for authentication with a username and password.
Info	Commented information on the printer.
Location	Commented location of the printer.
MakeModel	Make and model associated with the printer driver.
DeviceURI	Network location of the printer.
State	Current printer status.
StateTime	Number of seconds since the UNIX epoch for the last change to the queue.
Filter	Filter program associated with a printer PPD file.
Accepting	Status on whether the printer is accepting job requests from clients.
Shared	Whether the printer is local or accessible to the network.
JobSheets	Banner pages before and after the print job.
QuotaPeriod	A period for limits in seconds; 0 means no quota. If there's a quota such as 86400 (one day), it should be coupled with a directive such as **PageLimit** or **KLimit**.
PageLimit	Limit in number of pages, per **QuotaPeriod**.
KLimit	Limit in number of KB, per **QuotaPeriod**.
AllowUser	User who is allowed to print to the specified printer. Multiple **AllowUser** directives can be included. Other users are not allowed.
OpPolicy	Access control limits.
ErrorPolicy	Action when there is an error.
AllowFrom	Host or network from which access is allowed. Access is denied to other systems.
DenyFrom	Host or network from which access is denied. Access is allowed from all other systems.
DenyUser	User who is not allowed to print to the specified printer. Multiple **DenyUser** directives can be included. All other users are allowed to send jobs to that printer.

TABLE 15-7. *CUPS Printer Configuration Directives*

In contrast, the following directives deny access to two users; all others are allowed access:

```
DenyUser katie
DenyUser dickens
```

Further limitations are possible, beyond what can be configured with the Printer Configuration tool. For example, the following directive limits access to users in the group named supervisors:

```
AllowUser @supervisors
```

In addition, the following directive limits access to systems on the noted network:

```
AllowFrom 192.168.0.*
```

Finally, if you wanted to limit the number of jobs sent to, say, a high-resolution color printer, the following directives would limit the size of the jobs sent to a printer to 100MB per hour:

```
QuotaPeriod 3600
KLimit 100000
```

Configured Groups of Printers

If you've configured a class of printers with the Printer Configuration or the web-based tools, the results are documented in the /etc/cups/classes.conf file. In general, the directives described in this file are the same as those in the /etc/cups/printers.conf file. One example is shown in Figure 15-16.

The differences are straightforward. The **Printer** directive specifies the name of printers that are members of the class. The directive should reference printers in the printers.conf file.

Printers Shared via Samba

Samba is the UNIX software that allows Solaris to communicate on networks primarily populated by Microsoft Windows computers. This section provides just an overview of those Samba configuration options associated with printing. For a detailed discussion of Samba, see Chapter 21.

Although Microsoft uses IPP for printer configuration and sharing, some networks have already been configured with Samba. In such cases, you'll want to set up sharing via Samba.

```
# Class configuration file for CUPS v1.4.2
# Written by cupsd on 2011-08-12 13:33
# DO NOT EDIT THIS FILE WHEN CUPSD IS RUNNING
<Class Class_of_Printers>
Info Some group of printers
Location In the print room
State Idle
StateTime 1313181165
Accepting Yes
Shared Yes
JobSheets none none
Printer NewOfficePrinter
Printer OfficePrinter
QuotaPeriod 0
PageLimit 0
KLimit 0
OpPolicy default
ErrorPolicy retry-current-job
</Class>
~
~
~
~
"classes.conf" 19 lines, 424 characters
```

FIGURE 15-16. *The CUPS classes.conf file*

The Samba configuration file is smb.conf in the /etc/samba directory. Printer-related directives start with the following, which loads a list of printers to be shared:

```
load printers = yes
```

The comment here is based on the LP system, which sets up shared printers in the /etc/printcap file. If the local system is a SystemV-based LP print server, you could include them in the Samba share with the following directive:

```
printcap name = lpstat
```

Alternatively, if you need to share printers configured only on CUPS servers, you could set the **printcap** accordingly:

```
printcap name = cups
```

In many cases, printers on the local system will be detected automatically; some trial and error is often appropriate. Later in the configuration file, you'll see the following stanza, which documents /var/spool/samba as the directory reserved for print spools processed through this service. The comment about "BSD-style print" system should not be a concern for CUPS users, because there is no need to specifically define individual printers in the Samba configuration. You've already done that work with the Printer Configuration or web-based tools. Because CUPS maintains its own job list, there's no need to make the print jobs in the /var/spool/samba directory browseable. Of course, any non-print files that are written to the directory would throw a wrench into the works associated with a printer.

```
# NOTE: If you have a BSD-style print system there is no need to
# specifically define each individual printer
[printers]
    comment = All Printers
    path = /var/spool/samba
    browseable = no
# Set public = yes to allow user 'guest account' to print
    guest ok = no
    writable = no
    printable = yes
```

Print Server Log Files

Log files associated with CUPS are sent to the /var/log/cups directory. It's an excellent place to find information if problems arise. If there's a particularly stubborn issue, you may choose to change the **LogLevel** directive in the cupsd.conf file from warn to a level with more detail, such as notice, info, or even debug. Of course, once the problem is solved, you generally should restore the original warn level, to avoid creating log files that are too large.

Typically, you'll find three CUPS-related log files in the /var/log/cups directory:

- **access_log**   Documents every access to the CUPS server, including the creation of print jobs
- **error_log**   Lists problems such as authentication errors, driver issues, and inaccessible printers
- **page_log**   Specifies print jobs, with printer, along with the name of the file printed

Summary

With the release of Solaris 11, CUPS is now the default print service. Because CUPS is the default print service on several other UNIX-based operating systems, that move makes sense.

CUPS is based on IPP, and it supports printers that allow users to send print jobs over the Internet, using TCP and UDP protocols over port number 631. Although it includes a number of commands from the LP service, don't expect to fully configure CUPS with LP administrative commands. However, you can set up individual users as printer administrators, first with the **roleadd** command and then with membership in a **SystemGroup**, as defined in the /etc/cups/cupsd.conf and /etc/group files.

CUPS includes two GUI tools for configuration: the Printer Configuration tool and a web-based tool. With either tool, you can create a new printer that's customized in useful ways. You can create a print class, where multiple printers are represented by a single name. Also, you can administer CUPS remotely using either tool if this feature is enabled on the CUPS server.

All of this configuration primarily affects files in the /etc/cups directory. The main CUPS configuration file is cupsd.conf. Individual printers are configured in stanzas in printers.conf. Print classes are configured in classes.conf. With the help of /etc/printcap, such printers can be shared via Samba over a network with Microsoft systems. When problems arise, you may be able to identify them in log files in the /var/log/cups directory.

CHAPTER
16

DNS and DHCP

wo of the essential services for a LAN are associated with the Domain Name Service (DNS) and the Dynamic Host Configuration Protocol (DHCP). With a DNS server, you can configure a database of hostnames and IP addresses that's authoritative for a local network. With a DHCP server, you can ration IPv4 addresses. Even if your networks are configured to use IPv6 addresses, a DHCP server can help configure consistent network settings.

The standard DNS server for Solaris is based on the software of the Berkeley Internet Name Domain (BIND), developed under the umbrella of the Internet Systems Consortium. BIND is the focus of a number of security issues because black-hat hackers may be motivated to redirect traffic from major websites. One way they do so is by attacking insecure BIND servers.

In this chapter, you'll create DNS and DHCP servers for a sample local network. Just be aware that this chapter provides sufficient information only for basic operation.

The Domain Name Service

DNS is a distributed database of domain names such as mheducation.com and the corresponding IP addresses of 12.163.148.101. Even with current computing power, it's not realistic to maintain the entire database of Internet domain names on a single system. In addition, domain names vary by country, and every country wants to keep control over its domains. So there are DNS servers that are "authoritative" for different countries, as well as individual domains such as mcgraw-hill.com.

Although you probably already understand the concepts behind DNS, this chapter includes a short introduction to how DNS was developed. Standard DNS client packages should already be installed. After you install DNS server packages, you'll see how to configure DNS as a server in a number of configurations. If you're setting up a master DNS server, you'll also need to configure a database of hostnames and IP addresses. That database may be limited to a local private network, or it may be used by others on the Internet to find your websites and more.

DNS Background

DNS is part of the TCP/IP protocol suite. The IP part is the Internet Protocol, which is based on binary numbers. The dominant form of IP addressing is known as *IP version 4 (IPv4)*, which dates back to 1981. The developers who worked on the TCP/IP protocol suite included protocols for hostnames and IP addresses. Hostnames such as mheducation.com are part of the TCP protocol. In contrast, numbers such as 12.163.148.101 are part of the IP protocol.

In the early years of the DARPA network, computers were expensive and rare. Access to networked computers was limited to a very few large-scale organizations. For those years, hostnames and IP addresses were maintained in a static hosts.txt file distributed to the administrator of each system. By the early 1980s, this file was already being overloaded. That spurred the development of DNS.

NOTE
DARPA refers to the Defense Advanced Research Projects Agency. The network that they sponsored evolved into the Internet.

DNS Configuration Concepts

As a distributed database, DNS is organized in a top-down fashion. Take a look at the "mheducation .com." URL. It's organized from right to left; in other words, the root domain is the dot at the end of the .com. (It's not a period.) Elements such as .com, .net, and .uk are subdomains of root. Names such as mheducation are subdomains of .com. We know that there's a web server associated with the mheducation.com URL; www.mheducation.com is a subdomain of mheducation.com. If there's an FTP server associated with the domain, it is also a subdomain of mheducation.com., as depicted next. (We've included the dot at the end of each domain name in this paragraph just to make the point that it's the root domain. It's also required in DNS-related configuration files. In the rest of the book, we'll use the standard format for domain names.)

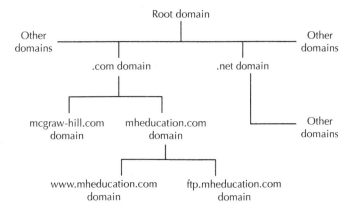

In the distributed database of hostnames, administrators are responsible for configuring and maintaining DNS servers that are authoritative for a particular zone. The root zone is administered by a group known as the Internet Assigned Numbers Authority (IANA). The master database of DNS servers authoritative for the root domain is maintained by the Internet Corporation for Assigned Names and Numbers (ICANN), which also oversees IANA. The file with these root servers can be downloaded from ftp.rs.internic.net. Each of these root servers is itself based on systems distributed in a variety of locations, often in different nation-states.

For users within McGraw-Hill, their systems may be configured to use DNS servers that are authoritative for the McGraw-Hill.com domain. Of course, the authority of that DNS server is likely limited to that domain, or possibly allied domains such as mheducation.com. If a McGraw-Hill user is searching for a URL outside that zone of authority, such as the Library of Congress at loc.gov, that McGraw-Hill DNS server should normally pass the request to another DNS server.

A Key Solaris Difference

Although DNS on many operating systems includes a series of configuration files, the Solaris 11 Service Management Facility (SMF) now generates many of them automatically. For example, although you could configure a DNS client by directly editing the /etc/resolv.conf configuration file, you can also have Solaris 11 generate that file with appropriate edits through SMF. You'll see how this works in the following sections.

Different DNS Servers

You can configure several different types of DNS servers, as listed next. Of course, you can create a master DNS server, with direct access to data for the local network.

- **Master** A master DNS server includes direct access to the database of hostnames and IP addresses. It may be configured as the authoritative DNS server for the network.

- **Secondary** A secondary DNS server can serve as a backup to the master DNS server, taking its information from zone transfers. It is sometimes also called a *slave* DNS server.

- **Caching** A caching DNS server forwards requests to others, while storing recently searched information in a local database. If the request is available in the local database, that information is served. You may want to "flush" information from a caching DNS server periodically. A caching DNS server is sometimes also called a *proxy* DNS server.

- **Forwarding** A forwarding DNS server forwards all requests to other DNS servers.

Some DNS servers may fall into multiple categories. For example, master and secondary servers can be configured to cache data collected from other DNS servers. Closely related to caching is recursion, where a DNS server sends a request not already in its database to another DNS server. The results of such recursive searches may themselves be cached. All DNS servers should be able to forward requests as needed to at least the root DNS servers. Yes, such features are subject to security attacks, especially when the DNS server is publicly available online.

In many cases, DNS administrators designate the secondary (slave) DNS server as the authoritative server for the network, authorized to receive requests from other DNS servers for your network. As the public face of the network, it can help protect the data configured for the master server. If the secondary server is compromised, you should be able to re-create it with a zone transfer from the master server.

Closely related are the multicast DNS services. Multicast DNS works as a distributed database of available services for the local network.

DNS Packages

The packages associated with DNS are straightforward. First, two basic packages are associated with DNS clients:

- **network/dns/bind** Basic DNS-related commands, including **host**, **dig**, **nslookup**, and **rndc**.

- **mdns** Multicast DNS libraries, which help the system discover shared services from other systems. Because MDNS is beyond the normal DNS database, we do not cover the configuration of this service.

Both are normally installed by default. If you need to set up a DNS server, you'll also need the following package:

- **service/network/dns/bind** DNS server libraries in the /lib/svc directory, along with DNS utilities in the /usr/sbin directory.

Key DNS Commands

One can think about DNS commands from two points of view: the client's and the server's. Appropriate client commands can be used to test DNS servers in different ways, from within the network as well as from outside the network. The following sections describe the basic commands from both the BIND client and server packages.

DNS Client Commands

The network/dns/bind package includes several client commands that can help you diagnose issues with DNS servers. First, the **dig** command requests information from the default DNS server defined in the /etc/resolv.conf file. If you configure a DNS server on a local system such as 192.168.0.1, you can query that server for information with a command like the following:

```
$ dig @192.168.0.1 mheducation.com
```

It's the successor to the **nslookup** command, which is also available for legacy support. In a similar fashion, you can use the **host** command to direct a request to a specific DNS server:

```
$ host mheducation.com 192.168.0.1
```

The **host** command is a bit more versatile because it can also be used to verify the reverse pointer, which specifies the FQDN associated with an IP address:

```
$ host 12.163.148.101 192.168.0.1
```

Finally, there are a couple of remote nameserver control utilities. Although they're part of the DNS client package, they're used to manage DNS servers and are therefore covered in subsequent sections.

DNS Server Management Commands

Some DNS server management commands are part of the BIND client tools package; others are part of the server package. We describe them briefly in Table 16-1; specific examples are provided later in this chapter.

A New Way to Configure a DNS Client

With Solaris 11, you have two ways to configure a client for DNS. You can directly edit key configuration files, or you can use the service configuration tool. In this section, you'll see how to use the service configuration tool to set up a DNS client, along with the changes it has made to the DNS client configuration file, /etc/resolv.conf.

Although the resolv.conf and nsswitch.conf files in the /etc/ directory have been deprecated, they're still generated from the Service Management Facility (SMF) database discussed in this chapter. Although you can still directly edit these files, the work you do to configure DNS in SMF is saved and can be restored to these files at your convenience.

The key command is **svccfg**. As an administrative user, use the **svccfg** command to set properties for the local system as a DNS client. You can open the prompt associated with the DNS client with the following command:

```
# svccfg -s network/dns/client
```

Here, the **-s** selects the Fault Management Resource Identifier (FMRI).

If the previously mentioned DNS client package is installed, you'll see the following prompt:

```
svc:/network/dns/client>
```

Command	Description
dns-sd	Runs the DNS service discovery test tool.
dnssec-dnsfromkey	Confirms a digital signature, created by the **dns-keygen** command.
dnssec-keyfromlabel	Creates an encryption key for a secure DNS server. Its functionally is similar to **dnssec-keygen**.
dnssec-keygen	Creates an encryption key for a secure DNS server.
dnssec-sigzone	Signs a zone with a key created by the **dnssec-keygen** command.
named	Specifies the main DNS daemon.
named-checkconf	Checks the syntax of DNS configuration files. Defaults to /etc/named.conf.
named-checkzone	Checks the syntax of DNS zone files, as defined in /etc/named.conf.
named-compilezone	Checks the syntax and integrity of a DNS zone file.
nscfg	Imports or exports legacy name service configuration files.
nsupdate	Updates the DNS database of hostnames and IP addresses.
rndc	Short for remote nameserver daemon control tool, the **rndc** command is used to manage DNS servers in various ways.
rndc-confgen	Generates DNS key configuration files, commonly rndc.conf.

TABLE 16-1. *DNS Server Management Commands*

At that point, you can set appropriate properties for the DNS client, refresh the configuration to implement the changes, and then exit from the **svccfg** utility. The following command sets the search properties for hostnames. When complete, this command adds the **search example.org** command to the /etc/resolv.conf configuration file:

```
svc:/network/dns/client> setprop config/search = astring: ("example.org")
```

The command that follows specifies IP addresses for remote DNS servers:

```
svc:/network/dns/client> setprop config/nameserver = net_address:
(8.8.8.8 8.8.4.4)
```

To verify the changes that you just made, run the following command:

```
svc:/network/dns/client> listprop config
```

The **select** command shown here applies the changes to the default DNS client configuration:

```
svc:/network/dns/client> select network/dns/client:default
```

The prompt changes to confirm that you're working with the default configuration:

```
svc:/network/dns/client:default>
```

Now the following command refreshes the local DNS client with the noted settings:

`svc:/network/dns/client:default>` **refresh**

Finally, return to the regular shell prompt:

`svc:/network/dns/client:default>` **quit**

To confirm the changes, review the contents of the /etc/resolv.conf file. Based on the commands used in this section, it should resemble Figure 16-1.

Now let's repeat the process for the name service search order. It's a hierarchy formerly configured through the /etc/nsswitch.conf file. Although that file is still in use, the database for that file is now also part of the SMF. In this case, the command that accesses the SMF name service switch database is

`# svccfg -s system/name-service/switch`

Because the nsswitch.conf file is part of the core-os package, it is almost certainly already installed on your system. Therefore, the noted command should always bring up the following prompt:

`svc:/system/name-service/switch>`

At this point, you can set the search order for hosts with the following command:

`svc:/system/name-service/switch> setprop config/host = astring: "files dns mdns"`

If you're not using multicast DNS, set **astring: "files dns"**.

Once again, verify the changes you just made. Because the category was config/host, you could apply the **listprop** command to that. But it's time to do a bit more. The following command lists all configuration values associated with the name service switch database:

`svc:/system/name-service/switch>` **listprop config**

```
#
# Copyright (c) 2011, Oracle and/or its affiliates. All rights reserved.
#

#
# _AUTOGENERATED_FROM_SMF_V1_
#
# WARNING: THIS FILE GENERATED FROM SMF DATA.
#   DO NOT EDIT THIS FILE.  EDITS WILL BE LOST.
# See resolv.conf(4) for details.

search  example.org
nameserver      8.8.8.8
nameserver      8.8.4.4
~
~
```

FIGURE 16-1.   *The /etc/resolv.conf file as modified with the **svccfg** utility*

As before, you'll want to set this in the default network configuration for this category:

```
svc:system/name-service/switch> select system/name-service/switch:default
```

When the new prompt appears, refresh the local name-service database with the noted settings:

```
svc:/system/name-service/switch:default> refresh
```

Now, return to the regular shell prompt:

```
svc:/system/name-service/switch:default> quit
```

Confirm the result in the /etc/nsswitch.conf file. Even though you just set the configuration for hostnames, you should see the same entries for the **ipnodes** directive.

DNS Client Configuration Files

When a client system searches for the IP address associated with a name such as mheducation.com, it searches local files and DNS servers based on a setting in the /etc/nsswitch.conf file, specifically:

```
hosts: files dns
ipnodes: files dns
```

This is based on the entries made in the previous section with the **svccfg** utility. If you use the /etc/nsswitch.dns file, it includes multicast DNS in the search order:

```
hosts: files dns mdns
ipnodes: files dns mdns
```

In either case, Solaris 11 configures **hosts** and **ipnodes** as the same databases. The **ipnodes** directive is included for legacy reasons. The search order based on these directives is as follows:

1. The database of hostnames and IP addresses listed in /etc/hosts.
2. DNS servers configured in the /etc/resolv.conf file.
3. Multicast DNS discovery, based on multicast searches.

The default contents of the /etc/hosts file include the localhost and local hostnames, along with the associated IPv4 and IPv6 loopback and network addresses. You can add the hostnames and IP addresses of your choice. Some may choose to document the hostnames and IP addresses in a small LAN in that file.

DNS Server Configuration

Although you may want to configure every networked system as a DNS client, you'll want to configure only a few systems as a DNS server. The basic configuration process for a caching DNS server is fairly simple. Assuming the DNS server package has been previously installed, you can set up such a server by taking the following steps:

1. If you've just installed the DNS server package and haven't yet configured it, the service should be disabled. Just to be sure, run the following command:

   ```
   # svcadm disable network/dns/server
   ```

2. Make sure the standard DNS server configuration file exists. The following command creates it, or just modifies the last access time if it already exists. It doesn't change anything already in the /etc/named.conf file.

```
# touch /etc/named.conf
```

3. The following command checks for connectivity to the root DNS servers. It doesn't matter that the named.conf file is empty. Because it also serves as a syntax checker, it may identify issues with the contents of /etc/named.conf.

```
# named-checkconf -z /etc/named.conf
```

4. Although not required, you should enhance security with the following command. It creates a digital key that authenticates commands sent to this server. That key is saved in the /etc/rndc.key file.

```
# rndc-confgen -a
```

5. Now start DNS services:

```
# svcadm enable network/dns/server
```

6. Test the result. One way to do so is with the **dig** command. For example, the following command uses the DNS server on the local system to look up DNS information for oracle.com:

```
# dig @localhost oracle.com
```

A caching-only nameserver works with the help of the root nameservers included as a part of the Solaris code for DNS. These are the root nameservers configured around the world, and are described at www.root-servers.org.

There's one weakness. Without local database files, a search for the local system or IP address will return a blank result. For example, Figure 16-2 illustrates a search for the localhost address

```
michael@solaris-test1:~$ dig @localhost localhost

; <<>> DiG 9.6-ESV-R4-P3 <<>> @localhost localhost
; (3 servers found)
;; global options: +cmd
;; Got answer:
;; ->>HEADER<<- opcode: QUERY, status: NXDOMAIN, id: 3869
;; flags: qr rd ra; QUERY: 1, ANSWER: 0, AUTHORITY: 1, ADDITIONAL: 0

;; QUESTION SECTION:
;localhost.                     IN      A

;; AUTHORITY SECTION:
.                       5720    IN      SOA     a.root-servers.net. nstld.verisi
gn-grs.com. 2011120401 1800 900 604800 86400

;; Query time: 1 msec
;; SERVER: 127.0.0.1#53(127.0.0.1)
;; WHEN: Sun Dec  4 21:09:55 2011
;; MSG SIZE  rcvd: 102

michael@solaris-test1:~$ █
```

FIGURE 16-2. *When a DNS search turns up nothing*

that doesn't turn up anything from the top-level root DNS servers. You know that the IP address associated with the localhost system is 127.0.0.1 (or ::1 in IPv6 notation). Later in this chapter, you'll see what files to add to the database to return appropriate IP addresses for the localhost system.

TIP
Whenever you make a change to a DNS configuration file, make sure to refresh the service with the **svcadm refresh network/dns/server** *command.*

DNS Server Configuration in SMF

To review the current SMF database associated with the local DNS server, run the following command:

```
$ svcprop dns/server
```

It returns a list of over 50 variables. If desired, you can use the **svccfg** command, described earlier, to change some of them. Several important DNS variables are highlighted in Table 16-2.

Creating a DNS Forwarding Name Server

More configuration options are available besides the ones listed in SMF. If you want to set up even a forwarding DNS server, you'll want to include several directives in the /etc/named.conf file. Those directives need to point to other files at least for the localhost system. If you're setting up a database for a local DNS server, you should also set up a separate directory for this purpose. Unless you're configuring DNS in a chroot jail, one sample directory that would work is /var/named. We describe a sample configuration file for /etc/named.conf in this section.

Even though the intent of a Forwarding DNS server is to forward all DNS requests, it can't forward all requests. It needs a local database for the loopback address. In other words, when a user on a local system searches for the local name or IP address, the DNS server should have

Variable	Value
options/chroot_dir	Sets to an **astring** value for the desired chroot directory.
options/configuration_file	Assigns to a configuration file other than the default, /etc/named.conf.
options/ip_interfaces	Supports limits to IPv4 or IPv6 networking; the default is both.
options/listen_on_port	Assigns communications to a different port number.
general/action_authorization	Specifies the role to be assigned to DNS administrators.
start/exec	Notes the executable file used to start the service.

TABLE 16-2. *Selected DNS Server SMF Variables*

authoritative information. The **forwarders** directive points to the IP address of a remote DNS server. If you want to test the result online, Google has reportedly made DNS servers available at IP addresses 8.8.8.8 and 8.8.4.4. You'd substitute those addresses for 192.168.0.1 in the stanza shown here:

```
options {
        directory "/var/named";
        allow-transfer {
                none;
        };
        forwarders {
        192.168.0.1;
        };
};
```

NOTE
If you're new to DNS configuration files, be careful. Even an extra space at the end of a line can lead to errors.

No separate directives are required to refer to root nameservers. If you've set up a different DNS server as a forwarder, that server should forward appropriate requests to the root DNS servers.

For every kind of DNS server, it should be authoritative for the local system. To that end, you should set up the following stanzas. The localhost zone specifies the response to a search for the localhost address:

```
zone "localhost" {
    type master;
    file "/var/named/db.local";
};
```

The stanza that follows specifies the response to a reverse search. Databases go both ways. Because the "127." covers the loopback network, in most cases, there will be only one datapoint in that file.

```
zone "127.in-addr.arpa" {
        type master;
        file "/var/named/db.127";
};
```

We'll return to the /etc/named.conf file shortly. In any primary or secondary nameserver, you'll want to set up a database of addresses for the "zone of authority," normally the local network.

Extending DNS for a Primary or Secondary Server

For a relatively small network, you could maintain a database of hostnames and IP addresses in each local /etc/hosts file. But for larger networks, that can be cumbersome. In that case, you'll want to set up at least a primary DNS server for a network. Sometimes also known as a master

DNS server, the following in stanzas /etc/named.conf creates the authoritative system for some sample example.com network

```
zone "example.com" IN {
        type master;
        file "/var/named/db.example.com";
        allow-transfer {
                none;
        };
};
```

The first line specifies the zone of authority for the example.com domain. As suggested by the **type master;** directive, this is the master or primary DNS for that zone. The **file** specifies the full path to the database file for that zone.

Because transfers to all other DNS servers are allowed by default, it's normal to set the **allow-transfer { none; }** option to disable it. Any black-hat hacker who gets a list of systems on your local network can then attack each component of that network systematically. If you're also enabling communication with a secondary DNS server, you'll want to substitute the IP address of that server for **none**. Conversely, if this /etc/named.conf file is on a secondary DNS server, you'll want to set **type slave**.

The **allow-update { none; }** option is no longer necessary because dynamic updates from system hosts are disabled by default.

Of course, you'll also need a stanza for reverse searches. The same provisions apply to the **allow-transfer** directive here as well:

```
zone "0.168.192.in-addr.arpa" IN {
        type master;
        file "/var/named/db.0.168.192.in-addr.arpa";
        allow-transfer {
                none;
        };
}
```

DNS Logging

If you're administering a DNS server, you'll want it to produce appropriate information for logs. If something goes wrong, you'll see it in the logs. If someone has a problem getting information from your the DNS server, you may see it in the logs. To configure logs, you'll want to add an appropriate stanza to the /etc/named.conf configuration file:

```
logging {
        channel some_standard {
                file "/var/log/named.log";
                severity info;
                print-time yes;
        };
        category "default" {
                "another_standard";
        };
};
```

The directives in this stanza are described here:

- **logging** Directive for a stanza that defines how log information is collected.
- **channel** Sets a name for the logging channel; substitute as desired for *some_standard*.
- **file** Specifies the full path to the file used to collect logging information.
- **severity** Defines the level of logging information sent to the configured logging file.
- **print-time** Includes a timestamp for each logged event.
- **category** Specifies categories of log data to collect and record in the specified log file. The **default** category shown specifies all nondefault logs. Substitute as desired for *another_standard*.

This information is over and above the standard Solaris logs in the /var/svc/log directory. As shown in the output to the **svcs -l dns/server** command, the Solaris DNS server log file is network-dns-server\:default.log. For more information, see the "Troubleshooting" section later in this chapter.

DNS Database Files

This section addresses the contents of database files associated with a DNS server. Most of the files are related to the local system because each DNS server has to be the authority for itself. These files can be configured on all DNS servers, including those that are configured as "forwarding-only" and "caching."

Just be careful, because each database includes "forward" and "reverse" databases. A forward database returns an IP address based on a search for a fully qualified domain name (FQDN) such as solaris11.example.com. A reverse database identifies the FQDN from the IP address.

Four files are at the heart of an authoritative DNS server because it is the database for the systems on an associated network. It includes two files each for the localhost system, and two files for the local network administered through the DNS server. Each set of files includes databases for forward and reverse address searches. These files can be found on primary and secondary DNS servers (also known as master and slave servers).

Although the names of these files as well as their locations can vary, you should specify them in the main DNS configuration file, /etc/named.conf. Even though this section assumes that you've used the filenames described earlier, all that matters is that you maintain the same filenames in the named.conf file and the associated directory. For the purpose of this chapter, we've named the files as follows, in the /var/named directory:

- **Forward localhost** db.local
- **Reverse localhost** db.127
- **Forward zone** db.example.com
- **Reverse zone** db.122.168.192

The files described in this section are taken in part from the Oracle Solaris Jumpstart Server Setup documentation. Each of these files includes a number of acronyms and abbreviations, as described in Table 16-3.

Variable	Description
TTL	Specifies Time To Live, which is the expatriation time for data in the local file, in seconds.
@	Notes the zone origin, such as localhost or example.com.
IN	Denotes the standard class of the record. **IN** is short for Internet.
NS	Specifies the location of the authoritative nameserver.
A	Designates an IPv4 address record.
AAAA	Designates an IPv6 address record.
MX	Specifies a mail server.

TABLE 16-3. *Commonly Used DNS Database Variables*

The Forward localhost Database

The file shown in Figure 16-3 specifies the forward database associated with the loopback address. The "localhost." in the SOA line specifies the full generic hostname of the local system. All DNS hostnames, including regular Internet addresses, are supposed to end with a dot. Other key entries are explained in Table 16-4. Unless otherwise noted, the times described in DNS database files are shown in seconds.

With the data in Table 16-4 in mind, the key information is in the last three lines. The first line here specifies the nameserver that is authoritative for the localhost system, which is and should be localhost:

```
@    IN    NS    localhost.
```

```
;
; BIND data file for local loopback interface
;
$TTL    604800
@       IN      SOA     localhost. root.localhost. (
                              2         ; Serial
                         604800         ; Refresh
                          86400         ; Retry
                        2419200         ; Expire
                         604800 )       ; Negative Cache TTL
;
@       IN      NS      localhost.
@       IN      A       127.0.0.1
@       IN      AAAA    ::1
~
~
"db.local" 14 lines, 474 characters
```

FIGURE 16-3. *The db.local Forward localhost Database*

Entry	Description
localhost.	The name of the local system, which requires a dot at the end.
root.localhost.	Specifies the e-mail address for the server administrator; this gets translated to root@localhost. If you have a dedicated DNS administrator, you may want to change this address accordingly.
Serial	For regular DNS database files, a 10-digit field, in yyyymmddss format, where yyyy is the four-digit year, mm is the month, dd is the day, and ss is the serial number. If you change the database more than once in a day, you should specify a revised serial number.
Refresh	Sets the period between searches for DNS master server databases.
Retry	Assigns a waiting time to retry the connection if there is a problem.
Expire	Configures an expiration time for data in the current file, if no connections are made to other DNS servers. It's normally set to four weeks.
Negative Cache TTL	Sets a minimum cache time for information in this database.

TABLE 16-4. *Important Entries in the db.local File*

The A record that follows assigns the well-known loopback address of 127.0.0.1 to the localhost hostname:

```
@    IN    A    127.0.0.1
```

Finally, the AAAA record specifies the IPv6 address:

```
@    IN    AAAA    ::1
```

Now save the file, and use a command such as **svcadm refresh dns/server** to reread all changes. To verify the result, run an appropriate **host** command. The command uses the following format:

```
$ host hostname dns_server
```

The Reverse localhost Database
The file shown in Figure 16-4 specifies the reverse database associated with the loopback address. The information shown in this database is nearly identical to the forward database. The db.127 file introduces one new directive, the pointer (PTR).

Take a look at the last line in the file:

```
1.0.0    IN    PTR    localhost.
```

```
;
; BIND reverse data file for local loopback interface
;
$TTL    604800
@       IN      SOA     localhost. root.localhost. (
                            1        ; Serial
                        604800       ; Refresh
                         86400       ; Retry
                       2419200       ; Expire
                        604800 )     ; Negative Cache TTL
;
@       IN      NS      localhost.
1.0.0   IN      PTR     localhost.
~
~
```

FIGURE 16-4. *The db.127 reverse localhost database*

You may realize that the first entry shows the last three numbers of the loopback address, in reverse order. When DNS recognizes the request for information about address 127.0.0.1, it should be translated to the hostname. Now save the file, and use a command such as **svcadm refresh dns/server** to reread all changes.

So the following command searches for the IP address of the localhost system, searching the database of the DNS server on IP address 127.0.0.1:

```
$ host localhost 127.0.0.1
```

If you've properly configured the aforementioned database files, you'll get the following entries in the output:

```
localhost has address 127.0.0.1

localhost has IPv6 address ::1
```

Now search for the 127.0.0.1 address in the database with the following command:

```
$ host 127.0.0.1 127.0.0.1
```

If successful, you'll see the following output, which starts with the inverse of the IP address:

```
1.0.0.127.in-addr.arpa domain name pointer localhost.
```

The Forward Zone Database

With the models of the forward and reverse databases for the localhost system, you can set up forward and reverse databases for the systems on a network. For the purpose of this section, we assume that IP addresses on the local network have been assigned statically.

For the forward zone, we start here with an arbitrary file named db.local. To that end, we create a simple DNS server that specifies the IP address of two systems. To do so, we take the following steps:

1. Navigate to the /var/named directory.

2. Use the db.local file as a template. Based on the files listed in the /etc/named.conf file described earlier, copy it to db.example.com.

3. Edit the db.example.com file. Substitute the name of the nameserver and appropriate e-mail address of the server administrator. The SOA line might read something like

```
@    IN    SOA    solaris11.example.com.    admin.example.com.
```

where the DNS host is nameserver.example.com, with an administrative e-mail address of admin@example.com.

4. Specify an appropriate serial number. As described earlier, it should include the current date; for example, the following entry might be the second version of this database created on July 13, 2012:

```
2012071302 ; Serial
```

Whenever you make additional changes to the file, revise the serial number. Other DNS servers that take data from this server won't read the file unless there's a different serial number.

5. You may wish to modify directives such as TTL, Refresh, Retry, and so on. You can specify these periods in minutes, hours, days, or weeks, as follows:

```
$TTL 3d
4h  ; Refresh
20m ; Retry
2w  ; Expire
3h  ; Negative Cache TTL
```

6. Make sure to change the first entry, which specifies the hostname of the local DNS server:

```
@    IN    NS    solaris11.example.com.
```

7. Mail servers on the local network get their own designation **(MX)** in the DNS forward database. For example, the following two entries designates the solaris11 and the maui systems as the first and second mail servers for the network:

```
@    IN    MX    10    solaris11.example.com.
@    IN    MX    20    maui.example.com.
```

8. Specify the names and IP addresses of the systems on the local network; here is one example:

```
solaris11    IN    A    192.168.122.74
maui         IN    A    192.168.122.1
```

9. This is an excellent opportunity to configure other uniform resource locators (URLs) as part of the database; the following example configures www.example.com and ftp.example.com, with the help of the canonical name **(CNAME)** directive:

```
www    CNAME    solaris11.example.com.
ftp    CNAME    maui.example.com.
```

10. Now save the file, and use a command such as **svcadm refresh dns/server** to reread all changes.

11. Verify the result with the **host maui.example.com 127.0.0.1** command. If successful, you'll see the following output:

```
maui.example.com has address 192.168.122.1
```

12. Test the DNS server for all the other information in the forward zone database file.

The Reverse Database

Now that you've created a forward database, it's time to complete the process. In this section, you'll create a reverse database, with an arbitrary file named db.122.168.192. The name is based on the inverse of the 192.168.122.0 network address. To be consistent with the forward database, we use the same IP addresses and the same two systems used in the earlier section, with the following steps:

1. Navigate to the /var/named directory.

2. Use the db.127 file as a template. Based on the files listed in the /etc/named.conf file described earlier, copy it to db.122.168.192.

3. Edit the db.122.168.192 file. As you did with the forward database, substitute the name of the nameserver and appropriate e-mail address of the server administrator. The SOA line might read something like this:

   ```
   @       IN      SOA     solaris11.example.com.      admin.example.com.
   ```

4. As before, include an appropriate serial number:

   ```
   2012071302 ; Serial
   ```

   To repeat, don't forget to change the serial number whenever you make additional changes to this file.

5. As with the forward database file, you may wish to modify directives such as TTL, Refresh, Retry, and so on. If you've made such changes to the forward database file, you may want to make similar changes here.

6. Once again, change the first entry to specify the hostname of the local DNS server:

   ```
           IN      NS      solaris11.example.com.
   ```

7. Now you can set up the components of the network. The first column is the system address on the network, in reverse order. Because it's just one number on the 192.168.122 network, reverse order doesn't matter in this particular case. It is set up as a PTR record associated with a specific URL:

   ```
   1       IN      maui.example.com.
   74      IN      solaris11.example.com.
   ```

8. Now save the file, and use a command such as **svcadm refresh dns/server** to reread all changes.

9. Verify the result with the **host 192.168.122.1 127.0.0.1** command. If successful, you'll see the following output:

   ```
   1.122.168.192.in-addr.arpa domain name pointer maui.example.com.
   ```

10. Test the DNS server for all the other information in the forward zone database file.

Troubleshooting

If problems arise with the DNS server, you'll eventually want to read the associated log file, defined from /etc/named.conf. But first, you should check the basics, with respect to networking and the DNS service. Once you've confirmed connectivity via physical means as well as with

```
02-Dec-2011 10:08:15.164 zone 0.in-addr.arpa/IN: loading from master file /var/n
amed/db.0 failed: file not found
02-Dec-2011 10:08:15.164 zone 0.in-addr.arpa/IN: not loaded due to errors.
02-Dec-2011 10:08:15.164 zone 127.in-addr.arpa/IN: loading from master file /var
/named/db.127 failed: file not found
02-Dec-2011 10:08:15.164 zone 127.in-addr.arpa/IN: not loaded due to errors.
02-Dec-2011 10:08:15.164 zone 0.168.192.in-addr.arpa/IN: loading from master fil
e db.0.168.192.in-addr.arpa failed: file not found
02-Dec-2011 10:08:15.164 zone 0.168.192.in-addr.arpa/IN: not loaded due to error
s.
02-Dec-2011 10:08:15.164 zone 255.in-addr.arpa/IN: loading from master file /var
/named/db.255 failed: file not found
02-Dec-2011 10:08:15.164 zone 255.in-addr.arpa/IN: not loaded due to errors.
02-Dec-2011 10:08:15.165 zone example.com/IN: loading from master file db.exampl
e.com failed: file not found
02-Dec-2011 10:08:15.165 zone example.com/IN: not loaded due to errors.
02-Dec-2011 10:08:15.165 zone localhost/IN: loading from master file /var/named/
db.local failed: file not found
02-Dec-2011 10:08:15.165 zone localhost/IN: not loaded due to errors.
02-Dec-2011 10:08:15.165 running
02-Dec-2011 10:12:18.214 shutting down
02-Dec-2011 10:12:18.214 stopping command channel on 127.0.0.1#953
02-Dec-2011 10:12:18.214 stopping command channel on ::1#953
02-Dec-2011 10:12:18.215 no longer listening on 127.0.0.1#53
02-Dec-2011 10:12:18.215 no longer listening on 192.168.122.74#53
02-Dec-2011 10:12:18.289 exiting
:
```

FIGURE 16-5. *Sample DNS log information*

commands such as **ping**, you should then make sure the current DNS service is running. One way to do so is with the following command:

```
$ svcs dns/server
```

There are three basic options for output. Either the DNS server service is online, disabled, or configured in maintenance mode. In most cases, maintenance mode is a result of some failure when trying to enable DNS.

If the system should be running, but isn't, you could check the system log for the DNS server. As described earlier, it is the network-dns-server\:default.log file. But that log file provides only basic information, such as an /etc/named.conf file that doesn't exist.

Of course, you should use the **named-checkconf** command described earlier to check the syntax of any configuration files you created.

For additional information, you can use the log file defined in the /etc/named.conf file. It's defined in that file as /var/log/named.log. The messages in this file are more descriptive. Look at the excerpt from this log shown in Figure 16-5. It identifies problems such as files that are not found, database files that can't be loaded because of errors, as well as TCP/IP ports in use.

The Dynamic Host Configuration Protocol (DHCP)

A DHCP service supports the automatic configuration of hosts on a network. DHCP is primarily used for IPv4 addresses, to ration and assign them as needed. However, automatic configuration can also ease administrative requirements on an IPv6 network. If IPv4 networks are sufficient, Solaris 11 includes a GUI-based configuration tool, **dhcpmgr**, based on a package of the same name. In this chapter, you'll explore this tool and how it sets up appropriate configuration files.

It's a "quick and easy" way for less experienced administrators to set up DHCP. Unfortunately, its abilities are limited to IPv4 addressing.

If you prefer a more traditional form of DHCP, or need to set up automated configuration for IPv6 networking, install the isc-dhcp package. It includes a standard sample dhcpd.conf configuration file in the /etc/inet directory. Linux administrators may find this option more familiar. In any case, the isc-dhcp package is preferred, and will be the only choice for DHCP server configuration in the future, perhaps even for a later release of Solaris 11.

The DHCP Management Tool

In this section, you'll explore the workings of the DHCP management tool. You'll configure a DHCP server on a local system. If you're working on a network that already includes a DHCP server, such as many routers, you'll want to disable it first. Although the DHCP management tool is deprecated for Solaris 11, it is still the one GUI-related tool available for this service, and is therefore one that can help illustrate the configuration of a DHCP server for administrators who are more comfortable with the GUI. If you see an issue with this GUI tool, we suggest that you learn to configure a DHCP server from the command line, as described shortly, in the /etc/dhcpd .conf configuration file.

Now open a command-line interface in a Solaris 11 GUI. Run the **dhcpmgr** command to start the configuration process. As shown in Figure 16-6, you can use this tool to configure a local DHCP server or a Bootstrap Protocol (BOOTP) relay for a DHCP server configured on a remote network. Select Configure As DHCP and click OK to continue. If this is the first time you've run **dhcpmgr**, this should start the DHCP Configuration Wizard, shown in Figure 16-7. (If **dhcpmgr** has been run on this system before, you'll see the DHCP Manager window shown in Figure 16-12. In that case, you can start the DHCP Configuration Wizard by "unconfiguring" the current DHCP server. To do so, click Service | Unconfigure and then click OK in the window that appears; then run **dhcpmgr** again.) At that point, take the following steps:

1. The DHCP Configuration Wizard, as shown, summarizes the steps you'll take in the left pane. To continue, you'll have to accept the one option for storing DHCP configuration data: Text Files. Only then will you be able to click Next to continue.

2. You're taken to step 2, where the wizard suggests that you use the /var/dhcp directory to store DHCP. This chapter assumes you accept that default. Do so and click Next to continue.

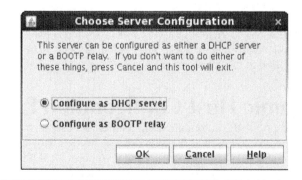

FIGURE 16-6. *The DHCP management tool*

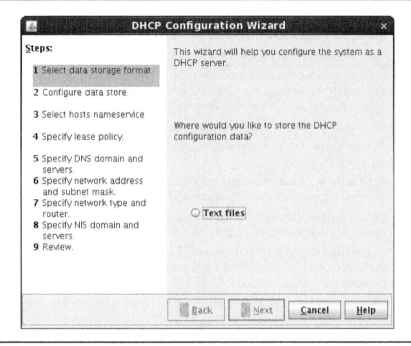

FIGURE 16-7. *The DHCP Configuration Wizard*

3. In step 3, you'll just need to accept the Do Not Manage Hosts Records option, because this DHCP server can't manage /etc/hosts. Do so and click Next to continue.

4. Now you can specify the length of the lease for IP addresses and more assigned to DHCP clients. The standard is one day; you can set lease times in hours or weeks. In general, you should retain the Clients Can Renew Their Leases option; otherwise, clients would have to reboot to renew a DHCP lease. Select a lease length and click Next to continue.

5. Next, you add the domain and IP addresses of a DNS server for the network. That information is included in the DHCP lease. You can add a domain such as example.com and the IP addresses of the DNS servers of your choice. Do so and click Next to continue.

6. Now you specify the network from which the DHCP server will assign IP addresses. Because it assumes IPv4, you'll enter addresses in dotted-quad notation. Enter the desired network address and subnet mask and then click Next to continue.

7. In this step, you configure the network type and whether to use the Router Discovery Protocol (RDP).

   Two network types are available: Local Area Network (LAN) and Point-to-Point. LAN is well known and should be the standard in the great majority of cases. Point-to-Point is an option for a network with just two systems.

RDP automatically discovers available routers for remote communications. If you have multiple routers and want to specify the gateway for communications, you'll want to specify the IP address for that router.

Make the appropriate selections and click Next to continue.

8. If there's a Network Information Service (NIS) server with user and host information, you can specify the name of the NIS domain as well as the IP address of NIS servers in this screen. If applicable, enter that information; when finished, click Next to continue.

9. You can now review the settings you've configured. One example is shown in Figure 16-8.

10. If you're satisfied with the configuration, click Finish. Files are written to the /var/dhcp directory.

11. If this is the first time you've run the DHCP Configuration Wizard, the DHCP Manager shown in Figure 16-9 opens, with an offer to start the Address Wizard.

12. Click Yes in the Start Address Wizard window. It should open the Add Addresses to Network window shown in Figure 16-10.

13. As shown in the figure, you're prompted to specify the number of IP addresses to allow the DHCP server to assign. Make a selection and add a comment if desired. Click Next to continue.

The Generate Client Names option is not currently active for the DHCP Address Wizard. Given the deprecated status of the GUI tool, it may not become active in the future. Make any desired changes and click Next to continue.

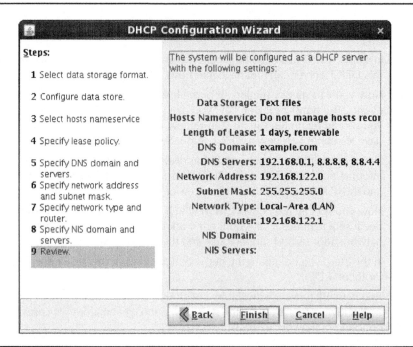

FIGURE 16-8. *Proposed configuration*

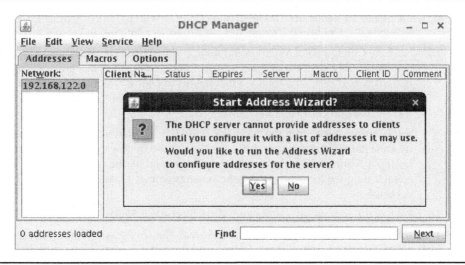

FIGURE 16-9. *The DHCP Manager*

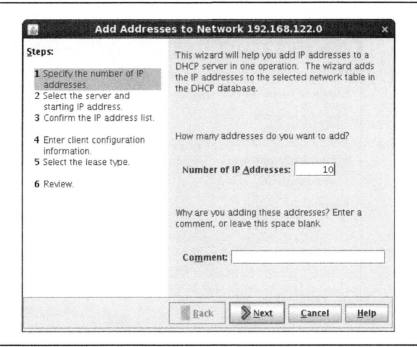

FIGURE 16-10. *The DHCP Address Wizard*

14. Review the IP addresses to be designated for assignment. The numbers should start with the first legal available IP address, and continue with the previously selected number of IP addresses. Confirm the result and click Next to continue.

15. Note the Configuration Macro from the drop-down text box, as shown in Figure 16-11. The default should reflect the options you've configured so far in this process. Other available options would omit data such as DNS servers in DHCP client assignments. Click View for details of a macro. This section assumes you find the default macro satisfactory. Make sure it's selected and click Next to continue.

    You can now select from the two basic lease types: dynamic and permanent. As suggested by their names, the dynamic lease type is limited by the length of the lease described in step 4. Permanent leases, while they are available, mean that the same IP address is always assigned to the same system, when possible. Make a selection and click Next to continue.

16. Review the settings just configured. If satisfied, click Finish.

17. You should now see the DHCP Manager with the configured DHCP parameters, including assignable IP addresses, status, server, and more. Explore the options available from the window, as shown in Figure 16-12. When finished, click File | Exit.

18. The DHCP server should already be running. To confirm, execute the following command:

    ```
    $ svcs dhcp-server
    ```

19. The DHCP server should now be ready for use.

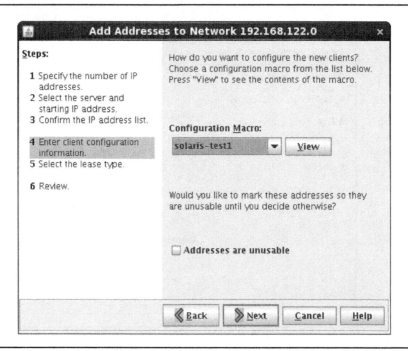

FIGURE 16-11. *Select a configuration macro.*

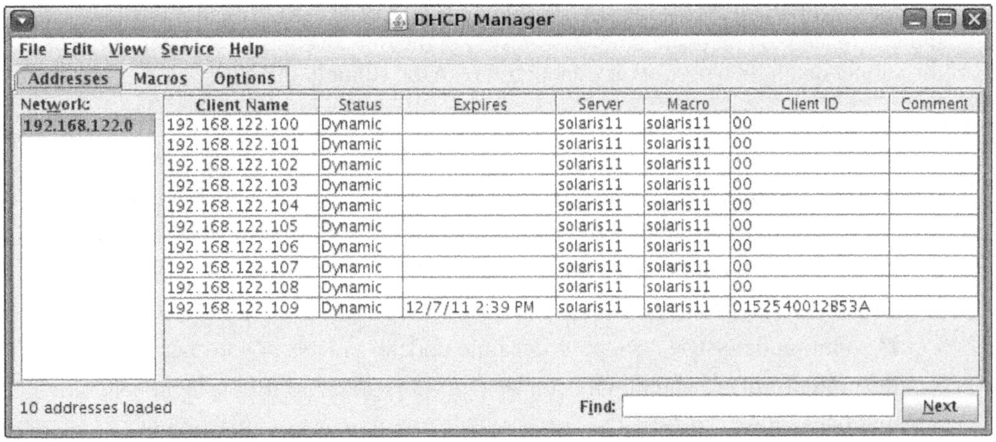

FIGURE 16-12. *The DHCP Manager, as configured*

The next time you run the **dhcpmgr** command, you'll be taken to the DHCP Manager screen shown in Figure 16-12. If you want to run the Address or Network Wizard again, they're available from the Edit menu.

DHCP Configuration Files

The steps you just took to set up a DHCP server should now be recorded in configuration files in the /var/dhcp directory. For the 192.168.122.0 network, these files are SUNWfiles1_192_168_122_0 and SUNWfiles1_dhcptab.

The comments in these files discourage editing "by hand"; therefore, if you want to change the associated parameters, rerun the appropriate wizard from the DHCP Manager window.

The ISC DHCP Server

If you need to set up IPv6 networking, if you prefer a more "standard" DHCP server with a dedicated configuration file, or if you just want to be ready for when the GUI **dhcpmgr** tool is no longer available for Solaris 11, install the **isc-dhcp** package. It includes a sample configuration file in the /etc/inet directory: dhcpd.conf.example. You can use it as a template.

The ISC DHCP server relies on separate configuration files for IPv4 and IPv6 networking. The server looks for the dhcpd4.conf and dhcpd6.conf files, respectively, in the /etc/dhcp directory.

Once you've configured these files, you can activate the ISC DHCP server on the IPv4 and IPv6 networks with the following commands:

```
# svcadm enable dhcp/server:ipv4
# svcadm enable dhcp/server:ipv6
```

If you've configured BOOTP relays, you can also activate those services:

```
# svcadm enable dhcp/relay:ipv4
# svcadm enable dhcp/relay:ipv6
```

Now we'll review the standard options in the dhcpd.conf.example configuration file. Because this file is written for IPv4 addressing, you may need to adjust to configure IPv6 networking. When directly related to addressing, the IPv6 version of the directive has a "6" at the end. For example, the subnet on an IPv6 network is configured with the **subnet6** directive.

- **option domain-name**   Specifies the domain name associated with the networks configured for this server.
- **option domain-name-servers**   Provides information on available DNS servers for the network. Normally you should change this to IP addresses.
- **default-lease-time**   Sets the standard time for a DHCP lease.
- **max-lease-time**   Configures a lease time after which it has to be renewed.
- **ddns-update-style**   Supports dynamic updates of DNS, if you change "none" to "interim."
- **authoritative**   Signifies the authoritative DHCP server for the local network.
- **log-facility**   Defines a log category for DHCP messages. Because this is set to **local7**, you may want to set this up in a specific log file in /etc/syslog.conf with a **local7.* /var/log/dhcpd.log** directive.
- **subnet**   Specifies the network address to be configured.
- **netmask**   Specifies the network mask associated with the network address.
- **range**   Sets the range of IP addresses within the given network to be assigned.
- **option routers**   Defines the gateway between the local network and remote networks. Normally you should change this to IP addresses.
- **option broadcast-address**   If needed, defines a nonstandard broadcast address for the network.
- **host**   Defines a hostname; normally associated with dedicated DHCP information.
- **hardware ethernet**   Specifies the hardware address of the network card in question.
- **fixed-address**   Associated with the IP address to be assigned; you should replace it with an actual IP address.

The DHCP Client

The Solaris 11 DHCP client is configured in the /etc/default/dhcpagent file. Open it on your system and review the options, commented and otherwise.

If you enable a network interface with **VERIFIED_LEASE_ONLY**, that interface discards the lease. The IP address is then made available to other systems. This feature may be useful for portable devices such as laptops, which may need to frequently connect to different networks. Based on the examples, if your wireless card is associated with device file net1, the following directive requires the verified lease feature:

```
net1.VERIFIED_LEASE_ONLY=yes
```

In contrast, the following directive specifies that lease information from an Ethernet card associated with device file net0 is stored in the /etc/dhcp directory:

```
net0.VERIFIED_LEASE_ONLY=no
```

Without the device file preface, the directive is applied to all other network interfaces, associated with IPv4 networking. The **.v6.VERIFIED_LEASE_ONLY** directive is applied to IPv6 networking.

As suggested in the file, DHCP clients send **DISCOVER** messages looking for DHCP servers. By default, they wait three seconds to collect **OFFER** messages from any DHCP servers that might be listening. You can change the waiting period by setting the following directive to a desired number of seconds:

```
OFFER_WAIT=
```

The **CLIENT_ID** is used to send a specific identifier to a DHCP server; the specification for this directive is associated with IPv6 networking.

```
CLIENT_ID=
```

For IPv4 networks, a DHCP client looks for a hostname locally. For the net0 network device, it would look for the hostname in the /etc/hostname.net0 file, in a format such as this:

```
net0 my_hostname
```

The next two directives specify what the DHCP client wants from the DHCP server. The numbers in the list are taken from the /etc/dhcp/inittab and /etc/dhcp/inittab6 files, respectively. As suggested by the second prefix, you can set up a different list for IPv4 and IPv6 networks.

```
PARAM_REQUEST_LIST=1,3,6,12,15,28,43
.v6.PARAM_REQUEST_LIST=7,12,23,24,27,29
```

Summary

In this chapter, you examined some methods for configuring the Solaris 11 implementation of the DNS and DHCP services. They are interrelated because dynamic DNS updates on a DHCP server can be used to keep the DNS database up to date.

DNS is a distributed database of FQDN and IP addresses. It's normally configured in the /etc/named.conf file, with references to database files in the /var/named directory. On Solaris 11, DNS clients can be configured with SMF, with the help of the **svccfg** utility. With an empty named.conf file, Solaris 11 DNS code supports easy configuration of a DNS caching-only nameserver. Of course, with the help of various DNS configuration options in /etc/named.conf, you can set up a primary, a secondary, or a forwarding nameserver. With appropriate options, you can enhance the log information available from DNS in any file you specify.

Although DHCP was originally developed to ration available IPv4 addresses, it has been enhanced as a way to configure networks with a variety of network-related information. You can configure DHCP with wizards associated with the GUI DHCP Manager. Alternately, you can configure DHCP in a more traditional way. Once the ISC DHCP package is installed, you can set up DHCP configuration files for IPv4 and IPv6 networks.

References

The BIND 9 Administrator's Manual on the Internet Systems Consortium (ISC) website is www.isc.org.

The BIND 9 Migration Notes documentation is available from the Solaris 11 BIND package in the following file: /usr/share/doc/bind/migration.txt.

Listings of BIND features, known bugs and defects, and links to additional material can be found on the ISC website at www.isc.org.

The oracle of domain name services is perhaps *DNS and BIND, Fifth Edition*, written by Paul Albitz and Cricket Liu (O'Reilly 2006).

Oracle Solaris System Administration: IP Services is available online from http://docs.oracle .com/cd/E23824_01/html/821-1453/index.html.

CHAPTER
17

Mail Services

he focus of this chapter is on the Solaris implementation of the Simple Mail Transfer Protocol (SMTP). The one relevant service available for Solaris 11 is known as sendmail. Although other SMTP services are available for other UNIX-based operating systems, sendmail is perhaps the traditional e-mail server service for such systems.

Once installed and configured, sendmail can be used as an e-mail server for everything from individual systems to entire enterprises. It's also a common SMTP option for Linux systems. If you're looking for the commercially supported version of sendmail, look for the Sentrion Message Processing Platform, available from www.sendmail.com. However, that support may not be necessary because the software released as a part of Solaris 11 is supported by Oracle.

In this chapter, you'll examine the installation of sendmail, the ways you can customize its configuration files, the aliases you can configure, as well as the management of sendmail e-mail queues. Just be aware that this chapter provides sufficient information only for basic operation. It is intended to help you learn how to configure sendmail on Solaris 11. Because sendmail is a topic covered in books of up to 1,000 pages, you may want to explore additional options before putting such a server into production.

A sendmail Configuration Plan

This section provides an overview of what you need to do to configure sendmail. Of course, the first thing to do is to make sure that sendmail is installed and is up to date with the latest version available from the Solaris repositories. One way to perform that task is with the following command:

```
# pkg install sendmail
```

The sendmail packages include a variety of configuration files in the /etc/mail directory. The actual configuration files have a .cf extension. You'll configure those files with the help of macros. As is common with other services, sendmail can be configured in separate servers, as virtual hosts. With appropriate aliases, you can associate users and real e-mail addresses. With a few tips, you should also be able to administer mail queues to make sure users get their communications with a minimum of interruption.

Customizing sendmail

The default sendmail configuration supports communication between users on the local system. In fact, that's how log messages that highlight problems are sent to users such as root. But it's only when you configure sendmail to serve multiple systems on a network that sendmail show its full capabilities. To that end, in this section, you'll configure sendmail configuration files, set up sendmail in virtual hosts, set up Transport Layer Security (TLS) to secure e-mail transmissions, and work with forwarding files to make sure appropriate users get important communications. But first, you'll examine how to configure sendmail on a local system, connected to others in a Network Information Service (NIS) database.

Basic Procedures

In general, you'll want to disable the sendmail service before making any changes with a command such as the following:

```
# svcadm disable network/smtp:sendmail
```

When you're ready to test sendmail again, run the following command:

```
# svcadm enable network/smtp:sendmail
```

Once this is complete, you'll want to test the sendmail system locally. One way to do so is with the following command, which send the contents of /etc/hosts to the root user:

```
$ sendmail -v root < /etc/hosts
```

If you've enabled sendmail for network communication, you'll want to use this command to test messages to remote accounts such as an appropriate Internet e-mail address.

Customizing the Configuration for a Local System

The main sendmail configuration files in the /etc/mail directory are already configured for a local system. This section applies if you haven't configured a DNS server for this system or network, as discussed in Chapter 16.

In this section, you'll change the /etc/hosts configuration file. If you haven't already made some changes, chances are you'll see a line similar to the following:

```
127.0.0.1 solaris-vm1 localhost loghost
```

The sendmail service requires that hosts use fully qualified domain names (FQDNs). To that end, you'll need to include some domain name for systems on the local network. If you don't already have one, the example.com domain is reserved for documentation and can be used for that purpose:

```
127.0.0.1 solaris-vm1 solaris-vm1.example.com localhost loghost
```

Once this is complete, save /etc/hosts and check the result with the **check-hostname** command. If the command is successful, you'll see a message similar to the following:

```
Hostname solaris-vm1 OK: fully qualified as solaris-vm1.example.com
```

Mail Clients on a Network

In this section, you'll set up the structure of an e-mail server for a local network. Specifically, you'll set up /etc/hosts to accommodate an NIS network and then share the /var/mail directory so all users can get their e-mail from appropriate files on that directory.

Every system that participates in an NIS network needs a mailhost entry in the /etc/hosts file. For the solaris-vm1.example.com system described earlier, that entry would be as follows:

```
192.168.0.111   solaris-vm1  mailhost  mailhost.example.com
```

Of course, if you've configured a DNS server on a network, you'd give the solaris-vm1 .example.com system an appropriate MX entry in the forward DNS database file for that network.

On the server, you'll share the /var/mail directory. Although you can do so with the /etc/dfs/ dfstab file, that file is deprecated. The preferred method is with the **share** command; one way to do so is with the following command, where **-F nfs** specifies sharing the noted directory through the Network File System (NFS), with the read/write option (**-o rw**):

```
# share -F nfs -o rw /var/mail
```

NOTE
NFS and the automounter is covered in more detail in Chapter 19.

On each client, you'll need an empty /var/mail directory that can then mount the /var/mail directory from the mail server. One way to do so is with the help of the automounter; you could add the following entry to one of the files referenced by /etc/auto_master:

```
/var/mail  -rw,soft,actimeo=0 solaris-vm1.example.com:/var/mail
```

The options are read/write, soft mount, and disable caching. Although soft mounting reduces the risk of hangs based on a troubled network connection, some administrators prefer hard mounting to minimize the risk of data corruption. The solaris-vm1.example.com system is the host of the sendmail server used in this chapter.

Creating a New Configuration File

Although the sendmail service reads configuration files in the /etc/mail directory, it also includes template macro files (with .mc extensions) in various /etc/mail/cf subdirectories. Even though this section uses the files in the /etc/mail/cf/cf directory as a template, you could just as easily use some of the templates in one of the other /etc/mail/cf subdirectories. Just be sure to follow good practices with respect to backing up current working configuration files, and all will be fine. Whatever macro file you use, it'll be processed with the **make** command, with the help of the options shown in the file named Makefile in the /etc/mail/cf/cf directory.

NOTE
For a more complete description of the sendmail file configuration process, see the README file in the /etc/mail/cf directory.

Take the current sendmail.mc file and use it as a template. Make a copy in the current directory in a file with a name such as test.mc, and then open that file in a text editor. Take a look at the default settings.

First, be aware that in the sendmail macro language, **dnl** is like a comment character, but is used at the end of each line. Although it isn't required at the end of every line, it's a good practice to place it there. In addition, the quotes don't match in the normal sense because they always start with a back quote (`) and end with a single quote (') character.

The Existing sendmail Configuration File

Now let's analyze the default configuration file. In slight contrast to Linux, sendmail macro files start with the following **divert** directive:

```
divert(0)dnl
```

The **VERSIONID** directive that comes next sets a label for the current configuration:

```
VERSIONID(`sendmail.mc (Sun)')
```

The **OSTYPE** specifies the operating system:

```
OSTYPE(`solaris11')dnl
```

The **DOMAIN** directive includes the directives from a file in the /etc/mail/cf/domain subdirectory. It's useful if you're configuring multiple systems with the same fundamental directives, such as with virtual hosts. We'll come back to the macros in solairs-generic.m4 shortly. In this case, the file is solaris-generic.m4:

```
DOMAIN(`solaris-generic')dnl
```

The next directive defines a fallback e-mail server host, for when there are DNS problems that prevent the identification of the mail server responsible for the local network. In that case, the fallback is to send e-mail to the server on the local system, as defined by mailhost.example.com (defined earlier):

```
define(`confFALLBACK_SMARTHOST', `mailhost$?m.$m$.')dnl
```

The **MAILER** directives that follow use the local system and the SMTP protocol. One common option is procmail (this mail delivery agent is not covered in the book).

```
MAILER(`local')dnl
MAILER(`smtp')dnl
```

The **LOCAL_NET_CONFIG** option supports the direct creation of rules in a sendmail.cf file. One intent of a sendmail macro is to avoid detailed explanations of actual sendmail rules. Therefore, we'll just say that the sendmail rules shown here are customized for local mail delivery:

```
LOCAL_NET_CONFIG
R$* < @ $* .$m. > $*    $#esmtp $@ $2.$m $: $1 < @ $2.$m. > $3
```

The Solaris Generic sendmail Configuration

As defined in the **DOMAIN** directive, the default Solaris 11 sendmail configuration file includes the directives from the solaris-generic.m4 file in the /etc/mail/cf/domain directory. It's time to analyze that file.

The solaris-generic.m4 file starts with the same **divert** directive used earlier; good practice suggests that you add a **dnl** to the end of the line:

```
divert(0)dnl
```

The **VERSIONID** directive that follows is essentially just a label; in this case, it adds the hostname and time to the label:

```
VERSIONID('%W% (Sun) %G%')
```

The **define** directive that follows points to a file associated with forwarded e-mail. In this case, **$z** represents the user home directory, **$w** specifies the local hostname, and **$h** includes detail about the user.

```
define('confFORWARD_PATH', '$z/.forward.$w+$h:$z/.forward+$h:$z/.
forward.$w:$z/.forward')dnl
```

Several **FEATURE** directives follow. The first one redirects sendmail to aliases for obsolete e-mail addresses, with the help of the aliases.db file in the /etc/mail directory:

```
FEATURE('redirect')dnl
```

This directive means the local sendmail server is authoritative for systems listed in the /etc/mail/local-host-names file:

```
FEATURE('use_cw_file')dnl
```

This directive points to the /etc/mail/trusted-users file for a list of trusted users:

```
FEATURE('use_ct_file')dnl
```

NOTE
*When the sendmail macro file is compiled, the **FEATURE** directives include the contents of specified files in the /etc/mail/cf/feature directory.*

Normally, sendmail requires e-mails from senders with accounts in normal user@domain_name format. This directive means the local sendmail server accepts e-mails from users without a domain name, such as users on a local system:

```
FEATURE('accept_unqualified_senders')dnl
```

Normally, sendmail uses DNS to check that the domain name associated with an e-mail actually exists. This directive disables the check, which may be appropriate for systems where access to DNS is blocked or unreliable:

```
FEATURE('accept_unresolvable_domains')dnl
```

This directive supports access from any system on the local domain. For example, if the local domain is example.net, access is allowed from maui.example.net, kauai.example.net, oahu.example.net, and so on.

```
FEATURE('relay_entire_domain')dnl
```

Some users are secured by masquerading. However, the root user is well known and may be "exposed" with the following directive:

```
EXPOSED_USER('root')
```

Changes to the sendmail Configuration File

In this section, we'll demonstrate a simple change to the basic sendmail configuration. It takes advantage of the template files in the /etc/mail/cf/cf directory. Assume that you have a reliable connection to a DNS server that can resolve the domains of all legal e-mail addresses. In that case, you could use the solaris-antispam.m4 file in the **DOMAIN** directive. To make and implement that change, use the following steps:

1. Deactivate the sendmail service, with a command such as **svcadm disable network/smtp:sendmail**.

2. Navigate to the /etc/mail/cf/cf directory.

3. Make a copy of the template sendmail.mc file. Use a different filename, such as antispam.mc.

4. Open the antispam.mc file and change the **DOMAIN** directive to read as follows:

   ```
   DOMAIN('solaris-antispam')
   ```

5. Save the changes. Note the existence of the Makefile in the current directory. It supports the use of the **make** command, as follows, to build the revised macro file:

   ```
   # make antispam.cf
   ```

6. Test the changes with the sendmail service. In this case, you can do so with a command such as the following, which sends the contents of the /etc/hosts file to the local root user:

   ```
   # sendmail -C antispam.cf -v root < /etc/hosts
   ```

   If this is successful, you'll see messages similar to those shown in Figure 17-1.

```
050 >>> .
050 250 2.1.5 root OK
050 root... Sent
050 MAILER-DAEMON... aliased to postmaster
050 postmaster... aliased to root
050 postmaster... aliased to root
050 >>> RSET
050 250 2.0.0 ok
050 root... Using cached LMTP connection for local...
050 >>> MAIL From:<>
050 250 2.5.0 ok
050 >>> RCPT To:<root>
050 >>> DATA
050 250 2.1.5 ok
050 354 go ahead
050 >>> .
050 250 2.1.5 root OK
050 root... Sent
250 2.0.0 pBD790af002146 Message accepted for delivery
root... Sent (pBD790af002146 Message accepted for delivery)
Closing connection to [127.0.0.1]
>>> QUIT
221 2.0.0 solaris-vm1 closing connection
michael@solaris-vm1:~$ █
```

FIGURE 17-1.   *Messages generated by sendmail*

7. Back up the current sendmail configuration file:

   ```
   # cp /etc/mail/sendmail.cf /root/sendmail.cf
   ```

8. Implement the new configuration file:

   ```
   # cp /etc/mail/cf/cf/antispam.cf /etc/mail/sendmail.cf
   ```

9. Restart the sendmail service with a command such as **svcadm enable network/smtp:sendmail**.

If this is not the configuration you want, now is a good time to restore the original sendmail configuration file from the /root directory.

Virtual Hosts and sendmail

The sendmail service supports the configuration of virtual hosts. These are not quite the same as virtual hosts for services such as Apache. In the context of sendmail, virtual hosts take advantage of a feature in a file named virtusertable to forward e-mail from now obsolete e-mail addresses. The format of that file in the /etc/mail directory is as follows:

```
user1@olddomain.com  user1@newdomain.com
```

Substitute accordingly for the noted domains.

Alternatively, all mail from an old domain can be forwarded to a specific user, in a similar format:

```
@olddomain.com  admin1@newdomain.com
```

To set that up forwarding in this manner, you'd take the following steps:

1. Repeat the first two steps from the previous section; deactivate sendmail and navigate to the /etc/mail/cf/cf directory.

2. Make a copy of the sendmail.mc file in the noted directory, saving it to a file with a name such as virt.mc.

3. Add the following directive to the virt.mc file:

   ```
   FEATURE('virtuser_entire_domain')dnl
   ```

4. Save your changes. Repeat the intent of steps 5–8 from the previous section (substitute appropriately for antispam.cf). Don't restart sendmail yet.

5. Create a virtusertable file in the /etc/mail directory, in the noted format.

6. Process the changes into a hash readable by sendmail with the following command:

   ```
   # makemap hash virtusertable.db < virtusertable
   ```

7. Reactivate the sendmail service.

To repeat, if this is not the configuration you want, now is a good time to restore the original sendmail configuration file from the /root directory.

sendmail and Transport Layer Security

Security is an important part of any e-mail service. To that end, sendmail supports cryptographic security, with the help of certificates created to the requirements of the Transport Layer Security

(TLS) protocol. In this section, you'll create a TLS certificate and then revise and recompile the sendmail macro file to point to that certificate.

1. Deactivate sendmail. Again, one way to do so is with the following command:

   ```
   # svcadm disable network/smtp:sendmail
   ```

2. Create appropriate certificate subdirectories for sendmail. One way to do so is with the following commands:

   ```
   # cd /etc/mail
   # mkdir certs
   # mkdir certs/CA
   # cd certs/CA
   # mkdir private newcerts crl certs
   ```

   Red Hat Linux users may realize that is the same directory structure that exists in a standard /etc/pki directory.

3. Copy the openssl.cnf file from the /etc/sfw/openssl directory:

   ```
   # cp /etc/sfw/openssl/openssl.cnf /etc/mail/certs/CA/
   ```

4. Edit the openssl.cnf file from its new location in a text editor. Look for the **dir** directive; in the default version of the openssl.cnf file, you'll find it on line 42. Revise the **dir** directive to point to the /etc/mail/certs/CA directory:

   ```
   dir = /etc/mail/certs/CA
   ```

5. You may also want to revise the conditions associated with certificate policies. The options shown in Figure 17-2 are most permissive. If you need to be careful, you'll want to change more of the policy options shown.

```
# A few difference way of specifying how similar the request should look
# For type CA, the listed attributes must be the same, and the optional
# and supplied fields are just that :-)
policy          = policy_match

# For the CA policy
[ policy_match ]
countryName             = match
stateOrProvinceName     = match
organizationName        = match
organizationalUnitName  = optional
commonName              = optional
#commonName             = supplied
emailAddress            = optional

# For the 'anything' policy
# At this point in time, you must list all acceptable 'object'
# types.
[ policy_anything ]
countryName             = optional
stateOrProvinceName     = optional
localityName            = optional
organizationName        = optional
organizationalUnitName  = optional
commonName              = optional
#commonName             = supplied
emailAddress            = optional
```

FIGURE 17-2. *A view of certificate policies*

6. With the following command, set up a TLS certificate:

```
# openssl req -new -x509 -keyout private/mikekey.pem \
-out mikecert.pem -days 60 -config openssl.cnf
```

This command creates certificate requests (**req**) that are new (**-new**) and self-signed (**-x509**). It outputs (**-keyout**) a private key name of mikekey.pem in the private/ subdirectory, with an output file (**-out**) of mikecert.pem. The certificate is good for 60 days (the default is 30 days). It generates the key based on parameters in the local openssl.cnf file.

7. Once you run the **openssl** command from step 6, it generates a 1,024-bit key, encrypted to the algorithm developed by Rivest, Shamir, and Adelman (RSA), writing a private key to the noted file:

```
Generating a 1024 bit RSA private key
..++++++
................................++++++
writing new private key to 'private/mikekey.pem'
```

8. You're prompted to enter a passphrase and then are prompted again to confirm. As you should already know, passphrases are typically complete sentences, with spaces between words.

9. You're prompted to enter more information for the self-signed certificate. That includes the following:

- Two-letter country name
- State or province name
- Locality, such as city or town
- Organization name
- Organizational unit name
- Common name
- E-mail address

10. The **openssl** utility writes the certificate to the specified file (in this case, mikecert.pem).

11. Now you need to set up a couple files in the same /etc/mail/certs/CA directory to accommodate and sign the new certificate:

```
# touch index.txt
# echo '01' > serial
```

12. If you need to set up a new secure connection, you could do so with the following command. For our purposes, the **-nodes** option means the key is not encrypted and is shown in the noted donnareq.pem file. You're prompted for the same information listed in step 9.

```
# openssl req -nodes -new -x509 -keyout donnareq.pem -out donnareq.pem -days¬
60 -config openssl.cnf
```

13. Now sign the new certificate with the previously created certificate authority:

```
# openssl x509 -x509toreq -in donnareq.pem -signkey donnareq.pem -out temp.pem
```

If this is successful, you'll see the following messages:

```
Getting request Private Key

Generating certificate request
```

14. Use the temp.pem file, with reference to the policy_anything stanza shown earlier in Figure 17-2.

```
# openssl ca -config openssl.cnf -policy policy_anything -out donnacert.pem¬
-infiles temp.pem
```

15. Enter the passphrase when prompted and then confirm that the certificate will be signed at the following prompt by typing **y**:

```
# Sign the certificate? [y/n]:y
```

16. Remove the temporary certificate created in step 13:

```
# rm temp.pem
```

17. Include the newly defined certificate in the appropriate *.mc file in the /etc/mail/cf/cf directory. The following directives define the location of various certificate files:

```
define('confCACERT_PATH','/etc/mail/certs/CA')dnl
define('confCACERT', '/etc/mail/certs/CA/CAcert.pem')dnl
define('confSERVER_CERT', '/etc/mail/certs/CA/MYcert.pem')
dnl define('confSERVER_KEY', '/etc/mail/certs/CA/MYkey.pem')
dnl define('confCLIENT_CERT', '/etc/mail/certs/CA/MYcert.pem')dnl
define('confCLIENT_KEY', '/etc/mail/certs/CA/MYkey.pem')dnl
```

You can either substitute accordingly for the noted files or create links to these files after changes to the sendmail configuration are complete. The directives are straightforward, as shown in Table 17-1.

To repeat, if this is not the configuration you want, now is a good time to restore the original sendmail configuration file from the /root directory.

Directive	Description
confCACERT_PATH	Defines the path to the directory that contains certificates.
confCACERT	Specifies the actual certificate.
confSERVER_CERT	Notes the public certificate.
confSERVER_KEY	Directs to the private certificate.
confCLIENT_CERT	Notes the public certificate; this normally should be the same as **confSERVER_CERT**.
confCLIENT_KEY	Directs to the private certificate; this normally should be the same as **confSERVER_KEY**.

TABLE 17-1. *Macro Directives for sendmail Certificates*

NOTE
You could also use the kernel SSL accelerator described in the "Oracle System Administration Guide: Network Services" document. If you do so, make sure to set the SSL port appropriately, such as 465 for the secure version of the Simple Mail Transport Protocol (SMTPS).

Files that .forward

Each user can set up e-mail forwarding based on a .forward file located in his or her home directory. A typical forward file might look like the following:

```
\mjang
michael@example.com
```

The backslash prevents an infinite loop of e-mails, by preventing the expansion of the first line into an alias. A copy of e-mail that is sent to user mjang is forwarded to the noted michael@example.com e-mail address.

Before the .forward can work, you'll need an /etc/shells file. Although Solaris documentation suggests that you download a script to generate that file from www.sendmail.org/vendor/sun/gen-etc-shells.html, it's actually a simple file that contains the full path to available shells on a Solaris 11 system, with the following lines:

```
/bin/csh
/bin/jsh
/bin/ksh
/bin/sh
/sbin/jsh
/sbin/sh
/usr/bin/bash
/usr/bin/csh
/usr/bin/jsh
/usr/bin/ksh
/usr/bin/pfksh
/usr/bin/pfsh
/usr/bin/sh
```

Some administrators believe that giving users control over forwarding is a security risk. If you want to disable forwarding on a sendmail server, you'd add the following line to an appropriate sendmail macro file:

```
define('confFORWARD_PATH','')dnl
```

Alias Management in sendmail

Some people change e-mail addresses frequently. Users with multiple e-mail addresses may want your help to redirect e-mails to a single address. Although it's possible for individuals to set up forwarders in .forward files, not everyone knows how to do so. In any case, it's often more efficient to set up aliases on a network scale. In this section, you'll see how to set up aliases for the generic postmaster address, for local users, and with NIS user maps. Some aliases are already configured in the /etc/mail/aliases file.

Whenever you make a change to that file, you'll need to rebuild the database that's actually read by the sendmail server. To that end, the following command creates or updates an aliases.db file in the /etc/mail directory:

```
# newaliases
```

Postmaster Aliases

One of the standards associated with sendmail (RFC 2821) requires developers to support the postmaster@domain e-mail address. The following entry in the default /etc/mail/aliases file forwards e-mail that is sent to that address to the root administrative user:

```
postmaster: root
```

You can change the postmaster alias to the real e-mail address of the administrator of the sendmail server.

Local Aliases

Most users will want to receive e-mail on accounts configured in "regular" address formats (with the @). To that end, you can set up aliases for all appropriate local users. For example, if the users donna, mike, katie, and dickens are configured on a local Solaris 11 system, you might add the following entries to the end of the /etc/mail/aliases file:

```
donna:      donna@example.net
mike:       mike@example.net
katie:      katie@example.net
dickens:    dickens@example.net
```

If each of these users has been configured on different systems on the local network, you could copy the processed aliases.db database to the /etc/mail directory on each system on that network.

Alias Maps and NIS

As with other files, NIS can take advantage of changes you make to local files. Assuming you've created aliases for the postmaster and regular user accounts, and the system is configured as an NIS client, you can use NIS to set up mail aliases for the network.

If you haven't yet configured NIS, you'll need to install the NIS service package with the following command:

```
# pkg install service/network/nis
```

You would then need to set up an NIS server. For more information on NIS, see Chapter 12. You can then include the aliases.db file in the /etc/mail directory by rebuilding the NIS database. To do so, navigate to the /var/yp directory and run the **make** command to process appropriate entries via the Makefile file in that directory.

Mail Queue Management

One common problem for sendmail administrators is the management of mail queues. Mail may get "stuck" in queues for various reasons, which can range from network problems to misspelled e-mail addresses. To that end, as a sendmail administrator, you need to know how to look at the mail queue, how to force it to process messages, how to manage a subset of that queue, and, if necessary, how to move the queue to a different directory.

Contents of the Mail Queue

The contents of the sendmail mail queue are contained in the /var/spool/mqueue directory. You can review the current contents of that queue with the **mailq** command. If messages are stuck in the queue, this command will provide the following information:

- Queue identifiers for e-mail messages
- Size
- Date
- Status
- Sender and recipients

Processing the Mail Queue

If e-mail is stuck in the queue, you can force processing with the **sendmail** command, enhanced with appropriate switches. Well, the **-q** switch itself is sufficient to force sendmail to process the current contents of the queue. If an extra push is required, you might try a command like the following, which tries to process the queue every 60 seconds, until the queue is empty:

```
# sendmail -q 60
```

Many administrators prefer to add the **-v** switch to the **sendmail** command, to run in verbose mode. If additional problems exist, verbose mode can help you diagnose them.

Alternatively, if e-mail to a certain user is urgent, such as all e-mail to mcgraw-hill.com addresses, you could run the following command:

```
# sendmail -qRmcgraw-hill.com -v
```

Note the lack of a space between the **-qR** switch and the domain name.

Changing Mail Queues

At some point in time, you may just have to set a mail queue aside. Just be aware that it's important to disable sendmail before starting this process, so e-mail is not lost in the queue during the transition. To set a current mail queue aside for later processing, take the following steps:

1. Deactivate the sendmail server:

   ```
   # svcadm disable network/smtp:sendmail
   ```

2. Navigate to the /var/spool directory.

3. Change the name of the current mail queue directory. This command sets the current mail queue aside in the /var/spool/later directory:

   ```
   # mv /var/spool/mqueue /var/spool/later
   ```

4. Create a new mail queue directory:

   ```
   # mkdir /var/spool/mqueue
   ```

5. Set up appropriate ownership and permissions to match those of the now-moved /var/spool/later directory:

```
# chown root.bin /var/spool/mqueue
# chmod 750 /var/spool/mqueue
```

6. Restart the sendmail service:

```
# svcadm enable network/smtp:sendmail
```

If you want to try processing the /var/spool/later queue at a later date, run the following command:

```
# sendmail -oQ/var/spool/later -q -v
```

This command selects additional options (**-o**) from the quarantined (**-Q**) queue in the /var/spool/later directory, just once (**-q**) and in verbose mode (**-v**). As suggested earlier, you could add a time period to the **-q** switch to try processing the spool at certain intervals.

Troubleshooting sendmail

In this section, you'll review available procedures for troubleshooting sendmail as an e-mail server. Some of the commands and techniques described in this section were already used, at least in part, elsewhere in this chapter. In this section, you'll see what can be done to test changes to the configuration file, to review the functionality of mail aliases, as well as to make sure that rules created through sendmail actually work.

In some cases, you may need to go through the operation of sendmail in more detail. To that end, you'll see how to set up the logging daemon to collect additional information. Additional sources of diagnostic information are available.

Testing Basic Operation

Perhaps the simplest way to test the operation of most services is with the **telnet** command. Assuming you've retained the default port for sendmail, 25, you can connect with a local operational sendmail server with the following command:

```
$ telnet localhost 25
```

NOTE
*Although **telnet** as a client is an excellent way to test the connectivity of remote services, Telnet as a server is insecure—it even sends passwords in clear text.*

If the sendmail server is operational, you'll see something similar to the following message, which happens to connect via the IPv6 loopback address of ::1. The system is solaris-test1 .example.com, and the version of sendmail in use is as shown.

```
Trying ::1...
Connected to solaris-test1.
Escape character is '^]'.
220 solaris-test1.example.com ESMTP Sendmail 8.14.5+Sun/8.14.5; Mon, 19 Dec 2011¬
18:57:37 -0800 (PST)
```

Then you'll see a blank line, with no prompt. Alternatively, you could run the **telnet 127.0.0.1 25** command, with the same essential result. One way to test remote connectivity to a sendmail server to run a similar **telnet** command from a remote system. Of course, you'd have to substitute the IP address or hostname of the sendmail server for localhost or 127.0.0.1.

You can still execute commands at that blank prompt. For a full list of available commands, see the sendmail.hf file in the /etc/mail directory.

Try the following command:

```
HELO example.com
```

In most cases, you'll get a response similar to the following:

```
250 solaris-test1.example.com Hello solaris-test1 [127.0.0.1], pleased to¬
meet you
```

In contrast, if you run an extended hello, the **EHLO** command, you'll get a series of commands and options. You can even send e-mail from this interface, with the help of commands such as **MAIL From** and **SEND From**. But given the option to send e-mail directly from the **sendmail** command, as discussed next, it may be more efficient to test sendmail in that way.

When desired, you can return to the command line with just a couple steps:

1. Press the CTRL-] key combination and then press ENTER. If this is successful, you'll see the following prompt:

   ```
   telnet>
   ```

2. You can then exit the telnet connection with the **quit** command.

Testing the Configuration

The simplest way to test a sendmail configuration is to see whether it actually sends e-mail messages. Once you've configured sendmail, processed any databases, and restarted the service, the following command uses verbose mode to send the contents of the /etc/hosts file to the noted e-mail address. If desired, substitute a real e-mail address.

```
# sendmail -v michael@example.com < /etc/hosts
```

The output can be valuable; some receiving e-mail servers may reject the message as spam, with messages such as the following:

```
050 <michael@example.com>... Closing connection to mx00.example.com.
050 554 RBL rejection: http://www.spamhaus.org/query/bl?ip=192.168.100.200
```

If the sendmail server is configured for a network, you'll want to repeat this test from other systems on the network.

Reviewing Aliases

Once you've configured aliases in the /etc/mail/aliases.db file, and reactivated the sendmail service, it should be available for use. You can test the database with the **mconnect** utility. If you're testing from a remote system, include the IP address of the sendmail server. The format of the command is

```
$ mconnect -p port hostname
```

When the **mconnect** command is run alone, it assumes the default port 25 on the local system. In a fashion similar to a **telnet** connection (described earlier), the prompt is a blank line. You can then use a command such as **expn** (short for expansion) to test the alias database. Based on the aliases created earlier in this chapter, user michael is associated with e-mail address michael@example.com. So if you run the **expn michael** command, it should return something similar to the following message:

```
250 2.1.5 <michael@example.com>
```

You can test this for each or all of the aliases configured in the aliases.db file in the /etc/mail directory. If the user is missing from the database, you'll see a message similar to the following:

```
550 5.1.1 mike... User unknown
```

When you're ready to exit from the **mconnect** utility, type the following command to return to the command-line prompt:

```
quit
```

Mail Logs

First, a default option is associated with log messages from the Solaris 11 e-mail server. It's part of the default log configuration file, /etc/syslog.conf, where messages at the debug level are sent to some undefined system named loghost. Well, nothing happens unless a loghost system is defined in the local /etc/hosts file:

```
mail.debug        ifdef('LOGHOST', /var/log/syslog, @loghost)
```

To set up logs for mail messages, you could set up a central logging server, specifying a loghost system. Alternatively, you could set up logs using one or more of the priorities described in the /etc/syslog.conf file. For example, if you wanted to isolate mail-related messages at the alert level, you could add the following directive to that file:

```
mail.alert        /var/adm/mailalerts
```

Just be aware, if there are no such messages, that file remains empty. For test purposes, you could set up debug-level messages in a different local file with a directive such as the following:

```
mail.debug        /var/adm/maildebug
```

Just be sure to restart the Solaris system logging service with a command such as the following:

```
# svcadm restart svc:/system/system-log:default
```

Then you can use a test e-mail message, such as the one used to send the /etc/hosts file to the root user, described earlier in this chapter.

Error Messages

As for errors, you can go beyond the log files, but it's a place to start. As shown in Figure 17-3, log messages written to the /var/log/syslog file may include the facility (mail) and the severity of the message (crit, alert, info, and warning are shown). In addition, as you may already know, parts of

```
Dec 20 16:32:52 solaris-test1 sendmail[25393]: [ID 801593 mail.info] pBL0WpVp025
393: pBL0WpVq025393: DSN: Service unavailable
Dec 20 16:32:52 solaris-test1 sendmail[25393]: [ID 801593 mail.info] pBL0WpVq025
393: to=michael@n        s.com, delay=00:00:00, xdelay=00:00:00, mailer=esmtp, p
ri=31405, relay=mx       .com., dsn=5.0.0, stat=Service unavailable
Dec 20 16:32:52 solaris-test1 sendmail[25393]: [ID 801593 mail.info] pBL0WpVq025
393: pBL0WpVr025393: return to sender: Service unavailable
Dec 20 16:32:52 solaris-test1 sendmail[25393]: [ID 801593 mail.info] pBL0WpVr025
393: to=michael@r        s.com, delay=00:00:00, xdelay=00:00:00, mailer=esmtp, p
ri=32429, relay=mx00.1and1.com., dsn=5.0.0, stat=Service unavailable
Dec 20 16:32:52 solaris-test1 sendmail[25393]: [ID 801593 mail.alert] pBL0WpVq02
5393: Losing ./qfpBL0WpVq025393: savemail panic
Dec 20 16:32:52 solaris-test1 sendmail[25393]: [ID 801593 mail.crit] pBL0WpVq025
393: SYSERR(root): savemail: cannot save rejected email anywhere
Dec 20 16:33:58 solaris-test1 sendmail[25397]: [ID 702911 mail.warning] gethostb
yaddr(192.168.0.201) failed: 1
Dec 20 16:33:58 solaris-test1 sendmail[25397]: [ID 801593 mail.info] pBL0XwRM025
397: from=michael, size=381, class=0, nrcpts=1, msgid=<201112210033.pBL0XwRM0253
97@solaris-test1.example.com>, relay=root@localhost
Dec 20 16:33:59 solaris-test1 sendmail[25397]: [ID 801593 mail.info] pBL0XwRM025
397: to=mjang@        s.com, ctladdr=michael (60004/10), delay=00:00:01, xdelay=
00:00:01, mailer=esmtp, pri=30381, relay=mta3.am0.        .net. [98.137.54.238],
 dsn=2.0.0, stat=Sent (ok dirdel)
```

FIGURE 17-3. *Logged error messages from sendmail*

the message can be used as a search term online, to identify other administrators with similar problems. As defined in the previous section, you can use definitions in the /etc/syslog.conf file to divide these messages into different categories.

Before you get lost in the details of sendmail logs, don't forget the other information associated with troubled e-mail:

- *Look at the headers of the e-mail.* Sometimes addresses are misspelled, and sometimes black-hat hackers don't bother to mask their address information.

- *Pay attention to any messages that come from a MAILER-DAEMON.* Sometimes there's an attachment to that message, similar to that shown here. Note the example.mistake domain in the following message:

```
Reporting-MTA: dns; solaris-test1.example.com
Arrival-Date: Wed, 21 Dec 2011 08:50:32 -0800 (PST)
Final-Recipient: RFC822; mjang@example.mistake
Action: failed
Status: 5.1.2
Remote-MTA: DNS; mailhost.example.com
Last-Attempt-Date: Wed, 21 Dec 2011 08:50:32 -0800 (PST)
```

- *Use the **mailstats** program.* To do so, you'll need to run the following command to create an associated statistics file:

```
# touch /etc/mail/statistics
```

You can then run the following command to display information about successful and discarded messages:

```
# mailstats -f /etc/mail/statistics
```

Solaris 11 documentation includes information on a number of error messages. Sometimes the most direct way to identify those error messages is in the output to a test command such as the following:

```
# sendmail -v michael@example.com < /etc/hosts
```

For completeness, it's worth describing them here. Sometimes, there's a problem with reading a message before a timeout, leading to the following error message:

```
451 timeout waiting for input during source
```

In that case, you may want to change a macro variable such as **confTO_INITIAL**. Because the default is five minutes, a problem with this measure may also indicate a connectivity problem.

Sometimes the problem is a bit more straightforward; the following suggests a problem with one of the name databases, such as DNS, NIS, or the local /etc/hosts file:

```
550 hostname... Host unknown
```

A similar problem may relate to a misspelled or an obsolete e-mail address, such as the following:

```
550 username... User unknown
```

Sometimes it's related to the following error:

```
user unknown
```

In either case, if the e-mail address is properly spelled, you may want to check the aliases as defined in the /etc/mail/aliases file. Just remember that sendmail reads aliases from the aliases.db file, and you can update any aliases configured in the database with the **newaliases** command.

Summary

This chapter focused on the Solaris SMTP service for e-mail delivery: sendmail. Because it's perhaps the most complex service, sendmail includes a group of macros in dedicated files that are easier to configure. All you need to do is make minor modifications to these files and then process them into the actual sendmail configuration file, sendmail.cf, in the /etc/mail directory.

By default, sendmail is configured to manage e-mail on the local system. With some minor changes, you can set up sendmail for clients on a network. In addition, you can set up virtual hosts to forward e-mail from once-obsolete e-mail addresses, and even all e-mail addresses from a specific domain. You can secure sendmail by configuring it with a TLS certificate. Individual users can set up forwarding in the .forward file in their home directories.

You can also set up aliases for local systems in the aliases file in the /etc/mail directory. Important aliases such as postmaster are already preconfigured in that file. Before aliases can be read by sendmail, you'll need to process them into a .db database file with the **newaliases** command. If NIS is configured on a system, you can also set up alias maps in an NIS database with the help of the **make** command in the /var/yp directory.

Sometimes, e-mail messages get stuck. That's where administration begins. If e-mail is stuck in the queue, you'll be able to review messages in the queue with the **mailq** command, process the queue with commands such as **sendmail -q 60**, or move the mail queue to a different directory for later analysis and processing.

Sometimes, you may have to troubleshoot a sendmail system. You can test connectivity with an appropriate **telnet** command. You can test the configuration with **sendmail** commands that send the contents of files to specific users, and you can test aliases with the **mconnect** utility. You can configure logs for mail-related issues in the /etc/syslog.conf file, and diagnose problems through a variety of messages.

References

For a more detailed look at sendmail, see *sendmail, Fourth Edition*, by Brian Costales, Claus Assmann, George Jansen, and Gregory Neil Shapiro, published by O'Reilly Media (2007).

For more information on how sendmail works as a network service, see "Oracle Solaris Administration: Network Services" (November 2011) which is available online from http://docs.oracle.com/cd/E23824_01/html/821-1454.

For more information on the commands used to manage systems like sendmail, see "Oracle Solaris Administration: Common Tasks" (December 2011) which is available online from http://docs.oracle.com/cd/E23824_01/html/821-1451.

CHAPTER
18

Solaris Trusted Extensions

erhaps one of the least well-known and sparsely documented areas of Solaris is Trusted Extensions. Even the name itself gives one pause. What is it? It's a good thing we've covered zones in Chapter 14, because zones and Trusted Extensions are so close they might as well be brother and sister. If you've grasped the concepts of zones, you're three-quarters of the way to understanding Trusted Extensions (TX). Indeed, zones are TX without the security label hierarchy and mandatory enforcement.

Overview of Trusted Extensions

Trusted Extensions has its roots in Trusted Solaris 8—an OS that was based on, but different and distinguishable from, Solaris 8. In Solaris 10 and Solaris 11, the "Extensions" refers to extending the OS with additional packages and enforcement policies applied to a typical installation. The packages and policies configure the OS as a multilevel system with mandatory access control. It's a mouthful, but don't worry, we'll break it down.

Systems have users and data. Who can read, modify, and transport which data is defined by the access control policy. There are two types: discretionary and mandatory. Discretionary Access Control (DAC), the first kind, is implemented by UNIX file ownership and permission (discussed in Chapter 12). The Solaris OS enhances basic DAC with Access Control Lists (ACLs), which are more fine-grained discretionary access controls. DAC enables the owner of data to set the correct access policy (the **chmod** and **chown** bits). For example, the owner can add +rwx to their directories and files. At the owner's discretion, read, modify, or execute permission can be granted to groups or the world. If the owner fails to set the correct permissions, someone can access a piece of data that should not be accessed.

Mandatory Access Control (MAC) separates the users from the data. It's no longer just *their* data. It's their *labeled* data. A label is a security tag. Labels go on directories and files, network endpoints, as well as the users and processes invoked by the users. Labels go on data and the things that act on the data, which are usually processes. A user has a clearance, which specifies the highest rung of the label hierarchy that they are allowed to access. Devices such as cameras, DVD writers, and USB drives are also labeled and must be allocated by a privileged user before they can be turned on. MAC allows access if the user has a clearance equal to or higher than the label of the data.

Everything has a label, and the label of the data (sometimes called the *object)* and of the processes (sometimes called the *subject)* are compared. Access is granted if the label of the subject is equal to or greater than the label of the object. You may encounter the term *label dominance* in the official literature, but for now we try to keep it simple: Labels are greater than, less than, or equal to each other when being compared. MAC policies are transparent and transparently enforced; even better, if the user does not have a clearance equal to or greater than the label of the data, they will never know about the existence of that data.

A vanilla Solaris 11 installation operates at one level; there's no label enforcement, and the only measure of access control is DAC. Solaris 11 with Trusted Extensions is a multilevel system; it contains data tagged with different security labels, and it allows the use of that data by users with different clearances.

Trusted Extensions is, at first, weird and unwieldy. It's not something that can just be "turned on" like a firewall. Trusted Extensions fits into a framework where there's a formal security policy, possibly an LDAP server where users and their clearances are defined, as well as network access points that are labeled. It requires a lot of planning. Despite several pushes to make Trusted

Solaris and Trusted Extensions a more common OS in the commercial world, labeled systems remain the province of government and military use, where controlling access to sensitive data is very serious business.

Enabling Trusted Extensions

Remember that improbable hacking scene from the first *Mission: Impossible* movie when Tom Cruise penetrates a super-secret security installation and hangs from the ceiling while copying the NOC list onto a floppy disk? Secure fortress, sound-sensitive to a whisper, temperature-sensitive to a degree, pressure-sensitive floor—but no Trusted Extensions. We don't have the money for all that cutting-edge technology, but let's see if we have the means to protect a fictional NOC list.

Zones and Trusted Extensions

You've been acquainted with zones in Chapter 14. Trusted Extensions provides an OS where all zones have unique security labels. Data in that zone and processes executing in that zone have the zone's label. Data access is granted by the user's clearance. Data movement is permitted or denied by comparing the label of the source and destination of the data.

In addition to modifying zones, TX modifies the kernel in other ways that are hidden from the administrators. Solaris provides a GUI, the **txzonemgr**, to configure and create labeled zones.

Instead of **zonecfg** and **zoneadm**, use the GUI. Official Solaris 11 documentation uses the **txzonemgr** GUI, and even though we can create labeled zones using **zonecfg** and **zoneadm**, we are going to do it the officially sanctioned way—at least until you've attained the 12th-level Zone Ninja Master Class.

Enabling Trusted Extensions

Verify that the system on which you are about to install Trusted Extensions has no non-global zone. Remove any existing zones. From the global zone, list the available zones and then halt and uninstall them. Then delete the configuration. Remember that you cannot delete the global zone. Review Chapter 14 to refresh your memory.

```
# zoneadm list -cv
  ID NAME              STATUS       PATH                        BRAND    IP
   0 global            running      /                           native   shared
   4 web               running      /zone/web                   native   shared
   - db                installed    /zone/db                    native   shared
# zoneadm -z web halt
# zoneadm -z web uninstall; zoneadm -z db uninstall
# zonecfg -z web delete -F; zonecfg -z web delete -F
# zoneadm list -cv
  ID NAME              STATUS       PATH                        BRAND    IP
   0 global            running      /                           native   shared
```

NOTE

We've simplified some of the administrative tasks to keep the material on point and accessible. A real-life installation of Trusted Extensions in a secure environment typically requires two teams—one to design the security policy and the other to implement it. Users assume roles to do their work, and there's an audit trail that verifies the implementation.

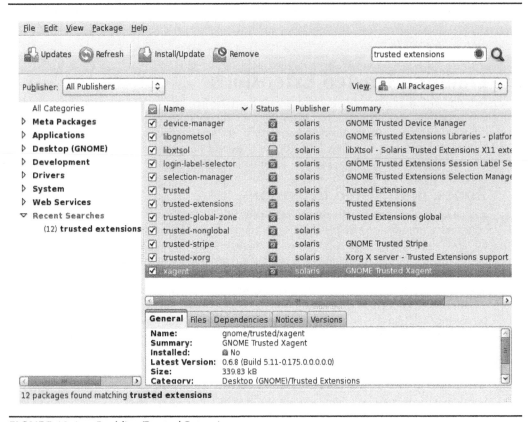

FIGURE 18-1.   *Enabling Trusted Extensions*

Open the Package Manager (System | Administration | Package Manager), select All Publishers on the left, and then search for "Trusted Extensions" in the search box. Check all the boxes and choose Install/Update, as shown in Figure 18-1.

The label_encodings File

After installing the Trusted Extensions packages, you should find in the directory /etc/security/tsol several versions of a file called label_encodings. This file contains the security labels to be used on this system as well as instructions to the kernel on how to interpret and apply the labels. The file is human-readable but cryptic, because it was designed to be interpreted by the kernel.

You're going to need to have a valid label_encodings file before you enable the SMF service labeld, which turns your machine from a typical OS to a Trusted OS. We will be using a different label_encodings file than the simple ones provided. It's more sparse to get right to the point of the example. Let's examine the file we will be using for our example:

```
* Components in TS
VERSION= Solaris 11 TX Example
CLASSIFICATIONS:
```

```
name= PUBLIC; sname= P; value= 1;
name= SECRET; sname= S; value= 4;
name= TOP SECRET; sname= TS; value= 7; initial compartments= 1;
INFORMATION LABELS:
WORDS:
name= :; prefix;
name= NEED TO KNOW; compartments= 1;
minclass= TS;
name= EYES ONLY; compartments= 2;
minclass= TS;
REQUIRED COMBINATIONS:
COMBINATION CONSTRAINTS:
SENSITIVITY LABELS:
WORDS:
name= :; prefix;
name= NEED TO KNOW; compartments= 1;
minclass= TS; prefix= :
name= EYES ONLY; compartments= 2;
minclass= TS; prefix= :
REQUIRED COMBINATIONS:
COMBINATION CONSTRAINTS:
CLEARANCES:
WORDS:
name= NEED TO KNOW; compartments= 1;
minclass= TS;
name= EYES ONLY; compartments= 2;
minclass= TS;
REQUIRED COMBINATIONS:

COMBINATION CONSTRAINTS:
CHANNELS:
WORDS:
PRINTER BANNERS:
WORDS:
ACCREDITATION RANGE:
classification= P; all compartment combinations valid;
classification= S; all compartment combinations valid;
classification= TS; all compartment combinations valid;
minimum clearance= P;
minimum sensitivity label= P;
minimum protect as classification= P;

*
* Local site definitions and locally configurable options.
*
LOCAL DEFINITIONS:
Classification Name= Classification;
Compartments Name= Sensitivity;
Default User Sensitivity Label= P;
Default User Clearance= S;
COLOR NAMES:
```

```
label= Admin_Low;          color= #bdbdbd;
label= P;                  color= green;
label= S;                  color= yellow;
label= TS : NEED TO KNOW;  color= orange;
label= TS : EYES ONLY;     color= red;
label= Admin_High;         color= #636363;
```

Under **CLASSIFICATIONS** we have the following:

```
name= PUBLIC; sname= P; value= 1;
name= SECRET; sname= S; value= 4;
name= TOP SECRET; sname= TS; value= 7; initial compartments= 1;
```

The encodings identify three classifications and assign to each of them an integer: $7 > 4 > 1$, and hence the label **TOP SECRET** > **SECRET** > **PUBLIC**. The **sname** value is the short name; sometimes the name is really long (for example, **INTERNAL RESTRICTED PARTNERS NDA ONLY**). 1, 4, and 7 are chosen for the same reason that old BASIC code began with 10, 20, 30—to leave room to add labels in between existing labels in the future.

You see something new called *initial compartments.* Classifications define hierarchies; compartments group things together in nonhierarchical ways. Together they define a security label. Compartments define access for groups. Compartments can also provide handling instructions for a classification (for example, **EYES ONLY** means no copying and transmission of materials in that compartment). Classifications do not require compartments; you can have a valid label with classification only.

In our example, the classifications **PUBLIC** and **SECRET** have no compartments. The initial compartment designation for **TOP SECRET** says that for every material classified at **TOP SECRET**, put it in a compartment (in this case, compartment number 1). This is the default compartment for **TS** materials.

Skip the next section, **INFORMATION LABELS**. We'll get back to that. We now come to **SENSITIVITY LABELS**. This block associates the compartment number with a name and specifies a minimum classification for that compartment. We have two compartments, **NEED TO KNOW** and **EYES ONLY**.

```
name= NEED TO KNOW; compartments= 1;
minclass= TS; prefix= :
name= EYES ONLY; compartments= 2;
minclass= TS; prefix= :
```

REQUIRED COMBINATIONS and **COMBINATION CONSTRAINTS** are used to narrow how a label can be found valid. For example, we may require that any **TS** compartment 1 must include compartment 2. Our example will not require combinations or make combination constraints.

We leave these blocks blank, but we have to include them in the label_encodings file. The syntax checker called **chk_encodings** will complain if they are not found, and the label_ encodings file will not work.

Come back up one block. Whatever is defined for the **SENSITIVITY LABELS** block, copy and paste that under the **INFORMATION LABELS** and **CLEARANCES** block. It's redundant but necessary to have a valid encodings file.

ACCREDITATION RANGE defines the valid range of labels from low to high that can be granted to users and roles. It specifies a system-wide bound on the clearances granted to users, to even further constrain the **REQUIRED COMBINATIONS**, if they were defined. For example, if we had created **SECRET** compartments **ARMY NAVY AIR MARINES**, we may see an accreditation range of

S ARMY MARINES, meaning the only valid compartment combination for **S** is **ARMY** and
MARINES, not **ARMY NAVY** or any other. To keep it simple, we specify that all combinations are
valid. We only use two compartments in our example.

```
ACCREDITATION RANGE:
classification= P; all compartment combinations valid;
classification= S; all compartment combinations valid;
classification= TS; all compartment combinations valid;
```

The next section is self-explanatory: The minimum clearance a user has to have is **PUBLIC**,
and the minimum sensitivity label for data on this system is tagged at **PUBLIC**. It's a pretty
welcoming system, allowing access to low classification data and low clearance users.

```
minimum clearance= P;
minimum sensitivity label= P;
minimum protect as classification= P;
```

Under **LOCAL DEFINITIONS**, we find the default sensitivity label and default clearance for
materials and users not explicitly tagged. We also find the color keys for windows that display
information tagged at each sensitivity and compartment.

```
LOCAL DEFINITIONS:
Classification Name= Classification;
Compartments Name= Sensitivity;
Default User Sensitivity Label= P;
Default User Clearance= S;
COLOR NAMES:
        label= Admin_Low;          color= #bdbdbd;
        label= P;                  color= green;
        label= S;                  color= yellow;
        label= TS : NEED TO KNOW;  color= orange;
        label= TS : EYES ONLY;     color= red;
        label= Admin_High;         color= #636363;
```

We write this information into a dummy file named something other than label_encodings,
we check its syntax, and after that goes well we replace the original label_encodings file with it.

```
# chk_encodings -a /etc/security/tsol/mission
No errors found in mission.
```

You'll see other informational output, but we're only concerned with whether or not it parses.

A TX desktop shows a Trusted Path bar at the top. It displays the user ID as well as the label
and color of the user's workspace. You will need to modify Solaris to put the Desktop panel at the
bottom. If you don't, the Trusted Path bar on top occludes the Desktop panel and you won't be
able access the Desktop menu. To enable TX, we're going to follow these steps:

1. Move the Desktop panel to the bottom of the user's screen.
2. Back up the original (and working) label_encodings file.
3. Copy over the new label_encodings file called "mission" that we've created.
4. Enable labeld.

We're going to step you through this, but first, some tips.

Trusted Extensions Tips and Pitfalls

You must be at the machine console for these steps. If you've ever worked remotely and enabled the firewall on a remote machine, killing your own connection, you can appreciate turning on TX on a remote machine and locking yourself out. Configure everything locally and make sure your remote connection works with Trusted Extensions while you still have local access to the box.

In addition, the Trusted Path in Trusted Extensions makes itself known by a bar at the top of the screen after you've logged in. It takes up the space typically used by the control panel, where important stuff such as Logout and Shutdown live. You have to move the original control panel to the bottom. If you do not do this before turning on labeld, your login session turns into Hotel California, and you can never leave.

Log in as root. Right-click the control panel (which is by default on the top) and select Properties. For Orientation, select Bottom, as shown next. Close the dialog box.

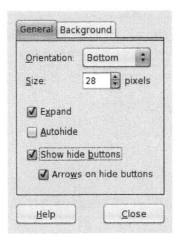

You can fix this for the entire system by editing the file /etc/gconf/schemas/panel-default-setup. entries. Find line 96 and change the word *top* to *bottom*. Restart the GNOME cache service, svc:/application/desktop-cache/gconf-cache:default:

```
93        <key>toplevels/top_panel/orientation</key>
94        <schema_key>/schemas/apps/panel/toplevels/orientation</schema_key>
95        <value>
96          <string>top</string>
97        </value>
```

Here's a short shell script to do that:

```
#!/bin/sh -x
cd /etc/gconf/schemas
cp panel-default-setup.entries panel-default-setup.entries.orig
sed 's/<string>top<\/string>/<string>bottom<\/string>/' panel-default-
setup.entries > foo
cp foo panel-default-setup.entries; rm foo
svcadm restart gconf-cache
```

We need to enable direct root login. Up until now the /etc/user_attr file has looked like this:

```
root::::type=role
ctran::::type=normal;lock_after_retries=no;profiles=System
Administrator;roles=root
```

This means root is a role that can only be assumed after a user login. We will be enabling Trusted Extensions without creating any labeled zone, which is the working environment for regular users. We have not created any new users with special clearance.

We do this for the sake of simplifying the explanation of how to enable Trusted Extensions, as well as conform to the way Solaris 11 works. In Solaris 10, Trusted Extensions allows a user with a Default Sensitivity Label of Public to log in, even though there's no matching security zone. Trusted Extensions in Solaris 11 will lock you out.

The only way to gain access to the global zone (the administrative zone) after enabling Trusted Extensions is to log in as root. We modify the user_attr file to allow root to log in and configure Trusted Extensions directly. Currently, root is a role, as we see here:

```
# getent user_attr root
root::::type=role
# usermod -K type=normal -A solaris.*,solaris.grant -P all root
```

The /etc/user_attr file should now look like this:

```
root::::type=normal;auths=solaris.*,solaris.grant;profiles=All
ctran::::type=normal;lock_after_retries=no;profiles=System Administrator
```

If you get locked out or stuck, force a hard reset, boot to single-user, log in as root, give the root password for maintenance, and disable labeld. Reboot again, and you should be back to where you were before you enabled Trusted Extensions.

We resume at enabling Trusted Extensions. Back up the working label_encodings file, copy the new "mission" label_encodings file, and enable labeld:

```
# cd /etc/security/tsol; cp label_encodings label_encodings.orig
# cp missions label_encodings
# svcadm -s enable labeld
# svcs labeld
STATE          STIME       FMRI
online         0:03:38     svc:/system/labeld:default
# init 6
```

Creating and Installing a Labeled Zone

Log in as root. Before a workspace appears, the system presents you with a dialog box that contains your security information: your available roles, rights, minimum label (ADMIN_LOW), and maximum clearance (ADMIN_HIGH).

These are the absolute lower and upper range of the label hierarchy. Do not check the box labeled "Restrict Session to a Single Label."

We'll be working with zones, but instead of using the **zonecfg** and **zoneadmd** CLI like you did in Chapter 14, we'll use a GUI-based tool called **txzonemgr**, the Labeled Zone Manager tool, to create them. Open a terminal window and run the following command:

```
# txzonemgr &
```

You'll be greeted with the following window. Select Main Menu (the other two options will create zones for you using default options).

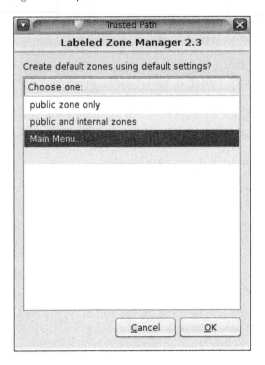

Select Create a New Zone. Walk through the prompts. For the zonename, enter **public**. Click on Select Label and select PUBLIC, as shown next. The label is now PUBLIC.

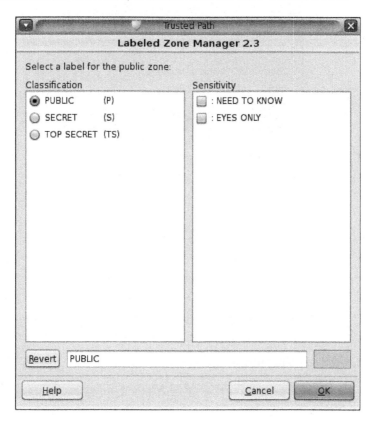

Next, select Configure Network Interfaces, as shown here.

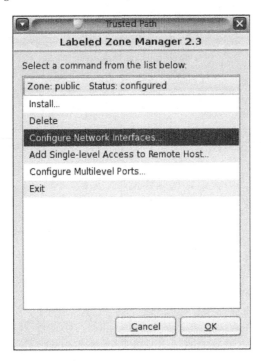

Now select Add an IP Instance, as shown next.

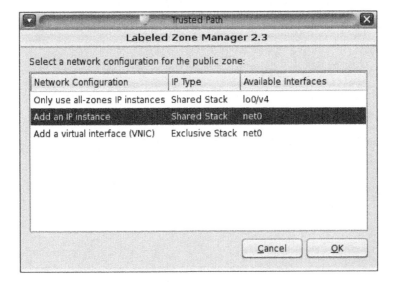

Add an IP address and a netmask in CIDR notation (for example, 192.168.0.20/24).

Select the interface on which to plumb this IP address. My system only has one available interface, net0, as shown here.

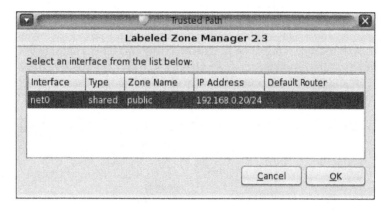

Make sure you add a default router, even though your test scenario may take place all on one segment. Without the definition of a default router, Solaris will not plumb a virtual interface for you.

Click on OK, which will bring you back to the configuration menu. Click on Install and then OK.

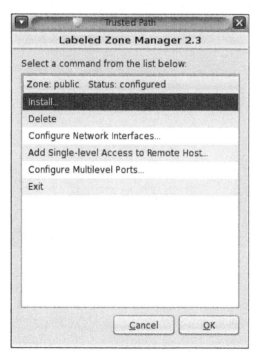

You'll be prompted for the zonename; enter in anything you wish. I used "public" to keep everything consistent and tidy, but it's worth emphasizing that the zonename "public" and the label **PUBLIC** pertain to different things.

The zone begins the installation phase and starts downloading IPS packages. If this is a new zone, it'll take about 20 minutes, depending on the speed of your connection to the package repository.

After this is done, repeat the same process to create two other zones, with labels **SECRET** and **TOP SECRET** and with compartments **EYES ONLY** and **NEED TO KNOW**. The **NEED TO KNOW** compartment is automatically selected because of what was specified in the label_encodings file. Use available IP addresses, but from the same subnet as the global zone.

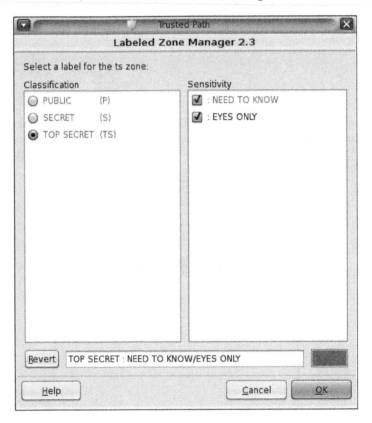

While the zone is installing, you may want to poke around to see what's going on under the hood. **zoneadm list –cv** shows you that there's a new zone called "public" on the zonepath /zone/ public. **txzonemgr** did not give us the option to change the zonepath, but that can be changed later if you wish. **zonecfg –z public info** shows you an output slightly different from what you've seen:

```
# zonecfg -z public info
zonename: public
zonepath: /zone/public
brand: labeled
```

```
autoboot: true
bootargs:
file-mac-profile:
pool:
limitpriv:
scheduling-class:
ip-type: shared
hostid:
fs-allowed:
fs:
        dir: /etc/passwd
        special: /etc/passwd
        raw not specified
        type: lofs
        options: [ro]
fs:
        dir: /etc/shadow
        special: /etc/shadow
        raw not specified
        type: lofs
        options: [ro]
net:
        address: 192.168.0.20/24
        allowed-address not specified
        configure-allowed-address: true
        physical: net0
        defrouter: 192.168.0.1
```

The brand of the zone is "labeled," and the ip-type is shared. The /etc/passwd and /etc/shadow files are **LOFS**-mounted back into the zone as read-only.

A Detour into the Shared-ip and Exclusive-ip Zones

You've been exposed to exclusive-ip zones in Chapter 14. There's another kind of zone, called shared-ip, on which Trusted Extensions depends to provide multilevel service. TX zones are typically shared-ip zones. Shared-ip zones share a single IP stack, which all IP traffic passes through, even if each zone has its own IP address. CIPSO, the Commercial IP Security Option, is the header written onto IP packets to identify their security label. By *multilevel service,* we mean that a service such as HTTP can use one "elevator shaft" to deliver packets to zones at different security labels. For this to work, labeled zones communicate through one address called *all-zones.* The global zone acts as an elevator operator and delivers the labeled packet to the correct labeled zone. Using one all-zones address also cuts down on the use of unique IPs for labeled zones.

Exclusive-ip zones are their own self-contained entity. They manage their own IP stack and name service, and they have their own routing table instead of inheriting the routing table from the global zone. They own their own packet filtering rules, IPSec, and IKE. They also manage their own data-link layer. Because the global zone is not involved in running the common elevator, multilevel service is not possible.

Some Observations, More Tips, and Pitfalls

After the zones have finished installing, boot them from the menu. It's very important that you do not configure your zones to use their own name service daemon (nscd). In my installation, Trusted Extensions turns this on by default.

You only need to run per-zone nscd if each zone is attached to a different network at a different label, and there's a trusted name server per network. The typical scenario is that each zone uses the nscd in the global zone through an IPC mechanism unique to Solaris called *doors*. The **txzonemgr** menu for the global zone should look like this:

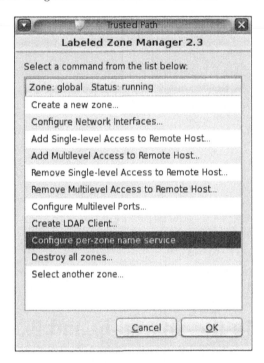

If this item reads "Unconfigure per-zone name service" instead of "Configure per-zone name service," you've gone down the wrong path. This is one of the most frequent rookie mistakes. Per-zone nscd requires all users to authenticate themselves again at their zone, called workspace. You must have set an LDAP server for account service or else create local accounts. Don't do this; make sure your zones all use the nscd in the global zone.

As we have seen, the /etc/passwd and /etc/shadow files are read-only copies from the global zone. If you look at the LOFS mounts from inside the zone, you'll see the **doors** mount:

```
# zlogin public df -F lofs
/etc/gconf-global    (/etc/gconf-global ):305508222 blocks 305508222 files
/etc/passwd          (/etc/passwd       ):305508222 blocks 305508222 files
/etc/security/tsol/doors(/etc/security/tsol/doors)¬
:305508222 blocks 305508222 files
/etc/shadow          (/etc/shadow       ):305508222 blocks 305508222 files
/lib/libc.so.1       (/usr/lib/libc/libc_hwcap1.so.1) :305508222 blocks 305508222 files
```

A ZFS dataset is created for each zone, the same as for nonlabeled zones we've seen previously.

```
# zfs list -r rpool/zones/public
NAME                                       USED   AVAIL  REFER  MOUNTPOINT
rpool/zones/public                         1.28G  146G    33K   /zone/public
rpool/zones/public/rpool                   1.28G  146G    37K   /zone/public/root/rpool
rpool/zones/public/rpool/ROOT              1.28G  146G    31K   legacy
rpool/zones/public/rpool/ROOT/solaris      1.28G  146G   1.22G  /zone/public/root
rpool/zones/public/rpool/ROOT/solaris/var  65.2M  146G   63.3M  /zone/public/root/var
rpool/zones/public/rpool/export             75K   146G    38K   /zone/public/root/
                                                                 export
rpool/zones/public/rpool/export/home        37K   146G    37K   /zone/public/root/
                                                                 export/home
```

New entries are defined in the files /etc/security/tsol/tnrhdb, /etc/security/tsol/tnrhtp, and /etc/security/tsol/tnzonecfg.

The hex number is the interpretation of the labels in hex. These entries are under-the-hood work that **txzonemgr** did for us, instead of us having to manually specify them through **zonecfg** and **zoneadm**.

Adding Roles and Users

We've been doing everything as root. We've added the TX packages, enabled labeld, created zones, and tagged them with labels. At this point, we adopt a safer practice of adding a Security Admin role with an accreditation range between the minimum and maximum the system allows. Then we can add users and designate who can assume this role, so every action can be subjected to audit.

```
# roleadd -c 'Security Admin' -m -u 101 ¬
-K profiles='System Administrator,Information Security,User Security' -S files ¬
-K lock_after_retries=no -K min_label=ADMIN_LOW -K clearance=ADMIN_HIGH secadm
# passwd -r files secadm
# useradd -c Alice -d /export/home/alice¬
-K lock_after_retries=no -K roles=secadm alice
# passwd -r files alice
```

You will be prompted to change the password for alice. Change it.

We've created user alice, who is able to assume the role secadm, which includes three profiles. Recall that the label_encodings file specifies label **PUBLIC** and clearance **SECRET** for all users without explicit label and clearance. When alice logs in, she can choose between the **PUBLIC** and **SECRET** workspaces, until she assumes the secadm role, which has a label of **ADMIN_LOW** and a clearance of **ADMIN_HIGH**. When alice leaves the secadm role, she also leaves that administrative label range and returns to her user label range.

The /etc/security/policy.conf files set the default key/value pair for things such as default auths, profiles, idle time, lockout, and so on. They can be overridden per user by the administrator.

User Logins and Roles

Log out of the system as root and then log in as alice. You can set up your desktop environment now, or click on Skip Setup and do it later.

You'll be greeted with the window that displays your roles, label, and clearance. Click on OK.

At the next screen, select SECRET for this login session. It should already be the default. There should be a yellow rectangle at the lower-right corner of the window. Click on OK. If you choose to log in at PUBLIC, you cannot "switch up" to SECRET, but if you log in at SECRET, you can "switch down" to PUBLIC.

You'll be presented with a typical desktop with the panel bar at the bottom. At the top is the Trusted Path bar, your name, the session label, and the color (called stripe) for PUBLIC. This is alice's minimum sensitivity label.

A quick look through the menu will reveal that some applications have been removed—for example, the ability to take a screen grab. Under Administration there's only the Time Slider tool; the rest have disappeared.

On the Trusted Path menu bar, you should see a workspace label; it is green, with the word PUBLIC in it. For any application you open in this workspace, a green stripe appears at the top of the window, making it clear that processes in this window are running at the PUBLIC label. Right-click and open up a terminal. Alice's home directory is mounted in the labeled zone public, at the label PUBLIC.

Multilevel Workspace

From the global zone, we see that in addition to alice's home directory in the global zone, the system has created an alice home directory inside the zones public and secret, and has mounted the directories inside those zones. Alice has three distinct home directories; in a labeled workspace, there's no shuffling your home directory around from label to label like an auto-mounted home directory from an NFS server. Home directories are labeled, and they exist as different directories at every label.

```
# zfs list |grep alice
rpool/export/home/alice                      1.03M   146G   1.03M   /export/home/alice
rpool/zones/public/rpool/export/home/alice   4.23M   146G   4.23M   /zone/public/root/
export/home/alice
rpool/zones/secret/rpool/export/home/alice    58K    146G    58K    /zone/secret/root/
export/home/alice
```

Switch your workspace label by clicking on the label PUBLIC and then click on the drop-down menu Change Workspace Label. Select SECRET and then open a terminal. You now are in a multilevel workspace, with two terminals opened: PUBLIC and SECRET. The current workspace is SECRET, denoted by yellow.

Try to cut and paste some text from one window to another. You'll be greeted with a friendly screen saying you are not authorized to transfer material from one label to another. A *write-down* is copying material from a higher label to a lower label. This is not permitted because it would constitute a leak (for example, from TOP SECRET to SECRET). A *write-up* is the opposite, transferring information from a lower label to a higher label. In some cases, this is desirable, such as one-way flow of tamper-resistant logs—or using our NOC list example, an addition of a name to the list. A read-down is possible, because a TOP SECRET label dominates a SECRET label. A read-up is not permitted because that would constitute a leak. This subject is advanced and geared toward developers, so we will not be covering it in this book.

Switching Roles

At the top left-corner you should see the user name alice. Clicking on it drops down a menu with secadm; click on secadm to assume that role. You'll be prompted to close your terminal windows and then for the secadm passwd. The stripe is now gray, and the current workspace label is TRUSTED PATH. This label is used for all administrative work.

If you open a terminal and check hostname and id, you will find you are logged into the global zone as secadm (a role, not a user), and the label of the window is ADMIN_LOW. Let's add another user, whose job it is to maintain the NOC list.

First, let's convert the clearance for the highest labeled zone to hex, because the string is a bit long:

```
secadm:~$ atohexlabel -c " TS NEED TO KNOW/EYES ONLY "
0x0007-08-60
secadm:~$ useradd -c Maintainer -d /export/home/bob -K lock_after_retries=no¬
-K min_label=0x0007-08-60 -K clearance=0x0007-08-60 bob
secadm:~$ passwd -r files bob
```

You'll be prompted to change bob's password. Change it.

Log out as alice and then log in as bob for the first time and ensure that his home environment is set up. Note that bob operates at label **TS NEED TO KNOW/EYES ONLY**, he has one home directory only, and that in the TS zone, his workspace stripe is red. Log out as bob, log back in as alice, and assume the secadm role as before.

Managing Devices in Trusted Extensions

The usual administrative tools have returned to the panel. On the Trusted Path drop-down menu, select Allocate Device. You'll find a list of devices such as audio0, cdrom0, rmdisk0, and so on, as shown in Figure 18-2.

A case can be made that on a system with mission-critical data, it's probably not a good idea to have any writable devices to prevent leaks. On the other hand, Trusted Extensions is a compromise to an absolute airgap; it allows a modicum of normal user activity while enforcing access to data.

NOTE
This is where this chapter earns its money. You can spend an hour reading the official documentation and another three hours trying to make it work, or you can read the next few paragraphs.

In Trusted Extensions, access to a device is granted per user, per zone, one at a time. The implication of more than one user, possibly at different labels, would be at odds with everything Trusted Extensions was designed to prevent. A CD-ROM tray can contain a CD labeled SECRET or TOP SECRET; the device does not know.

NOTE
The following example is by necessity an oversimplification to show how to list devices and allocate them to users. It's highly unlikely that a USB drive stick would be found attached to an unattended TX installation.

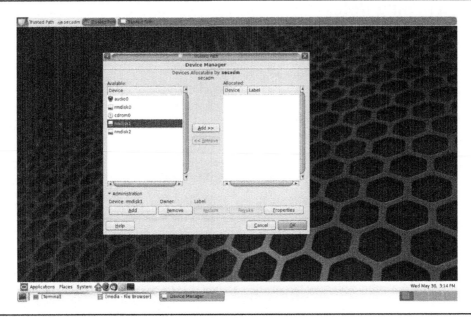

FIGURE 18-2. *Managing devices in Trusted Extensions*

To grant user bob in the zone ts the ability to read from or write to a USB drive stick (highly unlikely in the real world), use the following command:

```
secadm:~$ allocate -U bob -z ts rmdisk1
Insert disk in rmdisk1. (y to continue, n to cancel) y
Do you want rmdisk1 mounted? (y/n) y
Device rmdisk1 mounted for user bob in ts zone.
Volume                Mount Point
/dev/dsk/c5t0d0p0:1   /media/bob-rmdisk1/TravelDrive
```

On my system, rmdisk1 is the USB port; it may be different on another system, such as rmdisk0 or rmdisk2.

User bob would log in at label TOP SECRET/EYES ONLY, and the drive would be available at that same label. He would access the drive, which shows up as an icon, and copy our fictional NOC list from the drive to wherever the maintainer keeps his secret list.

When user bob is done, the secadm removes the USB drive allocation:

```
secadm:~$ deallocate -F -z ts rmdisk1
Please remove the disk from rmdisk1.
```

The device will no longer be available to user bob. To see the devices that are allocatable, use the following command:

```
secadm:~$ list_devices -l
```

However, be prepared for a long listing of many slices of block and raw devices. For device allocations and deallocations, the CLI provides an easier and more efficient alternative interface.

Network Access with Trusted Extensions

To recap, we have a standalone TX system with this zone configuration:

- **global (administrative zone)**   192.168.0.5/24
- **public (label PUBLIC)**   192.168.0.20/24
- **secret (label SECRET)**   192.168.0.21/24
- **ts (label TOP SECRET)**   192.168.0.22/24

Trusted Extensions systems talk to each other using a secret handshake called CIPSO (Commercial IP Security Option). The secret handshake is written into the header of the IP packets and allows machines at the same level of classification to talk to one another across a trusted network.

Machines not using Trusted Extensions are defined as unlabeled. Unlabeled hosts can talk to a trusted host if the Security Administrator makes special provisions to allow it. In the real world, this is rare. Trusted hosts live on trusted networks with other trusted hosts. Unlabeled hosts that connect to trusted host are the exceptions, not the rule. They usually perform a specific function, and the unlabeled-to-trusted connection has other checks.

NOTE
The following example should be considered a last resort, a break-glass pull-alarm example. We do not actually advocate that you do this, and it's very rare that you would ever have to do this. What you're about to do totally defeats the purpose of Trusted Extensions. Don't do this... until you have to.

In real life, sometimes there exists a broken Trusted Extensions box in a remote and inaccessible location, and the only human within typing distance is the janitor. You need to service the box, but you don't have the credentials, and the guy with all the right credentials can't be found. As a last resort, you need to allow an unlabeled host to connect to the TX machine.

To allow an unlabeled host to connect, it's as simple as removing a line from /etc/pam.conf. At the bottom of /etc/pam.conf, find and remove or comment out this line:

```
# Entries for Trusted Extensions
other    account required                pam_tsol_account.so.1
```

Without this line, any host can connect to the global zone, and any user can log in if they have an account.

To allow a specific host to connect to the global zone, perform the following steps. Add the **allow_unlabeled** entry to the previous line in /etc/pam.conf:

```
other    account required                pam_tsol_account.so.1 allow_unlabeled
```

My desktop is 192.168.0.2. To allow it to connect to the trusted host, I do the following:

1. Add 192.168.0.2 and its hostname to /etc/hosts.

2. Add it to the TX database:

   ```
   # tncfg -t admin_low add host=192.168.0.2/32
   A new template will be created
   ```

3. Restart the service tnctl, which reads the Trusted Networking Templates:

   ```
   # svcadm restart tnctl
   ```

At this point, the host 192.168.0.2 can connect to the Trusted Extensions host. The access policy is still very relaxed, even though it has been restricted to one host. To tighten it even more, and restrict logins from an unlabeled host only to zones at a specific label, add the remote host with the tag **public_unlab**, **secret_unlab**, or **ts_unlab**. These unlabeled tags are already defined for you in /etc/security/tsol/tnrhtp.

For example, if I want to grant access from an unlabeled host to the zone public, I would execute this:

```
# tncfg -t secret_unlab add host=192.168.0.4/32
# svcadm restart tnctl
```

What you're doing is modifying /etc/security/tsol/tnrhdb under the covers. This enables a user from the unlabeled host 192.168.0.4 to **ssh** to the public zone 192.168.0.20 as himself, if he has a valid clearance.

Summary

Trusted Extensions provides Mandatory Access Control. Users and data are assigned labels within a hierarchy, and the interactions between user and data and data endpoints are enforced according to the levels of the labels. Our examples have necessarily been demo exercises that give a flavor of the restrictions on what a user can and cannot do. In fact, Solaris with Trusted Extensions is a powerful and transparent tool to segregate and control access to information. It is not a turnkey proposition; it makes little sense to configure a Trusted Extensions system within a network of unlabeled OSes. TX takes careful planning, and it requires the humans who work with it to follow good security practice (for example, role segregation, audit trail, and media management). When deployed with other security measures such as RBAC, IPSec, IP Filter, and secure LDAP, Trusted Extensions is the preeminent enforcer and keeper of secrets.

References

The Trusted Extensions User's Guide, December 2011 Revision is found at http://docs.oracle.com/cd/E23824_01/pdf/821-1484.pdf.

The Trusted Extensions Developer's Guide, December 2011 Revision is found at http://docs.oracle.com/cd/E23824_01/pdf/821-1483.pdf.

The Trusted Extensions Configuration and Administration, December 2011 Revision is found at http://docs.oracle.com/cd/E23824_01/pdf/821-1482.pdf.

The Trusted Extensions Label Administration, December 2011 Revision is found at http://docs.oracle.com/cd/E23824_01/pdf/821-1481.pdf.

The Compartmented Mode Workstation Labeling: Encodings Format, November 2011 Revision is found at http://docs.oracle.com/cd/E23824_01/pdf/821-1480.pdf.

CHAPTER
19

The Network File System

he Network File System (NFS) is a standard method for sharing files and directories on networks with UNIX-based operating systems. Other operating systems include methods to join NFS networks. Even Microsoft recognizes the importance of NFS, with its Microsoft Services for NFS.

Although NFS Version 4 (NFSv4) is preferred for its security, Solaris 11 supports client and server versions of NFS Version 2 (NFSv2) and NFS Version 3 (NFSv3). Backward compatibility is often important in the enterprise. Linux users should pay attention because the basic commands and configuration files associated with NFS are different. The Automounter plays a larger role on Solaris systems. Of course, various methods are available to mount shared NFS directories during the boot process.

Available Versions

With the development of client/server networking in the 1980s, Sun Microsystems found that protocols such as FTP and HTTP weren't enough. There was a need for a networking protocol where the network would be invisible to the user. For that reason, Sun released NFSv2 back in 1984. Because a number of systems are configured to all three versions of NFS, Solaris 11 supports them all. As might be expected, NFSv4 is the most secure. However, the way it works is quite different from NFSv2 or NFSv3.

NOTE
NFS version 1 was never released for public use.

NFSv3 and NFSv4 support POSIX-style Access Control Lists (ACLs). POSIX is a group of standards, short for Portable Operating System Interface for UNIX.

NFS Version 2

Sun first released NFSv2 back in 1984. At that time, the 2GB limit on file sizes seemed generous. The filesystem formats of the time, such as DOS, could only handle files up to 16MB. But those limits were eventually shattered. However, NFSv2 is still available on a substantial number of systems. In fact, Solaris releases before version 2.5 supported only NFSv2.

NFS Version 3

With the release of Solaris 2.5 in 1995, Sun introduced NFSv3. With the introduction of Solaris 2.6, maximum file sizes were effectively raised to 4GB. NFSv3 provided the following features:

- **More efficient writes**   NFSv3 supports asynchronous writes, which improve performance with the help of memory caching, at the expense of filesystem reliability.
- **Caching file attributes**   Because the attributes of files on remote systems are now cached, performance is improved.
- **Larger transfer sizes**   NFSv3 increased the transfer size from 8KB to 32KB.
- **Move to TCP**   NFSv3 introduced TCP to shared directories; the TCP protocol is more firewall friendly.

One common feature of NFSv2 and NFSv3 is their use of the User Datagram Protocol (UDP), a "best effort" protocol. Despite the use of UDP, interruptions in NFS communications often led to systems that "hung," thus frustrating users. Nevertheless, NFSv3 also remains in fairly common use today.

NFS Version 4

NFSv4 was first introduced in 2000, using some different paradigms. In some ways, it is actually simpler because it does not use several daemons required by previous versions. As such, it uses fewer TCP/IP ports. It also uses different communications protocols. The following features are included in NFSv4:

- **Communication over TCP**   TCP verifies the delivery of network data.
- **Fewer protocols**   Does not use the **mountd**, **nfslogd**, and **statd** daemons.
- **Fewer ports**   Requires access through ports 111 and 2049.
- **More complete ACLs**   Supports NFSv4 ACLs.

Additional Common Features

NFS on Solaris 11 includes additional common features. In some fashion, all three versions can work with Kerberos for authentication. Logging can be configured through the /etc/nfs/nfslog.conf configuration file. The Automounter supports "on-demand" mounting. All of these features, except Kerberos, will be described later in this chapter.

The Solaris implementation of NFS supports Kerberos-based security in one format or another. Whereas support for the less secure Kerberos version 4 was included in Solaris 2, support for Kerberos version 5 was incorporated starting with Solaris version 2.6. Although you can refer to Chapter 12 for an overview of Kerberos, you can find a detailed discussion of this "single sign-on" authentication mechanism in the "System Administration Guide: Security Services" document referenced at the end of this chapter.

Solaris 11 has moved toward configuring NFS with the help of the Service Management Facility (SMF) described in Chapter 6. In addition, NFS configuration is now supported in non-global ZFS zones, based on the **sharenfs** property described in Chapter 9. The configuration options described next supersede the settings normally configured in /etc/default/autofs and /etc/default/nfs in Solaris 10.

NFS Service Configuration

The Solaris 11 NFS software includes a number of services, as shown in the following output to the **svcs -a | grep nfs** command:

```
online     Mar_26    svc:/network/nfs/status:default
online     Mar_26    svc:/network/nfs/nlockmgr:default
online     Mar_26    svc:/network/nfs/mapid:default
online     Mar_26    svc:/network/nfs/rquota:default
online     Mar_26    svc:/network/nfs/server:default
online     Mar_28    svc:/network/nfs/cbd:default
online     12:47:13  svc:/network/nfs/client:default
```

Service	Description
status	NFS Status Monitor. Based on the **statd** daemon.
nlockmgr	NFS Lock Manager, for file locking to prevent multiple users from opening the same file. Based on the **nlockd** daemon.
mapid	NFS ID mapper, which maps user and group IDs between NFS servers and clients. Based on the **nfsmapid** daemon.
rquota	NFS remote quota service, which can limit resources taken from an NFS share by user. Based on the **rquotad** daemon.
server	Main NFS server. Associated with the **nfsd** daemon.
cbd	NFSv4 callback program. Based on the **nfs4cbd** daemon.
client	NFS client. Based on the **mount_nfs** command. Although convenient for test purposes, there is no requirement to enable an NFS client on a system with an NFS server.

TABLE 19-1. *NFS Services*

Table 19-1 highlights some of the settings associated with each service. Of course, you can use a command such as **svccfg -s** to review and modify associated settings. Options are frequently described in the noted man page for the daemon or command.

In general, you configure any of these services via SMF, with the help of the **svccfg -s** command. For example, the following command accesses the SMF configuration interface for the NFS server:

```
# svccfg -s network/nfs/server
```

You can then list the current properties for NFS with the **listprop** command. The following subsections analyze the default properties, in appropriate categories. The settings available for the NFS server generally encompass those listed for other NFS daemons listed in the table. The following subsections reflect the output to the **listprop** command. Many of these services are collected in a manifest, in a server.xml file in the /lib/svc/mainfest/network/nfs directory.

Firewall Configuration

The default NFS firewall configuration uses settings as defined for the system as a whole. However, exceptions can be made, as described in Table 19-2.

Network Configuration

As with other services, the network configuration is dependent on a number of other factors. The SMF network characteristics as they relate to NFS are shown in Table 19-3. These characteristics are common to several other services, as discussed shortly.

The network/grouping option can be set to one of four values:

- **require_all**   All related systems must be online, or degraded.
- **require_any**   One or more systems must be online, or degraded.

Option	Description
firewall_config	Can take the Solaris 11 configuration when set to two properties: **com.sun,fw_configuration**.
firewall_config/apply_to	Can limit the firewall policy to a specific address, network, pool, or interface.
firewall_config/exceptions	Supports exceptions to specific firewall policies, based on the **apply_to list**.
firewall_config/policy	Inherits from the default (**use_global**) or some custom policy.
firewall_config/value_authorization	Designates value for firewall administrators, such as **solaris.smf.value.firewall.config**.
firewall_context	Can take the Solaris 11 configuration when set to **com.sun,fw_configuration**.
firewall_context/ipf_method	Specifies the script for filtering rules. Normally set to /lib/svc/method/nfs-server.

TABLE 19-2. *NFS Firewall Options*

- **optional_all** All related systems must be online, disabled, degraded, or in maintenance mode.
- **exclude_all** All related systems must be online, or degraded.

Configuration of the NFS Lock Manager
As noted earlier, the NFS lock manager service adds "locks" for files that may be in use over a shared NFS directory. Such locks in general are used to at least warn users who may open a file that

Option	Description
network	Specifies "dependency," which confirms NFS is dependent on networking.
network/entities	Points to network interfaces online via svc:/milestone/network.
network/grouping	Notes dependencies to be satisfied for NFS. **require_any** allows the use of any dependency (contrast with **require_all**).
network/restart_on	Specifies conditions for restarting the service. May be set to **error**, **none**, **all**, **restart**, or **refresh**.
network/type	Normally set to **service**.

TABLE 19-3. *NFS Network Options*

is already in use. Although the base options fall into the same categories as the network options, they differ in two respects:

- **FMRI**   The Fault Management Resource Identifier (FMRI) for the NFS Lock Manager is svc:/network/nfs/nlockmgr.
- **nlockmgr/grouping**   The service is set to **require_all**.

Configuration of the NFS ID Mapper

As noted earlier, the NFS ID mapper matches user and group IDs between NFS clients and servers. The SMF options differ from the network service in two respects:

- **FMRI**   The Fault Management Resource Identifier (FMRI) for the NFS ID mapper is svc:/network/nfs/mapid.
- **mapid/grouping**   The service is set to **optional_all**, which suggests that a failure in mapping is a nonfatal error.

Configuration of the rpcbind Service for NFS

The **rpcbind** service is a mapper that associates universal addresses to Remote Procedure Call (RPC) program mapper numbers. As with the other services, the base options fall into the same categories as the network options, except in three respects:

- **FMRI**   The Fault Management Resource Identifier (FMRI) for the RPC bind service is svc:/network/rpc/bind.
- **rpcbind/grouping**   The service is set to **require_all**.
- **rpcbind/restart_on**   The service is set to restart on command.

Additional SMF-based configuration options are listed in the man page for **rpcbind**.

Encryption Keys and NFS

NFS, as originally configured, is inherently insecure. Solaris 11 integrates a Kerberos-based key server to address this issue. It works hand in hand with the RPC service. For SMF configuration, the difference with the network service is as follows:

- **FMRI**   The Fault Management Resource Identifier (FMRI) for the **keyserv** service is svc:/network/rpc/keyserv.
- **keyserv/grouping**   The service is set to **optional_all**, which means sharing proceeds even if there's a key server failure.
- **keyserv/restart_on**   The service is set to **restart**.

Additional SMF-based configuration options are listed in the man page for **keyserv**.

GSS and NFS

The Generic Security Service (GSS) is used to validate credentials, such as those created by the Kerberos key server. Therefore, it makes sense that GSS is configured in the same way as the key server, with the obvious exception of the relevant FMRI, svc:/network/rpc/gss.

The Reparse Daemon and NFS

NFS referrals use symbolic links to redirect clients to the actual location of shared NFS directories. Such referrals are associated with the NFS referral utility, **nfsref**. The Reparse daemon, reparsed, is a filesystem service. The FMRI is svc:/system/filesystem/reparse.

NFS and Filesystem Services

NFS is a filesystem. Therefore, it makes sense that it depends on local filesystem services. The advantage of NFS is that, when properly configured, the files on a shared NFS directory look just like local files to the end user. Related filesystem services are as follows:

- ■ **FMRI** The Fault Management Resource Identifier (FMRI) for the local filesystem service is svc:/system/filesystem/local.

- ■ **filesystem-local/grouping** The service is set to **require_all**.

- ■ **filesystem-local/restart-on** The service is set to **restart** when it encounters errors.

NFS Configuration Files

NFS is configured in a number of different files on a Solaris 11 system. Most of the files shown in Table 19-4 are defaults and do not need to be changed. If you're new to NFS on Solaris, take a look at the contents of these files. Several of them are still available for legacy purposes, based on Solaris 10.

File	Description
/etc/default/nfslogd	Specifies logging defaults, including cycle time, maximum size, and number of previous logs to preserve.
/etc/nfs/nfslog.conf	Configures NFS server log files, private file handles, and buffers.
/etc/nfs/nfslogtab	Includes NFS log information in progress.
/etc/dfs/dfstab	Notes a legacy file no longer used for Solaris 11. If you still have information in this file, replace it. Use the **share -F nfs** scripts in the file to add shares to the /etc/dfs/sharetab file.
/etc/dfs/fstypes	Includes the default filesystems for directories mounted from remote locations.
/etc/dfs/sharetab	Configures shared directories for both NFS and Samba/CIFS. Configured with the **share** command.
/etc/mnttab	Lists the currently mounted filesystems.
/etc/netconfig	Notes applicable transport-level protocols.
/etc/nfssec.conf	Includes NFS security modes.

TABLE 19-4. *NFS Configuration Files*

Options for Sharing

You can configure shared directories for NFS in a number of ways. With the right commands, you can set up basic file sharing in a static configuration file. The share is automatically loaded from networked servers during the boot process. Alternatively, you could set up NFS shares as part of the Automounter service described later in this chapter. Despite the information in the official Solaris 11 documentation, WebNFS services are no longer supported.

Towards the end of this section, you'll see how to activate logging, as well as how the Shared Folders tool can be used to set up shared directories.

NOTE
The use of the /etc/dfs/dfstab file for shared NFS directories has been deprecated. You can find shared directories mounted during the boot process in the sharetab file in the same /etc/dfs directory.

Basic NFS Filesystem Sharing

The discussion on e-mail in Chapter 17 includes an example of NFS filesystem sharing. The following command shares the /var/mail directory, which is frequently configured with spools of e-mail messages for individual users. To review, the **-F nfs** shares via NFS, with the option of read/write mode (**-o rw**):

```
# share -F nfs -o rw /var/mail
```

Other options, which you can also assign with the **-o** switch, are shown in Table 19-5. For the complete list, see the share_nfs man page. You can set up multiple options in a comma-separated list. Don't include a space between the options.

Option	Description
aclok	Supports access control for NFSv2 clients.
anon=uid	Specifies the user ID of an unknown user who connects.
noaclfab	Avoids fabricating ACLs. Needed for filesystems such as the standard implementations of the Linux extended filesystems.
none=*list*	Specifies a list to prohibit access to.
nosub	Denies mount access to subdirectories of shared directories.
nosuid	Prevents access to the SUID (super user ID) or SGID (super group ID) permission bits.
ro	Enables read-only access.
rw	Enables read-write access.
rw=*list*	Enables read-write access from the given *list* of hosts.
root=*list*	Allows root access from systems specified in the *list*.

TABLE 19-5. *NFS Options for the **share** Command*

For example, you can set up a read-write share for the 192.168.0.0/24 network of a directory named /project with the following command:

```
# share -F nfs -o rw=@192.168.0/24 /project
```

Note the modified form of the IP address that's used (yes, even though 192.168.0/24 violates standard Classless Inter-Domain Routing notation, it is correct). Assuming hostname resolution such as DNS is working properly, you could also use an entry such as @.example.com for systems on the example.com network. Once all desired shares are configured, you can review them with the following command:

```
# share -F nfs
```

From a remote system, you should also review available shares. It's possible with the **showmount -e *hostname*** command.

TIP

*If you configure both an NFS client and server on the same system, make sure to specify the background (**bg**) option to the **share** command. If an attempt to mount an NFS directory has trouble connecting, the **bg** option can keep NFS from locking up a system.*

Unsharing a Share

You can reverse the process with the **unshare** command. For example, if a project is completed and you want to remove the /project directory share from the NFS server, you could run the following command:

```
# unshare /project
```

Changes made with the **share** and **unshare** commands are reflected in the /etc/dfs/sharetab file.

Limiting a Share with Netgroups

If you've set up the netgroups feature in a network database such as the Network Information Service (NIS) or the Lightweight Directory Access Protocol (LDAP), you can use it to limit access to specific shares. Let's say you wanted to limit access to the /var/mail share. If you've set up network groups, the following command would limit access to the netgroup named emailhosts:

```
# share -F nfs -o rw=emailhosts /var/mail
```

Alternatively, the following command would share the /var/mail directory for use by only the specified users, super1 and super2:

```
# share -F nfs -o rw=super1,super2 /var/mail
```

Client Configuration Options

You can browse the shares available from remote systems with the aforementioned **showmount** command. With that information, you can mount such shares from the command line, set them up for mounting during the boot process, or configure them to mount on demand with the help of the Automounter.

Mount from the Command Line

To determine how you should mount an NFS share from the command line, take a look at this sample output from the **showmount -e** *NFSserver* command; in this case, the *NFSserver* is named solaris-test1:

```
export list for solaris-test1:
/export/group  (everyone)
/export/home   (everyone)
/var/mail      (everyone)
/project       @192.168.0/24
```

You should be able to mount any of the shared directories. For example, the following command mounts the /var/mail share on the local directory of the same name. To review, the **-o rw** option mounts in read-write mode; however, that can't override a share that was created in read-only mode.

```
# mount -F nfs -o rw solaris-test1:/var/mail /var/mail
```

During the Boot Process

The configuration file that defines local filesystems to be mounted during the boot process is /etc/vfstab. Although its functionality for local filesystems has been deprecated in favor of ZFS and the Automounter, it's still used to mount NFS shares from remote systems. In addition, the file is well labeled because it includes options in seven categories, described in Table 19-6. For more information on ZFS, see Chapter 9.

The following example illustrates a share from the system named server1, of the /shared/project1 directory. Because it's a network share, it's set with a dash (-) since it's inappropriate to apply the **fsck** command over a network. The share is mounted on the local /share/project directory, using the NFS filesystem. The next column also has a dash (-) because you don't want to apply the **fsck** command over a network. The final two columns mean the share is mounted during the boot process (**yes**), with no specific options (**no**).

```
server1:/shared/project1 - /share/project nfs - yes no
```

Option	Description
Device to mount	Device name
Device to fsck	Device name to check and repair if needed
Mount point	Mount directory
Filesystem type	Filesystem format or type
Filesystem check info	Flag on whether to check the filesystem automatically
Mount point	Flag on whether to mount the filesystem during the boot process
Mount options	Filesystem mount options

TABLE 19-6. */etc/vfstab Options*

If desired, you may want to substitute appropriate permissions for the last column, such as **ro** or **rw** for read-only or read-write access. Just pay attention to the note earlier in this chapter about the background (**bg**) option. Otherwise, if you specify a mount in /etc/vfstab of a share without that option, a system could lock up.

Automount on Demand

In this section, you'll examine the Automounter as well as how it relates to the autofs package. You'll then review the basic Automounter configuration files as well as how they interact. Finally, you'll create a slight variation on the existing Automounter options, to show what you learned.

The Automounter Package

If desired, you can still use the "traditional" method to configure automated mounts of shared directories. The process starts with the basic Automounter package, autofs. If it isn't already installed, you can do so with the following command:

```
# pkg install system/file-system/autofs
```

As always, a system must be enabled before it actually runs. To enable the Automounter, you'd run the following command:

```
# svcadm enable system/filesystem/auotfs:default
```

Automounter Configuration Files

Once the autofs package is installed, you'll find the auto_master and auto_home configuration files in the /etc directory. The options shown in Figure 19-1 are straightforward; they include three shares, each configured with three basic options:

- **Mount point**   Access to automounted directories is configured on the noted directory (/net, /home, /nfs4) as a mount point.

- **Mapping**   The mapping specifies how a share is read from a remote system. It can refer to other files, such as /etc/auto_home, for additional information. It may also be based on a name service switch order, as defined in the /etc/nsswitch.conf file.

- **Mount options**   The mount options are based on options associated with the **mount** command, given the **mount -F nfs** command. Options are defined in the mount_nfs man page.

```
#
# Copyright (c) 1992, 2011, Oracle and/or its affiliates. All rights reserved.
#
# Master map for automounter
#
+auto_master
/net            -hosts          -nosuid,nobrowse
/home           auto_home       -nobrowse
/nfs4           -fedfs          -ro,nosuid,nobrowse
~
~
(END)
```

FIGURE 19-1.   */etc/auto_master*

Now examine the lines in the /etc/auto_master file. The first line indicates a master Automounter map:

```
+auto_master
```

The next line specifies the /net directory for mounting, based on the **-hosts** setting in the /etc/nsswitch.conf file. The mount options disable SUID permissions as well as browsing.

```
/net    -hosts  -nosuid,nobrowse
```

So based on the following excerpt from the /etc/nsswitch.conf file, you can search based on hostnames in /etc/hosts or fully qualified domain names (FQDNs) in an authoritative DNS server for the network:

```
hosts:   files dns
```

For a remote system named kauai.example.com, you could browse shared NFS directories from that system with the following command:

```
$ ls /net/kauai.example.com
```

The FQDN may not be required; all you need to do is match a name from the **-hosts** database. Alternatively, you could substitute the IP address of the target NFS server.

The next line is used for regular home directories, and it mounts them on the /etc/auto_home directory, in nobrowse mode. You'll explore that file in a moment.

```
/home   auto_home  -nobrowse
```

The final line is associated with mounts of an NFS version 4 filesystem, also in read-only, no SUID permissions, and no browse mode:

```
/nfs4    -fedfs  -ro,nosuid,nobrowse
```

Here, **-fedfs** refers to the Federated File System Server, which is included in the labels for an NFS server within a DNS database.

Now take a look at the /etc/auto_home file. Upon installation, it should be fairly simple; the first line confirms the auto_home map. It's followed by a line that mounts the michael/ subdirectory, taken from the localhost system, on the directory /export/home/michael.

```
+auto_home
michael   localhost:/export/home/michael
```

For systems with multiple users, you may find a line for each user. For example, the following lines may be associated with an anonymous and guest user on an FTP server, as described in Chapter 20:

```
anonymous  localhost:/export/home/anonymous
guest1  localhost:/export/home/guests/guest1
```

You can set up a more direct association between the NFS client and server with the help of the /etc/auto_direct file. First, you'd have to add the following entry to the /etc/auto_master file:

```
/-    /etc/auto_direct
```

Then you can set up the /etc/auto_direct file with direct maps from local directories and those shared from remote systems. The following example sets up the /corp/local/policies and /corp/local/template directories in read-only format from the server1.example.com system:

```
/corp/local      -ro \
     /policies          server1.example.com:/export/local/policies \
     /template          server1.example.com:/export/local/template
```

Just make sure to use actual mount points. For example, if you've set up home directories from the server1.example.com system in /etc/auto_direct, and you want to set up that configured automount on the local /remotehome directory, use the following format:

```
/remotehome/michael -rw  server1.example.com:/export/home/michael
```

Add to the Automounter Configuration

Now you'll take a few steps to add more to the Automounter configuration. Before starting, you'll back up key Automounter files. In addition, you'll need a shared NFS directory; if necessary, it can come from a system configured with a different UNIX-based operating system, such as Linux. Alternatively, you can set up a regular shared NFS directory, as defined later in this chapter. In either case, make sure the NFS service on the server is active. If that shared NFS directory is on a remote system, make sure that communications with that server are not blocked by a firewall.

To add to the Automounter configuration, take the following steps:

1. Back up the /etc/auto_master and /etc/auto_home files.
2. Open the /etc/auto_master file in a text editor.
3. Set up a system to be shared on the /share directory, configured in /etc/auto_share, in read-only mode. (This assumes auto_share doesn't already exist.) One way to do so is to add the following line to the /etc/auto_master file:

   ```
   /share  auto_share  -ro
   ```
4. Save your changes and exit from the /etc/auto_master file.
5. Open the new /etc/auto_share file in a text editor.
6. Add the following lines to the file, to first validate it as an auto_share map and then to specify mounting of the /tmp directory from the localhost system on the /share/solaris directory. If you have a different shared directory from a different system, substitute accordingly.

   ```
   solaris -soft  localhost:/tmp
   ```
7. Save your changes to the auto_share file; make sure it's saved to the /etc directory.
8. Run the **ls /share/solaris** command. Compare the output to the **ls /tmp** command. Run the **umount /share/solaris** command to unmount the share. (Alternately, you can wait the default mount time of 600 seconds.)
9. Open the auto_share file again. Substitute an NFS share from a remote system for localhost:/tmp. Save your changes.
10. Run the **ls /share/solaris** command again. If it worked, you now have a connection to the remote NFS share.

Log Management

You can use the **share** command to set up a shared NFS directory, with log messages sent to a file in the /etc/nfs directory. For example, the following command shares the /export/group directory in read-write mode, using the background option, with logs configured through the nfslog.conf file in the /etc/nfs directory:

```
# share -F nfs -o rw,bg,log=global /export/group
```

If successful, you'll see an nfslog_workbuffer_log_in_process file in the /var/nfs directory. It's configured through a single line in the /etc/nfs/nfslog.conf file. The **defaultdir** is the default directory for log files, and the **log** specifies the name of the file :

```
global   defaultdir=/var/nfs \
         log=nfslog fhtable=fhtable buffer=nfslog_workbuffer
```

But that is not enough to actually get logging information for connected systems. To set that up, you need to set the **logformat** directive to **basic** or **extended**. The following directive shows how we add it to the **global** tag:

```
global   defaultdir=/var/nfs \
         log=nfslog fhtable=fhtable buffer=nfslog_workbuffer \
         logformat=extended
```

Additional log files are associated with the different services upon which NFS depends. As suggested earlier, you can get a list of these dependent services with the following command:

```
$ svccfg -s network/nfs/server listprop
```

You'll then have to identify log files for individual services; for example, the following command identifies the log file for the NFS Lock Manager service, which may help you identify problems related to locked files:

```
$ svcs -x svc:/network/nfs/nlockmgr
```

Version Control

Although NFSv4 is the default, Solaris 11 does support the previous two versions of NFS. If you want to limit clients to a specific version, you can assign it on the client as a property. For example, the following command supports access to NFS versions 3 and 4:

```
# sharectl set -p client_versmin=3 nfs
```

In contrast, the following command limits access to NFS versions 2 and 3:

```
# sharectl set -p client_versmax=3 nfs
```

If you put the two commands together, access from the client is limited to directories shared from an NFSv3 server. If you want to transition away from these older versions of NFS, you may want to set **client_versmin=4 nfs**.

Firewall Considerations

Directories shared over NFSv4 communicate over TCP port 2049. If you want to browse NFS shares from remote systems, you'll also need to open TCP port 111 on the NFS server.

Summary

NFS is still a core network sharing service for Solaris. It has been updated for Solaris 11 to promote integration with SMF. Although it still supports the use of NFSv2 and NFSv3, the focus is on NFSv4. And that's as it should be because NFSv4 requires fewer services, fewer protocols, fewer open ports. It also supports more complete ACLs, larger files, and Kerberos-based security.

You can set up shared NFS directories when you configure a ZFS filesystem, or you can set them up with the **share -F** command. When shared NFS directories are configured with **share -F**, you can limit them by user or host with the help of the netgroups feature available through NIS or LDAP. The configuration of these directories is documented in the /etc/dfs/sharetab file.

You can customize NFS based on its service properties in a number of areas, including firewalls, network configuration, the lock manager, the RPC mapper, encryption keys, the GSS for key-based credentials, and different filesystem services. You can find most NFS configuration files in the /etc/nfs and /etc/dfs directories.

From a client, you can review shared directories over an open port 111 from a remote NFS server with the **showmount** command. You can mount those directories directly with the **mount** command. You can set up such mounts during the boot process in the /etc/vfstab file. You can configure such mounts with the help of the Automounter, starting in the /etc/auto_master file.

Related log files are normally stored in the /var/nfs directory, as defined in the /etc/nfs/nfslog. conf file.

References

For more information on the Solaris implementation of NFS, see the document "Oracle Solaris Administration: Network Services." Available online from http://docs.oracle.com/cd/E23824_01/html/821-1454/.

Security options such as Kerberos as well as how they relate to authentication are covered in the document "Oracle Solaris Administration: Security Services." Available online from http://docs.oracle.com/cd/E23824_01/html/821-1456/.

CHAPTER
20

The FTP and
Secure Shell Services

emote connections are an essential part of any modern network. The first remote connection protocols transmitted data in clear text. Today, protocol analyzers, colloquially known as *sniffers,* can allow a black-hat hacker to read everything that's transmitted in clear text, including usernames and passwords. As an administrator of an enterprise-level operating system, you should assume that threats exist everywhere, internally and externally. Yet, you want to give your users network access to internal files and external sites. When allowing access to data, you need to consider whether the data requires protection. FTP and Secure Shell allow access to data across the network. FTP, a clear-text protocol, is a good choice for providing access to public information, whereas Secure Shell, which provides encryption and authentication between client and server, is necessary for data that requires protection.

With the release of Solaris 11, Oracle has changed the default FTP server. Whereas Solaris 11 Express used the WU-FTP server, the official Solaris 11 release uses the ProFTPD service. In contrast, the SSH service used for Solaris 11 continues to be an enhanced version of OpenSSH, customized for Oracle service features, such as RBAC, SMF, and auditing.

TIP
For administrators who are converting from WU-FTPD, Solaris provides a file to help with migration, proftpd_migration.txt, in the /usr/share/doc/proftpd directory.

Secure and Insecure Communications

In earlier days of UNIX, users connected to remote systems with clear-text protocols such as Telnet, which supports easy connections to remote systems. It was appropriate on networks where users could be trusted and networks were slow. Today, you as an administrator do need to set up secure access for sensitive data. But there are times when it's best to make data freely available.

For example, open source developers commonly want to share entire copies of their software with the widest possible audience. Many developers want to be able to share their drivers and firmware with everyone who has their hardware. As long as the developers (and their sponsors) understand that anyone can have access to their shared software or documents, anonymous-only FTP servers are an excellent option.

Insecure Remote Connections

The TCP/IP protocol suite is filled with utilities that support insecure connections. Many users have a relatively high comfort level with these connections because they aren't concerned about the security of their user accounts. And if they don't keep personal data on their accounts, then perhaps that is somewhat justified.

But as an administrator of an enterprise-level operating system, security is and should be a prime concern. Breaches in security from individual users can lead to legal consequences, especially if private data of any sort is put at risk. Although compromises in user accounts may not put that user's personal data at risk, it can be a platform from which a black-hat hacker can put your entire network at risk.

It is therefore important for you as an administrator to evangelize the virtues of secure options such as the Secure Shell. Otherwise, if your users demand to use insecure protocols such as Telnet, and those users have influence, you may not have a choice in the matter.

FTP and SFTP Client Commands

FTP does not secure data transmissions. Nevertheless, FTP is still a popular way to share files. For that reason, you may need to be an educator. If policy so dictates, you may even need to be an enforcer. When security is important in the realm of FTP, you may want to present SFTP as an alternative. You can access remote FTP servers with the **ftp** client command. You can also access remote SSH servers with an FTP-like client with the **sftp** command. For example, we've configured an FTP and an SSH server to receive such connections on the solaris1 system. We access these servers with the following commands:

```
$ ftp solaris1
$ sftp solaris1
```

 NOTE
Many excellent FTP client utilities are available, at both the command line and the GUI. The reference to the ***ftp*** *and* ***sftp*** *clients are just for comparison only.*

Many of the same commands are available to both clients. Some of these commands are also used at the regular shell prompt. The place to start with these commands is the present working directory, which you can confirm with the **pwd** command. One common element with both clients is the availability of the local shell with the bang character (!). For example, to list the files in the current local directory, run the following command from the **sftp** or **ftp** prompt:

```
!ls
```

 NOTE
One disadvantage of ***sftp*** *is that anonymous access is not allowed.*

Use the **!pwd** and **pwd** commands to verify the directories. The **pwd** is on the local and remote systems. Information on the local and remote directories is especially important because it determines the upload and download directories for file transfers. Other commands of interest that work on both clients are shown in Table 20-1. Most of these commands work in the same way as their cousins at the regular shell prompt. Some commands not listed require administrative access, which is not encouraged over a regular FTP connection.

One advantage of a regular FTP client (relative to **sftp**) is its access to commands such as **mget** and **mput**, which can download and upload multiple files.

Command	Description
cd	Change the remote directory
lcd	Change the local directory
get *download*	Download the local file named *download*
put *upload*	Upload the local file named *upload* to the remote FTP server

TABLE 20-1. *Common FTP Client Commands*

Configure an FTP Server

The FTP server included with Solaris 11 is quite flexible. In this chapter, you'll see how to set it up for anonymous access, for guest users as well as for regular users. If it's already installed on a system, you'll see it in the following output to the **svcs -a | grep ftp** command:

```
svc:/network/ftp:default
```

If you don't see any output, you can install the FTP service. In any case, you may want to run the following command. Depending on current status, it either installs the package, or it checks for updates if the package is already installed:

```
# pkg install service/network/ftp
```

If the FTP service is disabled, you can enable it in the normal fashion with the following **svcadm** command:

```
# svcadm enable network/ftp:default
```

In the sections that follow, you'll look at key files associated with the FTP server, along with what you would do to configure anonymous, guest, and regular users with various levels of security. If you're already familiar with the Apache Web server, you'll be familiar with a number of directives in the file.

If security is important in FTP communications, consider the **sftp** command feature associated with the SSH service, described later in this chapter.

FTP Server Files and Utilities

The FTP server package includes configuration files in the /etc/ftpd directory, as well as daemons and utilities in the /usr/sbin directory. The package creates a user named ftp and a group that is also named ftp. Detailed examples follow in coming sections.

For the ProFTPD server, there are two basic configuration files. The main configuration file is proftpd.conf in the /etc directory. The ftpusers file lists usernames that are automatically denied access to the FTP server. In addition, you can configure a virtual host in a hidden .ftpaccess file in specific directories.

In addition, the ProFTPD server includes a variety of commands, some of which are listed in Table 20-2.

The ProFTPD server includes a number of defaults compiled into Solaris 11. To review those defaults, use the executable daemon, found in the /usr/lib/inet directory. In other words, run the following command:

```
$ /usr/lib/init/proftpd -V
```

The output lists the version in use, the location of the configuration file, the PID file, as well as the directory with ProFTPD headers.

Review the Default FTP Server Configuration File

In this section, you'll examine the default version of the FTP server configuration file, proftpd, in the /etc directory. With this information in hand, you'll better understand the requirements and options associated with configuring an FTP server on Solaris 11. Just be aware that the proftpd file

Command	Description
ftpcount	Lists the number of users, in each service class, defined in the ftpaccess file.
ftpdctl	Controls various FTP modules. For more information, run the **ftpdctl help** command.
ftprestart	Restarts an FTP server that was shut down with the **ftpshut** command.
ftpscrub	Scrubs the FTP scoreboard file, /var/run/ftpscoreboard.
ftpshut	Shuts down an FTP server at a given time.
ftptop	Shows the status of connections to the FTP server.
ftpwho	Displays process information for each connected user.

TABLE 20-2. *Common FTP Server Commands*

configures the standard Solaris 11 server and does not affect any other FTP-style servers you may configure on this operating system, including the SSH service described later in this chapter.

When reviewing these directives, think in terms of virtual servers. In other words, while you can set one option for the overall ProFTPD service, you can configure a different option for a specific virtual server.

NOTE
A full list of ProFTPD directives is available online from the ProFTPD website at www.proftpd.org/docs/directives/configuration_full.html.

The first directives set the stage for the server. The first two directives go together. Normally, the **ServerName** should specify the FTP server name that is shown to the client. However, it has no effect unless the **ServerIdent** option is activated.

```
ServerName  "FTP Server"
ServerIdent off
```

In other words, if we changed the first two directives to

```
ServerName  "Mike's FTP Server"
ServerIdent on
```

then users who connect remotely would see the following entry when they log into the server with a regular **ftp** command-line client:

```
220 ProFTPD 1.3.3e Server (Mike's FTP server) [::1]
```

The **ServerType** directive should normally stay as is:

```
ServerType standalone
```

The **DefaultServer** directive specifies the response if a request is sent to an IP address on the local system not configured for the FTP server. Naturally, this applies only if a system has multiple IP addresses. The standard Solaris 11 configuration file changes the default by enabling the **DefaultServer** directive:

```
DefaultServer on
```

The **Port** specifies the TCP/IP communications port used for this service. The standard shown here is the default FTP port number:

```
Port 21
```

The **Umask** directive applies to servers where logged-in users are allowed to create files and directories. In that case, the value of **Umask** is applied to the permissions for the file or directory:

```
Umask   022
```

The following **User** and **Group** directives specify the user and group associated with the running ProFTPD server. Since the root account is the default, the following settings limit the risk to the rest of the system:

```
User   ftp
Group  ftp
```

If you allow regular users to log in through ProFTPD, the following **AllowOverwrite** option makes sense (of course, it comes with security risks):

```
AllowOverwrite   on
```

Speaking of security risks, the following stanza prevents users from running the **chmod** command to change the permissions on a file or directory:

```
<Limit SITE_CHMOD>
  DenyAll
</Limit>
```

The following **AuthOrder** directive connects ProFTPD to the Pluggable Authentication Modules described in Chapter 12. In essence, it supports a connection to the regular user authentication database.

```
AuthOrder mod_auth_pam.c* mod_auth_unix.c
```

However, that's in slight contrast to the following **PersistentPassword** directive, which is normally disabled to allow authentication via the Network Information Service (NIS):

```
PersistentPassword  off
```

Logins by the root account via ProFTPD are disabled by default. And that's as it should be, because such communications proceed in clear text. So even though the following directive is available, it is commented out:

```
#RootLogin   on
```

Set Up a Basic Anonymous FTP Server

In this section, you'll create an anonymous user, set up an appropriate directory for that user, and modify the ftpaccess configuration file to limit the server to anonymous-only access. An anonymous account is generic, and it's often potentially used by multiple, perhaps even hundreds of users (if supported by the settings of the server). To that end, the following commands create a dedicated directory for the purpose, with ownership given to the appropriate user and group:

```
# mkdir /export/home/ftp
# chown -R ftp:ftp /export/home/ftp
```

The **chown** command shown here assigns ownership of the /export/home/ftp directory, as well as its files, to the user and group named ftp. If you haven't already set up files in the noted directory, you'll have to remember to assign ownership to the appropriate user and group at that time.

You can then set up allowed access to the previously noted directory in the /etc/proftpd.conf file. For example, the following stanza denies access to regular users:

```
# Deny regular login access
<Limit LOGIN>
  DenyAll
</Limit>
```

Next, the following stanza sets up anonymous logins in a specific directory. With the **UserAlias** directive, someone who logs in as the user named anonymous is actually logged in as the user ftp:

```
# Allow anonymous login access
<Anonymous /export/home/ftp>
    UserAlias anonymous ftp
<Limit LOGIN>
    AllowAll
</Limit>
</Anonymous>
```

One more item: The user named ftp is listed in the /etc/ftpusers file and therefore is prohibited from accessing the ProFTPD server by default. To allow access, you'll need to remove or comment out the ftp user from the /etc/ftpusers file. If you want to make sure that there are no logins from regular users, use the **<Limit LOGIN>** stanza just described.

A chroot Jail for ProFTPD

In general, you don't want users who log into an FTP server to have access to the entire Solaris 11 directory tree. Especially if the ProFTPD server supports anonymous access, you should assume that anyone might log into that server. Of course, you could isolate the system with that FTP server in its own ZFS zone, or even in its own virtual machine (VM) such as VirtualBox. But even if you take that step, a chroot jail, associated with the **DefaultRoot** directive, can help protect that VM. The following directive is the simplest way to set up a chroot jail. Users who log into a ProFTPD system configured in this way will be sent to their home directories:

```
DefaultRoot ~
```

In addition, connected users will see their home directories on the FTP server as if it were the top-level root directory. They won't be able to navigate to a higher-level directory, at least not without some link. The documentation associated with **DefaultRoot** comes with the following warning: "if a user has write access to the symlink he could modify it so that it points to '/'," which would override any protections from the **DefaultRoot** directive.

Unlike other services, ProFTPD does not require device or executable files within the chroot jail. It should already have stored information on required executables within its cache.

Set Up Guest Users

Administrators who are used to the FTP server from Solaris 10 (or even Solaris 11 Express) may want to configure a guest user. In essence, a guest user is like an anonymous user, except a guest user has an account with a password. As such, the stanza for a guest user is just a bit different from that for an anonymous user. Of course, you could set up guest users with different names, in their own stanzas. Just don't forget to actually assign passwords to such users.

```
<Anonymous ~guest>
  User                      guest
  Group                     nobody
  AnonRequirePassword       on

  <Limit LOGIN>
    AllowAll
  </Limit>
</Anonymous>
```

Of course, that stanza assumes the existence of a guest username, along with an appropriate ID, group, home directory, and password. For more information, see Chapter 11.

Basic Security on FTP

Sometimes FTP host security starts with the way the server is presented to a client. As described earlier, the standard **ServerIdent on** directive means that that user sees the **ServerName** as defined. By default, you'll see a message similar to the following, identifying the server as ProFTPD:

```
220 ProFTPD 1.3.3e Server (FTP Server)
```

But that may not always work to your advantage. If there is ever a security breach in this release of ProFTPD, any black-hat hacker who sees that message would instantly know what server is vulnerable. You could set **ServerIdent off**, which would disable the message shown. For example, if we substitute the directive

```
ServerIdent on "I'm not telling!"
```

then users who connect would see the following message:

```
220 I'm not telling!
```

User Security

As suggested, user security on an FTP server refers to users who are explicitly allowed or denied access to that server. Of course, you can add users to the list who are not allowed to connect, as specified in the /etc/ftpusers file. But in general, this file is dedicated to users associated with various services.

You can regulate users who are allowed to or prohibited from making a connection to the ProFTPD server. Perhaps the most straightforward method is with the **AllowUser** and **DenyUser** directives. One of the flaws associated with ProFTPD is that users listed in the /etc/proftpd.conf file have to be listed one at a time, such as this:

```
AllowUser mike
AllowUser donna
```

For that reason, the corresponding group directives (**AllowGroup**, **DenyGroup**) may be more convenient. For example, the following directives deny access to users who are members of the noted hypothetical groups:

```
DenyGroup peons
DenyGroup starters
```

The full list should be put together in a **LOGIN** stanza. The following stanza may be more secure because it limits login access to just the specified users:

```
<Limit LOGIN>
    AllowUser mike
    AllowUser harry
    DenyAll
</Limit>
```

Host Security

Of course, host security specifies limits based on the hostname or IP address of the client system. The options are similar to those just described for user security. Host security options are embedded in a **LOGIN** stanza, with **Order**, **Allow**, and **Deny** directives. One relatively secure option that limits access to two different IP addresses is shown here:

```
<Limit LOGIN>
    Order allow,deny
    Allow from 192.168.0.50,192.168.0.51
    Deny from all
    DenyAll
</Limit>
```

You could substitute partial IP addresses or domains. For example, 192.168.0. would represent the 192.168.0.0/24 network, and .example.net would represent all systems on that domain.

Virtual Hosts on FTP

If you're familiar with the directives associated with the Apache Web server, this chapter so far should be familiar. ProFTPD and Apache share a number of directives. But there's one difference that may disappoint Apache administrators: ProFTPD supports only IP-address-based virtual hosting. Therefore, unlike what you can do with Apache, you'll need at least one IP address per virtual FTP server.

The directives within a **VirtualHost** stanza can be unique, and they can vary from that of the main FTP server. You can set it up with one or more IP addresses or domain names. Two examples of the start of such stanzas are as follows:

```
<VirtualHost 192.168.0.100 192.168.0.101>
<VirtualHost ftp1.example.com ftp2.example.com>
```

Of course, you'll need to set configuration directives within the stanza, and end the stanza with the following directive:

```
</VirtualHost>
```

The Configuration of an SSH Server

The use of an SSH server for remote connections is encouraged. Unlike other remote connection protocols, communications over SSH are encrypted. In other words, potential black-hat hackers with protocol analyzers can't just read the passphrases that are sent over a network. They would need appropriate keys. Good SSH keys can be 1,024 bits or more, so they are difficult to decrypt.

SSH is so secure that it's enabled by default on Solaris 11 systems. It's also enabled by default on other UNIX-based operating systems, including a number of Linux distributions. It's a secure way for administrators to work on systems in remote locations, saving time and travel.

Of course, with the reliance of UNIX administrators on SSH, black-hat hackers have focused a good deal of their power on finding weaknesses in this service. This chapter will show you how to minimize those weaknesses.

General Configuration

Generic configuration files associated with SSH are in the /etc/ssh directory. In general, the Solaris 11 installation automatically enables access through the SSH server. It's associated with three packages:

- **network/ssh** Specifies SSH client configuration files and utilities
- **network/ssh/ssh-key** Includes SSH tools for generating private/public key pairs
- **service/network/ssh** Adds the SSH server

Of course, because SSH is so important to system security, you'll want to make doubly sure that the latest versions of these packages are installed.

Secure Shell Client Commands

There are two elements to the configuration of an SSH client: the ssh_config file in the /etc/ssh directory, and the files created along with the files in each user's home directory, in the .ssh/ subdirectory. But as a client, you need to know how to connect to a remote system. The commands that follow specify three methods for connecting to a remote SSH server. In each case, if this is the first time you're using an SSH client command, when a connection is made, you'll be prompted in a fashion similar to Figure 20-1.

If you accept the request by typing **yes**, you'll see the following warning:

```
Warning: Permanently added '192.168.0.150' (RSA) to the list of known hosts.
```

Of course, although the IP address may vary, the message confirms that the public server key is genuine. If in doubt, you'll want to get a copy of that key. RSA refers to an algorithm for public key cryptography. The initials are those of its developers: Rivest, Shamir, and Adelman. The warning means that the contents of the ssh_host_rsa_key.pub file from the remote SSH server host (in this case, on IP address 192.168.0.150) has now been added to a local file, known_hosts, in the current user's home directory, in the .ssh/ subdirectory.

TIP

One potential weakness in SSH is the availability of connected hostnames or IP addresses in the known_hosts file of individual users. A black-hat hacker who reads this file gets more information about the target. You'll see shortly how you can minimize this potential weakness as well.

Then you're prompted for a password. If you didn't enter a username, SSH looks for an existing account with the same username on both the client and the server. You can set up a connection to a different username in two ways. The following examples assume you're connecting to the account named admin1 on the remote system:

```
# ssh admin1@192.168.0.150
# ssh -l admin1  192.168.0.150
```

NOTE

One of the little known bits about SSH is that password-based logins are still sent in clear text. It's only after the login is complete that the connection is encrypted. Later in this chapter, you'll see how to work around that flaw with passphrases.

```
michael@solaris-kvm-clone:~$ ssh 192.168.0.150
The authenticity of host '192.168.0.150 (192.168.0.150)' can't be established.
RSA key fingerprint is e2:de:1a:e6:bf:84:55:7f:f3:f3:54:07:65:16:3b:6c.
Are you sure you want to continue connecting (yes/no)?
```

FIGURE 20-1. *Confirm the authenticity of an SSH host system*

After the password for the specified account is entered, you are connected to the remote system at the command-line interface. If you prefer GUI tools, you can use the **-X** option, as follows:

```
# ssh -X -l admin1 192.168.0.150
```

And if the remote system has appropriate GUI administrative applications, such as the Printer Configuration tool described in Chapter 15, you could then run the **system-config-printer** command to start that tool, remotely. The client system uses its own graphical hardware to run the GUI tool.

But you may just want to copy a file, without bothering to start a command line on the remote system. That's one reason behind the **scp** command. It's fairly straightforward because it supports direct copying from client to remote server (or vice versa). For example, the following command copies the F20-01.tif file from the local system to the home directory user michael on the remote system with IP address 192.168.0.150:

```
$ scp F20-01.tif michael@192.168.0.150:
```

The colon is important because it indicates that the secure copy is to be made to a remote system. It's assumed that the copy will be made to the logged-in user's home directory. Alternatively, the file could be sent to a different directory with a command such as the following:

```
$ scp F20-01.tif michael@192.168.0.150:/home/michael/bookfiles
```

As described earlier, you can connect to a remote SSH server as if it were an FTP server with the **sftp** command. You'll then have access to the home directory of the remote system. One difference between SSH and a regular FTP server is that they communicate on different TCP/IP ports. As defined in the /etc/services file, FTP communicates on port 21 and SSH communicates on port 22.

Secure shell commands are in many ways a successor to remote shell (RSH) commands. Although the use of RSH commands is discouraged because they transmit data in clear text, the **rsync** command, with the **-e ssh** switch, can be used to transmit directories of data over the encrypted SSH connection. For example, the following command would back up the contents of michael's home directory to the /backups directory on the remote system named backup:

```
$ rsync  -aHvz  -e  ssh  /home/michael  michael@backup:/backups
```

Later in this chapter, you'll see how to set up an SSH server with passphrases. If you've already entered a passphrase during the current session, the backup would proceed automatically.

The Main Client Configuration File

The basic SSH client configuration file is ssh_config in the /etc/ssh directory. Although the original version of the file is commented out, it's still useful for instructional purposes because the commented directives are all defaults.

The first directive applies other directives in the file to client connections to all other systems:

```
# Host *
```

The **ForwardAgent** directive generally should not be activated because it could help a black-hat hacker decipher authentication on the remote system:

```
# ForwardAgent no
```

The GUI on UNIX-based systems is associated with the term X11. In general, you shouldn't automatically forward such connections. You can override that setting with the **ssh -X** command:

```
# ForwardX11 no
```

Normally, SSH connections are verified using public key authentication. Generic SSH public keys are stored in the /etc/ssh directory:

```
# PubkeyAuthentication yes
```

Until passphrases are actually configured, password-based authentication is required to complete a connection:

```
# PasswordAuthentication yes
```

Although **PasswordAuthentication yes** is the default, it goes hand-in-hand with the unstated **KbdInteractiveAuthentication** directive. After configuring passphrases later in this chapter, you may choose to disable both directives to disable password-based access. The setting in the ssh_config client file does not override any corresponding setting in the sshd_config file on the server system.

RSH is an alternative that you should not encourage since it sends data over the network in clear text. And that option is disabled with the following directives:

```
# FallBackToRsh no
# UseRsh no
```

If you actually want to use RSH, you'd also have to install and activate appropriate packages.

In general, you should not enable **BatchMode** because it disables requests for passwords or passphrases. Of course, if you enable this setting, you'd have to enable a corresponding option on the SSH server:

```
# BatchMode no
```

With the following directive, the SSH client checks the identity of remote systems against the IP address listed in the known_hosts file:

```
# CheckHostIP yes
```

As described earlier, that file, in the user's .ssh/ subdirectory, includes the public key of the remote system. Figure 20-2 includes the contents of a sample file that contains the IP address and public keys of two remote SSH servers.

The **StrictHostKeyChecking** directive can be set to **yes**, **no**, or **ask**. With the **ask** option, users are asked to confirm the first time a connection is made to a system with an unknown IP address. If this option is set to **no**, the user is asked every time because the public key is not saved in local user known_host files.

```
# StrictHostKeyChecking ask
```

The escape character is sort of a secret code for SSH:

```
# EscapeChar ~
```

```
192.168.0.150 ssh-rsa AAAAB3NzaC1yc2EAAAABIwAAAQEA6Oyae4zhcA8f9V4XFQqxFAyW6tJQplA
+BetQntVG1fao1ST1Y5gn421KCesje1fxTddH1k2909fffaUuW3wPOf1lnj5vFa89DVW3PMjGrTj2UEw5
lkAKvCTgPbWVGbLsK8UOx4w1IT08yBkKFOCJ1rODTGUR9/kO7Bt7p2wwz+iM4TQlpFK2Cb/RSXzilmWUi
QOT1MuHYA9smRWm4WPZs6vzVOe3YkJOm7WC1WbRCyfA1tHkxBvE8NTxBXJiMbsVS1CImgA1hTQxESho5q
I7m560pSJ+dvWbeqAul6x619K88x7Or8ujuHYCi9WsdIeM7DVMsaC9bmsyJzqMqs9x5Q==
192.168.122.1 ssh-rsa AAAAB3NzaC1yc2EAAAABIwAAAQEAxF+/mrkPCg0iOlLUgJBi45DvTtWV9+F
cJqHeSCMSzSOw6dbXuS/e/fWHtLReyHMaCikLyfPN/WIAKw1hoCMvVJZDwW9+Q8BSqCHkNOWbPDflOOnN
IFo/bOYJYyrnyQMG3JBf3l/yLy8vfJiMbSzgi6TuumtmJZLmr4hlCXVnFVeEqsNHDdr61gmHCODyhNpDL
wv8ggai5ZbZTDClx4iuDMocsyH2uOUziiyBXr5NNfYLhHAbx/ZQyR/HrhsLd16tIYuwTmGm904T1GtLOG
dnvMYOnObR4zeVUGFLGW8xr8rF/CJc3y8V7Sr69yO9hsYviuHyjVL+3oeSugUBJi5HyQ==
~
~
~
```

FIGURE 20-2. *The IP addresses and public keys of known hosts*

The next time you log into an SSH server, press the **EscapeChar** and the question mark together. In this case, it should be

~?

The key combination may not appear until after you press both characters. What you should see should appear similar to Figure 20-3.

NOTE
User-specific SSH client files may exist in user home directories, in the .ssh/ subdirectory. That directory and its files aren't created until an SSH client connection is made and private/public key pairs are created.

Additional Files in the /etc/ssh Directory

The main SSH server configuration file is sshd_config in the /etc/ssh directory. The d in the filename stands for *daemon,* and is the only difference between the server and the corresponding client configuration file, ssh_config. You'll examine that server file shortly. This section addresses

---

```
michael@solaris-kvm-clone:~$ ~?
Supported escape sequences:
  ~.  - terminate connection (and any multiplexed sessions)
  ~B  - send a BREAK to the remote system
  ~C  - open a command line
  ~R  - Request rekey (SSH protocol 2 only)
  ~^Z - suspend ssh
  ~#  - list forwarded connections
  ~&  - background ssh (when waiting for connections to terminate)
  ~?  - this message
  ~~  - send the escape character by typing it twice
(Note that escapes are only recognized immediately after newline.)
```

FIGURE 20-3. *Available SSH escape character sequences*

File	Description
modulii	Includes prime numbers and random keys to support the Diffie-Hellman exchange key method.
ssh_host_dsa_key	Specifies the standard private key for the host system, based on the DSA algorithm.
ssh_host_dsa_key.pub	Notes the public version of the ssh_host_dsa_key; it includes the information that's sent to remote clients, if DSA is configured as the default algorithm.
ssh_host_rsa_key	Specifies the standard private key for the host system, based on the RSA algorithm.
ssh_host_rsa_key.pub	Notes the public version of the ssh_host_rsa_key; it includes the information that's sent to remote clients, if RSA is configured as the default algorithm.

TABLE 20-3. *Nonconfiguration files in the /etc/ssh directory*

the other files in the /etc/ssh directory, in Table 20-3. The RSA acronym was previously explained; the DSA shown in some of the files (and upcoming command switches) refers to the Digital Signature Algorithm, commonly required for U.S. governmental communications.

Private and Public Key Pairs for SSH

Private and public keys may be stored in the /etc/ssh directory, as well as the .ssh/ subdirectory of every user's home directory. In principle, the private key is stored on the client, and the public key is designed to be shared with other systems. The public key encrypts a message. Only the private key can be used to decrypt that message. Therefore, that private key is important.

Read access to the private key must be limited to the user owner. If access is given to other users, SSH will not use that key. In addition, private keys in user home directories are further protected by passphrases. Users on client systems can use their passwords or passphrases to authorize use of that private key.

Shortly, you'll see how to use the **ssh-keygen** command to create a private/public key pair, protected by a passphrase. As strange as it sounds, you'll run the **ssh-keygen** command from a client system and then send a copy of the public key to a server you want to administer remotely.

The Main SSH Server Configuration File

The main configuration file for the SSH service is sshd_config, in the /etc/ssh directory. This section describes the settings in the packaged version of the file, along with some alternatives that could help better secure the configuration. The SSH server included for most UNIX-based systems can be configured to support connections using both SSH versions 1 and 2; however, version 1 is known to have security weaknesses. Fortunately, the SSH service shipped with Solaris 11 already specifies that version 2 is the default. Don't specify **Protocol 1,2** unless absolutely necessary.

The standard TCP/IP port for SSH is 22:

```
Port 22
```

Some administrators believe in "security through obscurity," where the port for services important to security are set to nonstandard numbers. If you choose a nonstandard number, be sure it doesn't conflict with the standard ports of any other network service that might be running on the local network. One possible guide to such ports is the /etc/services file. In our opinion, the ports listed in the Solaris 11 version of this file are somewhat incomplete. A more complete list is available from IANA at www.iana.org/assignments/port-numbers.

TIP
*To determine the TCP/IP ports in use, run a command such as **nmap localhost** from the local system. The output should reveal the ports currently in use by network services.*

By default, SSH is configured to listen to all network cards configured on the local system. The following directives may be used on systems that are limited to IPv4 networks and systems that communicate using both IPv4 and IPv6, respectively:

```
#ListenAddress 0.0.0.0
ListenAddress  ::
```

If you do believe in "security through obscurity," the following **GatewayPorts** directive is especially important. If you plan to tunnel a network service through an SSH connection and you want to set up forwarding from a nonstandard port, such as from many routers, you'll want to change the value of this directive from **no** to **yes**:

```
GatewayPorts  no
```

The three directives that follow all start with X11, a reference to the older title for the GUI server software for UNIX-based operating systems. The **X11Forwarding** directive simply authorizes forwarding of GUI clients over SSH, for users who log in with the aforementioned **ssh -X** command. (If you set **X11Forwarding** to **no**, remote users who log in with **ssh -X** won't have access to GUI clients.) The **X11DisplayOffset** directive specifies the first available display number for such connections. If you configure 10 or more GUIs locally, you'll need to raise that number. The last X11 directive binds the display to the localhost address.

```
X11Forwarding  yes
X11DisplayOffset  10
X11UseLocalHost  yes
```

The commented **MaxStartups** directive that follows is a bit complex. By default, up to 10 connections to the local server are authorized. If you activate the directive, the SSH server will refuse 30 percent of any attempts to connect over and above the limit of 10; no more than 60 connections are allowed:

```
# MaxStartups  10:30:60
```

When users try to connect, the following directive supports a warning message prior to a remote login:

```
# Banner /etc/issue
```

As suggested by the documentation, "In some jurisdictions, sending a warning message before authentication can be relevant for getting legal protection." For demonstration purposes, we've added a sample message to that file that probably wouldn't be approved by a lawyer for a production system. You can review the resulting output in Figure 20-4.

The **PrintMotd** directive is set to **no** because its functionality is duplicated by the script in the /etc/profile, described in Chapter 10:

```
PrintMotd   no
```

A login is a login, whether it's local or over an SSH connection.

The **KeepAlive** directive sends messages to connected clients, to make sure that the client is still running or the network connection is still available. If the connection to the client is lost, the following directive causes the server to close the connection:

```
KeepAlive yes
```

The following two directives work together. Authentication messages are sent at an information level. Based on these directives and the standard version of /etc/syslog.conf, such messages are sent to the /var/adm/messages file; connection messages are sent to the /var/adm/wtmpx file.

```
SyslogFacility   auth
LogLevel   info
```

NOTE
*With the **last** command, you can read the contents of the /var/adm/ wtmpx file, to display login information for users connected locally and over an SSH connection.*

The private host keys shown here are used to verify connections from remote systems, with public host keys in appropriate known_hosts files (these keys are associated with SSH version 2):

```
HostKey /etc/ssh/ssh_host_rsa_key
HostKey /etc/ssh/ssh_host_dsa_key
```

```
michael@Maui:~$ ssh 192.168.122.199
The /etc/issue file might be a good place for some login mumbo-jumbo

Password: █
```

FIGURE 20-4. *An SSH server displays a banner before a user logs in.*

The **KeyRegenerationInterval** directive shown here is the default; in other words, the key required to decrypt communications changes every hour (3,600 seconds):

```
KeyRegenerationInterval 3600
```

Permissions on the .ssh/ subdirectory should be limited to the user owner, with so-called 700 permissions. The following directive checks for such permissions:

```
StrictModes yes
```

You shouldn't allow users infinite time to complete their logins. In fact, you may consider reducing the amount of grace time (in seconds) allowed for logins, as shown here:

```
LoginGraceTime 120
```

The following two directives regulate the number of authentication attempts per connection. Per the following directives, users are allowed six attempts. However, the fourth through sixth attempts are logged. If you're especially leery about security, consider reducing these numbers:

```
MaxAuthTries   6
MaxAuthTriesLog  3
```

Although it's possible to allow empty passwords to access client accounts, it is not recommended. This can be disabled as follows:

```
PermitEmptyPasswords  no
```

Unless every user who is allowed access through this SSH server has been configured with a passphrase, passwords are required, and are enabled with the following:

```
PasswordAuthentication  yes
```

There are risks associated with transmitting passwords over the network, even if they're encrypted through SSH. However, the following directive suggests that such risks are not acceptable for the root user. You shouldn't need to change this setting; administrators can connect via SSH with regular accounts. If there's a need to assume the privileges of the root user on a remote system, it can be done after login, after communication has been encrypted.

```
PermitRootLogin  no
```

The following directive enables FTP-style client commands, based on the **sftp** client discussed earlier in this chapter. If the service is active, users who access the SSH server in this way have access to their accounts with those FTP-style commands. If you want to disable such access, comment out or delete this line.

```
Subsystem  sftp  internal-sftp
```

If you comment out the **Subsystem sftp internal-sftp** directive, users who try to connect to this server with the **sftp** client get the following message, after entering a password or passphrase:

```
Request for subsystem 'sftp' failed on channel 0
Couldn't read packet: Error 0
```

The final directive in the Solaris 11 version of the standard configuration specifies whether SSH should use any RSA key that may be stored in the users' home directories, in the .ssh/ subdirectory, in the file named known_hosts.

Additional Security in the SSH Server Configuration

To enhance security, you can add a number of additional directives to the sshd_config file. First, you could change the default port from the standard of 22 to something else in both the server sshd_config and client ssh_config files. For example, the following directive would work in both files:

```
Port 2222
```

Yes, some port-scanning tools would detect a service open at this port, but that requires additional knowledge from would-be black-hat hackers, which may potentially reduce the number of attacks on your SSH server. To connect over a nonstandard port, users must specify the port number, as follows:

```
$ ssh -p 2222 user@remoteSSHserver
```

Just remember the warning earlier in this chapter about services that may be tunneled over an SSH connection along with the **GatewayPorts** directives.

User-based security is possible with the help of the following directives: **AllowUsers**, **DenyUsers**, **AllowGroups**, and **DenyGroups**. The directives are straightforward; for example, the following directive limits logins to the users listed:

```
AllowUsers admin1 supervisor1
```

If desired, users can be further restricted; the following example limits access to the users listed on the specified host IP addresses:

```
AllowUsers admin1@192.168.0.100 supervisor1@192.168.0.200
```

If the **AllowUsers** directive exists in the sshd_config file, access is limited to users specified by this directive.

Additional security is possible with the help of Pluggable Authentication Modules (PAM). Two relevant, mutually exclusive, directives are **PAMServiceName** and **PAMServicePrefix**. If you have both directives listed in the sshd_config file, the SSH service won't start. Available PAM services are listed in the SSH man page. Because the default value of **PAMServicePrefix** is **sshd**, all PAM modules are supported by default.

If you want to include LDAP authentication databases in PAM support of SSH passwords, the following directives in the PAM configuration file can help:

```
sshd  auth      sufficient  pam_openldap.so.1
sshd  account   sufficient  pam_openldap.so.1
sshd  password  sufficient  pam_openldap.so.1
```

More Security with TCP Wrappers

One of the services that is automatically protected by TCP Wrappers is SSH. You can create hosts. allow and hosts.deny files in the /etc directory to regulate access to these services. This assumes the security/tcp-wrapper package is already installed. In that case, you can open up the /etc/hosts.deny file in a text editor and add the following line:

```
sshd : ALL
```

Next, you could open /etc/hosts.allow in a text editor and then add the following line to limit access to a single IP address:

```
sshd : 192.168.0.200
```

Even though it's possible to add usernames to the TCP Wrappers configuration files, it's most straightforward to regulate account access with the help of the **AllowUsers** and **DenyUsers** directives in the SSH server configuration file. Nevertheless, additional layers of security are helpful, as long as they don't prevent authorized access.

More Security with Passphrases

Yes, we know, the password is transmitted over the network. A sharp black-hat hacker might realize that the username and password exist near the beginning of the network transmission. Given enough time, a determined black-hat could decrypt the start of an SSH datastream to find the username and password.

Therefore, you may want to make the process more difficult with passphrases. That's made possible with the **ssh-keygen** command, which can be used to set up a public/private key pair for individual users. You'll need to specify whether the encryption algorithm is RSA or DSA. For example, the following command starts the process of setting up an RSA passphrase:

```
$ ssh-keygen -t rsa
```

It proceeds to generate a unique private/public key pair, and then offers to save the key in the .ssh/ subdirectory, in the id_rsa file, as shown here:

```
Enter file in which to save the key (/home/./michael/.ssh/id_rsa):
```

You can accept the default shown by pressing ENTER. The corresponding public key, id_rsa.pub, would also be saved in the same subdirectory. You're then prompted for a passphrase:

```
Enter passphrase (empty for no passphrase):
```

Yes, empty passphrases are allowed. There are even appropriate uses for accounts with empty passphrases, such as those accounts responsible for automated scripts. But in general, empty passphrases should be avoided. A black-hat hacker with access to the public key associated with such an account can log into that account without a password or a passphrase. If you want to change the passphrase, the **ssh-keygen -p** command can help.

NOTE
Unlike passwords, passphrases can include spaces. In other words, you're free to include complete sentences in a passphrase. In fact, it's best to be a little cryptic about a passphrase; for example, "I eat 3 icb, every other T." could stand for "I eat three ice cream bars, every other Tuesday." That kind of passphrase is less susceptible to "social engineering" from black-hat hackers who know something about your personal life.

Once a passphrase is entered twice, the **ssh-keygen** command confirms the result with output similar to the following:

```
Your identification has been saved in /home/./michael/.ssh/id_rsa.
Your public key has been saved in /home/./michael/.ssh/id_rsa.pub.
The key fingerprint is:
e5:d6:84:73:00:d0:10:87:b1:6d:15:01:79:c6:6f:c9 michael@solaris-kvm-clone
```

In a moment, you'll use the public key to set up a client. But first, you should know some of the other options available to the **ssh-keygen** command, as listed in Table 20-4. Perhaps the most important options are **-b**, which specifies the number of bits used to create the encryption key (with the help of a random number generator), and **-t** (described earlier), which is needed to select DSA or RSA encryption.

Different Algorithms

At this point, you're probably wondering whether DSA or RSA is more secure. It depends on several factors—namely, the number of bits associated with the encryption key, along with potential attacks on each algorithm. Obviously, a larger number of bits is at least in some ways more secure. Just be sure to have the latest version of associated packages available.

NOTE
In 2008, a vulnerability was discovered with respect to SSH keys used on Debian-based Linux distributions (including Ubuntu). The associated random number generator was not truly random; black-hat hackers could use "brute-force" attacks to identify private SSH cryptographic keys. Even though the problem was addressed quickly by developers, it was up to responsible administrators to update appropriate software before black-hat hackers took advantage of the vulnerability.

Perhaps more important is the business done by your organization. If you do business with the U.S. government (and possibly many other governments), DSA is the established standard. In contrast, most commercial applications use RSA.

Option	Description
-b	Specifies the number of bits associated with the encryption key; the default is 2048 bits.
-e	Prompts for a private key location, and outputs the contents of the public key.
-F	Searches for the entry associated with a hostname hashed with the **ssh-keygen -H** command.
-H	Hashes the hostname entries in the current known_hosts file.
-p	Prompts for changes in the passphrase.

TABLE 20-4. *Important **ssh-keygen** Command Options*

In either case, based on the brute-force capabilities of "$10 million machines," 1,024-bit keys are no longer secure. Various papers suggest that encryption keys based on 2,048 or 3,072 bits should be secure through the year 2030. That depends on future computer developments, based on the rate at which processing power increases.

NOTE
The standard for a secure passphrase is based on whether a computer that currently costs about $10 million can decrypt that passphrase in a "reasonable" amount of time, using a brute-force attack.

Send That Passphrase to an SSH Server

One bit that's often confusing is that SSH passphrases are created on client systems. It's the public key on that system that gets transmitted to the SSH server. For example, when creating an RSA key on a local system, we have an id_rsa.pub file in the .ssh/ subdirectory. We need to get the contents of that file over to the server, in the authorized_keys file on the target user home directory. Of course, we could copy that file to some sort of portable media; in fact, that's probably more secure than the following process. Here are the steps to take based on the home directory, /home/michael (you should substitute as needed):

1. Use the **scp** command to copy the id_rsa.pub file to user michael's home directory on the remote server (in this case, the remote server is on IP address 192.168.0.150):

   ```
   $ scp .ssh/id_rsa.pub  michael@192.168.0.150:/home/michael/
   ```

2. Log into the remote system (in this case, on IP address 192.168.0.150). Navigate to the .ssh/ subdirectory. Write the contents of the file to the authorized_keys file. The following command appends it to that file, to avoid overwriting any previous public keys:

   ```
   $ cat id_rsa.pub  >>  .ssh/authorized_keys
   ```

3. Delete the id_rsa.pub file from the home directory. Be careful. If you've created an RSA key on the server, don't delete the id_rsa.pub file from the .ssh/ subdirectory.

   ```
   $ rm id_rsa.pub
   ```

Once you've set up passphrases, clients get three chances to enter that passphrase when trying to make a connection. If the attempts fail, the SSH server then prompts for a password. Although it's a viable backup authentication method, it would seem to defeat the purpose of the passphrase.

So if you want to enable access to an SSH server only with passphrases, you'll need to change or activate two directives in the /etc/ssh/ssh_config file on the SSH server. In that file, you'll want to include the following directives to both disable password- and keyboard-based authentication:

 ```
PasswordAuthentication  no
KbdInteractiveAuthentication no
```

NOTE
*Linux administrators should note that Solaris 11 also requires that the **KbdInteractiveAuthentication** directive be set to **no** to disable password-based access to an SSH server.*

FIGURE 20-5. *You're actually being prompted for a passphrase.*

Once the noted directives are changed, users who try to connect from clients without appropriate private keys aren't even prompted for a passphrase; they're just given the following error message:

```
Permission denied (gssapi-keyex,gssapi-with-mic,publickey).
```

Alternatively, if you try to connect to such a remote system from the command line within a GUI, you'll be prompted for a passphrase with a window similar to that shown in Figure 20-5. Even though the message suggests that the private key requires a password, it is actually looking for the passphrase created earlier with the **ssh-keygen** command.

More Security with Hashed Hosts

One additional feature of the **ssh-keygen** command, as noted in Table 20-4, is the ability to encrypt the hostnames found in the known_hosts file in a hash. As shown in Figure 20-6, each user's local known_hosts file identifies the IP address of SSH servers to which it has made a connection, as well as the RSA encryption associated with the connection.

```
192.168.0.150 ssh-rsa AAAAB3NzaC1yc2EAAAABIwAAAQEA60yae4zhcA8f9V4XFQqxFAyW6tJQpl
A+BetQntVG1fao1ST1Y5gn421KCesje1fxTddHlk2909fffaUuW3wPOf1lnj5vFa89DVW3PMjGrTj2UE
w5lkAKvCTgPbWVGbLsK8UOx4wlIT08yBkKF0CJ1rODTGUR9/k07Bt7p2wwz+iM4TQlpFK2Cb/RSXzilm
WUiQOTlMuHYA9smRWm4WPZs6vzVOe3YkJ0m7WC1WbRCyfA1tHkxBvE8NTxBXJiMbsVS1CImgA1hTQxES
hoSqI7m560pSJ+dvWbeqAul6x619K88x70r8ujuHYCi9WsdIeM7DVMsaC9bmsyJzqMqs9x5Q==
192.168.122.1 ssh-rsa AAAAB3NzaC1yc2EAAAABIwAAAQEAxF+/mrkPCg0i01LUgJBi45DvTtWV9+
FcJqHeSCMSzSOw6dbXuS/e/fWHtLReyHMaCikLyfPN/WIAKw1hoCMvVJZDwW9+Q8BSqCHkN0WbPDfl0O
nNIFo/bOYJYyrnyQMG3JBf3l/yLy8vfJiMbSzgi6TuumtmJZLmr4hlCXVnFVeEqsNHDdr61gmHC0DyhN
pDLwv8ggai5ZbZTDClx4iuDMocsyH2uOUziiyBXr5NNfYLhHAbx/ZQyR/HrhsLd16tIYuwTmGm9O4T1G
tLOGdnvMYOnObR4zeVUGFLGW8xr8rF/CJc3y8V7Sr69yO9hsYviuHyjVL+3oeSugUBJi5HyQ==
192.168.0.203 ssh-rsa AAAAB3NzaC1yc2EAAAABIwAAAQEAxF+/mrkPCg0i01LUgJBi45DvTtWV9+
FcJqHeSCMSzSOw6dbXuS/e/fWHtLReyHMaCikLyfPN/WIAKw1hoCMvVJZDwW9+Q8BSqCHkN0WbPDfl0O
nNIFo/bOYJYyrnyQMG3JBf3l/yLy8vfJiMbSzgi6TuumtmJZLmr4hlCXVnFVeEqsNHDdr61gmHC0DyhN
pDLwv8ggai5ZbZTDClx4iuDMocsyH2uOUziiyBXr5NNfYLhHAbx/ZQyR/HrhsLd16tIYuwTmGm9O4T1G
tLOGdnvMYOnObR4zeVUGFLGW8xr8rF/CJc3y8V7Sr69yO9hsYviuHyjVL+3oeSugUBJi5HyQ==
~
```

FIGURE 20-6. *Target hosts can be identified in standard known_hosts files.*

You can minimize that risk with the **ssh-keygen -H** command. When we run that command from our own account, it provides the following output:

```
/home/./michael/.ssh/known_hosts updated.
Original contents retained as /home/./michael/.ssh/known_hosts.old
WARNING: /home/./michael/.ssh/known_hosts.old contains unhashed entries
Delete this file to ensure privacy of hostnames
```

The original known_hosts file is copied to the known_hosts.old file. The hostnames (or IP addresses) are hashed, and written to the new known_hosts file, making the task that much more difficult for the black-hat hacker. If desired, you can determine if the hashed file contains an entry for a specific hostname with the **ssh-keygen -F *host*** command. For example, the following command searches for a hashed entry with the 192.168.122.1 IP address:

```
$ ssh-keygen -F 192.168.122.1
```

Summary

Functionally, the FTP and the SSH services are more similar than users might realize. In fact, there's a common SSH client (**sftp**) that uses many common FTP commands to access files in user home directories.

The Solaris 11 FTP server can be configured to accommodate anonymous, guest, and regular users. With appropriate configuration options, you can set up anonymous and guest users in chroot jails, to help protect the files on the main server. Although you can't hide files in top-level directories from regular users who log into the FTP server, you can protect them from being downloaded. Of course, you can regulate the commands that are run by users, send them login messages, and place other limits such as on the numbers of connected users and login time. The main configuration file is /etc/proftpd.conf.

In addition, you can set up partial or complete virtual hosts, if you have multiple IP addresses on the local system. Complete virtual hosts can include their own array of configuration files in a directory separate from /etc/ftpd.

From the moment a password is accepted, the Solaris SSH server can encrypt communication between a client and server system. Once a passphrase is created, and a public key is properly shared with a target system, you don't even need to transmit the password over the network. Standard SSH configuration files can be found in the /etc/ssh directory. Once you set up SSH for specific users, that's supplemented by files in each user's home directory, in the .ssh/ subdirectory.

References

More detailed information on the FTP service, as it operates on Solaris 11, is available from the Oracle Solaris Administration: Network Services document, available online from http://docs.oracle.com/cd/E23824_01/html/821-1454/index.html.

Additional information on the workings of the SSH service, as it operates on Solaris 11, is available from the Oracle System Adminstration Guide: Security Services document, available online from http://docs.oracle.com/cd/E23824_01/html/821-1456/index.html.

CHAPTER
21

Solaris and Samba

irst, let's clear something up. Solaris has two Sambas. Well, actually, Solaris has its own implementation of the Common Internet File System (CIFS). Although you can install the Samba services familiar to Linux administrators, Solaris engineers have created their own implementation, as a CIFS server integrated into the kernel.

With either implementation, UNIX-based operating systems such as Solaris can fully participate in Microsoft-based networks. The names Samba and CIFS are based on their heritages. Samba was built to communicate using the Server Message Block (SMB) protocol. Whereas Microsoft has updated SMB to the Common Internet File System (CIFS), UNIX developers have updated Samba with CIFS-compatible code without changing the name. The Solaris implementation was developed after CIFS came into common use on Microsoft-based networks.

Although Samba is well known in Linux, the Solaris implementation goes further. On Solaris 11, you can use Samba to set up shared home directories. Also, you can set up ZFS-based directories to be shared. In that way, Solaris 11 goes beyond the standard configuration options associated with the smb.conf file. So if you're a Linux user who is learning Solaris, you'll need to go beyond the standard options available from that file. In either case, Solaris systems can interact transparently on a Microsoft-based network.

Just be aware that, on a Solaris 11 system, you can't run both Samba and the Solaris CIFS services simultaneously. In this chapter, we'll explore the implementation of Samba based on the work of the open source Samba project at www.samba.org.

NOTE
In this chapter, we'll refer to the open source version of Samba as "UNIX Samba" and the Solaris kernel-based version as "Solaris CIFS." In addition, we refer to "Microsoft" as the alternative operating system, given that "Windows" is also the server associated with UNIX GUIs. Finally, whereas Microsoft operating systems are generally not case sensitive, UNIX-based operating systems see cat and CAT as two different files.

Basic Features

As Microsoft developed its implementation of networking based on the SMB protocol, the UNIX developers associated with the Samba project worked on mimicking the functionality of UNIX-based operating systems on such networks. As Microsoft's implementation evolved into CIFS, Samba developers revised their server accordingly. Because Samba enables Solaris to act as a member of a Microsoft-based network, it supports the following types of functionality on that network:

- **Membership in a workgroup or domain** With Samba, Solaris 11 systems can be configured as a member of a Microsoft-based workgroup or domain as a client, a member server, or a domain controller.

- **Sharing user home directories** The standard Samba configuration file is set up to share home directories, if the associated password database includes associated usernames and passwords.

- **WINS** Take the role of a Windows Internet Name Service (WINS) server.
- **Browsing** Work as a master browser, which maintains a list of resources accessible to the local network.

TIP
If you absolutely need to configure a master browser on a Solaris system, use UNIX Solaris. The kernel-based Solaris CIFS server can't be configured as a master browser.

For reference, you can identify the status of the UNIX Samba system with the **svcs -a | grep samba** command:

```
online    14:20:33 svc:/network/samba:default
```

Alternatively, you can identify the status of the Solaris CIFS system with the **svcs -a | grep smb** command:

```
disabled    14:20:20 svc:/network/smb/server:default
```

NOTE
Even if you intend to use the kernel-based version of Solaris CIFS, it may help to install the UNIX Samba package. It includes the Samba Web Administrative Tool (SWAT), which can be useful as a web-based tool to help configure either type of Samba. You'll see instructions later in this chapter on how to disable UNIX Samba.

One of the issues between UNIX and Microsoft systems is the case sensitivity of filenames. Unlike Solaris, Microsoft operating systems may not recognize a difference between the files README.txt and readme.TXT. Both UNIX Samba and the Solaris CIFS services handle that issue in different ways, as is described later in this chapter.

UNIX Samba on Solaris

We use "UNIX Samba" to refer to the work of the developers of open source Samba, which can be installed as part of Solaris 11. It can provide an easier transition for administrators who are converting from Linux. The associated configuration commands and files should be familiar to anyone who has administered Samba on Linux systems.

As with any Samba software, it is designed to work with Microsoft Windows networks. Originally, such networks were designed with NetBIOS names as hostnames, limited to 15 characters. Unfortunately, such networks were not "routable" and were therefore limited to 255 systems. To address this issue, Microsoft adapted SMB to the TCP/IP protocol suite. Windows networks also include an "elected" master browser to maintain the local database of hostnames and IP addresses. In the following sections, you'll see how Samba on Solaris can be configured with these roles in mind, and more.

The Basics of UNIX Samba

To make UNIX Samba work on your system, you'll need to make sure appropriate packages are installed, specifically service/network/samba. Once you've installed and configured UNIX Samba, you may need to disable the smb service and enable the samba service with the following commands:

```
# svcadm disable smb/server
# svcadm enable samba
```

When you install the packages, UNIX Samba includes a sample configuration file, along with the daemons, commands, and utilities required to manage the service. The following sections detail these elements.

Samba Configuration Files

You can find the standard Samba configuration file in the /etc/samba directory. Well, actually, when UNIX Samba is installed, you'll find an smb.conf-example file in that directory. You'll need to modify the file and then change its name to smb.conf before the UNIX Samba service will actually work.

Although there are workarounds, the Samba password database is separate from the standard local Solaris database. Alternatively, both Windows and Solaris can be configured to use a single LDAP database. The associated changes required for the smb.conf file will be described shortly.

The /etc/samba/private directory is designed for passwords. It's set up with two files. The smbpasswd file includes usernames and encrypted passwords. The secrets.tdb file is configured for usernames and passwords if you've configured a "trivial database."

Samba Daemons

You'll find three daemons associated with Samba in the /usr/sbin directory:

- **smbd** The main Samba daemon.
- **nmbd** The NetBIOS name service daemon, which responds to name service requests. It can be configured to display shared directories and printers, and can be used as a WINS server.
- **winbindd** The name service switch service, which manages connections and provides authentication services, with the help of a PAM module.

One important lesson from this section is that you need to make sure all three services are running to support Samba. One way to do so is with the following command:

```
# svcadm enable samba wins winbind
```

One way to confirm the result is with the **svcs samba wins winbind** command. If you've successfully started these services, you'll see something similar to the following output:

```
STATE          STIME    FMRI
online    14:20:33 svc:/network/wins:default
online    21:24:17 svc:/network/samba:default
online    21:24:51 svc:/network/winbind:default
```

But wait a second. The Samba Web Administration Tool (SWAT) is a service too. So if you prefer to configure Samba using that web-based tool, you'd add **swat** to the list of services to be enabled. Remember, UNIX systems are case sensitive, and the associated daemon is **swat** in the /usr/sbin directory. Once the swat service is online, which you can confirm with the **svcs swat** command, you can start SWAT by navigating to http://localhost:901 in a browser. You can read more about SWAT later in this chapter.

TIP
SWAT is one tool that can be used to configure either UNIX-based Samba or the kernel-based Solaris CIFS.

Samba Commands

The UNIX Samba package includes a series of commands and utilities in the /usr/bin directory. Table 21-1 summarizes these options to give you an overview of the capabilities of Samba, beyond editing of the basic configuration file.

Command	Description
eventlogadm	Pushes additional information into Samba logs, typically in /var/svc/log/ network-samba:default.log.
findsmb	Returns information on systems that respond to SMB name query requests.
ldbadd	Supports adding records to a Lightweight Directory Access Protocol (LDAP) database in LDAP Data Interchange Format (LDIF).
ldbdel	Supports deleting records from an LDAP database.
ldbedit	Enables changes to records in an LDAP database using the default editor.
ldbmodify	Supports changes to records in an LDAP database.
ldbrename	Supports changes to trees in an LDAP database.
ldbsearch	Allows record searches in an LDAP database.
net	Supports the use of various configuration and detection commands. To review the range of available subcommands, run **net** by itself.
nmblookup	Looks up IP addresses based on NetBIOS names.
ntlm_auth	Aids services such as proxies to access Microsoft's NT Lan Manager authentication.
pdbedit	Manages the Samba authentication database; for example, **pdbedit -L** lists current users.
rpcclient	Supports the management of Windows clients; includes a variety of query and configuration options.
sharesec	Allows changes to ACLs on shared directories.
smbcacls	Supports changes to ACLs.

TABLE 21-1. *UNIX Samba Commands and Utilities (Continued)*

Command	Description
smbclient	Searches for shared resources; can be used as an FTP-like client.
smbcontrol	Sends messages to the UNIX Samba daemons: smbd, nmbd, and winbindd.
smbget	Download tool. Functionally similar to **wget**.
smbpasswd	Supports changes to user passwords; does not change local Solaris 11 passwords.
smbprofiles	Manages security identifiers (SIDs).
smbquotas	Manages quotas associated with shared directories on NTFS filesystems.
smbspool	Transmits print files to print devices shared via Samba.
smbstatus	Lists current connections to shared Samba resources.
smbtar	Backs up selected shared directories, with the help of **smbclient**.
smbtree	Browses currently available shares.
tdbbackup	Backs up Samba .tdb files such as the secrets.tdb file of usernames and passwords in the /etc/samba/private directory.
tdbdump	Outputs .tdb files in human-readable format.
tdbtool	Supports management of .tdb file databases.
testparm	Checks the syntax of the current smb.conf file.
wbinfo	Asks the winbindd service for information; for example, **wbinfo -u** lists current users.

TABLE 21-1.   *UNIX Samba Commands and Utilities*

Given the number of LDAP-related commands, it's clear that LDAP is important to the effective operation of a Samba server. However, this is not ensured. For more information on the configuration of an LDAP authentication database, see Chapter 11. This chapter will address how to connect to such a database, not how to create it.

The Standard Samba Configuration File

This section explains the standard smb.conf-example file included with the standard Solaris 11 service/network/samba package. When it is properly installed, you can find this file in the /etc/samba directory. Before UNIX Samba can work, you'll need to modify this file as needed and then change the name of the file to smb.conf, in the same /etc/samba directory. Nominally, the file is split into two sections. Global settings apply to the server as a whole. Share definitions create the configuration and conditions for shared directories and printers.

NOTE
*Some directives in Samba configuration files work with multiple spellings. For example, **writable** and **writeable** work just as well for shared directories where connected users can write files.*

```
michael@solaris-kvm-clone:~$ testparm
Load smb config files from /etc/samba/smb.conf
rlimit_max: rlimit_max (256) below minimum Windows limit (16384)
Processing section "[homes]"
Processing section "[printers]"
Processing section "[secretstuff]"
Loaded services file OK.
Server role: ROLE_STANDALONE
Press enter to see a dump of your service definitions
```

FIGURE 21-1. *Initial run of **testparm***

If you want to test changes made to smb.conf, run the **testparm** command. It starts by processing the smb.conf file in its syntax checker. One example is shown in Figure 21-1.

TIP
*The default settings for many directives varies by operating system. If a directive isn't configured in the smb.conf file, you can determine the default with the **testparm -v** command.*

If you want to address the rlimit_max issue, run the following command (ideally in a boot script), which increases the limit on the number of open files:

```
# ulimit -n 16384
```

As you can see from Figure 21-1, the **testparm** command has processed the file, including share definitions. There are no syntax errors. You also know that the current Samba server is configured as a standalone system; it could also be a part of a domain. For information on directives that diverge from defaults, press ENTER. One view of the output is shown in Figure 21-2.

Although the following subsections describe a number of options, what you see in Figure 21-2 is what matters with respect to the current UNIX Samba configuration. It includes two comment characters: the pound sign (#) and the semicolon (;). This section explains the functionality of many commented directives. To actually put them into service, you'd delete the semicolon.

Global Settings

The introductory comments include links to additional documentation. A full list of directives, defaults, and options for the file is available in the associated smb.conf man page. If you want to read about the full range of Samba documentation (including the guides listed in the smb.conf-example file), navigate to www.samba.org/samba/docs.

Each section of the file is a stanza. The title is listed in brackets. Global settings for UNIX Samba are defined by the **[global]** title:

```
#======= Global Settings =============
[global]
```

Microsoft networks are organized in groups of computers. They may be workgroups, which are local peer-to-peer networks. They may be domains, where information such as home

```
Press enter to see a dump of your service definitions

[global]
        workgroup = MYGROUP
        server string = Mike's Samba Server
        passdb backend = smbpasswd
        log file = /var/samba/log/log.%m
        max log size = 50
        dns proxy = No

[homes]
        comment = Home Directories
        read only = No
        browseable = No

[printers]
        comment = All Printers
        path = /var/spool/samba
        printable = Yes
        browseable = No

[secretstuff]
        comment = Temporary file space
        path = /tmp
        read only = No
        guest ok = Yes
michael@solaris-kvm-clone:~$
```

FIGURE 21-2. *Active directives in the smb.conf file*

directories is centralized in a limited number of servers. To configure Samba, you'll want to set the **workgroup** directive to match that of the local workgroup or domain. If properly configured, the local system will detect and can work with systems on other workgroups or domains that are connected networks. The following line matches the current standard for Microsoft clients. If you deleted the line, Samba would assume that the current system is a member of the workgroup named WORKGROUP.

```
workgroup = MYGROUP
```

Although the server string is a comment, it can be important because it's the descriptive comment associated with the local server that appears in browse lists, such as that shown in the output to the **smbclient** command or a Microsoft "My Network Places" search. Therefore, you'll probably want to change the value of this directive to something more descriptive, such as "Super Sensitive Information." Then again, if security is an issue, it's an opportunity to set up a more obscure name.

```
server string = Samba Server
```

Many administrators add a NetBIOS name for the local server. Although it's limited to 15 characters, it can be the same as the regular hostname of the system. One way to do so is with the **netbios name** directive; the following is one example of how it could be set:

```
; netbios name = solaris11svr1
```

The standard security level determines the type of network associated with this particular server. The default shown here works for a system that uses the local password database, as well as a Samba server that works as a primary domain controller (PDC) on an NT-style network:

```
security = user
```

Alternatively, if you want to set this up as a member server of an NT or Active Directory network, you'll want to choose from a value of **server**, **domain**, or **ads** (it's related to the **password server** directive, described shortly):

- **server**   A value of **security = server** supports checks of password servers; however, if the first search fails, authentication fails.
- **domain**   A value of **security = domain** supports sequential checks of password servers.
- **ads**   Works like a value of **security = domain**; however, if you set up an Active Directory realm as suggested by the **ads** directive, Kerberos authentication is required.

The one option that should not be used is **security = share** because that protects a share with only a password. Because a username would not be required, it would be inherently insecure.

The **hosts allow** directive can limit access to the specified IP addresses or networks. Of course, this does not defeat a black-hat hacker who spoofs an allowed IP address. The following example, if active, would support access from hosts on the 192.168.1.0/24 and 192.168.2.0/24 networks, as well as the localhost system:

```
;    hosts allow = 192.168.1. 192.168.2. 127.
```

The following directive sets up printers, as discussed in Chapter 15:

```
load printers = yes
```

Although it goes hand in hand with either of the following directives, the default is CUPS:

```
printcap name = /etc/printcap
printing = cups
```

As noted in the comments, if you set the **guest account** directive to something like pcguest, you'll have to make sure that user has an appropriate account defined in the /etc/passwd file. You may want to configure such an account with an appropriate nonfunctional shell such as /bin/false. The default **guest account** is user nobody.

```
; guest account = pcguest
```

Sometimes, there are problems with individual clients. With that in mind, the **log file** directive shown here specifies the use of different log files for each client that connects. If a NetBIOS or hostname can't be found for the client, the IP address is used.

```
log file = /var/samba/log/log.%m
```

The directive that follows limits the size of logs associated with Samba; in this case, the limit is 50KB:

```
max log size = 50
```

If you've set up the system to look to others for password authentication, you'll want to activate one of the following directives. The first assumes an NT-style network; the second searches for available authentication servers; the third assumes a single authentication server is sufficient:

```
#    password server = My_PDC_Name [My_BDC_Name] [My_Next_BDC_Name]
#    password server = *
;    password server = <NT-Server-Name>
```

If you've specified **security = ads**, you'll need to activate this directive to set up this server as part of an Active Directory realm. Of course, you'll want to change MY_REALM to the name of the realm.

```
;    realm = MY_REALM
```

Passwords can be configured through the **passdb backend** directive:

```
passdb backend = smbpasswd
```

You can set this directive to one of three values, shown next. When passwords are stored locally, they're stored in the /etc/samba/private directory. Although the standard shown in the smb.conf-example file is **smbpasswd**, the default is **tdbsam**.

- **smbpasswd** Stores local clear-text information in the smbpasswd file.
- **tdbsam** Supports a "trivial database" of usernames and passwords; normally stored in the passdb.tdb file. Alternative locations can be specified with a **passdb backend = tdbsam:/etc/alternative/other.tdb** directive.
- **ldapsam** Enables access to an LDAP database. Can be configured with a **passdb backend = ldapsam:"ldap://*ldapserver*"** or **ldapsam:"ldaps://*ldapsecure*"**.

If desired, you can include additional options. The example in the file shows an entry by (client) machine. One alternative is **%u**, which substitutes the username.

```
;    include = /usr/sfw/lib/smb.conf.%m
```

Generally, you can leave this **interfaces** directive commented out. However, if more than one network interface is on the local system, you may want to specify the IP network address associated with the interface to be used. Just be aware that you can use the interface device name, such as rtls0.

```
;    interfaces = 192.168.12.2/24 192.168.13.2/24
```

The four directives that follow determine whether the local system will be the browse master. Unless you want the system to be designated as a local browse master, you should not activate this directive:

```
;    local master = no
```

The local server participates in browser "elections," based on the priority listed with the **os level** directive. Although Samba normally "wins" an election against all systems but a Microsoft domain controller, you could set the **os level** up to 255.

```
;    os level = 33
```

If so configured, the **domain master** system becomes the master browser for the domain or workgroup:

```
; domain master = yes
```

Alternatively, the **preferred master** directive forces an election, with preference given to the local system:

```
; preferred master = yes
```

In most cases, the following option won't be used. But if you're actually administering a network with Windows 95/98/NT workstations, you'll want to enable it with the following directive:

```
; domain logons = yes
```

Domain logons can sometimes be configured for XP systems. If you're configuring domain logons, you could activate the following batch files by workstation (**%m**) or user (**%U**), with roving profiles, given a NetBIOS name (**%L**):

```
;    logon script = %m.bat
;    logon script = %U.bat
;    logon path = \\%L\Profiles\%U
```

If you want to enable the local WINS server, you could enable the **wins support** directive. Just don't enable this directive on more than one system on any local network.

```
; wins support = yes
```

Alternatively, the following sets up the local system as a WINS client by pointing to a different IP address as the server. (You'd substitute the IPv4 address of the WINS server for **w.x.y.z**.)

```
; wins server = w.x.y.z
```

Some older clients may need the help of the local Samba server, to retransmit requests from a WINS server:

```
; wins proxy = yes
```

If active, the following add scripts create user, group, and machine accounts on the Samba server, the first time a client uses the local system as a domain controller. If these are successful, the appropriate accounts will be added to the locally managed authentication database.

```
;  add user script = /usr/sbin/useradd %u
;  add group script = /usr/sbin/groupadd %g
;  add machine script = /usr/sbin/adduser -n -g machines -c Machine -d /dev/null ¬
-s /bin/false %u
```

If these directives are active, when a command is used to delete users and groups from the local database, Samba executes the following scripts, as appropriate:

```
;  delete user script = /usr/sbin/userdel %u
;  delete user from group script = /usr/sbin/deluser %u %g
;  delete group script = /usr/sbin/groupdel %g
```

Options Related to ACLs

Although other options are available, two groups of options for the Samba configuration file relate to ACLs and case sensitivity. ACLs from Microsoft filesystems are often subtly different from those found on Solaris systems. Some ACL-related directives can be important, including the following:

- **acl check permissions** Supports the use of Microsoft Windows permissions for file deletion.

- **acl compatibility** Allows the use of different versions of ACLs associated with different releases of Microsoft Windows.

- **acl map full control** Supports maps of Microsoft "full control" to UNIX **rwx** permissions.

- **force unknown acl user** Maps ACLs of an unknown Microsoft user to the currently connected UNIX user.

- **inherit acls** Ensures emulation of Microsoft-based ACLsA.

There are a number of other directives in Samba may affect ACLs, as listed in the man page for smb.conf.

Case Sensitivity

One conflict between Microsoft and UNIX-based operating systems is the case sensitivity of filenames. In general, whereas filenames in Microsoft systems are not case sensitive, filenames in UNIX systems are. That relationship can be customized with the help of the following four directives:

- **case sensitive** Supports case-sensitive searches from clients. Can be set to **yes/no/auto**. Case sensitivity for Microsoft operating systems is set to **no** by default.

- **default case** Sets the standard for new filenames. Can be upper- or lowercase.

- **preserve case** Enables default case from the client system for new files.

- **short preserve case** Relates to older 8.3 filenames associated with Microsoft operating systems. Can be set differently from **preserve case**.

User and Group ID Maps

If you're using separate sets of user and group IDs for users based on Microsoft and UNIX operating systems, you'll want to designate an appropriate range of IDs in the UNIX Samba configuration file. The **idmap** in the directives refers to mapping between Microsoft SIDs and UNIX user IDs (UIDs) and group IDs (GIDs). The relevant directives are listed in Table 21-2.

LDAP Access

If you've configured **security = ldapsam** in the smb.conf file, you should consider including a number of related directives in the smb.conf file. Related directives are described in Table 21-3.

Share Definitions

Now you'll explore the second half of the smb.conf-example file—the share definitions. They define the individual directories shared over this server. Each share is associated with a stanza of directives. The first share shown, **[homes]**, is unique because it supports the sharing of all user home directories. Sharing works for users configured in the /home directory, as well as regular users configured in the /export/home directory. The default settings don't allow browsing by others. If access is granted, the user who mounts that directory can write files to that directory.

Authentication Directive	Description
idmap alloc backend	Provides a plug-in interface for the Winbind service to allocate UNIX UIDs and GIDs.
idmap backend	Supports a plug-in for mapping tables, such as the trivial database (tdb).
idmap cache time	Sets a cache time for accepted mapping queries, in seconds.
idmap config	Allows the configuration of multiple domains.
idmap gid	Assigns a range of UNIX GIDs to map to Microsoft SIDs. Synonymous with **winbind gid**.
idmap negative cache time	Sets a cache time for rejected mapping queries, in seconds.
idmap uid	Assigns a range of UNIX UIDs to map to Microsoft SIDs. Synonymous with **winbind uid**.

TABLE 21-2. *Samba User and Group ID Directives*

LDAP Directive	Description
ldap admin dn	Defines the distinguished name used to contact the authoritative LDAP server. May be a format such as "cn=Admin,dc=example,dc=com".
ldap connection timeout	Specifies the waiting time before possibly searching for an alternative.
ldap delete dn	Defines whether a deleted item affects just the Samba database or a common item in the LDAP database.
ldap follow referral	Allows following of referrals as defined in LDAP configuration files.
ldap group suffix	Defines an LDAP parameter that may be added to the end of an entry.
ldap idmap suffix	Defines an LDAP parameter that is added to an ID mapped user.
ldap machine suffix	Defines an LDAP parameter that's added to the end of a machine name.
ldap passwd sync	Specifies whether Samba syncs LDAP and NT password databases.
ldap ssl	Supports the use of SSL connections to an LDAP server.

TABLE 21-3. *Samba LDAP Directives*

NOTE
In general, on UNIX Samba the name of the stanza is the name of the share. The exception is the [homes] stanza, where the username associated with the home directory is the name of the share. This is more important when connecting from a client system.

```
[homes]
    comment = Home Directories
    browseable = no
    writable = yes
```

You can further limit access with additional directives. For example, you might replace the last directive with

```
read only = yes
```

Alternatively, you could limit access to the owner of the noted home directory with the following directive:

```
valid users = %S
```

You could substitute specific usernames if desired.

Next, if you want to set up a network logon service for Microsoft workstations such as Windows XP, you could activate the following stanza with appropriate login scripts:

```
; [netlogon]
;    comment = Network Logon Service
;    path = /usr/sfw/lib/netlogon
;    guest ok = yes
;    writable = no
;    share modes = no
```

As the files associated with a **[profiles]** stanza become part of the registry, you'd activate the following stanza with appropriate files for Microsoft workstation operating systems that require such. Roving profiles download part of the registry after a user connects:

```
; [Profiles]
;    path = /usr/local/samba/profiles
;    browseable = no
;    guest ok = yes
```

The stanza that follows provides a spool directory for printers that are shared via Samba. As suggested by the comment, one simple change allows guest users access to such printers; you'd substitute **public = yes** for **guest ok = no**.

```
[printers]
    comment = All Printers
    path = /var/spool/samba
    browseable = no
# Set public = yes to allow user 'guest account' to print
```

```
          guest ok = no
          writable = no
          printable = yes
```

Given the subject, scroll down in the file. There's another sample printer stanza available. The **[fredprn]** stanza would configure a printer with access limited to user fred, courtesy of the **valid users** directive. Because **public = no** is included, anyone but Fred who reviews available printers should not see that printer in the browse list. Just be aware that print jobs would be sent to user fred's home directory. Generally, that would have to be changed to a directory such as /export/home/fred. In addition, if you set **path** to a directory such as /export/home/fred/spool, print spools would be sent to a dedicated directory.

```
; [fredsprn]
;     comment = Fred's Printer
;     valid users = fred
;     path = /homes/fred
;     printer = freds_printer
;     public = no
;     writable = no
;     printable = yes
```

Now scroll back up in the smb.conf-example file. The following stanza provides a model for directories to be shared via Samba. The /tmp directory supports access by all users.

```
; [tmp]
;     comment = Temporary file space
;     path = /tmp
;     read only = no
;     public = yes
```

Remember, the name of the stanza is the name of the share. In other words, if you changed **[tmp]** to **[secretstuff]** in this stanza, a remote mount of the secretstuff share would still access the /tmp directory.

Some of the directives used in previous stanzas can be adapted here to change the character of the share. For example, you could set **browsable = no** to hide the share, **read only = yes** to prevent users from writing to the directory, and **guest ok = no** to disable access from guest users.

Access to shared directories can be limited to certain users. Although the following sample stanza is publicly viewable by all users, only members of the staff group have rights to write files to the shared directory:

```
; [public]
;     comment = Public Stuff
;     path = /home/samba
;     public = yes
;     writable = no
;     printable = no
;     write list = @staff
```

In a similar fashion, the following stanza sets up a set of shared directories by client system. Based on this stanza, you'd have to create the /usr/pc directory and subdirectories. Given the nature of the Solaris 11 directory structure, you may want to change that to some /export subdirectory, such as /export/pc/m%.

```
; [pchome]
;    comment = PC Directories
;    path = /usr/pc/%m
;    public = no
;    writable = yes
```

There are cases where you'll want to set up shared directories beyond the **[tmp]** stanza. The suggested **[public]** stanza goes further. Whereas files in the /tmp directory can in general be modified only by the file owner, files specified in the **[public]** stanza can be modified by any other user. Compare it to the **[public]** stanza described earlier with a **write list = @staff** directive.

```
; [public]
;    path = /usr/somewhere/else/public
;    public = yes
;    only guest = yes
;    writable = yes
;    printable = no
```

Finally, the last suggested stanza configures one more way to set up a directory, in this case for two specific users. It introduces one more directive, the **create mask**, which sets up default octal permission for files created by users mary and fred when connected to the share. Just be aware that some subdirectory of /export/home may be more suitable for user files than the /usr/somewhere/shared directory suggested in the stanza.

```
; [myshare]
;    comment = Mary's and Fred's stuff
;    path = /usr/somewhere/shared
;    valid users = mary fred
;    public = no
;    writable = yes
;    printable = no
;    create mask = 0765
```

Be aware that you can use any directive specified in the **[global]** section in each share stanza. If you do so, the setting in the share stanza supersedes that configured in the **[global]** section.

Client Commands

To use client commands, you may need to activate the associated service. Run the **svcs smb/client** command. If the associated service isn't already online, you can activate it with the following command (the **-r** may be required to also enable dependent services):

```
# svcadm enable -r network/smb/client
```

Once the client service is online, you'll be able to perform tasks such as browsing remote shares with the **smbclient** command. The basic format is as follows:

```
$ smbclient -L //sambaserver -U username
```

```
michael@solaris-kvm-clone:/home/michael$ smbclient -L localhost -U donna
Enter donna's password:
Domain=[MYGROUP] OS=[Unix] Server=[Samba 3.5.5]

        Sharename       Type       Comment
        ---------       ----       -------
        IPC$            IPC        IPC Service (Mike's Samba Server)
        secretstuff     Disk       Temporary file space
        Cups-PDF        Printer    Cups-PDF
        donna           Disk       Home Directories
Domain=[MYGROUP] OS=[Unix] Server=[Samba 3.5.5]

        Server              Comment
        ---------           -------
        SOLARIS-KVM-CLON    Samba Server

        Workgroup           Master
        ---------           -------
        MYGROUP             SOLARIS-KVM-CLONE
michael@solaris-kvm-clone:/home/michael$ ▮
```

FIGURE 21-3.   *A list of Samba shares*

You could substitute the IP address for the **sambaserver**; the username should be configured in the Samba-configured authentication database on the **sambaserver** system. One example is shown in Figure 21-3.

Once you've identified a desired share to mount, you can proceed from a client with the **mount** command. Key is the **-F smbfs** option, which specifies the mounting of a Samba filesystem share. You could then proceed with the domain, username, Samba server, share definition, and the local directory on which the share is to be mounted. For example, the command

```
# mount -F smbfs //[domain;][user[:password]@]sambaserver/share mount.point
```

mounts the Samba filesystem (smbfs). The domain (or workgroup) is not required, unless there are multiple versions of the same share on different domains. You can substitute the IP address for the name of the **sambaserver**. In most cases, the share is the title of the stanza. If in doubt, you can confirm it in the output to the **smbclient** command. The **share** name you use should correspond to what you see in the Sharename column output.

The SWAT Tool

If you've enabled the service associated with SWAT earlier in this chapter, open a browser and navigate to http://localhost:901. You'll be prompted for an administrative login, normally the first login on the local system, as shown in Figure 21-4.

Explore the tool on your own. It includes four sections:

- ■ **Home**   Includes links to man pages for relevant commands, along with access to additional Samba documentation.
- ■ **Status**   Notes the current status of the Samba daemon, along with connections to shared resources. Functionally equivalent to the **smbstatus** command.

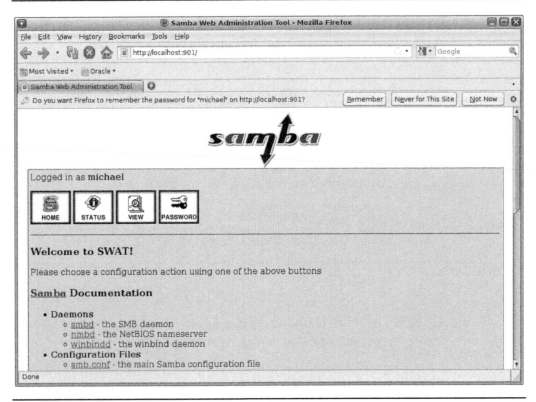

FIGURE 21-4. *The SWAT tool*

- **View** Lists relevant directives from the Samba configuration file; functionally equivalent to the **testparm** command.
- **Password** Supports changes to passwords on the server as well as in the local Samba database.

If desired, you can access SWAT from a remote location on the network.

Solaris CIFS

Now that you've looked at UNIX Samba on Solaris, you should understand its features better, how it can be configured on Linux, and how it can make Solaris a member of a Microsoft network, with appropriate links to Microsoft's authentication schemes. With all this in mind, why use the Solaris implementation of CIFS?

Because the code is integrated into the kernel, it's more efficient. Because the way it works is similar to NFS, it can help you set up two different files services with similar mechanisms. It supports automated shares of home directories, which provides one more way to set them up from a central server. It provides better interoperability with Microsoft-style ACLs. It can even be configured with NIS-based authentication mechanisms. If you don't have access to a network authentication database of usernames and passwords, you can even configure a connection between the local password authentication database and CIFS via pluggable authentication modules (PAM).

This section borrows heavily from the "Solaris CIFS Administration Guide," available from http://docs.oracle.com/cd/E19082-01/820-2429/index.html. In the sections that follow, you'll set up a mapping strategy for user and group IDs, configuring WINS, and possibly other associated services. Of course, you should think about whether this Solaris CIFS system should join a Microsoft domain or workgroup. You can then define directories and printers to be shared, possibly including user home directories.

NOTE
Shares created in this section can include most alphanumeric characters, but can't include the following elements of punctuation:
*" / \ [ ] : | + ; , ? * =*

Make Sure UNIX Samba Is "Off"

One problem with the two choices for networking with Microsoft systems is that they can't run simultaneously with Solaris CIFS. To that end, run the following commands:

```
# svcadm disable network/samba
# svcadm disable network/wins
# svcadm disable network/winbind
```

Now you can enable Solaris CIFS once the desired options are configured.

The Solaris CIFS Packages

Two packages relate to CIFS on Solaris. Just to be confusing, the names are

```
service/file-system/smb
system/file-system/smb
```

These are the Solaris 11 packages that integrate CIFS services into the kernel. These packages work together. For the service, options are configured in two files in the /lib/svc/manifest/network/smb directory: client.xml and server.xml. One regular command is associated with the client package: **smbutil**. It also includes its own versions of the **mount** and **umount** commands in the /usr/lib/fs/smbfs directory. In addition, it uses commands associated with sharing NFS directories, as discussed in Chapter 19, including **idmap**, **sharemgr**, and **zfs**, along with share definitions in the /etc/dfs/sharetab file.

Solaris CIFS client.xml

Read through the client.xml file in the aforementioned directory. It'll help you understand the workings of the Solaris 11 CIFS client. Here are some highlights:

- **Name** The client service is highlighted in network/smb/client.
- **Related services** Related dependent services are listed, including network, the Generic Security Service Application Programming Interface (GSSAPI), name services, ID mapping, and more.

■ **Execute method** Functionality is related to the **smb-client** script in the /lib/svc/method directory.

■ **Administrative access** Access is limited to users with appropriate rights.

Solaris CIFS server.xml

Take a close look at the server.xml file in the aforementioned directory. It'll help you understand the files associated with the Solaris 11 CIFS server. Although there are 10 categories of settings, some are blank in the standard version of the file. The following are highlights from our version of that file:

■ **Name** The server service is listed as network/smb/server.

■ **Default status** The Solaris 11 CIFS server is disabled by default.

■ **Instance** CIFS is set up as a single process.

■ **Dependencies** Several other services are listed as dependencies.

■ **Service management methods** Credentials, timeouts, and execute options are specified for starting, stopping, and refreshing the CIFS service.

■ **Faults to be ignored** By default, all faults are sent either to the screen or a log file.

■ **Service model** There are no changes in the standard server.xml file to the service model.

■ **More on dependencies** Special requirements help work with network attached storage (NAS).

■ **Service milestones** None at this time.

■ **Service template** Path to man pages included.

Basic CIFS Commands

As a user or even as an administrator, you should already be familiar with the regular **mount** and **umount** commands. As noted earlier, the CIFS client package includes these same commands for Solaris-based CIFS mounts, such as those related to home directories.

One of the strengths of Solaris CIFS is its use of commands available for other services. Many of the same commands used for NFS in Chapter 19 are also used here. But for now, review some of the options associated with the **smbutil** command. They're associated with the following functions:

■ View available shares

■ Create CIFS passwords in hashed format

■ Manage databases of NetBIOS names, IP addresses, and regular hostnames

Run the **smbutil** command by itself. The output shown in Figure 21-5 provides hints with respect to its capabilities.

Some associated procedures are listed in the following subsections.

```
michael@solarisdel:~$ smbutil

usage: smbutil [-hv] subcommand [args]
where subcommands are:
   crypt           slightly obscure password
   help            display help on specified subcommand
   login           login to specified host
   logout          logout from specified host
   logoutall       logout all users (requires privilege)
   lookup          resolve NetBIOS name to IP address
   print           print file to the specified remote printer
   status          resolve IP address or DNS name to NetBIOS names
   view            list resources on specified host

michael@solarisdel:~$ █
```

FIGURE 21-5.   *Basic options for the* **smbutil** *command*

Identify Basic Information   You can identify basic information about running CIFS servers with the following command; substitute the hostname or IP address of the server.

```
$ smbutil status hostname
```

The output is simple, identifying the domain or workgroup, along with the NetBIOS name.

Browse Shares with smbutil   The **smbutil** command can browse the list of resources currently shared by another Samba or CIFS server. The following example browses the noted system anonymously:

```
$ smbutil view -A //sambaserver
```

Alternatively, the following command specifies user michael on the remote *sambaserver* system, prompting for a password:

```
$ smbutil view //michael@sambaserver
```

Create a Password with smbutil   If you haven't connected the local CIFS server to a remote authentication database, you may need to set up local users and passwords. To create a password in encrypted format, the **smbutil crypt** command can help. By itself, it prompts for a password and then returns a hash of that password that can be configured. If you have an account with passwords on different servers, that password can be stored in your home directory, in the hidden .nsmbrc file. The following is an example we've run on our Solaris 11 systems:

1.   The user account is michael. Substitute your username, and the hostname or IP address of the remote CIFS server.

```
$ smbutil view //michael@192.168.122.1
```

2.   Enter a password when prompted. This process should eliminate the prompt.

3.   Run the **smbutil crypt** command. Enter the desired password at the prompt that appears. You should see a hash of that password, similar to $$17d4a4c2c2a2a0f47b2, in the output.

4. Copy the hash. Open the .nsmbrc file in the local home directory. Include the following lines and substitute the hash for your desired password. Save the result.

```
[default]
password=$$17d4a4c2c2a2a0f47b2
```

5. Try the command run in step 1 again. Believe it or not, if you see the following warning, it's a good sign:

```
Warning: .nsmbrc file not secure, ignoring passwords
```

6. Run the following command to make the file more secure. Like the SSH private key described in Chapter 20, the file won't be read if anyone but the user owner has permissions on this file.

```
$ chmod 600 .nsmbrc
```

7. Try the command run in step 1 one more time. It should reveal the shares on the remote server automatically, based on your username and the password stored in the .nsmbrc file.

To make this work on a permanent basis, you'll need to make a change to the /etc/pam.conf file. The following entry also works with the **smbutil login** command, described next:

```
login   auth    optional    pam_smbfs_login.so.1
```

Store a Password in the Local Cache   Now you'll set up the functionality of the .nsmbrc file in the local cache. When we do so on our own network, we run the **smbutil login** command and enter the password for the workgroup at the following prompt:

```
Password for WORKGROUP/michael:
```

You should now be able to run the **smbutil view** command described earlier to browse a remote CIFS server, with the username shown and the password just entered.

You can reverse the process with the **smbutil logout** command. As an administrator, you can disable the cache for all users with the **smbutil logoutall** command.

For the purpose of the remainder of this chapter, erase the .nsmbrc file.

More Functionality with smbutil   You can do more with the **smbutil** command. If there's a WINS server on the local network, you can use its database of NetBIOS names and IP addresses with the **smbutil lookup** *NetBIOSname* command. For example, the following command returns the IP address associated with the system named Kauai on our home network:

```
$ smbutil lookup Kauai
```

The Alternative Client Command: sharemgr   Later in this chapter, you'll see how the **sharemgr** command can be used to set up shared directories on a Solaris CIFS server. For now, run the following three commands and then compare their output on your system:

```
$ sharemgr show -p
$ sharemgr show -v
$ sharemgr show -x
```

```
michael@solaris-kvm-clone:~$ sharemgr show -p
default nfs=()
zfs
    zfs/rpool/export/home/michael smb=()
          /export/home/michael
    zfs/rpool/share1 smb=()
          /rpool/share1
smb smb=()
          /var/smb/cvol   smb=()
          IPC$    smb=()
group1 smb=()
          /tmp
          /export/home/donna
michael@solaris-kvm-clone:~$ sharemgr show -v
default
zfs
    zfs/rpool/export/home/michael
          rpool_export_home_michael=/export/home/michael
    zfs/rpool/share1
          rpool_share1=/rpool/share1
smb
      * /var/smb/cvol "Default Share"
              c$=/var/smb/cvol        "Default Share"
      * IPC$  "Remote IPC"
              IPC$=IPC$      "Remote IPC"
group1
          temps=/tmp
          guestdir=/export/home/donna
michael@solaris-kvm-clone:~$ █
```

FIGURE 21-6. *Showing local shares with the* **sharemgr** *command*

Take note of the differences. One example of the **-p** and **-v** switches is shown in Figure 21-6. Also note that the effect works only on the shares from the local system.

The **-x** switch appears most complex because it specifies each share in XML format. As befits XML, it includes all information required to fully define each shared directory.

Configure a Mapping Strategy

One more advantage of Solaris CIFS is the relative compatibility of ACLs in shared NFS (version 4) and ZFS directories, courtesy of the ID Mapping Service, known as **idmapd**. With that in mind, Solaris CIFS is able to map Microsoft users and groups with equivalent rights on the Solaris CIFS server. When you're mapping users and groups, there may already be a matching UID and GID. Alternatively, CIFS can dynamically allocate UIDs and GIDs as needed, also known as ephemeral ID mapping. In that way, the Microsoft Security Accounts Manager (SAM) database can be mapped appropriately. Three basic strategies are available, as discussed next.

Name-Based Mapping

A name-based mapping scheme associates Solaris users and groups with corresponding Microsoft users and groups. It can work when there's already an existing UNIX authentication database such as LDAP or NIS.

Directory-Based Mapping If there are a number of Solaris 11 servers configured in an environment with Microsoft systems, directory-based mapping is most appropriate. You can use an Active Directory (AD) naming service such as LDAP. You can set up such maps in AD-only or LDAP-only mode. AD-only mode is suitable for administrators who work from a Microsoft-based AD. You can also set up mixed mode.

Solaris engineers suggest the following command to enable directory-based mapping. Take care because the command requires a space after the last colon and the statement that follows.

```
# svccfg -s svc:/system/idmap setprop \
config/ds_name_mapping_enabled=boolean: true
```

The command selects the **idmapd** service and then activates the name-mapping property of the service. The next step depends on whether the network uses AD or LDAP. The following command tells the **idmapd** service about the AD attributes for hypothetical user1 and group1, respectively:

```
# svccfg -s svc:/system/idmap setprop \
config/ad_unixuser_attr=astring: user1

# svccfg -s svc:/system/idmap setprop \
config/ad_unixgroup_attr=astring: group1
```

Alternatively, the following command tells the **idmap** service about the Microsoft LDAP name attributes associated with some regular user's account:

```
# svccfg -s svc:/system/idmap setprop \
config/nldap_winname_attr=astring: MichaelJang
```

Note the commonality in the commands; in each case the service configuration command (**svccfg**) is used to activate some property of the ID Mapping service. As discussed shortly, the **idmap** command can also be used to add and remove mappings from appropriate Microsoft or Solaris user and group objects.

Rule-Based Mapping Rule-based maps can be configured and are suitable when there's only one Solaris server on a network. The rules would be stored on a single Solaris CIFS server. If there's more than one Solaris system on a network dominated by Microsoft servers, you'd have to duplicate the same rules on the other Solaris systems.

Ephemeral ID Mapping

In plain English, *ephemeral* means temporary. If you're in transition from a Microsoft server operating system, you don't have to do anything extra. If you haven't yet created a Solaris-type authentication scheme such as NIS, the standard for Solaris CIFS identity mapping already uses ephemeral IDs. These temporary IDs last only as long as the connection between the Microsoft and Solaris servers on your network.

Mapping via PAM

With the help of a single module in PAM, you can even configure CIFS to use the standard local password database in the /etc/passwd file. All you need to do is add the following line to the pam.conf file in the /etc directory:

```
other    password    required    pam_smb_passwd.so.1    nowarn
```

Set Up Membership in a Workgroup or Domain

Now it's time for a basic question. Will your Solaris 11 server be part of a workgroup or a domain? Of course, that depends on how the network is organized. For a small peer-to-peer network such as one you might be testing at home, a workgroup is appropriate. Assume you have an existing workgroup named MYGROUP. In that case, you can set up the local system to join that workgroup with the following command:

```
# smbadm join -w MYGROUP
```

When you try that command, it should prompt you as follows:

```
After joining MYGROUP the smb service will be restarted automatically.
Would you like to continue? [no]:
```

The default is **no**; you'll have to type in **yes** to implement the change. If you get an error similar to the following, the Solaris CIFS service may not be running:

```
failed to join MYGROUP: INTERNAL_ERROR
```

When you run the **svcs smb/server** command, it might show the following issue:

```
maintenance     9:09:38 svc:/network/smb/server:default
```

You still need to enable the service. One way to do so is with the following command:

```
# svcadm enable -r smb/server
```

TIP
If the target system includes multiple network adapters, you may see a message such as "svcadm: svc:/milestone/network depends on svc:/network/physical, which has multiple instances." This message can be ignored.

You'll also want to enable the service that actually does the sharing:

```
# svcadm enable shares/group:smb
```

You should be able to confirm operation with the **svcs -a | grep smb** command. If the Solaris CIFS server is still in "maintenance" mode, you may need to disable the server before running the **svcadm enable -r smb/server** command.

The **smbadm join** command should now work normally. As described earlier, you can confirm membership of the local system on a workgroup or domain with the following command:

```
# smbutil status localhost
```

In a mixed enterprise environment, it's more likely that you want this Solaris 11 system to join a domain. The associated command is slightly different; the following example assumes that the account authorized to accept new members of a domain is administrator, on hypothetical domain1:

```
# smbadm join -u administrator domain1
```

You may need the master password for the Active Directory. If successful, it'll restart the smb/ server service to implement the change. Also, a restart is needed, especially if the local system is currently a member of a workgroup. However, all of this is a bit premature because you should check a few things first:

- **AD controller**   Make sure an AD controller is currently active on the domain. It should be integrated with a DNS server, configured to dynamic DNS (DDNS). All of this depends on Kerberos.

- **Kerberos server**   Both AD and DDNS servers require access to Kerberos, specifically for any associated tickets. Make sure the default realm, the key distribution center (KDC), the administrative server, and password servers are properly configured in the associated configuration file (krb5.conf in the /etc/krb5 directory).

- **DNS lookups**   Lookups of DNS servers can be configured in /etc/nsswitch.conf and /etc/resolv.conf, as discussed in Chapter 16.

If all of these conditions are met, you should get the following response to the **smbadm join** request:

```
Successfully joined domain 'domain1'
```

Set Up WINS and Related Services

As noted earlier in this chapter, WINS is the name resolution service for Microsoft networks. In a Solaris 11 CIFS environment, you'll need to take the following steps:

1. Configure the local system to point to the address of the primary WINS server. The following command sets the property of the first WINS server (wins_server_1) to the noted IP address (substitute accordingly):

   ```
   # sharectl set -p wins_server_1=192.168.0.1
   ```

2. If you have a second WINS server on the local network, which is generally recommended for redundancy, you can point the local system to that second WINS server (wins_server_2) with a command similar to the following:

   ```
   # sharectl set -p wins_server_2=192.168.0.1
   ```

NOTE
Unlike the UNIX Samba service described in the first part of this chapter, the Solaris CIFS server cannot also be configured as a WINS server.

Configure CIFS Users and Groups

Given the special groups that exist on a Microsoft domain, you'll want to create several special groups on a Solaris 11 system to take full advantage of the capabilities assigned to users in such groups. With the **smbadm** command, you can create and configure these groups with desired users. They don't have to be special in any administrative sense; for example, the following command creates the local CIFS group named mechanics with the given description, courtesy of the **-d** switch:

```
$ smbadm create -d "Final assembly team members" mechs1
```

Be aware, CIFS group names are limited to eight lowercase alphanumeric characters. This particular command automatically also creates a new group called mechs1 in the /etc/group file. It also creates corresponding group information in the /var/smb directory, in the binary smbgroup .db file.

Now that you've created a Solaris CIFS group, you can add users to that group. The following sample command adds a user named larryl to the mechs1 group in the domain named domain 1. You can add multiple users in the same command.

```
# smbadm add-member -m domain1\\larryl mechs1
```

Then the following command removes user larryl from the noted group:

```
# smbadm remove-member -m domain1\\larryl mechs1
```

Mapping Users and Groups

In general, users and groups already exist in some database for the local network. The command you can use to create additional ID maps is **idmap**. But before setting up the map to a database, create the map for one user. For example, if you want to set up a map between the Microsoft and Solaris guest users, you could run the following command:

```
# idmap add winname:Guest unixuser:guest
```

Of course, that guest user has to exist in an appropriate database. If the **idmap** command is successful, you'll see the following in the output to the **idmap list** command:

```
add     winname:Guest@solarisde1    unixuser:guest
```

If needed, you can list current entries with the **idmap list** command and then remove the entry. The following command removes the noted guest user:

```
# idmap remove -t unixuser:guest
```

NOTE
One alternative to all of this is to have the AD admin enter the RFC 2307 schema (known as Services for UNIX by Microsoft). He can then authenticate against the AD via Kerberos, using the AD LDAP database for name services in the /etc/nsswitch.conf file.

Create a ZFS Share for Solaris CIFS

The Solaris CIFS server is designed for use with ZFS-based shares. Based on a standard installation, you should already have a group of ZFS-sharable directories available. To confirm what's available, run the following command:

```
# zfs list -r rpool
```

But you should do more. What you do depends on whether you want a regular ZFS share or one configured for guest users. When properly executed, these commands add settings to the /etc/dfs/sharetab file, which is normally read and shared during the boot process.

A Standard Solaris CIFS Share

The following command sets up a ZFS share more suited to Samba. Whereas UNIX-based operating systems are case sensitive, Microsoft-based operating systems are not. That's associated with the **casesensitivity=mixed** option. In addition, Microsoft and UNIX-based operating systems use different locking mechanisms on shared directories. In short, whereas UNIX normally uses "advisory" locking, Microsoft shares use "mandatory" locking. The **nbmand=on** option creates nonblocking mandatory locks, which straddle the difference.

```
# zfs create -o casesensitivity=mixed -o nbmand=on rpool/share1
```

Review the result with the **zfs list -r rpool** command. Relatively standard output is shown in Figure 21-7.

The following command is key. It adds the share to the /etc/dfs/sharetab file and ensures that the directory is shared once again if and when the system is rebooted. So, for the example just listed, set it up to share on a CIFS network like so:

```
# sudo zfs set sharesmb=on rpool/share1
```

Now you can confirm the share with the help of an appropriate **smbutil** command:

```
$ smbutil view //localhost
```

```
michael@solaris-kvm-clone:~$ zfs list -r rpool
NAME                        USED  AVAIL  REFER  MOUNTPOINT
rpool                       4.00G  3.81G  93.5K  /rpool
rpool/ROOT                  3.47G  3.81G    31K  legacy
rpool/ROOT/solaris          3.47G  3.81G  3.43G  /
rpool/export                838K  3.81G    32K  /export
rpool/export/home           806K  3.81G    32K  /export/home
rpool/export/home/michael   774K  3.81G   774K  /export/home/michael
rpool/share1                 31K  3.81G    31K  /rpool/share1
rpool/swap                  544M  4.22G   125M  -
michael@solaris-kvm-clone:~$ []
```

FIGURE 21-7. *ZFS-pools, including a CIFS share*

You should also confirm it in the contents of the /etc/dfs/sharetab file. The previous command adds the following entry to that file:

```
/rpool/share1    rpool_share1@zfs    smb
```

That share should now be available to clients connected to the current CIFS network. Although the server is efficiently run from the Solaris 11 kernel, the client can be a regular Samba client from a Solaris, a Linux, or even (of course) a Microsoft system.

Use the sharemgr Command to Create a CIFS Share

The **sharemgr** command can be used to create CIFS shares, based on the Solaris CIFS server associated with the kernel. First, use the **sharemgr list** command to confirm that appropriate shares can be created. You should see output similar to the following:

```
default
zfs
smb
```

Of course, if you don't see the smb group in the output, something else has to be done. Specifically, the following command adds the ability to create CIFS shares to the list:

```
# sharemgr create -P smb smb
```

Now you should be able to create a share group. For the moment, call it CIFSgroup1:

```
# sharemgr create -P smb CIFSgroup1
```

Next, you can add a share. The following command, with the **add-share** switch, adds a share named policies, associated with the /export/policies directory, as part of the newly defined group named CIFSgroup1:

```
# sharemgr add-share -r policies -s /export/policies CIFSgroup1
```

To confirm, run the **sharemgr show -v** command again. You should see the following entries in the output:

```
CIFSgroup1
          policies=/export/policies
```

You should be able to confirm the share in the /etc/dfs/sharetab file. If the Solaris 11 system is a member of an AD domain, you'll want to link the property of the container to the share. In this case, the AD container has an LDAP common name (**cn**) of "Company":

```
# sharemgr set -P smb -p ad-container=cn=Company -r policies \
  -s /export/policies CIFSgroup1
```

A Guest Share

Sometimes, it's appropriate to set up a CIFS share for guest access. In general, you'll want to set up a dedicated directory, perhaps in a dedicated zone. The following **sharemgr** command configures a new guest share, in a new group named CIFSguest1. This presumes you've already created that CIFSguest1 group with the **sharemgr create** command.

```
# sharemgr set -P smb -p guestok=true -r guest CIFSguest1
```

Mount a Share

The basic tools associated with mounting are the same as for the UNIX Samba server. The **mount** command mounts; the **umount** command disables the mount. One requirement for Solaris CIFS clients is appropriate settings in the exec_attr file in the /etc/security directory. Specifically, you'll want to add the following settings to that directory to support the mounting and unmounting of shares as a regular user:

```
Basic Solaris User:solaris:cmd::::/usr/lib/fs/smbfs/mount:privs=sys_mount
Basic Solaris User:solaris:cmd::::/usr/lib/fs/smbfs/umount:privs=sys_mount
```

Once you've identified a desired share to mount, you can proceed from a client with the **mount** command. Key is the **-F smbfs** option, which specifies the mounting of a Samba filesystem share. You could then proceed with the domain, username, Samba server, share definition, and the local directory on which the share is to be mounted. The following is a sample basic format used for the command:

```
$ mount -F smbfs //[domain;][user[:password]@]sambaserver/share mount.point
```

You may want to set this up with root privileges. Of course, all of this detail is generally not necessary. For example, the following command mounts the shared rpool_share1 from the system named server1, and mounts it on the local /home/michael/temp directory. The current username is assumed, and we're prompted for a password.

```
$ mount  -F  smbfs  //server1/rpool_share1  /home/michael/temp
```

As just suggested, the **umount** command reverses the process, and is simpler. All you need to do in this case is apply the **umount** command to the mount directory:

```
$ umount  /home/michael/temp
```

The Automouter and Home Directories

As discussed in Chapter 19, the automounter is configured in the /etc/auto_master and /etc/auto_home files. Those files can help you configure home directories on a central server, shared via NFS. But because this chapter is focused on CIFS, things are a bit different. The key Automounter configuration file is /etc/smbautohome. Entries in that file include two or three elements:

```
key    location    (container)
```

The key can be a username or a reference to name service switching. The location is a directory. Container entries, if used, are most frequently associated with characteristics in an LDAP database, such as one associated with an AD domain. The following would export the home directory for a personal account. The **?** is a wildcard associated with the username.

```
michael /export/home/?
```

The following entry could refer to any account:

```
* /export/home/?
```

In contrast, the following entry takes advantage of the /etc/nsswitch.conf file, which can search through authentication databases in a specific order, as configured in that nsswitch.conf file:

```
+nsswitch /export/home/?
```

The following entry includes containers associated with the distinguished name (**dn**), domain component (**dc**), and organizational unit (**ou**) components:

```
+nsswitch /export/home/?    dn=ads,dc=example,dc=com,ou=users
```

Troubleshooting Issues

This section is a simple list of troubleshooting issues collected by Solaris engineers as they relate to both the server and the client. Some of these issues are also addressed earlier in this chapter; others may appear with unexpected problems elsewhere in the network, workgroup, or domain. Some known server-related issues are listed in Table 21-4.

In contrast, some known client-related Solaris CIFS issues are shown in Table 21-5.

Issue	Description
Case sensitivity	Make sure to use the **-o case-sensitivity=mixed** option with the **zfs** command.
Unable to join Microsoft domain	Check four things: correct password for domain administrator, privileges for domain administrator, DNS, and Kerberos.
Problems with idmap	The idmap service can't connect to an AD in workgroup mode.
Connection to WINS	Specify a WINS server with the **sharectl set -p wins_server_1=ipaddress smb** command.
Shares not shown in browse lists	Configure the Solaris CIFS server on the same subnet as a master browser. (Solaris CIFS can't be configured as a master browser.)

TABLE 21-4. *Solaris CIFS Server Troubleshooting Issues*

Issue	Description
Access denied	Wrong password, unspecified domain.
Unable to view shares	Use the anonymous access option with a command similar to **smbutil view -A //cifs_server**.
Can't mount shares	Verify appropriate rights in the /etc/security/exec_attr file.

TABLE 21-5. *Solaris CIFS Client Troubleshooting Issues*

Summary

This chapter covered the two different services that can be used to connect Solaris 11 to a network based on the SMB and CIFS protocols, as implemented by Microsoft. UNIX Samba is the service developed by the Samba Foundation. For administrators who are more experienced with Linux, that service works equally well on Solaris 11 and includes many of the same options, including SWAT for configuration. It is based on the same smb.conf configuration file in the /etc/samba directory. You can set it up with users and passwords locally in a separate database, or you can set up a connection to Microsoft-based AD LDAP databases.

In contrast, Solaris engineers have created their own implementation of a service that communicates on a Microsoft network. Because Solaris CIFS is integrated in the kernel, it is more efficient. You can set up shared directories with the **zfs** command, assign shares with the **sharemgr** command, and browse shares with the **smbutil** command. But Solaris CIFS doesn't have all of the advantages because it can't be configured as a master browser for the network. It doesn't include lists of shared printers. However, Solaris CIFS makes it relatively easy to set up automounted home directories. It's not stuck with legacy support for older Microsoft operating systems. In any case, CUPS stands on its own for sharing printers.

Just be aware that Solaris 11 can't share directories using both UNIX Samba and the kernel-based Solaris CIFS. You'll have to make sure to disable one and enable the options associated with the other service.

References

The Solaris CIFS Administration Guide can be found at http://docs.oracle.com/cd/E19082-01/820-2429/index.html.

If you're using Samba in any sort of detail, it can be helpful to read "Samba, opening Windows to a Wider World," written by the main developers of the open source version of that server software. It's available online from the Samba website at www.samba.org.

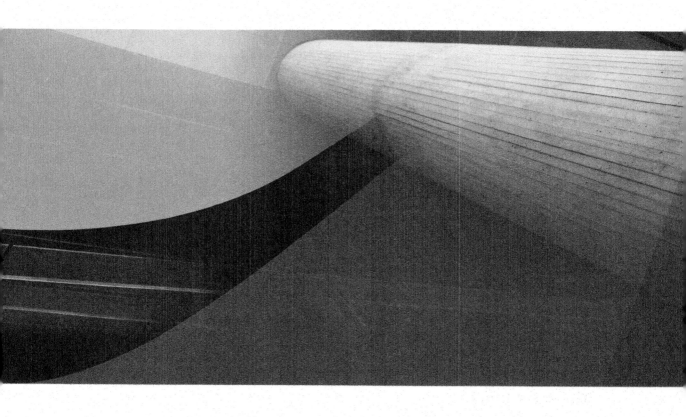

CHAPTER
22

Apache and
the Web Stack

pache has been the most widely used web server on the market for the last 17 years, and currently runs about two thirds of hostnames according to Netcraft's Web Server Survey. It was first launched in 1995 as open source software. Apache is well known for its security, flexibility, and robustness. Many commercial software vendors even incorporate it into their own products. Oracle provides Apache Web Server version 2.2.20 for the first release of Solaris 11. Version 2.2 is the most widely used, although the 2.4 branch was released in February 2012.

The Oracle Solaris package is compiled specifically for the Solaris OS and therefore takes advantage of Oracle Solaris features, such as the ZFS filesystem layout and the Service Management Facility (SMF).

These days, the web server is not alone. It is now the top layer in what has become known as the Web Stack. The Web Stack is a layered approach of three basic components: Web, application, and database.

Basic Components

Several products compete for their place within the Web Stack, but in the context of this book, we will be discussing the Apache web server, the MySQL database, and the PHP web programming language. We refer to this stack using its acronym—AMP. These three products are open source and freely available for download from their respective websites. This open source trio can be found in thousands, maybe millions of installations powering websites across the Internet.

The AMP Stack

Deploying the AMP stack on Solaris 11 and creating a secure, powerful online presence is made easy by its tight integration into the operating system. Any open source software provided with Solaris or from the Oracle repository is supported by Oracle for users who have a support contract. Starting with AMP on Solaris, often referred to as SAMP, allows an individual or small business to establish their web application and then easily scale it up as their needs grow. So, even if you start with a single CPU system in your basement, you can fairly easily upgrade. As server capacity needs increase, the AMP stack and applications can easily be migrated to larger x86, AMD64, or SPARC multicore, multiprocessor server environments while retaining the same familiar interfaces. The bottom line is your developers don't have to retool each time your business expands.

In order to use the AMP stack on your Oracle Solaris 11 system, you need to install Apache, MySQL, and PHP. Thankfully, installing the Solaris package for the AMP stack makes this easy. The AMP package is actually a metapackage that, when installed, will include the packages for Apache, MySQL, and PHP. This takes care of any dependencies that may exist between these packages as well as other packages that contain supporting binaries or libraries required for a fully functional AMP stack.

GUI AMP Installation

After logging in to the Solaris 11 Desktop Environment, open the Image Packaging System (IPS) Package Manager, which is easily accessed using the Add More Software icon located on the top-left side of the desktop and shown here. Use the search bar at the top right to search for "amp."

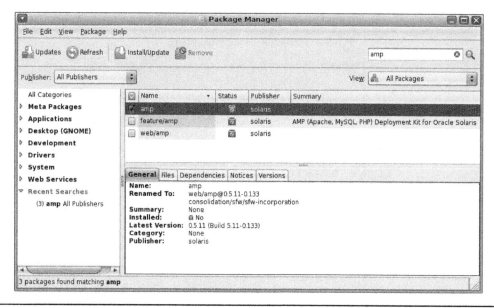

FIGURE 22-1.   *Selecting the amp package*

Now, let's install AMP. First, select the amp package and check the box next to it (see Figure 22-1). Second, click the Install/Update button.

A dialog appears to confirm installation (see Figure 22-2). Click Proceed. Installation will take a few minutes. Click Close once the package installation completes successfully (see Figure 22-3).

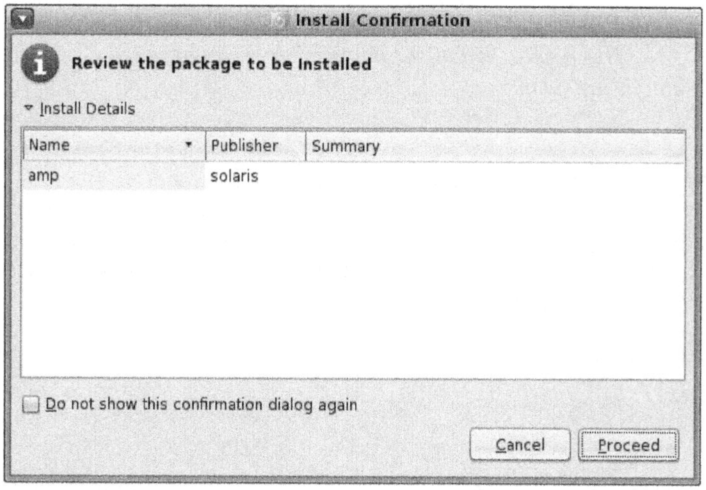

FIGURE 22-2.   *Install confirmation*

FIGURE 22-3. *Successful installation of amp*

NOTE
Reviewing the Package Manager will reveal that although we selected amp, the package feature/amp was actually installed, as shown in Figure 22-4. This is actually the current version of the package to which amp is just a link.

Command-Line AMP Installation

As has always been the case with Solaris, which is often run in a headless mode where no local GUI is available, the process of installing packages can be easily accomplished through the command-line interface. We will now repeat the steps of installing amp. First, check the availability of an amp package by searching:

```
# pkg search amp
```

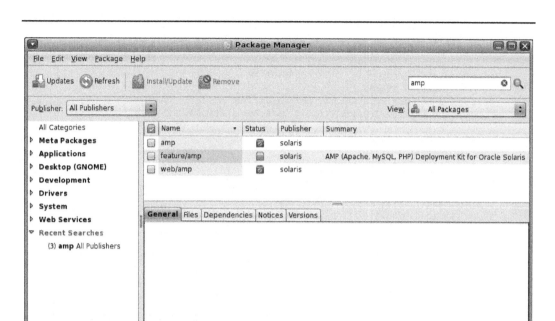

FIGURE 22-4. *AMP installed, shown in Package Manager*

This command shows the availability of the amp package, and we can get better information about the amp stack with the following command:

```
# pkg info -r amp
          Name: amp
       Summary:
         State: Not installed (Renamed)
    Renamed to: web/amp@0.5.11-0.133
                consolidation/sfw/sfw-incorporation
     Publisher: solaris
       Version: 0.5.11
 Build Release: 5.11
        Branch: 0.133
Packaging Date: October 27, 2010 06:31:05 PM
          Size: 0.00 B
          FMRI: pkg://solaris/amp@0.5.11,5.11-0.133:20101027T183105Z

          Name: group/feature/amp
       Summary: AMP (Apache, MySQL, PHP) Deployment Kit for Oracle Solaris
   Description: Provides a set of components for deployment of an AMP (Apache,
                MySQL, PHP) stack on Oracle Solaris
      Category: Meta Packages/Group Packages (org.opensolaris.category.2008)
                Web Services/Application and Web Servers (org.opensolaris.category.2008)
         State: Installed
```

```
      Publisher: solaris
        Version: 0.5.11
  Build Release: 5.11
         Branch: 0.175.0.0.0.2.2576
 Packaging Date: October 20, 2011 06:36:01 AM
           Size: 5.45 kB
           FMRI: pkg://solaris/group/feature/amp ¬
                 @0.5.11,5.11-0.175.0.0.0.2.2576:20111020T063601Z

           Name: web/amp
        Summary:
          State: Not installed (Renamed)
     Renamed to: group/feature/amp@0.5.11-0.174.0.0.0.0.0
                 consolidation/ips/ips-incorporation
      Publisher: solaris
        Version: 0.5.11
  Build Release: 5.11
         Branch: 0.174.0.0.0.0.0
 Packaging Date: September 21, 2011 07:15:02 PM
           Size: 5.45 kB
           FMRI: pkg://solaris/web/amp
 @0.5.11,5.11-0.174.0.0.0.0.0:20110921T191502Z
```

The output reveals the same three packages that were displayed in the Package Manager. Just as with the graphical Package Manager, we only need to specify the amp package. Use the following command:

```
# pkg install amp
            Packages to install: 1
          Create boot environment: No
Create backup boot environment: No

DOWNLOAD                              PKGS        FILES      XFER (MB)
Completed                             1/1          3/3        0.0/0.0

PHASE                                       ACTIONS
Install Phase                                17/17

PHASE                                         ITEMS
Package State Update Phase                     1/1
Image State Update Phase                       2/2
```

NOTE
*If you are not already logged in to an account with root or installation privileges, use the **sudo** command to temporarily escalate permissions to allow the **pkg install** command to be executed; otherwise, the installation will not succeed.*

```
# pkg install amp
pkg install: Could not operate on /var/pkg/lock
because of insufficient permissions. Please try the command again as a
privileged user.
```

We can now verify that the amp package is installed using the following command:

```
# pkg info amp
          Name: group/feature/amp
       Summary: AMP (Apache, MySQL, PHP) Deployment Kit for Oracle Solaris
   Description: Provides a set of components for deployment of an AMP (Apache,
                MySQL, PHP) stack on Oracle Solaris
      Category: Meta Packages/Group Packages (org.opensolaris.category.2008)
                Web Services/Application and Web Servers (org.opensolaris.category.2008)
         State: Installed
     Publisher: solaris
       Version: 0.5.11
 Build Release: 5.11
        Branch: 0.175.0.0.0.2.2576
Packaging Date: October 20, 2011 06:36:01 AM
          Size: 5.45 kB
          FMRI: pkg://solaris/group/feature/amp ¬
                @0.5.11,5.11-0.175.0.0.0.2.2576:20111020T063601Z
```

We can see that the amp stack is installed. Also, the package group/feature/amp was installed, just as it was when we used the GUI (note that the state is shown as "Installed").

Graphical Management: Webmin

Although it is certainly possible to fully manage the AMP stack from the command line, those who prefer having a GUI at their disposal may want to install Webmin, one of the best open source GUI management tools available for UNIX systems. Although not provided by or supported by Oracle, it is offered as a downloadable Solaris package from the Webmin website. Webmin is a full systems management tool that includes functionality for managing Apache, MySQL, and PHP.

To obtain the latest version of Webmin, you can browse to the home page www.webmin.com and click Solaris Package on the left side of the page. As of this writing, the current version is 1.580. Instructions for installation and usage are available on the Webmin website.

AMP Component Configuration

Now that the amp package has been installed, we need to do a few things to get it ready for use. Some basic configuration actions need to be performed. Apache and MySQL need to have their system services started, along with us verifying that each component is working correctly. Lastly, the PHP package needs to be verified.

Enabling MySQL   Enable the MySQL database server using SMF and verify that it started and is online:

```
# svcadm enable mysql
# svcs mysql
STATE     STIME    FMRI
online    14:15:37 svc:/application/database/mysql:version_51
```

The initial password for the MySQL root user is empty. Having a running MySQL database server with a blank root password is a huge risk to your systems' security and not recommended. Take the time to set one now by using the **mysqladmin** utility:

```
# /usr/mysql/bin/mysqladmin -u root password 'dbpasswd'
```

NOTE
The MySQL administrative user may be called root, but it should not be confused with your Solaris root user because it is separate.

We can now check the status of the MySQL database server with the command **mysqladmin**, as shown here:

```
# /usr/mysql/bin/mysqladmin status
Uptime: 30416 Threads: 1 Questions: 114 Slow queries: 0 Opens: 30 Flush tables: 1
Open tables: 4 Queries per second avg: 0.3
```

Enabling Apache   Enable the Apache web server using SMF and verify that it started and is online:

```
# svcadm enable apache22
# svcs apache22
STATE     STIME     FMRI
online    22:05:22  svc:/network/http:apache22
```

We can test our Apache web server by attempting to access it using our web browser. Open a browser (Firefox, for example) and in the address bar, type **http://localhost** and press ENTER. You should see the default index.html page "It works!" (see Figure 22-5).

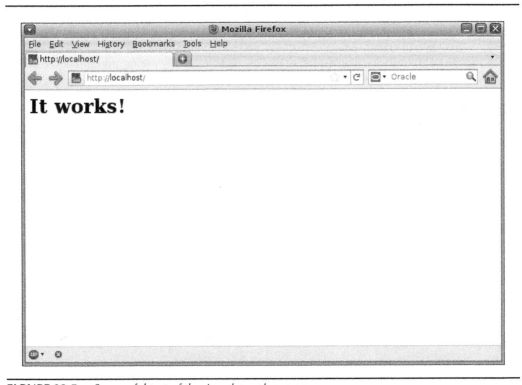

FIGURE 22-5.   *Successful test of the Apache web server*

Enabling PHP   PHP does not have an associated system service, but we can verify that it is installed and available by adding a test page to the Apache document root. Use the following command as a quick way to create this test page:

```
# echo "<?php\nphpinfo();\n?>" >>/var/apache2/2.2/htdocsphpcheck.php
# cat /var/apache2/2.2/htdocs/phpcheck.php
<?php
phpinfo();
?>
```

We can now test PHP by accessing the Apache web server using our web browser. Open a browser (Firefox, for example) and in the address bar, type **http://localhost/phpcheck.php** and press ENTER. You should see the PHP information page, as shown in Figure 22-6.

Keep Modules to a Minimum

One of the great features and advantages of Apache is modularity. Through a feature called dynamic shared object (DSO) support, Apache provides a mechanism for loading modules to do various things such as SSL encryption, URL redirects and rewrites, and user authentication. Dynamic shared

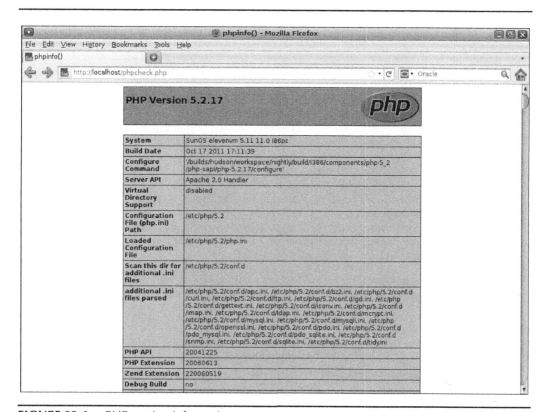

FIGURE 22-6.   *PHP version information page*

objects, also referred to as *modules,* make it easy for third-party vendors of other software applications to provide custom modules that improve the integration of their application with the Apache web server.

Information about DSO modules is stored in a configuration file that corresponds to your system architecture, 32 bit or 64 bit, located in the directory /etc/apache2/2.2/conf.d. Here is an excerpt of the file modules-64.load for the 64-bit platform:

```
# 64-bit Dynamic Shared Object (DSO) Support
#
# To be able to use the functionality of a module which was built as a
# 64-bit DSO you have to place corresponding 'LoadModule' lines at this
# location so the directives contained in it are actually available
# _before_ they are used.
# Statically compiled modules (those listed by 'httpd -l') do not need
# to be loaded here.
#
# Example:
# LoadModule foo_module libexec/64/mod_foo.so
#
LoadModule authn_file_module libexec/64/mod_authn_file.so
LoadModule authn_dbm_module libexec/64/mod_authn_dbm.so
LoadModule authn_anon_module libexec/64/mod_authn_anon.so
LoadModule authn_dbd_module libexec/64/mod_authn_dbd.so
LoadModule authn_default_module libexec/64/mod_authn_default.so
LoadModule authz_host_module libexec/64/mod_authz_host.so
LoadModule authz_groupfile_module libexec/64/mod_authz_groupfile.so
LoadModule authz_user_module libexec/64/mod_authz_user.so
LoadModule authz_dbm_module libexec/64/mod_authz_dbm.so
LoadModule authz_owner_module libexec/64/mod_authz_owner.so
LoadModule authnz_ldap_module libexec/64/mod_authnz_ldap.so
LoadModule authz_default_module libexec/64/mod_authz_default.so
LoadModule auth_basic_module libexec/64/mod_auth_basic.so
LoadModule auth_digest_module libexec/64/mod_auth_digest.so
LoadModule auth_gss_module libexec/64/mod_auth_gss.so
LoadModule file_cache_module libexec/64/mod_file_cache.so
LoadModule cache_module libexec/64/mod_cache.so
LoadModule disk_cache_module libexec/64/mod_disk_cache.so
LoadModule mem_cache_module libexec/64/mod_mem_cache.so
LoadModule dbd_module libexec/64/mod_dbd.so
```

Advanced administrators can use DSO to improve system performance by preventing Apache from loading unused modules to reduce memory usage and the number of running processes.

NOTE
Managing modules is an advanced exercise. Before disabling any module, make sure you have a good understanding of its function to be sure it will not be required.

Disabling a module is done by simply commenting out the **LoadModule** line associated with the module. Let's disable the module authn_anon_module as an example. The module is loaded with the following line in the configuration file. You can also take notice of how it appears in the file excerpt above.

```
LoadModule authn_anon_module libexec/64/mod_authn_anon.so
```

To comment out the line, add a # symbol to the beginning of the line using your favorite text editor. It should now appear as follows:

```
#LoadModule authn_anon_module libexec/64/mod authn_anon.so
```

As the Apache web server process starts up and reads its configuration files, it will ignore any line beginning with the # symbol. Therefore, this module will no longer be loaded. Repeat this process for each module that will not be needed to achieve a lean, mean, high-performance instance of Apache.

Any time we make a configuration change to the Apache configuration, especially when editing the configuration files directly, we risk a typo or other bad directive causing Apache to stop operating. If you have made changes and want to check that no errors exist before restarting, run the command **/usr/apache2/2.2/bin/apachectl –t** and Apache will check its configuration for syntax errors. If everything checks out, Apache will report "Syntax OK." You must restart Apache for the changes to take effect; you can use SMF for this by issuing the command **svcadm restart apache22**.

Basic Apache Configuration

Now that we have the Apache web server up and running in the default configuration, let's examine the configuration files and options available. We'll begin with the configuration files and work through several examples of different configurations that Apache can assume depending on the administrator's needs.

Configuration Files

The Apache web server's main configuration file, httpd.conf, is located in the directory /etc/apache2/2.2. The httpd.conf file is configured to provide a standard server instance by default. Also recall the /etc/apache2/2.2/conf.d directory, which contains the module configuration files covered in the previous section; this directory is where they are located. Other configurations can be added to this directory that will be automatically picked up by Apache as it starts up. This is made possible by the **Include** directive on line 391 of the main configuration file:

```
Include /etc/apache2/2.2/conf.d/*.conf
```

Configuration files can be added to the /etc/apache2/2.2/conf.d directory. Sample configuration files in the /etc/apache2/2.2/samples-conf.d directory can also be copied to it and edited accordingly.

The next several sections cover the details of Apache configuration. The directives provided can be added either to the bottom of the main configuration file or to separate configuration files in the conf.d directory.

Another important location to be familiar with is the directory where web content is stored, known as the *document root,* specifically /var/apache2/2.2/htdocs. From here, the Apache Web Server will serve content. Three files are provided by default, but the one that really matters is the index page, index.html. This is the default page a visitor will be served upon browsing to your website.

Apache as a Regular Host

At installation, the Apache web server can host one website only. Apache is configured to listen on all available network interfaces at the standard HTTP port, 80. This basic configuration is called a *regular host.*

NOTE
The HTTP, or Hypertext Transport Protocol, uses port 80 as defined by a standards body known as the Internet Assigned Numbers Authority (IANA), which is responsible for all protocol-to-port assignments.

If you are a home user hosting a personal site, a regular host is probably enough, but businesses both small and large often need to run more than one website. A business may have web-based applications for employee usage as well as its main corporate website. Any website-hosting provider will of course require multiple web servers.

A feature called *virtual hosting* enables a single installation of Apache to host multiple websites. Virtual hosting eliminates the requirement for each website to have its own individual installation of Apache or even a separate physical server. This greatly reduces the number of physical servers and Apache installations for administrators to maintain. Performance can also be better managed because it is usually more efficient to share server resources across services rather than the situation of one server having too little while another has too much.

From the network perspective, any given server is limited to one service per port (in this case, 80); therefore, each additional Apache installation would be forced to listen on a separate nonstandard port unless you added another IP address and/or interface to your server. Keeping track of multiple ports, interfaces, and IP addresses gets real messy.

The network operations teams that maintain routers, firewalls, load-balancers, and network routing maps will also be impacted by the increased complexity, but that is beyond the scope of this book. So, let's discuss the advanced approach to hosting multiple websites—virtual hosts.

Apache with Virtual Hosts

Virtual hosts enable more than one website to be hosted by a single instance of Apache web server. Each website is served from a virtual host. Adding a virtual host to your Apache server is quite simple, only requiring a few additional lines in what is known as the **<VirtualHost>** directive, also referred to as a *vhost*. The following is an example of a virtual host in its simplest form:

```
<VirtualHost *:80>
DocumentRoot "/var/apache2/2.2/htdocs_vhost"
</VirtualHost>
```

Let's take a look at the two ways virtual hosts can be implemented: IP based and name based.

IP-based Virtual Hosts

IP-based virtual hosting is one way that Apache can host multiple websites. This requires that each website use a different IP address. Solaris 11 can provide more than one IP address through either the addition of physical network interfaces or the configuration of virtual interfaces.

This section shows how to add an IP-based virtual host to your Apache web server. Before we begin, let's look at how Apache is configured by default using the command **apachectl -S**:

```
# /usr/apache2/2.2/bin/apachectl -S
VirtualHost configuration:
Syntax OK
```

As we can see from the output, no virtual hosts are configured for Apache web server at initial installation. To configure an IP-based virtual host, create the file vhosts.conf in the /etc/apache2/2.2/conf.d directory. The samples-conf.d directory also contains a sample vhosts.conf file for additional reference. Add the following virtual host code block to the new vhosts.conf file:

```
<VirtualHost *:80>
DocumentRoot "/var/apache2/2.2/htdocs2"
<Directory "/var/apache2/2.2/htdocs2">
allow from all
</Directory>
</VirtualHost>
```

After you add the new virtual host configuration and save the vhosts.conf file, **apachectl –S** will list details about it:

```
# /usr/apache2/2.2/bin/apachectl –S
VirtualHost configuration:
wildcard NameVirtualHosts and _default_ servers:
*:80            127.0.0.1 (/etc/apache2/2.2/conf.d/vhosts.conf:1)
Syntax OK
```

Because this virtual host will be listening on port 80, it will effectively override the main server. Recall that each website has a document root. Look in /var/apache/2.2/ and you'll see the directory htdocs. This directory is already being used by the main website, so we will create a new directory to be used as the document root for this new website to be served from our new virtual host:

```
# cd /var/apache/2.2
# cp -r htdocs htdocs2
# ls
cgi-bin  error  htdocs  htdocs2  icons  libexec  logs  proxy
```

Now, edit the index.html file located in the new directory to make it easier to determine that we are accessing the correct website when it comes time to test it:

```
# cd htdocs2
# vi index.html
<html><body><h1>Server 2 works!</h></body></html>
```

Restart the Apache web server:

```
# svcadm restart apache22
```

Now test the new virtual host. Open the web browser and enter the IP address of the server. The result is shown in Figure 22-7.

Name-based Virtual Hosts

Apache also supports the name-based virtual host, which has the big advantage of letting multiple websites share the same IP address. This greatly simplifies the network configuration. Apache directs browsers to the correct website based on the requested name.

NOTE
Assume the virtual host block created in the previous section has not been deleted. Also, assume that the server has a network interface configured with the IP address 10.0.4.15 and that you have some form of hostname resolution with the names server3 and server4 both registered to this IP address.

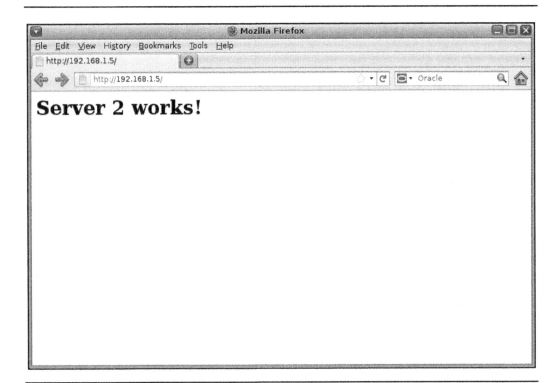

FIGURE 22-7.   *Successful test of the IP-based virtual host*

To demonstrate, the first thing to add is a **NameVirtualHost** directive to the vhosts.conf file that indicates that Apache will have a name-based virtual host listening on the IP address specified (in this case, 10.0.4.15):

```
NameVirtualHost 10.0.4.15:80
```

Now, let's create a name-based virtual host by adding the following virtual host code block to the vhosts.conf file:

```
<VirtualHost 10.0.4.15:80>
DocumentRoot "/var/apache2/2.2/htdocs3"
ServerName server3
<Directory "/var/apache2/2.2/htdocs3">
allow from all
</Directory>
</VirtualHost>
```

Create another document root for this website. First, copy another document root:

```
# cp -r htdocs htdocs3
# ls
cgi-bin   htdocs   htdocs3   libexec   proxy
error            htdocs2 icons    logs
```

Edit the index.html located in the new directory to make it easier to determine that we are accessing the correct website when it comes time to test it:

```
<html><body><h1>Server 3 works!</h></body></html>
```

After you have added the new virtual host configuration and saved the vhosts.conf file, **apachectl –S** will list details about it:

```
VirtualHost configuration:
10.0.4.15:80        is a NameVirtualHost
    default server server3 (/etc/apache2/2.2/conf.d/vhosts.conf:9)
    port 80 namevhost server3 (/etc/apache2/2.2/conf.d/vhosts.conf:9)
wildcard NameVirtualHosts and _default_ servers:
*:80            127.0.0.1 (/etc/apache2/2.2/conf.d/vhosts.conf:1)
Syntax OK
```

As shown, the name-based virtual host for server 3 is listed. Restart the Apache web server:

```
# svcadm restart apache22
```

One important distinction of a name-based virtual host is the need for a name that is declared using the **ServerName** directive. This name should match the name that will be used by the browser. Therefore, you will need to have working hostname resolution. The most common way is having a DNS server, where you can register an A record for the name, such as server 3, which is used for this demonstration. To test, point your browser at http://server3. Figure 22-8 shows that server 3 works.

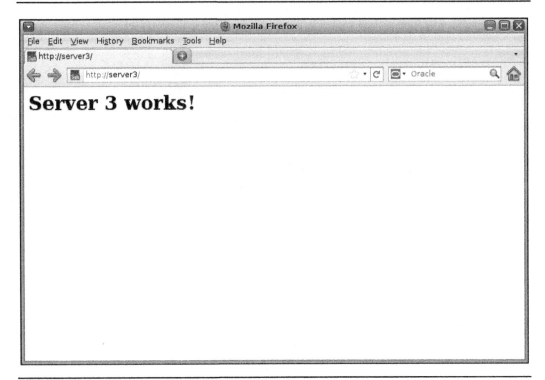

FIGURE 22-8. *Successful test of name-based virtual host "server 3"*

Adding more websites is just a matter of repeating this process and configuring each new name-based virtual host with a distinct name that is properly registered in your DNS. This can be a major benefit if you only have one external IP address from your Internet provider and would like to host more than one website.

The next **VirtualHost** code block shows the configuration for another website, server4, using the same IP address and port number:

```
<VirtualHost 10.0.4.15:80>
DocumentRoot "/var/apache2/2.2/htdocs4"
ServerName server4
<Directory "/var/apache2/2.2/htdocs4">
allow from all
</Directory>
</VirtualHost>
```

Again, **apachectl –S** lists each virtual server:

```
VirtualHost configuration:
10.0.4.15:80       is a NameVirtualHost
    default server server3 (/etc/apache2/2.2/conf.d/vhosts.conf:9)
    port 80 namevhost server3 (/etc/apache2/2.2/conf.d/vhosts.conf:9)
    port 80 namevhost server4 (/etc/apache2/2.2/conf.d/vhosts.conf:18)
```

```
wildcard NameVirtualHosts and _default_ servers:
*:80          127.0.0.1 (/etc/apache2/2.2/conf.d/vhosts.conf:1)
Syntax OK
```

Test by pointing the browser to http://server4. The result is shown in Figure 22-9.

NOTE
To properly administer virtual hosts—and in particular, name-based virtual hosts—it is very important to have a good understanding of how to configure the Domain Name System (DNS). An incorrect DNS can lead to weird behavior with potentially bad consequences. During this exercise, we mentioned that you should register an A record for the name of your website in DNS. This is only true for the first name registration. Each additional website should be registered as a canonical name (CNAME) record pointing to the first name. This is to avoid CNAME chains or CNAME loops, according to the Internet Engineering Task Force (IETF) Request for Comments (RFC) "Domain Names—Concepts and Facilities" (1034 3.6.2) for DNS. For example, web hosting providers often register the primary server with an A record for the name "www" (hence, the common usage http://www.somenetwork.com). Each subsequent website is then a CNAME to www.

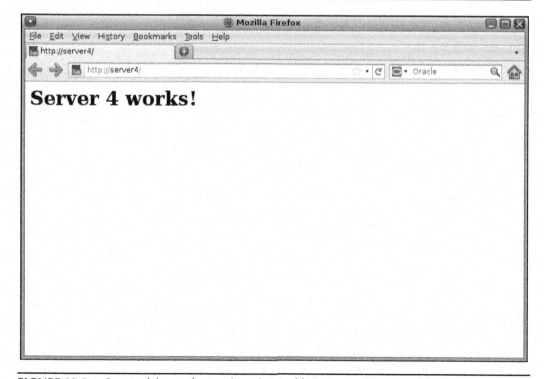

FIGURE 22-9. *Successful test of name-based virtual host "server 4"*

Secure Hosts

Like all Internet traffic, web server traffic must be secured from snooping, intercepting, and interjecting spurious packets. One way that network transmissions can be protected from unauthorized access is to apply encryption. Via certain algorithms and digital keys, data is scrambled so as to not be readable by someone else who might come to possess it unless they have been provided with the necessary algorithm and/or digital key to perform decryption. Web browser content requested by a browser can also be encrypted using Secure Sockets Layer (SSL) technology. You've most likely used an SSL-protected website, which is denoted by the https:// beginning to the URL. Most modern browsers will also display a small padlock icon to indicate the site is using encryption. Apache provides for SSL encryption and is fairly simple to configure.

There are just a few prerequisites. The first is that the module mod_ssl, which Solaris 11 provides by default, must be enabled. Second is the possession of a key file and certificate file, which both need to be generated using special commands. The process of generating certificates and keys is covered later in this chapter. Finally, your Apache web server needs to be configured with a few directives that turn on SSL and tell the server where your key and certificate files are located. First, add a **Listen** directive for the default SSL port, 443. The samples-conf.d directory contains a sample ssl.conf file for reference. It is a good idea to study this sample file closely to learn the many different configuration options available for SSL. For this demonstration, create a new ssl.conf file in the /etc/apache2/2.2/conf.d directory.

```
Listen 443
```

SSL can be enabled globally or within individual virtual hosts. Either way, only three lines are required:

```
SSLEngine on
SSLCertificateKeyFile /etc/apache2/2.2/SSL/elevenvm.key
SSLCertificateFile /etc/apache2/2.2/SSL/elevenvm.crt
```

That is all it takes to provide encryption to your Apache web server. Now, Apache can accept both SSL and standard non-SSL requests. An Apache virtual host with support for SSL is shown here:

```
<VirtualHost 192.168.1.5:443>
DocumentRoot "/var/apache2/2.2/htdocs5"
<Directory "var/apache2/2.2/htdocs5">
allow from all
</Directory>
SSLEngine on
SSLCertificateKeyFile /etc/apache2/2.2/SSL/elevenvm.key
SSLCertificateFile /etc/apache2/2.2/SSL/elevenvm.crt
</VirtualHost>
```

If we add this configuration to the ssl.conf file and run the **apachectl –S** command, the following listing is shown:

```
VirtualHost configuration:
10.0.4.15:80        is a NameVirtualHost
     default server server3 (/etc/apache2/2.2/conf.d/vhosts.conf:9)
     port 80 namevhost server3 (/etc/apache2/2.2/conf.d/vhosts.conf:9)
     port 80 namevhost server4 (/etc/apache2/2.2/conf.d/vhosts.conf:18)
```

```
192.168.1.5:443      elevenvm (/etc/apache2/2.2/conf.d/ssl.conf:3)
wildcard NameVirtualHosts and _default_ servers:
*:80          127.0.0.1 (/etc/apache2/2.2/conf.d/vhosts.conf:1)
Syntax OK
```

In a case where you would want to prevent unencrypted communications with your web server, ensuring that only SSL connections can be established, you can use another directive, **SSLrequireSSL**. Apache mod_ssl has many more available directives; for a full listing, consult the Apache HTTP Server documentation.

Apache Security

No other service is as important in terms of security as your web server. Some might be quick to say that it's your secure-shell (**ssh**) server, but we disagree. After all, **ssh** might be your front door, but your web server is your front window. Visitors to your site get to see some of what you've got inside, but you still need to prevent them from actually breaking in and taking anything. There are various ways to secure your Apache web server using features of both the Oracle Solaris 11 operating system and those within Apache itself. There are firewalls, and there are mechanisms for filtering based on incoming addresses and users and a combination of both. An entire Apache web server can also be isolated within a zone, which is a form of virtualization offered in Oracle Solaris 11. These capabilities are not mutually exclusive; all can be employed to provide a hardened web server instance. First, we'll review firewalls. Then we'll highlight Apache's filtering features and finally take a closer look at a zone.

Firewall Review

A firewall, in its basic form, is a software program installed at the perimeter of your system or network that provides a programmatic interface for creating rules used for filtering incoming and outgoing network traffic. The firewall is a very important component in a network security plan. Many years ago, firewalls didn't exist and computer systems relied on internal controls, often on a per-service basis, to prevent unauthorized access. As IT departments were tasked with maintaining and protecting networks of large and growing numbers of computers rather than one or two systems, as had been the case until the mid to late '90s, firewalls became the "one size fits all" solution because they could be placed at the network's egress/ingress points—usually at the gateway to their ISP and the Internet. Those were simpler times—there were no Wi-Fi access points, most applications used their own respective protocols and ports, and we trusted internal users. Today, firewalls are still very important and have gained many capabilities to better analyze the network traffic packets that flow through them. Most all modern operating systems have a built-in firewall as well, but with services such as Apache, we need to take additional steps to protect the system while maintaining the granularity needed to provide service to a varying dynamic user base.

IP Filter

Solaris 11 provides a firewall based on the open source program IP Filter. Two methods of administering IP Filter are included with Solaris 11: a GUI called Service Firewall and a set of command-line tools. The firewall can be enabled and configured from the System Firewall icon in the System menu, as shown in Figure 22-10.

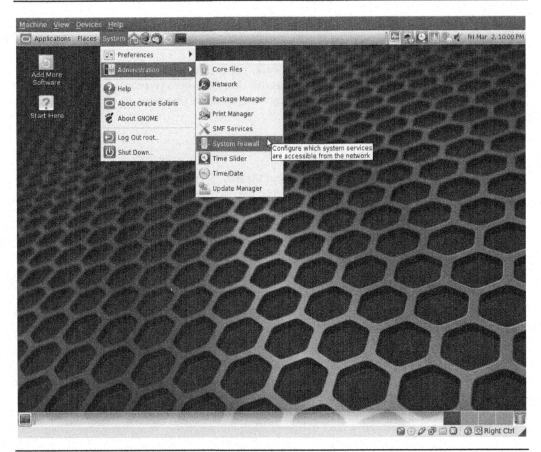

FIGURE 22-10. *Launching the system firewall*

Use the Add New Entry option under the Open Programs tab to quickly re-open access to the Apache web server by adding port 80, as shown in the following two illustrations.

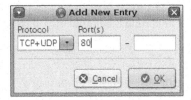

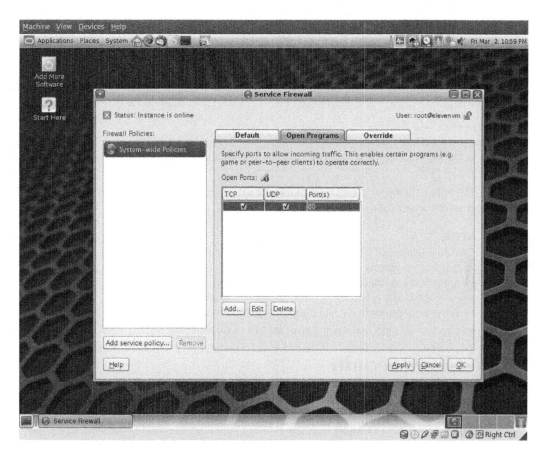

The firewall can also be turned on directly from the command line using SMF with **svcadm enable ipfilter**. Enabling **ipfilter** with this method doesn't configure any rules for incoming or outgoing traffic. We can view the currently active ruleset using the **ipfstat** command:

```
# ipfstat -io
empty list for ipfilter(out)
empty list for ipfilter(in)
```

To add a ruleset using the command line, edit the file /etc/ipf/ipf.conf. Be sure to include a line in the ipf.conf file that allows access for incoming HTTP traffic. A basic example is shown next. This example allows all outgoing traffic and blocks all incoming traffic, with the exception of incoming traffic to your Apache web server.

```
#
# ipf.conf
# IP Filter rules to be loaded during startup
#
# See ipf(4) manpage for more information on
# IP Filter rules syntax.
```

```
pass out quick all keep state
pass in quick from any to any port = 80
block in all
```

After saving the ipf.conf file, load and activate the new ruleset with the command **ipf –Fa –f /etc/ipf/ipf.conf**. Again, we can confirm that this new ruleset is currently active with the **ipfstat** command:

```
# ipfstat -io
pass out quick all keep state
pass in quick from any to any port = 80
block in all
```

The Solaris 11 firewall will now block any incoming connection that isn't destined for the Apache web server listening on port 80.

> **NOTE**
> *One nice feature of IP Filter is that your rules will follow the same format both in **ipfstat** output and a configuration file. This eases learning of the format and syntax and allows quick edits to running rulesets. Adding a rule to the current ruleset is as simple as piping it to a new configuration file, such as with **ipfstat –io >> ipf.newconf**, editing this file, and reloading it with **ipf –Fa –f ipf.newconf**.*

Host-based Security

Apache can filter incoming document requests based on client hostname or IP address. This is referred to as *host-based security*. Apache uses the **Allow**, **Deny**, and **Order** directives to accomplish this. If we suppose that we want to allow only connections from a system with the IP address of 192.168.1.65, we add an **Allow** directive into our virtual host section of the vhosts.conf file:

```
Allow from 192.168.1.65
```

Now we must prevent other systems from accessing our server using a **Deny** directive:

```
Deny from all
```

This **Deny** directive blocks all requests regardless of hostname or IP address; therefore, we should ensure that it is processed after the **Allow** directive. This is done using an **Order** directive:

```
Order allow,deny
```

After we have modified the first virtual host we created in this chapter, this is what our complete virtual host example looks like within the vhosts.conf file:

```
<VirtualHost *:80>
DocumentRoot "/var/apache2/2.2/htdocs2"
<Directory "var/apache2/2.2/htdocs2">
Order deny,allow
Deny from all
Allow from 192.168.1.65
</Directory>
</VirtualHost>
```

Connections from the allowed system will now succeed, while other systems attempting to access the web server will receive a 403 Forbidden response (see Figure 22-11).

Host-based access control can also use hostnames, fully qualified domain names, or networks. Here are just a few examples:

- Denying access from the "10.5" network:

  ```
  Deny from 10.5
  ```

- Allowing access from a system named professor.college.edu:

  ```
  Allow from professor.college.edu
  ```

- Denying access from a host named alfalfa:

  ```
  Deny from alfalfa
  ```

User-based Security

Another way Apache can control access is based on usernames and passwords. This is referred to as *user-based security* and is basically a process of password-protecting the web server. We'll take advantage of Apache's Basic Authentication, which uses two modules—mod_auth_basic and

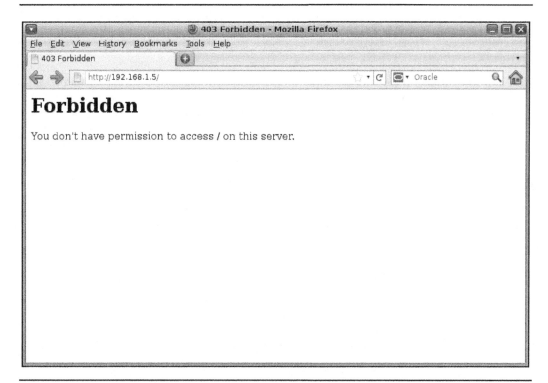

FIGURE 22-11. *403 Forbidden*

mod_authn_dbm—to provide password-protected access to a web server. Let's start with the virtual host created earlier:

```
<VirtualHost *:80>
DocumentRoot "/var/apache2/2.2/htdocs2"
<Directory "var/apache2/2.2/htdocs2">
allow from all
</Directory>
</VirtualHost>
```

Apache's Basic Authentication supports two options for storing your user information. The first uses a flat file (managed with the command **htpasswd**) that has scalability limitations when you get close to 100 users. The second uses a database file (known as a DBM file and managed with the command **htdbm**) that can support larger numbers of users. Because the two options function similarly and have an identical set of command-line options, let's use DBM. The first two directives define a name for the security realm and define that we are using Basic Authentication:

```
AuthName "protected server"
AuthType Basic
```

Because we will use a database rather than flat file, the next two directives declare the authentication type as such and provide the path to the .dbm file:

```
AuthBasicProvider dbm
AuthDBMUserFile /etc/apache2/2.2/dbm/Users.dbm
```

If we had chosen flat file storage, the provider would be set to **file**. The path to the dbm file is an administrator preference because the preceding dbm directory doesn't exist by default. A rule of thumb for locating any password database is to keep it away from the document root, because having it in the root opens the potential for someone to grab the file if they are able to exploit a vulnerability. The last directive we need to supply declares the actual users who are allowed to have access. This directive can be used in several ways. Specific users can be included, such as Harry and Christine, and would be declared by name:

```
Require harry christine
```

The **Require** directive can also be used to simply declare any user who has been authenticated, with the reserved word **valid-user**. This is how we will configure this example.

```
Require valid-user
```

The completed virtual host configuration section within the vhosts.conf file will appear as follows:

```
<VirtualHost *:80>
DocumentRoot "/var/apache2/2.2/htdocs2"
<Directory "var/apache2/2.2/htdocs2">
allow from all
AuthName "protected server"
AuthType Basic
AuthBasicProvider dbm
```

```
AuthDBMUserFile /etc/apache2/2.2/dbm/Users.dbm
Require valid-user
</Directory>
</VirtualHost>
```

Now we must create our user database and add accounts to it using the **htdbm** command. To create the database with an initial user, use the command **htdbm -c**:

```
# htdbm -c /etc/apache2/2.2/dbm/Users.dbm harry
```

This command will prompt for the password of user harry. Once the password is entered, the file is quickly created. Adding another user is just as easy as running **htdbm** again and specifying the new user:

```
# htdbm /etc/apache2/2.2/dbm/Users.dbm christine
```

Again, you are prompted for the password, and user christine is added. We can verify this by displaying the user database with the command **htdbm –l Users.dbm**:

```
Dumping records from database - - Users.dbm
Username            Comment
harry
christine
Total #records : 2
```

Once the virtual host is configured and we have created the user database, restart Apache and give it a try: **svcadm restart apache22**. The users Harry and Christine will be able to provide their username and password and access the site; any other username will not work.

Secure Certificates

A *certificate* is a file used to positively identify one system to another. Solaris includes the ability to generate secure certificate files by way of the OpenSSL Cryptography and SSL/TLS Toolkit. OpenSSL is another open source software product that is an enterprise-ready toolkit for implementing the SSL protocol. Solaris 11 includes version 1.0.0e. In order to provide SSL on the Apache web server, a secure certificate can be generated fairly easily using OpenSSL, available on your Solaris 11 system. The OpenSSL web page, www.openssl.org, includes documentation for administration of certificates. We'll now show you the set of commands used to generate the secure certificate used in our sample SSL-enabled Apache virtual host.

 NOTE
Make sure you're in the directory where you will create the files. This reduces the amount of typing needed.

To begin, a private key is required, so this is the first thing we need to generate:

```
# openssl genrsa -out elevenvm.key 2048
```

This command generates a private key with a size of 2048 bits. Just a few years ago, 1024 was an acceptable size; these days, 2048 or higher is recommended. Now, in order to have a certificate, we need a certificate signing request (CSR). The CSR is generated from the private key. This is the second command in the process.

```
# openssl req -new -key elevenvm.key -out elevenvm.csr
```

You will need to fill in the fields when prompted, making sure to provide the correct website name for the Common Name. For example, if your website is www.donut.net, that is what you should enter for the Common Name, despite the fact that the prompt reads "e.g., YOUR name." Leave the challenge password blank. The .csr file is submitted when you request a certificate from a domain registrar such as Network Solutions. The registrar will sign the CSR and use it to generate the secure certificate file, which you will load into Apache. This certificate will be recognized and accepted by all visitors. In this example, we won't submit the CSR to a registrar. Instead, let's sign our own. Doing so results in what is generally referred to as a *self-signed certificate*. This certificate will still work for your site's visitors, but they will be prompted with a warning concerning the authenticity of your self-signed certificate. If they choose not to accept, they cannot access the website. The last step is to issue the command to self-sign the certificate request:

```
# openssl req -x509 -key elevenvm.key -in elevenvm.csr -out elevenvm.crt
```

The OpenSSL toolkit also provides a shell in which all of these steps can be performed. The following shows a complete transcript of the certificate-creation process at an OpenSSL shell prompt:

```
# pwd
/etc/apache2/2.2/SSL
# openssl
OpenSSL> genrsa -out elevenvm.key 2048
Generating RSA private key, 2048 bit long modulus
....+++
...........................................................................
...........................................................................
...........................................................................
.........................................................+++
e is 65537 (0x10001)
OpenSSL> req -new -key elevenvm.key -out elevenvm.csr
You are about to be asked to enter information that will be incorporated
into your certificate request.
What you are about to enter is what is called a Distinguished Name or a DN.
There are quite a few fields but you can leave some blank
For some fields there will be a default value,
If you enter '.', the field will be left blank.
-----
Country Name (2 letter code) []:US
State or Province Name (full name) []:VIRGINIA
Locality Name (eg, city) []:RESTON
Organization Name (eg, company) []:WORK
Organizational Unit Name (eg, section) []:HR
Common Name (eg, YOUR name) []:elevenvm
Email Address []:root@elevenvm

Please enter the following 'extra' attributes
to be sent with your certificate request
A challenge password []:
```

```
An optional company name []:
OpenSSL> req -x509 -key elevenvm.key -in elevenvm.csr -out elevenvm.crt
OpenSSL> exit
# ls
elevenvm.crt    elevenvm.csr    elevenvm.key
```

Isolating Apache Within a Zone

Zones are a form of virtualization offered by the Oracle Solaris operating system. They provide a simple, elegant way to quickly deploy virtual machines and provide all of the benefits we've come to know and love with virtualization. Zones are covered in more detail in Chapter 14. This section will demonstrate how to isolate an Apache web server instance.

Let's assume we have an existing zone with Apache already installed, such as the webzone created in the exercises in Chapter 14. We can now apply various restrictions to the zone as well as modify the installed Apache instance within it to be much more resistant to break-in attempts. Or, in the event of a break-in, we can reduce the ability of the perpetrator to cause further damage to files or services running on the same server, either in other local zones or the global zone.

Protecting the Files

Various files required by your Apache web instance can be mounted from outside the local zone as read-only. For example, configuration files and HTML content files can effectively live outside the zone filesystem and in no way be modifiable from within the Apache web server or the zone.

Minimize Network Services

We can also reduce the network-facing attack surface of the zone by disabling unnecessary server daemons. Services such as sendmail, ftp, or nfs can be disabled. In fact, even the ssh service could be disabled, as there are other methods for system administrators to access the zone and no real need for anyone to use an access method that circumvents going through the global zone.

Minimize Privileges

Oracle Solaris 11 is configured by default to start as root and spawn subsequent Apache threads under the webservd user. This provides a little bit of security, but not enough. Viewing processes of Apache in the default configuration illustrates this.

```
# ps -aef |grep httpd |grep -v grep
webservd  9963  9961   0 22:35:00 ?          0:00 /usr/apache2/2.2/bin/httpd -k start
webservd  9964  9961   0 22:35:00 ?          0:00 /usr/apache2/2.2/bin/httpd -k start
webservd  9965  9961   0 22:35:00 ?          0:00 /usr/apache2/2.2/bin/httpd -k start

webservd  9968  9961   0 22:35:00 ?          0:00 /usr/apache2/2.2/bin/httpd -k start
webservd  9966  9961   0 22:35:00 ?          0:00 /usr/apache2/2.2/bin/httpd -k start
    root  9961  8609   0 22:34:58 ?          0:01 /usr/apache2/2.2/bin/httpd -k start
webservd  9967  9961   0 22:35:00 ?          0:00 /usr/apache2/2.2/bin/httpd -k start
```

So, we'd prefer not to see any Apache processes running as the root user. Therefore, modify the service start user to be webservd.

```
# svccfg -s apache22
svc:/network/http:apache22> setprop start/user = astring: webservd
svc:/network/http:apache22> setprop start/group = astring: webservd
svc:/network/http:apache22> end
```

Apache also is given a lot of privileges by default, as shown with the **ppriv** command.

```
# ppriv 9961
9961: /usr/apache2/2.2/bin/httpd -k start
flags = <none>

E: basic,contract_event,contract_identity,contract_observer,file_chown,file_
  chown_self,file_dac_execute,file_dac_read,file_dac_search,file_dac_write,file_
  owner,file_setid,ipc_dac_read,ipc_dac_write,ipc_owner,net_bindmlp,net_
  icmpaccess,net_mac_aware,net_observability,net_privaddr,net_rawaccess,proc_
  audit,proc_chroot,proc_lock_memory,proc_owner,proc_setid,proc_taskid,sys_
  acct,sys_admin,sys_audit,sys_flow_config,sys_ip_config,sys_iptun_config,sys_
  mount,sys_nfs,sys_ppp_config,sys_resource,sys_share

< some output deleted for brevity>
```

This privilege set should be drastically reduced and replaced with just the three privileges that are actually needed for Apache to run and bind to the listening port.

```
# svccfg -s apache22
svc:/network/http:apache22> setprop start/privileges = astring:
basic, !proc_session, !proc_info, !file_link_any,net_privaddr
svc:/network/http:apache22> setprop start/limit_privileges = astring: :default
svc:/network/http:apache22> setprop start/use_profile = boolean: false
svc:/network/http:apache22> setprop start/supp_groups = astring: :default
svc:/network/http:apache22> setprop start/working_directory = astring:

:default
svc:/network/http:apache22> setprop start/project = astring: :default
svc:/network/http:apache22> setprop start/resource_pool = astring: :default
svc:/network/http:apache22> end


# svcadm -v refresh apache22
```

Now, start Apache and take another look at the running processes and the privileges. There should no longer be any processes running as root. The list of privileges will be much shorter.

```
# svcadm -v enable -s apache22
# ps -aef | grep httpd | grep -v grep
webservd 10297 10295  0 23:03:56 ?      0:00 /usr/apache2/2.2/bin/httpd -k start
webservd 10295  8609  0 23:03:55 ?      0:01 /usr/apache2/2.2/bin/httpd -k start
webservd 10298 10295  0 23:03:56 ?      0:00 /usr/apache2/2.2/bin/httpd -k start
webservd 10299 10295  0 23:03:56 ?      0:00 /usr/apache2/2.2/bin/httpd -k start
webservd 10300 10295  0 23:03:56 ?      0:00 /usr/apache2/2.2/bin/httpd -k start
webservd 10301 10295  0 23:03:56 ?      0:00 /usr/apache2/2.2/bin/httpd -k start
webservd 10302 10295  0 23:03:56 ?      0:00 /usr/apache2/2.2/bin/httpd -k start

# ppriv -S 10295
10295:    /usr/apache2/2.2/bin/httpd -k start
flags = <none>
     E: basic, !file_link_any,net_privaddr, !proc_info, !proc_session
```

```
I: basic,!file_link_any,net_privaddr,!proc_info,!proc_session
P: basic,!file_link_any,net_privaddr,!proc_info,!proc_session
L: zone
```

 NOTE
*Make sure that wherever you have located the Apache log files,
the webservd user has write access to the directory and log files or
Apache will fail to start.*

Summary

This chapter has provided insight into the AMP Web Stack. We've seen how quickly and easily anyone can get a website up and running using AMP on Solaris 11. The Solaris 11 operating system makes a great platform on which to deploy AMP applications. It provides well-designed administrative capabilities and a high level of integration with open source software.

We covered the Apache HTTP server in good detail. The chapter walked through the process of installing, configuring, and securing an Apache web server. Solaris has always been known for a high level of security, and this is reinforced once more using IP Filter to provide a full system-level firewall to not only protect our Apache web server, but all other services running on Solaris 11 as well. We further isolated Apache within a Solaris zone.

The Solaris Service Management Facility was demonstrated for its tight integration with Apache and MySQL, which makes managing and monitoring these services reliable and intuitive. Last but not least, this chapter showed how to secure the Apache web server using SSL without the need for third-party and/or additional commercial software purchases. Together with some of the other topics covered in this book, it should be clear that Solaris 11 can provide a rock-solid and secure hosting option for dynamic websites of all sizes.

References

The Oracle Solaris 11 Information Library can be found at http://docs.oracle.com/cd/E23824_01/index.html.

The Webmin home page is found at www.webmin.org.

Apache Foundation Documentation for 2.2 is found at www.apache.org.

Oracle White Paper: How to Eliminate Web Page Hijacking Using Oracle Solaris 10 Security (May 2010)

The Netcraft Web Server Survey can be found at http://news.netcraft.com/archives/category/web-server-survey/.

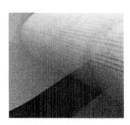

APPENDIX
A

Oracle Solaris 11 11/11 Quick Command Reference

he tables in the following sections categorize and list many of the most frequently used system administration commands for the Oracle Solaris 11 11/11 release.

System Information

Task	Command or File	Example[1]
Display hostname	/usr/bin/hostname	$ hostname
Display OS version	/etc/release	$ cat /etc/release
Display processor type	/usr/bin/isainfo /usr/sbin/psrinfo	$ isainfo $ psrinfo -v
Display system configuration	/usr/sbin/prtconf	$ prtconf -v
Unconfigure a system	/usr/sbin/sysconfig	# sysconfig unconfigure
Display host identifier	/usr/bin/hostid	$ hostid

[1] If a command can be run as an unprivileged user, the $ prompt is used; if the root role is required, the # prompt is used. The most commonly used/useful command options are listed. Multiple related commands are shown.

Services (SMF)

Task	Command or File	Example
List services	/usr/bin/svcs	$ svcs -a
List failed services	/usr/bin/svcs	$ svcs -xv
Enable or disable a service	/usr/sbin/svcadm	# svcadm enable sendmail # svcadm disable sendmail
Restart a service	/usr/sbin/svcadm	# svcadm restart sendmail

Package Management (IPS)

Task	Command or File	Example
List repository publisher	/usr/bin/pkg	$ pkg publisher

Add/delete a publisher	/usr/bin/pkg	$ pkg set-publisher -g¬
		{publ-url} {publ-name}
		$ pkg unset-publisher¬
		{publ-name}

Install/uninstall a package	/usr/bin/pkg	# pkg install gimp # pkg uninstall gimp
Search for a package	/usr/bin/pkg	$ pkg search gcc
List installed packages	/usr/bin/pkg	$ pkg list

Task	Command or File	Example
Update a package	/usr/bin/pkg	# pkg update gimp
Display package info	/usr/bin/pkg	$ pkg info gcc-45
Display package contents	/usr/bin/pkg	$ pkg contents ssh
Verify package contents	/usr/bin/pkg	$ pkg verify $ pkg verify apache-22

Boot Environments

Task	Command or File	Example
Create a new boot environment (BE)	/usr/sbin/beadm	# beadm create MyNewBE
Activate a boot environment	/usr/sbin/beadm	# beadm activate MyNewBE
List boot environments	/usr/sbin/beadm	$ beadm list

ZFS Filesystem

Task	Command or File	Example
Create a ZFS pool	/usr/sbin/zpool	# zpool create MyPool c2t1d0
Create a mirrored ZFS pool	/usr/sbin/zpool	# zpool create MyPool¬ mirror c2t1d0 c2t1d1
Add disks to a ZFS pool	/usr/sbin/zpool	# zpool add MyPool c2t1d2¬ c2t1d3
Display ZFS pool info	/usr/sbin/zpool	# zpool list # zpool status
Create a ZFS filesystem	/usr/sbin/zfs	# zfs create MyPool/MyFS1
Set a ZFS filesystem quota	/usr/sbin/zfs	# zfs set quota=2G¬ MyPool/MyFS1
Set a ZFS filesystem reservation	/usr/sbin/zfs	# zfs set reservation=1G¬ MyPool/MyFS1
List ZFS filesystems	/usr/sbin/zfs	# zfs list -H
Set ZFS filesystem property	/usr/sbin/zfs	# zfs set encryption=on¬ MyPool/MyFS1
Create a ZFS filesystem snapshot	/usr/sbin/zfs	# zfs snapshot¬ MyPool/MyFS1@June04
Recover to a ZFS filesystem snapshot	/usr/sbin/zfs	# zfs rollback¬ MyPool/MyFS1@June04
Verify pool checksums	/usr/sbin/zpool	# zpool scrub MyPool

Users and Roles

Task	Command or File	Example
Add a new user or group	/usr/sbin/useradd /usr/sbin/groupadd	# useradd -m johndoe # groupadd mynewgroup
Remove a user or group and files	/usr/sbin/userdel /usr/sbin/groupdel	# userdel -r johndoe # groupdel mynewgroup
Modify a user's info	/usr/sbin/usermod	# usermod -R mailadm johndoe
Set root as normal user	/usr/sbin/rolemod	# rolemod -K type=normal root
Set root as role	/usr/sbin/usermod	# usermod -K type=role root
List a user's roles	/usr/bin/roles	$ roles johndoe

Network Administration

Task	Command or File	Example
Show physical NICs	/usr/sbin/dladm	$ dladm show-phys $ dladm show-link
Create an IPv4 interface	/usr/sbin/ipadm	# ipadm create-ip net0 # ipadm create-addr -T static¬ -a 192.168.1.16 net0
Show network interfaces Show interface addresses	/usr/sbin/ipadm	$ ipadm show-if $ ipadm show-addr
Add a default route	/usr/sbin/route	# route -p add default¬ 192.168.1.1
List network profiles	/usr/sbin/netadm	# netadm list
Enable manual network configuration	/usr/sbin/netadm	# netadm enable -p ncp¬ DefaultFixed
Enable Automatic network configuration (DHCP)	/usr/sbin/netadm	# netadm enable -p ncp¬ Automatic
Display network status	/usr/bin/netstat	$ netstat -rn

Performance Monitoring

Task	Command or File	Example
Display memory and OS statistics	/usr/bin/vmstat	$ vmstat 5
Monitor process statistics	/usr/bin/prstat	$ prstat -Lm
Monitor process statistics	/usr/bin/top	$ top
Monitor I/O statistics	/usr/bin/iostat	$ iostat 5
Monitor per-processor statistics	/usr/bin/mpstat	$ mpstat 5
Observe OS activity	/usr/sbin/dtrace	# dtrace -s mydtscript.d

Zones (Containers[2])

Task	Command or File	Example
Create a new zone	/usr/sbin/zonecfg	# zonecfg -z MyNewZone
Install a zone	/usr/sbin/zoneadm	# zoneadm -z MyNewZone install
Boot a zone	/usr/sbin/zoneadm	# zoneadm -z MyNewZone boot
Shutdown or halt a zone	/usr/sbin/zoneadm	# zoneadm -z MyNewZone¬ shutdown # zoneadm -z MyNewZone halt
List all zones	/usr/sbin/zoneadm	$ zoneadm list -cvi
Log into zone console	/usr/sbin/zlogin	# zlogin -C MyNewZone

Monitor zones	/usr/bin/zonestat	$ zonestat 4
		$ zonestat -z MyNewZone 4
		$ prstat -Z
		$ prstat -z MyNewZone

Display current zone name	/usr/bin/zonename	$ zonename
Execute a command in a zone	/usr/sbin/zlogin	# zlogin MyNewZone df -H

[2] A container is a resource-managed zone; the two terms are often used interchangeably.

References

Additional Quick References and "Cheat Sheets" can be found at:

- ■ **Oracle Solaris 11 Cheat Sheet: General Administration**   www.oracle.com/technetwork/server-storage/solaris11/documentation/solaris-11-cheat-sheet-1556378.pdf

- ■ **Oracle Solaris 11 Cheat Sheet: Installation and Deployment Administration**   http://oracle.com/technetwork/server-storage/solaris11/documentation/solaris-11-install-cheat-sheet-1609420.pdf

- ■ **Oracle Solaris 11 Cheat Sheet for Image Packaging System**   www.oracle.com/technetwork/server-storage/solaris11/documentation/ips-one-liners-032011-337775.pdf

APPENDIX
B

Oracle Solaris 11 11/11
Information Library Files

ocumentation files in PDF format can be downloaded from http://docs.oracle.com/cd/E23824_01/index.html for local access; the following table will help you find the file you need.

Document Title	File Name
Oracle Solaris 11 Release Notes	E23811.pdf
Transitioning From Oracle Solaris 10 to Oracle Solaris 11	E24456.pdf
Installing Oracle Solaris 11 Systems	E21798.pdf
Creating and Administering Oracle Solaris 11 Boot Environments	E21801.pdf
Transitioning From Oracle Solaris 10 JumpStart to Oracle Solaris 11 Automated Installer	E21799.pdf
Creating a Custom Oracle Solaris 11 Installation Image	E21800.pdf
Adding and Updating Oracle Solaris 11 Software Packages	E21802.pdf
Copying and Creating Oracle Solaris 11 Package Repositories	E21803.pdf
Booting and Shutting Down Oracle Solaris on SPARC Platforms	821-2731.pdf
Booting and Shutting Down Oracle Solaris on x86 Platforms	821-2726.pdf
Oracle Solaris Administration: Common Tasks	821-1451.pdf
Oracle Solaris Administration: Devices and File Systems	821-1459.pdf
Oracle Solaris Administration: IP Services	821-1453.pdf
Oracle Solaris Administration: Naming and Directory Services	821-1455.pdf
Oracle Solaris Administration: Network Interfaces and Network Virtualization	821-1458.pdf
Oracle Solaris Administration: Network Services	821-1454.pdf
Oracle Solaris Administration: Oracle Solaris Zones, Oracle Solaris 10 Zones, and Resource Management	821-1460.pdf
Oracle Solaris Administration: SAN Configuration and Multipathing	E23097.pdf
Oracle Solaris Administration: Security Services	821-1456.pdf
Oracle Solaris Administration: SMB and Windows Interoperability	821-1449.pdf
Oracle Solaris Administration: ZFS File Systems	821-1448.pdf
Oracle Solaris Tunable Parameters Reference Manual	821-1450.pdf
Oracle Solaris 11 Security Guidelines	819-3195.pdf
Developer's Guide to Oracle Solaris 11 Security	819-2145.pdf
Trusted Extensions Configuration and Administration	821-1482.pdf
Trusted Extensions User's Guide	821-1484.pdf
Trusted Extensions Label Administration	821-1481.pdf

Document Title	File Name
Trusted Extensions Developer's Guide	821-1483.pdf
Compartmented Mode Workstation Labeling: Encodings Format	821-1480.pdf
Oracle Solaris 11 Accessibility Guide for the GNOME Desktop	E24675.pdf
Oracle Solaris 11 User's Guide for the GNOME Desktop	E24676.pdf
Optimizing the Oracle Solaris 11 Desktop for a Multiuser Environment	E26032.pdf
Introduction to Oracle Solaris 11 Developer Environment	820-0696.pdf
Linker and Libraries Guide	819-0690.pdf
ONC+ Developer's Guide	821-1671.pdf
Resource Management and Oracle Solaris Zones Developer's Guide	821-1499.pdf
Oracle Solaris Dynamic Tracing Guide	E22973.pdf
Programming Interfaces Guide	821-1602.pdf
Writing Device Drivers	819-3196.pdf

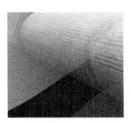

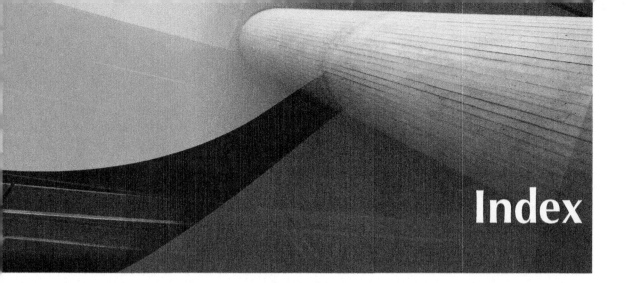

Index

O

P

Q

R

U